G. Enderle   K. Kansy   G. Pfaff

Computer Graphics Programming

GKS – The Graphics Standard

With 93 Figures, Some in Color

Springer-Verlag
Berlin Heidelberg NewYork Tokyo
1984

Dr. Günter Enderle
Standard Elektrik Lorenz AG
Hellmuth-Hirth-Str. 42
D-7000 Stuttgart 40

Dr. Klaus Kansy
Gesellschaft für Mathematik
und Datenverarbeitung
Schloß Birlinghoven
5201 St. Augustin 1

Dipl.-Inform. Günther Pfaff
Technische Hochschule Darmstadt
Alexanderstraße 24
6100 Darmstadt

ISBN 3-540-11525-0
Springer-Verlag Berlin Heidelberg New York Tokyo
ISBN 0-387-11525-0
Springer-Verlag New York Heidelberg Berlin Tokyo

Library of Congress Cataloging in Publication Data
Enderle, Günter, 1944–
Computer graphics programming.
(Symbolic computation. Computer graphics)
Bibliography: p.
Includes index.
1. Computer graphics–Standards. I. Kansy, Klaus, 1945–
II. Pfaff, Günther, 1951–   . III. Title. IV. Series.
T385.E53 1984   001.64′43   83-12438
ISBN 3-540-11525-0
ISBN 0-387-11525-0 (U.S.)

Typeset by Universitätsdruckerei H. Stürtz AG, Würzburg
Printed and bound by Halliday Litho, West Hanover, Massachusetts.
Printed in the United States of America.

9 8 7 6 5 4 3 (Third printing, 1985)

FOREWORD

For several years the authors of this book have been involved in the design and the national and international review of the forthcoming graphical standard. When the end of this process could be foreseen and the International Standard "Graphical Kernel System" (GKS) was cast into its final form, the urgent need arose for detailed information to the graphics community about this standard and for the education of graphics programmers. One major goal of GKS, besides the portability of graphical application programs and the device independence, is "programmer portability" by establishing a common base for training of graphics programmers. Having accompanied the path of GKS from the very early stages of defining the basic concepts and designing its first versions up to the final draft of the International Standard, we felt it worthwhile to start the venture of a text book on computer graphics programming based on GKS.

This book is aimed, at one hand, at graphics users, experts and managers who want to get an overview of the new standard and a better understanding of its concepts. On the other hand, it addresses the graphics programmers who want to use GKS for realizing their graphical applications. It can serve as the base for teaching and studying functions, concepts and methods of GKS. Additionally, it will be a valuable source of information for implementors of GKS.

One of the main application areas for computer graphics is Computer Aided Design (CAD). GKS can serve as an excellent base on which portable CAD systems can be designed. A thorough introduction into CAD is presented in another book of this SYMBOLIC COMPUTATION series: CAD — Fundamentals and System Architectures — by J. L. Encarnação and E. G. Schlechtendahl [ENCA82a].

The standard document defining GKS has to be complete and consistent, it uses a formal description where possible, and it has to adhere to certain formal rules for the specification of the standard. Only rarely it gives informal introductions, examples, or explanations for the decisions taken. For an overview, however, an informal and incomplete presentation will be the better way, and teaching has to use examples, figures and explanations. We want to offer an easy access to the GKS building and to the graphics environment in which it is situated.

Of course, in a book dealing with a standard, it is unavoidable to use information from the standard document. The authors were members of the editorial team that, up to GKS version 4.8 [DIN79] was designing GKS. Since then we were taking part in developing the following versions of the GKS document up to the GKS standard. However, the GKS document is the result of combined contributions from many different persons. It is an excellent document and, in several parts, there is no better way to describe the GKS standard. In these cases parts of the document are reproduced in this book with no or little change.

The book is divided into four main parts. In Part I, an overview of the integration of GKS into the Computer Graphics framework is given and the principles and basic concepts of GKS are introduced and explained. Part II describes the process of the GKS design. GKS, designed by the committee NI/UA-5.9 of the DIN (Deutsches Institut für Normung), has been reviewed and refined in a long international process that was carried on by experts in the working group TC97/SC5/WG2 of the ISO (International Organization for Standardization). The groups participating in this process, important events and major design decisions are presented as well as the methods used for handling the review and the revision of the standard draft and for resolving conflicts.

Part III of the book is devoted to explaining the GKS functions and their application. All GKS functions and their parameters are described, both in the language-independent form presented in the standard document, and in the FORTRAN subroutine version. Various examples are given both in the FORTRAN and Pascal programming languages. Exercises can serve for deepening the understanding of the functions and they can be a guide for teaching Computer Graphics programming on the basis of GKS.

The last part of the book covers the various interfaces of the standard within the Computer Graphics environment. Before a standardized graphics system can be used, it has to be implemented on existing hardware and operating systems. There is a desire that such implementations be validated and that their conformity to the standard be certified. The application of the standard in a given programming language is made possible by adapting the standard functions to the rules of that language. We describe the FORTRAN binding of GKS. Further interfaces exist to graphical input and output devices, and to graphics metafiles for storage of pictures. The communication between humans is made possible by a common graphics terminology developed parallel to the GKS standard. Finally, expected extensions of GKS in the areas of 3D-graphics applications are outlined.

Novices to the Computer Graphics field and persons that want to get an overview over GKS concepts should read Part I and then use the table of contents or the index at the end of the book to find information of special interest to them. Part II addresses itself to persons interested in standards and how they are created. Programmers and scientists designing graphics applications will find a detailed description of the GKS functions in Part III. This part will also be the main reference for training Computer Graphics programming on the ground of GKS. Part IV will be of special importance to GKS implementors.

We hope this book will help to disseminate the application of the Graphical Kernel System, to understand its principles and concepts, and to assist in Computer Graphics education on the base of the first standard in Computer Graphics.

Karlsruhe, Bonn, Darmstadt, July, 1983

Günter Enderle   Klaus Kansy   Günther Pfaff

DEDICATION

The subject of this book — the Graphical Kernel System — has been developed in a long process since 1976 and finally evolved as an International Standard. This book is dedicated to the graphics experts that designed GKS within the DIN (Deutsches Institut für Normung) and that accompanied its evolution in the international review process within the working group TC97/SC5/WG2 "Computer Graphics" of the ISO (International Organization for Standardization) and various national standardization organizations. More than 100 scientists from all over the world invested probably more that 50 man-years in this adventure, making GKS to the consistent and complete graphics standard it is today, developing a concise terminology for Computer Graphics, establishing the firm base of a methodology for Computer Graphics, and cooperating in a spirit of mutual confidence and friendship.

Members and experts of DIN-NI/UA-5.9 "Computer Graphics" 1975-1982: R. Anderl, E. Bauböck, H. Borik, H.-G. Borufka, L. Brandenburger, H. Brüggemann, P. Dobrowolski, R. Eckert, P. Egloff, J. Encarnação, G. Enderle, B. Fink, H. Flegel, R. Gnatz, M. Gonauser, H. Grauer, I. Grieger, Th. Johannsen, E. Jungmann, K. Kansy, R. Karg, W. Klingenberg, R. Konkart, H. Kuhlmann, G. Lang-Lendorff, St. Lewandowski, G. Mittelstraß, G. Nees, H. Nowacki, D. Otto, K. Pasemann, G. Pfaff, F.-J. Prester, K. Reumann, J. Rix, H.-J. Rosenberg, F.-K. Roth, E. G. Schlechtendahl, J. Schönhut, R. Schuster, D. Stroh, D. Völkel, J. Weiss, J. Weskott, H. Wetzel, P. Wißkirchen.

Members and experts of ISO TC97/SC5/WG2 "Computer Graphics" 1977-1982: J. Bettels (CH), K. Bö (N), P. Bono (USA), H.-G. Borufka (D), K. Brodlie (UK), L. Brown (NL-C), F. Canfield (USA), St. Carson (USA) J. Chin (USA), U. Cugini (I), J. Daabeck (DK), G. Dettori (I), F. de Witte (NL), D. Duce (UK), A. Ducrot (F), R. Dunn (USA), R. Eckert (D), P. Egloff (D), J. Encarnação (D), G. Enderle (D), J. Ero (NL), D. Fisher (UK), A. Francis (UK), J. Gallop (UK), P. Gauriat (F), R. Gnatz (D), T. H. Gossling (UK), I. Grieger (D), R. Guedj (F), Y. Gueniot (F), Ch. Hatfield (USA), W. Herzner (A), B. Herzog (USA), F. R. A. Hopgood (UK), M. Hosaka (J), K. Kansy (D), R. Kessener (NL), F. Kimura (J), J. Kivi (SF), A. Kotzauer (GDR), G. Krammer (H), H. Kuhlmann (D), R. Langridge (UK), M. Lucas (F), V. Lvov (USSR), J. Matthijs (B), J. Michener (USA), L. Moltedo (I), G. Nees (D), H. Newman (C), Ch. Osland (UK), Ch. Pellegrini (CH), G. Pfaff (D), A. Planman (SF), M. Polisher (USA), F.-J. Prester (D), R. Puk (USA), T. Reed (USA), K. Reumann (D), J. Rix (D), D. S. H. Rosenthal (UK), J. Rowe (USA), J. Schönhut (D), B. Shepherd (USA), E. Sonderegger (USA), R. Spiers (UK), D. Stroh (D), R. Sulonen (SF), D. Sutcliffe (UK), Z. Tolnay-Knefely (H), P. ten Hagen (NL), J. van der Star (NL), H. van Velden (NL), A. Warman (UK), M. Wein (C), J. Weiss (A), M. Whyles (USA), K. Willet (USA), A. Williams (UK), G. Williams (C), R. Williams (USA), P. Wißkirchen (D).

CONTENTS

Part I

INTRODUCTION TO COMPUTER GRAPHICS BASED ON GKS

Part I gives an introduction to basic concepts of computer graphics and to principles and concepts of GKS. The intention of this part is twofold: The computer graphics novice will be supplied with an overview of terms and concepts of computer graphics, shown on the base of GKS. The computer graphics expert will get an introduction to the GKS standard. In the first chapters of this part, main areas of computer graphics, different types of computer graphics users, the interfaces of GKS and the underlying design concepts for the GKS development are explained. Important terms are defined. The last chapters give an informal introduction to the main concepts of GKS and their interrelation: Output, attributes, coordinate systems, transformations, input, segments, metafile, state lists, and error handling. This introduction to the GKS system framework will prepare the grounds for the detailed description of GKS functions in Part III.

1 WHAT IS COMPUTER GRAPHICS?

1.1 Definition of Computer Graphics

The Data Processing Vocabulary of the International Organization for Standardization (ISO) [ISO82a] defines Computer Graphics as follows:
"Methods and techniques for converting data to and from a graphic display
via computer."

This definition refers to three basic components of any computer graphics
system — namely "data", "computer", and "display". However, the most
important aspect of computer graphics, and the main reason for the explosive
increase in computer graphics applications, is not mentioned in the above definition:
Computer graphics is the most versatile and most powerful means of communication between a computer and a human being.

Visually presented information can be accessed by human perception in
a most natural way. Complex structures and relations can be perceived in less
time, in greater number, and with less errors than in any other way. Models
of the real world or models of abstract concepts are hardly dealt with by humans
without taking resort to visual representations. This is the reason why computer
graphics is in first place a means of adapting the interface between computers
and men to the specific needs of men. Even in communications between men
on data originating from computers and on data processed by computers, computer graphics presentations are an important carrier of information.

1.2 Areas of Computer Graphics

Dependent on the direction in which data are converted and transferred between
a computer, the visual representation, and on the types of objects dealt with
by the computer graphics system, three computer graphics areas can be identified:
— generative computer graphics;
— picture analysis;
— picture processing.

Table 1.1 gives an overview of these areas. The table follows a scheme
set up by Giloi [GILO78].
With generative computer graphics, pictures are created from picture descriptions
given by computer programs and data. The data can originate from primary input

Table 1.1 Main areas of computer graphics

	Computer Graphics		
area	generative computer graphics	picture analysis	picture processing
input:	formal description	visual presentation	visual presentation
output:	visual presentation	formal description	visual presentation
objects:	lines, pixels, areas, texts or sets thereof	generated or scanned pictures	scanned pictures
purpose:	picture generation, presentation, segmentation, transformation	pattern analysis, structure analysis, scene analysis	picture enhancement

given by a user, it can be generated by computations, or it may originate from commands and actions of an operator at a graphical workstation. Basic objects like lines, raster elements (pixels), text strings, or filled polygons (areas) are created and their visual representation displayed on the display surface of a graphical output device. Pictures may be divided into parts (segments), pictures or parts thereof can undergo transformations. For the purpose of interactions with an operator, generative computer graphics also includes methods for handling operator input and identification of picture segments.

With picture analysis, basic objects and their relations are to be extracted from a picture given in unstructured form. Normally the pictures to be analysed are passed to the graphics system by digitizing (scanning) a photographic or television picture. Examples for picture analysis are the recognition of written characters, or the analysis of the type and situation of a mechanical part on a conveyer belt by the scene analysis system of a robot.

Picture processing is used to change the visual presentation of a picture in a way that human perception of the data contained in the picture is improved. Methods used are filtering, contrast improvement, or noise suppression. An example is the replacement of the gray scale values of a radiograph by corresponding colour hues. In this way the structures within the pictures are better accessible to human perception.

Naturally, there are various transitions between the three areas of computer graphics, and systems designed for one area may well have functional capabilities useful for one of the other areas. One common aspect of the whole field of computer graphics is that it deals with pictures, and that pictures have to be presented on a device for human perception. Thus a picture analysis system could well use a generative computer graphics system to present the pictures to be analysed and the results of the analysis.

1.3   Impact of the Graphical Kernel System on Computer Graphics

The Graphical Kernel System (GKS) [GKS82], which is the subject of this book, is covering the most significant parts of the area of generative computer graphics. It also lends itself for use with applications out of the areas of picture analysis and picture processing. The Graphical Kernel System is the first international standard for programming computer graphics applications. It offers functions for picture generation, picture presentation, segmentation, transformations and input. However, the extent of the functional capabilities is not the only important aspect of the standardization of the Graphical Kernel System. An even more important advantage of the GKS standardization is the following:

> For the first time, a methodological framework for the various concepts within the field of computer graphics has been developed. This is the base for a common understanding and a common terminology for creating computer graphics systems, for using computer graphics, for talking about computer graphics and for educating students in computer graphics methods, concepts and applications.

2   INTENTION AND CONTENTS OF PART I

Part I of this book gives an overview of principles and concepts of computer graphics on the basis of the Graphical Kernel System. Although the concepts described are closely related to GKS, most of them are general to a wide spectrum of computer graphics systems. This is true for the description of interfaces, including the interface to computer graphics users, and for the principles and goals of computer graphics standards as well as for the basic concepts of GKS. The dealing with concepts and methods has to be based on a common understanding. This requires a suitable terminology. The terminology used in this book is taken from the ISO Data Processing Vocabulary [ISO82a]. The set of terms defined in the GKS standard document [GKS82] is overlapping the ISO definitions for computer graphics to a great extent. Terms from both documents that are most important in our context are defined and explained in the following chapters. Most definitions are taken literally from the GKS document.

The intention of this part is twofold: The newcomer to computer graphics is addressed as well as the designer, user or teacher of computer graphics. The computer graphics novice will be supplied with an overview of terms and concepts of computer graphics. The computer graphics expert will get an introduction to the GKS standard. The integration of the special GKS functionality into the general context of computer graphics will be shown. A framework is to be established that is a sound base for the detailed description and the application of GKS functions in Part III.

3   THE COMPUTER GRAPHICS USER

Computer graphics is "used" in many different ways, for different purposes and by people of different skill and education. A person struggling with space invaders in a video game arcade is a computer graphics user as well as a programmer calling plotting routines in order to generate a diagram on a plotter. Three important types of users can be identified: the system implementors, the application programmers, and the graphical workstation operators. Figure 3.1 shows the relationship between the different types of computer graphics users.

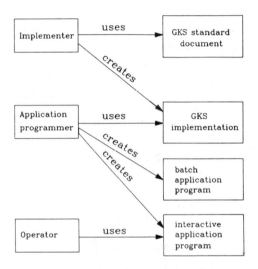

Figure 3.1 Computer graphics users

Implementor — Definition
   The implementor of a graphics system realizes the system defined by a specification. He uses basic software like programming language processors, linkers and loaders, or input/output routines. He makes the capabilities of graphics hardware (e.g., plotters or displays) available to the application programmer.

For GKS, the specification for the system design is given by the standard document. The GKS functions are grouped in different levels from minimal capabilities to the complete set of functions, with increasing functionality. The implementor has to choose the GKS level he wishes to realize and to specify implementation dependent aspects of the system. He has to stay within the bandwidth the standard leaves open for the implementor. The requirements of the GKS level structure must especially be followed (see Chapters I.6, III.2), and system interfaces that are not explicitly defined in the standard have to be designed. Implementation guidelines and implementation dependencies are summarized in Chapter IV.3.

Application programmer — Definition
> In the context of this book, we shall restrict the use of the term "application
> programmer" to applications containing computer graphics tasks. An appli-
> cation programmer uses a computer graphics system by writing programs
> that use computer graphics functions.

In most cases, computer graphics systems are realized as subroutine packages
callable from one or more programming languages (e.g., [GINO75, GSPC79,
BOS77, BO79]). GKS also is defined as a set of subroutines or procedures.
However, in some graphics systems graphics capabilities are integrated into
the constructs (data types, operations, statements) of the language (e.g.,
[HURW67, SMIT71, SOOP72, GILO72]). The application programmer uses
these constructs or the subroutine calls within a programming language together
with other application specific program parts. He creates a program that realizes
his application needs, including the graphics aspects of the application.

Operator — Definition
> An operator of a graphical workstation is a person manipulating physical
> input devices so as to change the measures of logical input devices and
> cause their triggers to fire.

This definition is taken from the GKS standard document. At this point,
the reader may simply visualize the operator to be a person sitting in front
of a display screen and manipulating input devices, e.g., a crosshair cursor
moved by a joystick. By his actions, the operator changes logical input values
that can be read in by the application program. The terms "measure" and
"trigger" are explained in Chapter III.8. Which input devices the operator
is allowed to manipulate, and in which order he may do so, is defined by
the application program that calls input functions for this purpose.

4 INTERFACES
OF THE GRAPHICAL KERNEL SYSTEM

The GKS standard document defines a set of functions performing graphical
tasks in a language-independent way. However, in an implementation of the
system these functions have to be realized as subroutines (or procedures) in
a given programming language. Such a language-specific realization, in which
the language-independent system nucleus is embedded, is called a language layer.
Language layers for FORTRAN and Pascal are available (see examples in Part
III and Chapter IV.4). The functions provided by the language layer can be
used by the application programmer, together with operating system functions.

Special application-dependent layers can be built on top of the GKS language layer. An application using an application layer for data representation graphics is shown in Figure C7, an example for a mapping application is shown in Figure C8 (page 503). Figure C3 (page 499) shows a CAD application.

The layer model represented in Figure 4.1 illustrates the role of GKS in a graphical system. Each layer may call the functions of the adjoining lower layers. So an application program will have access to a number of application-oriented layers, the language-dependent GKS layer, and operating system resources. All graphical functions should be performed only by calling GKS functions.

The top interface of the GKS nucleus is the language-independent application interface. It is defined by the GKS standard. The interface between the language-dependent layer and the application layers is the language-dependent application interface, e.g., the FORTRAN- or the Pascal-interface. These interfaces are currently under consideration for national and international standardization.

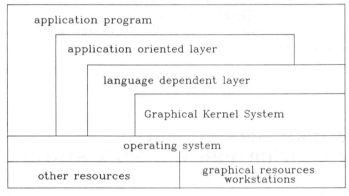

Figure 4.1 Layer model of GKS

GKS is a system nucleus not only in the sense that it provides basic graphical capabilities for many different applications. It also provides the graphical functions independently of specific graphical devices. Therefore, an important interface exists between the system nucleus and various graphical devices attached to it. In GKS, a graphical output device and the input devices connected to it are called a graphical workstation (see Chapter 9). The translation of the device-independent representations of functions within the nucleus to and from the different workstation-specific representations is performed by device drivers.

Device driver — Definition
    The device-dependent part of a GKS implementation intended to support a graphics device. The device driver generates device-dependent output and handles device-dependent interaction.

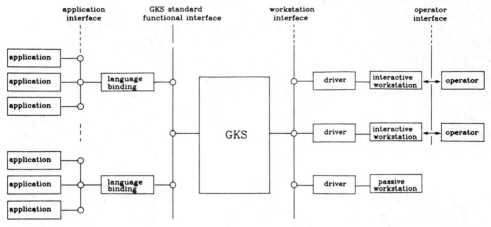

Figure 4.2 GKS interfaces

Device drivers of GKS are also called workstation drivers. Figure 4.2 shows the Graphical Kernel System as a nucleus between the application interface and the workstation interface. If the workstation is an interactive workstation with an operator, he is communicating with the system via the operator interface.

5   PRINCIPLES AND GOALS
OF THE GRAPHICAL KERNEL SYSTEM

The information contained in this chapter was first presented in a paper of the DIN Computer Graphics group [ENDE81]. Later it was included in the GKS draft standard in order to offer explanations and justifications for design decisions during the GKS development. GKS was designed to provide a set of functions for computer graphics programming that can be used by the majority of applications that produce computer generated pictures.

The main reasons for introducing a standard for basic computer graphics are:

— to allow application programs involving graphics to be easily portable between different installations;
— to aid the understanding and use of graphics methods by application programmers;
— to serve manufacturers of graphics equipment as a guideline in providing useful combinations of graphics capabilities in a device.

In order to reach these main objectives, the GKS design was based on the following requirements:

— GKS has to include all the capabilities that are essential for the whole
  spectrum of graphics, from simple passive output to highly interactive applications;
— the whole range of graphics devices, including vector and raster devices,
  microfilm recorders, storage tube displays, refresh displays and colour displays must be controllable by GKS in a uniform way;
— GKS must provide all the capabilities required by a majority of applications
  without becoming unduly large and complex.

These requirements have been used to formulate a number of principles
that were used to judge specific design alternatives. Thus it was possible to
contribute to the overall design goals while focusing on certain aspects. Five
design aspects have been identified, each having a group of principles: design
goals, functional capabilities, user interface design, graphics devices, and implementation aspects.

Design Goals
The following principles must not be violated by any technical design:
consistency: none of the mandatory requirements of GKS must be mutually
    contradictory;
compatibility: no other standards or commonly accepted rules of practice must
    be violated;
orthogonality: the functions or modules of GKS should be independent of each
    other, or the dependency must be structured and well-defined.

Functional Capabilities
The following principles were used to define the extent of GKS:
completeness: all functions which are used by most applications at a given
    level of functionality must be included;
minimality: no functions shall be provided that are unnecessary for applications
    of a given level of functionality;
compactness: an application must be able to achieve a desired result by a set
    of functions and parameters that is as small as possible;
richness: a rich set of functions offers an extensive range of facilities that
    stretches beyond the basic functions and includes higher order capabilities.

It is obvious that there must be a trade off between the principles in this
group. Therefore, the functions of GKS are grouped into levels. While the
lowest level contains only a minimal set of functions, higher levels are allowed
to extend beyond the basic needs towards greater richness.

User Interface Design
The following principles were used to define the user interface design:
user friendliness: GKS must allow the design of a desirable user interface;

clarity: the concepts and functional capabilities of GKS must be easily understandable, especially by the application programmer;

error handling: failure of system functions or modules, caused by errors of the system itself or by the application program, must be treated in such a way that the error reaction is clearly understandable and informative to the application programmer and that the impact on the system and the application program is as small as possible.

Clarity and a sound error handling are essential parts of user friendliness. The specification of error handling is an integral part of GKS. To aid clarity, the system and its state can be presented to the user in an easily comprehensible manner.

Clarity applies not only to the system design but also to the system description. To this end, the GKS specification is divided into a general description, a description of the underlying logical data structures representing the state of the system, and a description of the functions and their effects on these data structures.

Graphics Devices

The following principles are associated with the range of graphics devices that can be addressed by GKS:

device independence: GKS functions must be designed to allow an application program, using these functions, to address facilities of different types of graphics output and input devices without modification of the program structure;

device richness: the full capabilities of a wide range of different graphics output and input devices must be accessible from the functions of GKS.

These principles have led to a fundamental concept underlying the GKS architecture: the concept of multiple independent graphical workstations connected to and driven by GKS. The application program can inquire the capabilities of every workstation.

Implementation

The last group of principles is related to the implementation of GKS:

implementability: it must be possible to support the GKS functions in most host languages, on most operating systems and with most graphics devices;

language independence: it must be possible to access the standard facilities of GKS from all standard programming languages;

efficiency: the standard must be capable of being implemented without time-consuming algorithms;

robustness: the operator and application programmer must be protected in the best possible way from hardware or software failure of the system.

The five groups of principles are interconnected. For example, design goals and functional capabilities both contribute to user friendliness. Efficiency is also important when considering response time in an interactive environment. Some principles may be conflicting, such as richness versus minimality, comprehensive error handling versus efficiency, and compactness versus device richness. Compromises need to be made to achieve the overall design objective: GKS should have an easily comprehensible structure and a set of functions that enables a vast majority of computer graphics users to design portable, device independent application programs addressing the whole range of computer graphics equipment.

6   MAIN CONCEPTS
OF THE GRAPHICAL KERNEL SYSTEM

The main concepts of a graphics system are closely related to the tasks of such a system. Among these tasks are:
— generation and representation of pictures;
— routing parts of the pictures created in different user coordinate systems to different workstations and transforming them into the respective device coordinate systems;
— controlling the workstations attached to the system;
— handling input from workstations;
— allowing the structuring of pictures into parts that can be manipulated (displayed, transformed, copied, deleted) separately;
— long time storage of pictures.

Further concepts that result from the need to present the standard in a concise manner and to ease implementation and application of the system are system states represented in state lists, grouping of the functions into distinct levels with growing capabilities, and the error treatment. An important aspect of a graphics system is the dimensionality of the graphical objects it processes. The current GKS standard defines a purely two-dimensional (2D) system. However, it can be expected that an extension of the standard to three dimensions (3D) will be defined.

Output: One of the basic tasks of a graphics system is to generate pictures. The concept corresponding to this task is graphical output. The objects from which a picture is built up are output primitives, their visual appearance on the display surface of a workstation is controlled by a set of attributes (e.g., colour, linewidth).

Coordinate systems and transformations: The output primitives are created in one or several user coordinate systems. These primitives have to be placed on the display surface of different workstations having different device coordinate systems.

The way of graphical output from the application program to the display surface of a graphical device is called the "viewing pipeline". The routing and the transformation of output primitives along this viewing pipeline is performed by the graphics system. By using appropriate functions, the output transformations can be controlled by the application program. In 3D-systems, the viewing transformation from 3D-coordinates onto a 2D viewing surface is part of the viewing pipeline.

Workstations: The output devices and several input devices are assembled into groups called "graphical workstations" or just "workstations". They are usually operated by one operator. A workstation is, e.g., a plotter or a display with a keyboard or a tablet connected to it. The workstation concept is one of the original contributions of GKS to the methodology of graphics system design.

Input: In order to be able to communicate with a workstation operator, the application program has to be provided by means of obtaining input from a workstation. Besides input that is specific for graphical applications (coordinate data or the identification of a part of the picture), GKS also handles alphanumeric input, choice devices like function keys, and value-delivering devices like potentiometer dials. GKS handles input in a device-independent way by defining logical input devices.

Segmentation: The task of manipulating parts of the pictures leads to the concept of segmentation. A picture is composed of parts called segments that can be displayed, transformed, copied, or deleted independently of each other. Segments can be identified by an operator and their identification passed to the application program. GKS contains a very powerful segment facility, primarily by providing a workstation-independent segment storage together with functions for copying segments to workstations or into other segments.

Metafile: The metafile is a means for storing pictures for archiving purposes and for the transfer of pictures to a different location or different system. The GKS metafile interface allows for long-term storage and retrieval of pictures. It adds considerably to the flexibility of the system.

State lists: At every point in time, GKS is in an operating state that is represented by the values in a number of state lists. These values are changed by GKS functions called by the application program. The state includes, e.g., the set of workstations connected to the system at a given time, or the segments that are in existence. The concept of states and state lists has been developed during the design of GKS to allow for a clear and precise presentation of the effect of functions and to give assistance to implementors.

Levels: The GKS functions are grouped into 9 different levels. At the lowest level only a minimal set of output functions is present, while the highest level includes all GKS functions. This allows an implementor to realize only that level of functionality that is needed for his range of applications.

Error handling: GKS defines, together with the functions, a number of error conditions that could be raised when processing the function. The application program can control the error reaction or it can use a standard built-in error treatment.

Dimensionality: For the majority of computer graphics applications a 2D-system, as GKS in its present form, will be sufficient. All output and input coordinates are two-dimensional. Some applications, however, require 3D-output primitives, like lines or areas in 3D-space or even 3D-coordinate input. The Graphical Kernel System can be extended to three dimensions. This would add a set of 3D-functions, contained in separate levels, to the system. The definition of a 3D-extension to GKS is under way (see Chapter IV.9).

7 CREATING GRAPHICAL OUTPUT

7.1 Coordinate Graphics and Raster Graphics

If pictures are produced solely by output functions without interaction with an operator, we call the type of application passive output. The application programmer checks the result of his graphics program by looking at the picture and changing the program when he wishes a different result. The opposite of passive output is interactive computer graphics (see Chapter 10.). Dependent on the type of output device used, output can be divided into coordinate graphics and raster graphics.

Coordinate graphics — Definition
   Computer graphics in which display images are generated from display commands and coordinate data.

The basic elements of coordinate graphics pictures usually are vectors, or sequences of vectors. Examples for coordinate graphics devices are pen plotters or random scan displays. The typical property of coordinate drawing devices is a writing instrument (a pen, an electron beam) that can be positioned arbitrarily on the display surface. It can be moved to a different position with the writing instrument enabled or disabled (e.g., pen up or down), thus creating a visible vector or not. Refresh vector devices are permanently repeating the writing of all vectors of the picture in order to present a stable image to the human observer. The picture has to be stored for this purpose in a memory called display file. GKS has output primitives that allow the convenient addressing of coordinate graphics devices.

Raster graphics — Definition
>   Computer graphics in which a display image is composed of an array of
>   pixels arranged in rows and columns.

Pixel — Definition
>   The smallest element of a display surface that can be independently assigned
>   a colour or intensity.

The basic elements of a raster graphics picture are single dots of the display
surface that can be addressed independently of each other. Examples for raster
devices are raster colour displays (similar to television monitors) or electrostatic
plotters. Usually a raster device creates the picture line-by-line. Refresh raster
devices are writing all pixels of the screen repeatedly at a given refresh rate
(e.g., 25, 30, 50 or 60 times a second). The picture has to be stored for this
purpose in a memory called pixel storage or frame buffer.

GKS has special output primitives for addressing raster device capabilities.
However, raster primitives will be displayed on line graphics devices as well;
and line primitives will be displayed on raster devices.

Text can be displayed both on line and on raster graphics devices. The
graphical representation of characters will be broken down into the basic elements of the device (vectors or pixels) by a piece of hardware or software
called character generator. Figure 7.1 shows characters built up from vectors
and pixels.

Character generator — Definition
>   A functional unit that converts the coded representation of a character into
>   the graphical representation of the character for display.

**Characters built up   Characters built up from
from vectors   pixels**

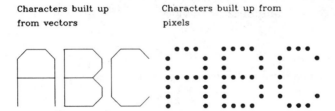

Figure 7.1 Character generation from vectors and pixels

7.2   Output Primitives and Attributes

The basic elements from which a picture is built up at the functional interface
of a graphics system are called output primitives. They are specified by their
geometry and by the way they appear on the display surface of a workstation.
These aspects are controlled by a set of attributes that belong to a primitive.
Certain attributes may vary from one workstation to the other, e.g., a line

may appear on one workstation black and dashed, on the other one red and solid. These aspects of a primitive are called workstation-dependent attributes. In GKS, functions are present for the creation of primitives and for the setting of attributes. For a number of attributes, the application program can select whether or not a specific attribute (e.g., linetype, polyline colour) is to be set in a workstation-dependent way.

Output primitive — Definition
   A basic graphic element that can be used to construct a display image. Output primitives in GKS are POLYLINE, POLYMARKER, TEXT, FILL AREA, CELL ARRAY, and GENERALIZED DRAWING PRIMITIVE.

Display image — Definition
   A collection of display elements or segments that are represented together at any one time on a display surface.

Attribute — Definition
   A particular property that applies to an output primitive or a segment. Examples: highlighting, character spacing. Note: In GKS some properties of workstations are called workstation attributes.

7.2.1   Output Primitives

GKS provides six output primitives; one line-primitive, one point-primitive, one text-primitive, two raster-primitives and one general purpose primitive serving as an entry point for specific workstation capabilities.

Line-primitive

POLYLINE: GKS generates a set of straight lines connecting a given point sequence.

Point-primitive

POLYMARKER: GKS generates symbols of some type centred at given positions. The symbols are called markers; these are glyphs with specified appearances which are used to identify a set of locations.

Text-primitive

TEXT: GKS generates a character string at a given position.

Raster-primitives

FILL AREA: GKS generates a polygon which may be hollow or filled with a uniform colour, a pattern, or a hatch style.

CELL ARRAY: GKS generates an array of rectangular cells with individual colours. This is a generalization of an array of pixels on a raster device. However, the cells of this primitive need not map one-to-one with the pixels defined by the display hardware.

General Purpose Primitive

GENERALIZED DRAWING PRIMITIVE(GDP) : GKS addresses special geometrical output capabilities of a workstation such as the drawing of spline
curves, circular arcs, and elliptic arcs. The objects are characterized by an
identifier, a set of points and additional data. GKS applies all transformations to the points but leaves the interpretation to the workstation.

Examples for the different output primitives are shown in Figure 7.2. This
figure was produced on a vector type workstation. Examples for the different
output primitives generated on a raster type workstation are shown in Figure
C1 (page 498).

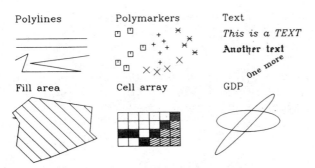

Figure 7.2 Examples for GKS output primitives

7.2.2   Output Primitive Attributes

In Table 7.1, for every type of primitive, the set of attributes that control
their appearance is given.
    The attributes describe the following aspects of output primitives:

Pick identifier — Definition
    A number assigned to individual output primitives within a segment and
    returned by the pick device. The same pick identifier can be assigned to
    different output primitives.

Pick identifiers have only a significance together with the input functions
used for identification of segments by an operator (see Chapter 10.)

Linetype — Definition
    Linetypes are used to distinguish different styles of lines. A line may be,
    e.g., solid, dashed, or dashed-dotted. Different linetypes are shown in Figure
    7.3.

Linewidth scale factor — Definition
    The actual width of a line is given by a nominal linewidth multiplied by
    the linewidth scale factor. Different linewidths are shown in Figure 7.3.

Table 7.1 Output primitive attributes

Primitive	Attributes	
POLYLINE	PICK IDENTIFIER LINEWIDTH SCALE FACTOR	LINETYPE COLOUR
POLYMARKER	PICK IDENTIFIER MARKER SIZE SCALE FACTOR	MARKER TYPE COLOUR
TEXT	PICK IDENTIFIER CHARACTER HEIGHT CHARACTER UP VECTOR CHARACTER EXPANSION FACTOR TEXT PATH CHARACTER SPACING	TEXT FONT TEXT PRECISION COLOUR TEXT ALIGNMENT
FILL AREA	PICK IDENTIFIER PATTERN SIZE PATTERN REFERENCE POINT PATTERN ARRAY	INTERIOR STYLE HATCH STYLE COLOUR
CELL ARRAY	PICK IDENTIFIER	COLOUR
GENERALIZED DRAWING PRIMITIVE	PICK IDENTIFIER dependent on the type of GDP	

Colour — Definition
    The colour is specified by the red-, green-, and blue-intensities defining a particular colour (RGB-values).

    The RGB colour model can be visualized by a colour cube (see Figure C5, page 502). The three axes of a 3D coordinate system in one corner of the cube represent the red-, green-, and blue-intensities. Every intensity can vary between 0 and 1. Every point within the cube (including its surface) represents a specific colour. RGB values (0,0,0) represent black, (1,1,1) is white.

Marker type — Definition
    The marker type is a number specifying the particular glyph used for identification of the polymarker positions.

Marker size scale factor — Definition
    The actual marker size of a line is given by a nominal marker size multiplied by the marker size scale factor.
    Different marker types and marker sizes are shown in Figure 7.3.

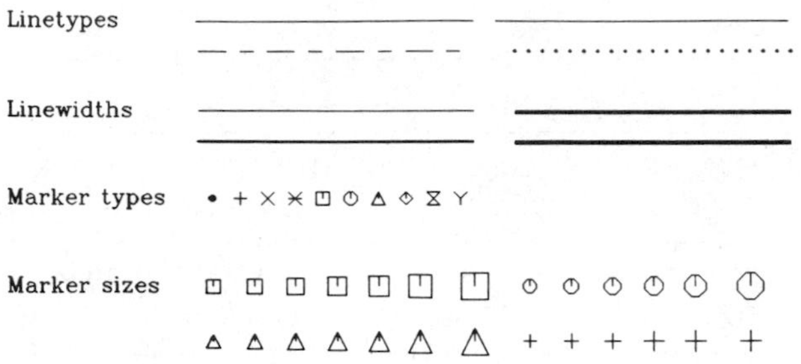

Linetypes

Linewidths

Marker types   • + × ✳ ⊡ ⊙ △ ◇ ⊠ Υ

Marker sizes   ⊡ ⊡ ⊡ ⊡ ⊡ ⊡ ⊡   ○ ○ ○ ○ ○ ○

                △ △ △ △ △ △ △   + + + + + +

Figure 7.3 Examples for polyline and polymarker attributes

Text font — Definition
The text font is a number selecting one representation for the text string characters out of the possibilities present on a workstation. Different text fonts are shown in Figure 7.4.

Text precision — Definition
An attribute describing the fidelity with which character position, character size, character orientation, and character font of text output match those requested by an application. In order of increasing fidelity, the precisions are: string, character, and stroke.

Normally, text generated by hardware character generators will only be available at restricted sizes or orientations, e.g., if text can only be displayed horizontally in one of three different character sizes, this is text precision "string". "Stroke" precision text usually will require a software character generator.

Character height — Definition
The vertical extend of a character.

Character up vector — Definition
The "UP"-direction of a character.

Character expansion factor — Definition
The deviation of the width/height-ratio of a character from the ratio defined by the text font designer.

Text path — Definition
The writing direction of the character sequence. The normal path used in this book is "right", i.e., the text you are reading is written from left to right. GKS allows also the text path values: left, up, and down.

Character spacing — Definition
Space to be inserted between adjacent characters of a text string, additional to the space defined by the font designer.

Character alignment — Definition
   A text attribute describing how the text string is positioned relative to the reference point of the text primitive (e.g., left aligned, centred).

Figure 7.4 gives examples for different values of character height, character-up-vector, expansion factor, path, spacing, and alignment.

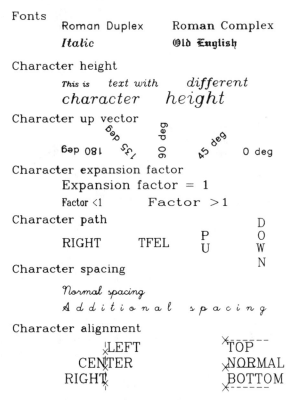

Figure 7.4 Examples for text attributes

Interior style — Definition
   The interior style is used to determine in what style an area should be filled. It has one of the values: hollow, solid, pattern, or hatch.

Figure 7.5 gives examples of different interior styles. This figure was generated on black and white raster plotter. Examples for fill areas of different interior style generated on a colour raster workstation are shown in Figure C2 (page 498). Fill areas with interior style FILLED were used for creating Figures C4 (page 499) and C5 (page 502). For the interior style "pattern", a pattern that is defined by the pattern size, the pattern reference point and the pattern array, is repeated for filling the area.

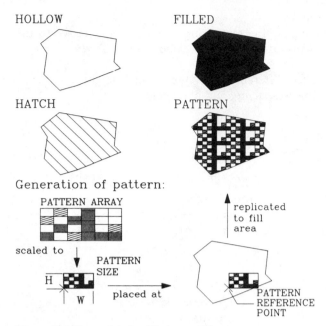

Figure 7.5 Examples for fill area attributes

Pattern size — Definition
   The pattern size specifies the size of the basic pattern rectangle.

Pattern reference point — Definition
   The pattern reference point specifies the origin of the basic pattern rectangle.
   The lower left corner of the rectangle is placed at the reference point. Then
   the pattern is repeated in both directions until the whole area is filled.

Pattern array — Definition
   A pattern is defined by an array of rectangular cells, each cell having a
   colour assigned to it. These values are used to assign colours to the basic
   pattern rectangle and to all replications of it. Figure 7.5 gives an example
   for a fill area primitive with a pattern.

Hatch style — Definition
   Hatching is specified by a number selecting one hatch style defined by the
   implementor and present on a workstation.

7.3   Indices, Bundles and Tables

Some attributes are always specified in a workstation-independent way. Some
other attributes are always workstation-dependent. For most attributes, how-

ever, the application program can specify whether or not it chooses to set the attributes workstation-dependent. The workstation-independent attributes are modally set by GKS functions, i.e., after an attribute has been set, it is used for all subsequently generated primitives as long it is not changed.

Example:

SET CHARACTER HEIGHT (hvalue)   {stores the value "hvalue"}

                                       {this text will be generated using
TEXT (point, 'ABC')   character height "hvalue"}

The workstation-dependent attributes (with the exception of colours and patterns) are specified by an index associated with the primitive. This index points into a table present on each workstation for different types of primitives. The set of workstation-dependent attributes for a primitive type is called a bundle, the table that contains the attributes is called a bundle table, e.g., for polylines, the POLYLINE INDEX points into a polyline bundle table that contains linewidth, linetype and a colour index (see Figure 7.6). The indices POLYLINE INDEX, POLYMARKER INDEX, TEXT INDEX, and FILL AREA INDEX can be set modally, they are used for displaying subsequently created primitives of the respective type.

A global switch is present for every one of those attributes that can be workstation-dependent or not. It selects the "attribute binding mode". The switches are called "aspect source flags", they can have either one of the two values "BUNDLED" (workstation-dependent) or "INDIVIDUAL" (workstation-independent).

Bundle index — Definition
    An index into a bundle table for a particular output primitive. It defines the workstation-dependent aspects of the primitive.

Bundle table — Definition
    A workstation-dependent table associated with a particular output primitive. Entries in the table specify all the workstation-dependent aspects of a primitive. In GKS, bundle tables exist for the following output primitives: polyline, polymarker, text and fill area.

Polyline bundle table — Definition
    A table associating specific values for all workstation-dependent aspects of a polyline primitive with a polyline bundle index. In GKS, this table contains entries consisting of linetype, linewidth scale factor, and colour index.

Polymarker bundle table — Definition
    A table associating specific values for all workstation-dependent aspects of a polymarker primitive with a polymarker bundle index. In GKS, this table contains entries consisting of marker type, marker size scale factor, and colour index.

Text bundle table — Definition
A table associating specific values for all workstation-dependent aspects of a text primitive with a text bundle index. In GKS, this table contains entries consisting of text font, text precision, character expansion factor, character spacing, and colour index.

The entries in the bundle tables are predefined by the system implementor according to the capabilities of the workstation. However, the entries can be changed by GKS functions. Also, the initial setting of the attribute source flags is implementation dependent. They can be reset individually at any time by the application program. An important property of workstation-dependent attributes is that they may influence the picture already present on the display surface. If such an attribute is changed, e.g., a RGB-value in the colour table, primitives already in existence and using these attributes will change their appearance accordingly (this only works properly for primitives contained in segments). Attributes assigned to primitives in the "INDIVIDUAL" attribute binding mode cannot be changed at a later stage.

Colour is a workstation-dependent attribute that is addressed via a colour index in the attribute bundle tables. The colour index points into a colour table that associates RGB-values with the colour indices. If entries in the colour table are changed while a picture is displayed on a workstation, the colours of the displayed primitives will change accordingly. Figure C6 gives an example (see page 502).

Colour table — Definition
A workstation-dependent table, in which the entries specify the values of the red, green and blue intensities defining a particular colour.

Figure 7.6 gives the set of attributes and their interrelation for polyline output primitives when all the attribute source flags for the polyline primitive are set to "BUNDLED". A similar figure could be drawn for polymarkers and texts.

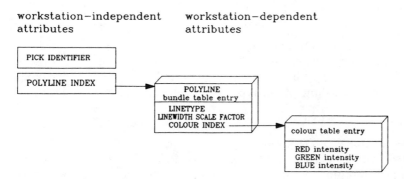

Figure 7.6 Relationship between polyline attributes for BUNDLED attribute binding mode

Figure 7.7 gives the set of attributes and their interrelation for polyline output primitives when all the attribute source flags for the polyline primitive are set to "INDIVIDUAL".

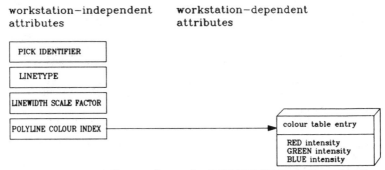

Figure 7.7 Relationship between polyline attributes for INDIVIDUAL attribute binding mode

The basic scheme for the fill area primitive is similar, however, the fill area bundle (and the alternate set of individual attributes) contains a style index that is used for selection of a pattern or a hatch style. For the interior style "pattern", the style index points into a table containing dimensions and colour indices of pattern arrays. The pattern identified by the style index will be used, together with the modal fill area attributes pattern size and pattern reference point, to fill the area. If the interior style is "hatch", the style index is used to select one of the hatch styles supplied by the implementation. Besides the implementation-defined hatch styles, no other hatching is available.

Fill area bundle table — Definition
A table associating specific values for all workstation-dependent aspects of a fill area primitive with a fill area bundle index. In GKS, this table contains entries consisting of interior style, style index, and colour index.

Figure 7.8 gives an overview of the relationship between the different fill area attributes when all the attribute source flags for the fill area primitive

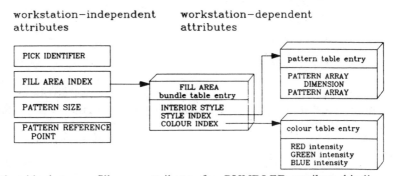

Figure 7.8 Relationship between fill area attributes for BUNDLED attribute binding mode

workstation–independent   workstation–dependent
attributes   attributes

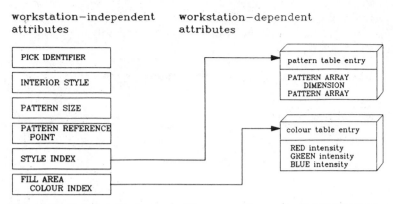

Figure 7.9 Relationship between fill area attributes for INDIVIDUAL attribute binding mode

are set to "BUNDLED". Figure 7.9 gives an overview over the fill area attributes when all the attribute source flags for the fill area primitive are set to "INDIVIDUAL".

Cell arrays use a different scheme; they provide a set of colour indices together with the primitive function. These colour indices refer directly to the colour table (see Figure 7.10). Figure C3 (page 499) shows a cell array generated on a colour raster workstation.

Primitive function   workstation–
contains parameter   dependent

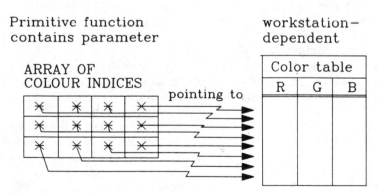

Figure 7.10 Colour specification for the cell array primitive

The generalized drawing primitive uses whichever attribute bundles or individual attributes that the implementor of a specific GDP chooses. There is no special GDP bundle.

8   COORDINATE SYSTEMS AND TRANSFORMATIONS

8.1   Coordinate Systems

The application programmer wants to define his graphical elements in a coordinate system that is related to his application. Output devices that are used for presenting the visual image of the elements, however, normally require the use of a device specific coordinate system. In order to meet these requirements while maintaining device independence, three coordinate systems have been defined in GKS. The application programmer uses the world coordinate (WC) system for specifying picture elements. The world coordinate system is the standard user coordinate system.

World coordinate (WC) — Definition
   A device-independent Cartesian coordinate system used by the application program for specifying graphical input and output.

If the application program wants to use other kinds of coordinate systems (e.g., polar coordinates), it has to do the necessary transformations before entering GKS. Conceptually, every output primitive is defined with its own world coordinate system.

Since different output devices have different device coordinate systems, GKS defines, as an abstraction of these device coordinate systems, one single normalized device coordinate (NDC) space. The relative positioning of output primitives is defined by mapping all the defined world coordinate systems onto the NDC space.

Normalized device coordinate (NDC) — Definition
   A coordinate specified in a device-independent intermediate coordinate system, normalized to some range, in GKS, typically 0 to 1.

Although NDC space conceptually extends to infinity, the part of NDC space in which the viewport must be located and that can be viewed at a workstation is the closed range [0,1]x[0,1]. The normalized picture in NDC space can be stored and manipulated via the segment mechanism; it can also be stored on a metafile.

The NDC space is mapped onto the device coordinates (DC) of every workstation that is to display the picture. Every type of workstation may have a different device coordinate space and a different mapping. The device coordinate space is always a bounded space since it represents the extension of the display surface of a physical, and hence bounded, device. DC units normally are metres in GKS, however, functions are available to enquire the correspondence between the specific device units and metres.

Device coordinate (DC) — Definition
A coordinate expressed in a coordinate system that is device-dependent.
Note: In GKS, DC units are metres on a device capable of producing a
precisely scaled image and appropriate workstation-dependent units otherwise.

8.2   Transformations

A set of normalization transformations define the mappings from the world
coordinate systems onto the single NDC space. A set of workstation transformations define the mapping of NDC space to every one of the active workstations.
These transformations define the viewing pipeline from the application transformation onto the display surface of the workstation and the input pipeline for
locator input devices from the locator position in DC to the application program. Other types of transformations can be applied to segments; these transformations take place in the NDC space. Figure 8.1 shows the coordinate systems
and the applicable transformations. The normalization transformation is explained below, the workstation transformation in Section 9.3, and the segment
transformations in Section 11.4.

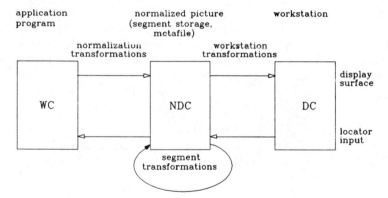

Figure 8.1 Coordinate systems and transformations

8.3   The Normalization Transformation

For output, a single normalization transformation is current at any one time
and this is used to transform world coordinates specified in output primitives
or geometric attributes into normalized device coordinates. A normalization
transformation is specified by defining the limits of an area in the world coordinate system (window) which is to be mapped onto a specified area of the normalized device coordinate space (viewport), see Figure 8.2.

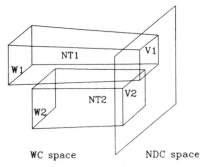

WC space   NDC space

W=Window,V=Viewport,NT=Normalization Transformation

Figure 8.2 Normalization transformation

Normalization transformation — Definition

A transformation that maps the boundary and interior of a window to the boundary and interior of a viewport. Note: In GKS this transformation maps positions in world coordinates to normalized device coordinates.

Window — Definition

A predefined part of a virtual space. Note: In GKS this definition is restricted to a rectangular region of the world coordinate space used for the definition of the normalization transformation.

Viewport — Definition

An application program specified part of normalized device coordinate space. Note: In GKS, this definition is restricted to a rectangular region of normalized device coordinate space used in the definition of the normalization transformation.

Window and viewport limits specify rectangles parallel to the coordinate axes in WC and NDC. The normalization transformation performs a mapping from WC onto NDC that includes translation and differential scaling with positive scale factors for the two axes. A number of normalization transformations can be defined in GKS at any one time. One of the normalization transformations defined is selected for generating graphical output. Each normalization transformation is identified by a transformation number which is an integer between 0 and an implementation dependent value n. The normalization transformation with transformation number 0 is the unity transformation which maps [0,1]x[0,1] in world coordinates to [0,1]x[0,1] in normalized device coordinates. It cannot be reset.

Initially, all other normalization transformations are set to a default transformation which is the same as transformation number 0. They may be reset to different transformations at any time when GKS is open. Since GKS provides a number of different normalization transformations, it is possible for the application program to specify them prior to outputting the graphical picture. The separate parts of the picture are output by selecting a particular normalization transformation before outputting the associated graphical primitives. However, redefining a normalization transformation while the graphical output is taking place is allowed.

8.4 Clipping

The application program may ask GKS to only show those parts of the picture that lie within the viewports that are associated with the picture elements. Cutting away all parts outside the viewport is called clipping (another type of clipping takes place on the the workstation, see Section 9.3). Clipping can be turned on or off by the application program.

Clipping — Definition
Removing parts of display elements that lie outside a given boundary, usually a window or viewport.

Clipping does not take place when the normalization transformation is performed but is delayed until the output primitives are to be displayed on the view surface of a workstation. Output primitives stored in segments will have had their coordinates transformed to NDC and the associated clipping rectangle will be stored with the primitives.

9 THE GRAPHICAL WORKSTATION

GKS is based on the concept of graphical workstations that are an abstraction of physical devices. An abstract graphical workstation can have the following set of properties (in practice, the workstation may or may not be equipped with all of these capabilities):
— It has one addressable display surface of fixed resolution;
— It allows only rectangular display spaces (the display space cannot consist of a number of separate parts);
— It permits the specification and use of smaller display spaces than the maximum while guaranteeing that no display image is generated outside the specified display space (this guaranteed behaviour is referred to as "workstation clipping");
— It supports several linetypes, text fonts, character sizes, etc., to allow output primitives to be drawn with different attributes;
— It has one or more logical input devices for each input class and permits different input modes (see following chapter);
— It stores segments and provides facilities for changing and manipulating them (see Chapter 11).

GKS allows the appearance of output primitives to vary between workstations, thus allowing advantage to be taken of their differing capabilities. The facilities which allow this variation are the attribute bundles (described in Section 7.5) and the indices pointing to bundle entries and the workstation transformation that can be set individually for every workstation. A deferral state allows for controlling the point in time when the updating of the display surface is required (e.g., a plotter may be driven by buffered output while an interactive workstation will display picture changes as soon as possible).

On a workstation, display images will be presented within the display space on the display surface of a display device (e.g., a picture will be displayed within that part of the screen defined as workstation viewport of a storage tube display.)

Display device — Definition
A device (for example, refresh display, storage tube display, plotter) on which display images can be represented.

Display image (picture) — Definition
A collection of display elements or segments that are represented together at any one time on a display surface.

Display surface — Definition
In a display device, that medium on which display images may appear.

Display space — Definition
That portion of the device space corresponding to the area available for displaying images.

9.1   Routing Output to Workstations

The workstations are identified by the application program by using a workstation identifier. In order to establish a connection between the application program and a workstation, that workstation has to be opened. The connection is released and no interactions are possible any longer if the workstation is closed. Output primitives are sent to an open workstation only after it has been activated for output. A function is available for clearing the display surface, i.e., erasing the display image. After deactivation, output will no longer be sent to the workstation. Input can be performed on all open workstations.

The following sequence of functions illustrates workstation selection, it includes the functions for opening and closing GKS:

```
   OPEN GKS;                              {start working}
     OPEN WORKSTATION (N1,...);           {open workstations}
     OPEN WORKSTATION (N2,...);
       ACTIVATE WORKSTATION (N1);         {allow output on N1}
```

Output functions;	{generated only on N1}
Input functions;	{possible on N1,N2}
ACTIVATE WORKSTATION (N2);	{output also on N2 }
Output functions;	{generated on N1,N2}
DEACTIVATE WORKSTATION (N1);	{no more output on N1}
Output functions;	{generated only on N2}
Input functions;	{possible on N1,N2}
DEACTIVATE WORKSTATION (N2);	{no more output}
CLOSE WORKSTATION (N2);	{close workstations}
CLOSE WORKSTATION (N1);	
CLOSE GKS;	{finish working}

9.2   Types of GKS Workstations

Each workstation type falls into one of six categories:
— output workstation, having a display surface for displaying output primitives (e.g., a plotter);
— input workstation, having at least one input device (e.g., a digitizer);
— output/input workstation (having a display surface and at least one input device, also called an interactive graphical workstation);
— workstation-independent segment storage (WISS, see Section 11.5);
— GKS Metafile(GKSM) output (see Chapter 12);
— GKSM input (see Chapter 12).

The last three (workstation-independent segment storage, GKSM output and GKSM input) are special GKS facilities that provide a means for temporarily or permanently storing graphical information. They are treated as workstations for the purposes of control, but otherwise have quite different characteristics.

9.3   The Workstation Transformation

For each open workstation, the application program can select independently some part of the NDC space in the range [0,1]x[0,1] to be displayed somewhere on the workstation display surface. A workstation transformation is a uniform mapping from NDC space onto the device coordinates (DC) for that workstation. Figure 9.1 completes Figure 8.2 to include the workstation transformation.

Whereas the normalization transformation is used for picture composition, the workstation transformation allows different aspects of the composed picture to be viewed on different workstations. For example, a drawing could be output to a plotter at the correct scale and simultaneously some part of the drawing could be displayed on the full display surface of an interactive workstation.

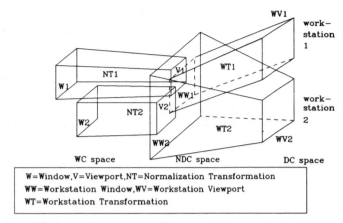

Figure 9.1 Normalization transformation and workstation transformation

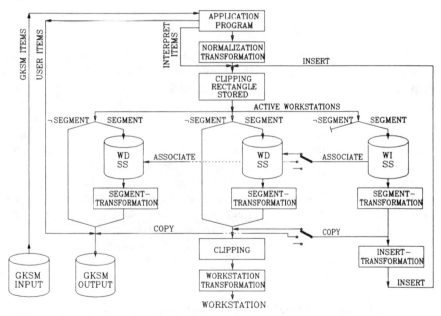

Figure 9.2 Data flow chart for GKS output

The workstation transformation can be reset at any time after the workstation has been opened.

A workstation transformation is specified by defining the limits of an area in the normalized device coordinate system within the range [0,1]x[0,1] (workstation window) which is to be mapped onto a specified area of the device coordinate space (workstation viewport). Workstation window and workstation viewport limits specify rectangles parallel to the coordinate axes in NDC and DC.

Workstation transformation — Definition
   A transformation that maps the boundary and interior of a workstation
   window into the boundary and interior of a workstation viewport (part
   of display space), preserving aspect ratio. Note: In GKS, this transformation
   maps positions in normalized device coordinates to device coordinates.

Workstation window — Definition
   A rectangular region within the normalized device coordinate system which
   is represented on a display space.

Workstation viewport — Definition
   A portion of display space currently selected for output of graphics.
   A complete data flow chart for graphical output is given in Figure 9.2
which is taken from the GKS standard document. For parts of this figure
related to segments and metafiles, refer to Chapters 11 and 12.

9.4   The Deferral State

The display of a workstation should, as far as possible, reflect the actual state
of the picture as defined by the application program. However, to use the
capabilities of a workstation efficiently, GKS allows a workstation to delay,
for a certain period of time, the actions requested by the application program.
During this period, the state of the display may be undefined. A workstation
state variable controlling if and how long such a delay of picture updates is
allowed, is called the deferral state of the workstation. The application program
can change the deferral state. However, appropriate default values are supplied
by the implementation for each workstation type, taking into account the workstation characteristics, e.g., plotter output normally can be buffered, a refresh
display should be updated as quickly as possible, and with a storage tube the
erasing of the screen and redrawing the actual picture may be optimised. The
updating of the display can be forced by the application program (using the
UPDATE WORKSTATION function).

9.5   Addressing Special Workstation Capabilities

Actual workstations may provide more capabilities than those listed in the
workstation description table. These cannot be used by GKS. However, if the
workstation itself provides sufficient intelligence, the additional capabilities may
be accessed via special functions. One such function, already introduced, is
the GENERALIZED DRAWING PRIMITIVE (GDP) that can be used for
creating geometrical output on a workstation. A function to address workstation
capabilities that must not be used for geometrical output is the ESCAPE function. It is a standard way of addressing non-standard features. It could be
used, e.g., to ring a bell at the workstation or to address raster-op hardware.

Escape — Definition
> A function within GKS which is the only access to implementation-dependent or device-dependent support for non-GKS functionality other than graphic output.

Another function that is realized in a workstation-specific way is the MESSAGE-function. It allows a character string to be sent to a workstation. The application program program has no control over the position and appearance of the character string, however, the message has to reach the operator.

10   INPUT

10.1   Interactive Computer Graphics

If a graphics system not only generates pictures on the display surface of a graphical output device, but also obtains input that an operator has entered at a graphical workstation, a new dimension is added to the computer graphics world. It is the dimension of interaction that causes the ever faster growing use of computer graphics devices and systems. The actions of pointing, selecting, sketching, placing or erasing in a direct manner and the instantaneous system response to these actions are truly adapted to the human way of dealing with his environment. Interactive computer graphics allows for such interactions. It is the most powerful instrument to adapt the human-computer interface to human needs. GKS contains functions that allow the input of values from different classes of input devices in different operating modes. The characteristics of different types of physical input devices are mapped on logical input devices in order to address a wide range of equipment in a device-independent way. GKS uses an input model that describes input devices in terms of logical and physical input devices and mappings between them. This model (including measures and triggers of logical input devices) is explained completely in Chapter III.8.

10.2   Logical Input Device Classes

A logical input device provides to the application program a logical input value. The type of input value is determined by the input class.

Logical input device — Definition
> A logical input device is an abstraction of one or more physical devices which delivers logical input values to the program.

Logical input value — Definition
   A value associated with a logical input device, which is determined by one
   or more physical input devices, together with a mapping from the values
   delivered by the physical devices.

Input class — Definition
   A set of input devices that are logically equivalent with respect to their
   function.

Input classes — Definition

   LOCATOR: provides a position in world coordinates. The position is sup-
      plied by the operator by positioning a locator input device (e.g., moving
      a crosshair by a joystick or by positioning a pen on a tablet).

   STROKE: provides a sequence of positions in world coordinates. The posi-
      tions are supplied by the operator by positioning a locator input device
      to a number of different locations.

   VALUATOR: provides a real number. This value is supplied by the operator
      by operating a valuator input device (e.g., by adjusting a potentiometer
      or by entering a number into the keyboard).

   CHOICE: provides a non-negative integer which represents a selection from
      a number of choices. A choice value is supplied by the operator by
      a choosing one possibility at a choice input device (e.g., by pressing
      one of a number of buttons or by pointing at one of the items of a
      menu).

   PICK: provides a segment name and a pick identifier. A segment is picked
      by the operator by pointing at a part of the picture displayed to him
      by the system (e.g., he may use a lightpen or the crosshair positioned
      by a joystick to point to a primitive at the screen). Pick identifiers are
      explained in Chapter 11.

   STRING: provides a character string. A character string is entered by the
      operator via a string input device (the most common string input device
      being an alphanumeric keyboard).

   Of these logical input device classes, only the locator, the stroke, and the
pick input can be called truly graphical. However, for the design of a powerful
interactive communication interface between an application program and an
operator all these classes of input will probably be needed. Therefore, they
have been included in the GKS functionality so that no other additional system
is required for handling the non-graphical interactions.

10.3   Operating Modes

Each logical input device can be operated in one of three different operating
modes. The operating mode is selected by the application program. Only one

of the modes can be used to obtain input from a given logical input device at one time. The three operating modes are REQUEST, SAMPLE and EVENT. Depending on the mode, input values can be entered by the operator and passed to the application program in different ways:

Operating modes — Definition

REQUEST: A specific invocation of an input function in REQUEST mode causes an attempt to read a logical input value from a specified logical input device. GKS waits until the input is either entered by the operator or a break action is performed by the operator. The break action is dependent on the logical input device and on the implementation.

SAMPLE: A specific invocation of a SAMPLE mode input function causes GKS, without waiting for an operator action, to return the current logical input value of a specified logical input device. The device must be in SAMPLE mode.

EVENT: GKS maintains one input queue containing temporally ordered event reports. An event report contains the identification of a logical input device and a logical input value from that device. Event reports are generated asynchronously, by operator action only, from input devices in EVENT mode. The application program can remove the oldest event report from the queue and examine its contents. The application can also flush from the queue all event reports from a specified logical input device.

The request input mode reads input from a graphical workstation in very much the same way as a normal FORTRAN READ would read text input from the terminal. The application program can only request an input from one specific input device at a time. This leads to a dialogue that is completely controlled by the application program, e.g., an operator does not have the freedom to enter a locator or a choice at a given point in time, when using request input. The operator can interrupt the input request by performing an implementation-dependent break action. This could be, e.g., pressing a "break"-key at the workstation. In this case, the application program will be notified that a break has occurred and no valid input value will be supplied.

With the sample and event input modes, the operator can be given the possibility to operate one of several input devices at his own choice. All logical input devices being in sample or event mode are eligible for operator actions. The difference is, that the current value of sample devices can be interrogated by the application program, whether or not the operator has changed the value (or even touched the device), while in event input mode, distinct operator actions are needed to transfer the value of a device to the event queue.

For example, in sample mode, an operator uses a joystick to change the value of a locator input device. The application program can sample this value in a loop to use it to generate a new transformation matrix and to apply it to a group of segments. If the loop is executed fast enough, the operator will have the impression that the segment transformations are directly caused by his operating the joystick. If at the same time the keyboard and a function keyboard are in event mode, the operator may notify the program by these input devices if he wants to modify or finish the ongoing operation. For this purpose, the application program will inspect the event queue every time the loop is executed.

10.4   Echos, Prompts, and Input Device Initialisation

When the application program wants the operator to input an input value, it has to notify him that an action is expected (in request mode) or possible (in sample or event mode). Such an advice to the operator to do something is called a prompt. Prompting could be done by displaying graphics primitives on the display surface, e.g., by a text "enter value", or by the message function. However, there are special prompting capabilities associated with graphical input devices. These capabilities can be controlled by the application program. For locator devices, the prompt may be the appearance of a crosshair or tracking cross, for text the appearance of the alphanumeric cursor, or for a choice device realized by a function keyboard it may be the blinking of the prompting lights.

Prompt — Definition
> Output to the operator indicating that a specific logical input device is available.

If an interaction with an input device is going on, the input device has a value that can be changed by the operator. The operator has to be notified about the current setting of the value. This notification is called the echo. For locator and stroke input devices, the echo could be, e.g., a crosshair or a tracking cross being positioned at the current locator position, for text the visual representation of the text string characters on the screen, for a pick input device the blinking of the currently picked segment. Examples for locator and valuator echoes are shown in Figure 10.1.

Echo — Definition
> The immediate notification of the current value provided by an input device to the operator at the display console.

For request input, the transfer of the current value to the application program has to be caused by a distinct action of the operator, e.g., he presses a button after positioning the locator. For event input, also a distinct action is necessary to cause the transfer of the current value to the event queue. The echo that notifies the operator that such a distinct action has been received is called an acknowledgement.

Acknowledgement — Definition
> Output to the operator of a logical input device that an operator action to indicate a distinct point of time has been received.

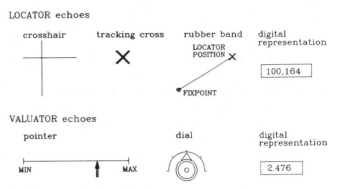

Figure 10.1 Examples for locator and valuator echoes

The echo and the acknowledgement, as well as the prompt, are realized by logical input devices mapped onto physical input devices. The application program can control these indicators as it can turn echoes and prompts on or off and select one of different echo/prompt types present at a particular input device. However, it cannot generate its own new echo/prompt types. If an echo is generated by displaying output primitives after interpretation of the input value by the application program, such an echo is called feedback. In the above example, where segment transformations are derived from a locator input value, the change of the size, orientation or position of segments on the screen is a feedback of the locator movements.

Feedback — Definition
Output indicating to the operator the application program's interpretation of a logical input value.

When an interaction starts with an input device, i.e., an input is requested or sample or event mode is enabled, the logical input value is initialised with an initial value. This value can be set by the application program. If echoing/prompting is turned on, it will reflect the initial value until the value is changed by operator actions.

11   SEGMENTS

11.1   Structuring Pictures

A picture is composed of output primitives. They may be grouped in parts that can be addressed and manipulated as a whole. These picture parts are called segments.

Segment — Definition
A collection of output primitives that can be manipulated as a unit.

If primitives are not collected in segments, the only possible structure is the grouping of primitives in different pictures. A new picture is started when GKS is opened or when the display surface is cleared (the latter may also result automatically when the picture has to be updated).

Each segment is stored on all workstations active at the time the segment is created. "Stored" means, that it is sent to the workstation and that it behaves on that workstation according to the segment manipulations requested by the application program. If a workstation has no real storing capability for segments, the GKS system has to manage the segments for this workstation in such a way that it behaves as if a workstation segment store were present. (This is referred to as a conceptual capability of the workstation).

Segments are identified by a unique name called segment identifier. All output primitives are collected in a segment after it has been created and until it is closed. After a segment is closed, no primitives can be added to or deleted from the segment. No new segment can be created as long as the previous segment is not closed. The output primitives within a segment can have an additional identification that need not be unique. This identification is called a pick identifier. It is part of the input value delivered by a pick input device when a segment is picked. The segment names are specified by the application program when a segment is created. The pick identifiers for the primitives inside the segment are given by a modally set output primitive attribute. The following example illustrates creation and closing of segments as well as the specification of pick identifiers:

```
SET PICK IDENTIFIER (pi4);
CREATE SEGMENT (sega);
    Output functions;                      {segment = sega, pick identifier = pi4}
SET PICK IDENTIFIER (pi2);
    Output functions;                      {segment = sega, pick identifier = pi2}
CLOSE SEGMENT;
    Output functions;                      {primitives not pickable}
                                           {pick identifier = pi2}

SET PICK IDENTIFIER (pi5);
    Output functions;                      {primitives not pickable}
                                           {pick identifier = pi5}

CREATE SEGMENT (segb);
    Output functions;                      {segment = segb, pick identifier = pi5}
SET PICK IDENTIFIER (pi3);
    Output functions;                      {segment = segb, pick identifier = pi3 }
CLOSE SEGMENT;
```

11.2 Manipulating Segments

Segments can be manipulated as a whole by:
— changing their transformation (see Section 11.4);

— changing their priority or by turning off or on their visibility, detectability, or highlighting (see Section 11.3);
— copying them to different workstations or inserting them into other segments (see Sections 11.5, 11.6);
— deleting them;
— renaming them.

Either a segment can be deleted on all workstations on which it is stored or on a specific workstation only. If a segment is deleted from all workstations, it is no longer known to GKS or a workstation and its name may be re-used. Renaming a segment means to replace its name by a new name that is not already used for an existing segment.

11.3   Segment Attributes

Segment attributes are state values that affect all the primitives in a segment as a whole. The segment attributes are visibility, highlighting, detectability, segment priority and the segment transformation. The segment attributes are unique for each segment and may not vary on different workstations. The attributes may be changed for any existing segment, including the open segment.

Segment attributes — Definition
   Attributes that apply only to segments.

Highlighting — Definition
   A device-independent way of emphasising a segment by modifying its visual attributes.

Detectability — Definition
   A segment attribute indicating whether or not a segment is eligible for the pick input function.

Visibility — Definition
   A segment attribute indicating whether or not a segment is displayed on the display surface of workstations. Invisible segments cannot be picked.

Segment priority — Definition
   A segment attribute used to determine which of several overlapping segments takes precedence for graphic output and input.

Segment priority affects segments being displayed only. If parts of primitives overlap with others of a visible segment with higher priority, these parts may be invisible. The realization of this feature is implementation-dependent. When primitives of segments overlapping each other are picked, the segment with higher priority shall be selected. Filled or patterned areas displayed on raster devices will be the most important case for a sensible evaluation of the segment priority. On those devices the picture is composed of an array of pixels, each pixel can only belong to one segment.

11.4   Segment Transformations

The segment transformations are mappings from NDC onto NDC. They perform translation, scaling and rotation.

Segment transformation — Definition
    A transformation which causes the display elements defined by a segment
    to appear with varying position (translation), size (scale), and/or orientation
    (rotation) on the display surface.

Translation — Definition
    The application of a constant displacement to the position of all or part
    of a picture. Note: In GKS, this capability is restricted to segments.

Scaling — Definition
    Enlarging or reducing all or part of a picture by multiplying the coordinates
    of display elements by a constant value. Note: For different scaling in two
    orthogonal directions two constant values are required. Note: In GKS this
    capability is restricted to segments.

Rotation — Definition
    Turning all or part of a picture about an axis. Note: In GKS, this capability
    is restricted to segments.

Segment transformations are specified by a transformation matrix that is
associated with the segment. The transformation matrix is a 2x3 matrix consisting of a 2x2 scaling and rotation portion and a 2x1 translation portion.
Utility functions are available to the application program for setting up the
transformation matrices. Initially, the transformation will be set to the identity
mapping. Because the transformation matrix is stored as part of the segment
state, the original state can be restored by resetting the transformation matrix
back to identity.

The segment transformation takes place after the normalization transformation, but before any clipping. If clipping is turned on, the primitives of the
transformed segment are clipped against the viewport (of the normalization
transformation), which was selected when the primitives were put into the segment (see Figure 9.2 on page 31).

11.5   Workstation-Dependent and Workstation-Independent
Segment Storage

The (conceptual) segment storage on an output or output/input workstation
that allows for change of the segment attributes, including transformation, and
for the deletion of the segment, is called the workstation-dependent segment

storage (WDSS). To allow primitives within a segment to be transferred from one workstation to another or to be inserted into the open segment, one workstation-independent segment storage (WISS) is defined where segments can be stored for use by the copying and insert functions. Only one WISS is permitted in a GKS implementation. The implementor has the choice to realize the WISS in the workstation-independent part of GKS or to utilize the capabilities of an appropriate physical workstation.

The point in the viewing pipeline at which primitives are recorded in the WISS, immediately follows the point at which data are distributed to workstations (see Figure 9.2 on page 31). This is one of the reasons for treating the WISS like a workstation, as far as control functions are concerned. The other reason is that no special functions need to be provided for the control of the WISS, and the programmer does not need to remember another set of function names. Segments are stored in the WISS as long as the WISS is open and active. They are eligible for copying by copy-functions as long as the WISS is not closed (in which case, all stored segments will be deleted). Besides opening and closing, activating and deactivating the WISS workstation, the clear function can be used for the WISS. It will delete all stored segments.

Primitives are transformed from world coordinates to NDC before they are recorded in the WISS. The clipping rectangle (viewport of the normalization transformation) is stored together with the primitives contained in a segment. When the segment is sent to a workstation for display, the recorded clipping rectangles are used to clip the primitives of the segment, if clipping is on.

11.6 Copying Segments

Three functions can use the data in segments in the WISS. None of these functions modify the contents of segments to which they are applied.

COPY SEGMENT TO WORKSTATION makes a copy of each primitive and its associated clipping rectangle in a segment in the WISS, transforms the primitives by the segment transformation and puts the clipping rectangles and the transformed primitives into the viewing pipeline at the place equivalent to the one where the segment was taken off, but on the pathway to the workstation specified in the function call.

ASSOCIATE SEGMENT WITH WORKSTATION sends the segment to the specified workstation to obtain the situation that would hold had the workstation been active when the segment was created.

INSERT SEGMENT copies the primitives in a segment from the WISS and applies the segment transformation followed by a special transformation given in the insert function. The second transformation is called the insert transformation. The primitives are then inserted into the viewing pipeline at the point before data is distributed to the workstations. Thus, inserted information may re-enter the WISS if the WISS is active and a segment is open. All clipping rectangles in the inserted segment are ignored. Each primitive processed is assigned a new clipping rectangle which is the viewport of the currently selected

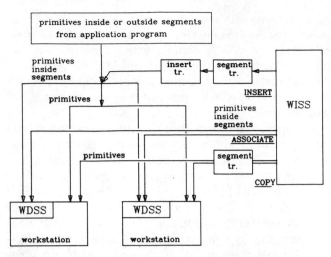

Figure 11.1 COPY-, ASSOCIATE-, and INSERT-function

normalization transformation if clipping is on, i.e., the inserted primitives are treated like directly generated primitives with respect to clipping.

Figure 11.1, which is an excerpt from Figure 9.2, shows the data flow for the copy functions available in GKS.

12   THE GKS METAFILE

12.1   Graphics Metafiles

GKS offers functions for writing a picture on an external file and for retrieving it from there as an integral part of the system. Files that are used for storing pictures are called graphics metafiles. Within the International Organization for Standardization (ISO), working group TC97/SC5/WG2 "Computer Graphics" has set up a metafile subgroup that defined graphics metafiles as follows [ISO81a]:

Graphics metafile — Definition
A graphics metafile is a mechanism for the transfer and storage of graphics data that is both device and application independent.

The metafile that is used by GKS is called the GKS metafile, GKSM.

GKS metafile (GKSM) — Definition

A sequential file that can be written or read by GKS; used for long-term storage (and for transmittal and transferral) of graphical information.

Main reasons for the introduction of graphics metafiles together with graphics systems are:

— The graphics data must be displayable on a number of different display devices. The user should be able to choose among different plotters, output on microfilm, or display screens for the representation of his pictures;

— Graphics data must be retainable for later use. They must be stored in a device independent way, so that the output device can be chosen after the generation of the data;

— Graphics data must be transportable, both by transmitting them over lines and by transporting a storage medium, e.g. a tape;

— Several sources of graphics data exist in most computing environments. Pictures produced as the result of picture processing techniques, of simulation computations or experimental records, using a number of different graphics packages, must be merged into a uniform representation;

— Finally, some way must be provided for editing graphics data that have previously been produced and stored. Editing means: changing, deleting or adding parts of pictures, modifying the visualization of parts of pictures, and merging of pictures.

The main impact of graphics metafiles results from the fact that they are able to interconnect various graphical devices and graphics systems in a standardized and straightforward way. They allow cost-efficient use and sharing of expensive graphical equipment.

The Graphical Kernel System GKS has an interface to the GKS metafile. As part of the standard, the GKS document contains a complete definition of the interface to and from the GKSM. The contents and the format of the GKSM are described in an appendix that is not part of the standard. This separation was done in order to allow for a development of standardized graphics metafile independently of specific systems or devices (without any time pressure).

12.2 The Metafile Interface

The graphics items of the GKSM are generated as the result of the invocation of graphical GKS functions. The user records are written by the function "WRITE USER ITEM TO GKSM". Reading the metafile is performed by GKS under user control. The items are passed to the application program; they can be completely processed there, or they can be skipped. The interpretation of graphics GKSM records can also be left to GKS. In this case, the application program passes them back to GKS and GKS will perform the

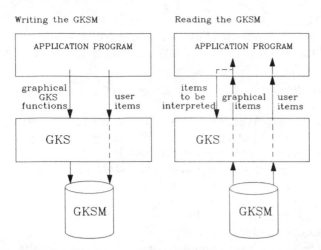

Figure 12.1 Writing and reading the GKSM

function that originally generated the GKSM record (see Figure 12.1). The flexibility and the generality of GKS has gained a great amount by the addition of the metafile interface.

12.3   The Metafile Format

The GKS metafile contains two dimensional pictures. Every picture is represented by a series of data records ("items") that are generated as the result of GKS functions invoked. The GKSM contains items for the output primitives, attributes, together with file header, picture header and end record. Additional to the graphical items, the GKSM contains non-graphical, application dependent data.

The GKSM is built up of a sequence of logical variable length data records. Every record starts with a key denoting the record type. It is followed by the length of the data record, so it can be skipped easily if an interpreter is not interested in a particular record type. The data format for the data values in the GKSM can be chosen in a flexible way. Internal machine code representation is possible as well as formatted representation by ASCII strings. Which format a given GKSM uses is specified in the file header, which is the first record of each metafile. The logical data records are arranged one after the other on physical records that have card image format.

13   STATES AND STATE LISTS

13.1   The GKS Operating State

At any time during execution of a program using GKS, GKS will be in a precisely defined state. The state is given by the operating state and by the values of state variables contained in a number of state lists present in a GKS system. The effects of functions are partly defined as the change of values in state lists that is caused by their invocation. The operating state has one of the following five values:
— GKS closed;
— GKS open;
— At least one workstation open;
— At least one workstation active;
— Segment open.

The transition from one state to the other is caused by control functions called by the application program, e.g., the function OPEN GKS will change the GKS state from "GKS closed" to "GKS open" (if the state is "GKS closed" when the function is called). Depending on the operating state, calling a specific GKS function is allowed or not. Figure 13.1 summarizes the state transitions and the functions allowed in every one of the states.

13.2   The State Lists

Whereas the GKS operating state is a global value that is available even if GKS is closed, the other state variables are allocated, initialised, and freed as an effect of GKS function calls. The following state lists are present in GKS:

GKS state list: Allocated and initialised by OPEN GKS, deleted by CLOSE GKS, present once in a GKS implementation;

Segment state list: Allocated and initialised by CREATE SEGMENT, deleted when the segment is deleted, present for every existing segment;

Workstation state list: Allocated and initialised by OPEN WORKSTATION, deleted by CLOSE WORKSTATION, present for every open workstation;

Error state list: Allocated and initialised by OPEN GKS, deleted by CLOSE GKS, present once in a GKS implementation;

Input queue: Allocated and initialised by OPEN GKS, deleted by CLOSE GKS, present once in a GKS implementation that offers event input capabilities.

The values in the state lists describe the state of GKS at any one time. In the course of a GKS application, the state list values will change. Additionally, GKS contains description tables with static values that will not change during a GKS application. The GKS description table contains information about the GKS implementation, e.g., GKS level. The workstation description table contains information about the workstations available in an implementation:

— GKS description table: Static table set up by the implementation, present once;
— Workstation description table: Static table set up by the implementation, present for every available workstation type (except WISS and GKSM workstations).

13.3   Inquiring State List Values

All values contained in one of the GKS state lists or in one of the description tables can be interrogated by the application program. The functions used for this purpose are called inquiry functions. As an example, a subroutine that belongs to the application layer of a program package can inquire the state of the system and save the state variables. It can then change the state, e.g., by changing attribute values. Before returning to the calling program, it could use the saved variables to reset the system to the previous state.

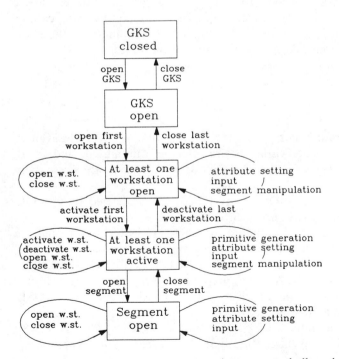

Figure 13.1 Transitions between operating states and allowed functions

14   ERROR HANDLING

With every GKS function, errors that are anticipated are listed together with
the function description. Every GKS implementation must realize an error handling facility that is able to discover these errors and record at least one of
the errors that have occurred in a message file. There the identification of
the error and the identification of the GKS function detecting the error will
be filed. The application program can replace the GKS standard error handling
procedure by its own routine that can perform specific error reactions. The
user error procedure is supplied by GKS with the error identification and the
identification of the error detecting GKS routine. It can also inspect the GKS
state list by using inquiry functions.

Part II

THE PROCESS OF GENERATING A STANDARD

Part II describes the process of GKS design. Chapter 1 traces the development of computer graphics to the state allowing a successful effort for standardization. Chapter 2 lists in detail the series of steps taken in developing and processing GKS until reaching the status of a standard. This development, by far, was not straightforward. Concepts and functionality, laid down in existing graphics systems and in literature, were examined carefully to select those which would be included in the standard kernel system. Chapter 3 attempts to describe the major points of discussion and the design decisions which were passed in establishing the contents of GKS. This chapter gives useful background information to understand why some features are included in GKS, why other useful concepts and features have been omitted, and why some features are included in a particular form.

1   THE EVOLUTION OF COMPUTER GRAPHICS

Before a standard can be established, a field must mature:
— a sufficiently large constituency for a standard must exist to justify the effort;
— common understanding of the field and commonly accepted practices must exist as a basis for standardization.

Computer graphics has existed a long time without formal standards. In the early days of computers, cathode ray tubes and plotters were the only graphics devices. Cathode ray tubes had only restricted capabilities and were expensive and, therefore, were rare. The users of plotting devices could live with the software provided by the vendors. The software interface provided by the main vendors became a 'de facto' standard in computer graphics.

By the advent of low cost interactive graphics devices in the 1960s, the situation of computer graphics changed drastically. The new devices offered interesting capabilities but it was not clear how these capabilities should be addressed. The integration of graphics in interactive programming was a challenge for many research workers and led to the development of a variety of graphics systems. This point can be regarded as the outset of computer graphics as a discipline.

1.1   Graphical Devices

The first interactive displays were cathode ray tubes (CRT) with vector generator and lightpen or tablet as interactive devices. These *vector refresh displays* possess deflection and intensity control circuitry which permits the drawing of a vector between any two addressable points on the screen. To get a stable image, the whole drawing has to be refreshed at least every 1/30 second. Therefore, the number of vectors is limited to that number which can be generated within 1/30 second. To increase the number of displayable vectors, fast vector generators had to be constructed which made the systems very expensive. Furthermore, the refresh necessity requires high data transfer rates which can be provided by expensive high speed channel interfaces only. Therefore, vector refresh display systems were used typically in special applications where the price was not the decisive factor, e.g., in turnkey systems for computer-aided design (CAD) in automobile and aerospace industries.

In the late 1960s, inexpensive *storage tubes* came onto the market which made interactive graphics affordable for many people. Storage tubes also use

CRTs but the displayed image is stored as electrostatic charges on a mesh within the tube which makes refreshing of the image obsolete. Slower vector generator circuitry can be used as there is no necessity of generating the whole image within 1/30 second. Furthermore, inexpensive terminal interfaces with low baud rates connected to a timesharing computer are sufficient. The number of displayable vectors is no longer limited and vectors are drawn with higher precision. The main disadvantage of storage tubes is that information on the screen can be removed only by erasing the whole screen and redrawing that information which is to be retained. As a consequence of the slow interfaces, the redrawing may take some time. Dynamic manipulations in real time are not possible.

In the mid 1970s, *raster displays* on television technology appeared which added new features to computer graphics. Whereas vector refresh displays and storage tubes are calligraphic devices which build up an image from line elements, raster displays accept a matrix of intensity values. These values are stored in a frame buffer from which they are permanently read out; a video signal is generated from the intensity values and fed to a standard television monitor. With raster devices it is possible to display solid areas and provide a full colour facility. Colour can be manipulated dynamically via a colour table. Line drawings have to be converted into raster format before they can be stored in the frame buffer. Raster devices accept an arbitrary number of vectors limited only by the resolution of the device which usually is smaller than that of other device types. The capabilities for dynamic image manipulations are better than for storage tubes as the frame buffer can be updated locally. Changes which affect the whole frame buffer, however, still take some time and cannot be done within one refresh cycle.

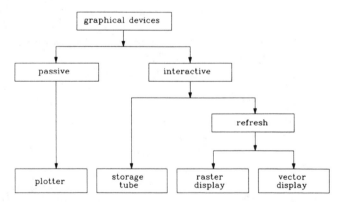

Figure 1.1 Major types of graphical devices

1.2 Graphics Software

The different types of graphics hardware offer a variety of capabilities, which, at first glance, seem to be incompatible. At the outset, it was not clear what were the primitive functions of each device and how these primitive functions could be correlated. Therefore, the graphics software developed for different types of equipment looked quite different as peculiarities of equipment became visible at the functional interface. For efficiency reasons, application-specific requirements were implemented within the graphics system and special features of an operating system were integrated. The lack of a common model of a graphics system and its functionality gave rise to the formation of different "schools" of graphics system design [NEWM78]. The graphics systems at that time tended to be:

— device-dependent;
— application-dependent;
— environment-dependent.

As a consequence, graphics software could be used exclusively at the installation where it was developed. The introduction of graphics devices with new features often resulted in a reprogramming of large parts of the graphics software.

A further point of divergence was the way graphics functionality was offered to the application program. Three main strategies were used:

— designing a graphics language;
— designing a graphics extension to an existing high level language;
— designing a subroutine package callable from existing high level languages.

The design of a new graphics language gives full freedom in providing any comfort to the programmer. However, the introduction of a new programming language is a difficult task as a sufficient large constituency must be found which supports the new language. Experience has shown that this way did not work.

The design of a graphics extension is a less complex task. Therefore, language extensions have been made for all major programming languages. The inclusion of graphics commands within the body of a programming language has the advantage that a thorough error check at compile time is possible and that the compiler has more possibilities to optimise the code.

The problem appears that the compiler must be modified. This reasonably can be done by the compiler provider only as future compiler versions should include the additional functionality. It is not easy to convince the clientele of a programming language to accept new features as the overhead has to be paid by all users whether they use graphics or not. The programming language BASIC is an example where the attempt is made to include graphics feature into the standard definition.

A subroutine package is the less elegant solution. The definition of graphical objects and operations via parameter list is not very appealing, errors will be detected mostly at run time only, and the performance will not be optimal. However, this way is the only which can be taken without interfering with other interests. Therefore, this way is anticipated when designing the standard.

In the beginning of interactive graphics, typically each owner of a graphics device developed his own graphics software with the intention of using the available resources in an optimal way. Graphics conferences were overwhelmed by presentations of new graphical systems. A typical question from the audience was: "Are you the only living user of your system?", a question which often had to be affirmed [NAKE72]. This waste of software was tolerable as long as the software investment was smaller than the expenses for hardware, as long as each new language really could offer some slight improvements, and as long as common agreement on the functionality of graphics systems could not be found.

However, by the advent of low cost devices and by a widespread use of graphics devices, this situation was no longer tolerable. People wanted to use their graphics devices instead of developing graphics systems. Furthermore, they wanted to exchange programs with colleagues rather than rewriting each routine for their local installation. This was reasonable as, in the meantime, a convergence in graphics systems functionality had become visible. Graphics seemed to be mature for standardization.

The standardization efforts started with a discussion about the objectives of standardization. Two alternatives were considered [ENCA81b]:
— standardize output primitives, input primitives and data structures starting from the current body of knowledge;
— develop a common model and design methodology before standardizing details of a graphics system.

The first approach considered the main interfaces within a graphical system. Some agreement surely could be found and would improve portability of graphics programs.

The second approach naturally would take more time. However, a common model and terminology would facilitate the task of defining primitives and data structures and would secure a higher degree of consistency.

1.3   SEILLAC I

In this situation, the Graphics Subcommittee WG 5.2 of the International Federation for Information Processing (IFIP) began an effort to establish a graphics methodology. Some 25 experts from Europe and Northern America were invited to participate at a workshop about "Methodology in Computer Graphics" which took place in Seillac (France) and became known under the title SEILLAC I [GUED76]. This workshop discussed a series of central issues of graphics standardization and formulated some principles which influenced the subsequent standardization efforts.

The discussion about the objectives of a standard led to a more precise definition of the term 'portability'. Portability can be achieved in at least four different areas:
— portability of application programs;
— device independency;
— portability of picture data;
— portability of education.

The portability of application programs was the primary target of the standardization effort. It can be achieved by standardizing the interface between kernel system and application program. By defining logical input/output primitives as abstractions of the available device capabilities, it is possible to specify a second interface, the interface between kernel system and device driver. This will make the kernel system device independent (see Figure 1.2). Devices may be exchanged without disastrous consequences.

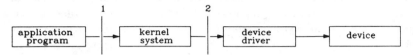

Figure 1.2 Interfaces of a graphics system

Another discussion concerned what functions should be included in the kernel and what functions should be in the application program area. The distinction was characterized by the terms:
— graphics system and
— modelling system.

The modelling system allows objects to be defined in their own coordinate system. A model of the viewed object is generated in a reference coordinate system called world coordinate system (WC). The task of the graphics system is the mapping of the model onto a display surface.

When discussing the functionality of the graphics system in detail, two strategies can be adopted:
— define a basic graphics system;
— define a rich graphics system.

In the first case, only a minimum set of functions necessary to access the facilities of the graphics devices would be included. In the latter case, graphics functions would be included according to the principle "what is good for most programmers and most interactive displays most of the time" [NEWM78].

Another important goal discussed at SEILLAC I was whether a formal specification technique should be adopted for the specification of the planned standard. The value of such techniques was well understood and further work in this area was encouraged (cf. Part IV, Chapter 7).

The SEILLAC I workshop gave a strong impulse for the standardization work undertaken in the Graphics Standard Planning Committee of ACM-SIG-GRAPH and in diverse national and international standardization bodies.

2 COMMITTEES, PEOPLE AND EVENTS

2.1 Graphics Standardization Committees

On the background of the evolution of different graphics packages and based on the desire to start activities in the field of Computer Graphics standardization, working groups and formal committees started working about 1975. Major efforts were untertaken in the United States, in Germany, in the United Kingdom, and internationally in the International Organization for Standardization (ISO).

Influenced by the hardware and the software developments in the Computer Graphics area and by international discussions on Computer Graphics methodology and terminology, the Standardization Committee for Information Processing (Normenausschuß Informationsverarbeitung, NI) of the DIN (Deutsches Institut für Normung) founded the subcommittee DIN-NI/UA-5.9 "Computer Graphics" in 1975. It was directed to promote the development of Computer Graphics standards [ENCA81b]. The committee originally had 13 members, the first chairman was José Encarnação. He was the moving force of the GKS development — accompanying, directing and protecting it with dedication and persistence until it reached maturity (he truly can be called the "Kernel of the Kernel System"). José Encarnação held this office until October 1981. He was followed by Günter Enderle. DIN-NI/UA-5.9 presented the first draft of GKS in 1977, since then the committee invested an enormous effort into redesigning, extending and reviewing GKS. The history and the background of the committee is best documented by the contributions in [ENCA81a].

In the United States, standardization efforts first were concentrated in the Special Interest Group "Computer Graphics" of the Association for Computing Machinery (ACM-SIGGRAPH). It founded in 1974 the "Graphics Standards Planning Committee" (GSPC) that was chaired since then by Bob Dunn, Robert Heilmen and Bert Herzog. In the years 1975 to 1979, GSPC designed two versions of a three-dimensional graphical system called GSPC or "Core System" [GSPC77, GSPC79]. In 1979, the graphics standardization activities in the United States were taken over by the American National Standards Institute that established the Committee ANSI X3H3 "Computer Graphics" with Peter Bono as chairman. The transfer of activities from SIGGRAPH to ANSI has caused an interruption in graphics standardization in the United States, however, the SIGGRAPH know-how was transferred to the ANSI X3H3 committee by a group of experts that were members of GSPC and became members of X3H3. X3H3 was one of the major contributors to the long, and sometimes controversial, reviewing process of GKS.

In the United Kingdom, graphics standardization is the task of the working group OIS/5/WG5 "Computer Graphics" (formerly DPS/13/WG5) of the British Standards Institute (BSI). The working group was established in 1978, chaired by David Fisher. Since 1980, David Rosenthal is chairman of OIS/5/WG5. The committee co-ordinates UK opinions on graphics standards and is one of the important contributors to the work on computer graphics within

ISO. BSI contributed largely to the GKS review and editing process and to the task of bringing the GKS document into an excellent form.

Many other standardization bodies have contributed to the GKS design and review process. This process was concentrated in a working group of the International Organization for Standardization (ISO) that was established in 1977. Mainly influenced by the Seillac I workshop on Computer Graphics Methodology [GUED76], by the SIGGRAPH Graphics Standards Planning Committee, and by the work started in the DIN-NI/UA-5.9 (in the context of this book: DIN), the working group TC97/SC5/WG2 "Computer Graphics" of the ISO was founded. TC97 is the ISO Technical Committee for Data Processing, TC97/SC5 is the Subcommittee that covers all aspects of programming, the scope of TC97/SC5/WG2 (in the context of this book: WG2) is Computer Graphics. The founding chairman of WG2 was David Fisher (UK), followed by Paul ten Hagen (NL) in August 1977. He led the working group until 1983, and without his outstanding leadership, his integrity and devotion, we would not have a graphics standard today.

The member countries of WG2 are: Austria, Canada, Finland, France, Germany F.R.G., Hungary, Italy, Netherlands, Norway, Switzerland, United Kingdom, and United States of America. Also, experts from the following countries participated: Belgium, Denmark, Germany G.D.R., and Japan.

In 1978, WG2 reviewed both the GSPC and GKS proposals, then, 1979, GKS was selected as the starting point for an international standard (however, many concepts and functions of GKS originate from the GSPC proposal). Since then, WG2 was the focal point of Computer Graphics standardization.

In order to create an international standard, certain formal rules must be followed. A standard is developed in several successive steps; formal votes are required to reach the next step towards a standard. The voting is done by letter ballot. Only official member bodies of the ISO committees are allowed to vote. For GKS, these are the member bodies of ISO TC97 and of ISO TC97/SC5. The following are the steps to reach an international standard [HAGE81]:

1. *Exploration:* The need for a standard in some area is recognized, the state of the art is analysed.
2. *Work Item:* A subject for standardization has to be accepted by a Letter Ballot. In most cases, a first draft is already available.
3. *Working Draft:* A draft is available. A national body (the sponsoring body) is responsible for updating, changing and distributing the draft.
4. *Draft Proposal (DP):* A working group (e.g., WG2) considers the draft to be sufficiently complete for a standard. The Subcommittee (e.g., SC5) asks the ISO secretariat to register the draft as a DP.
5. *Draft International Standard (DIS):* All technical objections against a DP have been resolved. There are no violations of existing standards. A Letter Ballot on the Subcommittee-level is required (e.g., within SC5).
6. *International Standard (IS):* All comments received on the DIS Letter Ballot have been answered. The DIS is approved in a final Letter Ballot both on the Subcommittee and the Technical Committee level (e.g., SC5 and TC97). The draft is registered as an ISO standard. The draft must be available in English and French.

To pass on from one of these steps to the next, an agreement is necessary within the body concerned. Obviously, it is not an easy or trivial task to reach agreement amongst the international community in such a fast developing and spreading field.

2.2 People

About 100 experts from 16 nations participated in the GKS design and review. Naturally, there was an active kernel of about 30 persons that brought GKS on the way to be an international standard. An enormous amount of work was invested in the design and review process of GKS. In the first years, this work was conducted primarily by the editorial subgroup of the DIN committee. Later the GKS review subgroup of WG2 and in the final stage the editorial subgroup of WG2, assisted by the English language and typesetting experts of BSI, were doing the bulk of the workload. Most of the group meetings were characterized by working hours extending well past midnight and a common commitment to produce in time a result acceptable to all participants. Conflicts arose where one participating country or another declared it impossible to support the standard if certain technical changes were not incorporated in the draft. It is the outstanding achievement of experts within WG2 that created a standard acceptable to all, and yet still kept it consistent and based on clear and clean concepts.

There is another aspect of international cooperation within WG2 during the GKS design process that surely deserves our attention, but that cannot be dealt with in a technical book like this: The social relations within a group of people that over the years work hard together on a subject that often gives rise to conflicts. The stories about the GKS people, their ups and downs, their interrelation in the technical and in the non-technical field, their victories and defeats and their endeavours to humanize the work, could well fill another book. A network of deep friendship and common understanding has been established between the WG2 experts spanning over borders and oceans. This was one basis for resolving conflicts, removing obstacles and accomplishing results towards the first international standard in Computer Graphics.

2.3 Overview over Main Events

The following is a schedule of meetings, major events and decisions in the development of the Graphical Kernel System (partly taken from [ENCA81b]). Whereas in the first years, the main activities favoured the side of the DIN-NI/ UA-5.9, since 1979, the GKS design centred more around ISO TC97/SC5/WG2.

April 1975 DIN-NI/UA-5.9 founded	The DIN subcommittee 5.9 is directed to promote Computer Graphics standardization and to develop Computer Graphics concepts based on existing Computer Graphics systems.

1976 Seillac I workshop (France)	In Seillac (France), IFIP working group WG5.2 organizes a workshop on Computer Graphics Methodology. A reference model for a Computer Graphics system is developed. The separation of "core" and "modelling" capabilities is advocated.
1977 ISO TC97/SC5/WG2 founded	Working group "Computer Graphics" of ISO is established. First chairman: D. Fisher (UK).
July 1977 GKS version 1	GKS version 1 is presented to an international community. It contains output only.
August 1977 WG2 meeting Toronto (Canada)	Proposals considered by WG2 are GSPC, GKS and IDIGS (proposed by Norway). Paul ten Hagen is elected chairman.
September 1978 WG2 meeting Bologna (Italy)	GKS version 2 containing output and event input is presented. The editorial board is established. Principles and concepts for evaluating Computer Graphics system proposals are formulated.
November 1978 GKS version 3	GKS version 3 containing output and request input is distributed within WG2.
February 1979 WG2 Editorial Board meeting Amsterdam (The Netherlands)	Evaluation of GSPC and GKS version 3; 24 recommendations are made to GKS, 10 to GSPC.
March 1979 DIN workshop Pulvermühle (Bavaria/Germany)	GKS version 4.8 is designed on the base of version 3, on WG2 recommendations, and DIN decisions. Inclusion of levels, inquiry-functions, GDP, raster primitives, two-stage transformation, metafile, event and sample input.
June 1979 ANSI X3H3 founded	The ANSI committee "Computer Graphics" is established. Chairman: Peter Bono. Takes GSPC as a base for Computer Graphics standardization.
October 1979 WG2 meeting Budapest (Hungary)	WG2 recommends to DIN to forward the GKS proposal as a work item to the ISO. BSI starts efforts on certification. Level 0 GKS is introduced. As a result of Budapest, DIN prepares GKS version 5.2.
Early 1980 GKS version 6.0	DIN gets 307 international comments on GKS version 5.2. They are used to create GKS version 6.0.
June 1980 WG2 meeting Tiefenbach (Bavaria/Germany)	GKS review based on version 6.0 and the international comments. As a result of agreed changes, DIN prepares GKS version 6.2.

July 1980 WG2 Editorial Board meeting Seattle (USA)	A procedure is agreed on to process GKS to an international standard. The GKS review subgroup of WG2 is established. Chairmen: Rens Kessener (NL) and David Rosenthal (UK).
October 1980 GKS is Work Item	ISO/TC97 "Computers and Information processing" accepts in a Letter Ballot without any negative votes GKS as an ISO Work Item.
Fall 1980 German translation of GKS 6.2	Version 6.2 of GKS is translated into German in order to prepare a DIN national standard.
December 1980 GKS Association founded	As a GKS users organization, and for GKS dissemination and education, the GKS Association (GKS-Verein) is founded in Germany (F.R.G.).
January 1981 WG2 review meeting Melbourne (Florida/USA)	The GKS review subgroup of WG2 processes 165 comments ("issues") raised by the WG2 member bodies on GKS version 6.2.
May 1981 working draft	GKS version 6.4 is registered by SC5 as first working draft.
May 1981 GKS version 6.6	Based on the resolved issues of the WG2 review meeting in Melbourne, the new GKS version 6.6 is prepared by DIN and finalized at an editorial meeting in Amsterdam.
October 1981 WG2 meeting Abingdon (UK)	GKS 6.6 is reviewed based on 152 international issues. All issues are solved and during the meeting, resulting in GKS version 7.0. This version is the base for the DIS Letter Ballot.
March 1982 DIN FORTRAN Interface for GKS 7.0	DIN prepares a proposal for a FORTRAN binding of GKS 7.0. This FORTRAN interface is distributed for commenting by WG2.
March 1982 French Translation of GKS 7.0	The French translation is started. It is additionally required to the English version for every ISO standard.
May 1982 GKS is DIS	In a Letter Ballot, ISO TC97/SC5 approves GKS as Draft International Standard (ISO DIS 7942).
June 1982 WG2 meeting Steensel (The Netherlands)	WG2 considers and answers 71 comments received with the DIS Letter Ballot. Final changes to the GKS document are agreed on (dual attribute binding model, stroke input, character alignment).
June 1982 German translation of GKS 7.0	Within DIN, the German translation of GKS is updated to version 7.0.

July 1982 GKS is DIN Draft	Version 7.0 of GKS is issued in its original English version Standard as a DIN Draft Standard (Entwurf DIN ISO 7942).
October 1982 GKS accepted for ANSI standardization	The American National Standards Institute committee X3H3 "Computer Graphics" votes to forward GKS as a draft proposed American National Standard.
December 1982 Final GKS document	The final version of the GKS standard is prepared at Rutherford Laboratories (UK).
Spring 1982 Final Letter Ballot	The Letter Ballot procedure for the GKS International Standard is started. All member bodies of ISO TC97 and TC97/SC5 have the opportunity to vote.
1983 GKS is IS	The GKS International Standard (ISO IS 7942) is scheduled before the end of 1983. For the final approval by ISO, the French translation is mandatory.

3   GKS REVIEW — ISSUES AND THEIR SOLUTION

In the beginning, the GKS document was developed within DIN according to the following scheme:
— The DIN committee comprising some 20 people discussed major design issues of the GKS concept and gave directives to an editorial board.
— An editorial board comprising four persons of the DIN committee discussed the consequences of the global decisions and worked out in detail the changes to the document.
— The document was compiled and maintained by one person.

This scheme gave the DIN committee the means to control the global direction of the GKS design. It gave sufficient freedom to the editorial board to choose the best way of implementing the concepts. If new aspects or implications became visible during elaboration, the editorial board had the authority to decide it on its own. The integrity of the whole document was controlled by one person having exclusive access to the document.

Thus, the conceptual integrity of the document was guaranteed while allowing relatively easy development of the document as only four persons had to find a common position. However, this scheme had some disadvantages:
— The only response the DIN committee got on its directives was the new document. This was feasible as long as the document was of a moderate size. When the document grew from version to version, it became more and more difficult to see how a specific feature had been implemented and what parts of the document had been affected.

— When new persons became involved with GKS, many decisions had to be rediscussed because the history of decision finding, the alternatives which had been considered and the arguments which led to the final decision, were not available.

These problems became more pronounced when GKS was discussed within WG2. In ISO, much work is done by correspondence and meetings take place once a year. Furthermore, ISO puts some importance on unanimous agreement. When processing a standard, each member is asked to give his comments on the draft. Each comment must be processed and a satisfactory (not necessarily a positive) answer must be given to the originator of a comment.

To support the commenting process, a formal reviewing procedure was established [ROSE80] which helped to structure the discussion within WG2 and made transparent to everybody the decisions taken. The reviewing procedure was adopted from a scheme proven successful in developing the GSPC CORE proposal.

At first, the right of the sponsoring body (i.e., the national standardization body submitting the document) to change arbitrarily the document was restricted: One version of the document was declared by WG2 the *current draft* which was the working base of the next work and which, therefore, had to remain unchanged until one stage of the reviewing procedure had been passed and WG2 explicitly requested the sponsoring body to generate a new version.

After a current draft had been established, all interested individuals were invited to comment the document. To secure quality of comments, an issue presented by an individual had to be filtered by a national body before it could be passed to WG2. The comments were collected in an *active issue list*. Each entry in this list had to conform to a given format containing the following items:

1. a title expressed as a question which briefly describes the issue;
2. at least one search key taken from the established graphics terminology (see Appendix 2) identifying the subject area;
3. a category selected from:

   disagreement: The commentator prefers a change of the content of the document.

   omission: The commentator suggests the addition of some feature or description to the document.

   inconsistency: The commentator identifies conflicting features in the document.

   ambiguity: The commentator believes that some parts of the document can be interpreted in multiple ways.

   question: The commentator requests to clarify incomprehensible parts of the document.

4. a detailed explanation of the issue;
5. an enumeration of possible alternatives to be taken for solving the issue;
6. list of arguments for or against some alternative resolution;
7. originator and date.

Items 4, 5, and 6 were optional.

When all comments had been gathered, WG2 had a technical discussion of all issues. The originator, as well as other parties, were invited to add material and arguments to any issue and refine it until a decision could be taken. The decision taken was added as item 8 to the issue and the issue was moved from the active issues list to the *resolved issues list*. All changes to the document required by a resolution of an issue had to be written down explicitly in a *change list*.

The resolved issue list documented all areas where a consensus had been reached. It contained all arguments considered in taking a specific decision. People with different opinions had the possibility to inspect this list as to whether all relevant aspects had been taken into account. For later stages, this list helped to avoid rediscussion of resolved issues. A resolved issue could be revisited only if completely new arguments could be provided.

The objective of the technical discussion was to move as many issues as possible from the active issues list to the resolved issue list. After a discussion round, WG2 requested the sponsoring body to generate a new version of the document containing all changes from the change list. This new version then became the current draft and was subject to another commenting phase. This process was iterated until the active issue list became empty.

During processing GKS in WG2, 307 issues were created in the exploratory stage; 165 and 152 issues were discussed in two stages of formal reviewing; 71 comments were produced during the formal voting procedure for GKS. The sets of issues partially overlapped as unresolved issues automatically reappeared in the subsequent stage. All issues were processed successfully.

To understand well the background of the GKS concept, a look to the development of GKS is very helpful. In the following sections, some major issues discussed during GKS design will be traced. The alternatives inspected and the arguments taken into consideration, together with the final decisions taken, will clarify the underlying concepts of GKS and explain how a specific solution has been found.

More information will be found in DIN and ISO documents. An overview about people and application areas contributing to the GKS design is given by [ENCA81a]. Major parts of the GKS design were evaluated by an early GKS implementation [WISS78], the experiences of which stimulated the development of GKS. For example, the removal of the current position, primitives outside segments, and a two-stage transformation pipeline were demanded in [WISS79]. The major steps of ISO GKS review are documented in [HAGE79, ISO80, ISO81b,c,d]. As GKS has many features in common with the GSPC CORE proposal, the issues discussed in this context [GSPC77, GSPC79, MICH78] will mostly apply also for GKS, although some issues have been decided in a different way.

3.1 Scope of the Standard

The initial points of discussion were focused around the problem of how to define the scope of the intended standard. Criteria like "what is good for most programmers on most existing interactive displays most of the time" [GSPC77] gave guidelines but no strict rules for inclusion or exclusion of concepts.

Graphics Versus Modelling: How Can the Graphics System Be Separated from Application-Specific Parts?

An important result of the SEILLAC I workshop [GUED76] was the distinction between the *graphics system* and the *modelling system*. The modelling system allows objects to be defined in their own coordinate system and to create a model in world coordinates. This modelling will depend strongly on the data structures and operations used in a specific application area. Therefore, different modelling systems will be required. The graphics system is responsible for the mapping of the model onto the display surface. To describe its functionality, the paradigm of a synthetic camera is used in the GSPC Core Proposal [GSPC77].

However, as useful as this distinction between graphics system and modelling system was at the beginning of standardization, as impeding were the long discussions whether a function was modelling or graphics each time a new function was to be included. It was found that the modelling issue cannot be kept completely separate from graphics design [NEWM78]. As a result, some basic modelling functions are included in the kernel and the questions, "what is modelling?" and "what is graphics?" were postponed until the design of the kernel had been finished. Then a precise definition of modelling and graphics can be given: Everything inside the kernel is graphics; everything outside is modelling.

2D Versus 3D: Should GKS Support Three-Dimensional Primitives?

Another important issue of the first days was whether the intended standard should serve 2D graphics only, or should include 3D graphics also. It was agreed that in the future compatible standards for both were required. However, it was not clear whether 2D should be standardized first and a 3D extension subsequently or whether a 3D standard was needed first from which a 2D subset could be extracted easily. Some arguments from this discussion are:

Pro 2D:
— Majority of applications require 2D only; this majority should not pay the extra cost for 3D.
— Almost all display surfaces are 2D; when using a 2D display finally, 3D can be built as a modelling system on top of a 2D system.
— There are many 3D applications where the application-dependent part extends to the 2D interface.
— Agreement can be achieved more easily for 2D graphics than for 3D.

Pro 3D:
— The constituency of 3D graphics is growing rapidly and will be a majority within a few years.
— Defining 3D first secures a full compatibility between 2D and 3D.

Con 2D:
— How can it be secured that the 2D standard can be extended to 3D?

The resolution was to deal with 2D only and postpone 3D. The work of GSPC on the 3D Core Proposal provided sufficient information about the requirements from 3D which could be considered in defining the 2D standard.

3.2 Output Primitives

Should GKS Support the Concept of a Current Position (CP)?

Many graphics systems maintain a register containing the current position of the drawing utensil. Primitives may be defined relatively to this position, e.g., LINE_TO (X,Y) draws a line from the current position to the specified position which is stored in the register as new current position. Some arguments from this discussion are:

Pro CP:
— CP is accepted practice.
— CP allows an easy concatenation of character strings.
— CP takes advantage of the capabilities of vector devices where a CP is defined by the device.
— CP permits the use of relative coordinates. In particular, a subroutine for drawing symbols can profit from the possibility of relative drawing.
— CP is useful when mixing 2D and 3D output primitives.
— CP decreases the number of parameters of output primitives.

Con CP:
— There are many possible definitions for a CP: CP can be maintained in WC, NDC, or DC and, furthermore, CP can be taken from the clipped or unclipped primitive. Most effective is a clipped CP in DC. However, there will be a different CP for different devices. Well-defined is an unclipped CP in WC. However, this CP gives no access to the device's CP; it is a syntactic abbreviation rather than a semantic concept.
— CP means some overhead for non-vector devices where the CP has to be calculated rather than be taken from a device's register.
— CP is not clearly defined after TEXT, FILL AREA, or CELL ARRAY primitives. If CP is not affected by these primitives, it cannot be used, e.g., to concatenate character strings which removes one 'pro' argument.
— Change of transformations may affect the CP.
— By the CP, one output primitive influences subsequent output primitives. Provision must be taken that this side effect does not carry over segment boundaries as the deletion of a segment shall not influence other segments.
— CP is equivalent to an accumulator in assembly language programming. Output primitives should be defined at a higher level. The definition of a primitive should be more self contained.

It was agreed that having no CP is cleaner, more consistent, and less confusing. Therefore, GKS does not include the concept of a CP.

Should GKS Have Optional Output Primitives like CIRCLE and INTERPOLATING CURVE ?

From the very beginning of GKS, people had required more output primitives than provided by GKS. CIRCLE and INTERPOLATING CURVE are two prominent examples requested by sufficiently large user groups.

However, it needs some efforts to implement these functions if not provided by the workstation. A CIRCLE may degenerate to an ellipse by transformations. This mandates implementation of ellipses rather than circles. Interpolation usually requires the solution of systems of linear equations. Besides these implementation cost arguments, another argument against the introduction of new primitives was the difficulty to draw a line against further requests.

On the other hand, these primitives cannot easily be built on top of the kernel system. The approximation of these curves by POLYLINE should be done workstation-dependent according to the current setting of transformations and the resolution and type of the display surface (low quality approximation for interactive workstations; high quality approximation for plotter).

The compromise, having optional output primitives for some workstations, contradicts several design principles of GKS and reduces the portability of programs. However, it was decided to adopt the compromise as it is better to have limited portability with well identified incompatibilities than programs totally ignoring the standard. The optional primitives were collected into one output primitive called GENERALIZED DRAWING PRIMITIVE (GDP). By this decision, the possible incompatibilities were concentrated in one primitive. If new optional primitives are required, the GDP can be extended easily.

Strict rules were formulated to insure that the optional primitives behave like the other output primitives with respect to transformations, clipping, and segment storage.

Should CELL ARRAY Be an Output Primitive?

The CELL ARRAY primitive had been introduced to respond to the growing importance of raster devices within computer graphics. CELL ARRAY is the basic raster primitive, however, it cannot be simulated reasonably on non-raster devices. This would infer, that CELL ARRAY is just another optional primitive within GDP to be accepted only from specific workstations. Furthermore, FILL AREA together with the PATTERN attribute could provide the whole functionality of CELL ARRAY.

Another objection was that, usually, the cells defined by CELL ARRAY are mapped one-to-one onto the pixels of the raster device as otherwise undesired effects may occur by pixel rounding. This implies that CELL ARRAY inherently is defined in DC rather than in WC as are the other primitives.

According to the importance of raster graphics, it was decided to include the CELL ARRAY primitive. It was clarified that CELL ARRAY is defined in WC like other primitives and that transformations (including rotation) and clipping are applied. It is left within the responsibility of the application program to enquire the raster resolution of a workstation and to set the transformations appropriately to avoid undesired pixel rounding effects (e.g., by securing integer mapping of CELL ARRAY cells to pixels on the display surface).

How Should Attributes Be Assigned to Primitives?

Output primitives are associated with a set of attributes controlling the appearance of the primitive, e.g., the attributes linetype, linewidth, and colour apply for the POLYLINE primitive. The attribute concept of GKS was under continual discussion during the whole reviewing process. In these discussions, many aspects of attribute definition and binding were considered.

An attribute can be specified
— directly, i.e., the value itself is bound to the primitive;
— indirectly, i.e., an index is bound to the primitive which points to a value stored in a table. The attribute is called table driven.

An attribute may be
— static, i.e., the specified attribute cannot be changed retroactively;
— dynamic, i.e., the specified attribute may be changed retroactively.

Usually, direct attributes will be static and indirect attributes will be dynamic.

In GKS, several workstations may be active simultaneously. In this case, an attribute may be specified
— workstation-dependent, i.e., the value can be set independently for each workstation;
— workstation-independent or global, i.e., one value is valid for all workstations.

A further distinction can be made whether attributes are specified
— individually, i.e., one attribute at a time;
— bundled, i.e., a set of related attributes is specified with one invocation.

GKS started with a concept including two non-overlapping sets of attributes:
— static global attributes specified directly and individually;
— dynamic workstation-dependent attributes which were table driven and were collected in one bundle called 'pen'.

One discussion considered the issue whether there should be workstation-dependent attributes at all. In cartography, for instance, there are strict rules, in which colour or in which linetype some line has to be drawn, and it makes no sense to have these attributes dynamic. Nevertheless, if a picture which uses such well-defined colours has to be drawn on a black-and-white display, the missing capabilities have to be simulated. The workstation concept of GKS mandates that all workstation-dependencies should be under control of the application program. This means that the simulation of colour on a black-and-white display should be specifiable by the application program rather than be determined by some implicit algorithm.

The grouping of attributes into workstation-dependent and -independent attributes turned out to be very difficult. The initial distribution was done according to the experience of the people involved. During review the following rule was established: geometric attributes should be global; non-geometric attributes should be workstation-dependent. This assured that all geometrical information about a primitive was available at generation time which permitted the specification in WC and a proper performance of transformations and clipping. Unfortunately, it was found out that this rule could not decide all cases as there are attributes which cannot be properly classified. Text font, for example, clearly is a non-geometric attribute as long as all characters are equally spaced. For proportionally spaced character sets, the character width may differ from character to character and, thus, the font will affect geometry.

The pen concept had been introduced for proper separation of device-dependent and -independent aspects of primitives. In a first step, only a symbolic attribute, the 'pen', was bound to the primitive which allowed to distinguish different classes of primitives. In a second step, it could be specified explicitly on a workstation basis what aspects each class of primitives was to be assigned. The pen concept with some overhead included the functionality of direct attributes, whereas direct attributes could not cover the full functionality of the pen concept.

In the discussion, the pen concept was refined. Instead of one pen governing all types of primitives, one bundle for each of the primitives POLYLINE, POLYMARKER, TEXT, and FILL AREA was introduced. This gave greater independence between different types of primitives and avoided the difficulty that some aspects of the pen did not apply to all types of primitives. However, it was not clear whether all these bundles should be table driven. Table driven attributes are more complicated than direct attributes and have higher implementation costs even for moderate applications. Tables need storage capacity the size of which cannot be well estimated a priori. The bundle approach deprecates this situation. If several aspects of one bundle are used simultaneously a multiplication effect occurs, e.g., if POLYLINES are to be drawn with 32 colours, 8 linetypes and 2 linewidths, a table of size 512 is necessary to allow all possible combinations of these aspects of the polyline bundle. The tables have to be maintained even if the entries are never re-used or redefined later on. This puts a heavy burden on some applications. Furthermore, if entries of a table are changed, this means a retroactive change of attribute values which must be performed by the driver if the workstation has no appropriate facilities. As the program cannot know a priori whether a retroactive change will occur later or not, it must be prepared for it. This extra cost must be paid by all applications whether they use retroactive change or not.

The problems were solved by allowing all bundled attributes to be used as unbundled static attributes, too.

3.3   Segmentation

Should Segmentation Be Optional?

Segmentation is a powerful facility within GKS which must be paid for in terms of complexity and implementation costs. There are classes of applications which will not use GKS segmentation as it is not needed or is not adapted for the specific requirements of an application. In these cases, the picture will be generated from an application program maintained data structure, directly. For these applications, GKS segmentation is only a burden without any use and a GKS level without segmentation would be preferred.

On the other hand, it was proposed to allow primitives to be generated within segments only. The arguments in favour of this strict segmentation were:
— segmentation corresponds to structured programming and, therefore, would improve programming style;
— explicit opening and closing is used elsewhere within GKS and, therefore, should be used for graphical output also.

If the concept of a current position (see Section 3.2) had been included in GKS, more arguments could be added.

The resolution was to have segmentation optional. This permits GKS levels with and without segmentation. If segmentation is present, primitives may be generated inside and outside segments. It is left to the application program to stick to strict segmentation or not.

What Is the Purpose of Segment Storage?

Segmentation is a means for structuring a picture such that structure elements can be manipulated. As interactive graphics is gaining more and more importance, it was clear from the very beginning that segmentation was to be an important part of the graphics standard.

The following purposes of a segment storage were identified:

re-use of segments on the same workstation: Redrawing of segments on a series of frames, deletion of segments, setting visibility, detectability and highlighting attributes, transforming segments;

re-use of segments on another workstation: Transfer of a picture generated on an interactive workstation to a plotter;

symbol facility: Symbols (e.g., resistors, transistors, capacitors) are defined as separate segments. Several instances of one segment are generated to form a picture (e.g., circuit drawing).

Re-use on the same workstation was readily accepted. It models the functionality available with the display files of high performance interactive workstations. This functionality is needed by interactive graphics and cannot be built on top of GKS as response time requirements mandate an implementation on or close to a workstation (workstation-dependent segment storage WDSS).

Transfer of graphics data to a second workstation or a symbol facility could be built on top of GKS as the real time requirements are less important. Furthermore, data must be stored in workstation-independent format as the content of a segment has to be accessed to perform the proper transformations on coordinates and attributes. If segments are transferred to another workstation, coordinates must be mapped onto the respective device coordinates and attributes to the available attributes. If multiple instances of a symbol are generated, they will differ in size, location, and attributes. This suggests that these purposes are high level facilities which could be regarded as 'modelling' and which, therefore, should be left outside the standard.

The transfer of graphical data to another workstation was accepted as a valid purpose within a graphical kernel system. With WDSS capabilities only, this is difficult to realize. If a picture is to be edited at an interactive workstation and only the final result is to be sent to a plotter workstation for making a hard copy, both workstations have to be active during the whole session. The interactive workstation is supposed to react immediately to each command, whereas, the plotter workstation is supposed to record all commands in the segment storage without generating any visible output. When the session is finished, an UPDATE command allows the plotter workstation to draw the current state of the picture while skipping all intermediate states and the respective commands. Such a scheme is difficult to explain and to understand. It seemed to be a more natural way to have the plotter deactivated as long as the picture is edited on the interactive workstation and to allow segments to be copied from the interactive workstation to the plotter when needed.

Both approaches are expensive. In the first case, all intermediate states of the picture and all interactive segment operations carefully have to be performed in the segment storage of the plotter although only the last state is needed. In the second case, segments have to be kept in workstation-independent format which may be less efficient than workstation-dependent formats.

The resolution was to allow copying of segments from one workstation to another. The argument of high costs of storing all segments in workstation-independent form was met by introducing a special workstation called workstation-independent segment storage (WISS). Only segments generated for this workstation are eligible for transfer to another workstation.

Having allowed segment transfer, a limited symbol facility was present. One segment can be transferred several times to the same workstation. However, not all meaningful manipulations of the content of a copied segment are possible. For example, the bundle representation can be changed. As the bundle index is bound to the primitives in the WISS, all instances of a segment use the same bundle indices and, therefore, the same representations. This means that it is impossible to have one instance red and another instance green within one frame.

At what Position Should Information Leave and Rejoin the Transformation Pipeline for Segment Storage?

Coordinates can leave the transformation pipeline
— before the normalization transformation is applied. Coordinates are in WC.
— after the normalization transformation and before clipping associated with the normalization transformation are applied. Coordinates are unclipped in NDC.
— after the normalization transformation and clipping are applied. Coordinates are clipped in NDC.

Storing coordinates in WC is an acceptable high level storage. It ensures that the user knows precisely what coordinates are stored. However, it is difficult for a workstation to handle such kind of data efficiently as the current setting of the GKS state list is needed to interpret the data. There is also an argument that a WC segment storage can be built on top of GKS.

Storing coordinates after transformation and before clipping gives valuable flexibility in clipping. If the clipping rectangle is stored rather than being applied immediately,
— segment transformation can be applied without data leaving the clipping rectangle;
— clipping can be combined with the clipping to the workstation window;
— if segments are used as a symbol facility, the stored clipping rectangle can be discarded and be replaced by the current clipping rectangle which is exactly what people would expect in this case.

Storing transformed and clipped coordinates improves the performance of a workstation. However, transformation of clipped segments may generate curious effects. If a segment is expanded, it will go beyond the clipping rectangle. If a segment is scaled down, it will fill only a part of the clipping rectangle. Primitives previously clipped away will not become visible although they now fit inside the clipping rectangle.

The resolution was to store data after transformation and before clipping.

Should INSERT SEGMENT Allow the Redefinition of Primitive Attributes?

As long as the segment storage is used for storage of complete pictures, there is no need to access primitive attributes. The bundle concept for attributes gives sufficient freedom to manipulate attributes on the same workstation or to select different attributes for different workstations.

However, when used as a symbol facility, the segment storage needs more flexibility in redefining primitive attributes. With a symbol facility, several instances of the same segment may be displayed on the same display surface. These instances may differ with respect to size and primitive attributes. For example, if a segment describes a resistor symbol, it should be possible to draw this symbol in different sizes and colours.

The segment transformation in GKS provides for copying of segments under different scaling. But there is no means to have two instances of a segment with different attributes on the same display surface, e.g., to have a red and a green resistor. Also the PICK identifier cannot be different for different instances of the same segment. Therefore, it was proposed to have a facility to redefine bundle indices and PICK identifier during insertion of a symbol.

One proposal was to specify an offset with the insert function which was to be added to bundle index and PICK identifier to generate new values. The proposal was rejected as it presented an ad hoc solution which complicated the GKS attribute model considerably without providing a fully satisfying facility. A full symbol facility was considered outside the scope of GKS.

Should INSERT SEGMENT Act like a Macro or like a Subroutine?

When a segment is inserted into another segment, it can be realized in two ways:

— copying the content of the segment;
— providing a pointer to the specified segment.

The first way compares with a macro facility of programming languages; the latter compares with subroutining. When constructing a symbol facility, subroutining with appropriate attribute redefinition capabilities would be the best solution because all instances of a symbol should refer to the same definition. If the definition of a symbol is modified, all instances should be modified accordingly. However, the macro facility puts less burden on an implementation and seems to be sufficiently powerful for a kernel system.

How Can a Segment Storage Be Structured?

The benefit of a segment storage can be increased if a structure present in a picture can be mapped onto a respective structure in segment storage. If nesting of segments was allowed, a tree structure could be generated. If INSERT SEGMENT just inserts a reference to a segment rather than a copy of the segment's content, linked structures can be built up. However, it was felt that such structures are useful but outside the scope of a kernel system and belong to a modelling system. Therefore, only a one level segment structure was included in GKS.

3.4   Input

For graphical input, a lot of devices with different characteristics may be used, e.g., for coordinate input a lightpen, a crosshair cursor, a mouse, a stylus on a tablet, etc. Although these physical input devices must be handled in different ways, it was clear from the very beginning that the application program should address logical input devices only and that it was the task of GKS to map the logical input devices onto the available physical input devices. Logical input devices are distinguished by the data type they deliver to the application program. Physical devices delivering the same type of data are grouped to form one logical input device. Wallace [WALL76] had proposed the following five input classes:

> PICK, delivering segment names;
> LOCATOR, delivering positions;
> VALUATOR, delivering real numbers;
> STRING (keyboard), delivering character strings;
> BUTTON, delivering no data;

Starting from this concept, the following issues were discussed:

Should CHOICE or BUTTON Input Be Provided?

The BUTTON device is the single input device delivering no data value but only the fact whether the device was touched or not. This suggests that the BUTTON device was defined on too low a level compared with the other input devices, e.g., if the keyboard device would have been split into some

50 devices, one for each key, the same effect would occur. To find out the logical data value behind BUTTON applications, the main purposes of BUTTON devices were identified:
— trigger for another input device which allows the identification of a specific value to be transmitted to the application program;
— program control or menu selection via programmable function key boards or light buttons.

The first purpose was refused as a trigger should be part of the respective device rather than be addressed as a separate input device. In the second case, buttons always are grouped. By pressing a specific button, the operator selects one entry from a menu containing commands, symbols, etc. To indicate this purpose, the corresponding logical input device was named CHOICE. The data value delivered is a positive integer giving the number of the chosen alternative.

Having defined a CHOICE input device, good programming style requires that all menu handling and command input is done via the CHOICE input device. Menu handling and command input are important tasks within interactive programs. In existing programs, comfortable facilities to handle elaborated menus with graphical symbols have been built on top of a PICK input device and command interpreters with syntax checking have been built on top of a STRING input device. It seemed very difficult to subsume such facilities in a CHOICE device which at the same time had to support simple programmable function keyboards. The solution found was to include the comfortable command/menu handling as special prompt/echo techniques (see Section III.8.3).

Should GKS Support STROKE Input?

The STROKE device is capable of returning a sequence of positions as a single input. A LOCATOR device only delivers single positions. When digitizing curved lines, a series of positions is to be delivered which describe the shape of the curve. Should these points be collected individually by a sequence of LOCATOR invocations or as an entity by a single STROKE invocation?

Pro STROKE:
— STROKE is an inherently graphical input device. GKS should elaborate graphical input at least as it does non-graphical input;
— STROKE corresponds to POLYLINE output (input/output symmetry);
— STROKE bears more semantics than a series of LOCATOR inputs. Within a series of LOCATORs, it may be meaningful to digitize the same point twice, consecutively. Within one STROKE input, however, data reduction may be performed at device driver level to eliminate points lying too close to the previous point. When simulating STROKE by LOCATOR, data reduction can be performed above GKS only. This reduces efficiency considerably. It may even prevent support of continuous input from tablet if no sufficient computing power is available to empty the buffers in real time.
— STROKE allows efficient operation in a stand-alone or fixed-function environment.

Con STROKE:
— For environments having no tablets, implementation of STROKE with other input classes may be unsatisfactory.
— STROKE could be built on top of the LOCATOR device. This contradicts the minimality principle of GKS. Only one of them should be present in GKS.
— STROKE input will jump if it leaves the viewport of the normalization transformation used for coordinate transformation from NDC to WC.

The resolution was to include STROKE input in addition to LOCATOR input.

Are EVENT and SAMPLE Input Disjoint Classes?

In SAMPLE mode, GKS reads the state of a device register. This is the usual way to work with continuous input devices like potentiometers. Potentiometers often are used for LOCATOR and VALUATOR devices.

In EVENT mode, the operator generates an interrupt to enter a specific input value to the application program. This is the usual technique to work with discrete input devices like STRING, PICK, CHOICE, STROKE.

These facts suggest that LOCATOR and VALUATOR should be used in SAMPLE mode only and the other devices in EVENT mode only.

Pro disjoint classes:
— Reading of STRING, PICK and CHOICE in SAMPLE mode is not very meaningful.
— EVENT is difficult to realize with potentiometer based devices.
— Disjoint classes allow the association of several SAMPLE devices to one EVENT device.

Con disjoint classes:
— Physical characteristics should not shine up into the concept of logical input devices.
— If an operating mode is accepted, it should be accepted for all devices.
— Uniform treatment of all devices is more elegant.
— Lightpen LOCATOR is an EVENT device.
— LOCATOR and VALUATOR usually possess a button (integrated in hardware or assigned by software) to generate an EVENT. This button should be regarded part of the respective device.

The resolution was that all operating modes should be applicable to all input devices.

Should it Be Possible to Build up Compound Input Devices?

For output primitives, GKS provides segments as compound output. For symmetry reasons, also compound input should be supported. Compound input is demanded by many interactive applications where the input does not consist of one single input primitive but where a set of actions is required to define a graphical object or a complex manipulation. Quality of interaction can be increased considerably if compound input facilities can be provided.

As long as the set of actions can be split up into a sequence of input primitives, a compound input device can easily be built on top of GKS. In this case, GKS should not carry the burden of additional input capabilities. However, there are compound input devices which cannot be built on top of GKS. For example, when editing a drawing, a common technique is to use one input device like a mouse with some buttons which by one activation
— identifies a line (PICK),
— inputs a position (LOCATOR) for distinguishing begin and end of the line,
—· selects the desired kind of manipulation by pressing a specific button (CHOICE).

Such a compound input device PICK + LOCATOR + CHOICE which by one operator action generates three inputs usually cannot be built on top of GKS. In this case, GKS can issue a series of three input function calls only. This does work properly only if it can be guaranteed that no noticeable time delay occurs between the different function calls. Otherwise, a LOCATOR value sampled after the PICK input may deliver a value different from that valid at the time of PICK input. If a compound input device is part of GKS, the device driver will do the task of gathering the different input values which usually can be done with negligible time delay.

It was found that there was not enough experience with advanced input concepts to allow standardization of a general mechanism for defining compound input devices at the application program interface. However, compound input devices may be implemented at a workstation to serve the needs of some application. From the GKS point of view, these compound input devices are equivalent to a set of single input devices. However, when EVENTS are stored in the input queue, a flag signals whether some input primitives are generated simultaneously. By this feature, an implementor has sufficient freedom to implement compound input devices without putting additional conceptional burden on the GKS design.

3.5   Transformations

Can the Normalization Transformation Be Changed while a Segment is Open?

The GSPC CORE [GSPC77, GSPC79] uses a 'synthetic camera' analogy to describe the functionality of the viewing pipeline. In this conceptual framework, the transformation process compares with taking a 'snapshot' of an object. The snapshot only can be taken from the object as a whole. The only picture parts known to GKS are segments. Therefore, the parameters for the snapshot should be valid for the whole segment. Further arguments in favour of this opinion are:
— If transformation parameters are set outside segments only, the consistency of transformation parameters can be checked at the beginning of a segment instead for each output primitive individually.

— Segment transformations apply for whole segments. Other transformations should behave accordingly for consistency reasons.

Arguments against this concept were:
— Segmentation and transformation are independent concepts and should be held apart.
— Segments are units for manipulation. This does not necessarily imply that they are to be constructed with the same normalization transformation.
— Resetting the normalization transformation between primitives does not yield surprising results as the current position has not been included in GKS.

The resolution was to keep segmentation apart from transformation and allow setting of the normalization transformation at any time.

How Should Normalization Transformation Clipping Be Defined?

There was no doubt that clipping should be available with the normalization transformation. Although some applications require clipping to an arbitrary outline, it was agreed that a kernel system should clip only to rectangles parallel to the axes. However, there was a long discussion whether
— the clipping rectangle should be defined by the window of the current normalization transformation (window clipping) or whether
— the clipping rectangle should be specified independently of the normalization transformation.

Arguments in favour of window clipping were:
— window clipping is accepted practice;
— in the synthetic camera analogy, clipping and transformation are combined also;
— less data must be kept by GKS;
— setting of a separate clipping rectangle affords an extra function.

Arguments for a separate clipping rectangle were:
— transformation and clipping are independent concepts which should be kept apart;
— linking of clipping and transformation may confuse the user.

Following accepted practice, window clipping was adopted. This decision was taken early in the discussion of GKS. Later on, it was decided to separate transformation from clipping and to postpone clipping until primitives are displayed on a workstation. May be that a different resolution had been taken if both decisions had been discussed at the same time.

What Coordinate System Should Be Used to Return LOCATOR/STROKE Input Data to the Application Program?

Coordinates delivered by LOCATOR or STROKE device must be converted from DC to some device-independent coordinate system. Within the GKS concept, coordinates might be delivered in WC or NDC.

Pro WC:
— Symmetry of input and output. The application defines output in WC and, therefore, also will expect coordinate input in WC.
— Most application need WC data.
— NDC can be regarded a special case of WC.

Pro NDC:
— Compatibility with 3D. In 3D a position cannot be retransformed to WC because there is no unique transformation from 2D to 3D. (This applies to a 2D LOCATOR, not to a 3D LOCATOR.)

Against NDC:
— GKS has the philosophy that as little as possible should be specified in NDC.

The resolution was to transform back LOCATOR and STROKE by the inverse of a normalization transformation.

Should GKS Be Able to Use Several Normalization Transformations Simultaneously?

The original GKS design included only one normalization transformation which, however, could be redefined at any time. The normalization transformation was used for input and output. This simple scheme seemed to be sufficiently flexible for most applications. Other applications could use the default normalization transformation, which delivered NDC values, and could build more comfortable transformation mechanisms outside GKS.

In this issue, it was proposed to have several normalization transformations defined simultaneously which could serve for different purposes:
— To facilitate the switching between normalization transformations.
   The normalization transformations to be used could be defined once. If a specific normalization transformation was required, it could be referenced by number rather than by repeating the full definition of window and viewport.
— To consider all normalization transformations used for output for transformation of coordinate input.
   Output primitives are generated by different normalization transformations. All these normalization transformations could be candidates for transforming back coordinate input. By storing all normalization transformations, GKS can choose that normalization transformation the viewport of which contains the position to be transformed. If viewports overlap, a viewport input priority attribute gives a scale of preference.
— To introduce a shielding capability.
   Shielding is an inverse clipping: While clipping removes everything outside a clipping rectangle, shielding removes everything inside a shielding rectangle. Shielding is used extensively for technical drawings to suppress drawing in areas where an inscription will be inserted thus securing legibility.
   Shielding can be introduced in the following way: A priority is assigned to output primitives, e.g., the priority of the current normalization transfor-

mation. Output primitives are transformed by the current normalization transformation. The viewports of all normalization transformations with higher priority will serve as a shield, viewports with same priority will serve for clipping, viewports with lower priority will be ignored.

Allowing the normalization transformation to change at any time enables the application program to build up complex pictures from different world coordinate spaces. This can be regarded as a modelling facility which should not be supported by GKS. The major position in the discussion was either to remove this modelling aspect or to provide a rich capability as described above.

The modelling aspect can be removed, e.g., by not allowing the normalization transformation to change at any time but only between segments or between pictures. In the latter case, a resetting of the normalization transformation would result in a CLEAR WORKSTATION operation. Such a restriction would narrow down the functionality of GKS beyond the capabilities present in most graphics systems. Therefore, the rigid position of cutting down the normalization transformation was refused.

On the other hand, the shielding requirement was eliminated as it was recognized that applications usually require shielding for hundreds of inscriptions which surely goes beyond the capabilities to be provided by a kernel system.

The main argument for a single normalization transformation was simplicity of concept and simplicity of implementation.

The main argument for multiple normalization transformations was that many applications generate graphical output in non-overlapping areas of the display surface from different WCs. These applications expect that coordinate input is delivered in the correct WC which can be provided without too much an overhead by the above concept. If only one normalization transformation can be used for input, the resulting coordinates will sometimes be in the correct WC and sometimes not which may be worse than having no transformation at all.

The resolution was a compromise. Multiple normalization transformations may be defined. One of them will be selected explicitly by the application program for output. One of them will be selected automatically on a viewport priority basis for input. Details are described in Chapter III.5.

3.6 Workstation Concept

Should GKS Support only One Workstation at a Time?

The first GKS versions allowed only one workstation at a time to be addressed. Arguments in favour of this concept were:
— Most applications only use one workstation at a time.
— Simplicity. Multiple workstations need multiple transformation pipelines; device drivers must be resident simultaneously. This increases complexity and costs of implementation considerably.

— The parameter 'workstation identifier' can be removed from the parameter list of many GKS functions. Otherwise, all applications have to reference the workstation explicitly in all workstation-relevant GKS functions although only one workstation is used.
— One idea behind the definition of a kernel system was to implement the kernel on a chip within the graphics workstation. This can be achieved more easily if GKS addresses only one workstation at a time.

Although only one workstation at a time is required in many cases, interactive programs will use at least two workstations in succession: an interactive workstation for the generation and editing of a drawing and a passive workstation (plotter, metafile) for saving the final result. A facility had to be provided to transfer graphical data from one workstation to the other. The segment storage already had been designed to store a description of the drawing for interactive manipulation. To allow transfer of graphical data to other workstations, an INSERT function was defined which could copy segments to any workstation (including the same workstation).

The INSERT function was attacked from many sides. Arguments were:
— INSERT requires maintenance of all segments in workstation-independent format whether they will be copied or not. This is a considerable overhead imposed on the kernel system.
— INSERT allows generation of several instances of a segment on the same workstation. This is a high level (modelling) function which should not be present in a kernel system.
— INSERT provides three different functionalities which should be separated:
   a) Copying of segments from one workstation's segment storage into another workstation's segment storage.
   b) Copying of primitives within a segment to the display surface of another workstation without touching the segment storage.
   c) Generation of several instances of a segment on the same display surface.

Another discussion independent of the INSERT issue led to the result that multiple workstations are not that uncommon (e.g., training programs with teacher and student before separate displays, control of film plotter output on a display, games). It was stated that it should be possible to address multiple workstations on a lower level than INSERT and without the necessity to store segments in workstation-independent format.

As a resolution, multiple workstations were accepted. This was facilitated by the evolution of the workstation concept of GKS. This concept made evident all workstation dependencies which, before, had been hidden within an implementation.

The INSERT function was kept and split into three functions INSERT SEGMENT, ASSOCIATE SEGMENT WITH WORKSTATION, and COPY SEGMENT TO WORKSTATION each serving exactly one purpose as indicated above. The application program can open several workstations if simultaneous output really is required or can use one of the above functions if a transfer of the picture to another workstation is desired.

GRAPHICS KERNEL SYSTEM PROGRAMMING

Part III gives a detailed description of the functional capabilities of GKS. It is the basic reference for the application programmer using GKS, for teachers and students. For every one of the different areas of the system, a detailed explanation of the concept is given. Every GKS function and GKS data structure relevant to that area is explained at large. For all functions, both the language-independent definition from the GKS standard and the FORTRAN programming language interface are given. Examples are used to clarify the GKS functions, they are presented both in the Pascal and the FORTRAN programming languages. Exercises are included in order to give assistance to GKS education.

1 FORMAT AND STRUCTURE OF PART III

1.1 Contents of Part III

Whereas Part I of this book presented a general overview of the principles and concepts of the Graphical Kernel System, and Part II described the process of creating this standard, Part III gives a detailed description of the functional capabilities of GKS. Therefore, this part is the basic reference for the application programmer using GKS. It also serves as the framework for teaching and learning computer graphics on the base of GKS. For every one of the different areas of the system, a detailed explanation of the concept is given. Every GKS function and GKS data structure relevant to that area is explained at large. For functions, both the language-independent definition from the GKS standard and the FORTRAN programming language interface are given.

Examples are used extensively throughout Part III to clarify the application of GKS functions. They are an important complement to the definition of the functions both for the application programmer and for the novice learning the use of GKS. The examples are presented in two versions corresponding to each other: one version uses Pascal as a programming language and the second version uses FORTRAN. In the Pascal version, the GKS functions are spelled as in the GKS standard document (e.g., OPEN GKS). In the FORTRAN version the function names are taken from the FORTRAN language interface (e.g., CALL GOPKS). Since the program constructs in Pascal are more powerful and allow for a presentation of examples following the principles of structured programming, they are generally more easily readable than the FORTRAN examples. Therefore, the Pascal version is valuable not only for the Pascal programmer but also for the FORTRAN programmer and the GKS student. However, it is possible to work with the following chapters without looking at the language-independent functional definitions or the Pascal version of the examples.

At the end of the following chapters, additional examples are given covering typical tasks within the respective GKS area. They are given in two language versions, too. These examples are meant primarily for teachers and students. Exercises are added after each chapter in order to give assistance to GKS education. Most, but not all, of the examples and the exercises have been tested by students during computer graphics courses at Darmstadt Technical University. Since the GKS implementations could not always keep up with the latest changes of the GKS document, some examples could not be tested in their final version.

1.2 Format of GKS Function Definitions

The definition of functions is given in two versions. The language-independent definition is taken almost literally from the GKS standard document [GKS82]. The FORTRAN binding for the given function is taken from the FORTRAN interface definition developed by DIN and refined within ISO WG2 [DIN82b]. Chapter IV.4 gives the complete FORTRAN binding. It is based on the FORTRAN 77 standard [FORT77].

1.2.1 Example for the Definition of GKS Functions

REQUEST CHOICE   WSOP,WSAC,SGOP   L0a

Parameters:

Input	workstation identifier		N
Input	choice device number	(1..n)	I
Output	status	(OK,NONE)	E
Output	choice number	(0..n)	I

Effect:

GKS performs a REQUEST on the specified CHOICE device. If the break facility is invoked by the operator, the status will be returned NONE, otherwise OK is returned together with the logical input value which is the current measure of the CHOICE device. The choice number zero means 'no choice'.

Errors:

7	GKS not in proper state: GKS shall be in one of the states WSOP, WSAC or SGOP
20	Specified workstation identifier is invalid
25	Specified workstation is not open
38	Specified workstation is neither of category INPUT nor of category OUTIN
140	Specified input device is not present on workstation
141	Input device is not in REQUEST mode

———————————————— *FORTRAN-Interface* ————————————————

CALL GRQCH (WKID,CHDNR,STATUS,CHNR)

Parameters:

Input	WKID	workstation identifier		INTEGER
Input	CHDNR	choice device number	(1..n)	INTEGER
Output	STATUS	status	(1=OK,0=NONE)	INTEGER
Output	CHNR	choice number	(0..n)	INTEGER

1.2.2 Format of Language-Independent Definition

The language-independent definition taken from the GKS document contains the heading, the parameters, the description of the effect, and the errors that may occur when the function is called.

The heading of the function specifies:
— the function's name in the GKS document;
— the GKS states in which the function may be used (see Chapter 3);
— the GKS level up to which the function is available in a GKS implementation (see Chapter 2).

The parameter list indicates for each entry:
— whether the entry is an input (Input) or an output (Output) parameter (input parameters are passed from the application program to the function, output parameters are returned by the function to the application program);
— for coordinate data, the coordinate system (WC, NDC, DC) to be used in the function call (see Chapter 5);
— either, for enumeration type data, the permitted values, or for real and integer data, any restriction on their value range;
— the data type.

The effect of the function is described informally (by English sentences). However, when developing the GKS standard document, the description was set up in manner as concise as possible.

The error list contains the errors that can be raised when the function is called. Both the error number and the meaning of the error are given. There are additional errors that can occur during evaluation of any GKS functions. Errors and error handling in GKS are described in Chapter 9.

Data types in the definition of functions are either simple types or a combination of simple types. Simple types are:

I integer: whole number

R real: floating point number

S string: number of characters and character sequence

P point: 2 real values specifying the x- and y-coordinates of a location in WC-, NDC- or DC-space

N name: identification of a file, a procedure, a segment or a number of primitives (via PICK IDENTIFIER)

E enumeration type: a data type comprising an ordered set of values. The ordered set is defined by enumerating the identifiers which denote the values. This type is mapped, for example, onto scalar types in Pascal, or onto integers in FORTRAN.

D record: storage space of a given length

A combination of simple types can be one of the following:
— a vector of values, for example, 2xR;
— a matrix of values, for example, 2x3xR;
— a list of values of one type: the type can be a simple type or a vector, for example, nxI and nx4xR;

— an array of values of simple type, for example, nxnxI;
— an ordered pair of different types, for example, (I;E).

An occurrence of n merely indicates a variable integer value and does not necessarily relate to other occurrences of n.

Permitted values or value ranges can be specified by:
— a condition, for example, >0 or [0,1]; the latter implies that the value lies between 0 and 1 inclusively;
— a standard range of integer values, for example, (1..4);
— a range of integer values in which the maximum is determined by implementation or other constraints, for example (32..n). Note that an occurrence of n does not necessarily imply any relationship with other occurrences of n: n merely denotes a variable integer in this context;
— a list of values which constitute an enumeration type, for example, (SUPPRESSED,ALLOWED);
— an ordered list of any of the above.

1.2.3   Format of FORTRAN-Definition

The FORTRAN interface for the GKS function contains a prototype function call and the description of the parameters. The effect and the errors are not repeated, since they can be taken from the language-independent definition of the function. Also the GKS state in which the function may be called and the GKS level at which it is available are the same as in the language-independent definition.

The prototype function call contains the FORTRAN keyword CALL, the FORTRAN name of the function, and the parameter list enclosed in parentheses. The parameters are identified by symbolic names.

The parameter description contains for every parameter:
— whether the parameter is an input (Input) or output (Output) parameter;
— the symbolic name of the parameter;
— the name of the parameter taken from the language-independent definition;
— the value range of the parameters;
— the FORTRAN data type (REAL, INTEGER, CHARACTER or arrays thereof).

The FORTRAN parameters are not in all cases a one-to-one mapping of the language-independent parameters, e.g., the GKS document data type 'point' is mapped on two FORTRAN REAL values, 'name' is mapped on INTEGER, and 'enumerated value' is mapped on INTEGER. The mapping of the GKS data type 'data record' may differ from function to function, the mapping is described together with the function. The mapping of the permitted values of enumeration type parameters is a one-to-one correspondence of the values given in the language-independent and the FORTRAN definition. In the example above (Section 1.2.1), the INTEGER values (0,1) correspond to the enumerated values (NONE,OK).

1.3   Format of Examples

The examples given in Part III are all presented in two versions: the Pascal version and the FORTRAN version. In the Pascal version the syntax described in the Pascal User Manual and Report [WIRT71] is followed as closely as possible. However, in most cases the examples are no complete Pascal programs, procedures or functions, but parts thereof. In many instances, declarations and definitions are omitted. GKS functions are referred to in the Pascal examples using the names of the GKS standard document.

The FORTRAN version will have the same basic effect as the Pascal version. However, the statements of both versions will not have a one-to-one correspondence in every case. Whereas the Pascal version of the examples is used primarily for clarification of GKS functions and for teaching computer graphics on the base of GKS, the FORTRAN version should be readily executable on any GKS implementation of appropriate level that realizes the GKS FORTRAN language interface.

A line numbering is used in the examples for two reasons:
— it shows the correspondence between the Pascal version and the FORTRAN version, identical line numbers are used for corresponding parts of the examples;
— the line numbers serve for referencing parts of the examples in the explaining text.

1.3.1   Example for an Example

Example 1.1   GKS-control

Opening and closing GKS.

―――――――――――――――――― *Pascal* ――――――――――――――――――

L10   OPEN_GKS (ERROR_FILE,BUFFER);   {GKS is set into state GKS OPEN}
L20   CLOSE_GKS;   {GKS is set into state GKS CLOSED}

―――――――――――――――― *Fortran* ――――――――――――――――

L10   CALL GOPKS(FERROR)
         C   *** sets GKS into state GKS OPEN
L20   CALL GCLKS
         C   *** sets GKS into state GKS CLOSED

1.3.2   Format of Pascal Examples

The Pascal examples consist of a line numbering, and a Pascal part. The Pascal part may be a complete Pascal program, procedure or function, a part thereof or even a fragment thereof. Line numbers consist of the letter 'L' followed by a decimal number. They are arranged at the left margin of the example in ascending order. GKS functions are spelled as in the GKS standard document. If the function name consists of several words, the separating blanks are replaced by underscores (e.g., OPEN_GKS). Parameters of GKS functions are given in the same order as in the GKS document and in a one-to-one correspondence. Since at present there is no standardized language mapping defined, the examples use a mapping of parameters in a way best suited for the example. Comments are given to explain the statements of each example. In the Pascal version, they are enclosed between '{' and '}'.

1.3.3   Format of FORTRAN Examples

The FORTRAN version of the examples consists of the line numbering and the FORTRAN source part. The FORTRAN source may be a complete main program, a complete SUBROUTINE or FUNCTION or a part thereof. A statement that corresponds to a Pascal statement has the identical line number. If a series of FORTRAN statements corresponds to a Pascal statement, the first line number of the FORTRAN sequence will be identical to the Pascal line number. Function names, parameter sequence and parameter types are taken from the FORTRAN interface definition. Comments are inserted in between other statements. According to FORTRAN rules they start with the letter C. For better readability the comment text is preceded by '***', and within the comment text, lower case characters are used together with capital letters.

1.4   Exercises

Exercises are added to the chapters describing the major areas of GKS. They are arranged with ascending complexity. This also implies that the time needed for their realization may range from a few minutes to several hours. The exercises can serve for the intensive training of students in computer graphics programming on the base of the Graphical Kernel System. In order to do the exercises in a most profitable way, a GKS implementation of the appropriate level should be available.

2 LEVELS

2.1 Overview

GKS as general-purpose graphical kernel system is designed to address most of the existing graphics devices as well as most graphics applications. GKS implementations have to be usable by a wide range of application classes, from static plotting to dynamic motion and real time interaction. In addition, GKS systems have to support a large variety of graphics devices, from simple plotters, microfilms, storage tubes, to highly sophisticated vector devices and real-time raster-scan devices. Furthermore, they have to be installed on various processors with different qualities, like word length (starting from 8 bits/word), and storage handling facilities (restricted memory sizes, slow external storage media, up to virtual memory management).

Obviously, it is not sensible to use one fixed GKS system for all the different purposes. Rather, it is desirable to tailor GKS to the special qualities of the specific environments existing at each time. An important means for adapting a GKS system is provided by the definition of suitable subsystems, called levels.

The level concept was designed based on the following guidelines:

Generation of application-oriented subsets. For a representative set of application classes a suitable subset of graphics functions was selected; thus, no extra burden in acquiring, installing, learning, memorizing, and handling unnecessary functions is placed upon system and application programmers.

Implementation feasibility. The capabilities of the overall GKS are distributed among the levels in such a way that subsystems of considerably smaller program sizes can be implemented. This is accomplished by isolating specific concepts and assigning them to the single levels; thus, concepts can be integrated or omitted as a whole. This decreases compilation, linkage editor, and program performance time and supports the usage of small memory machines.

Upward-compatibility. All GKS functions are defined to have identical effects on all levels in which they exist. Regardless for which GKS level an application program is written, it will run on every higher level achieving the same results.

In GKS, capabilities are expressed by functions and by ranges of parameters. There are three different types of capability at each level:

an explicitly defined and required capability. Every GKS implementation at a specific level must support the capability at that level.

an explicitly defined and non-required capability. A GKS implementation may support the capability and, if it does, it must be implemented according to the explicit function definitions.

a conceptually defined and non-required capability. A GKS implementation may provide the capability. Its implementation has to follow general rules given by the GKS concepts and functional definitions.

Explicitly Defined and Required Capabilities

Obviously an application program using GKS has to rely on the existence of certain capabilities in every GKS implementation regarding both functions and possibilities within the functions addressed by parameters. To meet these requirements GKS exactly defines the minimal support which must be provided at each level by every implementation. All functions of a level belong to this type of capability in this specific level. Further examples are: the four linetypes "solid", "dashed", "dotted", and "dash-dotted", the marker types 1 to 5, text precision STROKE for the output levels 1 and 2 and a minimum of 10 settable normalization transformations at all levels higher than 0.

Table 2.2 exactly specifies the minimal support which must be provided at each level.

Explicitly Defined and Non-Required Capability

The minimal required capabilities are defined in such a way that a major number of applications are supported sufficiently in the respective levels. Of course, certain applications may need considerably more facilities, like a large number of attribute bundles or simultaneously available workstations, a set of hatchstyles for filling polygons or certain prompt/echo types for logical input devices in order to better support human operators for given interactive application problems. The set of explicitly defined and non-required capabilities includes: text precision STROKE at the output level 0, the interior styles SOLID, PATTERN, HATCH, and prompt/echo types above 1 that are defined in GKS.

General-purpose implementations should provide means to extend their features by application-required facilities within the single concepts. If, for example, high quality text fonts are implemented in a system on a stroke basis, then an extension by other stroke-based fonts should be easily possible. In general, it should be possible to describe application requirements to a GKS system and to adjust the implementation to an optimal support. This, of course, calls for some sophisticated design decisions and special implementation structures. Existing approaches to design configurable adaptive systems can be found in [PARN75] for the operating system area and in [PFAF82a] for the field of computer graphics. Furthermore, chapter IV describes implementation structures allowing for flexible implementations.

Conceptually Defined and Non-Required Capability

Furthermore, applications may need GKS facilities which are not explicitly defined in the standard; they are only conceptually provided and general rules for their effects are given. Examples are: linetypes above 4, marker types above 5, specific generalized drawing primitives like circle, ellipse, arcs, splines, etc., prompt/echo types above the defined set, and specific escape functions.

All of these features must not violate the GKS design, e.g., using a special linetype to draw invisible lines seems not to be a valid interpretation of the concept of linetypes. Moreover, it should be mentioned, that the use of these features may decrease the portability of programs to a great extent.

2.2 Functionality of the GKS Levels

In this section, the capabilities of each GKS level are described. Some application classes for each of the levels are illustrated and typical graphical devices
and hardware configurations for specific applications and levels are listed.

The functional capabilities of GKS can be grouped into the major areas:
a) output (minimal performance, full performance);
b) input (no input, REQUEST input, full input);
c) number of workstations (one workstation, multiple workstations);
d) attributes (predefined bundles and direct attributes, full attribute concept);
e) segmentation (none, basic segmentation, full segmentation);

Table 2.1 Capabilities of the levels

	NO INPUT	REQUEST INPUT	FULL INPUT
Minimal Output	All five output primitives; all direct attributes; GDP if workstation support is available; Predefined bundles; at least 5 polyline, 5 polymarker, 2 text, and 5 fill area bundles Multiple normalization transformation facility; (at least 1 settable transformation); Metafile functions optional Multiple workstation concept at least 1 output workstation	Request input functions for LOCATOR, STROKE, VALUATOR, CHOICE and STRING; Initialise and Set device mode functions; SET VIEWPORT INPUT PRIORITY function; at least one input workstation available	SAMPLE and EVENT input concept; Event queue concept;
Full Output and Basic Segmentation	Multiple workstations; Full bundle concept; (redefinition of predefined bundles possible, and at least 20 user-settable bundles required); Metafile functions and metafile workstations required; basic segmentation	Request pick input Initialise pick device; Set pick device mode;	Sample and event input for pick device
Segment Storage Output	Workstation-independent segment storage; INSERT SEGMENT; COPY SEGMENT TO WORKSTATION; ASSOCIATE SEGMENT WITH WORKSTATION		

If an arbitrary combination of capabilities were to be considered a valid GKS implementation, an almost unlimited number of different standard dialects would result (each one being a combination of one alternative in each axis). This would markedly decrease portability of application programs. Since every application uses a different set of capabilities, it requires a very specific GKS level on the target site. Therefore, nine valid levels of the GKS system have been defined in order to address the most common classes of equipment and applications.

As shown in Table 2.1, GKS separates its facilities into two independent axes which basically can be described as "input", and "all the other functions" summarized as "output".

The output level axis has the three possibilities:

0: Minimal output;

1: Basic segmentation with full output;

2: Workstation-Independent Segment Storage (full segmentation).

The input level axis also has three possibilities:

a: No input;

b: REQUEST input;

c: Full input.

Before describing the functionality of each level, the overall structure of Table 2.1 needs some comments. Each box represents a valid GKS level. It contains a description of the main capabilities of the level in a few keywords. In order to obtain all capabilities of a specific level, one has to add the functions of the lower levels (previous boxes of the same row and column) to the ones described in the specific box. This also expresses the functional compatibility: each function belongs automatically to all higher levels.

2.2.1   The Minimal or Lowest Level of GKS (Level 0a)

Functionality

The lowest GKS level contains a subset of the GKS functions only, but addresses quite a large graphics community. Its capabilities cover all output primitives, normalization transformations, predefined bundles and direct attributes, restricted control of workstations, and associated inquire functions.

One of the goals of this level is to provide the adequate set of graphics functions for "data representation graphics". Implementations of this level should represent small systems that are simple, easy to learn and memorize, and easy to handle even for unskilled, occasional users. The lowest level supports the drawing of polygons, lines, markers, and texts using attributes like colour, linetype, marker and character size, font, pattern and hatch style. Furthermore, higher more application-specific graphics functions, such as "axes", can easily be constructed using the basic GKS primitives POLYLINE, POLYMARKER, TEXT, FILL AREA, and CELL ARRAY, and the GENERALIZED DRAWING PRIMITIVE (GDP).

Table 2.2 Minimal support required at each level

CAPABILITY	Level								
	0a	0b	0c	1a	1b	1c	2a	2b	2c
Foreground Colours (intensity)	1	1	1	1	1	1	1	1	1
Linetypes	4	4	4	4	4	4	4	4	4
Linewidths	1	1	1	1	1	1	1	1	1
Predefined polyline bundles	5	5	5	5	5	5	5	5	5
Settable polyline bundles	—	—	—	20	20	20	20	20	20
Marker types	5	5	5	5	5	5	5	5	5
Marker sizes	1	1	1	1	1	1	1	1	1
Predefined polymarker bundles	5	5	5	5	5	5	5	5	5
Settable polymarker bundles	—	—	—	20	20	20	20	20	20
Character heights (see note 1)	1	1	1	1	1	1	1	1	1
Character expansion factors (see note 1)	1	1	1	1	1	1	1	1	1
String precision fonts	1	1	1	1	1	1	1	1	1
Character precision fonts	1	1	1	1	1	1	1	1	1
Stroke precision fonts	0	0	0	2	2	2	2	2	2
Predefined text bundles	2	2	2	6	6	6	6	6	6
Settable text bundles	—	—	—	20	20	20	20	20	20
Predefined patterns (see note 2)	1	1	1	1	1	1	1	1	1
Settable patterns (see notes 2 and 5)	—	—	—	10	10	10	10	10	10
Hatch styles (see note 3)	3	3	3	3	3	3	3	3	3
Predefined fill area bundles	5	5	5	5	5	5	5	5	5
Settable fill area bundles	—	—	—	10	10	10	10	10	10
Settable normalization transformations	1	1	1	10	10	10	10	10	10
Segment priorities (see note 4)	—	—	—	2	2	2	2	2	2
Input classes	—	5	5	—	6	6	—	6	6
Prompt/echo types per device	—	1	1	—	1	1	—	1	1
Length of input queue (see note 5)	—	—	20	—	—	20	—	—	20
Maximum string buffer size (characters)	—	72	72	—	72	72	—	72	72
Maximum stroke buffer size (points)	—	64	64	—	64	64	—	64	64
Workstations capable of output	1	1	1	1	1	1	1	1	1
Workstations capable of input	—	1	1	—	1	1	—	1	1
Workstation independent segment storage	—	—	—	—	—	—	1	1	1
Metafile output workstations	0	0	0	1	1	1	1	1	1
Metafile input workstations	0	0	0	1	1	1	1	1	1

0   indicates explicitly defined and non-required at that level
— indicates not defined at that level

Notes:

1) relevant only for character and string precision text
2) relevant only for workstation supporting pattern interior style
3) relevant only for workstation supporting hatch interior style
4) relevant only for workstation supporting segment priorities
5) since available resources are finite and entries have variable size, it may not always be possible to achieve the minimal values in a particular application.

Workstation-dependent predefined bundles exist as combinations of the workstation attributes. These can be selected by the application program. Dynamic changes are prevented since the bundles cannot be redefined. Furthermore, level 0a includes all direct output primitive attributes. To take advantage of the colour tables of many colour raster displays, the SET COLOUR REPRESENTATION function is also provided at this level. It allows for modification of colour entries addressing them by indices.

Level 0a requires only one graphics workstation. To support special application needs, metafile functions and metafile workstations may be available in the lowest level. If, however, a metafile input workstation is connected, then at least one output workstation must also be available. This allows for generating and interpreting metafiles and for transporting pictures between suitable level 0a installations.

Level 0a systems include the concept of multiple normalization transformations. However, systems are permitted to implement only one settable normalization transformation, besides the default transformation 0.

Finally, the inquire functions should be mentioned. Application programs may inquire information like predefined bundle contents and the maximum display size to adjust themselves to actual workstation qualities and to control the precise picture scale. Furthermore, a function to inquire the text extent for a given text output primitive on a specific workstation is present. It can be used to place and concatenate text strings within the picture.

Applications

Applications of level 0a can be characterized as to gather data from some source (external files or program) and display them in graphical form on a screen or on a plotter device. After a picture is generated, only its colours may be changed if the connected workstation is equipped with a colour look-up table. Other changes of the picture, or of parts of it, can only be performed by the application program: this has to erase the contents of the display surface (CLEAR WORKSTATION) and to regenerate the picture. Other applications may use a GKS level 0a system for low level output purposes. They utilize GKS as a device-independent graphics driver. Examples are image processing systems (supported by INQUIRE PIXEL, INQUIRE PIXEL ARRAY) and three-dimensional output packages built on top of GKS.

Configurations

L0a implementations can be installed on a variety of computers starting from 8 bit microprocessors with integer arithmetic, simple operating systems, and slow external storage devices. They typically support output-only devices without display files such as grey-scale or colour vector and raster plotters, microfilm devices, storage tube devices, and also simple raster and vector refresh displays.

2.2.2   Level 0b

Functionality

Level 0b was designed to allow simple interaction for about the same graphics community as addressed by level 0a systems, with only slightly higher costs. It contains all functions of L0a and additionally provides REQUEST input functions. The input of positions (LOCATOR), of point sequences (STROKE), of real values (VALUATOR), of integer-coded alternatives (CHOICE), and of texts (STRING) is possible. Furthermore, there are INITIALISE and SET DEVICE MODE functions to control the kind and place of the appearance of the logical input devices and the display of prompting and echoing. The locator/stroke coordinate transformations from device to world coordinates can be controlled (details about input are explained in Chapter 8).

Applications

Using this level, it is possible to enter the data (e.g., for diagrams and charts) via the graphical workstation during program execution. Applying the echo facilities in suitable ways, even simple correction facilities are applicable. Bar charts, for instance, may be constructed interactively using locator prompt/echo type 5, i.e., a rectangle is drawn from an initial point to the current locator position as the operator uses the input device.

Table 2.3 Applications ordered by levels

Level	Applications
L0a	Business Graphics; Microfilm and Metafile Output; Metafile input and interpretation; Low level output driver for higher graphics systems such as three-dimensional drawing systems;
L0b	Interactive business graphics; Process control; Simple picture generating systems; Input supply for higher graphics systems
L0c	Input-based systems with strong interaction requirements, such as digitizing applications; Optimal usage of physical input device qualities via predefined multiple input device associations;
L1a L1b L1c	Multiple workstation systems; Display of several pictures simultaneously; Interaction on and manipulation of picture subparts; Design applications and simulation systems;
L2a L2b L2c	Design and drafting systems with maximal usage of GKS facilities; Re-use of once-defined segments for picture construction; Copying of workstation contents to other workstations; Office automation systems; Graphical editors; CAD systems.

Configurations

Suitable configurations for level 0b must include workstations that have some input facilities connected to them. Alphanumeric and function keyboards are standard equipment. Extensions may be:
— thumb wheels;
— tracking balls;
— joysticks;
— lightpens connected to display devices;
— tablets;
— positioning and input facilities of plotters, etc. Most of these devices can be used to implement the five logical input devices of this level.

2.2.3   Level 0c

Functionality

With increasing capabilities of the input component, we come to level 0c. EVENT and SAMPLE input expand the application range to input-oriented systems with strong requirements for interaction processing. Stress is placed on real time input of large data sets which must not be obstructed by other computation tasks. The requirements for graphical output are considerably smaller than the input requirements at this level.

An input buffer (EVENT QUEUE) compensates for differing processing speeds of the application program, which takes the data from the queue and processes it, and the operator who enters the data into the queue.

An additional major point of the event and sample concept in this level, is the possibility to connect several logical input devices to one or more physical devices. This enables the operator to generate several input reports simultaneously and put them into the queue with one action. To draw full advantage of existing input devices and to construct good operator tools, this level of input should be chosen for high quality interactive applications. The crosshair device of some digitizers may serve as an example: it allows the generation of a locator position and an integer value (choice) simultaneously, as one of the alternative cursor buttons is hit.

Applications

Typical examples are digitizing applications in cartography, architecture, and similar areas, where the speed and sequence of input actions is controlled by the human operator.

Configurations

A typical configuration for a level 0c system and a digitizing application consists of a 16 bit processor with multi-tasking operating system, a digitizer, and a storage tube or an alphanumeric raster device for displaying the data entered on the digitizer as graphical feedback.

Table 2.4 Processors and graphical devices ordered by levels

Level	Processors	Graphical Devices
L0a	starting with 8 bit processors (8,16,20,32,36,..bits/word); static memory handler; slow external storage media sufficient;	Microfilm, raster and vector plotters, alphanumeric displays and printers, TV-monitors, simple storage tubes, simple raster and vector refresh devices;
L0b	as L0a	output devices as L0a; input devices like alphanumeric and function keyboards, tracking balls, lightpens, tablets, thumb wheels, joysticks;
L0c	starting with 16 bit processors; multitasking facilities or programmable interrupt handling possibly dynamic storage handling for event queue;	as L0b; plus digitizers, shape sampling devices;
L1a L1b L1c	starting with 16 bit processors dynamic storage or virtual memory management; fast access to secondary memory desirable;	vector devices with segmented display file; sophisticated features like clipping and transformations desirable; storage tubes with refresh components; raster devices with several picture planes; fast raster scan displays with microcomputer intelligence for e.g. hidden surface elimination; For 1b and 1c systems, lightpens which deliver segment identifiers calculated from display file addresses or by coordinate comparison on raster scan displays.
L2a L2b L2c	As level 1 systems with emphasis laid on effective storage management	

2.2.4   Levels 1a, 1b, 1c

Functionality

Continuing with increasing output capabilities we come to the levels 1a, 1b, and 1c. These levels cover all GKS concepts except the workstation-independent segment storage. The bundling concept of attributes is completed. Arbitrary combinations of attributes can be defined as representations for polylines, polymarkers, texts, and fill areas; and they can be selected as current ones. Changes of representations which have already been used for output are performed in retrospective ways, i.e., the appearance of output on a specific workstation changes according to the new attributes either dynamically or after an image regeneration.

Finally, the segmentation feature is introduced. Segments can be created, deleted, transformed, and manipulated. This level, however, restricts the usage of segments: no transportation from one workstation to other ones and no insertion of already defined segments into new ones is possible. Of course, the application program (or a system on top of GKS) may generate output on one workstation, check it, and generate (corrected) output on a second workstation. This restriction may avoid the potential overhead of a workstation-independent segment storage which has to keep the graphics primitives in a device-independent format.

Proceeding to the right hand direction in Table 2.1, first, request input and secondly, event and sample input are added. The input facilities of the levels 1b and 1c differ from that of 0b and 0c only by having the PICK input function additionally. This is caused by the segmentation facility of these levels: segments and primitive groups within segments which are separated by PICK IDENTIFIERS, can be identified by the pick input function.

Applications

Typical level 1 applications require one or several of the following features:
— Full attribute facilities (i.e., the bundling concept);
— Multiple workstations simultaneously needed in an installation;
— Graphical structures.

Multiple workstations are needed for:
— using several screens when displaying pictures in overview and details in parallel;
— generating pictures interactively and finally redrawing them on a plotter;
— using several planes of certain raster devices in order to display and manipulate different graphic informations independently;
— displaying the same information on several workstations simultaneously, e.g., in teacher-student systems.

Segment structure is needed for the identification and manipulation of picture subparts. This is necessary, e.g., for the design of printed circuit board layout, shipbuilding design, and generally in CAD systems.

Configurations

In general, devices of level 0 systems can also be used for level 1 implementations. Some extra facilities are desirable and are utilized by efficient GKS implementations, in order to avoid expensive software simulations:
— the ability to keep and identify segments, and possibly perform segment manipulations by hardware without picture regeneration. This is provided by many vector display devices and the upcoming raster-scan devices which keep a coordinate-oriented display file;

— Sophisticated hardware (or local firmware) facilities such as clipping, coordinate transformations, hidden line and hidden surface elimination for two-dimensional (and 2.5 dimensional) applications;
— Maintaining of attribute tables (for colours, linetypes, patterns, etc.), in order to perform retroactive attribute changes dynamically.

Note, that all missing device capabilities are simulated by the GKS system. The differences to hardware (or firmware) solutions are visible when looking at the performance time and the memory requirements.

2.2.5   Levels 2a, 2b, 2c

Functionality

The highest GKS levels 2a, 2b, and 2c integrate the workstation-independent segment storage and the level 1 facilities. There are three new functions, INSERT SEGMENT to re-use segments which are already defined for the creation of new segments, COPY SEGMENT TO WORKSTATION to display primitives of a segment on a workstation, and ASSOCIATE SEGMENT WITH WORK-STATION to transport segments from the segment storage to a workstation.

Applications

Applications of the highest GKS levels differ from those of level 1 systems by using the GKS facilities more extensively. Basically, there are two application types. The first one is completely or largely supported by GKS: two-dimensional pictures are generated interactively or read in from a metafile, edited using the input and segmentation functions, and finally copied to a plotter device and stored on a metafile for long-term storage.

The other application type uses higher graphics systems like three-dimensional design and drawing systems, simulation systems, etc. which themselves use GKS as a basis: Unstructured GKS input data are mapped to structured application data and the application object structure is mapped to GKS segments and primitives. In contrast to applications only using level 0 output functions and performing the modelling solely in the higher system, the object structure is realized by GKS segments and structure information in the modelling system. The manipulation task is split into modelling the structure information and performing the visual effect via GKS segment manipulation functions.

Configurations

Level 2 systems can be implemented on the same types of processors and graphical devices as level 1 systems. Some more emphasis is laid on the handling of the device-independent segment storage; fast storage handling is needed either in the form of a direct access file or by a large main memory. The latter can be supplied by a virtual memory management.

2.3   Impacts on Writing Portable Application Programs

Every GKS application program needs a specific set of capabilities expressed by a set of functions and a set of parameters for each function. The function of the highest level which is used by the application program, determines the required GKS level. The set of capabilities required by the application program defines the support which a GKS implementation has to provide.

If a program is to be transported to another GKS implementation, it has to be ensured that all capabilities needed are available on the target site. In order to avoid erroneous program executions, either the required capabilities are described in accompanying documentation and checked by an operator, or — more conveniently — an "Inquire Facility Program" is supplied. In the most simple case, this consists of the instructions of Example 2.1:

Example 2.1   Check GKS-level

```
———————————————————— Pascal ————————————————————
L10      REQUIRED_LEVEL := .....;
L20      INQUIRE_LEVEL_OF_GKS (ERROR,LEVEL);
L30      IF (LEVEL < REQUIRED_LEVEL) THEN BEGIN
L40        WRITE ("available GKS-level too low for program requirements");
L50        GOTO LEND;
L60      END {end if block};
L...
L...     {program code};
L...
L9999    LEND: END {end of program};
———————————————————— Fortran ————————————————————
L10              REQLEV = ....
L20              CALL GQLVKS (ERRIND,LEVEL)
L30              IF (LEVEL .GE. REQLEV) GOTO 70
L40              WRITE (ERRFIL,1)
L50              GOTO 9990
L55      1       FORMAT (53H available GKS-level too low for program requirements)
L70      70      CONTINUE
L...
L...             { program code }
L...
L9990    9990    STOP
L9999            END
————————————————————————————————————————————————
```

Example 2.2   Check GKS facilities

If more than the minimal required support of Table 2.2 is required to perform the application program, then Example 2.1 has to be extended; e.g.

─────────────────────── Pascal ───────────────────────

```
L70    INQUIRE_MAXIMUM_NORMALIZATION_TRANSFORMA-
       TION_NUMBER (ERROR,NUMBER);
L80    IF (NUMBER < REQUIRED_NUMBER) THEN BEGIN
L90       WRITE ("number of available norm. transformations too small");
L100      GOTO LEND;
L110   END {end if block};
L...
L...   {program code};
L...
L9999  LEND: END { end of program };
```

─────────────────────── Fortran ───────────────────────

```
L70            CALL GQMNTN (ERRIND,MAXTNR)
L80            IF (MAXTNR .GE. REQNB) GOTO 20
L90            WRITE (ERRFIL,2)
L100           GOTO 9990
L105     1     FORMAT (52H number of available norm. transformations too small)
L120     20    CONTINUE
L...
L...           { program code }
L...
L9990    9990  STOP
L9999          END
```

2.4   Exercises

Exercise 2.1   Checking capabilities of a GKS implementation

Assume an application program uses, among other functions, the following GKS capabilities:
— POLYLINE, SET POLYLINE INDEX (indices 1 to 6);
— SET WINDOW, SET VIEWPORT for keeping 5 normalization transformations simultaneously;
— REQUEST LOCATOR via LOCATOR device 2;

Which GKS level is needed ? Write a check program, which decides whether the application program can be performed on a given GKS implementation. It should also generate a message which lists the required but not available GKS capabilities.

Exercise 2.2   Determining the required GKS level

Write a program which automatically scans FORTRAN GKS-programs, to decide the required level of a GKS implementation. Restrict yourself to inspecting GKS-subroutine calls.

3   STATES AND STATE LISTS

This chapter deals with states of GKS and data structures describing them. The operating states of GKS are a central concept within GKS which forces a strict structure in graphics programming. For example, a workstation can be accessed only after a certain sequence of initialising functions have been invoked; output can be generated only after a workstation has been activated; workstation attributes can be set only after the workstation has been allocated. Therefore, the novice reader should read carefully Section 3.2 and 3.3 where the different operating states are introduced and those functions are listed which are allowed in the respective operating states. Section 3.4 describes the content of some state lists. It aims primarily at implementors and experienced users of GKS. Section 3.5 introduces the first two GKS functions: OPEN GKS and CLOSE GKS.

3.1   Introduction

GKS contains some 100 functions which in some way have an effect on its state. Output functions modify the state of display surfaces; attribute setting functions change the state of the GKS nucleus or of a workstation and thus influence the appearance of output primitives; input functions set and enquire the state of input devices.

To clarify the GKS states, GKS has defined explicitly some data structures which define the major aspects of GKS states and help users and implementors in understanding the effect of each GKS function and the relationship between different GKS functions. These data structures are grouped into the following subsets:
— operating state;
— error state list;
— GKS description table;
— GKS state list;
— workstation description table for every existing workstation type;
— workstation state list for every open workstation;
— segment state list for every existing segment.

The description tables contain entries which describe implementation restrictions or workstation characteristics. The table entries are constant within one implementation but may differ from one implementation to another. They will be set by the implementor rather than by the user of GKS. The state lists contain state variables which can be set by GKS functions. The state lists are initialised from the description tables or as specified by the implementor.

All values in the above state lists and tables may be interrogated by an application program. The description tables allow an application program to adapt its behaviour to the capabilities of an implementation or a workstation. The state lists reflect the current state of GKS. They are of importance, e.g., for complex application systems where subsystems independently use GKS. By inquiring and storing the current state of all affected state variables when entering the subsystem and by resetting them to the interrogated values before leaving the subsystem, a subsystem can use GKS without side-effects on other subsystems.

Some very important data structures are not contained in any state list: the data structures describing graphical output. Generally, graphical output cannot be retrieved after generation. However, for raster devices with readable pixel store, the state of the individual pixels can be interrogated. For output contained in segments, a data structure will be generated internally. The segment as a whole may be retrieved, primitives within the segment are not accessible. Furthermore, GKS contains an interface to a graphics metafile. This metafile can be used to store graphical output and to retrieve individual primitives and attributes.

3.2   Operating States

GKS functions will usually refer to entries of some state lists and, therefore, can only be invoked if the corresponding state list is available. To clarify when which functions are allowed, five different operating states of GKS have been defined:

GKCL = GKS closed;
GKOP = GKS open;
WSOP = At least one workstation open;
WSAC = At least one workstation active;
SGOP = Segment open.

GKS always exists in exactly one of these operating states. The operating states differ in what state lists are available and what data structures are built up. State lists and description tables made available in one operating state also are available in the subsequent ones.

The above five operating states of GKS, naturally, cannot cover all aspects of GKS. They only cover overall aspects but do not characterize the individual state of a workstation. Each workstation may be opened and activated individually. This is reflected precisely by GKS states only if, at most, one workstation is addressed. Otherwise, only the highest state reached by some workstation is reflected. Furthermore, each workstation may have several input devices which can be in one of the operating modes REQUEST, EVENT, and SAMPLE. The operating states only reflect whether a workstation is allocated and, therefore, input is possible but not whether input devices are available or what is the operating mode of an individual input device.

The initial state of GKS is *GKCL (GKS closed)*. If dynamic allocation of resources is possible, all graphical resources, state lists and description tables are deallocated. Only the operating state and the error state list exist. The operating state indicates that GKS is closed.

Usually, the first GKS function to be invoked will be OPEN GKS which moves GKS to the state *GKOP (GKS open)*. OPEN GKS generates and initialises the GKS state list and makes inquirable the GKS description table and the workstation description tables for all available workstation types. In state GKOP some global attributes (workstation-independent primitive attributes and normalization transformations) may be set and will be recorded.

If input or output capabilities are to be used, a workstation with the desired capabilities has to be addressed. By OPEN WORKSTATION a specified workstation is allocated. OPEN WORKSTATION is invoked individually for each workstation. Each invocation generates and initialises a workstation state list. When the first workstation is opened, GKS moves from state GKOP to *WSOP (at least one workstation open)*. Each subsequent invocation does not change the operating state. It may occur in the states WSOP, WSAC or SGOP.

After a workstation has been opened, its input devices are immediately available for input in REQUEST mode. Each input device can be set independently into one of the operating modes REQUEST, EVENT, and SAMPLE by SET < input class > MODE. However, these substates are not considered as separate GKS states.

The output capabilities of a workstation are enabled by ACTIVATE WORKSTATION. ACTIVATE WORKSTATION can be invoked individually for each open workstation. Output is routed to all active workstations. When the first workstation is activated, GKS moves from state WSOP to *WSAC (at least one workstation active)*. No new state list is generated or made available. Each subsequent invocation of ACTIVATE WORKSTATION does not change the operating state. It may occur in the state WSAC only.

CREATE SEGMENT moves GKS from state WSAC to *SGOP (segment open)*. In state SGOP, graphical output is recorded in segments which may be manipulated as described in Chapter 7. CREATE SEGMENT generates and initialises the segment state list of the specified segment.

CLOSE SEGMENT moves GKS back from state SGOP to *WSAC*. The segment data structure is finished. No more output may be added to the segment. The segment state list, however, containing global attributes for the whole segment, still is available for manipulations. More segments may be generated by reentering the state SGOP.

Each invocation of DEACTIVATE WORKSTATION disables the corresponding workstation for output. Only the deactivation of the last workstation moves GKS from state WSAC to *WSOP*. No more output may be generated. The output primitives contained within segments, however, are still retained and may be manipulated. The visible effect of segment manipulations, e.g., making a segment visible, will appear also on open workstations.

Each invocation of CLOSE WORKSTATION disables the corresponding workstation for input and deletes the corresponding workstation state list. The workstation identifier is deleted from the list of associated workstations of every segment containing it. The input queue is flushed of all events from all devices on the workstation being closed. Only the closing of the last workstation moves GKS from state WSOP to *GKOP*. No more input may be generated at all.

The segment storage is deleted and the input queue in the GKS state list is set empty.

CLOSE GKS moves GKS from state GKOP to *GKCL*. The GKS state list is deleted. The GKS description table and all workstation description tables are no more accessible. GKS can be reopened by invoking the function OPEN GKS.

Table 3.1 lists all functions controlling the state of GKS. Table 3.2 sums up all state lists and description tables together with the states where they are available and the functions allocating and deallocating each list or table. Figure I.13.1 on page 46 illustrates the transitions within and between states.

Table 3.1 Functions changing the state of GKS

OPEN GKS	GKCL → GKOP		
OPEN WORKSTATION			
(first workstation)		GKOP → WSOP	
ACTIVATE WORKSTATION			
(first workstation)			WSOP → WSAC
CREATE SEGMENT			WSAC → SGOP
CLOSE SEGMENT			WSAC ← SGOP
DEACTIVATE WORKSTATION			
(last workstation)			WSOP ← WSAC
CLOSE WORKSTATION			
(last workstation)		GKOP ← WSOP	
CLOSE GKS	GKCL ← GKOP		

Table 3.2 Availability of state lists and description tables

operating state (exists always)	GKCL,GKOP,WSOP,WSAC,SGOP
error state list (exists always)	GKCL,GKOP,WSOP,WSAC,SGOP
GKS description table	GKOP,WSOP,WSAC,SGOP
(made inquirable by OPEN GKS, deallocated by CLOSE GKS)	
workstation description table	GKOP,WSOP,WSAC,SGOP
(made inquirable by OPEN GKS, deallocated by CLOSE GKS)	
GKS state list	GKOP,WSOP,WSAC,SGOP
(generated by OPEN GKS, deallocated by CLOSE GKS)	
workstation state list	WSOP,WSAC,SGOP
(one list generated by each invocation of OPEN WORKSTATION; one list deallocated by each invocation of CLOSE WORKSTATION)	
segment state list	WSOP,WSAC,SGOP
(one list generated by each invocation of CREATE SEGMENT; deallocated individually by invocation of DELETE SEGMENT, etc.; deallocated all by invocation of CLOSE WORKSTATION for last workst.)	

3.3   Functions Allowed in Individual States

GKS functions only can be invoked in certain operating states indicated in the description of the individual function. This section gives an overview about functions allowed in the five operating states.

Most GKS functions may be invoked in several states. However, the effect may be different in different states, e.g., if output functions are invoked in state WSAC, output will be created only once and then will be discarded. If the same functions are invoked in state SGOP, output will be recorded in a segment and will be regenerated automatically on all subsequent frames until the respective segment is deleted or made invisible.

In *any state,* the inquiry functions and the error handling functions may be invoked. The inquiry functions, however, only can provide data if the respective data structure is available. The operating state is the only value properly set in any state. The GKS state list and the GKS description table and the workstation description tables are available in states GKOP, WSOP, WSAC and SGOP. However, some entries of the GKS state list are meaningful in certain states only: the set of segment names in use and the input queue can be non-empty only if at least one workstation is open (WSOP, WSAC, SGOP); the name of the open segment only can be set in state SGOP. The other tables and state lists are available in states WSOP, WSAC and SGOP.

In state *GKCL* OPEN GKS may be invoked.

In state *GKOP,* CLOSE GKS, OPEN WORKSTATION and some functions setting entries of the GKS state list (workstation independent primitive attributes and normalization transformations) may be invoked. The ESCAPE function as a standard way of performing non-standard functions within GKS also can be used.

In the states *WSOP, WSAC and SGOP* most of the GKS functions can be invoked. Therefore, it is more indicative to list the functions not permitted in each of these states.

In state *WSOP,* the functions OPEN GKS, DEACTIVATE WORKSTA-TION and CLOSE SEGMENT are meaningless and, therefore, are not admitted. CLOSE GKS requires all workstations to be closed properly. CREATE SEGMENT needs at least one workstation to be active for output. All output functions, INSERT SEGMENT and WRITE ITEM TO METAFILE generate output which is possible in states WSAC and SGOP only. Note, that ASSO-CIATE SEGMENT TO WORKSTATION and COPY SEGMENT TO WORKSTATION are considered segment manipulations rather than output generation and, therefore, are admitted in this state.

In state *WSAC,* the functions OPEN GKS, CLOSE GKS and CLOSE SEG-MENT are not admitted as above. Besides these three functions, all GKS functions can be used in state WSAC.

In state *SGOP,* the functions OPEN GKS and CLOSE GKS are not meaningful and, therefore, are not admitted.

In SGOP, one segment is generated for all active workstations. ACTIVATE/ DEACTIVATE WORKSTATION enable/disable a workstation for output. If this was admitted in state SGOP, the content of a segment could differ on

Table 3.3 Table of GKS functions and corresponding states

Control Functions	
OPEN GKS	GKCL
CLOSE GKS	GKOP
OPEN WORKSTATION	GKOP,WSOP,WSAC,SGOP
CLOSE WORKSTATION	WSOP,WSAC,SGOP
ACTIVATE WORKSTATION	WSOP,WSAC
DEACTIVATE WORKSTATION	WSAC
CLEAR WORKSTATION	WSOP,WSAC
REDRAW ALL SEGMENTS	
ON WORKSTATION	WSOP,WSAC,SGOP
UPDATE WORKSTATION	WSOP,WSAC,SGOP
SET DEFERRAL STATE	WSOP,WSAC,SGOP
MESSAGE	WSOP,WSAC,SGOP
ESCAPE	GKOP,WSOP,WSAC,SGOP
Output Functions	WSAC,SGOP
Output Attributes	
Workstation-Independent Primitive Attributes	GKOP,WSOP,WSAC,SGOP
Workstation Attributes (Representations)	WSOP,WSAC,SGOP
Transformation Functions	
Normalization Transformation	GKOP,WSOP,WSAC,SGOP
Workstation Transformation	WSOP,WSAC,SGOP
Segment Functions	
Segment Manipulation Functions	
CREATE SEGMENT	WSAC
CLOSE SEGMENT	SGOP
RENAME SEGMENT	WSOP,WSAC,SGOP
DELETE SEGMENT	WSOP,WSAC,SGOP
DELETE SEGMENT FROM WORKSTATION	WSOP,WSAC,SGOP
ASSOCIATE SEGMENT WITH WORKSTATION	WSOP,WSAC
COPY SEGMENT TO WORKSTATION	WSOP,WSAC
INSERT SEGMENT	WSAC,SGOP
Segment Attributes	WSOP,WSAC,SGOP
Input Functions	WSOP,WSAC,SGOP
Metafile Functions	
WRITE ITEM TO GKSM	WSAC,SGOP
GET ITEM TYPE FROM GKSM	WSOP,WSAC,SGOP
READ ITEM FROM GKSM	WSOP,WSAC,SGOP
INTERPRET ITEM	WSOP,WSAC,SGOP
Inquiry Functions	allowed in all states but meaningful only in:
Inquiry Function for Operating State Value	GKCL,GKOP,WSOP,WSAC,SGOP
Inquiry Functions for GKS Description Table	GKOP,WSOP,WSAC,SGOP

Table 3.3 (continued)

Inquiry Functions for GKS State List	GKOP,WSOP,WSAC,SGOP
except:	
INQUIRE NAME OF OPEN SEGMENT	SGOP
INQUIRE SET OF SEGMENT NAMES IN USE	WSOP,WSAC,SGOP
INQUIRE MORE SIMULTANEOUS EVENTS	WSOP,WSAC,SGOP
Inquiry Functions for Workstation State List	WSOP,WSAC,SGOP
Inquiry Functions for Workstation Description Table	GKOP,WSOP,WSAC,SGOP
Inquiry Functions for Segment State List	WSOP,WSAC,SGOP
Pixel Inquiries	WSOP,WSAC,SGOP
Inquiry Function for GKS Error State List	WSOP,WSAC,SGOP
Utility Functions	GKOP,WSOP,WSAC,SGOP
Error Handling	GKCL,GKOP,WSOP,WSAC,SGOP

different workstations. As the content of a segment should be the same for all associated workstations, it is not allowed to activate or deactivate a workstation in state SGOP. Note, that opening and closing of workstations is admitted as it does not affect active workstations.

CLOSE WORKSTATION and CLEAR WORKSTATION delete all segments on one workstation. If allowed in state SGOP, the open segment might be deleted which is not allowed for systematic reason: If an open segment could be deleted, a correct CLOSE SEGMENT would generate an error. For the same reason, DELETE SEGMENT and DELETE SEGMENT FROM WORKSTATION in state SGOP may address all segments except the open segment.

Also, the function CREATE SEGMENT is not allowed in the state SGOP. Otherwise a nesting structure of segments could be generated which is not supported by GKS.

ASSOCIATE SEGMENT WITH WORKSTATION and COPY SEGMENT TO WORKSTATION move graphical output data to a workstation. These data will not be included into a segment and, therefore, the corresponding functions are not admitted in state SGOP.

Table 3.3 gives a summary of all GKS functions together with the allowed states. A rough overview is given also by Figure I.13.1 on page 46.

3.4 State Lists

In this section, the content of the
— operating state;
— error state list;
— GKS description table;
— GKS state list;
will be discussed. The remaining
— workstation description table (see Table 4.1, page 119);

— workstation state list (see Table 4.2, page 125)
— segment state list for every existing segment (see Table 7.2, page 235)
are discussed in the respective context in later chapters.

The information for each entry in the state lists and description tables includes:
— the name of the entry;
— the coordinate system (if appropriate);
— the permitted values;
— the data type;
— the initial value (if appropriate).

The notation used is the same as used in the description of the parameters of GKS functions setting the corresponding entries (see Section 1.2.2 for details). In addition, an initial value is specified for each entry if applicable. The abbreviations used in this column are:

i.d: Implementation dependent. The respective value is determined when designing a specific implementation. Applies for the description tables.

w.d.t: Value is derived from the workstation description table.

undef: Undefined value indicating that the corresponding entry has not yet been set.

empty: A value indicating that the respective set is empty.

The *operating state* (see Table 3.4) contains only one value indicating the current state of GKS. The initial value is GKCL = "GKS closed" which is available for inquiry before GKS has been opened. The operating state is set by the state changing functions listed in Table 3.1.

Table 3.4 Operating state

Operating state value	(GKCL,GKOP,WSOP,WSAC,SGOP) E GKCL

The *error state list* (see Table 3.5) contains some data relevant in error situations. When GKS detects an error situation, it calls the ERROR HANDLING procedure which may be replaced by a user provided procedure (see Section 9.3). The main error information,
— the identification of the error condition;
— the identification of the GKS function which called the ERROR HANDLING procedure
is not stored in the error state list but passed directly to this procedure. To avoid recursive call of the ERROR HANDLING procedure, however, only some GKS functions not generating error messages may be called during error handling. This condition is controlled by the entry 'error state' which indicates whether error handling is going on or not.

The next entry contains the name of an error file as defined by OPEN GKS. Error messages will be printed to this error file by the ERROR LOGGING procedure.

The next entry will be used if an input queue overflow occurs. As this error occurs asynchronously, it cannot be reported immediately to the ERROR HANDLING procedure and, therefore, is stored in the error state list. When the error can be reported to the application program, it may obtain the information by calling INQUIRE INPUT QUEUE OVERFLOW which removes the respective entry.

Table 3.5 Error state list

error state	(ON,OFF)	E	OFF
error file		N	i.d
identification of one of the logical input devices that caused an input queue overflow:			
workstation identifier		N	undef
input class	(LOCATOR,STROKE,VALUATOR, CHOICE,PICK,STRING)	E	undef
device number	(1..n)	I	undef

The *GKS description table* (see Table 3.6) describes overall characteristics of the implementation. It contains the level of GKS indicating that subset of GKS functions available in this implementation (see Chapter 2).

The following two entries describe the set of admissible workstation types for this implementation. The capabilities available on a specific workstation type may be interrogated from the corresponding workstation description table. The names of workstation types may be chosen arbitrarily by the implementor.

Implementations may differ in how many workstations may be used simultaneously. The next three entries precisely say how many workstations may be simultaneously open, active in state WSAC, and active in state SGOP. In the lowest GKS level 0a, only one workstation may be used at a time.

The next entry describes how many normalization transformations may be defined simultaneously. For GKS levels 0a,0b,0c one normalization transformation is sufficient; otherwise, at least 10 normalization transformations have to be supported. The range of admissible normalization transformation numbers is 0 to the maximum normalization transformation number.

Table 3.6 shows the content of the GKS description table.

Table 3.6 GKS description table

level of GKS	(0a,0b,0c,1a,1b,1c,2a,2b,2c)	E	i.d
number of available workstation types	(1..n)	I	i.d
list of available workstation types		nxN	i.d
maximum number of simultaneously open workstations	(1..n)	I	i.d
maximum number of simultaneously active workstations	(1..n)	I	i.d
maximum number of workstations associated with a segment	(1..n)	I	i.d
maximum normalization transformation number	(1..n)	I	i.d

The *GKS state list* (see Table 3.7) contains state variables referring to the global state of GKS rather than to the state of a particular workstation.

Whereas the GKS description table records which workstation types are available in this implementation, the first two entries of the GKS state list indicate which workstations are currently open or active.

Furthermore, it contains the last setting of each normalization transformation. Each implementation provides a fixed number of normalization transformations as specified in the GKS description table. When initialising the GKS state list by OPEN GKS, all transformations are set to identity transformation, i.e., all windows and viewports are set to unit square, the viewport input priority is assigned to give a transformation with lower number precedence over a transformation with higher number. Clipping is initially switched on. However, as long as all viewports are set to unit square, this has no effect.

The next entries contain the current setting of all workstation-independent primitive attributes (see Chapter 6 for details about the meaning of these attributes).

If segmentation is available (depending on the GKS level), the name of the open segment is recorded. This name is defined only during GKS being in state SGOP. However, in any of the states WSOP, WSAC and SGOP, the set of names of all defined segments (including the open segment) is recorded. For each segment a segment state list is held. The content of the segment state list is described in Section 7.5.

If EVENT input is possible, an input queue is generated. The function AWAIT EVENT moves the oldest entry from the input queue into the entry 'current event report' of the GKS state list from where it can be obtained by the respective GET <class> function.

Table 3.7 shows the content of the GKS state list.

Table 3.7 GKS state list

set of open workstations			nxN	empty
set of active workstations			nxN	empty
normalization transformation				
current normalization transformation number	(0..n)		I	0
list of transformation numbers ordered by viewport input priority (initially in numerical order with 0 highest)				
for every entry:				
normalization transformation number	(0..n)		I	entry number
window	WC		4xR	0,1,0,1
viewport	NDC		4xR	0,1,0,1
clipping indicator	(CLIP,NOCLIP)		E	CLIP
POLYLINE				
current polyline index	(1..n)		I	1
current linetype	(1..n)		I	1

Table 3.7 (continued)

current linewidth scale factor		R	1.0
current polyline colour index	(0..n)	I	1
current linetype ASF	(BUNDLED,INDIVIDUAL)	E	note 1
current linewidth scale factor ASF	(BUNDLED,INDIVIDUAL)	E	note 1
current polyline colour index ASF	(BUNDLED,INDIVIDUAL)	E	note 1

POLYMARKER

current polymarker index	(1..n)	I	1
current marker type	(1..n)	I	3
current marker size scale factor		R	1.0
current polymarker colour index	(0..n)	I	1
current marker type ASF	(BUNDLED,INDIVIDUAL)	E	note 1
current marker size scale factor ASF	(BUNDLED,INDIVIDUAL)	E	note 1
current polymarker colour index ASF	(BUNDLED,INDIVIDUAL)	E	note 1

TEXT

current text index	(1..n)	I	1
current text font and precision	(1..n; STRING,CHAR,STROKE)	(I;E)	1;STRING
current character expansion factor	>0	R	1.0
current character spacing		R	0.0
current text colour index	(0..n)	I	1
current text font and precision ASF	(BUNDLED,INDIVIDUAL)	E	note 1
current character expansion factor ASF	(BUNDLED,INDIVIDUAL)	E	note 1
current character spacing ASF	(BUNDLED,INDIVIDUAL)	E	note 1
current text colour index ASF	(BUNDLED,INDIVIDUAL)	E	note 1
current character height WC	>0	R	0.01
current character up vector WC		2xR	0,1
current text path	(RIGHT,LEFT,UP,DOWN)	E	RIGHT
current text alignment (horizontal and vertical)	(NORMAL,LEFT,CENTRE,RIGHT; NORMAL,TOP,CAP,HALF,BASE,BOTTOM)	2xE	(NORMAL; NORMAL)

FILL AREA

current fill area index	(1..n)	I	1
current fill area interior style	(HOLLOW,SOLID,PATTERN,HATCH)	E	HOLLOW
current fill area style index	(1..n)	I	1
current fill area colour index	(0..n)	I	1

Table 3.7 (continued)

current fill area interior style				
ASF		(BUNDLED,INDIVIDUAL)	E	note 1
current fill area style index				
ASF		(BUNDLED,INDIVIDUAL)	E	note 1
current fill area colour index				
ASF		(BUNDLED,INDIVIDUAL)	E	note 1
current pattern size	WC	SX,SY > 0	2xR	1,1
current pattern reference				
point	WC		P	(0,0)
current pick identifier			N	language binding dependent

segments

name of open segment	N	undef
set of segment names in use	nxN	empty
set of segment state lists (one state list for every segment)		empty

input queue

input queue (one entry for each event report)	empty

each event report containing:

workstation identifier			N
device number			I
device class		(LOCATOR,STROKE, VALUATOR,CHOICE,PICK, STRING)	E
if LOCATOR			
normalization trans-			
formation number		(0..n)	I
position	WC		P
if STROKE			
normalization trans-			
formation number		(0..n)	I
number of points		(0..n)	I
points in stroke	WC		nxP
if VALUATOR			
value			R
if CHOICE			
choice number		(0..n)	I
if PICK			
status		(OK,NOPICK)	E
segment name			N
pick identifier			N

Table 3.7 (continued)

if STRING			
string		S	
more simultaneous events	(NOMORE,MORE)	E	
(a single event is indicated by NOMORE)			

	current event report containing:		
device class	(NONE,LOCATOR,STROKE,VALUATOR, CHOICE,PICK,STRING)	E	NONE
if LOCATOR			
normalization trans- formation number	(0..n)	I	
position	WC	P	
if STROKE			
normalization trans- formation number	(0..n)	I	
number of points	(0..n)	I	
points in stroke	WC	nxP	
if VALUATOR			
value		R	
if CHOICE			
choice number	(0..n)	I	
if PICK			
status	(OK,NOPICK)	E	
segment name		N	
pick identifier		N	
if STRING			
string		S	
more simultaneous events	(NOMORE,MORE)	E	NOMORE
(a single event is indicated by NOMORE)			

Note 1: All the initial ASF values are the same. It is implementation-dependent whether the initial ASF values are all BUNDLED or are all INDIVIDUAL.

3.5 Basic Control Functions

The basic control functions comprise all GKS functions necessary to generate graphical output in the lowest GKS level 0a:
— OPEN GKS
— OPEN WORKSTATION
— ACTIVATE WORKSTATION
— CLEAR WORKSTATION ·
— DEACTIVATE WORKSTATION
— CLOSE WORKSTATION
— CLOSE GKS

OPEN GKS normally will be the first GKS function called by the application program. In the parameter list, an error file is specified. If an error is detected by GKS, the standard error reaction will include printing an error message to this error file. The second parameter restricts the amount of memory space to be allocated dynamically by GKS. This parameter is only meaningful in programming environments where independent processes can be loaded dynamically and then compete for memory space. If one process allocates all available memory space, no other process can be started subsequently. Note that this parameter has been omitted in the FORTRAN-Interface of OPEN GKS. OPEN GKS allocates and initialises the GKS state list; the entry 'error file' in the GKS error state list is set; all workstation description tables are made accessible.

CLOSE GKS will be the last GKS function called by the application program in order to leave GKS properly. All tables and state lists except the operating state and the error state list are deallocated. Therefore, the sequence
— CLOSE GKS
— OPEN GKS
may be used to reset all GKS parameters to their default value and to clear all buffers.

The functions OPEN WORKSTATION, ACTIVATE WORKSTATION, CLEAR WORKSTATION, DEACTIVATE WORKSTATION, CLOSE WORKSTATION are presented in the subsequent chapter.

OPEN GKS   GKCL   L0a
    Input   error file   N
    Input   amount of memory units for buffer area   I
Effect:
    GKS is set into the operating state GKOP = "GKS open". The GKS state list is allocated and initialised as indicated in Table 3.7. The GKS description table and the workstation description tables are made available. The entry 'error file' in the GKS error state list is set to the value specified by the first parameter. The permitted buffer area which can be used by GKS for internal purposes is limited.
Note:
    Certain environments may not permit dynamic memory management. In this case, the buffer area may be limited in a static way to be described in the installation documentation.
Errors:
    1   GKS not in proper state: GKS shall be in the state GKCL

———————————— *FORTRAN-Interface* ————————————

CALL GOPKS (ERRFIL)
Parameters:
    Input   ERRFIL   error message file   INTEGER

CLOSE GKS   GKOP   L0a

Parameters: none

Effect:

GKS is set into the operating state GKCL = "GKS closed". The GKS state list and the workstation description tables become unavailable. All GKS buffers are released and all GKS files are closed.

Note:

GKS can be reopened by invoking the function OPEN GKS.

Errors:

2   GKS not in proper state: GKS shall be in the state GKOP

───────────────────────── *FORTRAN-Interface* ─────────────────────────

CALL GCLKS

Parameters: none

3.6   Examples

Example 3.1   Use of basic control functions

This example illustrates the use of the state changing functions listed in Table 3.1. The workstation functions are introduced in Chapter 4 and the segment functions in Chapter 7. The comments show the main function groups callable at the respective position in the program. See Table 3.3 for a complete listing.

───────────────────────────── *Pascal* ─────────────────────────────

```
L10   CONST error_file = 'GKS_ERRORS';
L11      display = 'T4014';
L12      connection_identifier = '';
L13      type = 'STORAGE_TUBE';
L14      segmax = 100;
L15   VAR index : INTEGER;
L16      segnr : ARRAY [1..100] OF NAME;
```
                              {Names must be initialised to distinct values}

                {GKS in state GKCL which allows}
                {Opening or reopening of GKS}
                {Inquiring the operating state, Error handling}

```
L20   OPEN_GKS (error_file,memory_limit);
```
                {GKS in state GKOP which allows}
                {Setting of workstation independent primitive attributes}
                {Setting of normalization transformations}
                {Inquiring the GKS state list and all description tables}

```
L30   OPEN_WORKSTATION (display,connection_identifier,type);
```
                {GKS in state WSOP which in addition allows}
                {Setting of workstation attributes}

{Setting of workstation transformation}
{Input functions}
{Inquiring the state list of workstation 'display'}

L40   ACTIVATE_WORKSTATION (display);
{GKS in state WSAC which in addition allows}
{Output functions}

L50   FOR index: = 1 TO segmax DO
L60   BEGIN

L70   CREATE_SEGMENT (segnr[index]);
{GKS in state SGOP which in addition allows}
{Output functions with output stored}
{Setting of segment attributes of segment 'segnr'}
{Inquiring the state list of segment 'segnr'}

L80   CLOSE_SEGMENT;
{GKS in state WSAC which allows}
{Handling of existing segments}
{Input/output functions}
L90   END;

L100 DEACTIVATE_WORKSTATION (display);
{GKS in state WSOP which allows}
{Handling of existing segments}
{No more output}

L110 CLOSE_WORKSTATION (display);
{GKS in state GKOP}
{All segments deleted}
{State list of workstation 'display' deleted}

L120 CLOSE_GKS;
{GKS in state GKCL}
{Description table of all workstations deallocated}
{GKS state list deleted}

Fortran

```
L10            INTEGER ERRFIL,DISPL,CONID,WTYPE,SEGMAX,SEGNR
L11            DATA ERRFIL/27/,DISPL/3/,CONID/0/,WTYPE/3/,SEGMAX/100/
L20            CALL GOPKS (ERRFIL)
L30            CALL GOPWK (DISPL,CONID,TYPE)
L40            CALL GACWK (DISPL)
L50            DO 90 SEGNR = 1,SEGMAX
L70            CALL GCRSG (SEGNR)
L80            CALL GCLSG
L90       90   CONTINUE
L100           CALL GDAWK (DISPL)
L110           CALL GCLWK (DISPL)
L120           CALL GCLKS
```

---

4 WORKSTATIONS

4.1 Introduction

GKS provides a set of output functions for computer graphics which may generate output on any device of the whole range of graphics devices, including plotter and interactive devices, vector and raster displays, storage tube and refresh displays, black-and-white and colour displays.

The set of GKS functions has been designed such that all essential capabilities of graphical devices can be addressed. However, the capabilities of the individual devices differ significantly, e.g.,
— black-and-white devices cannot generate colour images;
— storage tubes cannot generate images moving in real time;
— vector displays may have difficulties in displaying solid areas.

This fundamental contradiction between the comprehensive functionality offered at the application program interface and the restricted capabilities of an individual device cannot be eliminated. However, the workstation concept of GKS is a means to localize the workstation dependencies and to put them under full control of the application program.

GKS introduces the concept of an abstract graphical workstation with maximum capabilities which:
— has one addressable display surface of fixed resolution;
— allows only rectangular display spaces (the display space cannot consist of a number of separate parts);
— permits the specification and use of smaller display spaces than the maximum while guaranteeing that no display image is generated outside the specified display space;
— supports several linetypes, text fonts, character sizes, etc., allowing output primitives to be drawn with different attributes;
— has one or more logical input devices for each input class;
— permits REQUEST, SAMPLE and EVENT type input;
— allows logical input devices to be set in REQUEST, SAMPLE or EVENT mode independently of each other;
— stores segments and provides facilities for changing and manipulating them.

In practice, the workstation may or may not be equipped with all of these capabilities. The available capabilities are documented in the workstation description table, which may be interrogated by the application program to adapt its behaviour to the existing environment.

A workstation, at least, possesses one display surface or one input device. Regarding the output and input capabilities the following categories of workstations are possible:

OUTPUT: output workstation,
INPUT: input workstation,
OUTIN: output/input workstation.

An output workstation has only output capabilities. It can display all output primitives with the possible exception of the GDP which is optional. The appearance of output primitives may vary between workstations with respect to the workstation-specific aspects of primitive attributes and the workstation transformation. Workstation-specific aspects and minimal requirements for the display of the individual primitives are described in detail in Chapter 6. An example of an output workstation is a plotter.

An input workstation has at least one logical input device. An example of an input workstation is a digitizer. Within a GKS implementation supporting input, at least, one logical input device of each class must be present. However, it is not required that any workstation has more than one logical input device; they may be assigned arbitrarily by the implementor to the individual workstations. Input class PICK must be present only in GKS implementations supporting both, input and segmentation.

An output/input workstation has the characteristics of both an output and an input workstation. All interactive devices are output/input workstations.

The conjunction of output and input within one workstation not only reflects a physical conjunction of a display surface with some input devices. The output/input workstation allows the modelling of the fact that input mostly refers to the output on one specific display surface, e.g., PICK input only makes sense in conjunction with visible output primitives. Also, LOCATOR input usually is given relative to visible output primitives. The workstation concept is a means to establish such relationships.

Segments are created for specific workstations. However, the storage of segments is not a capability of an individual workstation which may be present for one workstation and which may be absent for another one; on the contrary, it is a capability of a specific output level of GKS. If present, it must be supported by all output and output/input workstations. There may be differences between workstations whether the segment storage is provided locally or whether the workstation uses capabilities of the GKS nucleus. As these differences only have effect on the efficiency but do not touch the functionality, they are not visible at the application program interface. Segments are explained in Chapter 7.

In addition to the three workstation categories listed above, GKS has three special facilities that provide a means for temporarily or permanently storing graphical information:

WISS: workstation-independent segment storage;
MO: GKS metafile output;
MI: GKS metafile input.

They are treated as workstations for the purpose of control and, therefore, could be regarded as special workstations. With respect to other GKS functions they have quite different characteristics, e.g., these special workstations only possess a very restricted workstation description table and, except GKS metafile output, only a shortened workstation state list. The WISS is discussed in detail in Section 7.7. The metafile concept is explained in Chapter 11.

The capabilities of workstations are described in detail by workstation description tables (see Section 4.2). One table may characterize a whole class of devices with similar features. The current state of an individual workstation is recorded in a workstation state list (see Section 4.3). The six workstation categories mentioned above are best characterized by the set of functions applicable to them (see Section 4.4). The Sections 4.2-4.4 give valuable informations for the advanced programmer but may be skipped by the novice reader.

4.2   Workstation Description Table

The implementor of GKS will classify all workstations according to their characteristics and capabilities. For each workstation type available in a given implementation, a *workstation description table (w.d.t)* must be implemented containing a description of all workstation features relevant for GKS. Several workstations may be described by one workstation description table as long as they do not differ in features given in the workstation description table. The entries of the workstation description table may be interrogated, but, naturally, may not be set by the application program.

The first entry gives the name of the workstation type. This name will be generated by the implementor of GKS. The second entry indicates the workstation category to which belong all workstations of this workstation type. The special workstations (WISS, MO, MI) have a workstation description table only consisting of these two entries as their behaviour is fully defined by GKS.

The next entries describe the device coordinate system (DC). The maximum display surface, i.e., the maximum value for the device coordinates, is given as width and height measured in metres. However, there may be devices where a precise measurement of the display surface is not possible, e.g., if the operator has the possibility to scale the display surface without notifying GKS. In this case, the implementor will use an average length unit and indicate by the value 'OTHER' that the length units not necessarily are metres.

For input workstations the extent of the available input area (e.g., size of a tablet) will determine the maximum value for the device coordinates. If both, a display surface and a tablet, are present in an output/input workstation, both must be assigned the same device coordinate system.

Furthermore, the resolution of the display surface will be given by two integers. For raster devices, these are the numbers of pixels corresponding to the width and height of the maximum display surface.

The rest of the table describes output or input capabilities. Entries exist for workstations with respective capabilities only.

The next entry indicates whether the workstation possesses a vector display, a raster display, or perhaps another type of display. This value should be interrogated before using the CELL ARRAY output primitive as vector displays are sure to make a very poor simulation only. Also for the FILL AREA primitive, this entry may be useful as it helps to select an appropriate interior style.

The subsequent entries describe capabilities with respect to the individual output primitives (see Chapter 6 for details on primitives and primitive attributes).

The available linetypes, marker types, font/precision pairs, interior styles, hatch styles, and generalized drawing primitives are given as a list rather than by the maximum number. This implies that the defined numbers on an individual workstation may be non-contiguous. That means, the implementor may uniquely assign linetypes, marker types, etc. within an implementation without being forced to implement the full set on each individual workstations.

The available linewidths, marker sizes, and character heights are characterized by minimum and maximum value and number of available values. If number of available values is 0, all values between the limits are valid. If the number of available values is positive, some discrete values are available. It cannot be concluded that these values are equally spaced in the interval. GKS will round unavailable values to the next available value. The table gives a nominal linewidth and marker size in DC to which refer the linewidth and marker size scale factor. Linewidth and marker size are not transformable; a change of linewidth and marker size is achieved by resetting the respective scale factor rather than by resetting any transformation.

The following entries describe the maximum size and the predefined entries of the bundle tables related with the output primitives. The predefined entries have a contiguous set of indices starting from 1 (colour table: 0).

One entry indicates whether colour is available on the workstation or whether the output device is monochrome. The entry 'number of colours' gives the number of different definable colours which may differ from the 'maximum number of colour indices' giving the size of the colour table. If the number of colours is less or equal the size of the colour table, the available colours presumably will all be predefined.

The colour table is of use for non-colour devices also. Monochrome devices may use it to specify intensities or, at least, the background colour (entry 0) and the foreground colour (entry 1). Therefore, the colour table has at least length 2.

The list of available generalized drawing primitives contains the set of primitive attributes individually selected by the implementor for each generalized drawing primitive.

The behaviour of the workstation in displaying primitives and in changing the display dynamically is described by the following entries. The deferral mode controls the buffering of output functions, e.g., to optimise data transfer. The implicit regeneration mode indicates whether a regeneration of the picture may be performed at any time when required by some function or whether it is suppressed until requested explicitly. For example, this suppression of implicit regeneration is of great importance when working interactively with storage tubes. The entries 'dynamic modifications accepted for ...' indicate in detail which actions may lead to an implicit regeneration. The entries 'deferral mode' and 'implicit regeneration mode' contain values selected by the implementor such that the device's capabilities are used optimally and that most applications are served in the best way.

Segment priority controls the overlapping of segments. This feature primarily is intended for raster devices with multiple bit planes. The entry 'number of segment priorities supported' indicates how far a specific workstation allows control of overlapping segments.

The last entries indicate which input devices are available and what are the initial settings of these devices.

Table 4.1 shows the content of the workstation description table. The information for each entry includes:

— the name of the entry;
— the coordinate system (if appropriate);
— the permitted values;
— the data type;
— the initial value (if appropriate).

The notation used is explained in Section 3.2.

Table 4.1 Workstation description table

Entries exist for all workstation categories			
workstation type		N	i.d
workstation category	(OUTPUT,INPUT,OUTIN,WISS,MO,MI)	E	i.d
Entries exist for categories OUTPUT,INPUT,OUTIN			
device coordinate units	(METRES,OTHER)	E	i.d
maximum display surface			
(visible area of the display surface or			
available area on tablet for input only workstations)			
in length units	DC >0	2xR	i.d
in device units	(integer by integer)	2xI	i.d
(for vector displays, for example, the device units			
give the highest possible resolution; for raster displays,			
the number of columns and lines of the raster array)			
Entries exist for categories OUTPUT,OUTIN			
DISPLAY TYPE			
raster or vector display (for output) (VECTOR,RASTER,OTHER)		E	i.d
(VECTOR = vector display, RASTER = raster device,			
OTHER = other device, e.g., vector + raster)			
POLYLINE			
number of available linetypes	(4..n)	I	i.d
list of available linetypes	(1..n)	nxI	i.d
number of available linewidths	(0..n)	I	i.d
(if the workstation supports continuous linewidth,			
the number will be zero)			
nominal linewidth	DC >0	R	i.d
minimum linewidth	DC >0	R	i.d
maximum linewidth	DC >0	R	i.d

Table 4.1 (continued)

maximum number of polyline bundle table entries	(5..n)	I	i.d
number of predefined polyline indices (bundles)	(5..n)	I	i.d
table of predefined polyline bundles, for every entry:			
linetype	(1..n)	I	i.d
linewidth scale factor		R	i.d
polyline colour index	(0..n)	I	i.d
(within range of predefined colour indices)			

POLYMARKER

number of available marker types		(5..n)	I	i.d
list of available marker types		(1..n)	nxI	i.d
number of available marker sizes		(0..n)	I	i.d
(if the workstation supports continuous marker sizes, the number will be zero)				
nominal marker size	DC	>0	R	i.d
minimum marker size	DC	>0	R	i.d
maximum marker size	DC	>0	R	i.d
maximum number of polymarker bundle table entries		(5..n)	I	i.d
number of predefined poly-marker indices (bundles)		(5..n)	I	i.d
table of predefined polymarker bundles, for every entry:				
marker type		(1..n)	I	i.d
marker size scale factor			R	i.d
polymarker colour index		(0..n)	I	i.d
(within range of predefined colour indices)				

TEXT

number of available character heights		(0..n)	I	i.d
(if the workstation supports continuous character heights, the number will be zero)				
minimum character height	DC	>0	R	i.d
maximum character height	DC	>0	R	i.d
number of font/precision pairs		(1..n)	I	i.d
list of font/precision pairs		(1..n; STRING,CHAR,STROKE)	nx(I;E)	i.d
number of available character expansion factors		(0..n)	I	i.d
(if the workstation supports continuous character expansion factors, the number will be zero)				
minimum character expansion factor	DC	>0	R	i.d
maximum character expansion facor	DC	>0	R	i.d
maximum number of text bundle table entries		(2..n)	I	i.d

Table 4.1 (continued)

number of predefined text indices (bundles)	(2..n)	I	i.d
table of predefined text bundles, for every entry:		at least one entry	
text font	(1..n)	I	i.d
text precision	(STRING,CHAR,STROKE)	E	i.d
character expansion factor	>0	R	i.d
character spacing		R	i.d
text colour index	(0..n)	I	i.d
(within range of predefined colour indices)			

FILL AREA

number of available fill area interior styles	(1..4)	I	i.d
list of available fill area interior styles	(HOLLOW,SOLID,PATTERN,HATCH)	nxE	i.d
number of available hatch styles	(0..n)	I	i.d
list of available hatch styles	(1..n)	nxI	i.d
maximum number of fill area bundle table entries	(5..n)	I	i.d
number of predefined fill area indices (bundles)	(5..n)	I	i.d
table of predefined fill area bundles, for every entry:		at least one entry	
fill area interior style	(HOLLOW,SOLID,PATTERN,HATCH)	E	i.d
fill area style index	(1..n)	I	i.d
(for interior style PATTERN must be within range of predefined pattern indices; for interior style HATCH must be within range of available hatch styles)			
fill area colour index	(0..n)	I	i.d
(within range of predefined colour indices)			
maximum number of pattern indices	(0..n)	I	i.d
number of predefined pattern indices (representations)	(0..n)	I	i.d
table of predefined pattern representations, for every entry:			
pattern array dimensions	(1..n)	2xI	i.d
pattern array	(0..n)	nxnxI	i.d

GENERALIZED DRAWING PRIMITIVE

number of available generalized drawing primitives	(0..n)	I	i.d
list of available generalized drawing primitives (may be empty): for every GDP:			
GDP identifier		N	i.d
number of sets of attributes used	(0..4)	I	i.d
list of sets of attributes used	(POLYLINE,POLYMARKER,TEXT,FILL AREA)	nxE	i.d

Table 4.1 (continued)

COLOUR TABLE

number of available colours or intensities (if workstation supports a continuous range of colours, the number will be zero)	(0,2..n)	I	i.d
colour available	(COLOUR,MONOCHROME)	E	i.d
maximum number of colour indices	(2..n)	I	i.d
number of predefined colour indices (representations)	(2..n)	I	i.d
table of predefined colour representations, for every entry:	at least entries zero and one		
colour(red/green/blue intensities)	[0,1]	3xR	i.d

SEGMENT PRIORITY

number of segment priorities supported (a value of 0 indicates that a continuous range of priorities is supported)	(0..n)	I	i.d

---

DYNAMIC CAPABILITIES

default value for:			
deferral mode	(ASAP,BNIL,BNIG,ASTI)	E	i.d
implicit regeneration mode	(SUPPRESSED,ALLOWED)	E	i.d
dynamic modification accepted for:			
polyline bundle representation	(IRG,IMM)	E	i.d
polymarker bundle representation	(IRG,IMM)	E	i.d
text bundle representation	(IRG,IMM)	E	i.d
fill area bundle representation	(IRG,IMM)	E	i.d
pattern representation	(IRG,IMM)	E	i.d
colour representation	(IRG,IMM)	E	i.d
workstation transformation	(IRG,IMM)	E	i.d
segment transformation	(IRG,IMM)	E	i.d
visibility (visible → invisible)	(IRG,IMM)	E	i.d
visibility (invisible → visible)	(IRG,IMM)	E	i.d
highlighting	(IRG,IMM)	E	i.d
segment priority	(IRG,IMM)	E	i.d
adding primitives to open segment overlapping segment of higher priority	(IRG,IMM)	E	i.d
delete segment	(IRG,IMM)	E	i.d
where:			

IRG: implicit regeneration necessary (may be deferred)
IMM: performed immediately

Entries exist for categories INPUT and OUTIN

INPUT DEVICES

for every logical input device of class LOCATOR:			
locator device number	(1..n)	I	i.d
default initial locator position	WC	P	i.d

Table 4.1 (continued)

number of available prompt and echo types	(1..n)	I	i.d
list of available prompt and echo types	(1..n)	n × I	i.d
default echo area	DC	4 × R	i.d
default locator data record		D	i.d
for every logical input device of class STROKE:			
stroke device number	(1..n)	I	i.d
maximum input buffer size	(64..n)	I	i.d
number of available prompt and echo types	(1..n)	I	i.d
list of available prompt and echo types	(1..n)	n × I	i.d
default echo area	DC	4 × R	i.d
default stroke data record containing at least:		D	i.d
input buffer size	(1..n)	I	i.d
for every logical input device of class VALUATOR:			
valuator device number	(1..n)	I	i.d
default initial value		R	i.d
number of available prompt and echo types	(1..n)	I	i.d
list of available prompt and echo types	(1..n)	n × I	i.d
default echo area	DC	4 × R	i.d
default valuator data record containing at least:		D	i.d
low value		R	i.d
high value		R	i.d
for every logical input device of class CHOICE:			
choice device number	(1..n)	I	i.d
maximum number of choice alternatives	(1..n)	I	i.d
number of available prompt and echo types	(1..n)	I	i.d
list of available prompt and echo types	(1..n)	n × I	i.d
default echo area	DC	4 × R	i.d
default choice data record		D	i.d
for every logical input device of class PICK:			
pick device number		I	i.d
number of available prompt and echo types	(1..n)	I	i.d
list of available prompt and echo types	(1..n)	n × I	i.d
default echo area	DC	4 × R	i.d
default pick data record		D	i.d
for every logical input device of class STRING:			
string device number	(1..n)	I	i.d
maximum input buffer size	(72..n)	I	i.d
number of available prompt and echo types	(1..n)	I	i.d
list of available prompt and echo types	(1..n)	n × I	i.d
default echo area	DC	4 × R	i.d
default string data record containing at least:		D	i.d
input buffer size	(1..n)	I	i.d
initial cursor position	(1..n)	I	1

4.3   Workstation State List

When accessing an individual workstation via OPEN WORKSTATION, a *workstation state list* is created which contains all aspects of a workstation which may be changed directly or indirectly by the application program. The main part of the workstation state list consists of tables describing the POLY-LINE, POLYMARKER, TEXT, and FILL AREA bundles together with the pattern and colour table. Furthermore, the state of each input device is recorded in the workstation state list. The main source of initial values for this list is the workstation description table indicated by w.d.t in the last column.

One workstation state list exists for every open workstation including the special workstations WISS, MO and MI. For MI and WISS, however, only the first three or five entries exist. For MO all entries exist except those describing input capabilities. The values marked w.d.t are undefined for MO as its workstation description tables does not include these entries.

The first three entries of the workstation state list are initialised by OPEN WORKSTATION (see Section 4.5).

The workstation state indicates whether the workstation is enabled for output. The set of stored segments describes the content of the WDSS or the WISS, respectively (see Section 7.7). This entry only exists in GKS levels supporting segments. Both entries only exist for workstations with output capabilities.

The next entries describe the bundle tables and the pattern and colour table. They are initialised from the workstation description table.

The entries deferral mode and implicit regeneration mode allow the control of possible delay of output or changes of the display. Since the application program has the possibility to suspend the deferral when needed by UPDATE WORKSTATION (see Section 4.4), it will be unnecessary in most cases to change the initial values determined by the implementor via the workstation description table.

The entries workstation transformation update state and new frame action necessary at update give more information what actions have been deferred.

As a change of the workstation transformation may lead to an implicit regeneration which may be deferred, the transformation parameters are stored twice: the requested values, as specified by the application program, and the current values corresponding to the actual display. The requested and current values are initialised to the maximum possible values. If the current values specify rectangles with different aspect ratio, the workstation viewport internally is shrunken to a rectangle with the correct aspect ratio to achieve a workstation transformation with uniform scaling. This shrunken rectangle, however, is not stored in the workstation state list.

For workstations with input devices, the last entries record the current state of all input devices. See Chapter 8 for more details about input.

Table 4.2 Workstation state list

Entries initialised by OPEN WORKSTATION for all workstations

workstation identifier	N
connection identifier	N
workstation type	N

Entries for workstations of category OUTPUT,OUTIN,MO,WISS

workstation state	(ACTIVE,INACTIVE)	E	INACTIVE
set of stored segments for this workstation		nxN	empty

Entries for workstations of category OUTPUT,OUTIN,MO

POLYLINE

number of polyline bundle table entries	(5..n)	I	w.d.t
table of defined polyline bundles containing:			
polyline index	(1..n)	I	w.d.t
linetype	(1..n)	I	w.d.t
linewidth scale factor		R	w.d.t
polyline colour index	(0..n)	I	w.d.t

POLYMARKER

number of polymarker bundle table entries	(5..n)	I	w.d.t
table of defined polymarker bundles containing:			
polymarker index	(1..n)	I	w.d.t
marker type	(1..n)	I	w.d.t
marker size scale factor		R	w.d.t
polymarker colour index	(0..n)	I	w.d.t

TEXT

number of text bundle table entries	(2..n)	I	w.d.t
table of defined text bundles containing:			
text index	(1..n)	I	w.d.t
text font and precision	(1..n;STRING,CHAR,STROKE)	(I;E)	w.d.t
character expansion factor	>0	R	w.d.t
character spacing		R	w.d.t
text colour index	(0..n)	I	w.d.t

FILL AREA

number of fill area bundle table entries	(5..n)	I	w.d.t
table of defined fill area bundles containing:			
fill area index	(1..n)	I	w.d.t
fill area interior style			

Table 4.2 (continued)

	(HOLLOW,SOLID,PATTERN,HATCH)	E	w.d.t
fill area style index	(1..n)	I	w.d.t
fill area colour index	(0..n)	I	w.d.t
number of pattern table entries	(0..n)	I	w.d.t
table of pattern representations containing:			
pattern index	(1..n)	I	w.d.t
pattern array dimensions	(1..n)	2xI	w.d.t
pattern array	(0..n)	nxnxI	w.d.t

COLOUR TABLE

number of colour table entries	(2..n)	I	w.d.t
table of colour representations containing:			
colour index	(0..n)	I	w.d.t
colour (red/green/blue intensities)	[0,1]	3xR	w.d.t

DEFERRAL MODE

deferral mode	(ASAP,BNIL,BNIG,ASTI)	E	w.d.t
implicit regeneration mode	(SUPPRESSED,ALLOWED)	E	w.d.t
display surface empty	(EMPTY,NOTEMPTY)	E	EMPTY
new frame action necessary at update	(YES,NO)	E	NO

WORKSTATION TRANSFORMATION

workstation transformation update state	(PENDING,NOTPENDING)	E	NOTPENDING
requested workstation window	NDC	4xR	0,1,0,1
current workstation window	NDC	4xR	0,1,0,1
requested workstation viewport	DC	4xR	maximum display surface from w.d.t
current workstation viewport	DC	4xR	maximum display surface from w.d.t

Entries for workstations of category INPUT,OUTIN

LOCATOR

for every logical input device of class LOCATOR:			
LOCATOR device number	(1..n)	I	w.d.t

Table 4.2 (continued)

operating mode	(REQUEST,SAMPLE,EVENT)	E	REQUEST
echo switch	(ECHO,NOECHO)	E	ECHO
initial normalization transformation number	(0..n)	I	0
initial position WC		P	w.d.t
prompt/echo type	(1..n)	I	1
echo area DC		4xR	w.d.t
locator data record		D	i.d

STROKE

for every logical input device of class STROKE:

STROKE device number	(1..n)	I	w.d.t
operating mode	(REQUEST,SAMPLE,EVENT)	E	REQUEST
echo switch	(ECHO,NOECHO)	E	ECHO
initial normalization transformation number	(0..n)	I	0
initial number of points	(0..n)	I	0
initial points in stroke WC		nxP	empty
prompt/echo type	(1..n)	I	1
echo area DC		4xR	w.d.t
stroke data record containing at least:		D	i.d
input buffer size	(1..n)	I	w.d.t

VALUATOR

for every logical input device of class VALUATOR:

valuator device number	(1..n)	I	w.d.t
operating mode	(REQUEST,SAMPLE,EVENT)	E	REQUEST
echo switch	(ECHO,NOECHO)	E	ECHO
initial value		R	w.d.t
prompt/echo type	(1..n)	I	1
echo area DC		4xR	w.d.t
valuator data record containing at least:		D	i.d
low value		R	w.d.t
high value		R	w.d.t

CHOICE

for every logical input device of class CHOICE:

choice device number	(1..n)	I	w.d.t
operating mode	(REQUEST,SAMPLE,EVENT)	E	REQUEST
echo/prompt switch	(ECHO,NOECHO)	E	ECHO
initial choice number	(0..n)	I	0
prompt/echo type	(1..n)	I	1
echo area DC		4xR	w.d.t
choice data record		D	i.d

Table 4.2 (continued)

PICK

for every logical input device of class PICK:

pick device number		I	w.d.t
operating mode	(REQUEST,SAMPLE,EVENT)	E	REQUEST
echo switch	(ECHO,NOECHO)	E	ECHO
initial status	(OK,NOPICK)	E	NOPICK
initial segment		N	undef
initial pick identifier		N	undef
prompt/echo type	(1..n)	I	1
echo area	DC	4xR	w.d.t
pick data record		D	i.d

STRING

for every logical input device of class STRING:

string device number	(1..n)	I	w.d.t
operating mode	(REQUEST,SAMPLE,EVENT)	E	REQUEST
echo switch	(ECHO,NOECHO)	E	ECHO
initial string		S	'
prompt/echo type	(1..n)	I	1
echo area	DC	4xR	w.d.t
string data record containing at least:		D	i.d
buffer size	(32..n)	I	w.d.t
cursor position	(1..n)	I	1

4.4   GKS Functions Applying to Workstations

The characteristics of the different workstation types, especially the characteristics of the special workstations, is best described by the set of functions applicable to them.

Only four functions apply to all workstation types:
— OPEN WORKSTATION
— CLOSE WORKSTATION
— INQUIRE WORKSTATION CONNECTION AND TYPE
— ESCAPE

Output workstations are affected by all functions generating or controlling output. *Input workstations* are affected by all functions generating or controlling input except PICK input. *Output/input workstations* are affected by both groups of functions and, additionally, by all functions relating to PICK input. The special position of PICK is due to the fact that PICK input operates on images displayed on the display space and, therefore, requires output capabilities.

Metafile output is affected by the same functions as output workstations except INQUIRE TEXT EXTENT. This functions does not evaluate an entry in the workstation state list but uses also information associated with a certain font, e.g., character width for proportionally spaced fonts depends on the design of the font. As the assignment of a certain font is postponed for metafile output until metafile records are sent to an output or output/input workstation, which might happen at a different place with a different implementation of GKS, the text extent is not available for metafile output. Furthermore, as metafile workstations possess no workstation description table, all corresponding inquiry functions do not apply to metafile output. However, there exists one function which applies only to metafile output: WRITE ITEM TO GKSM.

Metafile input, in addition to the four functions mentioned above, is only affected by two special functions: GET ITEM TYPE FROM GKSM and READ ITEM FROM GKSM.

The *workstation-independent segment storage (WISS)* behaves like an output workstation except that functions relating to a display surface like: REDRAW ALL SEGMENTS TO WORKSTATION, UPDATE WORKSTATION, SET DEFERRAL STATE or specifying workstation attributes and workstation transformation do not apply. CLEAR WORKSTATION applies in so far as segments are deleted. The clearing of the display surface naturally is not relevant for WISS. COPY SEGMENT TO WORKSTATION needs the WISS as a source but may not use it as destination as this would have no effect. Furthermore, most entries of the workstation state list and the entire workstation description table do not exist for the WISS. Consequently, the respective inquiry functions do not apply.

All GKS functions with the workstation categories to which they apply, directly or indirectly, are listed in Table 4.3.

Table 4.3 List of all GKS functions and corresponding workstation types

GKS Function		Applies to				
Control Functions						
OPEN GKS		not applicable				
CLOSE GKS		not applicable				
OPEN WORKSTATION	WISS	MO	O	OI	I	MI
CLOSE WORKSTATION	WISS	MO	O	OI	I	MI
ACTIVATE WORKSTATION	WISS	MO	O	OI		
DEACTIVATE WORKSTATION	WISS	MO	O	OI		
CLEAR WORKSTATION	WISS	MO	O	OI		
REDRAW ALL SEGMENTS ON WORKSTATION		MO	O	OI		
UPDATE WORKSTATION		MO	O	OI		
SET DEFERRAL STATE		MO	O	OI		
MESSAGE		MO	O	OI	I	
ESCAPE	WISS	MO	O	OI	I	MI
Output Functions						
POLYLINE	WISS	MO	O	OI		
POLYMARKER	WISS	MO	O	OI		

Table 4.3 (continued)

TEXT	WISS	MO	O	OI	
FILL AREA	WISS	MO	O	OI	
CELL ARRAY	WISS	MO	O	OI	
GENERALIZED DRAWING PRIMITIVE (GDP)	WISS	MO	O	OI	

Output Attributes

SET POLYLINE INDEX	WISS	MO	O	OI	
SET LINETYPE	WISS	MO	O	OI	
SET LINEWIDTH SCALE FACTOR	WISS	MO	O	OI	
SET POLYLINE COLOUR INDEX	WISS	MO	O	OI	
SET POLYMARKER INDEX	WISS	MO	O	OI	
SET MARKER TYPE	WISS	MO	O	OI	
SET MARKER TYPE SCALE FACTOR	WISS	MO	O	OI	
SET POLYMARKER COLOUR INDEX	WISS	MO	O	OI	
SET CHARACTER HEIGHT	WISS	MO	O	OI	
SET CHARACTER UP VECTOR	WISS	MO	O	OI	
SET TEXT PATH	WISS	MO	O	OI	
SET TEXT ALIGNMENT	WISS	MO	O	OI	
SET TEXT INDEX	WISS	MO	O	OI	
SET TEXT FONT AND PRECISION	WISS	MO	O	OI	
SET CHARACTER EXPANSION FACTOR	WISS	MO	O	OI	
SET CHARACTER SPACING	WISS	MO	O	OI	
SET TEXT COLOUR INDEX	WISS	MO	O	OI	
SET FILL AREA INDEX	WISS	MO	O	OI	
SET FILL AREA INTERIOR STYLE	WISS	MO	O	OI	
SET FILL AREA STYLE INDEX	WISS	MO	O	OI	
SET FILL AREA COLOUR INDEX	WISS	MO	O	OI	
SET PATTERN SIZE	WISS	MO	O	OI	
SET PATTERN REFERENCE POINT	WISS	MO	O	OI	
SET ASPECT SOURCE FLAGS	WISS	MO	O	OI	
SET PICK IDENTIFIER	WISS	MO	O	OI	
SET POLYLINE REPRESENTATION		MO	O	OI	
SET POLYMARKER REPRESENTATION		MO	O	OI	
SET TEXT REPRESENTATION		MO	O	OI	
SET FILL AREA REPRESENTATION		MO	O	OI	
SET PATTERN REPRESENTATION		MO	O	OI	
SET COLOUR REPRESENTATION		MO	O	OI	

Transformation Functions

SET WINDOW	WISS	MO	O	OI	I
SET VIEWPORT	WISS	MO	O	OI	I
SET VIEWPORT INPUT PRIORITY	WISS	MO	O	OI	I
SELECT NORMALIZATION TRANSFORMATION	WISS	MO	O	OI	I
SET CLIPPING INDICATOR	WISS	MO	O	OI	
SET WORKSTATION WINDOW		MO	O	OI	I
SET WORKSTATION VIEWPORT		MO	O	OI	I

Table 4.3 (continued)

Segment Functions

CREATE SEGMENT	WISS	MO	O	OI
CLOSE SEGMENT	WISS	MO	O	OI
RENAME SEGMENT	WISS	MO	O	OI
DELETE SEGMENT	WISS	MO	O	OI
DELETE SEGMENT FROM WORKSTATION	WISS	MO	O	OI
ASSOCIATE SEGMENT WITH WORKSTATION	WISS	MO	O	OI
COPY SEGMENT TO WORKSTATION	(WISS)	MO	O	OI
INSERT SEGMENT	WISS	MO	O	OI
SET SEGMENT TRANSFORMATION	WISS	MO	O	OI
SET VISIBILITY	WISS	MO	O	OI
SET HIGHLIGHTING	WISS	MO	O	OI
SET SEGMENT PRIORITY	WISS	MO	O	OI
SET DETECTABILITY	WISS	MO	O	OI

Input Functions

INITIALISE LOCATOR	OI	I
INITIALISE STROKE	OI	I
INITIALISE VALUATOR	OI	I
INITIALISE CHOICE	OI	I
INITIALISE PICK	OI	
INITIALISE STRING	OI	I
SET LOCATOR MODE	OI	I
SET STROKE MODE	OI	I
SET VALUATOR MODE	OI	I
SET CHOICE MODE	OI	I
SET PICK MODE	OI	
SET STRING MODE	OI	I
REQUEST LOCATOR	OI	I
REQUEST STROKE	OI	I
REQUEST VALUATOR	OI	I
REQUEST CHOICE	OI	I
REQUEST PICK	OI	
REQUEST STRING	OI	I
SAMPLE LOCATOR	OI	I
SAMPLE STROKE	OI	I
SAMPLE VALUATOR	OI	I
SAMPLE CHOICE	OI	I
SAMPLE PICK	OI	
SAMPLE STRING	OI	I
AWAIT EVENT	OI	I
FLUSH DEVICE EVENTS	OI	I
GET LOCATOR	OI	I
GET STROKE	OI	I
GET VALUATOR	OI	I
GET CHOICE	OI	I

Table 4.3 (continued)

GET PICK		OI			
GET STRING		OI	I		

Metafile Functions

WRITE ITEM TO GKSM		MO			
GET ITEM TYPE FROM GKSM					MI
READ ITEM FROM GKSM					MI
INTERPRET ITEM	WISS	MO	O	OI	I

Inquiry Functions

INQUIRE OPERATING STATE VALUE		not applicable				
INQUIRE LEVEL OF GKS		not applicable				
INQUIRE LIST OF AVAILABLE WORKSTATION TYPES		not applicable				
INQUIRE WORKSTATION MAXIMUM NUMBERS		not applicable				
INQUIRE MAXIMUM NORMALIZATION TRANSFORMATION NUMBER		not applicable				
INQUIRE SET OF OPEN WORKSTATIONS		not applicable				
INQUIRE SET OF ACTIVE WORKSTATIONS		not applicable				
INQUIRE CURRENT PRIMITIVE ATTRIBUTE VALUES		not applicable				
INQUIRE CURRENT INDIVIDUAL ATTRIBUTE VALUES		not applicable				
INQUIRE CURRENT NORMALIZATION TRANSFORMATION NUMBER		not applicable				
INQUIRE LIST OF NORMALIZATION TRANSFORMATION NUMBERS		not applicable				
INQUIRE NORMALIZATION TRANSFORMATION		not applicable				
INQUIRE CLIPPING INDICATOR		not applicable				
INQUIRE NAME OF OPEN SEGMENT		not applicable				
INQUIRE SET OF SEGMENT NAMES IN USE		not applicable				
INQUIRE MORE SIMULTANEOUS EVENTS		not applicable				
INQUIRE WORKSTATION CONNECTION AND TYPE	WISS	MO	O	OI	I	MI
INQUIRE WORKSTATION STATE	WISS	MO	O	OI		
INQUIRE WORKSTATION DEFERRAL AND UPDATE STATES		MO	O	OI		
INQUIRE LIST OF POLYLINE INDICES		MO	O	OI		
INQUIRE POLYLINE REPRESENTATION		MO	O	OI		
INQUIRE LIST OF POLYMARKER INDICES		MO	O	OI		
INQUIRE POLYMARKER REPRESENTATION		MO	O	OI		
INQUIRE LIST OF TEXT INDICES		MO	O	OI		
INQUIRE TEXT REPRESENTATION		MO	O	OI		
INQUIRE TEXT EXTENT			O	OI		
INQUIRE LIST OF FILL AREA INDICES		MO	O	OI		
INQUIRE FILL AREA REPRESENTATION		MO	O	OI		
INQUIRE LIST OF PATTERN INDICES		MO	O	OI		
INQUIRE PATTERN REPRESENTATION		MO	O	OI		

Table 4.3 (continued)

	WISS	MO	O	OI	I	MI
INQUIRE LIST OF COLOUR INDICES		MO	O	OI		
INQUIRE COLOUR REPRESENTATION		MO	O	OI		
INQUIRE WORKSTATION TRANSFORMATION		MO	O	OI	I	
INQUIRE SET OF SEGMENT NAMES ON WORKSTATION	WISS	MO	O	OI		
INQUIRE LOCATOR DEVICE STATE				OI	I	
INQUIRE STROKE DEVICE STATE				OI	I	
INQUIRE VALUATOR DEVICE STATE				OI	I	
INQUIRE CHOICE DEVICE STATE				OI	I	
INQUIRE PICK DEVICE STATE				OI		
INQUIRE STRING DEVICE STATE				OI	I	
INQUIRE WORKSTATION CATEGORY	WISS	MO	O	OI	I	MI
INQUIRE WORKSTATION CLASSIFICATION			O	OI		
INQUIRE MAXIMUM DISPLAY SURFACE SIZE			O	OI	I	
INQUIRE DYNAMIC MODIFICATION OF WORKSTATION ATTRIBUTES			O	OI		
INQUIRE DEFAULT DEFERRAL STATE VALUES			O	OI		
INQUIRE POLYLINE FACILITIES			O	OI		
INQUIRE PREDEFINED POLYLINE REPRESENTATION			O	OI		
INQUIRE POLYMARKER FACILITIES			O	OI		
INQUIRE PREDEFINED POLYMARKER REPRESENTATION			O	OI		
INQUIRE TEXT FACILITIES			O	OI		
INQUIRE PREDEFINED TEXT REPRESENTATION			O	OI		
INQUIRE FILL AREA FACILITIES			O	OI		
INQUIRE PREDEFINED FILL AREA REPRESENTATION			O	OI		
INQUIRE PATTERN FACILITIES			O	OI		
INQUIRE PREDEFINED PATTERN REPRESENTATION			O	OI		
INQUIRE COLOUR FACILITIES			O	OI		
INQUIRE PREDEFINED COLOUR REPRESENTATION			O	OI		
INQUIRE LIST OF AVAILABLE GENERALIZED DRAWING PRIMITIVES			O	OI		
INQUIRE GENERALIZED DRAWING PRIMITIVE			O	OI		
INQUIRE MAXIMUM LENGTH OF WORKSTATION STATE TABLES			O	OI		
INQUIRE NUMBER OF SEGMENT PRIORITIES SUPPORTED			O	OI		
INQUIRE DYNAMIC MODIFICATION OF SEGMENT ATTRIBUTES			O	OI		
INQUIRE NUMBER OF AVAILABLE LOGICAL INPUT DEVICES				OI	I	
INQUIRE DEFAULT LOCATOR DEVICE DATA				OI	I	
INQUIRE DEFAULT STROKE DEVICE DATA				OI	I	
INQUIRE DEFAULT VALUATOR DEVICE DATA				OI	I	
INQUIRE DEFAULT CHOICE DEVICE DATA				OI	I	
INQUIRE DEFAULT PICK DEVICE DATA				OI		

Table 4.3 (continued)

INQUIRE DEFAULT STRING DEVICE DATA			OI	I
INQUIRE SET OF ASSOCIATED WORKSTATIONS	WISS	MO	O	OI
INQUIRE SEGMENT ATTRIBUTES	WISS	MO	O	OI
INQUIRE PIXEL ARRAY DIMENSIONS			O	OI
INQUIRE PIXEL ARRAY			O	OI
INQUIRE PIXEL			O	OI
INQUIRE INPUT QUEUE OVERFLOW		not applicable		

Utility Functions

EVALUATE TRANSFORMATION MATRIX	not applicable
ACCUMULATE TRANSFORMATION MATRIX	not applicable

Error Handling

EMERGENCY CLOSE GKS	not applicable
ERROR HANDLING	not applicable
ERROR LOGGING	not applicable

Key:
	WISS	workstation-independent segment storage
	MO	GKS metafile output
	O	output workstation
	OI	output/input workstation
	I	input workstation
	MI	GKS metafile input
	(WISS)	workstation-independent segment storage is fundamental to the operation of this GKS function, but the workstation identifier parameter cannot be workstation-independent segment storage

4.5 Workstation Control

Before the application program may use a workstation, it must be allocated by the GKS function OPEN WORKSTATION. This function associates a name, the workstation identifier, to the workstation by which it is referenced later.

The workstation is selected by a connection identifier which allows the operating system to establish the connection. The connection identifier may be a unit number in FORTRAN or a file name, a link name, etc. depending on the programming environment. The valid connection identifiers will be described in the installation manual.

A further parameter of OPEN WORKSTATION specifies the workstation type which selects the appropriate workstation driver and the workstation description table from which the workstation state list is to be initialised. The available workstation types are listed in the GKS description table (Table 3.5). They are implementation-dependent except three mandatory workstation types for metafile input, metafile output, and workstation independent segment storage the names of which will be defined with each language-dependent layer.

The selection of a workstation by connection identifier and workstation type offers a flexibility which may be redundant (e.g., if only one workstation of a given type exists) or which may not be supported by an operating system (e.g., if the connection must be determined prior to program starting). The installation manual will describe which combinations of both parameters are valid or whether one parameter will be ignored totally.

OPEN WORKSTATION allocates the workstation and the workstation state list which is now available for inquiry. Input devices may be used and segments may be manipulated on an open workstation.

To allow graphical output to be sent to an open workstation, it has to be made active by the function ACTIVATE WORKSTATION. Output primitives are sent to, and segments are stored on, all active workstations and no others. Naturally, only workstations possessing output capabilities may be activated.

A workstation must be opened before it may be activated. ACTIVATE WORKSTATION just enables an open workstation for output. There may exist open (i.e., not active) and active workstation at the same time.

An active workstation is made inactive by the function DEACTIVATE WORKSTATION; an open workstation is closed by the function CLOSE WORKSTATION; the workstation state list is cancelled and the connection to the workstation is released. Whether the workstation actually is deallocated and made available for another user, depends on the capabilities of the operating system.

Example 4.1 in Section 4.8 shows the use of the above functions. The functions OPEN/CLOSE GKS, OPEN/CLOSE WORKSTATION, and ACTIVATE/DEACTIVATE WORKSTATION have been defined as separate functions to clarify the transitions of states in GKS and to provide full flexibility for all environments. However, a usual case of a graphics workstation is a terminal used at the same time for alphanumeric dialogue with the operating system and for graphics. In this case, there is no need to inform the operating system which workstation is to be addressed, as this workstation is already allocated and active at the time of OPEN GKS. For such environments, it may be useful to have one single function which opens GKS and opens and activates this workstation in one step. Such a functions can easily be built on top of GKS.

OPEN WORKSTATION   GKOP,WSOP,WSAC,SGOP   L0a
Parameters:
   Input   workstation identifier   N
   Input   connection identifier   N
   Input   workstation type   N
Effect:
   If GKS is in operating state GKOP, it will be set into the state WSOP = "at least one workstation open". GKS requests the operating system to establish the specified connection for a workstation characterized in the workstation description table by

the 'workstation type'. The workstation state list is allocated and initialised as indicated in 4.3. The workstation identifier is added to the set of open workstations in the GKS state list. OPEN WORKSTATION ensures that the display surface is clear, but does not clear the surface needlessly.

Note:

The connection identifier is given in a form suitable for the application program language (for example, a 'unit number' in FORTRAN or a 'file identifier' in PL/1). There are three workstation categories 'metafile input', 'metafile output' and 'workstation-independent segment storage' which are mandatory at certain levels of GKS.

Errors:

8	GKS not in proper state: GKS shall be in one of the states GKOP, WSOP, WSAC or SGOP
20	Specified workstation identifier is invalid
21	Specified connection identifier is invalid
22	Specified workstation type is invalid
23	Specified workstation type does not exist
24	Specified workstation is open
26	Specified workstation cannot be opened
28	Workstation Independent Segment Storage is already open

———————————————— *FORTRAN-Interface* ————————————————

CALL GOPWK (WKID,CONID,WTYPE)

Parameters:

Input	WKID	workstation identifier	INTEGER
Input	CONID	connection identifier	INTEGER
Input	WTYPE	workstation type	INTEGER

CLOSE WORKSTATION   WSOP,WSAC,SGOP   L0a

Parameters:

Input	workstation identifier	N

Effect:

An implicit UPDATE WORKSTATION is performed for the specified workstation. The workstation state list is deallocated. The workstation identifier is deleted from the set of open workstations in the GKS state list and from the set of associated workstations in the segment state list of every segment containing it. If the set of associated workstations of a segment becomes empty, the segment is deleted. The input queue is flushed of all events from all devices on the workstation being closed. If the 'identification of one of the logical input devices that caused an input queue overflow' entry in the GKS error state list refers to this workstation identifier, then all the contents of that entry become undefined. The connection to the workstation is released. GKS is set into operating state GKOP if no workstations remain open. The display surface need not be cleared when CLOSE WORKSTATION is invoked, but it may be cleared.

Errors:

7	GKS not in proper state: GKS shall be in one of the states WSOP, WSAC or SGOP
20	Specified workstation identifier is invalid
25	Specified workstation is not open
29	Specified workstation is active
147	Input queue has overflowed

——————————————— *FORTRAN-Interface* ———————————————

CALL GCLWK (WKID)

Parameters:

Input   WKID   workstation identifier   INTEGER

ACTIVATE WORKSTATION   WSOP,WSAC   L0a

Parameters:

Input   workstation identifier   N

Effect:

GKS is set into the operating state WSAC = "At least one workstation active". The specified workstation is marked active in the workstation state list. The workstation identifier is added to the set of active workstations in the GKS state list.

Note:

Output primitives are sent to and segments are stored on all active workstations.

Errors:

  6   GKS not in proper state: GKS shall be either in the state WSOP or in the state WSAC

 20   Specified workstation identifier is invalid

 25   Specified workstation is not open

 29   Specified workstation is active

 33   Specified workstation is of category MI

 35   Specified workstation is of category INPUT

——————————————— *FORTRAN-Interface* ———————————————

CALL GACWK (WKID)

Parameters:

Input   WKID   workstation identifier   INTEGER

DEACTIVATE WORKSTATION   WSAC   L0a

Parameters:

Input   workstation identifier   N

Effect:

The specified workstation is marked inactive in the workstation state list. The workstation identifier is deleted from the set of active workstations in the GKS state list. GKS is set into the operating state WSOP = "At least one workstation open" if no workstation remains active.

Note:

While a workstation is inactive, primitives are not sent to it nor does it store new segments. Segments already stored on this workstation are retained.

Errors:

  3   GKS not in proper state: GKS shall be in the state WSAC

 20   Specified workstation identifier is invalid

 30   Specified workstation is not active

 33   Specified workstation is of category MI

 35   Specified workstation is of category INPUT

——————————————— *FORTRAN-Interface* ———————————————

CALL GDAWK (WKID)

Parameters:

Input   WKID   workstation identifier   INTEGER

To generate several images on the same workstation, a command is necessary which indicates the start of a new image. GKS provides the function CLEAR WORKSTATION which deletes entirely the previously generated primitives and allows the start of a new image on a cleared display surface. By calling this function, a series of pictures can be generated within one session (see Example 4.2).

If clearing of the display surface by CLEAR WORKSTATION is requested, two capabilities for clearing the display surface are recognized, namely
— clear the display surface even if it is empty;
— ensure that the display surface is clear without clearing the display surface unnecessarily.

The first capability allows the generation of empty images which is needed, e.g., when creating a pause within a film.

The second capability means that the display surface is only cleared when needed — this would normally be when the display surface was not clear. However, it is not trivial to find out whether the display surface is clear or not, e.g., a circle may have been generated via GDP with the midpoint within the display surface which has been clipped to non-existence. Therefore, GKS will avoid clearing a device unnecessarily only as far as it can be determined with reasonable effort.

CLEAR WORKSTATION   WSOP,WSAC   L0a
Parameters:
  Input   workstation identifier   N
  Input   control flag   (CONDITIONALLY,ALWAYS)   E
Effect:
All of the following actions are executed in the given sequence:
    a) All deferred actions (see Section 4.4) for the specified workstation are executed (without intermediate clearing of the display surface).
    b) The display surface is set to a clear state according to the control flag as follows:
        CONDITIONALLY: it is ensured that the display surface is clear without clearing it needlessly;
        ALWAYS: the display surface is cleared.
    c) If the 'workstation transformation update state' entry in the workstation state list is PENDING, the 'current workstation window' and 'current workstation viewport' entries in the workstation state list are assigned the values of the 'requested workstation window' and 'requested workstation viewport' entries; the 'workstation transformation update state' entry is set to NOTPENDING.
    d) For all segments stored on the specified workstation, the workstation identifier is deleted from the 'set of associated workstations' in the segment state list. If the 'set of associated workstations' of a segment becomes empty, the segment is deleted. The 'set of stored segments for this workstation' in the workstation state list is set to 'empty'.
    e) The 'new frame action necessary at update' entry in the workstation state list is set to NO.
    f) The 'display surface empty' entry in the workstation state list is set to EMPTY.
Errors:
    6   GKS not in proper state: GKS shall be either in the state WSOP or in the state WSAC

20   Specified workstation identifier is invalid
25   Specified workstation is not open
33   Specified workstation is of category MI
35   Specified workstation is of category INPUT

───────────────────────────── *FORTRAN-Interface* ─────────────────────────────
CALL GCLRWK (WKID,COFL)
Parameters:
   Input   WKID   workstation identifier   INTEGER
   Input   COFL   control flag   (0 = conditionally, 1 = always)   INTEGER

4.6   Deferring Picture Changes

The generation of pictures is a complicated and expensive task. Low performance devices will have difficulties to generate pictures fast enough which is a particular problem for interactive sessions. In this section the function SET DEFERRAL MODE is introduced which allows, to a certain degree, the tuning of a workstation in a way that the available resources are best used for a specific application.

The novice reader may skip this section as the default setting will serve best the most common needs. Some knowledge of the input and segment functions will be useful for the understanding of this section.

The display of a workstation should reflect as far as possible the actual state of the picture as defined by the application program. However, to use the capabilities of a workstation efficiently, GKS allows a workstation to delay, for a certain period of time, the actions requested by the application program. During this period, the state of the display may be undefined.

The function SET DEFERRAL STATE allows the application program to choose that deferral state which takes into account the capabilities of the workstation and the requirements of the application program. The deferral state of a workstation is controlled by two attributes: deferral mode and implicit regeneration mode.

Deferral mode controls the possible delay of output functions. For example, data sent to a device may be buffered to optimise data transfer. The deferral mode can be specified as follows:

ASAP: The visual effect of each function will be achieved on the workstation As Soon As Possible (ASAP).

BNIG: The visual effect of each function will be achieved on the workstation Before the Next Interaction Globally (BNIG), i.e., before the next interaction with a logical input device gets underway on any workstation (see Section 8.1). If an interaction on any workstation is already underway, the visual effect will be achieved as soon as possible.

BNIL: The visual effect of each function will be achieved on the workstation Before the Next Interaction Locally (BNIL), i.e., before the next interaction with a logical input device gets underway on that workstation (see Section

8.1). If an interaction on that workstation is already underway, the visual effect will be achieved as soon as possible.

ASTI: The visual effect of each function will be achieved on the workstation At Some TIme (ASTI).

Deferral applies to the following functions that generate output:
POLYLINE
POLYMARKER
TEXT
FILL AREA
CELL ARRAY
GENERALIZED DRAWING PRIMITIVE
INSERT SEGMENT
ASSOCIATE SEGMENT WITH WORKSTATION
COPY SEGMENT TO WORKSTATION
INTERPRET ITEM

Deferred output functions will be executed
— when a local or global interaction is initiated (for deferral mode BNIL and BNIG);
— when end of output for the current picture is indicated by the GKS functions CLEAR WORKSTATION or CLOSE WORKSTATION;
— before a new picture is initiated by REDRAW ALL SEGMENTS ON WORKSTATION;
— when required explicitly by UPDATE WORKSTATION or by setting the deferral mode to ASAP.

As long as none of these cases occurs, the workstation driver or GKS may decide arbitrarily when to send deferred output to a workstation's display surface.

Implicit regeneration mode controls the suppression of implicit regeneration of the whole picture. For example, change of colour by SET COLOUR REPRE-SENTATION may be performed immediately on a colour raster display by setting an entry of the device's colour table; the same function may be performed on a plotter only by putting new paper on it and redrawing the whole picture. The latter case is called implicit regeneration and controlled by the implicit regeneration mode. The mode can be specified as follows:
— implicit regeneration of the picture is SUPPRESSED;
— implicit regeneration of the picture is ALLOWED:
Suppression of implicit regeneration does not prevent an explicit regeneration initiated by REDRAW ALL SEGMENTS ON WORKSTATION or, possibly, by UPDATE WORKSTATION.

The purposes of the implicit regeneration mode are:
— efficient use of devices with poor dynamic capabilities like storage tubes;
— precise control of frames produced on hard copy devices.

For such devices, the initial setting of the implicit regeneration mode will be SUPPRESSED which secures that a new frame will be initiated only by

an explicit function call to REDRAW ALL SEGMENTS ON WORKSTA-
TION or UPDATE WORKSTATION.

The following functions change the picture and may imply an implicit regeneration:

SET POLYLINE REPRESENTATION
SET POLYMARKER REPRESENTATION
SET TEXT REPRESENTATION
SET FILL AREA REPRESENTATION
SET PATTERN REPRESENTATION
SET COLOUR REPRESENTATION SET WORKSTATION WINDOW
SET WORKSTATION VIEWPORT
SET SEGMENT TRANSFORMATION
SET VISIBILITY
SET HIGHLIGHTING
SET SEGMENT PRIORITY
DELETE SEGMENT
DELETE SEGMENT FROM WORKSTATION
ASSOCIATE SEGMENT WITH WORKSTATION
INTERPRET ITEM

In addition, the output of primitives (including INSERT SEGMENT), when
segment priority is important, may cause implicit regeneration, for example,
if primitives are generated within a segment overlapping another segment with
lower priority.

These functions can be performed immediately on some workstations, but
on others may imply a regeneration of the whole picture to achieve the effect.
The entries 'dynamic modification accepted' in the workstation description table
indicate which changes:
— can be performed immediately;
— lead to an implicit regeneration.

The effect of dynamic changes only is guaranteed for primitives within segments. The effect on primitives outside segments may be workstation-dependent.
If changes can be performed immediately, those changes may affect primitives
outside segments in addition to those inside segments. For example, changing
the colour table will affect primitives within and outside segments. On the other
hand, if changes are performed via an implicit regeneration, only primitives
inside segments will show the required attribute change. Primitives outside segments will be merely deleted from the display surface during regeneration. Therefore, for applications using primitives outside segments, it will be advisable
to suppress implicit regeneration and to control explicitly the deletion of primitives outside segments and the regeneration of the picture.

The concept of deferral refers only to visible effects of GKS functions. Effects
on the segment storage or on the state of the workstation are (conceptually)
not deferred. In none of the deferral states is it mandatory for the addition
of graphical data, or attribute changes, to be delayed. If this is required, it
should be achieved using the segment storage facility and the visibility attribute.

This restriction means that the buffer for deferred actions can be chosen in an implementation-dependent manner.

If segments of different priority are created on workstations that permit one segment to hide another, even the addition of data may cause an implicit regeneration, which can be deferred. Also in this case the buffer size may be limited. Since only segments have priority, this can happen to primitives within segments only which are already stored in the segment storage. Primitives outside segments need not be deferred on such workstations.

SET DEFERRAL STATE   WSOP,WSAC,SGOP   L1a

Parameters:

Input	workstation identifier		N
Input	deferral mode	(ASAP,BNIG,BNIL,ASTI)	E
Input	implicit regeneration mode	(SUPPRESSED,ALLOWED)	E

Effect:

The entries 'deferral mode' and 'implicit regeneration mode' for the specified workstation are set in the workstation state list. Depending on the new value of 'deferral mode', deferred output may be unblocked. If in the workstation state list, the new values of 'implicit regeneration mode' is ALLOWED and 'new frame action necessary at update' is YES, then an action equivalent to REDRAW ALL SEGMENTS ON WORKSTATION is performed.

Errors:

7	GKS not in proper state: GKS shall be in one of the states WSOP, WSAC or SGOP
20	Specified workstation identifier is invalid
25	Specified workstation is not open
33	Specified workstation is of category MI
35	Specified workstation is of category INPUT
36	Specified workstation is Workstation Independent Segment Storage

──────────────── *FORTRAN-Interface* ────────────────

CALL GSDS (WKID,DEFMOD,REGMOD)

Parameters:

Input	WKID	workstation identifier		INTEGER
Input	DEFMOD	deferral mode	(0=asap, 1=bnil, 2=bnig, 3=asti)	INTEGER
Input	REGMOD	implicit regeneration mode	(0=allowed, 1=suppressed)	INTEGER

The function SET DEFERRAL STATE should be used with care as a change of the values preset by the implementor may strongly influence the performance of the respective workstation. To secure that the display of a workstation shows the actual state at certain points in time, the function UPDATE WORKSTATION should be used.

UPDATE WORKSTATION performs two steps:
— If the deferral mode allows the delay of output functions and there are some functions actually delayed, these functions will be executed.
— If an implicit regeneration has been suppressed, the actual picture will be generated on the display surface.

The first step secures that all output underway to the workstation actually is generated on the display surface. Thus, UPDATE WORKSTATION defines an ultimate point until which output may be deferred. The second step allows performance of those changes which could not be made on the current picture but which require a full regeneration of the picture. If the second step is performed, the first step might seem useless. This may be true for interactive devices. For hard copy devices, however, it is essential to finish the current picture before initiating the next one.

UPDATE WORKSTATION   WSOP,WSAC,SGOP   L0a
Parameters:
  Input   workstation identifier   N
  Input   regeneration flag   (PERFORM,SUPPRESS)   E
Effect:
  All deferred actions for the specified workstation are executed (without intermediate clearing of the display surface). If the regeneration flag is set to PERFORM and the 'new frame action necessary at update' entry in the workstation state list is YES, then the following actions are executed in the given sequence:
a)   The display surface is cleared only if the 'display surface empty' entry in the workstation state list is NOTEMPTY. The entry is set to EMPTY.
b)   If the 'workstation transformation update state' entry in the workstation state list is PENDING, the 'current workstation window' and 'current workstation viewport' entries in the workstation state list are assigned the values of the 're-quested workstation window' and 'requested workstation viewport' entries; the 'workstation transformation update state' entry is set to NOTPENDING.
c)   All visible segments stored on this workstation (i.e. contained in the 'set of stored segments for this workstation' in the workstation state list) are redisplayed. This action typically causes the 'display surface empty' entry in the workstation state list to be set to NOTEMPTY.
d)   The 'new frame action necessary at update' entry in the workstation state list is set to NO.
Note:
  If the regeneration flag is PERFORM, UPDATE WORKSTATION suspends the effect of SET DEFERRAL STATE. In that case, it is equivalent to the following sequence of functions:
    INQUIRE WORKSTATION STATE;
    save deferral state;
    SET DEFERRAL STATE (ASAP,ALLOWED);
    set deferral state to saved value.
  If the value of the 'new frame action necessary at update' entry is NO or the regeneration flag is SUPPRESS, UPDATE WORKSTATION merely initiates the transmission of blocked data. If the value of the entry 'new frame action necessary at update' is YES and the regeneration flag is PERFORM, UPDATE WORKSTATION behaves as REDRAW ALL SEGMENTS ON WORKSTATION.
  The 'new frame action necessary at update' entry in a workstation state list is set to YES during deferred action generation if both of the following are true:
a) an action causing modification of the picture is actually deferred on that workstation;
b) the workstation display surface does not allow modification of the image without redrawing the whole picture (for example, plotter, storage tube display).

Errors:

7	GKS not in proper state: GKS shall be in one of the states WSOP, WSAC or SGOP
20	Specified workstation identifier is invalid
25	Specified workstation is not open
33	Specified workstation is of category MI
35	Specified workstation is of category INPUT
36	Specified workstation is Workstation Independent Segment Storage

———————————————— *FORTRAN-Interface* ————————————————

CALL GUWK (WKID,REGFL)

Parameters:

Input	WKID	workstation identifier		INTEGER
Input	REGFL	regeneration flag	(0 = suppress, 1 = perform)	INTEGER

4.7 Addressing Workstation Capabilities Not Covered by GKS

By setting the workstation state list, the application program may access and use a lot of workstation-specific features. However, there always will remain some particular features outside the scope of GKS. Knowing this limitation of GKS, some functions have been provided to give the application program a standardized way to access non-standard features. The use of these functions will reduce the portability of programs. Their use should be avoided as much as possible and be reserved for cases where important capabilities are available but their use is not provided for within GKS.

These additional functions are:
— GDP, to access additional output primitives on a workstation like circle, spline interpolation, etc.;
— MESSAGE, to address a human operator at a workstation and to give him some instructions like changing of paper on a plotter or change of camera in a microfilm recorder;
— ESCAPE, to call any installation- or hardware-specific features of a workstation or of the whole system

GDP is discussed in detail in Section 6.7. GKS knows the syntax of GDP which allows application of all GKS transformations to the geometrical parameters leaving the interpretation of the data to the individual workstation.

The MESSAGE function allows a character string to be sent to a workstation. The character string sent by MESSAGE is to be interpreted by an operator whose reaction is outside the scope of GKS. The application program has no control over the position and appearance of the character string and an implementation is allowed to place the string on a device, distinct from but associated with the workstation, e.g., on an alphanumeric terminal. The character string is not regarded as an output like the TEXT primitive belonging to the graphical output. Therefore, MESSAGE may apply also to input workstations. The WISS is the only workstation category which does not accept the MESSAGE function.

MESSAGE   WSOP,WSAC,SGOP   L1a
Parameters:
  Input   workstation identifier   N
  Input   message   S
Effect:
The message function:
a)   may display a message at an implementation-dependent location on the workstation viewport or on some separate device associated with the workstation.
b)   does not alter the GKS state list.
c)   may affect the workstation in a purely local way (for example, requesting the operator to change paper). Possible effects on the execution of the application program or on subsequent commands sent to the workstation by GKS must be stated explicitly in the implementation dependencies manual.

Errors:
   7   GKS not in proper state: GKS shall be in one of the states WSOP, WSAC or SGOP
  20   Specified workstation identifier is invalid
  25   Specified workstation is not open
  36   Specified workstation is Workstation Independent Segment Storage

———————————————— *FORTRAN-Interface* ————————————————

CALL GMSG (WKID,MESS)
Parameters:
  Input   WKID   workstation identifier   INTEGER
  Input   MESS   message   CHARACTER*(*)

    A standard cannot cover all requirements of all graphics applications. Nevertheless, it is desirable that all application programs stick as close as possible to the standard functionality. For this purpose, an ESCAPE function is provided as a standard way of being non-standard which allows to extend the functionality of GKS. Such an ESCAPE function naturally has negative consequences on the portability of programs. Therefore, it should be used exclusively if important capabilities are needed which, otherwise, are not covered by GKS.

    ESCAPE allows the addressing of all features of an GKS-implementation and of any hardware except that ESCAPE may not generate output. The generation of non-standard output primitives is solely reserved for GDP to allow GKS at least a minimal control of output. An example for the use of ESCAPE is a raster device which has firmware to perform logical operations (AND, OR, EXCLUSIVE OR) on raster matrices to generate the resulting raster image ("raster-op").

ESCAPE   GKOP,WSOP,WSAC,SGOP   L0a
Parameters:
  Input   specific escape function identification   N
  Input   escape data record   D

Effect:

The specified non-standard specific escape function is invoked. The form of the escape data record may vary for different functions. Also the GKS states allowing the invocation of a specific escape function may be restricted. The following rules govern the definition of a new specific escape function:

a) the GKS design concept is not violated;

b) the GKS state lists are not altered;

c) the function does not generate geometrical output;

d) any side effects must be well documented.

Specific escape functions may apply to more than one workstation, for example all open workstations or all active workstations. The escape data record can include a workstation identifier where this is required.

Note:

Examples of specific escape functions anticipated at present are:

a) support of raster devices allowing the display of more than one frame buffer;

b) use of raster-op hardware to manipulate data previously output by CELL ARRAY.

Errors:

8	GKS not in proper state: GKS shall be in one of the states GKOP, WSOP, WSAC or SGOP
180	Specified function is not supported
181	Contents of escape data record is invalid

———————————————— *FORTRAN-Interface* ————————————————

CALL GESC (FCTID,LDR,DATREC)

Parameters:

Input	FCTID	function identification	INTEGER
Input	LDR	length of data record	INTEGER
Input	DATREC (LDR)	data record	CHARACTER*80

The functions mentioned above allow the application program to access non-standard features. Besides that, additional features of a workstation may be used locally by the workstation operator without notifying GKS. For example, if a workstation has two display surfaces, the operator may switch locally from one to the other. More than one display surface can be controlled by GKS only by defining a separate workstation for each display surface. Such a local extension of functionality naturally does not affect program portability but operator portability.

4.8   Examples

Example 4.1   Workstation selection for input and output

This example illustrates how two workstations 'disp' and 'digi' can be selected independently for input and output. Note that OPEN_WORKSTATION can be called for any workstation whereas ACTIVATE_WORKSTATION requires the existence of some output capability on the respective workstation.

———————————————————— *Pascal* ————————————————————

L10   OPEN_GKS (error_file,memory_limit);
L20   OPEN_WORKSTATION (disp,conid1,vector_refresh_type);
          {Input possible on disp}
L30   OPEN_WORKSTATION (digi,conid2,digitizer_type);
          {Input possible on disp,digi}
L40   ACTIVATE_WORKSTATION (disp);
          {Input possible on disp,digi; Output generated on disp}
L50   ACTIVATE_WORKSTATION (digi);
          {Input possible on disp,digi; Output generated on disp,digi}
L60   DEACTIVATE_WORKSTATION (disp);
          {Input possible on disp,digi; Output generated on digi}
L70   CLOSE_WORKSTATION (disp);
          {Input possible on digi; Output generated on digi}
L80   DEACTIVATE_WORKSTATION (digi);
          {Input possible on digi}
L90   CLOSE_WORKSTATION (digi);
L100 CLOSE_GKS;

———————————————————— *Fortran* ————————————————————

L10   CALL GOPKS (ERRFIL)
L20   CALL GOPWK (DISP,CONID1,VECT)
        C   *** Input possible on DISP
L30   CALL GOPWK (DIGI,CONID2,DIG1)
        C   *** Input possible on DISP,DIGI
L40   CALL GACWK (DISP)
        C   *** Input possible on DISP,DIGI; Output generated on DISP
L50   CALL GACWK (DIGI)
        C   *** Input possible on DISP,DIGI; Output generated on DISP,DIGI
L60   CALL GDAWK (DISP)
        C   *** Input possible on DISP,DIGI; Output generated on DIGI
L70   CALL GCLWK (DISP)
        C   *** Input possible on DIGI; Output generated on DIGI
L80   CALL GDAWK (DIGI)
        C   *** Input possible on DIGI
L90   CALL GCLWK (DIGI)
L100   CALL GCLKS

Example 4.2   Generating a sequence of independent pictures

Assume that a procedure DRAW_PICTURE reads a file containing data describing a series of numbered pictures. This example shows the control functions which allocate and deallocate a plotter workstation and advance paper for each picture.

———————————————————— *Pascal* ————————————————————

L10   OPEN_GKS (error_file,memory_limit);
L20   OPEN_WORKSTATION (plot,connection,plotter_type);
L30   ACTIVATE_WORKSTATION (plot);

```
L40      FOR i:=1 TO max DO
L50      BEGIN
L60        CLEAR_WORKSTATION (plot, CONDITIONALLY);
L80          DRAW_PICTURE (i);                    {procedure draws i-th picture}
L90      END;

L100     DEACTIVATE_WORKSTATION (plot);
L110     CLOSE_WORKSTATION (plot);
L120     CLOSE_GKS;
```

─────────────────────────── *Fortran* ───────────────────────────

```
L10              CALL GOPKS (ERRFIL)
L20              CALL GOPWK (PLOT,CONNEC,TYPE)
L30              CALL GACWK (PLOT)

L40              DO 90 I=1,MAX
L60              CALL GCLWK (PLOT, CONDIT)
L80              CALL DRPICT (I)
      C                                    *** DRPICT draws i-th picture
L90          90 CONTINUE

L100             CALL GDAWK (PLOT)
L110             CALL GCLWK (PLOT)
L120             CALL GCLKS
```

4.9   Exercises

Exercise 4.1   Workstation description table

Write a workstation description table for one of the graphical input or output
devices available in your computing centre. Indicate which capabilities are immediately available on the device and which must be provided by additional software. Note that the minimal requirements depend on the GKS level (see Table
2.2). Furthermore, some requirements are valid for the set of all workstations
rather than for each individual workstation.

Exercise 4.2   Workstation state list

Describe in detail how the workstation state list of the workstation of Exercise 4.1 looks like immediately after initialisation. What entries do apply
and what are the values taken from the workstation description table?

5 TRANSFORMATIONS

5.1 Coordinate Systems

Pictures to be generated by GKS will be derived from data provided by the application program. These data may include results from measurements with arbitrary physical dimensions like temperature, weight, time, etc. By digitizing an object, data with metrical dimensions will be generated. Numerical calculations may generate unitless data. These *user coordinates* have to be mapped onto device coordinates describing the display surface of a workstation.

GKS only accepts Cartesian coordinates requiring solely linear scaling with positive scale factors and shifting to be transformed to device coordinates. These user coordinates are called *world coordinates (WC)*. Other user coordinates like polar or logarithmic coordinates cannot be handled by GKS and must be transformed by the application program before handing it over to GKS.

The transformation of world coordinates to device coordinates is done in two steps. In a first step, world coordinates are mapped onto an abstract display surface with *normalized device coordinates (NDC)*. This abstract display surface contains a workstation-independent representation of the picture. This intermediate step has been introduced to separate clearly workstation-dependent and -independent parts of a picture definition. Each workstation may show a different view of the workstation-independent picture. Furthermore, the NDC is used for the segment storage (see Chapter 7) and for the metafile (see Chapter 11). The NDC conceptually is unlimited. However, as long as no segment transformations are available, only that part of a picture lying in the range [0,1]x[0,1] can be displayed on a display surface. If segment transformations are available, parts of a picture can be moved from outside the range [0,1]x[0,1] back to the inside and thus become visible. If real numbers are used when storing coordinate data in segments there will be no difficulties to provide a sufficient large NDC-space. For smaller implementations using integer number representation, at least, an NDC of size $[-7, +7]$x$[-7, +7]$ must be supported. The number 7 has been selected somehow arbitrarily. It takes into account the resolution of common graphics devices and the word length of 16 bit used in many small computers.

The display space of each workstation is described by Cartesian coordinates called *device coordinates (DC)*. DC are metres on a device capable of producing a precisely scaled image and appropriate units, otherwise. The dimension 'metre' for DC makes it very easy to specify a transformation with a prescribed scale. This is a major use of DC in application programs. Whereas the NDC is quadratic, the display space of each workstation may be an arbitrary rectangle the size of which can be interrogated from the workstation description table.

5.2   Normalization Transformation

The application program may compose a picture from different sources which will have their own WC system. The *normalization transformation* is a means to relate the different coordinate systems by scaling and positioning the picture parts to form a picture in a single NDC. As WC systems may have axes with different dimensions, a different scaling may be specified for each axis. The normalization transformation is said to perform non-uniform scaling in such cases. The effect of non-uniform scaling is shown in Figure 5.1 where the right picture is obtained by non-uniform scaling of the left picture with the x-axis scaled by 1 and the y-axis scaled by 0.7.

A normalization transformation is defined by two rectangles, a *window* within WC space and a *viewport* within the range [0,1]x[0,1] of NDC space. Window and viewport define a transformation which maps the content of the window onto the viewport.

The window/viewport values of the normalization transformation are stored in the GKS state list. For high output levels, a minimum of ten normalization transformations may be specified and stored. The different transformations are identified by a normalization transformation number. This is an integer between 0 and n where n is an implementation-specific number which can be interrogated from the workstation description table. By default, all normalization transformations are set to identity, i.e., window and viewport are set to unit square.

Although several normalization transformations may be defined, only one of them can be active for output of primitives at any time. Initially, normaliza-

a   b

Figure 5.1 Effect of a non-uniform normalization transformation

tion transformation 0 is active. As far as output is concerned, the stored normalization transformations do not give additional functionality but only give some comfort for applications frequently switching between a fixed set of transformations. The purpose for this concept is the transformation of LOCATOR input. LOCATOR input is transformed back to WC. As different normalization transformations are used for generating a picture, it is reasonably to expect LOCATOR in the appropriate WC space. This can be done only if all transformations used for picture generation are still available. Section 5.5 describes in detail how the transformation to be applied for coordinate input is selected.

Different normalization transformations can be obtained also by redefining the window and/or viewport of the current normalization transformation. All normalization transformations (except transformation 0) may be redefined at any time thus allowing the definition of an unlimited number of transformations. This facility will be adequate for many applications and, in output level 0, is the only way of defining different normalization transformations.

SET WINDOW   GKOP,WSOP,WSAC,SGOP   L0a
Parameters:

| Input | transformation number | | (1..n) | I |
| Input | window limits XMIN < XMAX, YMIN < YMAX | WC | | 4xR |

Effect:
The window limits entry of the specified normalization transformation in the GKS state list is set to the value specified by the parameter.

Errors:

8	GKS not in proper state: GKS shall be in one of the states GKOP, WSOP, WSAC or SGOP
50	Transformation number is invalid
51	Rectangle definition is invalid

———————————— *FORTRAN-Interface* ————————————

CALL GSWN (TNR,XMIN,XMAX,YMIN,YMAX)
Parameters:

Input	TNR transformation number		(1..n) INTEGER
Input	XMIN,XMAX,YMIN,YMAX window limits		
	XMIN < XMAX, YMIN < YMAX	WC	4xREAL

SET VIEWPORT   GKOP,WSOP,WSAC,SGOP   L0a
Parameters:

| Input | transformation number | | (1..n) | I |
| Input | viewport limits XMIN < XMAX, YMIN < YMAX | NDC | | 4xR |

Effect:
The viewport limits entry of the specified normalization transformation in the GKS state list is set to the value specified by the parameter.

Errors:

8	GKS not in proper state: GKS shall be in one of the states GKOP, WSOP, WSAC or SGOP
50	Transformation number is invalid
51	Rectangle definition is invalid
52	Viewport is not within the Normalized Device Coordinate unit square

————————————— *FORTRAN-Interface* —————————————

CALL GSVP (TNR,XMIN,XMAX,YMIN,YMAX)
Parameters:
  Input   TNR   transformation number   (1..n) INTEGER
  Input   XMIN,XMAX,YMIN,YMAX viewport limits
              XMIN < XMAX,YMIN < YMAX   NDC   4xREAL

SELECT NORMALIZATION TRANSFORMATION
                                      GKOP,WSOP,WSAC,SGOP   L0a
Parameters:
  Input   transformation number   (0..n)   I
Effect:
  The 'current normalization transformation number' entry in the GKS state list is set
  to the value specified by the parameter.
Errors:
  8   GKS not in proper state: GKS shall be in one of the states GKOP, WSOP,
         WSAC or SGOP
  50   Transformation number is invalid

————————————— *FORTRAN-Interface* —————————————

CALL GSELNT (TNR)
Parameters:
  Input   TNR   transformation number   (0..n) INTEGER

5.3   Workstation Transformation

The NDC space can be regarded as a workstation-independent abstract display
surface. For display on a real workstation, the NDC must be mapped onto
the coordinate space of the specific workstation. This transformation is called
workstation transformation.

As different workstations may have different coordinate systems, the workstation transformation may be different for each workstation. The default setting
of this transformation secures that the range [0,1]x[0,1] in NDC is mapped
onto the largest square which fits within the workstation's display surface. The
application program may dynamically reset any workstation transformation.
The resetting of the workstation transformation requests a new frame action
on the respective workstation. Therefore, in contrast to the normalization transformation, the workstation transformation cannot be used to compose pictures
with different workstation transformations on the same display surface. Furthermore, a new frame action deletes all primitives outside segments. For applications not using the segment storage facility, it is recommended to reset the
workstation transformation only as long as no primitives are displayed, i.e.,
immediately after a CLEAR WORKSTATION.

The workstation transformation is specified in a similar manner as the normalization transformation by a window within the range [0,1]x[0,1] of the NDC,

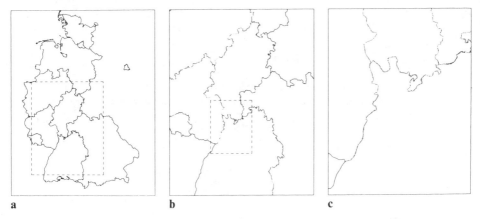

a   b   c

Figure 5.2 Zooming by resetting the workstation window

the *workstation window,* and by a viewport within the display surface, the *work-station viewport.* Workstation window and workstation viewport are rectangles which can be set independently. Hence, both rectangles may have different aspect ratios. However, the workstation transformation allows only uniform scaling. Therefore, GKS automatically will shrink the workstation viewport to a rectangle with the same aspect ratio as the workstation window. This rectangle is then positioned in the lower left-hand corner of the workstation viewport leaving unused space, if necessary, either at the top or right side of the workstation viewport.

The major objectives for setting the workstation transformation are:
— to completely use non-square display surfaces by selecting a workstation window in NDC with the same aspect ratio as the display surface;
— to zoom the whole picture by selecting a smaller workstation window in NDC for display;
— to draw a picture in proper scale by setting the appropriate size of the workstation viewport.

SET WORKSTATION WINDOW   WSOP,WSAC,SGOP   L0a
Parameters:
  Input   workstation identifier   N
  Input   workstation window limits
        XMIN<XMAX,YMIN<YMAX   NDC   4xR
Effect:
The 'requested workstation window' entry in the workstation state list of the specified workstation is set to the value specified by the parameter.
If the 'dynamic modification accepted for workstation transformation' entry in the workstation description table is set to IMM, or if the 'display surface empty' entry in the workstation state list is set to EMPTY, then the 'current workstation window' entry in the workstation state list is set to the value specified by the parameter and the 'workstation transformation update state' entry is set to NOTPENDING. Otherwise the 'workstation transformation update state' entry in the workstation state list is set to PENDING and the 'current workstation window' entry is not changed.

Errors:
- 7   GKS not in proper state: GKS shall be in one of the states WSOP, WSAC or SGOP
- 20   Specified workstation identifier is invalid
- 25   Specified workstation is not open
- 33   Specified workstation is of category MI
- 36   Specified workstation is Workstation Independent Segment Storage
- 51   Rectangle definition is invalid
- 53   Workstation window is not within the Normalized Device Coordinate unit square

———————————————— *FORTRAN-Interface* ————————————————

CALL GSWKWN (WKID,XMIN,XMAX,YMIN,YMAX)
Parameters:

Input	WKID workstation identifier			INTEGER
Input	XMIN,XMAX,YMIN,YMAX workstation window			
	limits XMIN < XMAX,YMIN < YMAX		NDC	4xREAL

SET WORKSTATION VIEWPORT   WSOP,WSAC,SGOP   L0a
Parameters:

Input	workstation identifier		N
Input	workstation viewport limits		
	XMIN < XMAX,YMIN < YMAX	DC	4xR

Effect:
The 'requested workstation viewport' entry in the workstation state list of the specified workstation is set to the value specified by the parameter.
If the 'dynamic modification accepted for workstation transformation' entry in the workstation description table is set to IMM, or if the 'display surface empty' entry in the workstation state list is set to EMPTY, then the 'current workstation viewport' entry in the workstation state list is set to the value specified by the parameter and the 'workstation transformation update state' entry is set to NOTPENDING. Otherwise the 'workstation transformation update state' entry in the workstation state list is set to PENDING and the 'current workstation viewport' entry is not changed.
Errors:
- 7   GKS not in proper state: GKS shall be in one of the states WSOP, WSAC or SGOP
- 20   Specified workstation identifier is invalid
- 25   Specified workstation is not open
- 33   Specified workstation is of category MI
- 36   Specified workstation is Workstation Independent Segment Storage
- 51   Rectangle definition is invalid
- 54   Workstation viewport is not within the display space

———————————————— *FORTRAN-Interface* ————————————————

CALL GSWKVP (WKID,XMIN,XMAX,YMIN,YMAX)
Parameters:

Input	WKID workstation identifier			INTEGER
Input	XMIN,XMAX,YMIN,YMAX workstation viewport			
	limits XMIN < XMAX,YMIN < YMAX		DC	4xREAL

5.4 Clipping

GKS provides a mechanism to clip graphical output to a clipping rectangle. All parts of primitives within or on the boundary of the clipping rectangle will be displayed, everything else will be discarded (see Figure 5.3). This applies to all output primitives.

For the POLYMARKER and the TEXT primitive, GKS relaxes the requirement for exact clipping as hardware facilities may be involved which cannot clip parts of a marker or a character. For POLYMARKER, the marker is visible if, and only if, the marker position is within the clipping rectangle. The clipping of partially visible markers can be done in a workstation-dependent way. For TEXT there exists a text precision attribute which specifies whether
— clipping is done exactly (precision STROKE);
— clipping is done at least on a character body by character body basis (precision CHAR);
— clipping is done in an implementation- and workstation-dependent way (precision STRING).

GKS allows both, the normalization transformation and the workstation transformation, to be associated with clipping. The respective clipping rectangles are the viewport and the workstation window. However, this does not imply that the clipping procedure has to be performed twice. The clipping associated with the normalization transformation is postponed. The clipping rectangle is sent like an attribute with the output primitives down the transformation pipeline and, if required, into the segment storage, too. Clipping is performed when

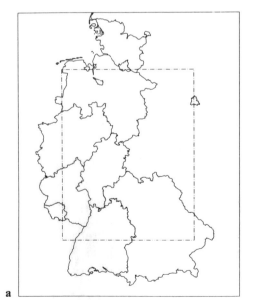
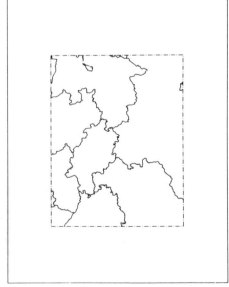

a   b

Figure 5.3 Effect of clipping at a clipping rectangle

output is displayed on a workstation. This allows the combination of both clipping processes by clipping to the intersection of viewport and workstation window.

The normalization transformation clipping is done to the viewport of the active normalization transformation. The normalization transformation may be changed arbitrarily during generation of a picture by selecting another normalization transformation or resetting the viewport of the current transformation. Then the respective clipping rectangle changes accordingly. This allows the clipping of primitives individually to different clipping rectangles and the building up of complex pictures from clipped subpictures. As it is such a high level facility, it is made optional within GKS. There exists one global switch, called 'clipping indicator', which enables and disables normalization transformation clipping.

The clipping associated with the workstation transformation clips to the workstation window. It cannot be switched off and, thus, ensures that no output outside the workstation window is displayed and no more space of the display surface is used than is asked for.

When segment transformations are applied, they affect coordinate data and geometrical attributes of output primitives but have no effect on the stored clipping rectangle. Thus, the clipping rectangle appears invariantly at the position it had during primitive generation. This allows a segment to be zoomed within a given clipping rectangle without interfering with the rest of the picture. There is one segment function which does affect the stored clipping rectangles: INSERT SEGMENT. When this function is performed, all stored clipping rectangles in the respective segment are replaced by the current clipping rectangle — the viewport of the active normalization transformation.

Some applications, like cartography, require more complicated clipping facilities, for example, clipping to an arbitrary polygon or shielding. Shielding is an inverse clipping securing that no drawing is inside a given rectangle which helps creating readable legends on maps. Such facilities, if necessary, must be provided above GKS.

SET CLIPPING INDICATOR   GKOP,WSOP,WSAC,SGOP   L0a
Parameters:
   Input   clipping indicator   (CLIP,NOCLIP)   E
Effect:
   The 'clipping indicator' entry in the GKS state list is set to the value specified by the parameter.
Errors:
   8   GKS not in proper state: GKS shall be in one of the states GKOP, WSOP, WSAC or SGOP

--------------------------- *FORTRAN-Interface* ---------------------------
CALL GSCLIP (CLSW)
Parameters:
   Input   CLSW   clipping indicator   (0 = noclip, 1 = clip) INTEGER

5.5 Transformation of LOCATOR and STROKE Input

When generating graphical output, GKS accepts coordinate data in several
WC systems which are transformed via NDC onto the display space of a workstation. When defining positions for the LOCATOR or STROKE input device,
the operator points to a position within the display space or tablet area. For
symmetry reasons, these DC positions are transformed back via NDC to WC
before handing them over to the application program. This scheme allows the
immediate use of LOCATOR or STROKE input for output primitive generation
at the same position the operator has pointed to. Furthermore, this transformation to WC conforms to the GKS design principle that all coordinate data,
as far as possible and reasonable, are specified in WC at the application program
interface.

At any time, exactly one workstation transformation is in effect for all
primitives visible on a specific workstation. Therefore, the transformation between NDC and DC is always well-defined and allows back transformation
of positions in DC to positions in NDC. To assure that positions do not leave
the range [0,1]x[0,1] in NDC, input is restricted to the image of the workstation
window which is equal to or smaller than the workstation viewport.

The mapping between WC and NDC cannot be found in a similar trivial
way as, generally, several normalization transformations have been used to
generate a picture. GKS arbitrates between concurring normalization transformations by comparing their viewports with the input positions. That normalization transformation will be used the viewport of which contains the NDC value
of the LOCATOR position or the NDC values of all STROKE positions (see
Figure 8.1, page 273).

However, this test is not sufficient to find exactly one normalization transformation as viewports of different normalization transformations may overlap.
For this reason, GKS has introduced the *viewport input priority* attribute which
defines a strict hierarchy between viewports. The priority of a normalization
transformation is specified relative to a reference normalization transformation
thus inserting it immediately below or above this transformation in the priority
scale. By default, all normalization transformations get viewport input priorities
according to their transformation number in decreasing order giving highest
priority to normalization transformation 0. If input positions are to be mapped
differently to normalization transformation 0, the priority of some normalization transformation must be set explicitly.

Now by testing all viewports in order of decreasing priority, a viewport
containing all input positions uniquely can be determined. It is obvious that
only stored transformations participate in this test. If a transformation is redefined, the previous setting is lost and cannot be considered for input transformation.

As long as input is generated synchronously (REQUEST or SAMPLE mode;
see Section 8.1.3), there is no doubt what is the last setting of transformations.
If input is generated in EVENT mode (see Section 8.1.3), positions are generated,
transformed, and stored in an input queue asynchronously to the retrieval of
the data by the application program. If transformations are reset during a

LOCATOR or STROKE device being in EVENT mode, the application program has no control what data are transformed with the old setting and what data are transformed with the new setting. To ensure, that the desired WC value is given back to the application program, transformations should not be reset while a LOCATOR or STROKE device is in EVENT mode or while there are still entries in the queue.

In practice, the workstation transformation will make no problems, as the operator will be aware of any change. Resetting of normalization transformations can be avoided as long as the number of storable transformation is not exceeded. The viewport input priority, however, cannot be used in EVENT mode although intended as a dynamic facility to give precedence to a transformation of actual interest in a certain situation.

As the selection of a normalization transformation for input transformation depends on positions and priorities, it not obvious for the application program to know which transformation has been applied. Therefore, GKS delivers the corresponding transformation number together with the respective WC values to the application program.

To secure that at least one viewport always is available for LOCATOR and STROKE transformation, a normalization transformation 0 exists which maps the WC unit square onto the NDC unit square. This viewport contains all possible NDC values of LOCATOR and STROKE input. Normalization transformation 0 cannot be reset; however, it may be selected and its viewport input priority may be changed.

Output primitives in segments may be subject to segment transformations before display. These transformations are not considered for input transformation.

SET VIEWPORT INPUT PRIORITY   GKOP,WSOP,WSAC,SGOP   L0b
Parameters:

Input	transformation number	(0..n)	I
Input	reference transformation number	(0..n)	I
Input	relative priority	(HIGHER,LOWER)	E

Effect:
The viewport input priority of the specified normalization transformation in the GKS state list is set to the next higher or next lower priority relative to the reference transformation according to the specified relative priority.
Errors:

8	GKS not in proper state: GKS shall be in one of the states GKOP, WSOP, WSAC or SGOP
50	Transformation number is invalid

--------------------------- *FORTRAN-Interface* ---------------------------
CALL GSVPIP (TNR,RTNR,RELPRI)
Parameters:

Input	TNR	transformation number	(0..n)	INTEGER
Input	RTNR	reference transformation number	(0..n)	INTEGER
Input	RELPRI	relative priority	(0 = higher, 1 = lower)	INTEGER

5.6 Examples

Example 5.1 Composition of a picture using one normalization transformation number

In this example, only normalization transformation 1 is used. Firstly, transformation is set to transform OUTLINE properly; then transformation 1 is reset to transform PIE.

───────────────────── *Pascal* ─────────────────────

```
L10   SELECT_NORMALIZATION_TRANSFORMATION (1);

L20   SET_WINDOW (1, 0.0, 5000.0, 0.0, 5000.0);
      {SET_VIEWPORT (1, 0.0, 1.0, 0.0, 1.0)                      set by default}
L30   OUTLINE;                                        {Procedure draws outline}

L40   SET_WINDOW (1, 0.0, 1.0, 0.0, 1.0);
L50   SET_VIEWPORT (1, 0.2, 0.3, 0.7, 0.8);
L60   PIE;                {Procedure draws pie showing some statistical numbers}
```

───────────────────── *Fortran* ─────────────────────

```
L10      CALL GSELNT (1)

L20      CALL GSWN (1, 0.0, 5000.0, 0.0, 5000.0)
      C  CALL GSVP (1, 0.0, 1.0, 0.0, 1.0)                      set by default
L30      CALL OUTLIN
      C  *** Procedure draws outline

L40      CALL GSWN (1, 0.0, 1.0, 0.0, 1.0)
L50      CALL GSVP (1, 0.2, 0.3, 0.7, 0.8)
L60      CALL PIE
      C  *** Procedure draws pie showing some statistical numbers
```

Example 5.2 Composition of a picture using different normalization transformation numbers

In this example, normalization transformation 1 is solely used for OUTLINE and transformation 2 for PIE. Therefore, both transformations are available for coordinate input.

───────────────────── *Pascal* ─────────────────────

```
L10   SET_WINDOW (1, 0.0, 5000.0, 0.0, 5000.0);
      {SET_VIEWPORT (1, 0.0, 1.0, 0.0, 1.0)                      set by default}

L20   SET_WINDOW (2, 0.0, 1.0, 0.0, 1.0);
L30   SET_VIEWPORT (2, 0.2, 0.3, 0.7, 0.8);
```

L40 SELECT_NORMALIZATION_TRANSFORMATION (1);
L50 OUTLINE;   {Procedure draws outline}

L60 SELECT_NORMALIZATION_TRANSFORMATION (2);
L70 PIE;   {Procedure draws pie showing some statistical numbers}

─────────────────────────── *Fortran* ───────────────────────────
L10   CALL GSWN (1, 0.0, 5000.0, 0.0, 5000.0)
    C   CALL GSVP (1, 0.0, 1.0, 0.0, 1.0)   set by default
L20   CALL GSWN (2, 0.0, 1.0, 0.0, 1.0)
L30   CALL GSVP (2, 0.2, 0.3, 0.7, 0.8)

L40   CALL GSELNT(1)
L50   CALL OUTLIN
    C   *** Procedure draws outline

L60   CALL GSELNT (2)
L70   CALL PIE
    C   *** Procedure draws pie showing some statistical numbers
──

Example 5.3   Layer which only allows uniform normalization transformations

For many applications, e.g., applications with metrical user coordinates, only mappings with uniform scaling are meaningful. In this example, two functions
— SET_WINDOW_WITH_UNIFORM_SCALING
— SET_VIEWPORT_WITH_UNIFORM_SCALING
are defined which secure that the viewport always is adapted by shrinking to have the same aspect ratio as the window. The GKS function INQUIRE_NORMALIZATION_TRANSFORMATION is used for obtaining the current values of windows. More details about this inquiry function can be found in Chapter 10.

─────────────────────────── *Pascal* ───────────────────────────
L10 VAR listvw: ARRAY [1..4,1..20] OF REAL;
                                        {listvw stores the requested viewports}

L20 PROCEDURE ADAPT_VIEWPORT (trnum:INTEGER;
             wxmin,wxmax,wymin,wymax,rxmin,rxmax,rymin,rymax: REAL);
             {ADAPT_VIEWPORT calculates a new viewport from the requested viewport
                                and the window given in the parameter list}

L30 VAR nxmin,nxmax,nymin,nymax, ratiow,ratiov,factor : REAL;
L40 BEGIN   {Assume that the x-extent has to be adapted}
L50   dx := (wxmax-wxmin) * (rymax-rymin)/(wymax-wymin);
                 {The adapted viewport will be centred within the requested viewport}
L60   nxmin := (rxmin + rxmax — dx) / 2.0;

```
L70     IF nxmin > rxmin THEN BEGIN
L80         nxmax := nxmin + dx;
L90         nymin := rymin;
L100        nymax := rymax;
L110    END

L120    ELSE BEGIN                              {The y-extent has to be adapted}
L130        dy := (wymax-wymin) * (rxmax-rxmin)/(wxmax-wxmin);
L140        nymin := (rymin + rymax — dy) / 2.0;
L150        nymax := nymin + dy;
L160        nxmin := rxmin;
L170        nxmax := rxmax;
L180    END;

L190    SET_VIEWPORT (trnum, nxmin,nxmax,nymin,nymax);
L200 END {ADAPT_VIEWPORT};

L210 PROCEDURE SET_WINDOW_WITH_UNIFORM_SCALING
        (trnum:INTEGER; wxmin,wxmax,wymin,wymax:REAL)
L220 VAR rxmin,rxmax,rymin,rymax : REAL;
L230 BEGIN
L240    SET_WINDOW (trnum, wxmin,wxmax,wymin,wymax);
L250    rxmin := listvw[1,trnum];          {get requested viewport rxmin,... from listvw}
L260    rxmax := listvw[2,trnum];
L270    rymin := listvw[3,trnum];
L280    rymax := listvw[4,trnum];

L290    ADAPT_VIEWPORT
           (trnum,wxmin,wxmax,wymin,wymax,rxmin,rxmax,rymin,rymax);
L300 END {SET_WINDOW_WITH_UNIFORM_SCALING};

L310 PROCEDURE SET_VIEWPORT_WITH_UNIFORM_SCALING
        (trnum:INTEGER; rxmin,rxmax,rymin,rymax:REAL)
L320 VAR wxmin,wxmax,wymin,wymax,dummy : REAL;
L330 BEGIN
L340    listvw[1,trnum] := rxmin;
L350    listvw[2,trnum] := rxmax;
L360    listvw[3,trnum] := rymin;
L370    listvw[4,trnum] := rymax;
                                        {enquire window wxmin,... from GKS state list}
L380    INQUIRE_NORMALIZATION_TRANSFORMATION
           (trnum, error_indicator,
           wxmin,wxmax,wymin,wymax, dummy,dummy,dummy,dummy);
L390    ADAPT_VIEWPORT
           (trnum,wxmin,wxmax,wymin,wymax,rxmin,rxmax,rymin,rymax);
L400 END {SET_VIEWPORT_WITH_UNIFORM_SCALING};
```

———————————————————— *Fortran* ————————————————————

```
L20           SUBROUTINE ADPTVP (TRNUM,WXMIN,WXMAX,
       +  WYMIN,WYMAX,RXMIN,RXMAX,RYMIN,RYMAX)
```

```
        C           *** ADPTVP calculates a new viewport from the requested viewport and
        C           *** the window given in the parameter list.

L30               INTEGER TRNUM
L31               REAL WXMIN,WXMAX,WYMIN,WYMAX,
            +           RXMIN,RXMAX,RYMIN,RYMAX,FACTOR
                        NXMIN,NXMAX,NYMIN,NYMAX, RATIOW, RATIOV

        C           *** Assume that the x-extent has to be adapted
L50               DX =
                    (WXMAX-WXMIN) * (RYMAX-RYMIN)/(WYMAX-WYMIN)
        C           *** The adapted viewport will be centred within the requested viewport
L60               NXMIN = (RXMIN + RXMAX − DX) / 2.0
L70               IF (NXMIN.LT.RXMIN) GOTO 330
L80               NXMAX = NXMIN + DX
L90               NYMIN = RYMIN
L100              NYMAX = RYMAX
L110              GOTO 390
        C           *** The y-extent has to be adapted
L130      330     DY =
                    (WYMAX-WYMIN) * (RXMAX-RXMIN)/(WXMAX-WXMIN)
L140              NYMIN = (RYMIN + RYMAX − DY) / 2.0
L150              NYMAX = NYMIN + DY
L160              NXMIN = RXMIN
L170              NXMAX = RXMAX
        C           *** Set adapted viewport for normalization transformation TRNUM
L190      390     CALL GSVP (TRNUM, NXMIN,NXMAX,NYMIN,NYMAX)
L200              RETURN
L201              END

L210              SUBROUTINE SWNUS
            +         (TRNUM, WXMIN,WXMAX,WYMIN,WYMAX)
        C           *** Set window WXMIN,... and adapt viewport of normalization trans-
        C           *** formation TRNUM to the window's aspect ratio.

L220              INTEGER TRNUM
L221              REAL WXMIN,WXMAX,WYMIN,WYMAX, RXMIN,RXMAX,
            +         RYMIN,RYMAX, LISTVW(4,20)
L222              COMMON LISTVW

L240              CALL GSWN (TRNUM, WXMIN,WXMAX,WYMIN,WYMAX)
        C           *** Get requested viewport RXMIN,... from LISTVW
L250              RXMIN = LISTVW(1,TRNUM)
L260              RXMAX = LISTVW(2,TRNUM)
L270              RYMIN = LISTVW(3,TRNUM)
L280              RYMAX = LISTVW(4,TRNUM)
L290              CALL ADPTVP(TRNUM,WXMIN,WXMAX,WYMIN,WYMAX,
            +         RXMIN,RXMAX,RYMIN,RYMAX)
L300              RETURN
L301              END
```

```
L310              SUBROUTINE SVPUS
            +        (TRNUM, RXMIN,RXMAX,RYMIN,RYMAX)
       C          *** Store requested viewport RXMIN,... and adapt this viewport to the
       C          *** aspect ratio of the window of normalization transformation
       C          *** TRNUM.

L320              INTEGER TRNUM
L321              REAL W(4),RXMIN,RXMAX,RYMIN,RYMAX
L322              REAL DUMMY(4), LISTVW(4,20)
L323              COMMON LISTVW

       C          *** Store the required viewport
L340              LISTVW(1,TRNUM) = RXMIN
L350              LISTVW(2,TRNUM) = RXMAX
L360              LISTVW(3,TRNUM) = RYMIN
L370              LISTVW(4,TRNUM) = RYMAX
       C          *** Inquire window WXMIN,... from GKS state list
L380              CALL GQNT (ERRIND,TRNUM,W,DUMMY)
L390              CALL ADPTVP(TRNUM,W(1),W(2),W(3),W(4),
            +        RXMIN,RXMAX,RYMIN,RYMAX)
L400              RETURN
L401              END
```

Example 5.4   Drawing in a given scale

A map of size 0.7 m x 0.9 m has been digitized. The digitizer delivers the data according to its resolution in units of 1/10 mm, i.e., data are in the space 7000 x 9000. These data are to be mapped onto the display of an interactive workstation by using as much as possible of the available display space while preserving the aspect ratio. The same data are to be drawn on a plotter in the same scale as the source map. The statements below show the required setting of transformations. Window describes the space 7000 x 9000 of the digitized data. Viewport and workstation window are set to a rectangle within [0,1] with same aspect ratio as the window to preserve aspect ratio and to select the full map for display. Workstation viewport is left undefined for workstation display to allow automatic adaptation to the available display surface; for workstation plotter, it gives the size of the plot in metres.

——————————————————— *Pascal* ———————————————————

```
                    {Set normalization transformation such that aspect ratio is preserved}
L10    SELECT_NORMALIZATION_TRANSFORMATION (1);
L20    SET_WINDOW (1, 0.0, 7000.0, 0.0, 9000.0);
L30    SET_VIEWPORT (1, 0.0, 7.0/9.0, 0.0, 1.0);

                                               {Generate picture on display}
L40    ACTIVATE_WORKSTATION (display);
       {The setting workstation_window = viewport secures that the whole map is
       mapped onto the display; by not setting the workstation-viewport, GKS is enabled
                              to use as much as possible of the display space. }
```

L50   SET_WORKSTATION_WINDOW (display, 0.0, 7.0/9.0, 0.0, 1.0);
L70   DRAW_FILE(FRG);
L120 DEACTIVATE_WORKSTATION (display);

                {Generate picture on plotter with precise scaling and using different colours}
L130 ACTIVATE_WORKSTATION (plotter);
          {Workstation_window is set as above; workstation_viewport is set to the desired
                                    size of the map measured in metres}
L140 SET_WORKSTATION_WINDOW (plotter, 0.0, 7.0/9.0, 0.0, 1.0);
L150 SET_WORKSTATION_VIEWPORT (plotter, 0.0, 0.7, 0.0, 0.9);
L170 DRAW_FILE(FRG);
L220 DEACTIVATE_WORKSTATION (plotter);

———————————————————————— *Fortran* ————————————————————————

      C   Set normalization transformation such that aspect ratio is preserved
L10   CALL GSELNT(1)
L20   CALL GSWN (1, 0.0, 7000.0, 0.0, 9000.0)
L30   CALL GSVP (1, 0.0, 7.0/9.0, 0.0, 1.0)

      C   *** Generate picture on display using different linetypes
L40   CALL GACWK (DISPL)
      C   The setting workstation_window = viewport secures that the whole map is
      C   mapped onto the display; by not setting the workstation-viewport, GKS
      C   is enabled to use as much as possible of the display space.
L50   CALL GSWKWN (DISPL, 0.0, 7.0/9.0, 0.0, 1.0)
L70   CALL DRFILE(FRG)
L120   CALL GDAWK (DISPL)

      C   Generate picture on plotter with precise scaling and using different colours
L130   CALL GACWK (PLOTTR)
      C   Workstation_window is set as above; workstation_viewport is set to
      C   the desired size of the map measured in metres
L140   CALL GSWKWN (PLOTTR, 0.0, 7.0/9.0, 0.0, 1.0)
L150   CALL GSWKVP (PLOTTR, 0.0, 0.7, 0.0, 0.9)
L170   CALL DRFILE(FRG)
L220   CALL GDAWK (PLOTTR)

_____

See Figure 5.1a for a sample output.

Example 5.5   Clipping mechanism

The normalization transformation of Example 5.4 is now defined by a
smaller window and viewport which, yet, define the same transformation. If
the clipping indicator is NOCLIP, the same picture is generated; if the clipping
indicator is CLIP, however, the results differ as the window of the normalization
transformation is used as a clipping rectangle.

———————————————————————————— *Pascal* ————————————————————————————

L90   SELECT_NORMALIZATION_TRANSFORMATION (1);
L100 SET_WINDOW (1, 1400.0, 5600.0, 1800.0, 7200.0);
L110 SET_VIEWPORT (1, 0.155, 0.622, 0.2, 0.8); {viewport := window limits / 9000}

L120 SET_CLIPPING_INDICATOR (NOCLIP);
L130 DRAW_FILE (FRG);   {See Figure 5.3a}

L140 SET_CLIPPING_INDICATOR (CLIP);
L150 DRAW_FILE (FRG);   {See Figure 5.3b}

———————————————————————— *Fortran* ————————————————————————

L90   CALL GSELNT(1)
L100   CALL GSWN (1, 1400.0, 5600.0, 1800.0, 7200.0)
L110   CALL GSVP (1, 0.155, 0.622, 0.2, 0.8)
     C   *** Viewport = window limits / 9000

L120   CALL GSCLIP (NOCLIP)
L130   CALL DRFILE (FRG)
     C   *** See Figure 5.3a
L140   CALL GSCLIP (CLIP)
L150   CALL DRFILE (FRG)
     C   *** See Figure 5.3b

Example 5.6   Setting of viewport input priority

On a display surface of an interactive workstation, a part of a map is zoomed. In addition, in the upper right corner of the display surface, a global view of that map is drawn. Regardless, whether the operator points to the zoomed map or to the global view, the correct user coordinates will be returned (see also Exercise 5.5).

User data are the same as in the above examples.

———————————————————————————— *Pascal* ————————————————————————————

                {This transformation zooms part of map onto full display}
L20   SET_WINDOW (1, 300.0, 6300.0, 300.0, 6300.0);
L30   SET_VIEWPORT (1, 0.0, 1.0, 0.0, 1.0);
L40   SELECT_NORMALIZATION_TRANSFORMATION (1);
L50   DRAW_FILE (FRG);   {see Example 6.1}

                {This transformation maps whole map onto a small viewport}
L60   SET_WINDOW (2, 0.0, 7000.0, 0.0, 9000.0);
L70   SET_VIEWPORT (2, 0.72, 1.0, 0.64, 1.0);
L80   SELECT_NORMALIZATION_TRANSFORMATION (2);
L90   DRAW_FILE (FRG);   {see Example 6.1}

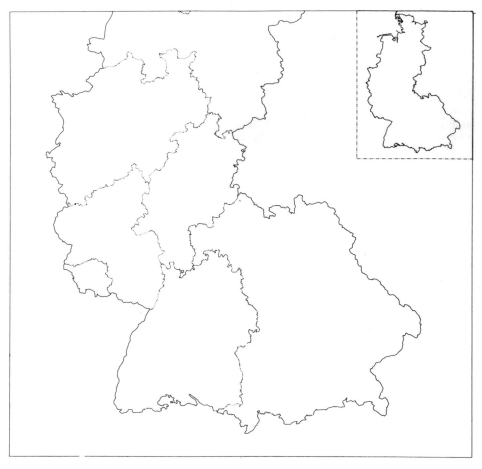

Figure 5.4 Global and zoomed view within one display space

{Set viewport input priority as vip0 < vip1 < vip2}
L100 SET_VIEWPORT_INPUT_PRIORITY (0, 1, LOWER);
L110 SET_VIEWPORT_INPUT_PRIORITY (1, 2, LOWER);

———————————————————————— *Fortran* ————————————————————————

```
      C    *** Draw zoomed part of map onto full display
L20        CALL GSWN (1, 300.0, 6300.0, 300.0, 6300.0)
L30        CALL GSVP (1, 0.0, 1.0, 0.0, 1.0)
L40        CALL GSELNT(1)
L50        CALL DRFILE (FRG)
      C    *** see Example 6.1

      C    *** Draw global view of map onto small viewport
L60        CALL GSWN (2, 0.0, 7000.0, 0.0, 9000.0)
L70        CALL GSVP (2, 0.72, 1.0, 0.64, 1.0)
```

L80   CALL GSELNT(2)
L90   CALL DRFILE (FRG)
   C   *** see Example 6.1

   C   *** Set viewport input priority as vip0 < vip1 < vip2
L100   CALL GSVPIP (0, 1, LOWER)
L110   CALL GSVPIP (1, 2, LOWER)

5.7   Exercises

Exercise 5.1   Setting of transformations

Assume WC coordinates in the range $0 < x < 7$, $0 < y < 11$ and a display surface of size 0.21m x 0.296m. Solve the following problems:
1. Secure that all data are displayed on the display surface.
2. Secure that the display surface is used optimally.
What is the minimum set of transformation setting functions needed in both cases? What are the effective values of normalization transformation and workstation transformation applied on the coordinate data?.

Exercise 5.2   Uniform scaling

Solve Exercise 5.1 under the restriction, that only transformations with equal scaling in x and y are allowed.

Exercise 5.3   Prescribed scaling

Assume that WC data in Exercise 5.1 are measured in inches. Generate a drawing in true scale.

Exercise 5.4   Clipping

Example 5.5 shows clipping in conjunction with the normalization transformation. The same effect can be achieved with the workstation transformation. Rewrite Example 5.5 such that lines L90-120 remain unchanged and the two pictures in Figure 5.3 are generated by two different workstation transformations.

Exercise 5.5   Shielding

If arbitrary transformations are applied to the zoomed part in Figure 5.4, Example 5.6, the zoomed drawing may penetrate into the small rectangle containing the global view. Although both normalization transformations defined in Example 5.6 may generate output within the small rectangle, the setting of the viewport input priority decides that in any case normalization transformation 2 will be used for LOCATOR input within the small rectangle. This may be confusing for casual users. It would be more convenient to suppress any output of normalization transformation 1 within the viewport of normalization transformation 2.

The blanking out of drawing within a given rectangle ("shielding") is not supported as a standard GKS facility. However, by use of three normalization transformations, it can be achieved that global view and zoomed view in Figure 5.4 do not interfere. Write a program.

6   OUTPUT PRIMITIVES

6.1   Introduction

The graphical output that is generated by GKS is built up from two groups of basic elements:
— output primitives;
— output primitive attributes.

The *output primitives* are abstractions of the basic actions that a graphical device can perform. GKS provides the following six output primitives:

POLYLINE: GKS generates a set of connected lines defined by a point sequence.

POLYMARKER: GKS generates symbols of one type centred at given positions.

TEXT: GKS generates a character string at a given position.

FILL AREA: GKS generates a polygon which may be hollow or filled with a uniform colour, a pattern, or a hatch style.

CELL ARRAY: GKS generates an array of pixels with individual colours.

GENERALIZED DRAWING PRIMITIVE (GDP): GKS addresses special geometrical output capabilities of a workstation such as the drawing of spline curves, circular arcs, and elliptic arcs. The objects are characterized by an identifier, a set of points and additional data. GKS applies all transformations to the points but leaves the interpretation to the workstation.

The definition of the primitives contains information about its geometrical shape. More geometrical details and information about the appearance of the primitives can be added to the primitives' definition via *output primitive attributes*. In GKS, attributes can be defined and are bound to the primitives in different ways. For a better understanding, these different schemes are explained

Table 6.1 Geometric attributes in GKS

TEXT:	CHARACTER HEIGHT
	CHARACTER UP VECTOR
	TEXT PATH
	TEXT ALIGNMENT
FILL AREA:	PATTERN SIZE
	PATTERN REFERENCE POINT

in this section. The meaning of attributes is explained in the context of the respective primitive in the subsequent sections.

GKS distinguishes geometric and non-geometric attributes. *Geometric attributes* affect the shape and size of a primitive. They are treated in the same way as are coordinates in the parameter list of a primitive. They are defined in world coordinates (e.g., CHARACTER HEIGHT gives the height of characters within the WC system) or are applied to the primitive in WC (e.g., TEXT PATH 'left' gives the writing direction in WC which is not necessarily the same on the display surface). They are subject to all transformations. Therefore, a different setting of transformations will yield different results. For example, if a segment is dynamically scaled by setting the segment transformation, this will affect the geometric attributes and, e.g., scale character height. The default character height 0.01 is 1/100 of the default window (unit square) and, if used with the default transformations, will generate characters with the size of 1/100 of the display space. After setting the window to (0.0, 0.0, 100.0, 100.0), illegible characters of 1/10000 of the display space will be generated until the character height is reset accordingly. Table 6.1 lists all geometric attributes in GKS.

Non-geometric attributes control aspects of a primitive which cannot be transformed, like COLOUR, or which shall not be transformed, like LINE-WIDTH and MARKER SIZE. The exclusion of LINEWIDTH from the set of geometric attributes was done due to the fact that the most common devices have no transformable LINEWIDTH and it seemed unreasonable to require such a facility within the standard. MARKER SIZE is not transformable as markers designate points with extension 0. However, independent of transformations, different linewidths and marker sizes, if available, can be selected via linewidth and marker size scale factor. CHARACTER SPACING and CHAR-ACTER EXPANSION FACTOR affect the geometry. As they are defined relative to CHARACTER HEIGHT, they change accordingly to CHARACTER HEIGHT without needing a transformation. They can be considered part of the definition of a specific text font rather than independently transformable geometric attributes.

An attribute may be bound *immediately* (i.e., at primitive definition time) to the primitive, or the binding can be *delayed* until display time. Figure 6.1 shows the different points in the transformation pipeline where attributes are bound. This figure also illustrates the binding of segment attributes. Segment attributes are discussed in detail in Chapter 7.

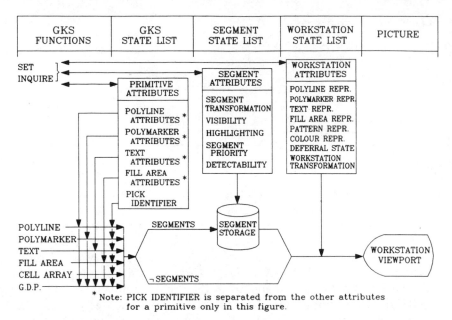

| GKS FUNCTIONS | GKS STATE LIST | SEGMENT STATE LIST | WORKSTATION STATE LIST | PICTURE |

Figure 6.1 Binding of attributes

An attribute can be specified *directly* by giving the attribute value, or *indirectly or indexed* by providing an index to the respective attribute. In GKS, geometric attributes are always specified directly. On the other hand, colour is an attribute which cannot be specified directly but only via an index pointing to a colour table. The following sequence is necessary for generating red polylines:

SET_POLYLINE_COLOUR_INDEX (1)
SET_COLOUR_REPRESENTATION (workstation, 1, 1.0, 0.0, 0.0)
POLYLINE (N, POINTS1)

Furthermore, there are attributes which can be used in both fashions, direct and indexed. Table 6.5 contains a list of these attributes.

The indexed attributes can be divided in two sets: those contained in implementation-provided static tables and those contained in adjustable workstation tables.

Table 6.2 lists all implementation-provided static tables. The value ranges are defined by the implementor. He has to provide a minimal set of entries as specified in the description of the individual attribute functions below. He may provide more entries than mandated on some workstations. However, if the same entry is present on different workstations, it must refer to the same capability.

The adjustable workstation tables include the
— polyline bundle table,
— polymarker bundle table,
— text bundle table,

Table 6.2 Indices pointing to implementation-provided static workstation tables

LINETYPE	→ linetype table (minimal length 4)
MARKER TYPE	→ marker type table (minimal length 5)
TEXT FONT AND PRECISION	→ text font and precision table
	(minimal requirement depends on level)
FILL AREA STYLE INDEX	→ hatch table (minimal length 3)
	(if FILL AREA INTERIOR STYLE
	= hatch and hatching supported on the
	workstation)

— fill area bundle table,
— pattern table,
— colour table.

Table 6.3 lists all indices pointing to these tables and all aspects of the indices which can be set in the respective bundle table. Indexing may occur in several stages. For example, the fill area index points to a bundle containing a fill area style index. This index may point to a pattern array. The pattern array contains colour indices pointing to the colour table.

The primary purpose of the workstation tables is the display of one picture on different workstations while using the specific capabilities of each workstation type. This can be achieved by setting the tables immediately after opening the workstation. In addition, GKS allows the workstation tables to be reset at any time. This adds a powerful dynamic functionality to GKS. For example, the dynamic capabilities of colour tables of raster displays can be addressed via this mechanism.

Attributes may be *static* or *dynamic*. The value of a static attribute is bound to a primitive at primitive generation time. This specific value cannot be changed during the whole lifetime of the primitive. The attribute itself can be redefined such that subsequently generated primitives get another value. Character height is a static attribute. Therefore, the sequence

SET_CHARACTER_HEIGHT (1.0)
TEXT (P,'First text')
SET_CHARACTER_HEIGHT (2.0)
TEXT (Q,'Second text')

generates two text strings in different sizes.

All aspects listed in the right column of Table 6.3 are dynamic attributes. If a dynamic attribute is changed, this change affects primitives generated previously and subsequently. As the attribute change of previously generated primitives requires the storage of graphical information, this effect is guaranteed only for primitives within segments.

The dynamic capabilities of workstation tables apply to any workstation independent whether they are supported well or not by that workstation. It can be imagined that some workstations, e.g., plotter workstations, will not show a good dynamic behaviour. However, it is not assumed that each workstation reacts immediately on the resetting of an entry in a bundle table. According

Table 6.3 Indices pointing to adjustable workstation tables

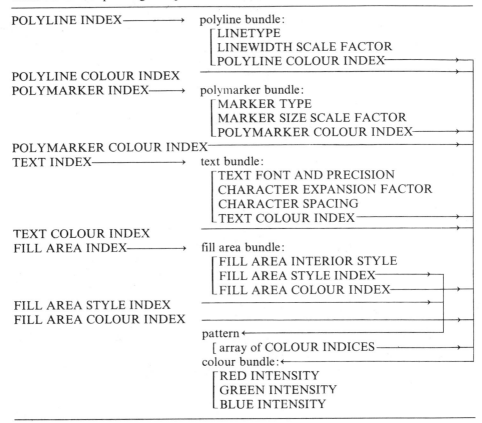

POLYLINE INDEX⟶ polyline bundle:
  ⌈LINETYPE
  |LINEWIDTH SCALE FACTOR
  ⌊POLYLINE COLOUR INDEX⟶

POLYLINE COLOUR INDEX
POLYMARKER INDEX⟶ polymarker bundle:
  ⌈MARKER TYPE
  |MARKER SIZE SCALE FACTOR
  ⌊POLYMARKER COLOUR INDEX⟶

POLYMARKER COLOUR INDEX
TEXT INDEX⟶ text bundle:
  ⌈TEXT FONT AND PRECISION
  |CHARACTER EXPANSION FACTOR
  |CHARACTER SPACING
  ⌊TEXT COLOUR INDEX⟶

TEXT COLOUR INDEX
FILL AREA INDEX⟶ fill area bundle:
  ⌈FILL AREA INTERIOR STYLE
  |FILL AREA STYLE INDEX⟶
  ⌊FILL AREA COLOUR INDEX⟶

FILL AREA STYLE INDEX
FILL AREA COLOUR INDEX

pattern⟵
  [array of COLOUR INDICES⟶
colour bundle:⟵
  ⌈RED INTENSITY
  |GREEN INTENSITY
  ⌊BLUE INTENSITY

Note: The FILL AREA STYLE INDEX points to the pattern table only if FILL AREA
  INTERIOR STYLE = pattern.

to its capabilities, the workstation may react immediately (which may also affect
primitives outside segments) or it may use the segment storage to regenerate
the display for achieving the desired effect. The latter case is called 'implicit
regeneration' which may be deferred arbitrarily by setting the deferral state
(see Section 4.6) appropriately. Whether a workstation is capable of performing
dynamic changes immediately or not, is described in the workstation state list
by the entry 'dynamic modification accepted'.
  Dynamic attributes are referred to via indices. The index itself may be a
static or a dynamic attribute. Colour is a typical dynamic attribute. The sequence
  SET_POLYLINE_COLOUR_INDEX (1)
  SET_COLOUR_REPRESENTATION (workstation, 1, 1.0, 0.0, 0.0)
  POLYLINE (N, POINTS1)
  SET_COLOUR_REPRESENTATION (workstation, 1, 0.0, 1.0, 0.0)
  POLYLINE (N, POINTS2)

at first, generates a red polyline. By redefining the colour representation, this polyline becomes green. The second polyline is generated with green colour.

Attributes can be *global* or *workstation-dependent*. For global attributes, one attribute value is valid for all workstations. Workstation-dependent attributes can be set individually for each workstation.

Geometric attributes are made global attributes as the geometry of a picture is not allowed to vary between workstations. Other attributes controlling the appearance of primitives may be workstation-dependent. For example, a map generated on a storage tube will use different linetypes to distinguish classes of lines. The same map generated on a plotter will use different colours for the same purpose. This can be achieved by using indexed attributes. A global index is bound to the primitive which points to workstation-specific tables containing the workstation-dependent aspects of that index.

Attributes may be set *individually* or *bundled*. In the first case, a separate function exists for each attribute such that one individual attribute can be set without affecting another one. In the second case, a whole bundle of aspects is defined with one function call. In GKS, all global attributes are set individually. The workstation-dependent attributes are set bundled. These attributes are stored in bundle tables where each entry describes several aspects. For example, the POLYLINE bundle table describes the aspects LINETYPE, LINEWIDTH SCALE FACTOR, and POLYLINE COLOUR INDEX. The whole bundle of aspects is defined with one function call, i.e., LINETYPE cannot be specified without specifying the two other aspects.

In GKS, one attribute usually applies exactly to one primitive class. The setting of the attributes of one primitive, therefore, cannot have side effects on the appearance of another primitive. Only the PICK IDENTIFIER attribute and the colour table are used by all primitives.

The PICK IDENTIFIER attribute does not describe visual aspects of a primitive but is used to identify single primitives or sets of primitives within segments. It is discussed in more detail in Chapter 7.3.

Only one colour table exists on each workstation which is used by all primitives displayed on that workstation. However, the COLOUR INDEX referencing the colour table is specific for each primitive class.

Table 6.4 gives a survey about output primitive attributes. The left column lists all global attributes. Global attributes are static attributes. The values are set individually and are bound immediately. The right column lists all workstation-dependent attributes. They are pointed to by indices. The aspects of a specific index are set bundled and are stored in adjustable workstation tables. The binding of the value is delayed and, therefore, redefinition of a table entry is possible and will cause a retroactive change of the appearance of all related primitives.

As shown in Table 6.4, some attributes occur twice, within a bundle on a workstation and as individual attributes. Therefore, the two uses are called BUNDLED and INDIVIDUAL. Bundled attributes are workstation-dependent, their binding is delayed, and their value can be changed dynamically. Individual attributes are global attributes, they are bound immediately, and their value is static and cannot be manipulated. This richness has been introduced to serve the needs of a small single workstation graphics system where the costs of workstation tables could be a serious problem and direct attributes are sufficient. The power of table-driven workstation-dependent attributes has effect primarily in multi-workstation systems or in dynamic manipulation.

However, if both types of use were to be admitted simultaneously, contradicting attributes could occur. Therefore, for each attribute, it must be defined what way of definition is used. This is done by a list of Aspect Source Flags (ASF) which, for each attribute, can have the value INDIVIDUAL or BUNDLED, therefore indicating that way the attribute is used.

By default, the implementation will have all these attributes either INDIVIDUAL or BUNDLED. This reflects the feeling that the two different concept should best kept apart. However, the application program may redefine the ASFs according to its needs. It may use some attributes BUNDLED and others INDIVIDUALLY, e.g., the polyline LINETYPE as a workstation-dependent attribute and the POLYLINE COLOUR INDEX as a global attribute. The assignment can be changed dynamically. This has no retroactive effect but only affects primitives generated later on. However, it seems to be no good programming style to manipulate the ASFs. It is recommended either to use a pure BUNDLED or INDIVIDUAL fashion or, at least, fix the ASF in the beginning of a session and never change it afterwards. Table 6.5 lists all attributes which can be used either BUNDLED or INDIVIDUALLY.

Table 6.4 Synopsis of attributes of GKS output primitives

global, static, immediate binding	workstation-dependent, dynamic, delayed binding
For all primitives: PICK IDENTIFIER	colour: ⌈RED INTENSITY ⎪GREEN INTENSITY ⌊BLUE INTENSITY
POLYLINE: POLYLINE INDEX LINETYPE LINEWIDTH SCALE FACTOR POLYLINE COLOUR INDEX	polyline bundle: ↔ ⌈LINETYPE ↔ ⎪LINEWIDTH SCALE FACTOR ↔ ⌊POLYLINE COLOUR INDEX
POLYMARKER: POLYMARKER INDEX MARKER TYPE MARKER TYPE SCALE FACTOR POLYMARKER COLOUR INDEX	polymarker bundle: ↔ ⌈MARKER TYPE ↔ ⎪MARKER TYPE SCALE FACTOR ↔ ⌊POLYMARKER COLOUR INDEX

Table 6.4 (continued)

global, static, immediate binding	workstation-dependent, dynamic, delayed binding

TEXT:

CHARACTER HEIGHT
CHARACTER UP VECTOR
TEXT PATH
TEXT ALIGNMENT
TEXT INDEX   text bundle:
TEXT FONT AND PRECISION   ↔ ⌈TEXT FONT AND PRECISION
CHARACTER EXPANSION FACTOR ↔ │CHARACTER EXPANSION FACTOR
CHARACTER SPACING   ↔ │CHARACTER SPACING
TEXT COLOUR INDEX   ↔ ⌊TEXT COLOUR INDEX

FILL AREA:

FILL AREA INDEX   fill area bundle:
FILL AREA INTERIOR STYLE   ↔ ⌈FILL AREA INTERIOR STYLE
FILL AREA STYLE INDEX   ↔ │FILL AREA STYLE INDEX
FILL AREA COLOUR INDEX   ↔ ⌊FILL AREA COLOUR INDEX
PATTERN SIZE
PATTERN REFERENCE POINT

                                           pattern:
                                           [array of COLOUR INDICES

CELL ARRAY:

(array of COLOUR INDICES)
(specified in the primitive's definition
rather than as a separate attribute)

GENERALIZED DRAWING PRIMITIVE (GDP):

No own attributes, may adopt attributes
from zero or more of the above primitives

Legend: ↔ indicates the presence of an additional global attribute, the ASPECT
         SOURCE FLAG (ASF), which for each of the respective attributes indicates,
         whether the global attribute on the left side or the workstation-dependent
         attribute in the bundle on the right side applies for this primitive.

    With regard to attributes, CELL ARRAY and GDP occupy a special position. Both have no attributes of their own other than PICK IDENTIFIER. CELL ARRAY is defined by an array of colour indices which specifies the colour attributes of the primitive. These colour indices are treated like the colour attributes of other primitives. GDP may use the most appropriate attributes of one or more of the other primitives or none at all. For each specific GDP function, the implementor may take another decision. The selection of attributes,

Table 6.5 Attributes to be used either INDIVIDUALLY or BUNDLED

POLYLINE:	LINETYPE
	LINEWIDTH SCALE FACTOR
	POLYLINE COLOUR INDEX
POLYMARKER:	MARKER TYPE
	MARKER TYPE SCALE FACTOR
	POLYMARKER COLOUR INDEX
TEXT:	TEXT FONT AND PRECISION
	CHARACTER EXPANSION FACTOR
	CHARACTER SPACING
	TEXT COLOUR INDEX
FILL AREA:	FILL AREA INTERIOR STYLE
	FILL AREA STYLE INDEX
	FILL AREA COLOUR INDEX

however, must be documented with the description of the GDP function. For example, an interpolating curve, implemented as a specific GDP function, is sure to use the polyline attributes. A solid circle, on the other hand, may use polyline attributes for the boundary and fill area attributes for the interior.

In the following sections, all output primitives, output primitive attributes, and workstation-specific aspects of a primitive are discussed in detail. Colour table, pick identifier, and aspect source flags are described in Section 6.8.

6.2   POLYLINE Primitive

POLYLINE generates a sequence of straight lines which connects the sequence of points given in the primitive's definition. The points are specified by absolute world coordinates. Relative coordinates are not supported by GKS. Also, the elementary primitives MOVETO and LINETO, used in many graphics packages for positioning a pen and drawing one straight line, are not present in GKS. The reasons for this decision were conceptual difficulties stemming from the concept of the so-called 'current position'. To draw one straight line, an array of two points must be given in the primitive's definition. This is the minimum number of points needed for a meaningful definition.

A POLYLINE only allows a series of straight lines with vertices to be drawn. If a smooth line is needed, it can be approximated by a POLYLINE consisting of many short straight lines, or interpolating capabilities of a workstation, if present, can be addressed via an appropriate GDP (see Section 6.7).

POLYLINE   WSAC,SGOP   L0a
Parameters:
   Input   number of points   (2..n)   I
   Input   coordinates of points   WC   nxP

Effect:
    A sequence of connected straight lines is generated, starting from the first point and ending at the last point. The current values of the polyline attributes, as given by the GKS state list (see Section 3.4), are bound to the primitive.

Errors:

5	GKS not in proper state: GKS shall be either in the state WSAC or in the state SGOP
100	Number of points is invalid

──────────────────────── *FORTRAN-Interface* ────────────────────────

CALL GPL (N,PX,PY)

Parameters:

Input	N	number of points	(2..n)	INTEGER
Input	PX(N),PY(N)	coordinates of points	WC	2xREAL

6.2.1 Global POLYLINE Attributes

POLYLINE can be drawn using some values of LINETYPE, LINEWIDTH, and POLYLINE COLOUR INDEX. The current setting of the ASF (see Section 3.8.2) decides individually for each of these attributes whether the current setting of the attribute in the GKS state list or the POLYLINE INDEX is bound to the primitive. In the latter case, the POLYLINE INDEX will be replaced at display time by values taken from a workstation-dependent table.

    By default, all attributes will be initialised to select the most common way of drawing lines in that environment. The default POLYLINE INDEX 1 will point to an entry in the polyline bundle table which describes the most natural way of drawing lines on each workstation.

    If lines are to be distinguished in their appearance, the application program may draw them with different POLYLINE INDICES. The first entries of each polyline bundle table will be predefined by the implementor to address the most common ways of drawing lines on that workstation, e.g., use different the pens on a plotter, different linetypes on a storage tube, or different colours on a colour raster display. At least, POLYLINE INDICES 1 to 4 will be predefined by any implementation of GKS. Specific workstation aspects can be selected by calling SET POLYLINE REPRESENTATION (see 6.2.2).

    The direct selection of the polyline attributes LINETYPE, LINEWIDTH, and POLYLINE COLOUR INDEX can be reasonable within environments having only one workstation or workstations of homogeneous capabilities. If a workstation cannot provide a specified feature, it will be replaced by some available feature selected by the implementor of GKS.

    LINETYPE allows the selection of a specific dash-dotting from a list defined at implementation time of GKS. Linetypes 1 to 4 are solid, dashed, dotted and dashed-dotted. These must be available on each output workstation and their described effects are mandatory. Linetypes greater than 4 may be available but are implementation dependent. The linetype specifies a sequence of line segments and gaps which are repeated in drawing a POLYLINE. For some application, it is of great importance whether this sequence is restarted or continued at the start of POLYLINE, at the start of a clipped piece of POLYLINE,

Figure 6.2 Different linetypes shown with two linewidths

or at each vertex of a POLYLINE. Yet, GKS leaves it to the implementor how to implement the linetypes. If a specific way of restarting is needed, it should be implemented as an additional linetype.

LINEWIDTH SCALE FACTOR allows the specification of the linewidth. The linewidth is calculated as a nominal linewidth multiplied by the linewidth scale factor. This value is mapped by the workstation to the nearest available linewidth. The nominal linewidth and the capabilities of a workstation generating different linewidths can be interrogated from the workstation description table. Linewidth is not affected by GKS transformations.

POLYLINE COLOUR INDEX selects a colour from the workstation's colour table (see Section 6.8).

SET LINETYPE   GKOP,WSOP,WSAC,SGOP   L0a
Parameters:
Input   linetype   (1..n)   I
Effect:
The 'current linetype' entry in the GKS state list is set to the value specified by the parameter. When the 'current linetype ASF' entry in the GKS state list is INDIVIDUAL, subsequently generated POLYLINE output primitives will be displayed with this linetype. When the 'current linetype ASF' entry in the GKS state list is BUNDLED, this function will not affect the display of subsequently created POLYLINE output primitives until the 'current linetype ASF' is reset.
Linetype values produce linetypes as indicated:
1. solid line
2. dashed line
3. dotted line
4. dashed-dotted line
>4. implementation-dependent
If the specified linetype is not available on a workstation, linetype 1 is used.
Errors:
    8   GKS not in proper state: GKS shall be in one of the states GKOP, WSOP, WSAC or SGOP
   62   Linetype is less than or equal to zero

---------------------------- *FORTRAN-Interface* ----------------------------

CALL GSLN (LTYPE)
Parameters:
Input   LTYPE   linetype   (1..n)   INTEGER

SET LINEWIDTH SCALE FACTOR   GKOP,WSOP,WSAC,SGOP   L0a
Parameters:
Input   linewidth scale factor   R

Effect:

The 'current linewidth scale factor' entry in the GKS state list is set to the value specified by the parameter. When the 'current linewidth scale factor ASF' entry in the GKS state list is INDIVIDUAL, subsequently generated POLYLINE output primitives will be displayed with this linewidth scale factor. When the 'current linewidth scale factor ASF' entry in the GKS state list is BUNDLED, this function will not affect the display of subsequently created POLYLINE output primitives until the 'current linewidth scale factor ASF' is reset.

The linewidth scale factor is applied to the nominal linewidth on a workstation; the result is mapped by the workstation to the nearest available linewidth.

Errors:

 8   GKS not in proper state: GKS shall be in one of the states GKOP, WSOP, WSAC or SGOP

—————————————————— *FORTRAN-Interface* ——————————————————

CALL GSLWSC (LWIDTH)

Parameters:

Input   LWIDTH   linewidth scale factor   REAL

SET POLYLINE COLOUR INDEX   GKOP,WSOP,WSAC,SGOP   L0a

Parameters:

Input   colour index   (0..n)   I

Effect:

The 'current polyline colour index' entry in the GKS state list is set to the value specified by the parameter. When the 'current polyline colour index ASF' entry in the GKS state list is INDIVIDUAL, subsequently generated POLYLINE output primitives will be displayed with this polyline colour index. When the 'current polyline colour index ASF' entry in the GKS state list is BUNDLED, this function will not affect the display of subsequently created POLYLINE output primitives until the 'current polyline colour index ASF' is reset.

The colour index is a pointer to the colour tables of the workstations. If the specified colour index is not present in a workstation colour table, a workstation-dependent colour index is used on that workstation.

Errors:

 8   GKS not in proper state: GKS shall be in one of the states GKOP, WSOP, WSAC or SGOP

 85   Colour index is less than zero

—————————————————— *FORTRAN-Interface* ——————————————————

CALL GSPLCI (COLI)

Parameters:

Input   COLI   colour index   (0..n)   INTEGER

SET POLYLINE INDEX   GKOP,WSOP,WSAC,SGOP   L0a

Parameters:

Input   polyline index   (1..n)   I

Effect:

The 'current polyline index' entry in the GKS state list is set to the value specified by the parameter. This value is used for creating subsequent POLYLINE output primitives.

Errors:

8   GKS not in proper state: GKS shall be in one of the states GKOP, WSOP,
        WSAC or SGOP
60   Polyline index is invalid

───────────────────── *FORTRAN-Interface* ─────────────────────

CALL GSPLI (INDEX)
Parameters:
Input   INDEX   polyline index   (1..n)   INTEGER

6.2.2 Workstation-Dependent POLYLINE Attributes

The GKS function SET POLYLINE INDEX REPRESENTATION, for each
workstation individually, allows the selection of polyline aspects LINETYPE,
LINEWIDTH SCALE FACTOR, and POLYLINE COLOUR INDEX. These
values are accessed via a POLYLINE INDEX if the respective aspect source
flag is BUNDLED.

The capabilities of each workstation with respect to these attributes can
be interrogated from the workstation description table. If capabilities are requested which are not supported on that workstation, GKS will generate an
error message. This contrasts with the treatment of global attributes where
sometimes an attribute has to be specified which is not supported on some
workstation and which, therefore, is mapped automatically to an appropriate
valid value.

───

SET POLYLINE REPRESENTATION		WSOP,WSAC,SGOP L1a
Parameters:		
Input workstation identifier		N
Input polyline index	(1..n)	I
Input linetype	(1..n)	I
Input linewidth scale factor		R
Input polyline colour index	(0..n)	I

Effect:
In the polyline bundle table of the workstation state list, the given polyline index
is associated with the specified parameters.
Linetype values produce linetypes as indicated:
    1. solid line
    2. dashed line
    3. dotted line
    4. dashed-dotted line
  >4. implementation-dependent
If the specified linetype is not available, linetype 1 is used.
Linewidth scale factor: a scale factor applied to the nominal linewidth. The result
    is mapped by the workstation to the nearest available linewidth.
Polyline colour index: pointer to the colour table of the workstation.
The polyline bundle table in the workstation state list has predefined entries taken
from the workstation description table; at least one shall be predefined for every

workstation of category OUTPUT and OUTIN. Any table entry (including the predefined entries) may be redefined with this function.

When polylines are displayed, the polyline index refers to an entry in the polyline bundle table. If POLYLINES are displayed with a polyline index that is not present in the polyline bundle table, polyline index 1 will be used. Which of the aspects in the entry are used depends upon the setting of the corresponding ASFs (see Section 6.8.2).

Errors:

7	GKS not in proper state: GKS shall be in one of the states WSOP, WSAC or SGOP
20	Specified workstation identifier is invalid
25	Specified workstation is not open
33	Specified workstation is of category MI
35	Specified workstation is of category INPUT
36	Specified workstation is Workstation Independent Segment Storage
60	Polyline index is invalid
62	Linetype is less than or equal to zero
63	Specified linetype is not supported on this workstation
86	Colour index is invalid

———————————————— *FORTRAN-Interface* ————————————————

CALL GSPLR (WKID,PLI,LTYPE,LWIDTH,COLI)

Parameters:

Input	WKID	workstation identifier		INTEGER
Input	PLI	polyline index	(1..n)	INTEGER
Input	LTYPE	linetype	(1..n)	INTEGER
Input	LWIDTH	linewidth scale factor		REAL
Input	COLI	polyline colour index	(0..n)	INTEGER

6.3 POLYMARKER Primitive

POLYMARKER is a means of identifying points on the display surface. A marker symbol is drawn centred at each position specified in the definition of the POLYMARKER. Figure 6.3 shows three sets of points connected by polylines in different linetypes and polymarkers with different marker types.

The marker facility should be well distinguished from a symbol facility which allows the drawing of several instances of a subpicture. For such purposes

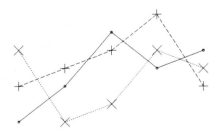

Figure 6.3 Example for a POLYLINE plus POLYMARKER output

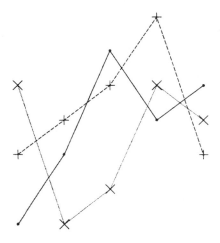

Figure 6.4
Marker not affected by transformation

the INSERT SEGMENT function (see Section 7.7) has been introduced. A symbol containing a subpicture should be properly transformed. With the PO-LYMARKER primitive only the positions are transformed. The size and the orientation of a marker symbol will not be affected. Figure 6.4 shows the output of Figure 6.3 with a different normalization transformation which affects the positions but not the marker size.

The size may be addressed, however, via the POLYMARKER SCALE FAC-TOR attribute (see Figure 6.6). This attribute allows the selection of different sizes of a marker symbol relative to a nominal size measured in device coordinates.

This approach to markers also has consequences on the clipping algorithm. A marker symbol is drawn if, and only if, the position is inside the clipping rectangle. If the position is inside and parts of the marker are outside, the implementation may choose to clip properly or not. If the position is outside and parts of the marker extend to the inside, no part of the marker may be drawn. Figure 6.5a shows the output of Figure 6.3 with the leftmost and right-most points lying on the clipping rectangle. The markers are clipped exactly. In Figure 6.5b the clipping rectangle is slightly shifted by a quarter of the marker size to the right. The markers at the left margin are omitted totally, the markers at the right margin are clipped properly.

POLYMARKER   WSAC,SGOP   L0a
Parameters:
   Input   number of points   (1..n)   I
   Input   coordinates of points   WC   nxP
Effect:
   A sequence of markers is generated to identify all the given positions. The current values of the polymarker attributes, as given by the GKS state list (see Section 3.4), are bound to the primitive.
Note:
   A marker is visible if and only if the marker position is within the clipping rectangle.

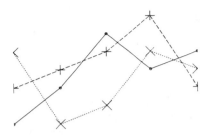

Figure 6.5a Clipping of POLYMARKER,
points inside clipping rectangle

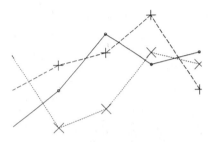

Figure 6.5b Clipping of POLYMARKER,
some points outside clipping rectangle

Errors:
  5   GKS not in proper state: GKS shall be either in the state WSAC or in
           the state SGOP
100   Number of points is invalid

———————————————————— *FORTRAN-Interface* ————————————————————

CALL GPM (N,PX,PY)
Parameters:
  Input   N   number of points   (1..n)   INTEGER
  Input   PX(N),PY(N) coordinates of points   WC   2xREAL

6.3.1 Global Polymarker Attributes

If specific symbols, symbol sizes, and colours are desired, the application pro-
gram may select the values for the polymarker attributes by the GKS functions
SET MARKER TYPE, SET MARKER SIZE SCALE FACTOR, and SET
POLYMARKER COLOUR INDEX.

Within one invocation of POLYMARKER, the same symbol is drawn at
all positions given as parameter. For different invocations of POLYMARKER,
different symbols may be selected by the MARKER TYPE attribute from an
implementation-provided table. GKS requires the implementation of the five
symbols   . + * 0 ×   which must be realized with recognizable shapes on
any output workstation. Further symbols can be added by an implementor
to serve the needs of his constituency.

The application program may ask GKS to draw markers with specified
MARKER SIZES. Marker type 1 always is displayed as the smallest displayable

Figure 6.6
The minimal set of markers in two sizes

dot and, therefore, is not affected by the size attribute. The size is specified as a factor applied to a workstation-specific nominal marker size; it is not affected by GKS transformations. As nominal sizes may be different on different workstations, the same scale factor may lead to different marker sizes.

It is not mandatory for a workstation to support different marker sizes. An implementor may implement any number of marker sizes according to the needs. This decision can be made different for each workstation. If a desired marker size is not realized on a workstation, GKS will select the nearest available marker size.

For colour devices, the colour of a marker can be selected by a colour index specific for POLYMARKER primitives.

If the above attributes are selected on a workstation basis, a POLY-MARKER INDEX can be used which points to workstation tables containing, for each index value, a triple of values for the above attributes. At least POLY-MARKER INDICES 1 to 5 can be used immediately as they are predefined by any implementation.

Whether global or workstation-dependent attributes are applied, is decided by the current (at primitive generation time) setting of the aspect source flags (see Section 3.8.2).

SET MARKER TYPE   GKOP,WSOP,WSAC,SGOP   L0a
Parameters:
    Input marker type   (1..n)   I
Effect:
The 'current marker type' entry in the GKS state list is set to the value specified by the parameter. When the 'current marker type ASF' entry in the GKS state list is INDIVIDUAL, subsequently generated POLYMARKER output primitives will be displayed with this marker type. When the 'current marker type ASF' entry in the GKS state list is BUNDLED, this function will not affect the display of subsequently created POLYMARKER output primitives until the 'current marker type ASF' is reset.

Marker type values produce centred symbols as indicated:
  1 .
  2 +
  3 *
  4 0
  5 X
> 5 implementation dependent

Marker type 1 is always displayed as the smallest displayable dot. If the specified marker type is not available, marker type 3 (*) is used on that workstation.

Errors:
    8   GKS not in proper state: GKS shall be in one of the states GKOP, WSOP, WSAC or SGOP
    66   Marker type is less than or equal to zero

―――――――――――――――――――― *FORTRAN-Interface* ――――――――――――――――――――

CALL GSMK (MTYPE)
   Input   MTYPE   marker type   (1..n)   INTEGER

―――

SET MARKER SIZE SCALE FACTOR   GKOP,WSOP,WSAC,SGOP   L0a
Parameters:
   Input   marker size scale factor   R
Effect:
The 'current marker size scale factor' entry in the GKS state list is set to the value specified by the parameter. When the 'current marker size scale factor ASF' entry in the GKS state list is INDIVIDUAL, subsequently generated POLYMARKER output primitives will be displayed with this marker size scale factor. When the 'current marker size scale factor ASF' entry in the GKS state list is BUNDLED, this function will not affect the display of subsequently created POLYMARKER output primitives until the 'current marker size scale factor ASF' is reset.
The marker size scale factor is applied to the nominal marker size on a workstation; the result is mapped by the workstation to the nearest available marker size.
Errors:
     8   GKS not in proper state: GKS shall be in one of the states GKOP, WSOP, WSAC or SGOP

―――――――――――――――――――― *FORTRAN-Interface* ――――――――――――――――――――

CALL GSMKSC (LWIDTH)
Parameters:
   Input   LWIDTH   marker size scale factor   REAL

―――

SET POLYMARKER COLOUR INDEX   GKOP,WSOP,WSAC,SGOP   L0a
Parameters:
   Input   polymarker colour index   (0..n)   I
Effect:
The 'current polymarker colour index' entry in the GKS state list is set to the value specified by the parameter. When the 'current polymarker colour index ASF' entry in the GKS state list is INDIVIDUAL, subsequently generated POLYMARKER output primitives will be displayed with this polymarker colour index. When the 'current polymarker colour index ASF' entry in the GKS state list is BUNDLED, this function will not affect the display of subsequently created POLYMARKER output primitives until the 'current polymarker colour index ASF' is reset.
The colour index is a pointer to the colour tables of the workstations. If the specified colour index is not present in a workstation colour table, a workstation-dependent colour index is used on that workstation.
Errors:
     8   GKS not in proper state: GKS shall be in one of the states GKOP, WSOP, WSAC or SGOP
   85   Colour index is less than zero

―――――――――――――――――――― *FORTRAN-Interface* ――――――――――――――――――――

CALL GSPMCI (COLI)
Parameters:
   Input   COLI   polymarker colour index   (0..n)   INTEGER

SET POLYMARKER INDEX   GKOP,WSOP,WSAC,SGOP   L0a
Parameters:
Input   polymarker index   (1..n)   I
Effect:
The 'current polymarker index' entry in the GKS state list is set to the value specified
by the parameter. This value is used for creating subsequent POLYMARKER output
primitives.
Errors:
   8   GKS not in proper state: GKS shall be in one of the states GKOP, WSOP,
           WSAC or SGOP
  64   Polymarker index is invalid

────────────────────────── *FORTRAN-Interface* ──────────────────────────

CALL GSPMI (INDEX)
Parameters:
Input   INDEX   polymarker index   (1..n)   INTEGER

6.3.2   Workstation-Dependent POLYMARKER Attributes

The GKS function SET POLYMARKER INDEX REPRESENTATION allows the selection of polymarker attributes MARKER TYPE, MARKER
WIDTH SCALE FACTOR, and POLYMARKER COLOUR INDEX for each
workstation individually. These values are accessed via a POLYMARKER IN-
DEX if the respective aspect source flag is BUNDLED.
    The capabilities of each workstation with respect to these attributes can
be interrogated from the workstation description table. If capabilities are requested which are not supported on the workstation, GKS will generate an
error message. This contrasts with the treatment of the global attributes where
sometimes an attribute has to be specified which is not supported on some
workstation and which, therefore, is mapped automatically to an appropriate
valid value.

SET POLYMARKER REPRESENTATION   WSOP,WSAC,SGOP   L1a
Parameters:
Input   workstation identifier   N
Input   polymarker index   (1..n)   I
Input   marker type   (1..n)   I
Input   marker size scale factor   R
Input   polymarker colour index   (0..n)   I
Effect:
In the polymarker bundle table of the workstation state list, the given polymarker
index is associated with the specified parameters.
Marker type: marker type values produce centred symbols as indicated:
     1 .
     2 +
     3 *
     4 0
     5 X
   >5 implementation dependent

Marker type 1 is always displayed as the smallest displayable dot.

Marker scale factor: a scale factor applied to the nominal marker size. The result is mapped by the workstation to the nearest available marker size.

Polymarker colour index: a pointer to the colour table of the workstation.

The polymarker bundle table in the workstation state list has predefined entries taken from the workstation description table; at least one shall be predefined for every workstation of category OUTPUT and OUTIN. Any table entry (including the predefined entries) may be redefined with this function.

When POLYMARKERS are displayed, the polymarker index refers to an entry in the polymarker bundle table. If POLYMARKERS are displayed with a polymarker index that is not present in the polymarker bundle table, polymarker index 1 will be used. Which of the aspects in the entry are used depends on the setting of the corresponding ASFs (see Section 6.8.2).

Errors:

7	GKS not in proper state: GKS shall be in one of the states WSOP, WSAC or SGOP
20	Specified workstation identifier is invalid
25	Specified workstation is not open
33	Specified workstation is of category MI
35	Specified workstation is of category INPUT
36	Specified workstation is Workstation Independent Segment Storage
64	Polymarker index is invalid
66	Marker type is less than or equal to zero
67	Specified marker type is not supported on this workstation
86	Colour index is invalid

———————————— *FORTRAN-Interface* ————————————

CALL GSPMR (WKID,PMI,MTYPE,MSZSF,COLI)

Parameters:

Input	WKID	workstation identifier		INTEGER
Input	PMI	polymarker index	(1..n)	INTEGER
Input	MTYPE	marker type	(1..n)	INTEGER
Input	MSZSF	marker size scale factor		REAL
Input	COLI	polymarker colour index	(0..n)	INTEGER

6.4 TEXT Primitive

Pictures usually contain inscriptions giving additional textual information. The TEXT primitive, in a convenient way, allows the generation of character strings on the display space. The application program specifies the character codes, and GKS automatically translates this code into geometrical data describing the shape of the individual characters. GKS, at least, provides the character set used in data processing and which is the well known ASCII-character set. This set has been standardized in the ISO 646 standard.

Besides the character string, a starting position in world coordinates also has to be specified. This allows the proper positioning of characters relative to other graphical primitives. The geometry of each individual character is maintained by GKS. GKS provides geometrical text attributes which allow a precise control of the overall size, shape and orientation of characters and character strings. Other attributes allow the selection of a specific font and the manipulation of font characteristics like spacing and aspect ratio. Text geometry is defined in world coordinates; the shape of a character will be transformed like other primitives. For efficiency reasons, this strict rule may be relaxed by a text precision attribute. More details about text attributes are given in the subsequent sections.

TEXT   WSAC,SGOP   L0a

Parameters:

  Input   starting point   WC   P
  Input   character string   S

Effect:

  A character string is generated. The current values of the text attributes, as given by the GKS state list (see Section 3.4), are bound to the primitive. The text position is given in WC and transformed by the current normalization transformation.

Note:

TEXT is clipped in a way that depends on the text precision.

Errors:

    5   GKS not in proper state: GKS shall be either in the state WSAC or in the state SGOP
  101   Invalid code in string

———————————————— *FORTRAN-Interface* ————————————————

CALL GTX (X0,Y0,CHARS)

Parameters:

  Input   X0,Y0   starting point   WC   2xREAL
  Input   CHARS   string of characters (ISO 646)   CHARACTER*(*)

6.4.1   TEXT Attributes for Beginners

GKS provides a variety of text attributes which allow a powerful control of the appearance of text on the display surface. To understand all effects which can be achieved by these attributes, a thorough knowledge of some typographical terms is necessary which will be given in the subsequent sections. However, the text attributes have been structured in such a way that a standard user does not have to deal with all these technical details. Therefore, in this section, a short description of those concepts is given which are of importance for the common user, the text attributes CHARACTER HEIGHT, CHARACTER UP VECTOR, TEXT COLOUR INDEX, and TEXT INDEX. This section should be read by a novice reader. The subsequent sections addresses advanced features of text generation and aim at the experienced user or the implementor of GKS.

By setting CHARACTER HEIGHT, the size of characters can be determined. CHARACTER HEIGHT specifies the height of a capital letter. CHARACTER HEIGHT also controls character width and spacing, as these values are specified relative to CHARACTER HEIGHT. This means that, by doubling

HEIGHT_1
HEIGHT_2
HEIGHT_3

Figure 6.7
TEXT with different CHARACTER HEIGHT values

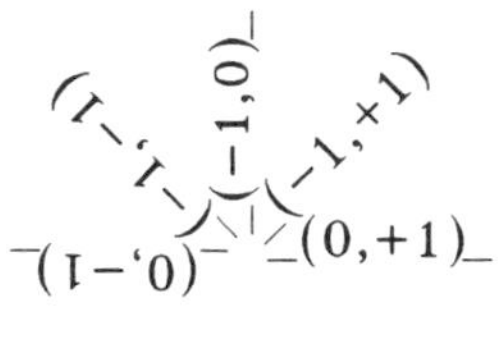

Figure 6.8
TEXT with different CHARACTER UP VECTOR
values

$(-1,0)$ $(-1,+1)$
$(1,-1)$
$-(1-'0)$ $(0,+1)-$

the character height, character width and spacing are also doubled implicitly (see Figure 6.7).

The height value is specified in world coordinates and, therefore, is influenced by transformations. For example, if the current normalization transformation is reset, subsequently generated text primitives may show a different character size on the display surface (see Figure 6.9). Segment transformations and workstation transformations influence text primitives in a similar way.

The default value specifies a CHARACTER HEIGHT of 0.01 which in conjunction with the default window and viewport (unit square) will specify something like the smallest legible character size. With a window of [0,100]x[0,100], illegible characters will be generated. It is therefore recommended to set explicitly CHARACTER HEIGHT for each normalization transformation used for TEXT output.

By default, strings are written along a horizontal baseline starting at the position specified as parameter of the TEXT primitive. The baseline may be rotated to allow strings to be written in other directions. For this purpose, a CHARACTER UP VECTOR must be set which specifies the vertical orientation of characters (see Figure 6.8). The baseline is perpendicular to this vector.

CHARACTER UP VECTOR and baseline are defined in world coordinate system and undergo all transformations. However, as they define angles only, most transformations will have no effect, i.e., the angles will be the same in world coordinate system and on the display surface. It is obvious, that a segment transformation specifying a rotation will rotate TEXT primitives accordingly. It is less evident, that a transformation performing different scaling in x- and y-direction (this is possible for the normalization and segment transformations), may affect angles and even may shear characters (see Figure 6.9). However, this can happen only if the CHARACTER UP VECTOR is not parallel to the axes. These latter effects may be irritating for novice users and applications where a text is regarded more in terms of device coordinates rather than world coordinates. However, the definition of text in world coordinates secures that text behaves like other output primitives. For example, if text is surrounded by a rectangle, both should be transformed in the same way as the text.

For colour devices, the colour of text can be selected by a TEXT COLOUR INDEX specific for TEXT primitives.

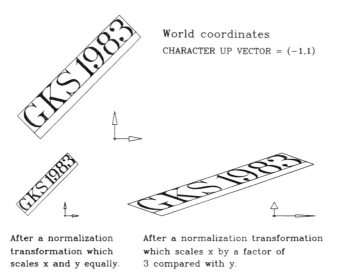

World coordinates

CHARACTER UP VECTOR = $(-1,1)$

After a normalization
transformation which
scales x and y equally.

After a normalization transformation
which scales x by a factor of
3 compared with y.

Figure 6.9 Text with different normalization transformations

Some text attributes can be selected on a workstation basis. A TEXT INDEX can be used which points to text bundles in tables on the individual workstations. See Section 6.4.6 for details about which attributes can be selected workstation-dependently.

6.4.2   Character Body

This section explains how the size and shape of the individual characters in world coordinates are determined. In the beginning, the terminology used for the description of character fonts is explained in detail.

Fonts are defined with respect to some horizontal and vertical lines. *Topline* and *bottomline* delimit characters in vertical direction. *Leftline* and *rightline* delimit characters in horizontal direction. All four lines define a rectangle, parallel to the axes of a 2D Cartesian font coordinate system, which is called the *character body* . It is assumed that the characters lie within their character body, except that kerned characters (see characters j and f in Figure 6.10) may exceed the side limits of the character body. The character body includes some spacing such that characters written with their bodies touching in the horizontal direction should give an appearance of good normal spacing, and characters with their bodies touching in the vertical direction should avoid ascender/descender clashing.

Topline and bottomline will have the same distance for all characters. The distance of leftline and rightline, however, may vary allowing narrow characters like i or l to occupy less space than broad characters like M and W. Fonts

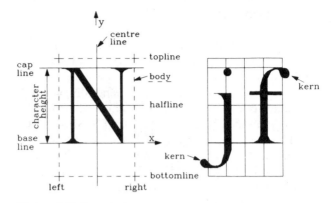

Figure 6.10 Font geometry

with character-dependent width of the character box are called *proportionally spaced fonts* in contrast to *monospaced fonts*.

   Baseline and *capline* must lie within the vertical extent of the character body and, usually, will limit the extent of a capital letter. *Halfline* and *centreline* bisect the character body in vertical and horizontal direction. The exact positions of these lines are specified by the font designer who, for example, may refer to aesthetical criteria for finding the best position rather than choosing the geometric mean.

   The size of the character body is affected by the CHARACTER HEIGHT and CHARACTER EXPANSION FACTOR attributes.

   CHARACTER HEIGHT specifies the nominal height of a capital letter character, i.e., the distance of baseline and capline, in world coordinates. The character body is scaled uniformly in x- and y-direction to achieve the desired CHARACTER HEIGHT. Therefore, the width/height ratio remains unchanged (see Figure 6.7).

   CHARACTER EXPANSION FACTOR allows the manipulation of the width/height ratio of the character body. The width of the character body is scaled by the specified factor. A factor of 1/2 narrows the body to half the width, a factor of 2 doubles the width.

```
Expansion_0.5
Expansion_1
Expansion_2
```

Figure 6.11 Text with different CHARACTER
EXPANSION FACTOR values

   The attributes CHARACTER HEIGHT and CHARACTER EXPANSION FACTOR in conjunction with the font geometry as determined by the font designer fully define the shape and size of the character body of each character in world coordinates.

6.4.3   Text Extent Rectangle

This section deals with the building up of a character string. The purpose of the character body and the horizontal and vertical lines related to the character body is to allow a precise and well defined positioning of characters with respect to their neighbouring characters. Generally, when drawing a string of characters, character bodies are placed adjacent to their neighbours unless additional spacing is demanded by the CHARACTER SPACING attribute (see below).

The side of the character body, where the next character body is placed, is selected by the text attribute TEXT PATH which has four values: RIGHT, LEFT, UP, DOWN. RIGHT is the usual writing direction. LEFT specifies that a 'string' is written backwards, i.e., 'gnirts'. UP and DOWN allow the writing of strings in vertical sequence; with UP the first character is at the bottom and with DOWN at the top of the string. The inter-character alignment is trivial for horizontal writing as all characters use the same baseline, capline, etc. For vertical writing problems occur with proportionally spaced fonts. Note that for vertical writing characters are aligned along the centre line.

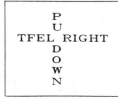

Figure 6.12 TEXT with different TEXT PATH values

The character body already includes some standard spacing of characters. The CHARACTER SPACING value specifies how much additional space is to be inserted between two adjacent character bodies. If the value of CHARACTER SPACING is zero, the character bodies are arranged one after the other along the TEXT PATH. A positive value of CHARACTER SPACING will insert additional space between character bodies. A negative value of CHARACTER SPACING will cause adjacent character bodies to overlap. CHARACTER SPACING is specified as a fraction of the font-nominal character height, i.e., a value of 1 will insert a spacing of the distance of baseline and capline, a value of -1 will backspace by the same distance. Note that this extra spacing applies for all writing directions as specified by TEXT PATH.

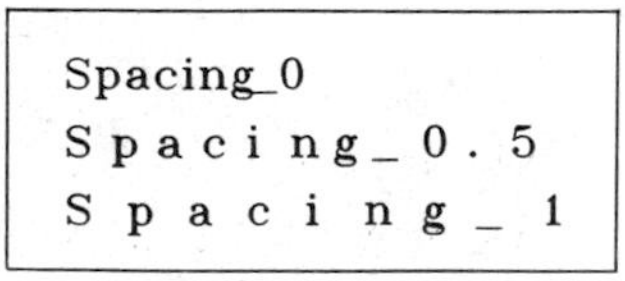

```
Spacing_0
S p a c i n g _ 0 . 5
S  p  a  c  i  n  g  _  1
```

Figure 6.13 TEXT with different CHARACTER SPACING values

TEXT PATH and CHARACTER SPACING in conjunction with the character body geometry as defined in the previous section fully define the geometry

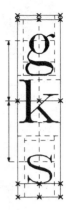

Figure 6.14 Text extent rectangle

of a string. The rectangle which encloses all characters of a string is called *text extent rectangle* . It is formed by
— the topline of the top-most character,
— the bottomline of the bottom character,
— the leftline of the left-most character,
— the rightline of the right-most character.

The lines introduced with the character body in Figure 6.10 are defined for the text extent rectangle similarly. However, depending on the TEXT PATH value, not each line is as meaningful as it was for single characters.

For horizontal writing, bottomline, baseline, halfline, capline, and topline of the text extent rectangle coincide with the respective lines of each character body. Leftline coincides with the leftline of the left-most character, rightline with the rightline of the right-most character, and centreline lies in the geometric mean of both.

For vertical writing, bottomline and baseline of the text extent rectangle coincide with the respective lines of the bottom character, capline and topline coincide with the respective lines of the top-most character, and halfline lies in the geometric mean of the halflines of the bottom and top-most character. Rightline, centreline and leftline coincide with the respective lines of all character bodies for monospaced fonts and with the respective lines of the widest character for proportionally spaced fonts.

These lines are introduced to allow a precise positioning of the text extent rectangle relative to the starting position given in the TEXT primitive invocation. The TEXT ALIGNMENT attribute has two components, a horizontal component with the three values LEFT, CENTRE, RIGHT and a vertical component with the five values TOP, CAP, HALF, BASE, BOTTOM which refer to the respective lines within the text extent rectangle (see Figure 6.14). The text string is positioned such that the starting point given in the parameter list of TEXT lies on the intersection of the selected vertical and horizontal lines.

To relieve the normal user from explicit setting of attributes which have no specific importance in his context, GKS should provide default values which satisfy the most common needs. However, as the natural alignment will depend on the value of the TEXT PATH attribute, it is impossible to give one default suited for all TEXT PATH values. For example, TEXT PATH value RIGHT will usually be combined with alignment to rightline and LEFT with alignment to leftline. This problem has been solved by introducing an additional value for horizontal and vertical alignment called NORMAL. By specifying this value, the programmer indicates that the most natural alignment for the effective TEXT PATH value should be taken. In detail, the following alignment values will be taken:

TEXT PATH value:	RIGHT	LEFT	UP	DOWN
Horizontal alignment NORMAL:	LEFT	RIGHT	CENTRE	CENTRE
Vertical alignment NORMAL:	BASE	BASE	BASE	TOP

Having positioned the text extent rectangle together with the enclosed characters in world coordinate space, it will be rotated such that the CHARACTER UP VECTOR is parallel to the direction of the vertical lines, e.g., the leftline, and points from the bottomline to the topline. See Figure 6.8 for an illustration of the effect.

The horizontal lines, e.g., the baseline, are perpendicular to this direction. Note for implementors: The perpendicular relation between vertical and horizontal font lines only holds in world coordinate system. Therefore, when characters are sent to a workstation, generally, it is not sufficient to send a transformed CHARACTER UP VECTOR with the text primitive but also a transformed baseline vector is needed.

The attributes presented in the above sections give a detailed functionality for specification of the text extent rectangle in world coordinate system. Nevertheless, it is generally not possible for the application program to determine in any case the effective size of the text extent rectangle. This difficulty is due to the fact, that the effect of the above attributes depends on the geometry of a specific font which is not readily available especially for proportionally spaced fonts. Their effect, furthermore, depends on the text precision (see Section 6.4.4) which allows the text attributes, which are too expensive for a workstation, to be ignored. Some of the text attributes can be chosen globally or on a workstation basis. Therefore, character body and text extent rectangle, although defined in world coordinates, are workstation-dependent.

A precise knowledge of the size of the text extent rectangle, in some cases, may be needed. To facilitate the application programmer in the control of the aggregated effects of workstation-dependent and -independent attributes, GKS provides an INQUIRE TEXT EXTENT function (see Section 10.2.4) which delivers on a workstation basis information about the text rectangle for any given text string. Furthermore, it delivers a concatenation point which permits the proper concatenation of strings on one specific workstation.

6.4.4   Text Font and Precision

The TEXT FONT attribute can be used to select a particular font. Every workstation must support at least one font that is able to create a graphical representation of the characters defined in ISO 646 Standard (ASCII-character set). This shall be font number 1. The fonts available for a workstation should be documented in the implementation manual.

The generation of text may be expensive for workstations having inadequate hardware. The TEXT PRECISION attribute is a means of indicating that a poorer realization of the text primitives should be made for efficiency reasons. The TEXT PRECISION value is used to select the 'closeness' of the text representation in relation to that defined by the above text attributes and the transformation/clipping currently applicable. The TEXT PRECISION has the following possible values:

STRING: The TEXT character string is generated in the requested text font and is positioned by aligning the TEXT output primitive at the given TEXT starting position. CHARACTER HEIGHT and CHARACTER EXPANSION FACTOR are evaluated as closely as reasonable, given the capabilities of the workstation. CHARACTER UP VECTOR, TEXT PATH, TEXT ALIGNMENT, and CHARACTER SPACING need not be used. Clipping is done in an implementation- and workstation-dependent way.

CHAR: Individual characters of the TEXT character string in the requested text font are positioned relative to each other according to the TEXT PATH, CHARACTER EXPANSION FACTOR, and CHARACTER SPACING. The writing direction is defined by the CHARACTER UP VECTOR and TEXT PATH. The position of the resulting text extent rectangle is determined by the TEXT ALIGNMENT and the text starting position. For the representation of each individual character, the attributes CHARACTER HEIGHT, the up direction of the CHARACTER UP VECTOR, and CHARACTER EXPANSION FACTOR are evaluated as closely as possible, in a workstation-dependent way. Clipping is done at least on a character body by character body basis.

STROKE: The TEXT character string in the requested text font is displayed at the text starting position by applying all text attributes. The character string is transformed and clipped exactly at the clipping rectangle. It should be recognized that STROKE precision does not necessarily mean vector strokes; as long as the representation adheres to the rules governing STROKE precision, the font may be realized in any form, for example by raster fonts.

Figure 6.15 shows the different behaviour of TEXT for text precision STRING, CHAR, and STROKE. The string 'TEXT DEMONSTRATION' is written with all three precisions; in Figure 6.15a, the string is clipped against the clipping rectangle; in Figure 6.15b, clipping is switched off and only clipping at the workstation window occurs.

A GKS output level 0 implementation must support TEXT precisions STRING and CHAR. Above output level 0, all TEXT precisions must be supported as defined below. A workstation may use a higher precision than the one requested for this purpose, i.e., if STROKE precision is supported in a particular font, the implication is that both STRING and CHAR precision are available in that font.

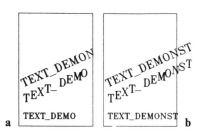

a   TEXT_DEMO   TEXT_DEMONST   b   **Figure 6.15** TEXT with different text precisions

Even when using STRING precision, the CHARACTER HEIGHT should be set. The use of CHARACTER HEIGHT is optional for STRING precision and the default value of CHARACTER HEIGHT will not always produce legible characters depending on the current normalization transformation.

TEXT font and precision are workstation mandatory. That is, for any GKS level supporting a STROKE precision font, every workstation of a particular installation has to support at least one STROKE precision TEXT font. This shall be font number 1, and should contain the character set defined by ISO 646. This implies that, for STROKE precision TEXT, some sort of software character generator will be required for those implementations that have inadequate hardware. Not all workstations need to support all fonts, but for those that do, the same font number shall be used to select that font on all workstations of a particular installation.

6.4.5   Setting Global Text Attributes

The previous sections gave an introduction into the semantics of text attributes. The following Figures 6.16 a,b illustrate, with a series of examples, the interdependence between the different text attributes.

Most of the attributes can be used as global attributes only. The attributes TEXT FONT AND PRECISION, CHARACTER EXPANSION FACTOR, CHARACTER SPACING, and TEXT COLOUR INDEX can also be selected on a workstation basis. In this case a TEXT INDEX can be used which points

Table 6.6 Initial values of the global text attributes

CHARACTER HEIGHT	WC	0.01 (i.e. 1% of the height of the default window)
CHARACTER UP VECTOR	WC	(0,1)
TEXT PATH		RIGHT
TEXT ALIGNMENT		(NORMAL;NORMAL)
TEXT INDEX		1
TEXT FONT AND PRECISION		(1;STRING)
CHARACTER EXPANSION FACTOR		1
CHARACTER SPACING		0
TEXT INDEX		1

to workstation tables containing, for each index value, a bundle of values for these attributes.

Whether global or workstation-dependent attributes are applied, is decided by the current (at primitive generation time) setting of the aspect source flags (see Section 6.8.2).

In the following, a description of all functions setting the global text attributes will be given. The initial values of these attributes are compiled in Table 6.6.

SET CHARACTER HEIGHT   GKOP,WSOP,WSAC,SGOP   L0a
Parameters:
Input   character height   WC   >0   R
Effect:
   The 'current character height' entry in the GKS state list is set to the value specified by the parameter. This value is used for creating subsequent TEXT output primitives.
Errors:
   8   GKS not in proper state: GKS shall be in one of the states GKOP, WSOP, WSAC or SGOP
   73   Character height is less than or equal to zero

———————————————— *FORTRAN-Interface* ————————————————

CALL GSCHH (CHH)
Parameters:
Input   CHH   character height   WC   >0   REAL

SET CHARACTER UP VECTOR   GKOP,WSOP,WSAC,SGOP   L0a
Parameters:
Input   character up vector   WC   2xR
Effect:
   The 'current character up vector' entry in the GKS state list is set to the value specified by the parameter. This value is used for creating subsequent TEXT output primitives.
Errors:
   8   GKS not in proper state: GKS shall be in one of the states GKOP, WSOP, WSAC or SGOP
   74   Length of character up vector is zero

———————————————— *FORTRAN-Interface* ————————————————

CALL GSCHUP (CHUX,CHUY)
Parameters:
Input   CHUX,CHUY   character up vector   WC   2xREAL

SET TEXT COLOUR INDEX   GKOP,WSOP,WSAC,SGOP   L0a
Parameters:
Input   text colour index   (0..n)   I
Effect:
   The 'current text colour index' entry in the GKS state list is set to the value specified by the parameter. When the 'current text colour index ASF' entry in the GKS state

Examples are illustrated with STROKE precision,
a character expansion factor of 1 and a zero
character spacing.

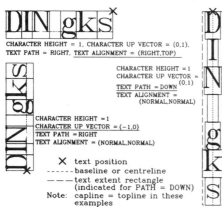

Figure 6.16a Samples for the effect
of text attributes

Figure 6.16b Samples for the effect
of text attributes (continued)

list is INDIVIDUAL, subsequently generated TEXT output primitives will be displayed with this text colour index. When the 'current text colour index ASF' entry in the GKS state list is BUNDLED, this function will not affect the display of subsequently created TEXT output primitives until the 'current text colour index ASF' is reset.

The colour index is a pointer to the colour tables of the workstations. If the specified colour index is not present in a workstation colour table, a workstation dependent colour index is used on that workstation.

Errors:

8   GKS not in proper state: GKS shall be in one of the states GKOP, WSOP, WSAC or SGOP

85   Colour index is less than zero

──────────────────── *FORTRAN-Interface* ────────────────────

CALL GSTXCI (COLI)

Parameters:

Input   COLI   colour index   (0..n)   INTEGER

SET TEXT INDEX   GKOP,WSOP,WSAC,SGOP   L0a

Parameters:

Input   text index   (1..n)   I

Effect:

The 'current text index' entry in the GKS state list is set to the value specified by the parameter. This value is used for creating subsequent TEXT output primitives.

Errors:

8   GKS not in proper state: GKS shall be in one of the states GKOP, WSOP, WSAC or SGOP

68   Text index is invalid

──────────────────── *FORTRAN-Interface* ────────────────────

CALL GSTXI (INDEX)

Parameters:

Input   INDEX   text index   (1..n)   INTEGER

SET TEXT PATH   GKOP,WSOP,WSAC,SGOP   L1a

Parameters:

Input   text path   (RIGHT,LEFT,UP,DOWN)   E

Effect:

The 'current text path' entry in the GKS state list is set to the value specified by the parameter. This value is used for creating subsequent TEXT output primitives.

Errors:

8   GKS not in proper state: GKS shall be in one of the states GKOP, WSOP, WSAC or SGOP

──────────────────── *FORTRAN-Interface* ────────────────────

CALL GSTXP (TXP)

Parameters:

Input   TXP   text path   (0 = right, 1 = left, 2 = up, 3 = down)   INTEGER

SET TEXT ALIGNMENT   GKOP,WSOP,WSAC,SGOP   L0a

Parameters:

Input   text alignment   (NORMAL,LEFT,CENTRE,RIGHT;
                                   NORMAL,TOP,CAP,HALF,BASE,BOTTOM)   2xE

Effect:

The 'current text alignment' entry in the GKS state list is set to the value specified by the parameter. This value is used for creating subsequent TEXT output primitives. Text alignment has two components: horizontal and vertical.

Errors:

    8   GKS not in proper state: GKS shall be in one of the states GKOP, WSOP,
        WSAC or SGOP

———————————————— *FORTRAN-Interface* ————————————————

CALL GSTXAL (TXALH,TXALV)

Parameters:

Input   TXALH   text alignment horizontal
                                   (0=normal, 1=left, 2=centre, 3=right)   INTEGER
Input   TXALV   text alignment vertical
                    (0=normal, 1=top, 2=cap, 3=half, 4=base, 5=bottom)   INTEGER

SET TEXT FONT AND PRECISION   GKOP,WSOP,WSAC,SGOP   L0a

Parameters:

Input   text font and precision   (1..n;STRING,CHAR,STROKE)   (I;E)

Effect:

The 'current text font and precision' entry in the GKS state list is set to the value specified by the parameter. When the 'current text font and precision ASF' entry in the GKS state list is INDIVIDUAL, subsequently generated TEXT output primitives will be displayed with this text font and precision. When the 'current text font and precision ASF' entry in the GKS state list is BUNDLED, this function will not affect the display of subsequently created TEXT output primitives until the 'current text font and precision ASF' is reset.

Text font and precision is a single text aspect; a particular text font can be available at some, but necessarily all, precisions. The text precision value determines the fidelity with which the other text aspects are used. The values of text precision, in order of increasing fidelity, are STRING, CHAR, and STROKE.

If the specified text font is not available on a workstation, the value (1;STRING) is used on that workstation.

Errors:

    8   GKS not in proper state: GKS shall be in one of the states GKOP, WSOP,
        WSAC or SGOP

   70   Text font is less than or equal to zero

———————————————— *FORTRAN-Interface* ————————————————

CALL GSTXFP (FONT,PREC)

Parameters:

Input   FONT   text font   (1..n)   INTEGER
Input   PREC   text precision   (0=string, 1=char, 2=stroke)   INTEGER

SET CHARACTER EXPANSION FACTOR

GKOP,WSOP,WSAC,SGOP   L0a

Parameters:

Input   character expansion factor   >0   R

Effect:

The 'current character expansion factor' entry in the GKS state list is set to the value specified by the parameter.

When the 'current character expansion factor ASF' entry in the GKS state list is INDIVIDUAL, subsequently generated TEXT output primitives will be displayed with this character expansion factor. When the 'current character expansion factor ASF' entry in the GKS state list is BUNDLED, this function will not affect the display of subsequently created TEXT output primitives until the 'current character expansion factor ASF' is reset.

Errors:

8   GKS not in proper state: GKS shall be in one of the states GKOP, WSOP, WSAC or SGOP

72   Character expansion factor is less than or equal to zero

————————————————————— *FORTRAN-Interface* —————————————————————

CALL GSCHXP (CHXP)

Parameters:

Input   CHXP   character expansion factor   >0   REAL

SET CHARACTER SPACING   GKOP,WSOP,WSAC,SGOP   L0a

Parameters:

Input   character spacing   R

Effect:

The 'current character spacing' entry in the GKS state list is set to the value specified by the parameter.

When the 'current character spacing ASF' entry in the GKS state list is INDIVIDUAL, subsequently generated TEXT output primitives will be displayed with this character spacing. When the 'current character spacing ASF' entry in the GKS state list is BUNDLED, this function will not affect the display of subsequently created TEXT output primitives until the 'current character spacing ASF' is reset.

Errors:

8   GKS not in proper state: GKS shall be in one of the states GKOP, WSOP, WSAC or SGOP

————————————————————— *FORTRAN-Interface* —————————————————————

CALL GSCHSP (CHSP)

Parameters:

Input   CHSP   character spacing   REAL

6.4.6 Workstation-Dependent TEXT Attributes

The GKS function SET TEXT REPRESENTATION allows the selection of text attributes TEXT FONT AND PRECISION, CHARACTER EXPANSION FACTOR, CHARACTER SPACING, and TEXT COLOUR INDEX for each workstation individually. These values are accessed via TEXT INDEX if the respective aspect source flag is BUNDLED.

The capabilities of each workstation with respect to these attributes can be interrogated from the workstation description table. If capabilities are requested which are not supported on the workstation, GKS will generate an error message. This contrasts with the treatment of the global attributes where sometimes an attribute has to be specified which is not supported on some workstation and which, therefore, is mapped automatically to an appropriate valid value.

SET TEXT REPRESENTATION   WSOP,WSAC,SGOP   L1a
Parameters:

Input	workstation identifier		N
Input	text index	(1..n)	I
Input	text font and precision	(1..n;STRING,CHAR,STROKE)	(I;E)
Input	character expansion factor	>0	R
Input	character spacing		R
Input	text colour index	(0..n)	I

Effect:

In the text bundle table of the workstation state list, the given text index is associated with the specified parameters.

Text font and precision: gives the text font to be used and determines the fidelity with which the other text attributes are used.

Character expansion factor: specifies the deviation of the width to height ratio of the characters from the ratio indicated by the font designer.

Character spacing: specifies how much additional space is to be inserted between two adjacent character bodies. Character spacing is specified as a fraction of the font-nominal character height.

Text colour index: a pointer to the colour table of the workstation.

The text bundle table in the workstation state list has predefined entries taken from the workstation description table; at least one shall be predefined for every workstation of category OUTPUT and OUTIN. Any table entry (including the predefined entries) may be redefined with this function.

When TEXT is displayed, the TEXT index refers to an entry in the text bundle table. If TEXT is displayed with a text index that is not present in the text bundle table, text index 1 will be used. Which of the aspects in the entry are used depends upon the setting of the corresponding ASFs (see Section 6.8.2).

Errors:

7	GKS not in proper state: GKS shall be in one of the states WSOP, WSAC or SGOP
20	Specified workstation identifier is invalid
25	Specified workstation is not open
33	Specified workstation is of category MI
35	Specified workstation is of category INPUT
36	Specified workstation is Workstation Independent Segment Storage
68	Text index is invalid
70	Text font is less than or equal to zero
71	Requested text font is not supported for the required precision on this workstation
72	Character expansion factor is less than or equal to zero
86	Colour index is invalid

————————————————————— *FORTRAN-Interface* —————————————

CALL GSTXR (WKID,TXI,FONT,PREC,CHXP,CHSP,COLI)
Parameters:

Input	WKID	workstation identifier		INTEGER
Input	TXI	text index	(1..n)	INTEGER
Input	FONT	text font	(1..n)	INTEGER
Input	PREC	text precision (0 = string, 1 = char, 2 = stroke)		INTEGER
Input	CHXP	character expansion factor	> 0	REAL
Input	CHSP	character spacing		REAL
Input	COLI	colour index	(0..n)	INTEGER

6.5 FILL AREA Primitive

FILL AREA generates a closed polygon which may be hollow or filled with a uniform colour, a pattern, or a hatch style. The primitive's purpose is the display of areas.

The FILL AREA primitive has gained increasing importance by the advent of colour raster displays where the display of solid areas is the main primitive. Areas have been of interest before. However, other devices did not provide adequate capabilities. Black-and-white raster displays can easily display solid areas but no colours are available to make adjacent areas distinguishable. This difficulty has been overcome by providing a set of characteristic patterns with which the areas can be filled. Vector devices use hatching for displaying areas, e.g., in cartography and in business graphics. However, the hatching algorithm has to be paid for so that interactive vector devices usually abandon hatching for efficiency reasons.

The different methods of area display have been combined into one FILL AREA primitive which, by use of workstation specific aspects, allows the addressing of the appropriate technique on each workstation.

Areas are defined by their bounding polygon. The polygon given in the parameter list is closed by connecting the last point with the first one. There are no restrictions concerning the shape of the polygon; it may define convex and nonconvex areas and may cross itself. Figure 6.18 shows how the interior of the polygon is defined in such cases. However, insular structures, i.e., areas with holes which need several separate polygons to be defined, have been excluded from GKS. Such structures were regarded as being outside the scope of a kernel system and, therefore, must be handled on top of GKS.

FILL AREA is clipped precisely to the clipping rectangle. Therefore, clipping may change the boundaries of the area and even generate multiple subareas from one area (see Figure 6.18).

A problem which does exist for all primitives but has special relevance for FILL AREA is the treatment of overlapping primitives. For line primitives, overlapping occurs only in points of intersection and, usually, is ignored. With FILL AREA, large portions of the display can be overlapped and a decision has be be taken as to what primitive is to be displayed and what primitive is to be suppressed partially.

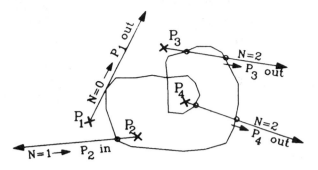

P_i :   **points to be tested**

N :   **intersection count**

Figure 6.17 Testing whether P lies inside a polygon

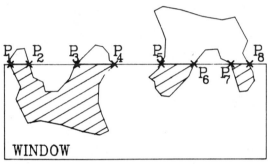

▨ **resulting AREAs after**
    clipping at the WINDOW

× P_i **points added to polygon**

Figure 6.18 Examples of FILL AREA clipping

For this reason, GKS has introduced the segment priority which, at least at the segment level, allows the specification of which primitives should be preferred (see Section 7.6 for details).

FILL AREA		WSAC,SGOP	L0a
Parameters:			
Input	number of points	(3..n)	I
Input	coordinates of points	WC	nxP

Effect:
 A FILL AREA primitive is generated. The current values of the fill area attributes, as given by the GKS state list (see Section 3.4), are bound to the primitive. The polygon defined by the points is filled according to the fill area interior style currently selected. The boundary is drawn for style HOLLOW and is not drawn for other interior styles.

If parts of the area are clipped, the resulting new boundaries generated become part of the area boundaries. Multiple subareas may be generated (see Figure 6.18).

The interior of a polygon is defined in the following way (see Figure 6.17): For a given point, create a straight line starting at that point and going to infinity. If the number of intersections between the straight line and the polygon is odd, the point is within the polygon, otherwise it is outside. If the straight line passes a polygon vertex tangentially, the intersection count is not affected.

For PICK input, a FILL AREA primitive with interior style HOLLOW may be picked by pointing at any point on the bounding polygon. A FILL AREA primitive with interior style SOLID or PATTERN may be identified by pointing at any point inside the polygon. Pointing at a hole in the area does not identify that area. A FILL AREA primitive with interior style HATCH may be picked by pointing at any point on any hatch line.

Errors:

5	GKS not in proper state: GKS shall be either in the state WSAC or in the state SGOP
100	Number of points is invalid

———————————————— *FORTRAN-Interface* ————————————————

CALL GFA (N,PX,PY)
Parameters:

Input	N	number of points		INTEGER
Input	PX,PY	coordinates of points	WC	NxREAL

6.5.1 Global FILL AREA Attributes

FILL AREA possesses the attributes FILL AREA INTERIOR STYLE, FILL AREA STYLE INDEX, and FILL AREA COLOUR INDEX which either can be set globally or workstation-dependently. Two further attributes, PATTERN REFERENCE POINT and PATTERN SIZE, are relevant only for a specific fill area interior style value.

The fill area interior style is used to determine in what style the area should be filled. It has the following values:

SOLID: Fill the interior of the polygon with the colour specified by the fill area colour index. This style typically is used with colour raster displays.

PATTERN: Fill the interior of the polygon with a pattern specified by the fill area style index. In this context, the style index points to an adjustable pattern table and, therefore, sometimes is referred to as the pattern index. Patterns are widely used with black-and-white raster devices as the only means for distinguishing different areas. Colour raster devices may use patterns for generating textures.

HATCH: Hatch the interior of the polygon using the colour specified by the fill area colour index. In this context, the style index points to an implementation-provided hatch table containing different hatch styles and, therefore, sometimes is referred to as the hatch index. Hatching is a technique primarily used with plotters.

Figure 6.19 Example of a map with hatching

HOLLOW: No filling, but draw the bounding polyline, using the fill area colour index. Linetype and linewidth are implementation-dependent. This style often is used with vector refresh displays having limited number of displayable vectors.

Fill area attributes on a colour raster display are shown in Figure C2, a map with solid area filling is shown in Figure C4, hatching on a flatbed plotter is illustrated in Figure C8 (all figures on pages 503). Figure 6.19 shows hatching in black and white.

For fill area interior style PATTERN, two global attributes PATTERN REFERENCE POINT and PATTERN SIZE define the geometry of the pattern rectangle. The PATTERN REFERENCE POINT defines the location of the lower left corner of the pattern rectangle and PATTERN SIZE gives the extent in x- and y-direction. The style index points to a pattern table on the workstation. The pattern can be set by SET PATTERN REPRESENTATION (see Section 6.5.2). Each entry contains an array of COLOUR INDICES.

The pattern rectangle is divided into a regular grid of cells according to the dimensions of the colour index array. Each cell is assigned the corresponding colour index. The pattern rectangle is repeated in directions parallel to the sides of the pattern rectangle until the interior of the polygon is covered completely. Then the cells are transformed and mapped to the pixels of the workstation. The pixels of a workstation are assigned colour indices by point sampling the transformed cells at the pixel's centrepoint: If a pixel's centrepoint lies inside the transformed polygon, it is assigned the colour index of that transformed cell the centrepoint lies in. Otherwise, the pixel is not touched. This scheme compares exactly with the scheme described for CELL ARRAY (see

Section 6.6) with the only difference that CELL ARRAY is limited by the cell array rectangle whereas FILL AREA is limited by the polygon.

Transformation of patterns is necessary if one wants to get a realistic view of transformed picture parts. If the pattern is not transformed, a viewer has the impression of a moving outline before a wall with a stationary wall-paper pattern.

Workstations are not required to perform all types of area display. The workstation description table indicates the capabilities supported by a specific workstation type. For a workstation which is able to display areas with patterns but cannot transform the patterns, a suitable action is to generate non-transformable patterns to fill a polygon.

For interior style HATCH, the style index selects the desired hatch pattern. Hatching is a workstation capability which may be present or not. In the latter case, the effect will be identical to specifying HOLLOW. Hatching may be affected by transformations but this is not required. The hatch patterns cannot be set by the application program. Only a choice between hatch patterns provided by the implementor of GKS can be made. The minimum number of hatch styles supported by a workstation is 1, and it may be identical to specifying HOLLOW. Whether hatching is affected by transformations or not, is workstation-dependent.

If a workstation is not capable of the interior style SOLID, PATTERN or HATCH, the minimal action required is the interior style HOLLOW.

The representation of FILL AREA at the workstation can be controlled by the current FILL AREA INDEX, which is a pointer to the fill area bundle table.

SET FILL AREA INTERIOR STYLE   GKOP,WSOP,WSAC,SGOP   L0a
Parameters:
   Input   fill area interior style   (HOLLOW,SOLID,PATTERN,HATCH)   E
Effect:
   The 'current fill area interior style' entry in the GKS state list is set to the value specified by the parameter. When the 'current fill area interior style ASF' entry in the GKS state list is INDIVIDUAL, subsequently generated FILL AREA output primitives will be displayed with this fill area interior style. When the 'current fill area interior style ASF' entry in the GKS state list is BUNDLED, this function will not affect the display of subsequently created FILL AREA output primitives until the 'current fill area interior style ASF' is reset.
   The fill area interior style is used to determine in what style the area is filled. If the requested interior style is not available on a workstation, HOLLOW will be used on that workstation.
Errors:
   8   GKS not in proper state: GKS shall be in one of the states GKOP, WSOP, WSAC or SGOP

--------------------------- *FORTRAN-Interface* ---------------------------
CALL GSFAIS (INTS)
Parameters:
   Input   INTS   interior style
                     (0 = hollow, 1 = solid, 2 = pattern, 3 = hatch)   INTEGER

SET FILL AREA STYLE INDEX   GKOP,WSOP,WSAC,SGOP   L0a
Parameters:
   Input   fill area style index   (1..n)   I
Effect:
   The 'current fill area style index' entry in the GKS state list is set to the value specified
   by the parameter. When the 'current fill area style index ASF' entry in the GKS
   state list is INDIVIDUAL, subsequently generated FILL AREA output primitives
   will be displayed with this fill area style index. When the 'current fill area style index
   ASF' entry in the GKS state list is BUNDLED, this function will not affect the
   display of subsequently created FILL AREA output primitives until the 'current fill
   area style index ASF' is reset.
   For interior styles HOLLOW and SOLID, the style index value is unused. For interior
   style PATTERN, it is a pointer to the pattern tables of the workstations. For interior
   style HATCH, its value determines which of a number of workstation-dependent hatch
   styles is used.
   If the requested style index is not available on a particular workstation, style index
   1 is used on that workstation. If style index 1 is not present on that workstation,
   the result is workstation-dependent.
Errors:
   8   GKS not in proper state: GKS shall be in one of the states GKOP, WSOP,
          WSAC or SGOP
   78   Style (pattern or hatch) index is less than or equal to zero

———————————————————— *FORTRAN-Interface* ————————————————————

CALL GSFASI (STYLI)
Parameters:
   Input   STYLI   fill area style index   (1..n)   INTEGER

SET FILL AREA COLOUR INDEX   GKOP,WSOP,WSAC,SGOP   L0a
Parameters:
   Input   fill area colour index   (0..n)   I
Effect:
   The 'current fill area colour index' entry in the GKS state list is set to the value
   specified by the parameter. When the 'current fill area colour index ASF' entry in
   the GKS state list is INDIVIDUAL, subsequently generated FILL AREA output
   primitives will be displayed with this fill area colour index. When the 'current fill
   area colour index ASF' entry in the GKS state list is BUNDLED, this function will
   not affect the display of subsequently created FILL AREA output primitives until
   the 'current fill area colour index ASF' is reset.
   The colour index is a pointer to the colour tables of the workstations. If the specified
   colour index is not present in a workstation colour table, a workstation-dependent
   colour index is used on that workstation.
Errors:
   8   GKS not in proper state: GKS shall be in one of the states GKOP, WSOP,
          WSAC or SGOP
   85   Colour index is less than zero

———————————————————— *FORTRAN-Interface* ————————————————————

CALL GSFACI (COLI)
Parameters:
   Input   COLI   colour index   (0..n)   INTEGER

SET FILL AREA INDEX   GKOP,WSOP,WSAC,SGOP   L0a
Parameters:
Input   fill area index   (1..n)   I
Effect:
The 'current fill area index' entry in the GKS state list is set to the value specified
by the parameter. This value is used for creating subsequent FILL AREA output
primitives.
Errors:
   8   GKS not in proper state: GKS shall be in one of the states GKOP, WSOP,
        WSAC or SGOP
  75   Fill area index is invalid

———————————————— *FORTRAN-Interface* ————————————————

CALL GSFAI (INDEX)
Parameters:
Input   INDEX   fill area index   (1..n)   INTEGER

SET PATTERN SIZE   GKOP,WSOP,WSAC,SGOP   L0a
Parameters:
Input   pattern size   WC   SX,SY > 0   2xR
Effect:
The 'current pattern size' entry in the GKS state list is set to the value specified
by the parameter. When the currently selected (either via the fill area bundle or individually, depending on the corresponding ASF) fill area interior style is PATTERN, this
value is used, where possible, in conjunction with the 'current pattern reference point'
entry in the GKS state list for displaying the FILL AREA output primitives.
Errors:
   8   GKS not in proper state: GKS shall be in one of the states GKOP, WSOP,
        WSAC or SGOP
  81   Pattern size value is not positive

———————————————— *FORTRAN-Interface* ————————————————

CALL GSPA (SX,SY)
Parameters:
Input   SX,SY   pattern size   WC   SX,SY > 0   REAL

SET PATTERN REFERENCE POINT   GKOP,WSOP,WSAC,SGOP   L0a
Parameters:
Input   reference point   WC   P
Effect:
The 'current pattern reference point' entry in the GKS state list is set to the value
specified by the parameter. When the currently selected (either via the fill area bundle
or individually, depending on the corresponding ASF) fill area interior style is PAT-
TERN, this value is used, where possible, in conjunction with the 'current pattern
size' entry in the GKS state list for displaying the FILL AREA output primitives.
Errors:
   8   GKS not in proper state: GKS shall be in one of the states GKOP, WSOP,
        WSAC or SGOP

—————————————————————— *FORTRAN-Interface* ——————————————————————

CALL GSPARF (RFX,RFY)
Parameters:
  Input   RFX,RFY   pattern reference point   WC   2xREAL

6.5.2   Workstation-Dependent FILL AREA Attributes

The GKS function SET FILL AREA REPRESENTATION allows the selection of the fill area attributes FILL AREA INTERIOR STYLE, FILL AREA STYLE INDEX, and FILL AREA COLOUR INDEX for each individual workstation. These values are accessed via a FILL AREA INDEX if the respective aspect source flag is BUNDLED.

The capabilities of each workstation with respect to these attributes can be interrogated from the workstation description table. If capabilities are requested which are not supported on the workstation, GKS will generate an error message. This contrasts with the treatment of the global attributes where sometimes an attribute has to be specified which is not supported on some workstation and which, therefore, is mapped automatically to an appropriate valid value.

If a workstation supports interior style PATTERN, there exists a pattern table on that workstation describing the patterns to be used for area filling. For GKS output levels 1 and 2, at least 10 entries must be present which can be redefined via the function SET PATTERN REPRESENTATION. The application program has to specify a colour index array which defines the pattern unit which is to be repeated to cover any given area. The location and the size of this pattern unit is determined by the global attributes PATTERN REFERENCE POINT and PATTERN SIZE introduced in the previous section.

SET FILL AREA REPRESENTATION   WSOP,WSAC,SGOP   L1a
Parameters:
  Input   workstation identifier   N
  Input   fill area index   (1..n)   I
  Input   fill area interior style   (HOLLOW,SOLID,PATTERN,HATCH)   E
  Input   fill area style index   (1..n)   I
  Input   fill area colour index   (0..n)   I
Effect:
  In the fill area bundle table of the workstation state list, the given fill area index is associated with the specified parameters.
  Fill area interior style: is used to determine in what style the area should be filled.
  Fill area style index: For interior styles HOLLOW and SOLID, this value is unused. For style PATTERN, it is a pointer to the pattern table of the workstation. For style HATCH, its value determines which of a number of workstation-dependent hatch styles is used.
  Fill area colour index: Pointer into the colour table of the workstation.
  The fill area bundle table in the workstation state list has predefined entries taken from the workstation description table; at least one shall be predefined for every

workstation of category OUTPUT and OUTIN. Any table entry (including the predefined entries) may be redefined with this function.

When fill area is displayed, the current fill area index refers to an entry in the fill area bundle table. If FILL AREAS are displayed with a fill area index that is not present in the fill area bundle table, fill area index 1 is used. Which of the aspects in the entry are used depends upon the setting of the corresponding ASFs (see Section 6.8.2).

Errors:

7	GKS not in proper state: GKS shall be in one of the states WSOP, WSAC or SGOP
20	Specified workstation identifier is invalid
25	Specified workstation is not open
33	Specified workstation is of category MI
35	Specified workstation is of category INPUT
36	Specified workstation is Workstation Independent Segment Storage
75	Fill area index is invalid
77	Specified fill area interior style is not supported on this workstation
79	Specified pattern index is invalid
80	Specified hatch style is not supported on this workstation
86	Colour index is invalid

──────────────────────── *FORTRAN-Interface* ────────────────────

CALL GSFAR (WKID,FAI,INTS,STYLI,COLI)

Parameters:

Input	WKID	workstation identifier		INTEGER
Input	FAI	fill area index	(1..n)	INTEGER
Input	INTS	fill area interior style		
		(0 = hollow, 1 = solid, 2 = pattern, 3 = hatch)		INTEGER
Input	STYLI	fill area style index	(1..n)	INTEGER
Input	COLI	fill area colour index	(0..n)	INTEGER

───

SET PATTERN REPRESENTATION	WSOP,WSAC,SGOP	L1a

Parameters:

Input	workstation identifier		N
Input	pattern index	(1..n)	I
Input	dimensions of pattern array DX,DY	(1..n)	2xI
Input	pattern array	(0..n)	nxnxI

Effect:

In the pattern table of the workstation state list, the given pattern index is associated with the specified parameters. A grid of DXxDY cells (DX horizontal, DY vertical) is specified. The colour is given individually for each cell by a colour index, a pointer to the colour table of the workstation.

If the workstation supports interior style PATTERN, the pattern table in the workstation state list has predefined entries taken from the workstation description table. Any table entry (including the predefined entries) may be redefined with this function. When a fill area is displayed, if the currently selected (either via the fill area bundle or individually, depending upon the corresponding ASF) interior style is PATTERN, the currently selected style index refers to an entry in the pattern table. If fill areas are displayed with a pattern index that is not present in the pattern table, pattern index 1 will be used. If pattern index 1 is not present, the result is workstation-dependent.

Errors:

7	GKS not in proper state: GKS shall be in one of the states WSOP, WSAC or SGOP
20	Specified workstation identifier is invalid
25	Specified workstation is not open
33	Specified workstation is of category MI
35	Specified workstation is of category INPUT
36	Specified workstation is Workstation Independent Segment Storage
79	Specified pattern index is invalid
83	Interior style PATTERN is not supported on this workstation
84	Dimensions of colour array are invalid
86	Colour index is invalid

—————————————————————— *FORTRAN-Interface* ——————————————————————

CALL GSPAR (WKID,PAI,N,M,DIMX,COLIA)

Input	WKID	workstation identifier		INTEGER
Input	PAI	pattern index	(1..n)	INTEGER
Input	N,M	dimensions of pattern array	(1..n)	2xINTEGER
Input	DIMX	first dimension of pattern array	(1..n)	INTEGER
Input	COLIA-(DIMX,M)	pattern array	(0..n)	INTEGER

6.6   CELL ARRAY Primitive

The output primitive CELL ARRAY serves for passing raster images to GKS. The raster image is defined by a colour index matrix and its size and position is determined by a rectangle in WC. All workstations must accept this primitive. However, it is not intended that workstations with inadequate capabilities simulate colour raster displays. The minimum reaction expected is to draw the boundaries of the cell rectangle.

Whereas the FILL AREA primitive introduced in the previous section allows only one colour or one pattern to be specified for the whole area, CELL ARRAY allows the specification of areas with varying colours where the dimensions of the colour array determine the resolution. Therefore, this primitive is suited for display of photographic images with some random colour distribution or of surfaces with continuously varying colours (see Figure C3 on page 499).

Because of the close relationship between the CELL ARRAY primitive and the hardware of raster devices, one could expect that the matrix given in the primitive's definition is immediately mapped to the pixels of the raster device. However, for consistency with other GKS primitives, the CELL ARRAY primitive is defined in WC space and has to be transformed by all GKS transformations. Otherwise, a CELL ARRAY cannot be used together with other primitives. However, this does not imply that transformation of CELL ARRAY is the usual case. If an application needs an immediate addressing of pixels on a specific workstation only, it will set transformations in a way that each cell of CELL ARRAY corresponds exactly to one pixel on the display.

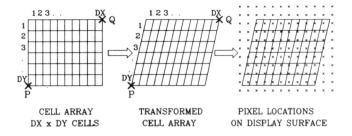

Cells are mapped on display surface.
If display location is within cell then
cell colour is assigned to pixel.

Figure 6.20 Mapping of CELL ARRAY

The cell rectangle is divided by a regular grid aligned with the world coordinate axes into congruent rectangular cells such that the number of cell rows and columns corresponds to the dimensions of the colour index array. Each cell is assigned the corresponding colour index.

The grid defined in WC is subject to all transformations, potentially rotating the grid and transforming the rectangular cells into parallelograms and to clipping. Then the colour index of a pixel on a workstations is set by point sampling the transformed cells at the pixel's centrepoint:

If a pixel's centrepoint lies inside a transformed cell, it is assigned the corresponding colour index. Otherwise, the pixel is not touched. (See Figure 6.20)

The simple point sampling approach of GKS has some disadvantages in comparison with area sampling or filtering. Transformed CELL ARRAYS may show unexpected distortions due to the rounding of transformed cells to the pixels available on the workstation. However, it is within the responsibility of the application program to avoid such effects by careful selection of transformations or by appropriate choice of resolution of the CELL ARRAY.

CELL ARRAY has no attributes other than PICK IDENTIFIER. The colours are specified via a matrix of colour indices in the definition of a cell array rather than as separate attributes. However, these colour indices are handled just like the colour indices used as attributes for other primitives.

CELL ARRAY   WSAC,SGOP   L0a
Parameters:

Input	cell rectangle (P,Q)	WC		2xP
Input	dimensions of colour index array DX,DY	(1..n)		2xI
Input	colour index array	(0..n)		nxnxI

Effect:

A CELL ARRAY primitive is generated using the cell rectangle corners, the dimensions of the colour index array and the colour index array.

A rectangle, which is taken to be aligned with the world coordinate axes, is defined by the points P and Q. This rectangle is conceptually divided into a grid in DXxDY cells. Each cell has a width of PX-QX /DX and a height of PY-QY /DY, where

(PX,PY) are the coordinates of the corner point P and (QX,QY) are the coordinates of the corner point Q. The colour of each cell is specified by the index of the corresponding element of the colour index array. If an index value is not present in the colour index table then a workstation-dependent index value is used.

The rectangular grid defined by P,Q,DX and DY is subject to all transformations, potentially transforming the rectangular cells into parallelograms. If part of a transformed cell is outside the window, the transformed cell is partially clipped. Mapping the transformed cells onto the cells of a raster display is performed by the following rules (see Figure 6.20):

a) If the centrepoint of a raster display cell lies inside the parallelogram defined by the transformed rectangle, its colour is set.

b) The raster display pixel will be assigned the colour of the cell which contains the pixel's centrepoint. Thus, the pixel colour is selected by point sampling the transformed rectangle at the pixel centrepoint, not by area sampling or filtering.

The minimal simulation required is to draw the transformed boundaries of the cell rectangle, using implementation-dependent colour, linewidth and linetype.

Errors:

5	GKS not in proper state: GKS shall be either in the state WSAC or in the state SGOP
84	Dimensions of colour array are invalid

──────────────────────── *FORTRAN-Interface* ────────────────────────

CALL GCA (PX,PY,QX,QY,N,M,DIMX,COLIA)
Parameters:

Input	PX,PY, QX,QY	two points (P, Q) WC		4xREAL
Input	N, M	dimensions of colour index array (1..n) (number of columns, number of rows)		INTEGER
Input	DIMX	first dimension of colour index array (1..n)		INTEGER
Input	COLIA(DIMX,M)	colour index array (0..n)		INTEGER

6.7   GENERALIZED DRAWING PRIMITIVE (GDP)

Generalized drawing primitive (GDP) is a standard way of providing additional non-standard output primitives. The purpose of GDP is to address special capabilities of a workstation like spline interpolation and circle interpolation.

A specific GKS implementation specifies how such additional capabilities are to be addressed. The geometric data have to be passed to the workstation separately from the non-geometric data, thus allowing GKS a proper transformation of the geometric data. This has the advantage that a user of such a non-standard feature makes efficient use of the transformation capability already present within GKS. Only the geometric data are transformed. This may lead to unexpected results in some cases. For example, if a non-uniform transformation is specified, a circle degenerates to an ellipse. This cannot be achieved by transforming the defining points of a circle, but has to be handled by defining the circle as a special case of an ellipse.

It is not necessary that a GDP is supported. If a workstation does not support a specific GDP function, an error message is generated. At least, a module generating the appropriate error messages must be implemented within GKS. A good implementation also should provide an appropriate default action, e.g., generating a POLYLINE with the geometric data of the GDP.

As the content of the GDP is undefined, no attributes can be assigned except the PICK IDENTIFIER. However, if a specific GDP is similar to one of the output primitives mentioned above, the implementor may use the corresponding primitive attributes. Further accompanying information may be specified in a data record in the primitive's parameter list.

GENERALIZED DRAWING PRIMITIVE (GDP)   WSAC,SGOP   L0a

Parameters:

Input	number of points		(0..n)	I
Input	points	WC		nxP
Input	GDP identifier			N
Input	GDP data record			D

Effect:

A Generalized Drawing Primitive (GDP) of the type indicated by the GDP identifier is generated on the basis of the given points and the GDP data record. The current values of the entries in the GKS state list for the sets of polyline, polymarker, text, or fill area attributes are bound to the primitive. When the GDP generates output at the workstation, zero or more of the sets of attributes are used. These are the sets of attributes most appropriate for the specific GDP function and are selected for the GDP as part of the definition of the GDP. (They are defined in the workstation description table.)

Note:

The parameters are transmitted to the workstation and interpreted in a workstation-specific way. In this way special capabilities of the workstation can be addressed. Even if error 104 occurs, the GDP is displayed on all active workstations capable of doing so. For example, some of the primitives anticipated at present are:

a) circle: points given are centre, peripheral point;
b) circular arc: points given are centre, start point, end point to be connected counter-clockwise in world coordinates;
c) ellipse: points given are 2 focal points, peripheral point;
d) elliptic arc: points given are 2 focal points, start point, end point to be connected counter-clockwise in world coordinates;
e) interpolating curve (for example, spline): points given are interpolated.

The recommended bundle to use for the above GDP examples would be the polyline attributes.

It should be pointed out that the points specified as parameters are transformed by GKS before the interpretation of the points as defining a spline curve or circle takes place by the active workstations. Though the points cannot be clipped, the resulting output of the GDP is clipped against the viewport if clipping is on and the workstation window. The data record attribute list may contain additional data for each point (for example, vertex order for splines) which remain untransformed. These have to be defined for a specific GDP. In defining a new GDP, the GKS design concepts must not be violated. The set of generalized drawing primitives implemented on a workstation may be empty.

Errors:

    5   GKS not in proper state: GKS shall be either in the state WSAC or in the state SGOP
  100   Number of points is invalid

102   Generalized drawing primitive identifier is invalid
103   Content of generalized drawing primitive data record is invalid
104   At least one active workstation is not able to generate the specified generalized
        drawing primitive

———————————————————— FORTRAN-*Interface* ————————————————————

CALL GGDP (N,PX,PY,PRIMID,LDR,DATREC)
Parameters:

Input	N	number of points		(0..n)	INTEGER
Input	PX(N),PY(N)	coordinates of points	WC		2xREAL
Input	PRIMID	GDP identifier		(1..n)	INTEGER
Input	LDR	length of data record		(0..n)	INTEGER
Input	DATREC (LDR)	data record			CHARACTER*80

6.8   Attribute Setting Functions Concerning All Primitives

6.8.1   Setting the Colour Table

Colour is an attribute of all primitives. It may be specified as a global attribute,
as a workstation-dependent attribute or in the pattern or CELL ARRAY definition (see Table 6.4). In any case, it is not possible to specify a colour directly.
A COLOUR INDEX must be used which points to a colour table located
at each workstation.

For each COLOUR INDEX value, the colour table contains an entry which
specifies colour in terms of red/green/blue intensities in the range [0,1]. This
colour table is modelled after the colour table present in many colour raster
devices. The colour table can be reset at any time so as to allow dynamic
colour changes which are a powerful feature of colour raster devices.

However, not all devices have such a comfortable colour manipulation facility. If a dynamic colour table is not available on the device, a colour table
must be held within the driver and a regeneration of the picture must be initiated
if a dynamic change of colour has been requested.

Some workstations are not capable of displaying colours but can generate
one colour in different intensities (monochrome devices). In this case, the colour
specified is mapped to an intensity according to:

intensity $= 0.5 \times (M + m)$

where $M = \max(red, green, blue)$, $m = \min(red, green, blue)$.

If colours or intensities are not available on a workstation, the requested
values are mapped to the nearest available value.

The colour table is set individually for each workstation so as to allow
the application program to address the specific colour capabilities of each workstation. The minimum size of the colour table is 2 entries. Entry 0 corresponds
to the background colour. Entry 1 is the default foreground colour. This corresponds exactly to the capabilities of black and white devices.

The colour table of a workstation will be predefined according to the available capabilities such that a number of well distinguishable colours are associated with different entries in the colour table. If a specific colour is required, it can be selected, if available, by SET COLOUR REPRESENTATION.

SET COLOUR REPRESENTATION   WSOP,WSAC,SGOP   L0a
Parameters:

Input	workstation identifier		N
Input	colour index	(0..n)	I
Input	colour (red/green/blue intensities)	[0,1]	3xR

Effect:

In the colour table of the workstation state list, the given colour index is associated with the specified colour. The colour is mapped by the workstation to the nearest available.

The colour table in the workstation state list has predefined entries taken from the workstation description table; at least indices 0 and 1 shall be predefined for every workstation of category OUTPUT or OUTIN. Any table entry entry (including the predefined entries) may be redefined with this function.

When output primitives are displayed, the colour index refers to an entry in the colour table. If output primitives are displayed with a colour index that is not present in the colour table, a workstation-dependent colour index will displayed with a colour index that is not present in the colour table, a workstation-dependent colour index will be used. The background colour is defined by colour index 0.

Note:

On monochrome devices, the intensity is computed from the colour values as follows: intensity $= 0.5 \times (M + m)$ where $M = \max(\text{red},\text{green},\text{blue})$, $m = \min(\text{red},\text{green},\text{blue})$.

Errors:

7	GKS not in proper state: GKS shall be in one of the states WSOP, WSAC or SGOP
20	Specified workstation identifier is invalid
25	Specified workstation is not open
33	Specified workstation is of category MI
35	Specified workstation is of category INPUT
36	Specified workstation is Workstation Independent Segment Storage
85	Colour index is less than zero
88	Colour is outside range [0,1]

———————————— *FORTRAN-Interface* ————————————

CALL GSCR (WKID,CI,CR,CG,CB)
Parameters:

Input	WKID	workstation identifier		INTEGER
Input	CI	colour index	(0..n)	INTEGER
Input	CR,CG,CB	red, green, blue	[0,1]	3xREAL

6.8.2 Setting the Aspect Source Flags

Some output primitive attributes can be set INDIVIDUALLY or BUNDLED. Table 6.4 on page 174 lists all these attributes. The individual attributes are bound directly and, therefore, cannot be manipulated. The bundled attributes are addressed via bundle indices pointing to bundle tables which are set workstation-dependently. The binding is delayed allowing the bundle entries to be set dynamically.

The function SET ASPECT SOURCE FLAG, for each of these attributes, sets a flag indicating in which way the attribute is to be applied. Any combination of bundled and individual attributes is admitted even for attributes belonging to one bundle. For example, the setting

linetype ASF = INDIVIDUAL
linewidth ASF = INDIVIDUAL
polyline colour index ASF = BUNDLED

specifies that linetype and linewidth of a POLYLINE should be taken from the current setting of the respective attributes in the GKS state list. The values are bound directly to each POLYLINE primitive. The colour is derived from the respective entry in the polyline bundle table. The latter value may be different for each workstation and may be changed dynamically.

The ASFs have been introduced for efficiency reasons. The powerful facility of attributes addressed via bundle tables involves some overhead. There are applications which rest content with limited attribute capabilities, e.g., if only one type of workstation is used, or which need more different attributes than can reasonably be stored in workstation tables. These application can be satisfied with direct attribute setting. They should not be forced to pay the overhead for capabilities which are not used.

The possibility of manipulating a specific attribute in two totally different ways can be very confusing. It is therefore recommended to use the function SET ASPECT SOURCE FLAG with care, e.g., by having all attributes either bundled or individual or by setting the ASFs only once after opening of GKS according to the needs. The application program may redefine the ASFs at any time; however, this will affect only subsequently generated primitives.

The default setting of the ASFs reflects the philosophy that bundled and individual attributes are two concept which should best be left apart. An implementor may choose to have all defaults for the ASFs either BUNDLED or INDIVIDUAL according to the needs of his constituency but may not provide a mixed set of defaults.

SET ASPECT SOURCE FLAG   GKOP,WSOP,WSAC,SGOP   L0a
Parameters:
   Input   list of Aspect Source Flags   (BUNDLED,INDIVIDUAL)   13xE
Effect:
  The Aspect Source Flags (ASFs) in the GKS state list are set to the values indicated by the parameter. The elements of the list of ASFs are arranged in the following order:

       1   linetype ASF
       2   linewidth scale factor ASF
       3   polyline colour index ASF
       4   marker type ASF
       5   marker size scale factor ASF

                   6   polymarker colour index ASF
                   7   text font and precision ASF
                   8   character expansion factor ASF
                   9   character spacing ASF
                  10   text colour index ASF
                  11   fill area interior style ASF
                  12   fill area style index ASF
                  13   fill area colour index ASF

Errors:

8   GKS not in proper state: GKS shall be in one of the states GKOP, WSOP, WSAC or SGOP

——————————————— *FORTRAN-Interface* ———————————————

CALL GSASF (LASF)
  Input   LASF(13)   list of aspect source flags
                         (0 = bundled, 1 = individual)   13 × INTEGER

6.8.3 Setting the Pick Identifier

The pick identifier is relevant only if a PICK input device and the segment storage is available. The reader of this section should be familiar with both concepts (see Chapter 7 and 8).

The pick identifier is different from other primitive attributes in the sense that it has no meaning for the graphical output but is stored for the purpose of the PICK input device. It has been introduced for applications which use their own data structure for manipulation purposes but want to use the PICK input device with minimal expenses for the segment mechanism. The pick identifier allows the identification of primitives within a segment and, thus, establishes a second level of naming. However, GKS provides no functions to access and manipulate primitives with a given pick identifier. Therefore, the use of pick identifiers is not as restricted as is the use of segment names. The same pick identifier may be assigned to non-contiguous groups of primitives within a segment. The pick identifier may be set outside segments but this setting becomes relevant only when GKS enters state SGOP. See Example 7.3 for the use of the pick identifier.

SET PICK IDENTIFIER   GKOP,WSOP,WSAC,SGOP   L1b

Parameters:
  Input   pick identifier   N
Effect:
  The 'current pick identifier' entry in the GKS state list is set to the value specified by the parameter.
Errors:

8   GKS not in proper state: GKS shall be in one of the states GKOP, WSOP, WSAC or SGOP

89   Pick identifier is invalid

——————————————— *FORTRAN-Interface* ———————————————

CALL GSPKID (PCID)
  Input   PCID   pick identifier   INTEGER

6.9   Examples

Example 6.1   Plotting coordinate data in a file by POLYLINE

Assume that coordinate data describing polylines are stored in a file. The procedure DRAW_FILE reads in one data record after the other and generates a polyline with each of them. Such a procedure was used for generation of Figures 5.1—5.4.

———————————————————— *Pascal* ————————————————————

```
L10    PROCEDURE DRAW_FILE (VAR input_file :TEXT);
                                    {Read data from FILE and draw polylines}
L20    VAR xarray,yarray :ARRAY[1..1000] OF REAL;          {Declarations}
L30      i,length :INTEGER;

L50    BEGIN
L60      RESET (input_file);
L60      WHILE NOT EOF(input_file) DO
L70      BEGIN
L80        READ(input_file,length);
L90        IF (length > 0) THEN
L100       BEGIN
L110         FOR i:=1 TO length DO READ(input_file,xarray[i],yarray[i]);
L120         POLYLINE (length,xarray,yarray);
L130       END;
L140     END;
L150   END {DRAW_FILE};
```

———————————————————— *Fortran* ————————————————————

```
L10            SUBROUTINE DRFILE (FILE)
       C                              *** Read data from FILE and draw polylines

       C                                              *** Declarations
L20            REAL XARRAY(1000), YARRAY(1000)
L30            INTEGER FILE, LENGTH, I

L110     110   READ(FILE,160,END=150)
              +    LENGTH,(XARRAY(I),YARRAY(I),I=1,LENGTH)
L120           CALL GPL (LENGTH,XARRAY,YARRAY)
L130           GOTO 110

L150     150   RETURN
L160     160   FORMAT (I10/(2F12.2))
L170           END
```

Example 6.2   Use of direct POLYLINE attributes

A map containing border lines, rivers, roads is to be drawn. The different classes of lines are distinguished by different line attributes. The map is drawn

on workstation 'display' with attributes: border lines = solid, rivers = dashed, roads = dotted, and then is drawn on workstation 'plotter' with attributes: border lines = red, rivers = blue, roads = black. It is assumed that on the plotter workstation there are predefined colour table entries:
1 = black; 2 = red; 3 = green; 4 = blue.

─────────────────────── *Pascal* ───────────────────────

                    {Setting of transformations see Example 5.4, L10—50}
                                              {Generate picture on display}

L40   ACTIVATE_WORKSTATION (display);

L60   SET_LINETYPE (1);   {Set linetype and draw line data in files}
L70   DRAW_FILE(borderlines);
L80   SET_LINETYPE (2);
L90   DRAW_FILE(rivers);
L100 SET_LINETYPE (3);
L110 DRAW_FILE(roads);

L120 DEACTIVATE_WORKSTATION (display);

                         {Generate picture on plotter using different colours}
L130 ACTIVATE_WORKSTATION (plotter);
                    {Setting of workstation transformation see Example 5.4, L140—150}
                                    {Set colour index and draw line data in files}
L160 SET_POLYLINE_COLOUR_INDEX (2);
L170 DRAW_FILE(borderlines);
L180 SET_POLYLINE_COLOUR_INDEX (4);
L190 DRAW_FILE(rivers);
L200 SET_POLYLINE_COLOUR_INDEX (1);
L210 DRAW_FILE(roads);

L220 DEACTIVATE WORKSTATION (plotter);

─────────────────────── *Fortran* ───────────────────────

```
        C        ***Setting of transformations see Example 5.4, L10—50
        C        ***Generate picture on display using different linctypes
L40              CALL GACWK (DISPL)
        C        *** Set linetype and draw line data in files 21, 22, 23
L60              CALL GSLN (1)
L70              CALL DRFILE(21)
L80              CALL GSLN (2)
L90              CALL DRFILE(22)
L100             CALL GSLN (3)
L110             CALL DRFILE(23)
L120             CALL DAWK (DISPL)


        C        ***Generate picture on plotter using different colours
L130             CALL GACWK (PLOTTR)
        C        ***Setting of workstation transformation see Example 5.4, L140—150
        C        ***Set colour index and draw line data in files 21, 22, 23
L160             CALL GSPLCI (2)
L170             CALL DRFILE(21)
```

L180	CALL GSPLCI (4)
L190	CALL DRFILE(22)
L200	CALL GSPLCI (1)
L210	CALL DRFILE(23)
L220	CALL GDAWK (PLOTTR)

Example 6.3   Use of indexed POLYLINE attributes

The same task as in Example 6.2 is performed with the use of polyline index. As the polyline representation is defined separately for each workstation, the picture can be generated simultaneously on both workstations which eliminates every second call for DRAW_FILE.

Indexed attributes can also be used for dynamic attribute change on the same workstation (see Example 7.1).

———————————————————— *Pascal* ————————————————————

{Initialising of POLYLINE INDEX REPRESENTATION}
{Using different linetypes for workstation display}

L10   SET_POLYLINE_REPRESENTATION (display, 1, 1, 1.0, 1);
L20   SET_POLYLINE_REPRESENTATION (display, 2, 2, 1.0, 1);
L30   SET_POLYLINE_REPRESENTATION (display, 3, 3, 1.0, 1);

{Using different colours for workstation plotter}

L40   SET_POLYLINE_REPRESENTATION (plotter, 1, 1, 1.0, 2);
L50   SET_POLYLINE_REPRESENTATION (plotter, 2, 1, 1.0, 4);
L60   SET_POLYLINE_REPRESENTATION (plotter, 3, 1, 1.0, 1);
L70   SET_COLOUR_REPRESENTATION (plotter, 1, 1.0, 1.0, 1.0);   {black}
L80   SET_COLOUR_REPRESENTATION (plotter, 2, 1.0, 0.0, 0.0);   {red}
L90   SET_COLOUR_REPRESENTATION (plotter, 4, 0.0, 0.0, 1.0);   {blue}

{Setting of transformations see Example 5.4, L10—50, L140—150}

L100 ACTIVATE_WORKSTATION (display);
L110 ACTIVATE_WORKSTATION (plotter);

L120 SET_POLYLINE_INDEX (1);   {Draw line data in data sets}
L130 DRAW_FILE(borderlines);
L140 SET_POLYLINE_INDEX (2);
L150 DRAW_FILE(rivers);
L160 SET_POLYLINE_INDEX (3);
L170 DRAW_FILE(roads);

L180 DEACTIVATE_WORKSTATION (display);
L190 DEACTIVATE_WORKSTATION (plotter);

——————————————————— *Fortran* ———————————————————

```
        C              *** Initialising of POLYLINE INDEX REPRESENTATION
        C                  *** Using different linetypes for workstation display
L10            CALL GSPLR (DISPL, 1, 1, 1.0, 1)
```

L20	CALL GSPLR (DISPL, 2, 2, 1.0, 1)
L30	CALL GSPLR (DISPL, 3, 3, 1.0, 1)
C	*** Using different colours for workstation plotter
L40	CALL GSPLR (PLOTTR, 1, 1, 1.0, 2)
L50	CALL GSPLR (PLOTTR, 2, 1, 1.0, 4)
L60	CALL GSPLR (PLOTTR, 3, 1, 1.0, 1)
C	*** Set colour table entries 1 = black, 2 = red, 4 = blue
L70	CALL GSCR (PLOTTR, 1, 1.0, 1.0, 1.0)
L80	CALL GSCR (PLOTTR, 2, 1.0, 0.0, 0.0)
L90	CALL GSCR (PLOTTR, 4, 0.0, 0.0, 1.0)
C	*** Setting of transformations see Example 5.4, L10—50, L150—160
L100	CALL GACWK (DISPL)
L110	CALL GACWK (PLOTTR)
C	*** Draw line data in files 21, 22, 23
L120	CALL GSPLI (1)
L130	CALL DRFILE(21)
L140	CALL GSPLI (2)
L150	CALL DRFILE(22)
L160	CALL GSPLI (3)
L170	CALL DRFILE(23)
L180	CALL GDAWK (DISPL)
L190	CALL GDAWK (PLOTTR)

Example 6.4   Drawing a chart with three histograms

Three different sets of values (e.g., returns of three companies over several years) are given in the arrays yarray1, yarray2, and yarray3. The array xarray contains the dates of the years. For each company, a POLYLINE, connecting the returns values, is drawn and the vertices of the POLYLINE are marked by marker symbols.

Sample output see Figure 6.3 on page 181.

———————————————————— *Pascal* ————————————————————

L10	SET_MARKER_TYPE (1); {Choose different marker type for each set of points}
L20	POLYMARKER (length,xarray,yarray1); {Draw symbol at given positions}
L30	SET_LINETYPE (1); {Choose different linetypes for each set of points}
L40	POLYLINE (length,xarray,yarray1);
	{Draw POLYLINE to connect given positions}
	{repeat the above statements with marker type and linetype 2 and 3 for yarray2 and yarray3}

———————————————————— *Fortran* ————————————————————

C	*** Choose different marker type for each set of points
L10	CALL GSMK (1)
C	*** Draw symbol at given positions
L20	CALL GPM (LENGTH,XARRAY,YARRAY1)

```
         C          *** Choose different linetypes for each set of points
L30                 CALL GSLN (1)
         C          *** Draw POLYLINE to connect given positions
L40                 CALL GPL (LENGTH,XARRAY,YARRAY1)
         C
         C          *** Repeat the above statements with marker type
                    *** and linetype 2 and 3 for YARRAY2 and YARRAY 3
```

Example 6.5   Effect of transformation and clipping on markers

This example illustrates the generation of Figures 6.3—6.5 (pages 181–183) which show the effect of clipping and transformations on POLYMARKER. Figure 6.5 shows a very comfortable clipping. An implementor has some freedom in implementing clipping less comfortable.

The picture to be clipped has been defined in Example 6.4. Data are assumed to be in the range $1 \leq x \leq 5$, $1 \leq y \leq 5$.

─────────────────────── *Pascal* ───────────────────────

```
L10    SET_WINDOW (1, 1.0, 5.0, 1.0, 5.0);
L20    SET_VIEWPORT (1, 0.1, 0.5, 0.1, 0.5);
L30    SET_CLIPPING_INDICATOR (NOCLIP);
       {Insert Example 6.4;                          Figure 6.3 generated}

L40    SET_VIEWPORT (1, 0.1, 0.5, 0.1, 0.9);
       {Insert Example 6.4;                          Figure 6.4 generated}

L50    SET_VIEWPORT (1, 0.1, 0.5, 0.1, 0.5);
L60    SET_CLIPPING_INDICATOR (CLIP);
       {Insert Example 6.4;                          Figure 6.5a generated}

L70    SET_WINDOW (1, 1.05, 5.05, 1.0, 5.0);
       {Insert Example 6.4;                          Figure 6.5b generated}
```

──────────────────── *Fortran* ────────────────────

```
L01              INTEGER CLIP,NOCLIP
L02              DATA CLIP/1/, NOCLIP/0/

L10              CALL GSWN (1, 1.0, 5.0, 1.0, 5.0)
L20              CALL GSVP (1, 0.1, 0.5, 0.1, 0.5)

L30              CALL GSCLIP (NOCLIP)
         C       ***Insert Example 6.4;               Figure 6.3 generated

L40              CALL GSVP (1, 0.1, 0.5, 0.1, 0.9)
         C       ***Insert Example 6.4;               Figure 6.4 generated
```

L50		CALL GSVP (1, 0.1, 0.5, 0.1, 0.5)
L60		CALL GSCLIP (CLIP)
	C	***Insert Example 6.4;

Figure 6.5a generated

L70		CALL GSWN (1, 1.05, 5.05, 1.0, 5.0)
	C	***Insert Example 6.4;

Figure 6.5b generated

Example 6.6   Setting the TEXT attributes

This example illustrates some typical settings for different TEXT attributes.
The TEXT attributes are set directly. Generated figures are shown on pages
189–192.

———————————————————— *Pascal* ————————————————————

L10   SET_WINDOW (1, 0.0, 20.0, 0.0, 20.0);
{Set workstation viewport on plotter to 20 cm x 20 cm}
L20   SET_WORKSTATION_VIEWPORT (1, 0.0, 0.2, 0.0, 0.2);

L30   SET_CHARACTER_HEIGHT (0.9);   {Vary CHARACTER HEIGHT}
L40   TEXT (1.0, 1.0, 'HEIGHT_3');
L50   SET_CHARACTER_HEIGHT (0.6);
L60   TEXT (1.0, 2.2, 'HEIGHT_2');
L70   SET_CHARACTER_HEIGHT (0.3);
L80   TEXT (1.0, 3.1, 'HEIGHT_1');   {generates Figure 6.7}

{Vary CHARACTER UP VECTOR, character baseline is rotated accordingly}
L90   SET_CHARACTER_UP_VECTOR (0.0,-1.0) ;
L100   TEXT (10.0, 10.0, '_(0,-1)_');
L110   SET_CHARACTER_UP_VECTOR (-1.0,-1.0) ;
L120   TEXT (10.0, 10.0, '_(-1,-1)');
L130   SET_CHARACTER_UP_VECTOR (-1.0, 0.0) ;
L140   TEXT (10.0, 10.0, '_(-1,0)_');
L150   SET_CHARACTER_UP_VECTOR (-1.0, 1.0) ;
L160   TEXT (10.0, 10.0, '_(-1,+1)');
L170   SET_CHARACTER_UP_VECTOR (0.0, 1.0);
L180   TEXT (10.0, 10.0, '_(0,+1)_');   {generates Figure 6.8}

{vary CHARACTER EXPANSION FACTOR}
L190   SET_CHARACTER_EXPANSION_VECTOR (2.0);
L200   TEXT (10.0, 1.0, 'EXPANSION_2');
L210   SET_CHARACTER_EXPANSION_VECTOR (0.5);
L220   TEXT (10.0, 2.4, 'EXPANSION_0.5');
L230   SET_CHARACTER_EXPANSION_VECTOR (1.0);
L240   TEXT (10.0, 1.7, 'EXPANSION_1');   {generates Figure 6.11}

L250   SET_TEXT_PATH (UP); {TEXT PATH selects one from four writing directions}
L260   TEXT (15.0, 10.5,'UP');   {without rotating the individual characters}

L270 SET_TEXT_PATH (DOWN);
L280 TEXT (15.0, 9.8, 'DOWN');
L290 SET_TEXT_PATH (LEFT) ;
L300 TEXT (14.8, 10.0, 'LEFT');
L310 SET_TEXT_PATH (RIGHT) ;
L320 TEXT (15.2, 10.0, 'RIGHT');   {generates Figure 6.12}

                              {CHARACTER SPACING sets additional spacing}
L330 SET_CHARACTER_SPACING (1.0);
L340 TEXT (1.0, 5.0, 'SPACING_1');
L350 SET_CHARACTER_SPACING (0.5);
L360 TEXT (1.0, 5.7, 'SPACING_0.5');
L370 SET_CHARACTER_SPACING (0.0);
L380 TEXT (1.0, 6.4, 'SPACING_0');   {generates Figure 6.13}

─────────────────────────── *Fortran* ───────────────────────────

L10   CALL GSWN (1, 0.0, 20.0, 0.0, 20.0)
         C   *** Set workstation viewport on plotter to 20 cm x 20 cm
L20   CALL GSWKVP (1, 0.0, 0.2, 0.0, 0.2)

         C   *** Vary CHARACTER HEIGHT
L30   CALL GSCHH (0.9)
L40   CALL GTX (1.0, 1.0, 'HEIGHT_3')
L50   CALL GSCHH (0.6)
L60   CALL GTX (1.0, 2.2, 'HEIGHT_2')
L70   CALL GSCHH (0.3)
L80   CALL GTX (1.0, 3.1, 'HEIGHT_1')
         C   *** generates Figure 6.7

         C   *** Vary CHARACTER UP VECTOR, character baseline is rotated
                                                              accordingly
L90   CALL GSCHUP (0.0,-1.0)
L100   CALL GTX (10.0, 10.0, '_(0,-1)_')
L110   CALL GSCHUP (-1.0,-1.0)
L120   CALL GTX (10.0, 10.0, '-_(-1,-1)')
L130   CALL GSCHUP (-1.0, 0.0)
L140   CALL GTX (10.0, 10.0, '_(-1,0)_')
L150   CALL GSCHUP (-1.0, 1.0)
L160   CALL GTX (10.0, 10.0, '_(-1,+1)')
L170   CALL GSCHUP (0.0, 1.0)
L180   CALL GTX (10.0, 10.0, '_(0,+1)_')
         C   *** generates Figure 6.8

         C   *** vary CHARACTER EXPANSION FACTOR
L190   CALL GSCHXP (2.0)
L200   CALL GTX (10.0, 1.0, 'EXPANSION_2')
L210   CALL GSCHXP (0.5)
L220   CALL GTX (10.0, 2.4, 'EXPANSION_0.5')
L230   CALL GSCHXP (1.0)
L240   CALL GTX (10.0, 1.7, 'EXPANSION_1')
         C   *** generates Figure 6.11

```
        C                        *** TEXT PATH selects one from four writing directions
        C                             *** without rotating the individual characters
L250              CALL GSTXP (2)
L260              CALL GTX (15.0, 10.5, 'UP')
L270              CALL GSTXP (3)
L280              CALL GTX (15.0, 9.8, 'DOWN')
L290              CALL GSTXP (1)
L300              CALL GTX (14.8, 10.0, 'LEFT')
L310              CALL GSTXP (0)
L320              CALL GTX (15.2, 10.0, 'RIGHT')
        C                                              *** generates Figure 6.12

        C                        *** CHARACTER SPACING sets additional spacing
L330              CALL GSCHSP (1.0)
L340              CALL GTX (1.0, 5.0, 'SPACING_1')
L350              CALL GSCHSP (0.5)
L360              CALL GTX (1.0, 5.7, 'SPACING_0.5')
L370              CALL GSCHSP (0.0)
L380              CALL GTX (1.0, 6.4, 'SPACING_0')
        C                                              *** generates Figure 6.13
```

Example 6.7   Generating digits on a clock using TEXT_ALIGNMENT

Example 7.4 in the next chapter describes the generation of a clock. This example shows how the digits on the clock-face can be drawn. Digits are written horizontally. Text alignment is used to centre the digits to a position on a corresponding radial line at a distance of 0.85 from the centre. Character height for digits is 0.036. The clock time (hours) is transformed to an angle (radians) according to the following rules: 3 o'clock corresponds to angle 0 (angle := hours-3); 12 hours correspond to angle twopi (angle := twopi*(hours-3)/12); radians are measured counter-clockwise (angle := -twopi*(hours-3)/12).

——————————————————————— *Pascal* ———————————————————————

```
L10    PROCEDURE CLOCK_FACE_DIGITS;              {Draw digits on clock-face}
L20    CONST twopi = 6.2831852;
L25    TYPE char2 = ARRAY [1..2] OF CHARACTER;
L30    VAR i,j,length : INTEGER;
L40      init_x,init_y : REAL;
L50      digit : ARRAY [1..9] OF CHARACTER;
L52      digit2: ARRAY [10..12] OF CHAR2;

       {Initialising of 'digit' and 'digit2' with 12 characters strings '1',..,'12' is omitted}
L60    BEGIN
L70      SET_CHARACTER_HEIGHT (0.036);
                                                 {select high text precision}
L80      SET_TEXT_FONT_AND_PRECISION (1,STROKE);
L90      SET_TEXT_ALIGNMENT (CENTRE,HALF);       {text centred to position}
L100     FOR i:=1 TO 12 DO
L110       BEGIN
       {Compute centrepoint of string on clock; -twopi*(i-3)/12 gives angle in radians}
```

```
L120        init_x := 0.85 * COS(-twopi*(i-3)/12);
L130        init_y := 0.85 * SIN(-twopi*(i-3)/12);
L140      IF i<10 THEN TEXT (init_x,init_y, digit[i])
L141              ELSE TEXT (init_x,init_y, digit2[i]);
L150    END;
L160  END {CLOCK_FACE_DIGITS};
```

─────────────────────────── *Fortran* ───────────────────────────

```
L10          SUBROUTINE DIGITS
L20          INTEGER I,CENTRE,HALF,STROKE,FIRST
L30          REAL TWOPI,XI,YI
L35          CHARACTER*2 DIGIT
L40          DATA TWOPI/6.2831852/, CENTRE/2/, HALF/3/, STROKE/2/

L70          CALL GSCHH (0.036)
L80          CALL GSTXFP (1,STROKE)
L90          CALL GSTXAL (CENTRE,HALF)

L100         DO 1 I=1,12
     C       *** Compute centre of string on clock;
     C       *** -TWOPI*(I-3)/12.0 gives angle in radians
L120         XI = 0.85 * COS (-TWOPI*(I-3)/12.0)
L130         YI = 0.85 * SIN (-TWOPI*(I-3)/12.0)

L135         WRITE (UNIT = DIGIT, FMT = '(I2)') I
L136         FIRST = 2
L137         IF (I.GT.9) FIRST = 1
L140         CALL GTX (XI,YI, DIGIT (FIRST:2))
L150    1    CONTINUE
L160         RETURN
L161         END
```

6.10   Exercises

Exercise 6.1   Text in given DC size and orientation

Text geometry always is specified in WC to allow a full transformability of character strings. However, there are valid applications where the geometry of a character string ought to be defined in DC. For example, a temperature/time diagram is drawn and an inscription is to be written at a certain temperature/time position. Assume that no segment transformation applies and that the workstation transformation of workstation 'plot' is not changed.
a) Assume that the normalization transformation performs uniform scaling. Design procedures SET CHARACTER HEIGHT DC and SET CHARACTER UP VECTOR DC which accept DC-values and which call SET CHARACTER HEIGHT and SET CHARACTER UP VECTOR with appropriate WC values of character height and character up vector such that on workstation 'plot' characters are generated with the specified height and orientation in DC.

b) Assume an arbitrary normalization transformation with non-uniform scaling and restrict CHARACTER UP VECTOR to be parallel to the axes. Write a procedure SET CHARACTER HEIGHT DC for this constellation. Do we need a procedure SET CHARACTER UP VECTOR DC?
c) Consider the general case of an arbitrary normalization transformation and an arbitrary CHARACTER UP VECTOR. Design procedures SET CHARACTER HEIGHT DC and SET CHARACTER UP VECTOR DC which accept DC values and which secure that the specified character height and the baseline orientation as implicitly specified by character up vector are achieved in DC.
d) Consider all text attributes and discuss the effect which may occur to text under the assumptions of case c).

Exercise 6.2   Line formatting of text without hyphenation

The functionality provided with the GKS TEXT primitive allows the generation of high quality text. A common function provided with text system is the capability of line formatting with right-justification.

Given a routine GET WORD which reads one word at a time from a text file and given a fixed line length, write a program which reads the text file sequentially, puts as many words as possible (without hyphenation) into each line and positions each word such that the interword gaps in each line are of same size and that the first word is left-adjusted and the last word right-adjusted.

Note that the size of the text extent rectangle can be interrogated by the function INQUIRE TEXT EXTENT (see Section 10.2.4). Can this line formatting be done for several workstations simultaneously? Can the metafile be used for this purpose?

Exercise 6.3   Generating a RGB colour cube

Write a program which generates a RGB colour cube as shown in Figure C5 on page 502. Calculate a colour index array which can be passed to CELL ARRAY and set the colour table accordingly. Assume that the colour table can store a maximum of 256 colours. What is a reasonable size for the colour index array?

Exercise 6.4   Temperature flow

When heating an object, the temperature will increase differently in different parts of the object. For control purposes, an image of the object showing the temperature shall be generated (see Figure C6 on page 502).
a) Select a sequence of 16 RGB-values which represent well the colour transitions occurring when heating an object: black, blue, red, yellow, white (avoid green).
b) Given an array of 500 x 500 temperature values in the range [0,2000], calculate a colour index array to be passed to CELL ARRAY showing the temperature distribution within the object.

c) Even if only one array of measurements at a specific time is available, the temperature flow can be well demonstrated by merely manipulating the mapping of temperatures to colours. Let T traverse the full range of temperatures. For each value of T map the temperature interval $[T, T+100]$ on the full range of the above 16 RGB-values, making black all points with a temperature $t < T$, and making white all points with a temperature $t > T+100$. This reassignment of colours can be done in the colour table only. What is the initial value for T? Write a program.

d) Under the above assumptions, give reasonable estimates for the size of the colour table needed for b) and c).

Exercise 6.5   Building up of polygons for FILL AREA

If FILL AREA is generated in a style different from HOLLOW, the bounding polygon is not drawn. Note, that it is not good practice to generate the boundary just by combining the two functions
— FILL AREA (n, points);
— POLYLINE (n, points).

A line separating two areas occurs in the boundary of both areas and would be drawn twice.

Assume that the boundary network is cut at all points of intersection into small polylines. These polylines are numbered and stored in a file. A second file contains a description of each area consisting of a list of signed line numbers. By concatenating the lines in the sequence as specified by the list, the bounding polygon is constructed. The sign of the line number indicates whether the polyline must be traversed forward (+) or backward (-).

Write a program which reads the area description of each area, then collects all line pieces from a direct access storage device, and forms the bounding polygon for each area. Then generate a picture where the interior of each area is filled using colour index 1 and the polygons are drawn using colour index 2.

7   SEGMENTS

7.1   Introduction

A picture is built up of output primitives. After having generated the corresponding graphical output on a display, the primitives are no longer accessible. However, there are many applications where it is desirable to have access to previously generated output primitives, e.g.,
— to edit a picture and to redraw the modified picture,
— to send a picture edited at one workstation to a second one for making a hard copy,
— to have several instances of one subpicture (symbol) within one picture.

To allow such picture manipulations, a picture must be structured, the structure elements must be named, a description of the picture must be stored, and a set of manipulation functions must be provided.

A kernel system like GKS cannot satisfy all possible requests for picture structuring and manipulation. The GKS segment storage, however, provides some basic tools for picture structuring and manipulation which will be appropriate for many applications.

7.2   How are Segments Generated ?

When calling the GKS function CREATE SEGMENT, GKS enters the state SGOP (Segment Open) in which all output primitives and all related primitive attributes are recorded in a record called segment. The segment is closed by CLOSE SEGMENT which puts GKS back into the state WSAC (At Least One Workstation Active). The segment currently created in state SGOP is called the open segment. Each time GKS enters state SGOP, exactly one segment is created. It is identified by a unique segment name and is assigned a unique set of segment attributes. More segments may be generated by re-entering the state SGOP. Example 7.1 on page 252 shows the creation of several segments.

GKS supports one level of segmentation only. The brackets CREATE SEGMENT and CLOSE SEGMENT delimit a contiguous group of primitives from the stream of output primitives. Segments cannot contain references to other segments nor can segments be nested (i.e., call CREATE SEGMENT while another segment is open) which would allow the definition of segment hierarchies.

The PICK IDENTIFIER (see Section 6.8.3) is a primitive attribute which allows the naming of primitives inside segments thus establishing a second level of naming (see Example 7.3). However, the PICK IDENTIFIER can be used only with the PICK input device and offers no further manipulation possibilities.

It is not allowed to re-open an existing segment and append more primitives to it. Although such a feature is useful for some applications, it has not been included for simplicity reasons. As some primitive attributes are set modally, confusion may occur whether the attribute setting at segment closing time is re-established or the current setting of attributes is effective. The INSERT SEGMENT function, however, offers the functionality needed to build an append facility on top of GKS (see Exercise 7.3).

Output primitives are displayed at all workstations which are active at primitive generation time. Similarly, segments are assigned to all active workstations. To secure proper assignment, the activation and deactivation of any workstation in state SGOP is not allowed.

Conceptually, one instance of each segment is stored on each active workstation. This does not preclude a specific way of implementing the segment storage but serves as a model for describing the effects of segment manipulations. The manipulation of segment attributes affects all instances of a segment even on those workstations currently not active. Thus, segment manipulations may cause visible effects on an inactive workstation. This does not contradict the rule that graphical output is generated only for active workstations, as no new primitives are accepted by that workstation, but existing primitives are manipulated.

All primitives are affected by the workstation transformation and by the workstation specific tables which define the interpretation of the bundle index stored as a primitive attribute in the segment. These are the only aspects in which the appearance of a segment may differ on different workstations.

Primitives outside segments are displayed on a workstation only once. They are retained until the workstation performs a regeneration implicitly (see Section 4.6) or explicitly. Primitives within segments are retained until the segment is deleted.

7.3   What is Stored in a Segment ?

A segment contains all output primitives generated between CREATE SEGMENT and CLOSE SEGMENT. For each primitive, all corresponding primitive attributes must be stored irrespective of the time or GKS state in which they were set.

Segments may be transformed by a segment transformation. In contrast to the other GKS transformations, this transformation is a general affine transformation which includes rotation and shearing besides translation and scaling. As a consequence, rectangles like character body, pattern rectangle and cell rectangle may be sheared. To allow correct transformation of primitives, additional information has to be stored to permit the reconstruction of sheared rectangles.

As the clipping associated with the normalization transformation is delayed until a primitive is actually displayed, the clipping rectangles must also be stored.

Table 7.1 lists all items which may be stored in a segment. Of course, the implementor will store the attributes in the segment only if needed and if necessary, e.g., at the first instance of a primitive type and each time an attribute changes. Furthermore depending on the setting of the aspect source flags, either the direct attributes or the ⟨output primitive⟩ INDEX might be omitted.

After generation of a segment the application program has no longer access to the data contained in it. It is not possible to enquire, to modify, or to extend the contents of a segment. However, there are functions which allow the manipulation of the segment as a whole. The aspects of a segment that are changeable are described by the segment attributes which are stored in the segment state list.

7.4   When are Primitives Taken off the Transformation Pipeline ?

There are different locations on the transformation pipeline where primitives might be taken off to be stored in segments. In the beginning of the pipeline, the full definition of primitives and attributes is available and can be manipulated. However, if primitives are not pre-processed before stored in segment storage, efficiency will be poor. At the end of the pipeline, all transformations,

Table 7.1 Contents of a segment

A segment contains an arbitrary sequence of the following items:
CLIPPING RECTANGLE
PICK IDENTIFIER
ASPECT SOURCE FLAGS
LINETYPE
LINEWIDTH SCALE FACTOR
POLYLINE COLOUR INDEX
POLYLINE INDEX
POLYLINE

CLIPPING RECTANGLE
PICK IDENTIFIER
ASPECT SOURCE FLAGS
MARKER TYPE
MARKER TYPE SCALE FACTOR
POLYMARKER COLOUR INDEX
PICK IDENTIFIER
POLYMARKER INDEX
POLYMARKER

CLIPPING RECTANGLE
PICK IDENTIFIER
ASPECT SOURCE FLAGS
CHARACTER HEIGHT
CHARACTER UP AND BASELINE VECTOR
TEXT PATH
TEXT ALIGNMENT
TEXT FONT AND PRECISION
CHARACTER EXPANSION FACTOR
CHARACTER SPACING
TEXT COLOUR INDEX
TEXT INDEX
TEXT

CLIPPING RECTANGLE
PICK IDENTIFIER
ASPECT SOURCE FLAGS
FILL AREA INTERIOR STYLE
FILL AREA STYLE INDEX
FILL AREA COLOUR INDEX
FILL AREA INDEX
PATTERN RECTANGLE
FILL AREA

CLIPPING RECTANGLE
PICK IDENTIFIER
CELL ARRAY

CLIPPING RECTANGLE
PICK IDENTIFIER
optional (implementation-dependent): any of the above attributes
GDP

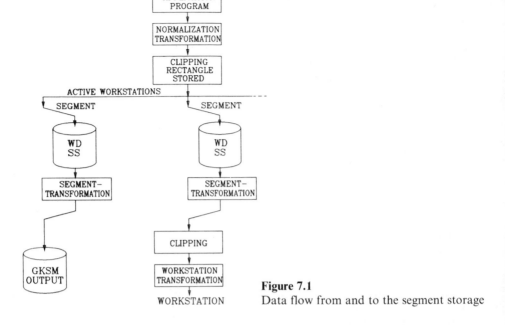

Figure 7.1
Data flow from and to the segment storage

clipping and attribute binding have been done. Therefore, pictures can be generated efficiently from this data structure. However, only limited segment manipulations are possible. GKS has chosen a solution in between.

In GKS, the transformation pipeline is split into two parts. The first part allows the definition of a workstation-independent picture and the second allows an adaptation to the workstation coordinate system. Similarly, the binding of the workstation-dependent aspects of the primitive attributes is split into two stages whereby in the first stage a symbolic attribute (an index) is bound to the primitive and in the second stage the aspects are assigned to the symbolic attributes. Thus, GKS has introduced in the centre of the pipeline an 'abstract viewing surface' on which a workstation-independent representation of a picture is defined. This is the point where the data describing segments are removed from the pipeline and where they are later put back.

Therefore, the segment storage contains primitives which have passed the normalization transformation. Global attributes are bound to the primitives. The effect of both operations cannot be changed. The clipping rectangles are stored allowing segment transformations to be performed before clipping. Also the clipping rectangles cannot be manipulated with the only exception of the INSERT SEGMENT function which just discards all stored clipping rectangles. On the other hand, workstation transformation and workstation attributes are related to the second part of the transformation pipeline which is applied after segment storage. They can be reset at any time and will have retroactive effects on all primitives stored in segments and displayed on the respective workstation.

7.5 Segment Creation and Deletion

CREATE SEGMENT sets GKS into the state SGOP in which all output primitives are collected to form a segment. This happens independently of the display
process, i.e., primitives inside and outside of segments are immediately sent
to the display surface for display except specified otherwise by the deferral
state (see Section 4.6).

For each segment, GKS creates a segment state list (see Table 7.2) which
describes the state of a segment, i.e., all aspects of a segment which may be
manipulated. A segment may be:
— renamed;
— deleted;
— made visible or invisible;
— made detectable or undetectable by the PICK input device;
— highlighted;
— ordered front-to-back;
— transformed.

The workstation-independent segment storage described in Section 7.7 provides additional capabilities, e.g., to copy segments from one workstation to
another and to form new segments with the help of previously defined segments.

The segment state list is created and initialised by CREATE SEGMENT
as described below.

The parameter of CREATE SEGMENT specifies the name of the segment
which must not be a segment name currently in use. GKS supervises all segment
names in use and allows the re-use of a segment name only after deleting or
renaming the segment.

The segment is recorded on all active workstations. These workstations are
listed in the set of associated workstations. To secure consistency of this set,
the activation and deactivation of workstations is forbidden until the state
SGOP is left by CLOSE SEGMENT. The manipulation of the set of associated
workstations is discussed in the context of the workstation-independent segment
storage in the Section 7.7.

Table 7.2 Segment state list

segment name		N	
set of associated workstations		nxN	active workstations at create time
segment transformation matrix (the elements M13 and M23 are in NDC coordinates and the other elements are unitless)		2x3xR	1,0,0 0,1,0
visibility	(VISIBLE,INVISIBLE)	E	VISIBLE
highlighting	(NORMAL,HIGHLIGHTED)	E	NORMAL
segment priority	[0,1]	R	0
detectability	(UNDETECTABLE,DETECTABLE)	E	UNDETECTABLE

Note: The notation is explained in Section 3.2.

The segment attributes are initialised as shown in Table 7.2. These attributes may be changed by the functions described in Section 7.6.

The segment state list exists only once for each segment, i.e., the entries are valid for all workstations where the segment is stored.

CREATE SEGMENT   WSAC   L1a

Parameters:

Input   segment name   N

Effect:

GKS is set into the operating state SGOP = "Segment open". The segment state list is set up and initialised as indicated in Table 7.2. The segment name is recorded as the 'name of the open segment' in the GKS state list (see Section 3.3). All subsequent output primitives until the next CLOSE SEGMENT will be collected into this segment. The segment name is entered in the 'set of stored segments for this workstation' in the workstation state list (see Section 4.3) for every active workstation. All active workstations are included in the 'set of associated workstations' of the segment state list of the newly opened segment. The segment name is entered into the 'set of segment names in use' in the GKS state list. Primitive attributes are not affected.

Errors:

3   GKS not in proper state: GKS shall be in the state WSAC

120   Specified segment name is invalid

121   Specified segment name is already in use

————————————————— *FORTRAN-Interface* —————————————————

CALL GCRSG (SGNA)

Parameters:

Input   SGNA   segment name   INTEGER

CLOSE SEGMENT puts GKS back into the state WSAC (At Least One Workstation Active). The definition of the segment is finished. It is not possible to add more primitives to the segment, to modify or to delete primitives stored in the segment. Only manipulations of the whole segment via the segment attributes are possible.

CLOSE SEGMENT   SGOP   L1a

Parameters: none

Effect:

GKS is put into the operating state WSAC = "At least one workstation active". Primitives may no longer be added to the previously open segment. The 'name of the open segment' in the GKS state list (see Section 3.2) becomes unavailable for inquiry.

Errors:

4   GKS not in proper state: GKS shall be in the state SGOP

————————————————— *FORTRAN-Interface* —————————————————

CALL GCLSG

Parameters: none

RENAME SEGMENT allows a new name to be assigned to an existing segment or to the open segment. The new name must not be in use. Subsequently the old name is available for re-use.

RENAME SEGMENT WSOP,WSAC,SGOP L1a
Parameters:
Input   old segment name N
Input   new segment name N
Effect:
Each occurrence of old segment name in the 'set of stored segments for this workstation' in a workstation state list (see Section 4.3) and in the 'set of segment names in use' in the GKS state list is replaced by new segment name. If old segment name is the name of the open segment, the 'name of the open segment' in the GKS state list is set to new segment name.
Note:
The old segment name may be re-used by the application program.
Errors:
   7   GKS not in proper state: GKS shall be in one of the states WSOP, WSAC or SGOP
 120   Specified segment name is invalid
 121   Specified segment name is already in use
 122   Specified segment does not exist

———————————————— *FORTRAN-Interface* ————————————

CALL GRENSG (OLD,NEW)
Parameters:
Input   OLD   old segment name INTEGER
Input   NEW   new segment name INTEGER

DELETE SEGMENT deletes the specified segment from all workstations' display surface and from the segment storage. The deletion is not reversible. For temporary deletion of segments from the display surface the function SET VISIBILITY may be used. The open segment may not be deleted. After deletion, the segment name is available for re-use.

DELETE SEGMENT WSOP,WSAC,SGOP L1a
Parameters:
Input   segment name N
Effect:
The segment and the entry in the 'set of stored segments for this workstation' in each workstation state list (see Section 4.3) which contains the segment name are deleted. The segment name is removed from the 'set of segment names in use' in the GKS state list. The segment's state list is cancelled.
Note:
The segment name may be re-used by the application program.

Errors:

7	GKS not in proper state: GKS shall be in one of the states WSOP, WSAC or SGOP
120	Specified segment name is invalid
122	Specified segment does not exist
125	Specified segment is open

———————————————— *FORTRAN-Interface* ————————————————

CALL GDSG (SGNA)
Parameters:
Input   SGNA   segment name   INTEGER

DELETE SEGMENT FROM WORKSTATION only deletes the segment from one specific workstation's display space and segment storage. If the segment is only present on this workstation, the effect is equivalent to DELETE SEGMENT. In some sense, DELETE SEGMENT FROM WORKSTATION can be regarded as a counterpart to ASSOCIATE SEGMENT TO WORKSTATION (see Section 7.7).

DELETE SEGMENT FROM WORKSTATION   WSOP,WSAC,SGOP   L1a
Parameters:
Input   workstation identifier   N
Input   segment name   N
Effect:
The segment is deleted from the specified workstation. The segment name is removed from the 'set of stored segments for this workstation' in the workstation state list (see Section 4.3). The workstation identifier is removed from the 'set of associated workstations' in the segment state list. If the 'set of associated workstations' becomes empty, the segment is deleted, i.e. the DELETE SEGMENT function is performed.
Errors:

7	GKS not in proper state: GKS shall be in one of the states WSOP, WSAC or SGOP
20	Specified workstation identifier is invalid
25	Specified workstation is not open
33	Specified workstation is of category MI
35	Specified workstation is of category INPUT
120	Specified segment name is invalid
123	Specified segment does not exist on specified workstation
125	Specified segment is open

———————————————— *FORTRAN-Interface* ————————————————

CALL GDSGWK (WKID,SGNA)
Parameters:
Input   WKID   workstation identifier   INTEGER
Input   SGNA   segment name   INTEGER

CLEAR WORKSTATION (see Section 4.4) clears the display surface of one specified workstation and deletes all segments from its segment storage. This allows a new picture to be generated on a fresh display surface.

Usually, the new picture will not start from scratch but will re-use the pictorial information stored in the segment storage. REDRAW ALL SEGMENTS

ON WORKSTATION clears the display surface like CLEAR WORKSTA-
TION. Then all segments stored for the specified workstation are redrawn.
This is an efficient way of generating a sequence of pictures with a constant
background and some changing parts in the foreground. The constant picture
parts can be stored in segments and will be regenerated automatically for each
picture by REDRAW ALL SEGMENTS ON WORKSTATION. Only the
changing parts have to be generated by the application program directly (see
Example 7.2).

REDRAW ALL SEGMENTS ON WORKSTATION
WSOP,WSAC,SGOP   L1a

Parameters:
Input   workstation identifier   N
Effect:
All of the following actions are executed in the given sequence:
a) All deferred actions for the specified workstation are executed (without intermediate
   clearing of the display surface).
b) The display surface is cleared only if the 'display surface empty' entry in the workstation state list is NOTEMPTY. The entry is set to EMPTY.
c) If the 'workstation transformation update state' entry in the workstation state list
   is PENDING, the 'current workstation window' and 'current workstation viewport'
   entries in the workstation state list are assigned the values of the 'requested workstation window' and 'requested workstation viewport' entries; the 'workstation transformation update state' entry is set to NOTPENDING.
d) All visible segments stored on this workstation (i.e. contained in the 'set of stored
   segments for this workstation' in the workstation state list) are redisplayed. This
   action typically causes the 'display surface empty' entry in the workstation state
   list to be set to NOTEMPTY.
e) The 'new frame action necessary at update' entry in the workstation state list is
   set to NO.
Errors:
7   GKS not in proper state: GKS shall be in one of the states WSOP, WSAC
        or SGOP
20   Specified workstation identifier is invalid
25   Specified workstation is not open
33   Specified workstation is of category MI
35   Specified workstation is of category INPUT
36   Specified workstation is Workstation Independent Segment Storage

—————————————————— *FORTRAN-Interface* ——————————————————

CALL GRSGWK (WKID)
Parameters:
Input   WKID   workstation identifier   INTEGER

7.6 Manipulation of the Segment Attributes

In the following section, the functions for manipulating the segment attributes
are described. The segment attributes include visibility, detectability, highlighting, segment priority, and segment transformation.

The visibility assumes two values: VISIBLE and INVISIBLE. In the former case, the primitives in the segment are stored and displayed. In the latter case, primitives are only stored and can be made visible later on. The default setting is VISIBLE. If a segment's visibility attribute changes from VISIBLE to INVISIBLE, the segment is erased from all display surfaces. On some workstations, this may lead to an implicit regeneration of the whole display. If a segment's visibility attribute changes to VISIBLE, the segment will be drawn on all workstations which were active during segment generation (not which are currently active!).

The visibility attribute is useful for complex picture where the display space is overloaded by graphical output. By setting the VISIBILITY attribute, those picture parts currently not of interest can be temporarily removed from the display surface.

The setting of the visibility attribute only affects the segment's state list and the display surface. The data structure in the segment storage is not affected. The attribute can be reset arbitrarily. This makes an important difference to the DELETE SEGMENT or DELETE SEGMENT FROM WORKSTATION functions.

SET VISIBILITY   WSOP,WSAC,SGOP   L1a
Parameters:
   Input   segment name   N
   Input   visibility   (VISIBLE,INVISIBLE)   E
Effect:
   The 'visibility' entry in the segment state list of the named segment is set to the value specified by the parameter.
Errors:
   7   GKS not in proper state: GKS shall be in one of the states WSOP, WSAC or SGOP
   120   Specified segment name is invalid
   122   Specified segment does not exist

——————————————————— *FORTRAN-Interface* ———————————————————

CALL GSVIS (SGNA,VIS)
Parameters:
   Input   SGNA   segment name   INTEGER
   Input   VIS   visibility   (0 = invisible, 1 = visible)   INTEGER

The detectability is used to select those segments which should be identifiable by the PICK input device. Therefore, it is supported only in those GKS levels where segments and input devices are present. The detectability can assume the values DETECTABLE and UNDETECTABLE. The default setting is UNDETECTABLE so that an explicit action by the application program is necessary to make a segment available for the PICK input device. The detectability is a subordinate attribute of the visibility. Invisible segments are treated as undetectable, regardless of the setting of the detectability attribute.

There are several reasons for the introduction of this attribute:
— to facilitate the identification of objects in complicated drawings;
— to avoid undesired identifications;
— to optimise the performance of the PICK input device.

The detectability attribute restricts the realm of the PICK input device to those objects the application program is interested in and is prepared to work with. The display may show much accompanying information which is helpful for decision finding. By making such accompanying information undetectable, the identification is not impeded even if the manipulated structure is overlapped by accompanying data. Furthermore, if the PICK input device is simulated by searching the entire segment storage for the segment lying closest to the picked position, the performance may be improved considerably.

An example for the use of the detectability is a map showing roads, railways, rivers, and towns. These four classes of objects may overlap or lie very close side by side. Even if the operator is editing one class of objects only, it is very helpful for him to see the full map as it improves his orientation on the map and the context may be important for the editing task.

SET DETECTABILITY   WSOP,WSAC,SGOP   L1b
Parameters:
  Input   segment name   N
  Input   detectability   (UNDETECTABLE,DETECTABLE)   E
Effect:
The 'detectability' entry in the segment state list of the named segment is set to the value specified by the parameter. If the segment is marked as DETECTABLE and VISIBLE, the primitives in it are available for PICK input. DETECTABLE but INVIS-IBLE segments cannot be picked.
Errors:
  7   GKS not in proper state: GKS shall be in one of the states WSOP, WSAC or SGOP
  120   Specified segment name is invalid
  122   Specified segment does not exist

——————————————— *FORTRAN-Interface* ———————————————

CALL GSDTEC (SGNA,DET)
Parameters:
  Input   SGNA   segment name   INTEGER
  Input   DET   detectability   (0 = undetectable, 1 = detectable) INTEGER

The highlighting attribute is used to emphasize a segment and to draw the attention of an operator to a specific part of the display. A standard application is the echo of the segment picked by the PICK input device. The highlighting attribute can assume the values HIGHLIGHTED and NORMAL. The default setting is NORMAL. The highlighting is a subordinate attribute of the visibility. Invisible segments are not highlighted regardless of the setting of the highlighting attribute.

The way a segment is highlighted depends on the capabilities of the respective workstation. Some devices can increase the intensity and use this technique to emphasize a segment. Others use blinking or repeatedly drawing of the segment.

SET HIGHLIGHTING   WSOP,WSAC,SGOP   L1a
Parameters:
   Input   segment name   N
   Input   highlighting   (NORMAL,HIGHLIGHTED)   E
Effect:
   The 'highlighting' entry in the segment state list of the named segment is set to the value specified by the parameter. If the segment is marked as HIGHLIGHTED and VISIBLE, the primitives in it are highlighted in an implementation dependent manner.
Errors:
   7   GKS not in proper state: GKS shall be in one of the states WSOP, WSAC or SGOP
   120   Specified segment name is invalid
   122   Specified segment does not exist

———————————————————— *FORTRAN-Interface* ————————————————————

CALL GSHLIT (SGNA,HIL)
Parameters:
   Input   SGNA   segment name   INTEGER
   Input   HIL   highlighting   (0 = normal, 1 = highlighted)   INTEGER

The segment priority allows the ordering of segments front-to-back. In the case of overlapping visible segments, the segment priority decides which segment should be preferred. This preference has an effect on the display of primitives and for the PICK input device. The segment priority lies in the interval [0,1]. The default value is 0, i.e., lowest priority.

If output primitives overlap on a display surface, the effect depends on the device. For many devices, e.g., plotter and vector devices, the effect is beyond the control of the graphics system or is very difficult to control. As long as only lines are drawn, the overlapping may be neglected.

However, there are devices today which are gaining more and more importance where the effect of overlapping primitives is under full control of the graphics software. These are raster devices where the picture is converted into a raster image stored in a frame buffer from where it is repeatedly displayed on a display surface. The overlapping takes place in the frame buffer and an implementor has to make a decision what to do. The segment priority is intended to address these capabilities. It is not intended that such capabilities should be simulated on vector devices.

Segment priority only applies to segments as a whole. If primitives within one segment overlap, the effect is not defined by GKS and, therefore, is implementation-dependent.

SET SEGMENT PRIORITY   WSOP,WSAC,SGOP   L1a
Parameters:
   Input   segment name   N
   Input   segment priority   [0,1]   R

Effect:

The 'segment priority' entry in the segment state list of the named segment is set to the value specified by the parameter. Segment priority affects the display of segments and PICK input if segments overlap, in which case GKS gives precedence to segments with higher priority. If segments with the same priority overlap, the result is implementation-dependent.

Note:

The use of segment priority applies only to workstations where the entry 'number of segment priorities supported' in the workstation description table is greater than 1 or equal to 0 (indicating an infinite number of priorities is supported).

If 'number of segment priorities supported' is greater than 1, the range [0,1] for segment priority is mapped to the range 1 to 'number of segment priorities supported' for a specific workstation before being used by a device driver. If 'number of segment priorities supported' is equal to 0, the implementation will allow all values of segment priority to be differentiated.

This feature is intended to address appropriate hardware capabilities only. It cannot be used to force software checking of interference between segments on non-raster displays.

The segment priority is also used for picking segments. When overlapping or intersecting segments are picked, the segment with higher priority is delivered as a result of the PICK input primitive. All workstations having PICK input should provide this mechanism.

Errors:

7	GKS not in proper state: GKS shall be in one of the states WSOP, WSAC or SGOP
120	Specified segment name is invalid
122	Specified segment does not exist
126	Segment priority is outside the range [0,1]

——————————————— *FORTRAN-Interface* ———————————————

CALL GSSGP (SGNA,PRIOR)
Parameters:

Input	SGNA	segment name		INTEGER
Input	PRIOR	segment priority	[0,1]	REAL

A segment transformation is a mapping from NDC onto NDC including translation, non-uniform scaling and rotation. The segment transformation is specified by a 2x3 transformation matrix consisting of a 2x2 scaling and rotation portion and a 2x1 translation portion. Utility functions (see Section 7.9) are available to the application program for setting up the transformation matrix. A fixed point for scaling and rotation, and a shift vector in either WC or NDC may be specified. In the former case, the WC values of the shift vector are first transformed using the current normalization transformation.

The segment transformation takes place after the normalization transformation but before any clipping. The primitives of the transformed segment are clipped against the clipping rectangle stored with the primitives. Note that the clipping rectangle itself is not transformed.

A segment transformation, specified by the SET SEGMENT TRANSFORMATION function, is not actually performed in the segment storage but only saved in the segment state list. Every time the segment is redrawn, this segment transformation will be applied before clipping. Successive SET SEGMENT TRANSFORMATION function calls for the same segment are not accumulated; each succeeding transformation matrix replaces its predecessor. By calling SET SEGMENT TRANSFORMATION with an identity transformation matrix, the original segment can be obtained without loss of information.

Note that LOCATOR input data is not affected by any segment transformation.

SET SEGMENT TRANSFORMATION   WSOP,WSAC,SGOP   L1a
Parameters:
  Input   segment name   N
  Input   transformation matrix   2x3xR
Effect:
The 'segment transformation matrix' in the segment state list is set to the value specified by the parameter. When a segment is displayed, the coordinates of its primitives will be transformed by applying the following matrix multiplication to them:

$$\begin{bmatrix} x' \\ y' \end{bmatrix} = \begin{bmatrix} M11 & M12 & M13 \\ M21 & M22 & M23 \end{bmatrix} \times \begin{bmatrix} x \\ y \\ 1 \end{bmatrix}$$

The original coordinates are (x,y), the transformed are (x',y'), both in NDC. The values M13 and M23 of the transformation matrix are in NDC coordinates, the other values are unitless. For geometric attributes which are vectors (for example, CHARACTER UP VECTOR), the values M13 and M23 are ignored.

This function can be used to transform a segment stored on a workstation. The transformation applies to all workstations where the specified segment is stored even if they are not all active.

The segment transformation (conceptually) takes place in NDC space. The segment transformation will be stored in the segment state list and will not affect the contents of the segment. The segment transformation is not cumulative, i.e., it always applies to the segment as originally created.

Note:
Applying the same segment transformation twice to a segment will give identical results. The identity transformation will show the segment in its original geometrical appearance.

Errors:
   7   GKS not in proper state: GKS shall be in one of the states WSOP, WSAC
           or SGOP
   120   Specified segment name is invalid
   122   Specified segment does not exist

───────────────────────────── *FORTRAN-Interface* ─────────────────────────────

CALL GSSGT (SGNA,M)
Parameters:
  Input   SGNA   segment name   INTEGER
  Input   M(2,3)   transformation matrix   2x3xREAL

7.7 The Workstation-Independent Segment Storage (WISS)

In the above description, it was assumed that there was a unique definition of each segment but one instance of this conceptual segment on each associated workstation. This model was chosen to clarify the fact that a segment is related to all workstations activated at segment generation time. However, GKS does not presume anything about the implementation of a segment storage. An implementor may implement the segment storage in different ways as long as the functional requirements are met.

All functions mentioned above only manipulate segments on that workstation for which they were created. This functionality can be met by decentralized segment storages as well as with one central segment storage and by segments stored in workstation-dependent as well as in workstation-independent format. If efficiency is desired, a local storage of segments will be preferred as no delay by transmission media can happen. Furthermore, data will be stored in a workstation-dependent format for improved performance.

Such a local *workstation-dependent segment storage (WDSS)* well serves for local manipulations. However, there are other requirements which cannot be met by a WDSS. If a segment is generated and edited at one workstation and then is to be sent to another workstation, a workstation-independent representation of the segment is required. This is also true if a segment storage is used as a symbol facility containing subpictures from which a picture shall be constructed. As some overhead is involved with the workstation-independent representation, GKS has introduced a special workstation called *workstation-independent segment storage (WISS)*. The WISS is only a conceptual scheme which need not necessarily be realized via a physical workstation. The WISS is a means to identify those segments which must be stored in a manner that the following functions can be provided:
— copying segments to another workstation for immediate output;
— copying segments as an entity into the segment storage of a workstation which has not been active during segment generation;
— symbol facility allowing the construction of pictures from previously defined segments.
As a conceptual scheme, there is only one WISS workstation within GKS.

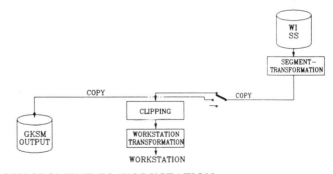

Figure 7.2 Data flow for COPY SEGMENT TO WORKSTATION

COPY SEGMENT TO WORKSTATION creates a copy of a segment stored in the WISS. The primitives and their geometric attributes are transformed by the segment transformation. The transformed data together with the other attributes and the associated clipping rectangles are inserted into the viewing pipeline at the same place where the information previously has left it. Then they are sent down the pathway to the workstation specified in the invocation. No segment can be open when this function is invoked.

The main purpose of this function is copying a picture generated and edited at an interactive workstation to a hard copy workstation for saving the final result of an interactive session.

COPY SEGMENT TO WORKSTATION   WSOP, WSAC   L2a
Parameters:
   Input   workstation identifier   N
   Input   segment name   N
Effect:
   The primitives in the segment are sent to the specified workstation after segment transformation and clipping. They are not stored in a segment.
Note:
   The specified segment must be present in workstation-independent segment storage. The specified workstation must not be workstation-independent segment storage. All primitives keep the values of the primitive attributes (for example, polyline index, text path, pick identifier) that are assigned to them when they are created, for their whole lifetime. In particular, when segments are copied, the values of the primitive attributes within the copied segments are unchanged.
Errors:
    6   GKS not in proper state: GKS shall be either in the state WSOP or in the state WSAC
   20   Specified workstation identifier is invalid
   25   Specified workstation is not open
   27   Workstation Independent Segment Storage is not open
   33   Specified workstation is of category MI
   35   Specified workstation is of category INPUT
   36   Specified workstation is Workstation Independent Segment Storage
 120   Specified segment name is invalid
 124   Specified segment does not exist on Workstation Independent Segment Storage

---
FORTRAN-Interface

CALL GCSGWK (WKID,SGNA)
Parameters:
   Input   WKID   workstation identifier   INTEGER
   Input   SGNA   segment name   INTEGER

ASSOCIATE SEGMENT WITH WORKSTATION sends the segment to the specified workstation. By this function the same situation is achieved as if the workstation had been active when the segment was created. Only segments contained in the WISS may be sent to other workstations. This function merely manipulates the entry 'set of associated workstations' in the segment state list of the specified segment. Whereas ASSOCIATE SEGMENT WITH WORK-STATION adds one new element to the 'set of associated workstations', the function DELETE SEGMENT FROM WORKSTATION (see Section 7.5) can be used to remove one element. This function cannot be invoked when a segment is open.

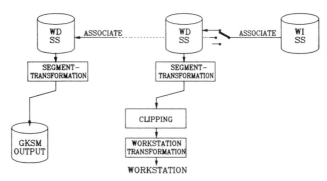

Figure 7.3 Data flow for ASSOCIATE SEGMENT WITH WORKSTATION

ASSOCIATE SEGMENT WITH WORKSTATION   WSOP, WSAC   L2a

Parameters:

Input	workstation identifier	N
Input	segment name	N

Effect:

The segment is sent to the specified workstation in the same way as if the workstation were active when the segment was created. The segment name is added to the in the workstation state list (see Section 4.3). The workstation identifier is included in the 'set of associated workstations' in the segment state list (see Section 7.5).

Note:

The specified segment must be present in the workstation-independent segment storage. If the segment is already associated with the specified workstation, the function has no effect.

Errors:

6	GKS not in proper state: GKS shall be either in the state WSOP or in the state WSAC
20	Specified workstation identifier is invalid
25	Specified workstation is not open
27	Workstation Independent Segment Storage is not open
33	Specified workstation is of category MI
35	Specified workstation is of category INPUT
120	Specified segment name is invalid
124	Specified segment does not exist on Workstation Independent Segment Storage

———————————— *FORTRAN-Interface* ————————————

CALL GASGWK (WKID,SGNA)

Parameters:

Input	WKID	workstation identifier	INTEGER
Input	SGNA	segment name	INTEGER

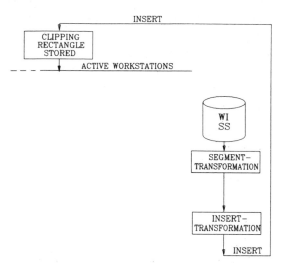

Figure 7.4 Data flow for INSERT SEGMENT

INSERT SEGMENT copies the primitives contained in a segment from the WISS, applies the segment transformation followed by the insert transformation and then inserts them into the viewing pipeline at the point before data is distributed to the workstations. Thus, inserted information may re-enter the WISS if the WISS is active and a segment is open. The primitives retain all their attributes except the clipping rectangle. The old clipping rectangles are discarded. Each primitive processed is assigned the current clipping rectangle which is the viewport of the currently selected normalization transformation if the clipping indicator is on, and is $[0,1]x[0,1]$ if the clipping indicator is off. In other words, inserted primitives are assigned clipping rectangles in the same manner as currently generated primitives.

An invocation of INSERT SEGMENT has no effect on output primitives passing through the pipeline before or after the invocation. For example, the attributes bound to the inserted primitives do not affect the current setting of attributes which are applied to primitives generated afresh. The INSERT SEGMENT function can be used when a segment is open. Note that the open segment itself cannot be inserted to avoid recursive copying.

The insert transformation is specified in the same way as is the segment transformation. For consistency, both transformations, the segment transformation and the insert transformation, will be applied. However, in practice, at most one of them will be set different from identity. The main advantage of the insert transformation is the possibility to copy one segment several times at different places and in different sizes. The same effect could be achieved by setting the segment transformation before inserting the segment. However, a separate insert transformation was included for simplifying the user interface and for avoiding annoying effects which might occur on workstations having no adequate capabilities for dynamic change of the segment transformation.

Example 7.7 shows the use of the insert transformation for generating 60 minute markers from two sample markers.

It is not allowed to re-open an existing segment and append more primitives. A major difference between COPY SEGMENT TO WORKSTATION and INSERT SEGMENT is that output of INSERT SEGMENT may be sent into another segment whereas COPY SEGMENT TO WORKSTATION generates only output outside segments. For example, INSERT SEGMENT can be used for extending segments. (see Exercise 7.3).

INSERT SEGMENT   WSAC,SGOP   L2a

Parameters:

  Input   segment name   N

  Input   transformation matrix   2x3xR

Effect:

Having been transformed as described below, the primitives contained in the segment are copied either (in state SGOP) into the open segment or (in state WSAC) into the stream of primitives outside segments. In both cases the transformed primitives are sent to all active workstations.

The coordinates of the primitives contained in the inserted segment will be transformed firstly by any segment transformation specified for it, and secondly by applying the following matrix multiplication to them:

$$\begin{bmatrix} x' \\ y' \end{bmatrix} = \begin{bmatrix} M11 & M12 & M13 \\ M21 & M22 & M23 \end{bmatrix} \times \begin{bmatrix} x \\ y \\ 1 \end{bmatrix}$$

The original coordinates are (x,y), the transformed coordinates are (x',y'), both in NDC. The values M13 and M23 of the transformation matrix are NDC coordinates, the other values are unitless. For geometric attributes which are vectors (for example, CHARACTER UP VECTOR), the values M13 and M23 are ignored.

The insert transformation (conceptually) takes place in NDC space. Other than the segment transformation, attributes of the inserted segment are ignored.

All clipping rectangles in the inserted segment are ignored. Each primitive processed is assigned a new clipping rectangle which is the viewport of the currently selected normalization transformation if the clipping indicator is ON and is [0,1]x[0,] if the clipping indicator if OFF. All primitives processed by a single invocation of INSERT SEGMENT receive the same clipping rectangle.

Note:

The specified segment must be in workstation-independent segment storage and must not be the open segment. All primitives keep the values of the primitive attributes (e.g., polyline index, text path, pick identifier) that are assigned to them when they are created for their whole lifetime. In particular, when segments are inserted, the values of the primitive attributes within the inserted segments are unchanged. The values of primitive attributes used in the generation of subsequent primitives within the segment into which the insertion takes place are unaffected by that insertion.

Errors:

     5   GKS not in proper state: GKS shall be either in the state WSAC or in the state SGOP

   27   Workstation Independent Segment Storage is not open

  120   Specified segment name is invalid

124   Specified segment does not exist on Workstation Independent Segment Storage

125   Specified segment is open

──────────────────────── *FORTRAN-Interface* ────────────────────────

CALL GINSG (SGNA,M)
Parameters:
  Input   SGNA   segment name   INTEGER
  Input   M(2,3)   transformation matrix   2 × 3 × REAL

7.8   Different Levels of Segmentation

The segment mechanism of GKS provides some powerful features which must be paid for in terms of implementation costs and performance. However, the segmentation capabilities are not satisfactory for all applications. There may be applications which do not need a segment storage at all, e.g., batch plotting programs generating complex maps from a consistent cartographical data basis. Here, interactive capabilities are not needed and the efficiency is very important. There may be applications having requirements not met by the GKS segment storage. These applications have to build their own comfortable data structure outside GKS and do not want to pay the overhead for a second data structure within GKS.

When defining the level structure of GKS, these requirements have been considered. GKS provides three segmentation levels:
0. no segmentation at all,
1. basic segmentation, including all functions which can be implemented only by workstation-dependent segment storages (WDSS),
2. full segmentation, including those functions referring to the workstation-independent segment storage (WISS).

To achieve compatibility between level 0 and 1, output primitives in GKS may be generated outside and inside of segments even in those levels supporting segmentation. Therefore, a programmer may optimise his program by storing in segments only those primitives to be re-used later on and generating outside segments all primitives to be displayed only once.

7.9   Utility Functions

The GKS functions SET SEGMENT TRANSFORMATION and INSERT SEGMENT allow to transform a segment. The transformation is defined by a 2x3 transformation matrix. This matrix is a compact means of specifying the full range of affine transformation capabilities but it is not suitable for a programmer. Therefore, GKS includes two utility functions which accept definitions of transformations in terms of shift, scaling, rotation and generate the respective transformation matrix to be passed to SET SEGMENT TRANS-FORMATION and INSERT SEGMENT. For scaling and rotation a fixed point must be specified relative to which scaling is performed or which is the centrepoint for rotation. Fixed point and shift vector can be specified either in world coordinates, which is the usual coordinate system for GKS users, or in normalized coordinates, which reflects the fact that segment transformations take place in NDC exclusively.

The order in which the single transformation operations take place is scale, rotate and shift. Note that a different order generally yields different results. The first utility function EVALUATE TRANSFORMATION MATRIX directly generates a matrix from the single operations specified in the parameter list. The second function ACCUMULATE TRANSFORMATION MATRIX allows to accumulate any number of shift, scale, rotate operations in any order and multiplicity within one transformation matrix. This function expects an input matrix which probably will be initialised by EVALUATE TRANSFORMATION MATRIX.

EVALUATE TRANSFORMATION MATRIX

GKOP,WSOP,WSAC,SGOP   L1a

Parameters:

Input	fixed point	WC/NDC	P
Input	shift vector	WC/NDC	P
Input	rotation angle in radians (positive if anti-clockwise)		R
Input	scale factors		2xR
Input	coordinate switch	(WC,NDC)	E
Output	segment transformation matrix		2x3xR

Effect:

The transformation defined by fixed point, shift vector, rotation angle, and scale factors is evaluated and the result is put in the output segment transformation matrix (for use by INSERT SEGMENT and SET SEGMENT TRANSFORMATION). The coordinate switch determines whether the shift vector and fixed point are given in WC coordinates or NDC coordinates. If WC coordinates are used, the shift vector and the fixed point are transformed by the current normalization transformation. The order of transformation is: scale, rotate (both relative to the specified fixed point), and shift. The elements M13 and M23 of the resulting 2x3 transformation matrix are in NDC coordinates, the other elements are unitless.

Errors:

8	GKS not in proper state: GKS shall be in one of the states GKOP, WSOP, WSAC or SGOP

--------------------------- *FORTRAN-Interface* ---------------------------

CALL GEVTM (X0,Y0,DX,DY,PHI,FX,FY,SW,MOUT)

Parameters:

Input	X0,Y0	fixed point	WC/NDC	2xREAL
Input	DX,DY	shift vector	WC/NDC	2xREAL
Input	PHI	rotation angle in radians		REAL
Input	FX,FY	scale factors		2xREAL
Input	SW	coordinate switch	(0 = WC, 1 = NDC)	INTEGER
Output	MOUT(2,3)	segment transformation matrix		2x3xREAL

ACCUMULATE TRANSFORMATION MATRIX

GKOP,WSOP,WSAC,SGOP   L1a

Parameters:

Input	segment transformation matrix		2x3xR
Input	fixed point	WC/NDC	P
Input	shift vector	WC/NDC	P
Input	rotation angle in radians (positive if anti-clockwise)		R
Input	scale factors		2xR
Input	coordinate switch	(WC,NDC)	E
Output	segment transformation matrix		2x3xR

Effect:

The transformation defined by fixed point, shift vector, rotation angle, and scale factors is composed with the input segment transformation matrix and the result is returned in the output segment transformation matrix (for use by INSERT SEGMENT and SET SEGMENT TRANSFORMATION). The coordinate switch determines whether the shift vector and fixed point are given in WC coordinates or NDC coordinates. If WC coordinates are used, the shift vector and the fixed point are transformed by the current normalization transformation. The order of transformation is: specified input matrix, scale, rotate (both relative to the specified fixed point), and shift. The elements M13 and M23 of the 2x3 input matrix and the resulting 2x3 transformation matrix are in NDC coordinates, the other elements are unitless.

Errors:

8   GKS not in proper state: GKS shall be in one of the states GKOP, WSOP, WSAC or SGOP

———————————————— *FORTRAN-Interface* ————————————————

CALL GACTM (MIN,X0,Y0,DX,DY,PHI,FX,FY,SW,MOUT)

Parameters:

Input	MIN(2,3)	segment transformation matrix		2x3xREAL
Input	X0,Y0	fixed point	WC/NDC	2xREAL
Input	DX,DY	shift vector	WC/NDC	2xREAL
Input	PHI	rotation angle in radians		REAL
Input	FX,FY	scale factors		2xREAL
Input	SW	coordinate switch	(0 = WC, 1 = NDC)	INTEGER
Output	MOUT(2,3)	segment transformation matrix		2x3xREAL

7.10   Examples

Example 7.1   Zoom with content of picture depending on scale

The primary purpose of zooming is making recognizable details present in the picture by changing the scale. Figure 5.2 on page 153 demonstrates this simple zoom.

The segment mechanism, however, allows for a more powerful zoom capability. In this example, a map is drawn showing political boundaries at different levels (national, state, county). According to these levels, boundaries are stored in different segments. After this initialisation stage, the map can be zoomed.

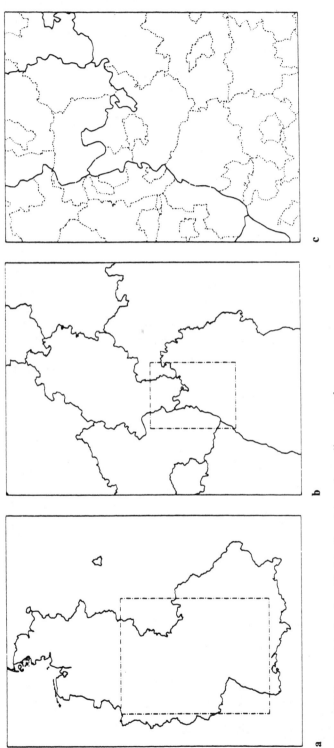

Figure 7.5 Zoom with details added to the picture depending on scale

Depending on the scale, some level of boundaries can be made visible or can be suppressed (see Figure 7.5). It is assumed that the operator when selecting the zoom region has the possibility of setting a switch 'interrupt'.

──────────────────────── *Pascal* ────────────────────────

```
L10    ACTIVATE_WORKSTATION(display);                    {select workstation}

L20    CREATE_SEGMENT (seg1);          {Segment 1 contains national boundaries}
L30      DRAW_FILE (borders_1);
L40    CLOSE_SEGMENT;                                       {See Figure 7.5a}

L50    CREATE_SEGMENT (seg2);             {Segment 2 contains state boundaries}
L60      SET_VISIBILITY (2,INVISIBLE);
L70      DRAW_FILE (borders_2);
L80    CLOSE_SEGMENT;
L90    CREATE_SEGMENT (seg3);            {Segment 3 contains county boundaries}
L100     SET_VISIBILITY (3,INVISIBLE);
L110     DRAW_FILE (borders_3);
L120   CLOSE_SEGMENT;

L130   REPEAT
L140             {Select interactively region to be zoomed; statements are omitted here.}
L150     SET_WORKSTATION_WINDOW (display, xmin,xmax,ymin,ymax);
L160     IF xmax-xmin < 0.5 THEN SET_VISIBILITY (seg2,VISIBLE)
                                                           {See Figure 7.5b}
L170     ELSE SET_VISIBILITY (seg2,INVISIBLE);
L180     IF xmax-xmin < 0.25 THEN SET_VISIBILITY (seg3,VISIBLE)
                                                           {See Figure 7.5c}
L190     ELSE SET_VISIBILITY (seg3,INVISIBLE);
L200   UNTIL interrupt;
```

──────────────────────── *Fortran* ────────────────────────

```
       C       *** select workstation
L10            CALL GACWK (DISPL)
       C       *** Segment 1 contains national boundaries
L20            CALL GCRSG (SEG1)
L30            CALL DRFILE (21)
L40            CALL GCLSG
       C       *** See Figure 7.5a

       C       *** Segment 2 contains state boundaries
L50            CALL GCRSG (SEG2)
L60            CALL GSVIS (SEG2,INVIS)
L70            CALL DRFILE (22)
L80            CALL GCLSG

       C       *** Segment 3 contains county boundaries
L90            CALL GCRSG (SEG3)
L100           CALL GSVIS (SEG3,INVIS)
L110           CALL DRFILE (23)
L120           CALL GCLSG
```

```
L130     130    CONTINUE
L140  C         *** Select interactively region to be zoomed;
      C         *** statements are omitted here.
L150            CALL GSWKWN (DISPL, XMIN,XMAX,YMIN,YMAX)
L160            IF (XMAX-XMIN .LT. 0.5) CALL GSVIS (SEG2,VISIBL)
L170            IF (XMAX-XMIN .GE. 0.5) CALL GSVIS (SEG2,INVIS)
      C         *** See Figure 7.5b
L180            IF (XMAX-XMIN .LT. 0.25) CALL GSVIS (SEG3,VISIBL)
L190            IF (XMAX-XMIN .GE. 0.25) CALL GSVIS (SEG3,INVIS)
      C         *** See Figure 7.5c
L200            IF (.NOT. INTRPT) GOTO 130
```

Example 7.2   Generating a sequence of pictures with invariant background

When generating an animated cartoon, the background often remains unchanged while the objects move. If the background picture is generated within
segments, GKS will automatically regenerate the background by REDRAW
ALL SEGMENTS ON WORKSTATION. The application program can focus
on the generation of the changing parts within the picture which is assumed
to be done by a procedure DRAW PICTURE.

──────────────────────────────── *Pascal* ────────────────────────────────

```
L10         {Assume that segments containing background picture have been generated}
L20    FOR i:=1 TO max DO
L30    BEGIN
L40       REDRAW_ALL_SEGMENTS_ON_WORKSTATION (plot);
                                                         {Draw background}
L50       DRAW_PICTURE(i);                               {draw i-th picture}
L60    END;
```

──────────────────────────────── *Fortran* ────────────────────────────────

```
L10   C         *** Assume that segments containing background picture have been
      C         *** generated.
L20             DO 60 I=1,MAX
      C         *** Draw background
L40             CALL GRSGWK (PLOT)
L50             CALL DRPICT (I)
L60      60     CONTINUE
```

Example 7.3   Illustration of the use of the pick identifier

The pick identifier establishes a second level of naming beside the segment
mechanism. However, the pick identifier is an output primitive attribute and,
therefore, is governed by the rules for attributes rather than by the naming

conventions for segments. This example demonstrates that the pick identifier can be assigned to non-contiguous groups of primitives and that its value is not affected by segment opening and closing.

――――――――――――――――――――― *Pascal* ―――――――――――――――――――――

```
L10   SET_PICK_IDENTIFIER (pi1);    {pick identifier = pi1, no effect on primitives}
L20   CREATE_SEGMENT (seg1);
L30   Output primitives;
                  {pick identifier pi1 associated to these primitives in segment storage}
L40   SET_PICK_IDENTIFIER (pi2);
L50   Output primitives;
                  {pick identifier pi2 associated to these primitives in segment storage}
L60   SET_PICK_IDENTIFIER (pi1);
L70   Output primitives;
                  {pick identifier pi1 associated to these primitives in segment storage}
L80   SET_PICK_IDENTIFIER (pi3);
L90   Output primitives;
                  {pick identifier pi3 associated to these primitives in segment storage}
L100  CLOSE_SEGMENT;
L110  Output primitives;                  {pick identifier = pi3, no effect on primitives}
```

―――――――――――――――――――――― *Fortran* ――――――――――――――――――――――

```
L10           CALL GSPKID (1)
      C       *** pick identifier = 1, no effect on primitives
L20           CALL GCRSG (SEG1)
L30           Output primitives
      C       *** pick identifier 1 associated to these primitives in segment storage
L40           CALL GSPKID (2)
L50           Output primitives
      C       *** pick identifier 2 associated to these primitives in segment storage
L60           CALL GSPKID (1)
L70           Output primitives
      C       *** pick identifier 1 associated to these primitives in segment storage
L80           CALL GSPKID (3)
L90           Output primitives
      C       *** pick identifier 3 associated to these primitives in segment storage
L100          CALL GCLSG
L110          Output primitives
      C       *** pick identifier = 3, no effect on primitives
```

Example 7.4   Clock with dynamic hands realized by CREATE, DELETE, RENAME

Three segments (seg1,seg2,seg3) are created which contain the hour, minute, and second hand of a clock. Every second, a new segment (temp) is created for each hand which shows the updated position. The old segment is deleted; the new segment is renamed to obtain the original name.

Procedure HAND contains the description of a standard hand showing upwards towards 12 on the clock-face. This hand is transformed to achieve different sizes for hour, minute, and second hand. Furthermore, the hand is rotated to point to the correct position on the clock-face. The rotation angle corresponds to the clock time in the following way: 12 hours correspond to angle twopi (angle := twopi*hours/12); 60 minutes correspond to angle twopi (angle := twopi*minutes/60); 60 seconds correspond to angle twopi (angle := twopi*seconds/60); radians are measured counter-clockwise (angle := -angle). The hour hand does not jump from one hour to the next but is moved slightly every minute with 60 minutes corresponding to one hour (angle := -twopi*(hours + minutes/60.0)/12).

———————————————— Pascal ————————————————

```
L630  PROCEDURE HAND (segment:NAME; angle,width,length:REAL)
      {Creates segment 'segment' containing a clock hand with width 'width' and length
                             'length' at angle 'angle'. 0 ≤ angle ≤ 1, clockwise}
L640  CONST twopi = 6.2831852;
L650  VAR hand_x,hand_y :REAL;
L660     x,y,xx,yy :ARRAY[1..5] OF REAL;
L670  BEGIN
                             {x,y describe hand with length 1 pointing upwards}
L680     x[1]: = 0.00; x[2]: = width; x[3]: = 0.0; x[4]: = -width; x[5]: = 0.00;
L690     y[1]: = 0.01; y[2]: = 0.15; y[3]: = 1.0; y[4]: = 0.15; y[5]: = 0.01;
                     {Compute complex number which is to be multiplied with x,y}
L700     hand_x := COS(-angle*twopi) * length; {to achieve proper scaling and rotation}
L710     hand_y := SIN(-angle*twopi) * length;

L720     FOR i: = 1 TO 5 DO
L730     BEGIN
L740       xx[i] := x[i]*hand_x — y[i]*hand_y;
L750       yy[i] := x[i]*hand_y + y[i]*hand_x;
L760     END;
L770     CREATE_SEGMENT (segment);
L780     POLYLINE (5,xx,yy);                              {Generating hand}
L790     CLOSE_SEGMENT;
L800  END {HAND};


L510  PROCEDURE HHAND (segment:NAME; hours,minutes:INTEGER)
                                                          {Draws hour hand}
L520  BEGIN HAND (segment, (hours + minutes/60.0)/12.0, 0.05, 0.6);
L540  END {HHAND};


L550  PROCEDURE MHAND (segment:NAME; minutes:INTEGER)
                                                          {Draws minute hand}
L560  BEGIN HAND (segment, minutes/60.0, 0.03, 0.8);
L580  END {MHAND};


L590  PROCEDURE SHAND (segment:NAME; seconds:INTEGER)
                                                          {Draws second hand}
L600  BEGIN HAND (segment, seconds/60.0, 0.01, 0.95);
L620  END {SHAND};
```

```
L10   PROCEDURE CLOCK1;
                    {Generating real time clock using CREATE, DELETE, RENAME}
L20   CONST error_file = ..... ;
L30        memory_limit = ..... ;
L40        display = ..... ;
L50        connection = ..... ;
L60        type = ..... ;
L70   VAR stop :BOOLEAN;
L80        hours,minutes,seconds,hours1,minutes1,seconds1 :INTEGER;
L90        seg1,seg2,seg3,temp,digits :NAME;
                              {Names must be initialised to distinct values}


L100  BEGIN                                              {Initialisation}
L110      OPEN_GKS (error_file,memory_limit);
L120      OPEN_WORKSTATION (display,connection,type);
L130      ACTIVATE_WORKSTATION (display);
                              {Set and select normalization transformation 1}
L140      SET_WINDOW (1, -1.0, +1.0, -1.0, +1.0);
L150      SELECT_NORMALIZATION_TRANSFORMATION (1);

L160      MINUTE_MARKERS;              {Draws minute markers, see Example 7.7}
L170      CREATE_SEGMENT(digits);
L171      CLOCK_FACE_DIGITS;              {Generates digits, see Example 6.7}
L172      CLOSE_SEGMENT;
L180      TIME (hours,minutes,seconds);    {Assume that TIME delivers clock time}
L190      HHAND (seg1, hours, minutes);                    {Generate hands}
L200      MHAND (seg2, minutes);
L210      SHAND (seg3, seconds);


L220      WHILE (NOT stop) DO                              {Loop forever}
                              {Wait for 1 second very useful here}
                    {Examine some input device here which sets 'stop'}


L230      BEGIN                                {Updating of real time clock}
L240        TIME (hours1,minutes1,seconds1);               {Get real time}

L250        IF NOT ((hours = hours1) AND (minutes = minutes1)) THEN
L260        BEGIN                              {Redraw hour hand once a minute}
L270          HHAND (temp, hours1, minutes1);
L280          DELETE_SEGMENT (seg1);
L290          RENAME_SEGMENT (temp,seg1);
L300          hours := hours1;
L310        END;
L320        IF NOT (minutes = minutes1) THEN
L330        BEGIN                            {Redraw minute hand once a minute}
L340          MHAND (temp, minutes1);
L350          DELETE_SEGMENT (seg2);
L360          RENAME_SEGMENT (temp,seg2);
L370          minutes := minutes1;
L380        END;
L390        IF NOT (seconds = seconds1) THEN
```

```
L400        BEGIN                        {Redraw second hand once a second}
L410          SHAND (temp,seconds1);
L420          DELETE_SEGMENT (seg3);
L430          RENAME_SEGMENT (temp,seg3);
L440          seconds := seconds1;
L450        END;
L460      END;
L470    DEACTIVATE_WORKSTATION (display);
L480    CLOSE_WORKSTATION (display);
L490    CLOSE_GKS;
L500    END {CLOCK1};
```

_____ *Fortran* _____

```
L10              PROGRAM CLOCK1
      C          *** Generating real time clock using CREATE, DELETE, RENAME
L70              LOGICAL STOP
L80              INTEGER HOUR,MIN,SEC,HOUR1,MIN1,SEC1
L81              INTEGER ERRFIL,DISP,CONID,TYPE
L82              DATA ERRFIL/9/,DISP/1/,CONID/0/,TYPE/3/

L110             CALL GOPKS (ERRFIL)
L120             CALL GOPWK (DISP,CONID,TYPE)
L130             CALL GACWK (DISP)
      C          *** Set and select normalization transformation 1
L140             CALL GSWN (1, -1.0, -1.0, 1.0, 1.0)
L150             CALL GSELNT (1)
      C          *** Generate clock digits and minute markers (see Examples 7.7 and
                     6.7)
L160             CALL MINMAR
L170             CALL GCRSG (80)
L171             CALL DIGITS
L172             CALL GCLSG
L180             CALL TIME (HOUR,MIN,SEC)
      C          *** Assume that TIME delivers real time
L190             CALL HHAND (100, HOUR, MIN)
L200             CALL MHAND (200, MIN)
L210             CALL SHAND (300, SEC)

      C          *** Loop forever
L220    1        CONTINUE
      C          *** Examine some input device here which sets STOP
L221             IF (STOP) GOTO 9
      C          *** Updating of real time clock
      C          *** Wait for 1 sec very useful here
L240             CALL TIME (HOUR1,MIN1,SEC1)
      C          *** Redraw hour hand once a minute
L250             IF (HOUR.EQ.HOUR1 .AND. MIN.EQ.MIN1) GOTO 2
L270             CALL HHAND (101, HOUR1, MIN1)
L280             CALL GDSG (100)
L290             CALL GRENSG (101,100)
L300             HOUR = HOUR1
```

```
        C           *** Redraw minute hand once a minute
L320                IF (MIN.EQ.MIN1) GOTO 2
L340                CALL MHAND (201, MIN1)
L350                CALL GDSG (200)
L360                CALL GRENSG (201,200)
L370                MIN = MIN1
        C           *** Redraw second hand once a second
L390    2           IF (SEC.EQ.SEC1) GOTO 1
L410                CALL SHAND (301, SEC1)
L420                CALL GDSG (300)
L430                CALL GRENSG (301,300)
L440                SEC = SEC1
L450                GOTO 1                                      ì

L470    9           CALL GDAWK (DISP)
L480                CALL GCLWK (DISP)
L490                CALL GCLKS
L500                STOP
L501                END


        C           *** Draw hour hand
L510                SUBROUTINE HHAND (SEGNR, HOUR, MIN)
L511                INTEGER SEGNR,HOUR,MIN
L530                CALL HAND (SEGNR, (HOUR + MIN/60.0)/12.0, 0.05, 0.6)
L540                RETURN
L541                END


        C           *** Draw minute hand
L550                SUBROUTINE MHAND (SEGNR, MIN)
L551                INTEGER SEGNR,MIN
L570                CALL HAND (SEGNR, MIN/60.0, 0.03, 0.8)
L580                RETURN
L581                END


        C           *** Draw second hand
L590                SUBROUTINE SHAND (SEGNR, SEC)
L591                INTEGER SEGNR,SEC
L610                CALL HAND (SEGNR, SEC/60.0, 0.01, 0.95)
L620                RETURN
L621                END


L630         .      SUBROUTINE HAND (SEGNR, ANGLE, WIDTH, LENGTH)
        C           *** Creates segment SEGNR containing a clock hand
                    with width WIDTH
        C           *** and length LENGTH at angle ANGLE (0 ≤ ANGLE ≤ 1, clockwise).
L640                INTEGER SEGNR
L641                REAL  X(5),Y(5),XX(5),YY(5),XR,YR,
             +            ANGLE,WIDTH,LENGTH,TWOPI
L650                DATA X/5*0.0/, Y/0.01,0.15,1.0,0.15,0.01/,TWOPI/6.2831852/
        C           *** X,Y describe hand with length 1 pointing upwards
        C           *** Setting width of clock hand
L660                X(2) = WIDTH
```

Figure 7.6 Clock at 8:03:27, 12:25:43, 15:59:39

L670		X(4) = -WIDTH
	C	*** Compute complex number (XR,YR) which is to be multiplied with
	C	*** hand (X,Y) to give proper length and angle
L700		XR = COS(-ANGLE*TWOPI) * LENGTH
L710		YR = SIN(-ANGLE*TWOPI) * LENGTH
	C	*** Compute hand rotated by ANGLE and scaled by LENGTII
L720		DO 10 I=1,5
L740		XX(I) = X(I)*XR — Y(I)*YR
L750		YY(I) = X(I)*YR + Y(I)*XR
L760	10	CONTINUE
L770		CALL GCRSG (SEGNR)
	C	*** Generate hand
L780		CALL GPL (5,XX,YY)
L790		CALL GCLSG
L800		RETURN
L801		END

Example 7.5   Clock with dynamic second hand realized via setting VISIBILITY

In this example, for efficiency reasons, the second hand is not generated afresh every second, but all 60 possible positions are predefined in 60 distinct segments and the current position is displayed by making visible the respective segment. As hour and minute hands are generated only every minute, they can be generated afresh without great loss of performance.

———————————————— *Pascal* ————————————————

L10	PROCEDURE CLOCK2;	{Same as Example 7.4 except:}
L11	VAR seg :ARRAY[1..60] OF NAME;	
		{Names must be initialised to distinct values}
.....		
		{Replace line L210 by}
L210	FOR i:=0 to 59 DO	

```
L211  BEGIN                                    {Generate all possible second hands}
L212    SHAND (seg[i], i);
L213    SET_VISIBILITY (seg[i], INVISIBLE);
L214  END;
L215  SET_VISIBILITY (seg[seconds], VISIBLE);
.....
                                               {Replace lines L410-430 by}
L410    SET_VISIBILITY (seg[seconds1], VISIBLE);
L420    SET_VISIBILITY (seg[seconds], INVISIBLE);
.....
```

────────────────────────────── *Fortran* ──────────────────────────────

```
L10             PROGRAM CLOCK2
.....    C      *** Same as Example 7.4 except:
         C      *** Replace line L210 by
         C      *** Generate all possible second hands
L210            DO 10 I = 0,59
L211            CALL SHAND (I, I)
L212            CALL GSVIS (I, 0)
L213    10      CONTINUE
L214            CALL GSVIS (SEC, 1)
.....
         C      *** Replace lines L410-430 by
         C      *** Make second hand visible
L410            CALL GSVIS (SEC1, 1)
L420            CALL GSVIS (SEC, 0)
.....
```

Example 7.6   Clock with dynamic hands realized via SET SEGMENT TRANSFORMATION

The immediate way of generating a clock with dynamic hands is by use of the segment transformation attribute. Only three segments, one for each hand, have to be maintained. The positions are updated just by setting the appropriate transformation value.

────────────────────────────── *Pascal* ──────────────────────────────

```
L10   PROCEDURE CLOCK3;                         {Same as Example 7.4 except:}
.....
                                                {Add line L92}
L92   VAR transf: ARRAY [1..2, 1..3] OF REAL;
.....
                                                {Replace lines L270-290 by:}
L270      angle := -twopi*(hours1 + minutes1/60.0)/12.0;
L280      EVALUATE_TRANSFORMATION_MATRIX
              (0.0,0.0,0.0,0.0,angle,1.0,1.0,0.0,transf);
L290      SET_SEGMENT_TRANSFORMATION (seg1, transf);
.....
```

{Replace lines L340-360 by:}
L340   angle := -twopi*minutes1/60.0;
L350   EVALUATE_TRANSFORMATION_MATRIX
　　　　　(0.0,0.0,0.0,0.0,angle,1.0,1.0,0.0,transf);
L360   SET_SEGMENT_TRANSFORMATION (seg2, transf);
.....

{Replace lines L410-430 by:}
L410   angle := -twopi*seconds1/60.0;
L420   EVALUATE_TRANSFORMATION_MATRIX
　　　　　(0.0,0.0,0.0,0.0,angle,1.0,1.0,0.0,transf);
L430   SET_SEGMENT_TRANSFORMATION (seg3, transf);
.....

―――――――――――――――――――― *Fortran* ――――――――――――――――――――

```
L10          PROGRAM CLOCK3
      C      *** Same as Example 7.4 except:
.....  C
      C      *** Add line L92
L92          REAL TRANSF(2,3)
.....  C
      C      *** Replace lines L270-290 by:
L270         ANGLE = — TWOPI * (HOUR + MIN/60.0)/12.0
L280         CALL GEVTM (0.0, 0.0, 0.0, 0.0, ANGLE, 1.0, 1.0, 0, TRANSF)
L290         CALL GTRSG (100,TRANSF)
.....  C
.....  C      *** Replace lines L340-360 by:
L340         ANGLE = — TWOPI * MIN/60.
L350         CALL GEVTM (0.0, 0.0, 0.0, 0.0, ANGLE, 1.0, 1.0, 0, TRANSF)
L360         CALL GTRSG (200,TRANSF)
.....  C
      C      *** Replace lines L410-430 by:
L410         ANGLE = — TWOPI * SEC/60.
L420         CALL GEVTM (0.0, 0.0, 0.0, 0.0, ANGLE, 1.0, 1.0, 0, TRANSF)
L430         CALL GTRSG (300,TRANSF)
.....
```

Example 7.7   Generating minute markers on a clock using INSERT SEGMENT

Whereas Example 7.4 explains the generation of clock hands, this example shows how the INSERT SEGMENT function can be applied to copy one minute marker and one hour marker to all the 60 positions around a clock-face. The minute and hour markers are at first generated within two distinct temporary segments stored in the workstation-independent segment storage (WISS). These segments are copied under appropriate transformations several times into a third segment which finally contains the description of all markers on the clock-face.

———————————————————————— *Pascal* ————————————————————————

```
L10    PROCEDURE MINUTE_MARKERS;    {Drawing of minute markers on clock}

L20    CONST twopi = 6.2831852;
L30      wiss = 'WISS';
L40      connection = ';
L50      type = 'WISS';
L60      display = '....';
L70    VAR x,y : ARRAY [1..2] OF REAL;
L80      transf : ARRAY [1..2, 1..3] OF REAL;
L90      angle : REAL;
L100     i : INTEGER;
L110     minute,hour,markers : NAME;    {Names must be initialised to distinct values}
L120   BEGIN
L130     DEACTIVATE_WORKSTATION (display);
L140     OPEN_WORKSTATION (wiss);                                {Activate WISS}
L150     ACTIVATE_WORKSTATION (wiss);

L160     x[1] := 0.95;
L170     x[2] := 1.0;
L180     y[1] := 0.0;
L190     y[2] := 0.0;
L200     CREATE_SEGMENT (minute);                    {Create one minute marker}
L210       POLYLINE (2,X,Y);
L220     CLOSE_SEGMENT;

L230     x[1] := 0.9;
L240     CREATE_SEGMENT (hour);                       {Create one hour marker}
L250       POLYLINE (2,X,Y);
L260     CLOSE_SEGMENT;

L270     DEACTIVATE_WORKSTATION (wiss);
                                 {No more segments recorded in WISS}
L280     ACTIVATE_WORKSTATION (display);         {Activate output device}

       {Create segment with minute markers by inserting segments hour and minute
                                        under appropriate rotation}
L290     CREATE_SEGMENT (markers);
L300       FOR i:=1 TO 60 DO
L310       BEGIN
L320       angle := twopi*i/60.0;                      {Angle corresponding to i}
L330         EVALUATE_TRANSFORMATION_MATRIX
                 (0.0, 0.0, 0.0, 0.0, angle, 1.0, 1.0, 0.0, transf);
L340         IF i DIV 5 * 5 = i DO INSERT_SEGMENT (hour,transf)
L350         ELSE INSERT_SEGMENT (minute,transf);
L360       END;
L370     CLOSE_SEGMENT;

L380     DELETE_SEGMENT (minute);
L390     DELETE_SEGMENT (hour);
L400     CLOSE_WORKSTATION (wiss);
L410   END {MINUTE_MARKERS};
```

Fortran

```
L10              SUBROUTINE MINMAR
       C         *** Drawing of minute markers on clock
L20              REAL X(2),Y(2),TRANSF(2,3),ANGLE,TWOPI
L30              INTEGER WISS,CONID,TYPE,DISP
L40              DATA X/0.95,1.0/, Y/0.0,0.0/, TWOPI/6.2831852/
L50              DATA WISS/7/, CONID/0/, TYPE/0/, DISP/1/
       C         *** Activate WISS
L130             CALL GDAWK (DISP)
L140             CALL GOPWK (WISS,CONID,TYPE)
L150             CALL GACWK (WISS)
       C         *** Create one minute marker
L200             CALL GCRSG (71)
L210             CALL GPL (2,X,Y)
L220             CALL GCLSG
       C         *** Create one hour marker
L230             X(1)= 0.9
L240             CALL GCRSG (72)
L250             CALL GPL (2,X,Y)
L260             CALL GCLSG
       C         *** No more segments recorded in WISS
L270             CALL GDAWK (WISS)
L280             CALL GACWK (DISP)
       C         *** Create segment with minute markers
       C         *** by inserting segments 71,72 under appropriate rotation
L290             CALL GCRSG (70)
L300             DO 1 I=1,60
       C         *** Angle corresponding to I
L320             ANGLE = TWOPI*I/60.0
L330             CALL GEVTM (0.0, 0.0, 0.0, 0.0, ANGLE, 1.0, 1.0, 0, TRANSF)
L340             IF (I/5*5 .EQ. I) CALL GINSG (72,TRANSF)
L350             IF (I/5*5 .NE. I) CALL GINSG (71,TRANSF)
L360     1       CONTINUE
L370             CALL GCLSG

L380             CALL GDSG(71)
L390             CALL GDSG(72)
L400             CALL GCLWK (WISS)
L410             RETURN
L420             END
```

7.11   Exercises

Exercise 7.1   Dynamic change of indexed attributes

In Example 6.3 indexed POLYLINE attributes were used during generation
of a map. Rewrite this program such that data are generated within segments
and the local segment storage of workstation 'display' can be used for dynamic
changes of the linetype attribute.

— Is workstation 'plotter' affected by the dynamic manipulations on workstation 'display?
— Has workstation 'plotter' to pay for the additional capabilities of workstation 'display'?

Exercise 7.2   Use of the WISS

In Exercise 7.1 both workstations are active at the same time. For a novice user, it may be difficult to imagine what happens at a passive workstation while interactive manipulations of a common picture take place at an interactive workstation. To simplify such situations, the WISS can be used.
— Rewrite Exercise 7.1 such that the interactive manipulations only take place on workstation 'display' and WISS and the final picture is copied to the plotter by COPY SEGMENT.
— Can the same be done with ASSOCIATE SEGMENT TO WORKSTATION or INSERT SEGMENT? Explain the differences.

Exercise 7.3   Append primitives to an existing segment

An existing segment cannot be reopened for adding more primitives to it. However, it is possible to create a second segment, to copy the first segment into the second one and to add primitives as desired. Then the first segment can be deleted and the second be renamed to have the name of the first segment. Write a program which
— generates segment 'segment1' containing a TEXT primitive using CHARACTER HEIGHT 1;
— generates segment 'segment2' containing a TEXT primitive using CHARACTER HEIGHT 2;
— replaces segment 'segment1' by a segment containing all primitives of old segment 'segment1' and an additional TEXT primitive using CHARACTER HEIGHT 1.

Which of the functions COPY SEGMENT, ASSOCIATE SEGMENT TO WORKSTATION and INSERT SEGMENT must be used for copying 'segment1'? Does the copying of segment 'segment1' influence the current setting of CHARACTER HEIGHT?

Exercise 7.4   Compare INSERT SEGMENT with COPY SEGMENT TO WORKSTATION

Example 7.7 shows the generation of minute markers by INSERT SEGMENT. Write a program which generates the minute markers from segments 'minute' and 'hour' with help of TRANSFORM SEGMENT and COPY SEGMENT TO WORKSTATION. Can your program also be used for a dynamic clock? (What may happen after the first clock update?)

Exercise 7.5   Segment transformations

In Example 7.7, two separate segments 'minute' and 'hour' are used for generating minute markers. However, segment 'hour' can be obtained from segment 'minute' by applying a segment transformation to it. Rewrite Example 7.7 such that all minute markers are generated by inserting segment 'minute' only.

8 INPUT

The GKS input concept represents a rather complex area of application and implementation details. In many cases, the reader of this book will need to know only some aspects. Therefore, we want to give some hints how to study this chapter.

— In any case, the reader should study the following Sections 8.1 and 8.2 very carefully. They contain detailed information about logical input data which form the basis for providing input to application programs.

— For simple input applications, a skip to Section 8.5 is then appropriate. There, the REQUEST input functions and some sample programs are presented that are sufficient for many applications. Using these functions and studying the examples, the reader will often notice the need for INITIALISE functions. The necessary details about those can be found in Section 8.3.

— For more sophisticated interactive applications, sample and event input is applicable. Then the Sections 8.6 and 8.7 should be read where SAMPLE and EVENT input and the concept of input queuing is described. Also Section 8.4 may be of value which describes how to set the operating modes of logical devices.

— If the reader wants to have more details about applications of input functions, he should read Section 8.8 which contains examples of flexible bindings of logical input devices to physical input devices.

— Chapter IV.2, finally describes the mapping from the logical input level to the physical equipment and the concept of measure/trigger devices from an implementation's point of view.

8.1   Introduction to Logical Input Devices

An application program obtains graphical input from an operator by controlling logical input devices which deliver logical input values to the program.

It has available a range of logical input devices and, thus, a range of associated logical data types. If, for instance, a position is required in an application program, a "LOCATOR" device is to be selected (instead of e.g., a physical cursor device), if a character string is required, the logical device "STRING" has to be used (instead of e.g., a physical keyboard). Whereas the application program can control the available logical input devices, the mapping of logical to physical devices is done by the implementation.

8.1.1   Identification

Each logical input device is identified by:
— a workstation identifier,
— an input class,
— and a device number.

The workstation identifier is a name for selecting the workstation; it is a parameter of the input functions. The input class specifies which one of the six logical device types is addressed (see below). For every class a specific set of input functions is present in GKS. The device number selects one of several logical input devices of the same class on the same workstation. It is an integer parameter of the input functions.

Logical input devices are connected to input or output/input workstations. To use a logical device, the corresponding workstation must be open. The logical input device is implemented in terms of a physical device or devices present on the workstation.

8.1.2   Logical Input Classes and Values

GKS provides six logical input classes: LOCATOR, STROKE, VALUATOR, CHOICE, PICK, and STRING. Each input class determines the type of logical input value that the logical input device delivers. The six input classes and the logical input values they provide are:

LOCATOR: a position in world coordinates (a pair of REAL values) and a normalization transformation number;

STROKE: a sequence of positions in world coordinates and a normalization transformation number;

VALUATOR: a REAL number

CHOICE: a non-negative INTEGER value which represents a selection from a number of choices. Zero indicates "no choice";

PICK: a PICK status (OK,NOPICK), a segment name and a pick identifier. Primitives outside segments cannot be picked;

STRING: a string of CHARACTERS.

8.1.3   Operating Modes

Each logical input device can be operated in three modes, called operating modes. At any time, it is in one, and only one, of the modes set by the invocation of a function in the group SET <input class> MODE. The three operating modes are REQUEST, SAMPLE and EVENT. Input from devices is obtained in different ways depending on the mode:

REQUEST: A specific invocation of REQUEST <input class> causes an attempt to read a logical input value from a specified logical input device, which must be in REQUEST mode. GKS waits until the input is entered by the operator or a break action is performed by the operator. The break action is dependent on the logical input device and on the implementation. If a break occurs, the logical input value is not valid.

SAMPLE: A specific invocation of SAMPLE <input class> causes GKS, without waiting for an operator action, to return the current logical input value of a specified logical input device, which must be in SAMPLE mode.

EVENT: GKS maintains one input queue containing temporally ordered event reports. An event report contains the identification of a logical input device and a logical input value from that device. Event reports are generated asynchronously, by operator action only, from input devices in EVENT mode.

The application program can remove the oldest event report from the queue, and examine its contents. The application can also flush from the queue all event reports from a specified logical input device.

Note, that in contrast to other systems, also STROKE, CHOICE, PICK, and STRING devices can be sampled; and that any LOCATOR and VALUA-TOR devices can generate events. The operating modes are independent of physical device characteristics: all logical input devices provide all three operating modes. This is made possible by the concept of measure/trigger devices which is explained in the next sections and in Chapter IV.2.

8.1.4 Logical Input Device Model

A logical input device contains a measure, a trigger, an initial value, a prompt/ echo type, an echo area and a data record containing details about the echo type. A logical input device's measure and trigger are parts of the implementation of the workstation containing the logical input device. Initial value, echo type, echo area, and data record can be supplied by the application program.

Interaction
A specific logical input device is said to be taking part in an interaction during the time that it is in SAMPLE or EVENT mode, but, when it is in REQUEST mode, only during the execution of a REQUEST function for that device. Many devices on many workstations may be taking part in interactions simultaneously.

Measure
The measure of a logical input device is a value determined by one or more physical input devices together with a "measure mapping" from physical to logical values. More than one measure can simultaneously be determined by a single physical device. A separate measure mapping applies for each measure. A measure can be seen as the state of an independent, active process (a measure process). Each state corresponds exactly with a logical input value.

The current state of the measure process (i.e. the device's measure) is available to GKS as a logical input value. The measure process is in existence while an interaction with the logical input device is underway. Under other conditions, this process does not exist.

When a measure process comes into existence, the data in the workstation state list entry for the logical input device is examined. The initial value is checked for legality according to input class dependent rules explained in Section 8.3. If the check succeeds, the initial value is used as the current state of the process; otherwise a value dependent on the logical input device is used.

Prompt/Echo

Prompting information is output to the operator to indicate the device is ready for use. Echoing indicates the current state of the measure process. While the measure process is in existence, echoing is provided to the operator, if the prompt/echo switch is ON. The prompt/echo technique for a device may be selected by calling the appropriate INITIALISE function. After prompting and displaying the echo of the initial values, the creation of the measure process is complete. For example, the crosshair of a LOCATOR device is a specific echo, its appearance when the LOCATOR is initialised may be seen as prompting at the same time. However, prompting could also be implemented independently from echoing as giving a message to the operator such as "please enter a position".

Trigger

The trigger of a logical input device is a physical input device or a set of them together with a "trigger mapping". The operator can use a trigger to indicate significant moments in time. At these moments, a message is sent to the measure process of the corresponding device (devices). The effect of doing this is dependent on the logical device's mode as follows:

— In REQUEST mode, the measure process returns its data value to the application, and then terminates;
— In SAMPLE mode, trigger messages are always ignored. The application may obtain the data value from the measure process whenever it pleases.
— In EVENT mode, the measure process attempts to add an event record to the input queue; if more than one logical device refers to the same trigger, all corresponding measure values are added to the queue as a "group of simultaneous event reports" when the trigger fires.

A single operator action (for example, pressing a button or a light pen tip switch) causes the firing of not more than one trigger. Several logical input devices can refer to the same trigger.

A trigger can be seen as an independent, active process (a trigger process) that sends a message to one or more recipients when it fires. A logical input device is a recipient of its trigger if there is a pending REQUEST for it or if it is in EVENT mode.

Acknowledgement

When a trigger fires, GKS provides the operator an acknowledgement which depends on the implementation of the logical input device. The acknowledgement is not controllable by a GKS function.

8.1.5   Setting the Logical Input Device Mode

Initially, a logical input device is in REQUEST mode which implies that its measure process does not exist and its identifier is not on its trigger's list of recipients.

The mode of a logical input device may be changed by invoking the appropriate SET <input class> MODE function. After a SET <input class> MODE invocation with parameter REQUEST no measure or trigger process exists for the specified device. After a SET <input class> MODE invocation with parameter SAMPLE a newly initialised measure process is in existence for the specified device, but the device is not on its trigger's list of recipients. After a SET <input class> MODE invocation with parameter EVENT, a newly initialised measure process is in existence for the specified device, and the device is on its trigger's list of recipients.

— While a device is in REQUEST mode, a logical input value may be obtained by invoking the appropriate REQUEST <device class> function. The effects of doing so are described in Section 8.5.

— While a logical input device is in SAMPLE mode, a logical input value can be obtained by invoking the appropriate SAMPLE <device class> function. The effect of doing so will set the logical input value to the current state of the measure process without waiting for a trigger firing.

— While a logical input device is in EVENT mode, logical input values are added as event records to the event queue, and may be obtained in sequence by invoking AWAIT EVENT, and then invoking the appropriate GET <device class> function.

The following Example 8.1 describes the operation of a logical LOCATOR device in the three operating modes. The LOCATOR may be implemented, for example, by using a tablet with a pointing device and a button attached to it.

Example 8.1   Use of a LOCATOR device in all operating modes

```
──────────────────────────── Pascal ────────────────────────────
                                            {LOCATOR in REQUEST mode}
L10   REQUEST_LOCATOR (DISPLAY,LC1,STATUS,TNR,POS);
                                             {LOCATOR in SAMPLE mode}
L20   SET_LOCATOR_MODE (DISPLAY,LC1,SAMPLE,ECHO);
L30   SAMPLE_LOCATOR (DISPLAY,LC1,TNR,POS);
                                              {LOCATOR in EVENT mode}
L40   SET_LOCATOR_MODE (DISPLAY,LC1,EVENT,ECHO);
L50   AWAIT_EVENT
        (TIMEOUT,WORKSTATION,INPUT_CLASS,DEVICE_NUMBER);
L60   IF (INPUT_CLASS = LOCATOR) THEN
L70      GET_LOCATOR (TNR,POS);
L80   SET_LOCATOR_MODE (DISPLAY,LC1,REQUEST,ECHO);
                                                   {DISABLE LOCATOR}
```

                                   Fortran

```
        C                                    *** LOCATOR in REQUEST mode
L10             CALL GRQLC (DISP,LC1,STATUS,TNR,PX,PY)
        C                                    *** LOCATOR in SAMPLE mode
L20             CALL GSLCM (DISP,LC1,GSAMPL,GECHO)
L30             CALL GSMLC (DISP,LC1,TNR,PX,PY)
        C                                    *** LOCATOR in EVENT mode
L40             CALL GSLCM (DISP,LC1,GEVENT,GECHO)
L50             CALL GWAIT (TOUT,WK,CLASS,DEVNB)
L60             IF (CLASS = GLOCAT) CALL GGTLC (TNR,PX,PY)
        C                    *** disable LOCATOR (put it into REQUEST mode)
L80             CALL GSLCM (DISP,LC1,GREQU,GECHO)
```

8.2   Details About Logical Input Devices

8.2.1   LOCATOR and STROKE Devices

GKS provides a LOCATOR device class, returning a position in world coordinates and a normalization transformation number. Let P and N denote these values.

Then P transformed to NDC by N lies within the workstation window. Also P must lie within the window specified by N and, in addition, P transformed to NDC by N must lie outside all viewports of higher priority than N.

GKS provides a STROKE device class, returning a sequence of positions in world coordinates and a normalization transformation number. Let P1 .... Pm be the positions and N be the transformation number.

Then P1 .... Pm transformed to NDC by N lie within the workstation window. Also P1 ... Pm must lie within the window specified by N and, in addition, P1 .... Pm transformed to NDC by N must lie outside all viewports of higher priority than N. Note that the normalization transformation N may change as points are added to the stroke.

Any invocation of SET WINDOW, SET VIEWPORT or SET VIEWPORT INPUT PRIORITY can cause a change in P (P1 .... Pm for STROKE) or N or both, but must preserve the condition just defined.

The rule implies that no normalization transformation having priority less than that of transformation 0 can appear in the state of a LOCATOR or STROKE measure process (note that, at the default setting of the viewport input priorities, normalization transformation 0 has the highest).

The LOCATOR and STROKE positions are transformed from device coordinates (DC) to world coordinates (WC) applying the following algorithm:

— When a physical locator returns a value, the workstation transforms it back to normalized device coordinates (NDC) using the inverse of the current workstation transformation;

Note that LOCATOR and STROKE input can be obtained only from positions within the part of the current workstation viewport into which the

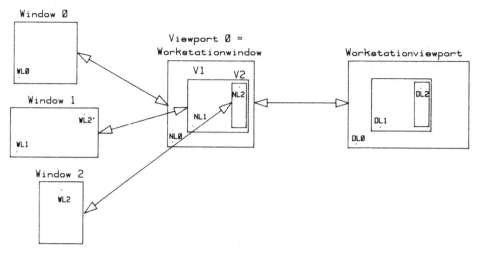

Figure 8.1 LOCATOR/STROKE input transformations

current workstation window is mapped. (If workstation window and work-station viewport both have the same aspect ratio, then the complete worksta-tion viewport can be used for LOCATOR and STROKE input). This ensures that LOCATOR and STROKE positions are within NDC space.
— In NDC space, the normalization transformation of highest priority is se-lected in whose viewport the NDC position lies. Each normalization transfor-mation has an associated viewport input priority which is used to arrange the normalization transformations into a priority-order.
— The inverse of the selected transformation is used to calculate a world coordi-nate value.
— Both the world coordinate value and the index of the selected transformation are stored as the current measure value of the logical device.

To ensure that the NDC position lies within at least one viewport, there is a default transformation which cannot be changed. It has number zero and both its window and its viewport are set to the unit square [0,1]x[0,1]. The world coordinates returned are NDC coordinates in effect in two cases:
— If no normalization transformation is defined with higher viewport input priority than that of transformation number 0. Transformation zero is initial-ised with highest priority;
— If the LOCATOR/STROKE positions, transformed to NDC space, lie out-side any application-defined viewport.

Figure 8.1 depicts an application of LOCATOR input; it is assumed that the application program defines two window/viewport transformations: T1 maps window 1 to viewport 1, and T2 maps window 2 to viewport 2 which lies within viewport 1. There is the default transformation T0 which performs the unity transformation (window 0 = viewport 0 = NDC space = [0,1]x[0,1]). Furthermore, this application uses a default workstation transformation, which maps the NDC space onto the largest rectangle that fits within the display surface while preserving the aspect ratio.

Let us further assume two application cases c1 and c2: the first one assigns viewport 2 higher priority than viewport 1 and than viewport 0. Case c2 assigns viewport 2 lower priority than viewport 1 but higher than viewport 0. Thus, the lists of normalization transformations are ordered with increasing viewport input priority as

— case c1: T0, T1, T2
— case c2: T0, T2, T1

Figure 8.1 demonstrates the following transformation cases:

1. Using a physical LOCATOR device, position DL0 is entered; it is transformed back to the NDC position NL0; NL0 only lies within the default viewport (outside any application-defined viewport) and, thus, is delivered back as tuple (NL0 = WL0, T0).
2. DL1 is entered and transformed to NL1; this lies within the two viewports V0 and V1. Since we assumed V1 to be of higher priority than V0, NL1 is transformed back using T1 and returned as (WL1, T1).
3. DL2 is entered and transformed to NL2; this lies within all three viewports; in the first case (c1), NL2 is transformed back to WL2 applying T2. In case c2 T1 is used to transform NL2 back to WL2'.

Obviously the viewport input priority can be used to "hide" world coordinate systems below other ones. The change of the viewport input priority can be performed dynamically using the function SET VIEWPORT INPUT PRIORITY as a means to navigate LOCATOR/STROKE input transformations within coordinate systems.

8.2.2   VALUATOR

GKS provides a VALUATOR class, returning a real number in a range specified by the application; for each valuator device a low, a high, and an initial value is given. Additionally, the resolution of the valuator device may be adjusted if the device is suitably implemented.

8.2.3   CHOICE

The CHOICE class is intended to provide a "menu" or a "function key" capability. It returns an integer value which indicates the selected alternative. Furthermore, zero as indication of "no choice" may be returned if, for example, the device is in a state where no buttons are depressed or a non-existing alternative is selected (e.g., marking outside the menu box). The number of choice alternatives defines the maximum integer value that can be returned. The choice device class represents a powerful input facility in that it provides potentially complex application-controlled prompting techniques, such as displaying a menu consisting of strings or of graphical symbols.

Choice input typically occurs when an operator presses a button (the numeric identification of the button determines the value) or combinations of buttons (the value is derived from the combinations of buttons pressed).

8.2.4 PICK

The PICK device class returns a PICK status, a segment name, and a pick identifier; the PICK status indicates OK (a valid PICK input has occurred), or NOPICK. NOPICK might, e.g., occur if the light pen was not pointing at any detectable segment. If the PICK status is OK, the segment name and pick identifier must obey the following rules:
— The segment exists and has VISIBILITY and DETECTABILITY on.
— The segment is present on the workstation containing the PICK device.
— The pick identifier is the pick identifier attribute of at least one output primitive in the segment, satisfying the following condition: part of the primitive is within the clipping rectangle in effect on the workstation when it arrived there. This rectangle is either the workstation window, if GKS is in the state clipping off, or the intersection of the workstation window and the primitive's normalization clipping rectangle, if GKS is in the state clipping on. Further, the primitive must not be completely overlapped by primitives in a segment of higher priority.

The PICK initial value is tested against the above rules whenever the PICK measure process is initiated. If the rules are not satisfied, the process state is set to NOPICK.
Note:
For certain workstations, testing rule c) when the PICK measure process is initiated, may be very expensive. In such cases, only rules a) and b) need be tested.
Note:
The PICK measure is defined using the properties of output primitives and segments. PICK devices can exist only on an output/input workstation.

8.2.5 STRING

The GKS STRING device class returns a character string, which may also be empty (null string). The operator is prompted by the initial string, and a cursor at an application-specified position within it. Replacement of characters starts at the cursor position, and may extend the string up to an application-specified maximum length.

8.3 Initialising Logical Input Devices

For each input class, there is an initialisation function which can only be called if the respective logical device is in REQUEST mode. The functions provide the following information to a device via the workstation state list. If the initialisation function is not called for a device, default values apply as defined in the workstation description table by the workstation implementor.

Initial Values
Initial values appropriate to the device class can be defined. If they violate the rules defined in Section 8.2, an error occurs and the workstation state list is unchanged. Initial values serve for starting the display of prompts and echos and for setting initial measure values. Each time a device is activated (a REQUEST function is invoked or the device is set into sample or event mode), the initial values are taken from the internal workstation state list.

The "initial values"-feature aims at easing the operation of input tools. The application program may adjust the input device to some "expected" value; the operator then needs only confirm that adjustment if he wishes so, otherwise he may change it to the desired value starting from a — perhaps nearby situated — initial value. Obviously, the calculation of initial values is highly application specific. Experience has shown, for example, that for locator input it is often convenient to initialise the locator device before each activation to that position, which was last entered via this device; thus the operator may continue entering coordinates where he had last stopped.

Prompt/echo Types
For each input device class, GKS defines a number of prompt/echo types. An implementation-dependent prompt/echo type (type 1) is required for all logical input devices. Further prompt/echo types appropriate to each class may be provided by an implementation following the definition of the INITIALISE functions; prompt/echo types above those are device-dependent. The echo appearance may be switched on and off using the SET <device> MODE functions.

Echo Area
For some prompt/echo types, an echo area is of importance; it may be used to control the location of the echo and prompting appearance, such as menus on a screen, prompt messages on a scroll area, display of digital values, or echo of STRING input devices. The echo area is defined in device coordinates in the form (left/right/bottom/top).

Data Record
Depending on the device class, the device implementation, and the selected prompt/echo type, the data record of the INITIALISE function may contain both certain required values and other additional information. Some input classes have mandatory control values in the data record. Some prompt/echo types within an input class also have mandatory control values in the data record. These values occupy well-defined places in the data record. In any data record used in initialising an input device, values mandatory to an input class, if any, must appear first followed by values mandatory to the prompt/echo type if any.

The items required by each class in the data record are:

for STROKE: input buffer size in number of points;

for VALUATOR: low value and high value;

for STRING, input buffer size and initial cursor position.

Prompt/echo types which have mandatory values are types 3 and 4 for STROKE and types 2,3,4 and 5 for CHOICE. These values and other optional values are listed with the INITIALISE functions in the following part.

Note that the FORTRAN language binding provides a special subroutine to pack data values into a data record. In this way, the number of parameters which represent the data type "data record" in FORTRAN is minimized. Applications of this mapping function are shown in the Sections 8.5, 8.6, and 8.7 together with applications of the INITIALISE functions.

This function is defined as follows:

PACK DATA RECORD GKOP,WSOP,WSAC,SGOP L0a

――――――――――――――― *FORTRAN-Interface* ―――――――――――――

CALL GPREC (IL,IA,RL,RA,LSTR,STR,MLDR,LDR,DATR)

Parameters:

Input	IL	length of integer array	(1..n)	INTEGER
Input	IA(IL)	integer array		nxINTEGER
Input	RL	length of real array	(1..n)	INTEGER
Input	RA(RL)	real array		nxREAL
Input	LSTR	number of characters in string	(0..n)	INTEGER
Input	STR	string array		CHARACTER*(*)
Input	MLDR	maximal length of data record	(1..n)	INTEGER
Output	LDR	actual length of data record	(0..n)	INTEGER
Output	DATR(MLDR)	data record		nxCHARACTERx80

Initialise Functions

INITIALISE LOCATOR WSOP,WSAC,SGOP L0b

Parameters:

Input	workstation identifier			N
Input	locator device number		(1..n)	I
Input	initial locator position	WC		P
Input	initial normalization transformation number		(0..n)	I
Input	prompt/echo type		(1..n)	I
Input	echo area XMIN<XMAX,YMIN<YMAX	DC		4xR
Input	data record			D

Effect:

The initial locator position, initial normalization transformation number, prompt/echo type, echo area and data record are stored in the workstation state list entry for the specified LOCATOR device.

For some LOCATOR prompt/echo types, two positions are required. One of the positions, which remains fixed during the input operation, is the initial locator position. The other position is the current locator position that varies dynamically as the operator uses the LOCATOR.

The prompt/echo area is required for prompt/echo type 6 only; other (implementation-dependent) techniques may also use it.

Prompt/echo type:

1: Implementation Standard

Designate the current position of the LOCATOR using an implementation defined technique; normally, hardware-provided facilities are used for this type; e.g., the display of position registers at some tablets and digitizers, or some of the prompt/echo types explained below.

2: Crosshair

A crosshair is displayed, i.e., the current position of the LOCATOR is designated, using a vertical line and a horizontal line spanning over the display surface or the workstation viewport intersecting at the current locator position. This technique should be used, if applications request positions which are horizontally or vertically dependent on other — possible already generated — parts of the picture. Examples are flow chart construction, electrical layout design, etc.

3: Tracking Cross

Designate the current position of the LOCATOR using a tracking cross symbol. This echo is mainly useful for applications which need quick and less precise free-hand drawings, e.g., architectural drafting systems.

4: Rubber Band

Designate the current position of the LOCATOR using a rubber band line connecting the initial LOCATOR position given by this function and the current locator position. A rubber band line may be used to determine intersections and local dependencies of picture components.

5: Rectangle

Designate the current position of the LOCATOR using a rectangle. The diagonal of the rectangle is the line connecting the initial LOCATOR position given by this function and the current locator position. The rectangle combines some advantages of the rubber band and cross hair echos. It helps indicating local geometrical dependencies, mainly in horizontal and vertical directions. It may be used to determine overlappings of parts of the picture or "contained conditions" of components.

6: Digits

Display a digital representation of the current LOCATOR position in LOCATOR device-dependent coordinates within the echo area. This echo is mainly aimed for precise determination of coordinates.

>6: Device-Dependent

Prompting and echoing is LOCATOR device-dependent. An example for a specific LOCATOR implementation is the grid-based input of discrete positions. The step width of the grid may be adjusted according to an entry in the locator data record. Each time the LOCATOR device is activated (requested, or put into sample or event mode), the grid is displayed. A cursor may be implemented such that it moves only from grid point to grid point or that it moves arbitrarily, and the closest grid-point is used to calculate world coordinate positions.

Errors:

7	GKS not in proper state: GKS shall be in one of the states WSOP, WSAC or SGOP
20	Specified workstation identifier is invalid
25	Specified workstation is not open
38	Specified workstation is neither of category INPUT nor of category OUTIN
51	Rectangle definition is invalid
140	Specified input device is not present on workstation

141	Input device is not in REQUEST mode
144	Specified prompt and echo type is not supported on this workstation
145	Echo area is outside display space
146	Contents of input data record are invalid
152	Initial value is invalid

———————————————— *FORTRAN-Interface* ————————————————

CALL GINLC (WKID,LCDNR,TNR,PX,PY,PET,EX1,EX2,EY1,EY2,IL,CA)
Parameters:

Input	WKID	workstation identifier		(1..n)	INTEGER
Input	LCDNR	locator device number		(1..n)	INTEGER
Input	TNR	initial normalization transformation number		(0..n)	INTEGER
Input	PX,PY	initial locator position	WC		2xREAL
Input	PET	prompt/echo type		(1..n)	INTEGER
Input	EX1,EX2,EY1,EY2	echo area XMIN < XMAX,YMIN < YMAX			
			DC		4xREAL
Input	IL,CA(IL)	data record			nxCHARACTERXx80

An application of the INITIALISE LOCATOR function is shown in Section 8.5 on page 294. The following Figure 8.2 demonstrates some prompt/echo types of the LOCATOR device.

INITIALISE STROKE   WSOP,WSAC,SGOP   L0b

Parameters:

Input	workstation identifier			N
Input	stroke device number		(1..n)	I
Input	number of points in initial stroke		(0..n)	I
Input	points in initial stroke	WC		nxP
Input	initial normalization transformation number		(0..n)	I
Input	prompt/echo type		(1..n)	I
Input	echo area XMIN < XMAX,YMIN < YMAX	DC		4xR
Input	stroke data record			D

Effect:

The initial stroke, initial normalization transformation number, prompt/echo type, echo area and stroke data record are stored in the workstation state list entry for the specified STROKE device.

For all prompt/echo types, the first entry in the stroke data record must be the input buffer size which is an integer in the range (0..n). This is compared against an implementation-defined 'maximum input buffer size for stroke devices' (contained in the workstation description table). If the requested buffer size is greater, the 'maximum input buffer size for stroke devices' is substituted in the stored data record. If the initial stroke is longer than the buffer size, an error is issued.

When a stroke measure process comes into existence, it obtains a buffer of the current input buffer size. The initial stroke is copied into the buffer, and the editing position is placed at the initial buffer editing position within it. Replacement of points begins at this initial position.

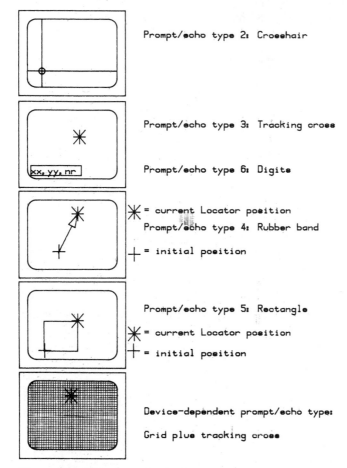

Figure 8.2 LOCATOR device prompts and echos

Prompt/echo types:
1: Implementation Standard
   Display the current STROKE using an implementation-defined technique; normally, hardware-provided facilities are used for this type; e.g., the display of position registers at some tablets and digitizers, or some of the prompt/echo types explained below.
2: Digits
   Display a digital representation of the current STROKE position within the echo area.
3: Marker
   Display a marker at each point of the current STROKE.
4: Line
   Display a line joining successive points of the current STROKE.
>4: Device-Dependent
   Prompting and echoing is STROKE device-dependent.
If the operator enters more points than the current input buffer size, the additional points are lost. It is anticipated that the operator would be informed of this situation.

It is anticipated that stroke data record entries for variables such as intervals in X, Y and time may be provided to constrain the number of points delivered.

Note:

For all prompt/echo types, the stroke data record may contain an initial buffer editing position, which may range from 1 to length of initial stroke plus 1.

Errors:

7	GKS not in proper state: GKS shall be in one of the states WSOP, WSAC or SGOP
20	Specified workstation identifier is invalid
25	Specified workstation is not open
38	Specified workstation is neither of category INPUT nor of category OUTIN
51	Rectangle definition is invalid
140	Specified input device is not present on workstation
141	Input device is not in REQUEST mode
144	Specified prompt and echo type is not supported on this workstation
145	Echo area is outside display space
146	Contents of input data record are invalid
152	Initial value is invalid

───────────────── *FORTRAN-Interface* ─────────────────

CALL GINSK (WKID,SKDNR,TNR,IN,IPX,IPY,PET,EX1,EX2,EY1,EY2,BUFLEN, IL,CA)

Parameters:

Input	WKID	workstation identifier		(1..n)	INTEGER
Input	SKDNR	stroke device number		(1..n)	INTEGER
Input	TNR	initial normalization transformation number		(0..n)	INTEGER
Input	IN	number of points in initial stroke		(1..n)	INTEGER
Input	IPX,IPY	initial stroke positions	WC		nxREAL
Input	PET	prompt/echo type		(1..n)	INTEGER
Input	EX1,EX2,EY1,EY2	echo area XMIN < XMAX,YMIN < YMAX			
			DC		4xREAL
Input	BUFLEN	buffer length for stroke		(1..n)	INTEGER
Input	IL,CA(IL)	data record			nxCHARACTERx80

───

INITIALISE VALUATOR	WSOP,WSAC,SGOP	L0b

Parameters:

Input	workstation identifier		N
Input	valuator device number		(1..n)	I
Input	initial value		R
Input	prompt/echo type		(1..n)	I
Input	echo area XMIN < XMAX,YMIN < YMAX	DC	4xR
Input	data record		D

Effect:

The initial value, prompt/echo type, echo area, and data record are stored in the workstation state list entry for the specified VALUATOR device.

For all VALUATOR prompt/echo types, the data record must include a low value and a high value, specifying the range. The values from the device will be scaled linearly to the specified range.

The data record may also contain a resolution value determining the desired precision of the valuator. The implementation of the device may support this technique; if it does not, the resolution value is ignored.

Prompt/echo types:

1: Implementation Standard

Designate the current VALUATOR value using an implementation defined'technique, e.g., use hardware-provided facilities like potentiometer devices, etc.

2: Dial

display a graphical representation of the current VALUATOR value within the echo area (for example, a dial or a pointer).

A lot of sophisticated techniques exist to adjust a desired value, both quickly and precisely. Most of them use different modes of operation allowing different speeds of value changes. The slowest mode can be used for precise adjustments.

Commonly used input devices are lightpen, control panels, function keyboards, potentiometers, track balls, etc.

3: Digits

Display a digital representation of the current VALUATOR value within the echo area.

This simple technique allows the use of alphanumeric keyboards additionally to the input devices supported by prompt/echo type 2.

>3: Device-Dependent

prompting and echoing is VALUATOR device-dependent.

Errors:

7	GKS not in proper state: GKS shall be in one of the states WSOP, WSAC or SGOP
20	Specified workstation identifier is invalid
25	Specified workstation is not open
38	Specified workstation is neither of category INPUT nor of category OUTIN
51	Rectangle definition is invalid

Errors:

140	Specified input device is not present on workstation
141	Input device is not in REQUEST mode
144	Specified prompt and echo type is not supported on this workstation
145	Echo area is outside display space
146	Contents of input data record are invalid
152	Initial value is invalid

———————————————— *FORTRAN-Interface* ————————————————

CALL GINVL (WKID,VLDNR,VAL,PET,EX1,EX2,EY1,EY2,LOVAL, HIVAL,IL,CA)

Parameters:

Input	WKID	workstation identifier	(1..n)	INTEGER
Input	VLDNR	valuator device number	(1..n)	INTEGER
Input	VAL	initial valuator value		REAL
Input	PET	prompt/echo type	(1..n)	INTEGER
Input	EX1,EX2,EY1,EY2			
		echo area XMIN < XMAX,YMIN < YMAX		
			DC	4xREAL
Input	LOVAL,HIVAL	low value, high value		2xREAL
Input	IL,CA(IL)	data record		nxCHARACTERx80

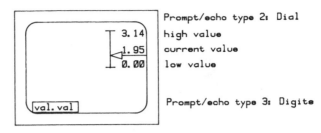

Figure 8.3 Valuator device prompts and echos

An application of the INITIALISE VALUATOR function is shown in Section 8.5 on page 298. Figure 8.3 demonstrates some prompt/echo types of the VALUATOR device.

INITIALISE CHOICE   WSOP,WSAC,SGOP   L0b

Parameters:

Input	workstation identifier		N
Input	choice device number	(1..n)	I
Input	initial choice number	(0..n)	I
Input	prompt/echo type	(1..n)	I
Input	echo area XMIN < XMAX,YMIN < YMAX	DC	4xR
Input	data record		D

Effect:

The initial choice number, prompt/echo type, echo area, and data record are stored in the workstation state list entry for the specified CHOICE device.

Prompt/echo types:

1: Implementation Standard

Designate the current CHOICE number using an implementation-defined technique.

2: Lamps

The physical input devices that are most commonly used to implement a CHOICE logical input device normally have a built-in prompting capability, e.g., lamps which can be switched on and off. This prompt/echo type allows the application program to invoke this prompting capability. If the value of the i-th element of 'prompt array' in the data record is OFF, prompting of the i-th alternative of the specified choice input device is turned off. An ON value indicates that prompting for that alternative is turned on.

This prompt/echo type may especially be used for skilled and frequent operators who do neither need nor want explicit dialogue guidance.

3: String Menu

Allow the operator to indicate a CHOICE number by selecting, using an appropriate technique, one of a set of CHOICE strings. The CHOICE strings are contained in the data record and are displayed within the echo area. The logical input value is the number of the string selected.

In that way, text strings may be displayed as screen command menus. Using a lightpen or a positioning device like track-ball or thumb wheels, the operator may identify the desired alternative. Example 8.4 demonstrates an application of this prompt/echo type.

4: String Commands

Allow the operator to indicate a CHOICE number by selecting, via an alphanumeric keyboard, one of a set of CHOICE strings. The CHOICE strings are contained in the data record and may be displayed in the echo area as a prompt. The string typed in by the operator is echoed in the echo area. The logical input value is the number of the string that has been typed in by the operator.

This prompt/echo type allows the proper use of alphanumeric keyboards, the largest used input device. The alternative commands may be displayed in the echo area, if the operator needs such help-facilities.

5: Symbol Menu

The segment named by the data record is interpreted during execution of INITIAL-ISE CHOICE for later use as a prompt of the specified CHOICE device. It will be displayed within the echo area by mapping the unit square [0,1]x[0,1] of NDC space onto the echo area. The pick identifiers in the segment are mapped to CHOICE numbers in a CHOICE device-dependent fashion. Picking these primitives selects the corresponding CHOICE value. After the interpretation, no logical connection between the specified segment and the specified CHOICE device exists.

This most powerful choice facility allows the graphical representation of menu alternatives which may be defined by the application program. Groups of graphical primitives contained in a segment and separated by primitive identifiers form the single alternatives.

>5: Device-Dependent

prompting and echoing is CHOICE device-dependent.

Errors:

7	GKS not in proper state: GKS shall be in one of the states WSOP, WSAC or SGOP
20	Specified workstation identifier is invalid
25	Specified workstation is not open
38	Specified workstation is neither of category INPUT nor of category OUTIN
51	Rectangle definition is invalid
140	Specified input device is not present on workstation
141	Input device is not in REQUEST mode
144	Specified prompt and echo type is not supported on this workstation
145	Echo area is outside display space
146	Contents of input data record are invalid
152	Initial value is invalid

———————————————— *FORTRAN-Interface* ————————————————

CALL GINCH (WKID,CHDNR,NR,PET,EX1,EX2,EY1,EY2,IL,CA)

Parameters:

Input	WKID	workstation identifier	(1..n)	INTEGER
Input	CHDNR	choice device number	(1..n)	INTEGER
Input	NR	initial choice number	(0..n)	INTEGER
Input	PET	prompt/echo type	(1..n)	INTEGER
Input	EX1,EX2,EY1,EY2			
		echo area XMIN<XMAX,YMIN<YMAX		
			DC	4xREAL
Input	IL,CA(IL)	data record		nxCHARACTERx80

An application of the INITIALISE CHOICE function is given in Section 8.5 on page 299. The following Figure 8.4 demonstrates some prompt/echo types of the CHOICE device.

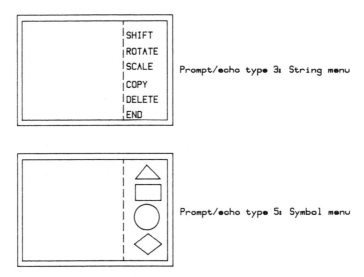

Figure 8.4 Choice device prompts and echos

INITIALISE PICK   WSOP,WSAC,SGOP   L1b

Parameters:

Input	workstation identifier		N
Input	pick device number	(1..n)	I
Input	initial status	(OK,NOPICK)	E
Input	initial segment		N
Input	initial pick identifier		N
Input	prompt/echo type	(1..n)	I
Input	echo area XMIN<XMAX,YMIN<YMAX	DC	4xR
Input	data record		D

Effect:

The prompt/echo type, echo area, initial status, initial segment, initial pick identifier and the data record are stored in the workstation state list entry for the specified PICK device.

Prompt/echo types:

Note that most prompt/echo types will echo the PICK device by a highlighting technique. The highlighting of a picked segment is performed as blinking of primitives, increasing their intensity, changing their colour, etc., for a short period of time.

Typical input devices suitable for PICK input are lightpen and positioning devices like the cursor of a digitizer or tablet, a mouse, a track-ball, thumb-wheels, or function-keyboards.

1: Implementation Standard

use an implementation-defined technique that at least highlights the "picked" primitive for a short period of time.

2: Pick Identifier Group

Echo the contiguous group of primitives with the same pick identifier as the "picked" primitive, or all primitives of the segment with the same pick identifier as the "picked" primitive.

3: Segment

Echo the whole segment containing the "picked" primitive.

> 3: Device-Dependent
     Prompting and echoing is PICK device-dependent
Errors:

7	GKS not in proper state: GKS shall be in one of the states WSOP, WSAC or SGOP
20	Specified workstation identifier is invalid
25	Specified workstation is not open
37	Specified workstation is not of category OUTIN
51	Rectangle definition is invalid
140	Specified input device is not present on workstation
141	Input device is not in REQUEST mode
144	Specified prompt and echo type is not supported on this workstation
145	Echo area is outside display space
146	Contents of input data record are invalid
152	Initial value is invalid

———————————— *FORTRAN-Interface* ————————————

CALL GINPK (WKID,PCDNR,STAT,SGNA,PCID,PET,EX1,EX2,EY1,EY2,IL,CA)
Parameters:

Input	WKID	workstation identifier	(1..n)	INTEGER
Input	PCDNR	pick device number	(1..n)	INTEGER
Input	STAT	initial status	(0 = ok,1 = nopick)	INTEGER
Input	SGNA	initial segment name	(1..n)	INTEGER
Input	PCID	initial pick identifier	(1..n)	INTEGER
Input	PET	prompt/echo type	(1..n)	INTEGER
Input	EX1,EX2,EY1,EY2			
		echo area XMIN<XMAX,YMIN<YMAX		
			DC	4xREAL
Input	IL,CA(IL)	data record		nxCHARACTERx80

—————————————————————————————————————

INITIALISE STRING   WSOP,WSAC,SGOP   L0b
Parameters:

Input	workstation identifier		N
Input	string device number	(1..n)	I
Input	initial string		S
Input	prompt/echo type	(1..n)	I
Input	echo area XMIN<XMAX,YMIN<YMAX	DC	4xR
Input	data record		D

Effect:
The initial string, prompt/echo type, echo area and data record are stored in the workstation state list entry for the specified STRING device.

For all prompt/echo types, the data record must contain an input buffer size, which is compared against an implementation-defined "maximum input buffer size for string devices" (contained in the workstation description table). If the requested buffer size is greater, the "maximum input buffer size for string devices" is substituted in the record. If the initial string is longer than the buffer size, an error is issued.

For all prompt/echo types, the data record must contain an initial cursor position, which may range from 1 to length of initial string plus 1.

When a STRING measure process comes into existence, it obtains a buffer of the current input buffer size. The initial string is copied into the buffer, and the cursor is placed at the initial cursor position within it. Replacement of characters begins at this cursor position.

Using the specific buttons, the cursor may be moved within the string without changing characters. Also, certain buttons may be used to "insert" a character (extending the string), or to "remove" a character (contracting the string).
Prompt/echo types:
1: Implementation Standard
   Display the current STRING value within the echo area.
> 1: Device-Dependent
   Prompting and echoing is STRING device-dependent
Note:
   if the operator enters more characters than the current input buffer size, the additional characters are lost.
Errors:

7	GKS not in proper state: GKS shall be in one of the states WSOP, WSAC or SGOP
20	Specified workstation identifier is invalid
25	Specified workstation is not open
38	Specified workstation is neither of category INPUT nor of category OUTIN
51	Rectangle definition is invalid
140	Specified input device is not present on workstation
141	Input device is not in REQUEST mode
144	Specified prompt and echo type is not supported on this workstation
145	Echo area is outside display space
146	Contents of input data record are invalid
152	Initial value is invalid

——————————————— *FORTRAN-Interface* ———————————————

CALL GINST (WKID,STDNR,STR,PET,EX1,EX2,EY1,EY2,BUFLEN,
INIPOS,IL,CA)
Parameters:

Input	WKID	workstation identifier	(1..n)	INTEGER
Input	STDNR	string device number	(1..n)	INTEGER
Input	STR	initial string		CHARACTER*(*)
Input	PET	prompt/echo type	(1..n)	INTEGER
Input	EX1,EX2,EY1,EY2			
		echo area XMIN < XMAX,YMIN < YMAX		
			DC	4xREAL
Input	BUFLEN			
		buffer length of string	(1..n)	INTEGER
Input	INIPOS	initial cursor position	(1.n)	INTEGER
Input	IL,CA(IL)	data record		nxCHARACTERx80

An application of the INITIALISE STRING function is shown in Section 8.5 on page 303.

8.4   Changing the Input Device Mode

All logical input devices of GKS can operate in each of the three modes, RE-QUEST, SAMPLE, and EVENT. Devices are initialised to REQUEST mode when the corresponding workstation is opened. SET <device class> MODE functions are provided to control the operating modes and the echo switch.

At any time, when the workstation is open, a device can be put into one of the three modes.

The effect of setting a device into REQUEST mode is to stop the current interaction with the specified device, if one is underway. This is always the case if the device is in SAMPLE or EVENT mode. Any possibly existing prompting or echoing output is deleted from the screen. The measure process is destroyed. The device's identifier is removed from its trigger's list of recipients. If the list becomes empty, the trigger process is destroyed.

A REQUEST function can only be issued if the logical input device it addresses is in REQUEST mode. The operating scheme and the effect of the REQUEST functions are described in Section 8.5.

If a device is put into SAMPLE or EVENT mode, the following actions are performed:

— The current interaction with the specified device is stopped (this is the case if the device is already in SAMPLE or EVENT mode).
— The measure process of the specified device is initiated; prompting and echoing if the echo switch is on, are started, using the initial values from the workstation state list.
— If the device is put into EVENT mode, its measure identification is added to its trigger's list of recipients.

SET LOCATOR MODE   WSOP,WSAC,SGOP   L0b

Parameters:

Input	workstation identifier		N
Input	locator device number	(1..n)	I
Input	operating mode	(REQUEST,SAMPLE,EVENT)	E
Input	echo switch	(ECHO,NOECHO)	E

Effect:

The given LOCATOR device is set to the specified operating mode and its echoing state is set to ECHO or NOECHO. Depending on the specified operating mode, an interaction with the given device may begin or end. The input device state defined by 'operating mode' and 'echo switch' is stored in the workstation state list for the given LOCATOR device.

Errors:

7	GKS not in proper state: GKS shall be in one of the states WSOP, WSAC or SGOP
20	Specified workstation identifier is invalid
25	Specified workstation is not open
38	Specified workstation is neither of category INPUT nor of category OUTIN
140	Specified input device is not present on workstation
143	EVENT/SAMPLE input mode is not available at this level of GKS

——————————— *FORTRAN-Interface* ———————————

CALL GSLCM (WKID,LCDNR,MODE,ESW)

Parameters:

Input	WKID	workstation identifier	(1..n)	INTEGER
Input	LCDNR	locator device number	(1..n)	INTEGER
Input	MODE	mode (0=REQUEST,1=SAMPLE,2=EVENT)		INTEGER
Input	ESW	echo switch	(0=OFF,1=ON)	INTEGER

SET STROKE MODE   WSOP,WSAC,SGOP   L0b

Parameters:

Input	workstation identifier		N
Input	stroke device number	(1..n)	I
Input	operating mode	(REQUEST,SAMPLE,EVENT)	E
Input	echo switch	(ECHO,NOECHO)	E

Effect:

The given STROKE device is set to the specified operating mode and its echoing state is set to ECHO or NOECHO. Depending on the specified operating mode, an interaction with the given device may begin or end. The input device state defined by 'operating mode' and 'echo switch' is stored in the workstation state list for the given STROKE device.

Errors:

7	GKS not in proper state: GKS shall be in one of the states WSOP, WSAC or SGOP
20	Specified workstation identifier is invalid
25	Specified workstation is not open
38	Specified workstation is neither of category INPUT nor of category OUTIN
140	Specified input device is not present on workstation
143	EVENT/SAMPLE input mode is not available at this level of GKS

———————————————— *FORTRAN-Interface* ————————————————

CALL GSSKM (WKID,SKDNR,MODE,ESW)

Parameters:

Input	WKID	workstation identifier	(1..n)	INTEGER
Input	SKDNR	stroke device number	(1..n)	INTEGER
Input	MODE	mode (0=REQUEST,1=SAMPLE,2=EVENT)		INTEGER
Input	ESW	echo switch	(0=OFF,1=ON)	INTEGER

SET VALUATOR MODE   WSOP,WSAC,SGOP   L0b

Parameters:

Input	workstation identifier		N
Input	valuator device number	(1..n)	I
Input	operating mode	(REQUEST,SAMPLE,EVENT)	E
Input	echo switch	(ECHO,NOECHO)	E

Effect:

The given VALUATOR device is set to the specified operating mode and its echoing state is set to ECHO or NOECHO. Depending on the specified operating mode, an interaction with the given device may begin or end. The input device state defined by "operating mode" and "echo switch" is stored in the workstation state list for the given VALUATOR device.

Errors:

7	GKS not in proper state: GKS shall be in one of the states WSOP, WSAC or SGOP
20	Specified workstation identifier is invalid
25	Specified workstation is not open
38	Specified workstation is neither of category INPUT nor of category OUTIN
140	Specified input device is not present on workstation
143	EVENT/SAMPLE input mode is not available at this level of GKS

――――――――――――― *FORTRAN-Interface* ―――――――――――――

CALL GSVLM (WKID,VLDNR,MODE,ESW)
Parameters:
Input	WKID	workstation identifier	(1..n)	INTEGER
Input	VLDNR	valuator device number	(1..n)	INTEGER
Input	MODE	mode (0=REQUEST,1=SAMPLE,2=EVENT)		INTEGER
Input	ESW	echo switch	(0=OFF,1=ON)	INTEGER

SET CHOICE MODE   WSOP,WSAC,SGOP   L0b
Parameters:
Input	workstation identifier		N
Input	choice device number	(1..n)	I
Input	operating mode	(REQUEST,SAMPLE,EVENT)	E
Input	echo switch	(ECHO,NOECHO)	E

Effect:
The given CHOICE device is set to the specified operating mode and its echoing state is set to ECHO or NOECHO. Depending on the specified operating mode, an interaction with the given device may begin or end. The input device state defined by "operating mode" and "echo switch" is stored in the workstation state list for the given CHOICE device.

Errors:
7	GKS not in proper state: GKS shall be in one of the states WSOP, WSAC or SGOP
20	Specified workstation identifier is invalid
25	Specified workstation is not open
38	Specified workstation is neither of category INPUT nor of category OUTIN
140	Specified input device is not present on workstation
143	EVENT/SAMPLE input mode is not available at this level of GKS

――――――――――――― *FORTRAN-Interface* ―――――――――――――

CALL GSCHM (WKID,CHDNR,MODE,ESW)
Parameters:
Input	WKID	workstation identifier	(1..n)	INTEGER
Input	CHDNR	choice device number	(1..n)	INTEGER
Input	MODE	mode (0=REQUEST,1=SAMPLE,2=EVENT)		INTEGER
Input	ESW	echo switch	(0=OFF,1=ON)	INTEGER

SET PICK MODE   WSOP,WSAC,SGOP   L0b
Parameters:
Input	workstation identifier		N
Input	pick device number	(1..n)	I
Input	operating mode	(REQUEST,SAMPLE,EVENT)	E
Input	echo switch	(ECHO,NOECHO)	E

Effect:
The given PICK device is set to the specified operating mode and its echoing state is set to ECHO or NOECHO. Depending on the specified operating mode, an interaction with the given device may begin or end. The input device state defined by "operating mode" and "echo switch" is stored in the workstation state list for the given PICK device.

Errors:

7	GKS not in proper state: GKS shall be in one of the states WSOP, WSAC or SGOP
20	Specified workstation identifier is invalid
25	Specified workstation is not open
37	Specified workstation is not of category OUTIN
140	Specified input device is not present on workstation
143	EVENT/SAMPLE input mode is not available at this level of GKS

———————————————— *FORTRAN-Interface* ————————————————

CALL GSPKM (WKID,PCDNR,MODE,ESW)

Parameters:

Input	WKID	workstation identifier	(1..n)	INTEGER
Input	PCDNR	pick device number	(1..n)	INTEGER
Input	MODE	mode (0 = REQUEST,1 = SAMPLE,2 = EVENT)		INTEGER
Input	ESW	echo switch	(0 = OFF,1 = ON)	INTEGER

SET STRING MODE   WSOP,WSAC,SGOP   L0b

Parameters:

Input	workstation identifier		N
Input	string device number	(1..n)	I
Input	operating mode	(REQUEST,SAMPLE,EVENT)	E
Input	echo switch	(ECHO,NOECHO)	E

Effect:

The given STRING device is set to the specified operating mode and its echoing state is set to ECHO or NOECHO. Depending on the specified operating mode, an interaction with the given device may begin or end. The input device state defined by "operating mode" and "echo switch" is stored in the workstation state list for the given STRING device.

Errors:

7	GKS not in proper state: GKS shall be in one of the states WSOP, WSAC or SGOP
20	Specified workstation identifier is invalid
25	Specified workstation is not open
38	Specified workstation is neither of category INPUT nor of category OUTIN
140	Specified input device is not present on workstation
143	EVENT/SAMPLE input mode is not available at this level of GKS

———————————————— *FORTRAN-Interface* ————————————————

CALL GSSTM (WKID,STDNR,MODE,ESW)

Parameters:

Input	WKID	workstation identifier	(1..n)	INTEGER
Input	STDNR	string device number	(1..n)	INTEGER
Input	MODE	mode (0 = REQUEST,1 = SAMPLE,2 = EVENT)		INTEGER
Input	ESW	echo switch	(0 = OFF,1 = ON)	INTEGER

8.5   Request Input

A specific invocation of a REQUEST function causes an attempt to read a logical input value from a specified logical input device which must be in RE-

QUEST mode. GKS waits until the input is entered by the operator or a break action is performed. If a break occurs, the logical input value is invalid.

In order to support a wide range of interactive graphics applications by simple input facilities, GKS defines three levels which contain the REQUEST input feature but not SAMPLE and EVENT input: L0b, L1b, and L2b. All REQUEST functions operate in a uniform scheme:

— After being invoked, a measure process is created for the specified device. Its value is set to the initial value from the workstation state list.
— The device's identifier is added to its trigger's list of recipients. If this list was previously empty, the trigger process is started.
— The operator is prompted for input, indicating both the logical value to be entered and the physical devices to be used; for example, a tracking cross is displayed at the initial LOCATOR position. Additionally, a message may be issued like "USE TABLET TO ENTER A POSITION", but normally the assignment of a specific LOCATOR device to the physical device(s) should be made known by accompanying system documentation.
— If the echo switch of the specified device is on, echoing is performed by the measure process starting with the initial values; in the above example, the appearing of the tracking cross represents prompting and initial echoing at the same time.
— GKS is suspended, while the operator adjusts a desired input value; the operator receives an immediate echo (if the echo switch is ON); e.g., the tracking cross moves according to the movement of a pen on the tablet.
— The operator terminates the adjusting loop by pressing a button (or more generally, by causing a trigger device to fire). This either indicates that the adjusted value should be entered into the system, or that a break should be caused without entering any value. He should receive an acknowledgement of his action, e.g., a short highlighting of the tracking cross symbol, to confirm the system's acceptance of the input value.
— The particular request function returns the value of the logical device or, in a separate STATUS parameter, the indication that the break facility was invoked. The measure process is destroyed. The device's identifier is removed from its trigger's list of recipients. If the list becomes empty, the trigger process is destroyed.

REQUEST LOCATOR   WSOP,WSAC,SGOP   L0b
Parameters:

Input	workstation identifier		N
Input	locator device number	(1..n)	I
Output	status	(OK,NONE)	E
Output	normalization transformation number	(0..n)	I
Output	locator position	WC	P

Effect:
GKS performs a REQUEST on the specified LOCATOR device. If the break facility is invoked by the operator the status will be returned NONE; otherwise, OK is returned together with the logical input value entered by the operator. This value consists of

a LOCATOR position in world coordinates and the normalization transformation number which was used in the conversion to world coordinates. The locator position is within the window of the normalization transformation.

Errors:

7	GKS not in proper state: GKS shall be in one of the states WSOP, WSAC or SGOP
20	Specified workstation identifier is invalid
25	Specified workstation is not open
38	Specified workstation is neither of category INPUT nor of category OUTIN
140	Specified input device is not present on workstation
141	Input device is not in REQUEST mode

———————————————————— *FORTRAN-Interface* ————————————————————

CALL GRQLC (WKID,LCDNR,STATUS,TNR,PX,PY)

Parameters:

Input	WKID	workstation identifier		(1..n)	INTEGER
Input	LCDNR	locator device number		(1..n)	INTEGER
Output	STATUS	status	(0=NONE,1=OK)		INTEGER
Output	TNR	normalization transformation nb		(0..n)	INTEGER
Output	PX,PY	LOCATOR position	WC		2xREAL

Example 8.2   Generating triangles using REQUEST and INITIALISE LO-CATOR

The following part of a program generates a triangle; its edge points are entered by an operator. Three positions are requested using the REQUEST LOCATOR function. The logical device with number 1 is used; it is connected to the work-station 'DISPLAY'. The workstation has to be previously opened. The coordinates are gathered and the POLYLINE function is invoked to display the triangle (see Figure 8.5).

———————————————————————— *Pascal* ————————————————————————

```
........
L10    FOR I:= 1 TO 3 DO
L20      REQUEST_LOCATOR (DISPLAY,LC1,STATUS,TNR,P[I]);
L30    END {end because of coming extensions} ;
L40    P[4] := P[1];
L50    POLYLINE (4,P[1:4]);
......
L999  999 END;
```

If the operator does not want to enter data when the REQUEST function is pending, he should invoke the "break facility". Normally, this is implemented by a special "break"-button. The REQUEST function then returns without a locator position, but the STATUS parameter is set to "NONE". Given this information, the application program may perform some exception handling,

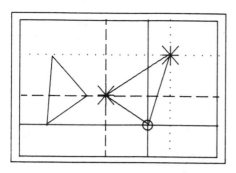

Figure 8.5
Generating triangles using crosshair echo

like terminating the loop of triangle generation and continuing with other program parts:

――――――――――――――― *Pascal* ―――――――――――――――

```
L25   IF STATUS = 'NONE' THEN BEGIN
L26      EXCEPTION_HANDLING;
L27      GOTO 999;
L28   END;
```

It might be possible that locator positions are returned in a different coordinate system than the one just active for output (see also Section 8.2.1). In order to apply the appropriate normalization transformation, the transformation TNR as delivered by the REQUEST function is selected as current one:

――――――――――――――― *Pascal* ―――――――――――――――

```
L35   IF TNR <> CURRENT_TNR THEN BEGIN
L36      SELECT_NORMALIZATION_TRANSFORMATION (TNR);
L37      CURRENT_TNR := TNR;
L38   END;
```

As a further extension, we want to provide different echos to give the operator convenient guidance. Often, it is meaningful to supply the last position entered by the operator (or a starting position before the first activation) as initial position for each new REQUEST invocation. The following four instructions realize the desired effect:

――――――――――――――― *Pascal* ―――――――――――――――

```
L5    P[0] := (0,0);                    { origin in the window of normalization }
                                        { transformation 0 }
L6    TNR := 0;
                      { current normalization transformation assumed to be 0 }
L7    CURRENT_TNR := 0;
L8    P_E_TYPE := 2;                     { use crosshair echo }
...
L15   INITIALISE_LOCATOR
         (DISPLAY,LC1,P[I-1],TNR,P_E_TYPE,ECHO_AREA,EMPTY);
```

―――――――――――――――――――――――――― *Fortran* ――――――――――――――――――――――――

```
.........
         C                          *** set origin in the window belonging to transformation 0
L5               PX(1) = 0.
L6               PY(1) = 0.
L7               TNR = 0
L8               CTNR = 0
L9               PET = 2
L10              DO 30 I = 2,4
L15              CALL GINLC (DISP,LC1,TNR,PX(I-1),PY(I-1),
                 PET,EX1,EX2,EY1,EY2,1,EMPTD)
L20              CALL GRQLC (DISP,LC1,STATUS,TNR,PX(I),PY(I))
L25              IF (STATUS .EQ. 0) GOTO 990
L30      30      CONTINUE
         C                          *** select normalization transformation tnr if not yet done
L35              IF (TNR.EQ.CTNR) GOTO 40
L36              CALL GSELNT (TNR)
L37              CTNR = TNR
         C                                                        *** complete triangle
L40      40      PX(5) = PX(2)
L45              PY(5) = PY(2)
         C                                                        *** draw triangle
L50              CALL GPL (4,PX(2),PY(2))
L60              GOTO 998
L990     990     CONTINUE
         C                                                        *** exception handling
........
L998     998     STOP
L999             END
```

The INITIALISE LOCATOR function is explained in detail in Section 8.3.1; here we want to describe two prompt/echo types briefly. Their appearance is shown in Figure 8.5.

Prompt/echo type 2: Crosshair

For the above example, a crosshair is displayed as prompting information at the initial position. A vertical and a horizontal line spanning over the screen intersect at this position. Both lines vary dynamically as the operator uses the input device, e.g., a tracking ball, a pair of thumb wheels, a pen on a tablet or digitizer, or a lightpen on a screen. They always intersect at the current LOCATOR position. This allows for construction of new triangles in dependence of the location of other already created triangles in orthogonal directions.

Prompt/echo type 4: Rubber Band

A rubber band line is displayed starting and being fixed at the initial position (in our example at the last entered position). As the operator uses the input device, it dynamically connects the current locator position with the initial position, thus demonstrating intersections with already generated triangles.

REQUEST STROKE   WSOP,WSAC,SGOP   L0b
Parameters:

Input	workstation identifier		N
Input	stroke device number	(1..n)	I
Output	status	(OK,NONE)	E
Output	normalization transformation number	(0..n)	I
Output	number of points	(0..n)	I
Output	points in stroke	WC	nxP

Effect:

GKS performs a REQUEST on the specified STROKE device. If the break facility is invoked by the operator, the status will be returned NONE; otherwise, OK is returned together with the logical input value which is the current measure of the STROKE device. This consists of a sequence of not more than 'input buffer size' (in the stroke data record) points in world coordinates, and the normalization transformation number used in the conversion to world coordinates. The points in the stroke all lie within the window of the normalization transformation.

Note:

If an operator enters more points than the stroke input buffer size (in the workstation state list) allows, the additional points are lost. It is anticipated that the operator would be informed of this situation.

Errors:

7	GKS not in proper state: GKS shall be in one of the states WSOP, WSAC or SGOP
20	Specified workstation identifier is invalid
25	Specified workstation is not open
38	Specified workstation is neither of category INPUT nor of category OUTIN
140	Specified input device is not present on workstation
141	Input device is not in REQUEST mode

———————————————— *FORTRAN-Interface* ——— ————————

CALL GRQSK (WKID,SKDNR,MNB,STATUS,TNR,NB,PX,PY)
Parameters:

Input	WKID	workstation identifier	(1..n)	INTEGER
Input	SKDNR	stroke device number	(1..n)	INTEGER
Input	MNB	maximum number of points	(1..n)	INTEGER
Output	STATUS	status	(0=NONE,1=OK)	INTEGER
Output	TNR	normalization transformation nb	(0..n)	INTEGER
Output	NB	number of points	(0..n)	INTEGER
Output	PX(MNB),PY(MNB)			
		STROKE positions	WC	nx2xREAL

REQUEST VALUATOR   WSOP,WSAC,SGOP   L0b
Parameters:

Input	workstation identifier		N
Input	valuator device number	(1..n)	I
Output	status	(OK,NONE)	E
Output	value		R

Effect:

GKS performs a REQUEST on the specified VALUATOR device. If the break facility is invoked by the operator, the status will be returned NONE; otherwise, OK is returned together with the logical input value entered by the operator. The value delivered is in the range specified in the workstation state list entry for this device. The application program may define the range using the INITIALISE VALUATOR function (see Section 8.3).

Errors:

7	GKS not in proper state: GKS shall be in one of the states WSOP, WSAC or SGOP
20	Specified workstation identifier is invalid
25	Specified workstation is not open
38	Specified workstation is neither of category INPUT nor of category OUTIN
140	Specified input device is not present on workstation
141	Input device is not in REQUEST mode

——————————————————— *FORTRAN-Interface* ———————————————————

CALL GRQVL (WKID,VLDNR,STATUS,VAL)

Parameters:

Input	WKID	workstation identifier	(1..n)	INTEGER
Input	VLDNR	valuator device number	(1..n)	INTEGER
Output	STATUS	status	(0 = NONE,1 = OK)	INTEGER
Output	VAL	value		REAL

Example 8.3   Adjusting picture size using REQUEST and INITIALISE VALUATOR

This part of a program interactively adjusts the size of a picture to be drawn. It prompts the operator to enter the desired x-scale by using the MESSAGE function, REQUESTS a real value from the operator and sets the workstation viewport to the size defined by the real value. Note, that in this first version of the example, the range of the real values is completely implementation-dependent.

——————————————————————— *Pascal* ———————————————————————

```
L10   MESSAGE (DISPLAY,'ENTER PICTURE SCALE IN X-DIRECTION');
L20   REQUEST_VALUATOR (DISPLAY,VL1,STATUS,VAL);
L30   SET_WORKSTATION_VIEWPORT (DISPLAY,0,VAL,0,VAL);
```

To prevent possible errors of too large or negative real values which might be entered, the range of the values should be defined. The data record of the INITIALISE VALUATOR function is assigned the range 0 as low value, and the maximum display surface size as high value; the latter may be inquired from the workstation description table. With that, a VALUATOR device prompting is displayed when the REQUEST function is invoked, indicating the range of possible values. An example is shown in the picture below.

─────────────────────────── Pascal ───────────────────────────

L5   MAXDISPLAYSIZEX := .... ;
L6   DATA := (0,MAXDISPLAYSIZEX);
L7   INITIALISE_VALUATOR
         (DISPLAY,VL1,MAXDISPLAYSIZEX,1,ECHO_AREA,DATA);

───

If the operator does not want to enter a precise value but wants to use a default adjustment instead, he may press the "break" button. The following statement ensures a correct program behaviour, in that case, adjusting the picture scale to the maximum size.

─────────────────────────── Pascal ───────────────────────────

L25   IF (STATUS = 'NONE') THEN VAL = MAXDISPLAYSIZEX;

─────────────────────────── Fortran ───────────────────────────

          C   *** set maximum display size and data record
L5   MAXDX = ...
L9   CALL GINVL (DISP,VL1,MAXDX,1,EX1,EX2,EY1,EY2,0.,
              MAXDX,1,EMPTD)
          C   *** prompt operator for input, request value
L10   CALL GMSG (DISP,34HENTER PICTURE SCALE IN X-DIREC-
              TION)
L20   CALL GRQVL (DISP,VL1,STATUS,VAL)
          C   *** if break occurs, set maximum length
L25   IF (STATUS .EQ. 0) VAL = MAXDX
          C   *** set workstation viewport
L30   CALL GSWKVP (DISP,0.0,VAL,0.0,VAL)
....

───

REQUEST CHOICE   WSOP,WSAC,SGOP   L0b
Parameters:

Input	workstation identifier		N
Input	choice device number	(1..n)	I
Output	status	(OK,NONE)	E
Output	choice number	(0..n)	I

Effect:
GKS performs a REQUEST on the specified CHOICE device. If the break facility is invoked by the operator, the status will be returned NONE; otherwise, OK is returned together with the logical input value which is the current measure of the CHOICE device . The choice number zero means 'no choice'.

Errors:

7	GKS not in proper state: GKS shall be in one of the states WSOP, WSAC or SGOP
20	Specified workstation identifier is invalid
25	Specified workstation is not open
38	Specified workstation is neither of category INPUT nor of category OUTIN

140   Specified input device is not present on workstation
141   Input device is not in REQUEST mode

————————————————— *FORTRAN-Interface* —————————————————

CALL GRQCH (WKID,CHDNR,STATUS,CHNR)
Parameters:

Input	WKID	workstation identifier	(1..n)	INTEGER
Input	CHDNR	choice device number	(1..n)	INTEGER
Output	STATUS	status	(0 = NONE,1 = OK)	INTEGER
Output	CHNR	choice number	(0..n)	INTEGER

Example 8.4 Command control using REQUEST and INITIALISE CHOICE

This program part demonstrates command control in an interactive system. The alternative commands of a menu are assigned to a data record. The logical CHOICE device is initialised to display the single commands as identifiable distinct buttons within the echo area defined by the area limits EX1 to EX2 and EY1 to EY2. The echo area coordinates must be specified in device coordinates.

————————————————————— *Pascal* —————————————————————

```
L5    ECHO_AREA := {right part of a rectangular screen};
L10   DATA := 'GENERATE,TRANSFORM,COPY,DELETE';
L20   INITIALISE_CHOICE (DISPLAY,CH1,1,3,ECHOAREA,DATA);
                                                    {string menu echo}
L30   REPEAT
L40   REQUEST_CHOICE (DISPLAY,CH1,STATUS,NB);
L50   IF (STATUS = 'OK') THEN BEGIN
L60     CASE NB OF
L70       1: PROCEDURE_GENERATE_OBJECTS;      {extension of example 8.5.1}
L80       2: PROCEDURE_TRANSFORM_OBJECTS;
L100      3: PROCEDURE_COPY_OBJECTS;
L110      4: PROCEDURE_DELETE;                {see Example 8.5.4}
L120:   END;
L130  END;
L140  UNTIL (STATUS = 'NONE');
```

————————————————————— *Fortran* —————————————————————

```
      C                        *** assign right part of a rectangular screen as echo area
L5          EX1 = ...
L6          EX2 = ...
L7          EY1 = ...
L8          EY2 = ...
      C                        *** define menu string in data record
L10         CALL GPREC (1,EMPTI,1,EMPTR,30,30HGENERATE,
            TRANSFORM,COPY,DELETE,MDL,IL,CA)
L11   1     FORM,COPY,DELETE,MDL,IL,IA)
```

L20	20	CALL GINCH (DISP,CH1,1,3,EX1,EX2,EY1,EY2,IL,CA)
L30		CALL GRQCH (DISP,CH1,STATUS,NB)
L40		IF (STATUS .EQ. 0) GOTO 130
L60		GOTO (70,80,100,110),NB
L70	70	CALL {PROCEDURE_GENERATE_OBJECTS} (extension of example 8.2)
L75		GOTO 20
L80	80	CALL {PROCEDURE_TRANSFORM_OBJECTS}
L90		GOTO 20
L100	100	CALL {PROCEDURE_COPY_OBJECTS}
L105		GOTO 20
L110	110	CALL {PROCEDURE_DELETE_OBJECTS} (see Example 8.5)
L120		GOTO 20
L130	130	CONTINUE

......

REQUEST PICK   WSOP,WSAC,SGOP   L1b

Parameters:

Input	workstation identifier		N
Input	pick device number	(1..n)	I
Output	status	(OK,NONE,NOPICK)	E
Output	segment name		N
Output	pick identifier		N

Effect:
GKS performs a REQUEST on the specified PICK device. If the break facility is invoked by the operator, the status will be returned NONE; if the measure of the PICK device indicates no pick, status will be returned NOPICK; otherwise, OK is returned together with a segment name and a pick identifier which are set according to the current measure of the PICK device. The pick identifier is associated with the primitive within the segment that was picked.

Errors:

7	GKS not in proper state: GKS shall be in one of the states WSOP, WSAC or SGOP
20	Specified workstation identifier is invalid
25	Specified workstation is not open
37	Specified workstation is not of category OUTIN
140	Specified input device is not present on workstation
141	Input device is not in REQUEST mode

——————————————————— *FORTRAN-Interface* ———————————————————

CALL GRQPK (WKID,PCDNR,STATUS,SGNA,PCID)

Parameters:

Input	WKID	workstation identifier	(1..n)	INTEGER
Input	PCDNR	pick device number	(1..n)	INTEGER
Output	STATUS	status	(0=NONE,1=OK)	INTEGER
Output	SGNA	segment name		INTEGER
Output	PCID	pick identifier		INTEGER

Example 8.5   Segment deletion using the REQUEST PICK function

The following program realizes the deletion of a set of segments. It is aimed at applications which, on the average, delete several segments in a sequence without forcing the operator to enter the "deletion" command each time anew. Furthermore, it provides user-control over erroneously picked segments: if the operator recognizes that the segment just picked must not be deleted, he may identify it a second time. The operator is given feedback by highlighting the currently picked segment. The operator terminates the loop using the "break" facility.

```
———————————————————————————— Pascal ————————————————————————————
L10   REQUEST_PICK (DISPLAY,PC1,STATUS,SEGMENT,PICKID);
L20   SET_HIGHLIGHTING (SEGMENT,ON);              {highlight picked segment}
L30   NEWSEGMENT := EMPTYNAME;                       {initialise newsegment}
L40   REPEAT
L50     REQUEST_PICK (DISPLAY,PC1,STATUS,NEWSEGMENT,PICKID);
L60     IF STATUS = OK THEN BEGIN
L70       SET_HIGHLIGHTING (NEWSEGMENT,ON);
          (* highlight picked segment *)
                            {if the same segment is picked twice, it is not deleted }
L80       IF SEGMENT = NEWSEGMENT THEN SET_HIGHLIGHTING
          (SEGMENT,OFF)
L90       ELSE BEGIN
L100        DELETE_SEGMENT (SEGMENT);
L110        SEGMENT := NEWSEGMENT;
L120      END; (* end else *)
L130    END; (* end "status = ok" *)
L140  UNTIL STATUS = NONE;
                         { after the loop is terminated the segment has to be deleted }
                              { which was picked at last (if it was not picked twice) }
L150  IF SEGMENT < > NEWSEGMENT THEN
      DELETE_SEGMENT (SEGMENT);
```

```
———————————————————————— Fortran  ————————————————————————
      C                         *** request first pick (segment) and highlight it
L10           CALL GRQPK (DISP,PC1,STATUS,SEGM,PCID)
L20           CALL GSHLIT (SEGM,1)
      C                                               *** initialise newsegment
L30           NSEGM = 0
      C                      *** start loop of segment picking and delayed deletion
L40       40  CALL GRQPK (DISP,PC1,STATUS,NSEGM,PCID)
      C                                      *** terminate loop if break occurs
L50           IF (STATUS .EQ. 0) GOTO 140
      C                                          *** highlight picked segment
L60           CALL GSHLIT (NSEGM,1)
      C                    **** if the same segment is picked twice, it is not deleted
L70           IF (SEGM .NE. NSEGM) GOTO 100
L80           CALL GSHLIT (SEGM,0)
L90           GOTO 120
L100     100  CALL GDSG (SEGM)
```

L110		SEGM = NSEGM
L120	120	CONTINUE
L130		GOTO 40
L140	140	CONTINUE
	C	*** after the loop is terminated the segment has to be deleted
	C	*** which was picked at last (if it was not picked twice)
L150		IF (SEGM .NE. NSEGM) CALL GDSG (SEGM)

REQUEST STRING   WSOP,WSAC,SGOP   L0b

Parameters:

Input	workstation identifier		N
Input	string device number	₍ (1..n)	I
Output	status	(OK,NONE)	E
Output	character string		S

Effect:

GKS performs a REQUEST on the specified STRING device. If the break facility is invoked by the operator, the status will be returned NONE; otherwise, OK is returned together with the logical input value which is the current measure of the STRING device.

Note:

The length of the returned string is less than or equal to the buffer size specified in the workstation state list entry (for this device) in the data record.

Errors:

7	GKS not in proper state: GKS shall be in one of the states WSOP, WSAC or SGOP
20	Specified workstation identifier is invalid
25	Specified workstation is not open
38	Specified workstation is neither of category INPUT nor of category OUTIN
140	Specified input device is not present on workstation
141	Input device is not in REQUEST mode

———————————————— *FORTRAN-Interface* ————————————————

CALL GRQST (WKID,STDNR,STATUS,L,STR)

Parameters:

Input	WKID	workstation identifier	(1..n)	INTEGER
Input	STDNR	string device number	(1..n)	INTEGER
Output	STATUS	status	(0=NONE,1=OK)	INTEGER
Output	L	length of string	(in character)	INTEGER
Output	STR	character string		CHARACTER*(*)

Example 8.6   Form editing using REQUEST and INITIALISE STRING

This program is used to fill in forms starting with given default text strings for the single form fields. The reference text is read in from an external file.

The text string is used as initial string for the STRING device and the field position serves for calculating a text box which defines the string echo area. Character replacement starts at the end of the actual string and may extend it up to the maximum permissible length. Of course, the operator may reset the cursor position to the previous characters, or depending on the application, the initial cursor position may be set to 1:

L30   D = (MAXSTLENGTH,1);

After the string is edited and reentered, it is stored in a second external form file.

──────────────────── *Pascal* ────────────────────

```
L10    REPEAT
L20      READ (POSITION,MAX_ST_LENGTH,ACT_ST_LENGTH,STRING);
L30      D := (MAX_ST_LENGTH, ACT_ST_LENGTH + 1);
L35      WITH ECHOAREA DO BEGIN
L40        EX1 := POSITION.X;
L50        EY1 := POSITION.Y;
L60        EX2 := EX1 + MAX_ST_LENGTH * CHARACTERWIDTH;
L70        EY2 := EY1 + CHARACTERHEIGHT;
L75      END;
L80      INITIALISE_STRING (DISPLAY,ST1,STRING,1,ECHOAREA,D);
L90      REQUEST_STRING (DISPLAY,ST1,STATUS,STRING);
L100     ACT_ST_LENGTH := LENGTH (STRING);
L110     WRITE (POSITION,MAX_ST_LENGTH,ACT_ST_LENGTH,STRING);
L120   UNTIL (end of file);
```

──────────────────── *Fortran* ────────────────────

```
      C                *** start loop of reading the given text with starting position,
      C                              *** maximum length, and actual length
L10    10   READ(INFIL,121,EOF=990) PX,PY,MAXLST,ACTLST,(STR(I),I=
                1,ACTLST)
L30         EX1 = PX
L40         EY1 = PY
L50         EX2 = EX1 + MAXSTL * CHARWI
L60         EY2 = EY1 + CHARHE
L70         CALL GINST (DISP,ST1,STR,1,EX1,EX2,EY1,EY2,MAXLST,
                ACTLST + 1,1,EMPTD)
L80         CALL GRQST (DISP,ST1,STATUS,ACTLST,STR)
L90         WRITE (OUTFIL,122)
                PX,PY,MAXLST,ACTLST,(STR(I),I= + 1,ACTLST)
L100        GOTO 10
L121  121   FORMAT (2F8.3,2I3,80A1)
L122  122   FORMAT (1H ,2F8.3,2I3,80A1)
.....
L990  990   STOP
L999        END
```

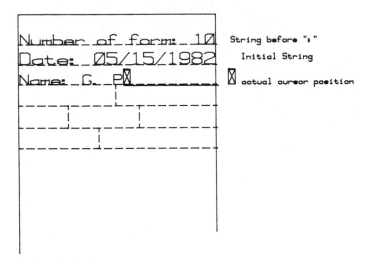

Figure 8.6 Form editing

8.6   Sample Input Functions

Activations of SAMPLE input functions cause GKS to return the current logical input value of a specified logical input device without waiting for an operator action. The logical input device must be in SAMPLE mode.

Typical applications of SAMPLE input can be characterized as to directly couple program operations to certain input device states which can be adjusted dynamically by an operator; in contrast to REQUEST and EVENT input, not the operator but the program performance determines the significant moments in time when input data is transferred to the application.

SAMPLE input may, for example, be used to perform dynamic picture changes via segment transformations, to apply zooming and windowing of complete pictures on workstations, to change attribute table entries; and also to control other, non-graphic parts of application programs.

The following parts of this chapter describe the SAMPLE input functions and demonstrate SAMPLE input applications.

SAMPLE LOCATOR		WSOP,WSAC,SGOP	L0c
Parameters:			
Input	workstation identifier		N
Input	locator device number	(1..n)	I
Output	normalization transformation number	(0..n)	I
Output	locator position	WC	P

Effect:
    The logical input value, which is the current measure of the specified LOCATOR device, is returned. The measure consists of a LOCATOR position in world coordinates and the normalization transformation number, which was used in the conversion to

world coordinates. The LOCATOR position is within the window of the normalization transformation.

Errors:

7	GKS not in proper state: GKS shall be in one of the states WSOP, WSAC or SGOP
20	Specified workstation identifier is invalid
25	Specified workstation is not open
38	Specified workstation is neither of category INPUT nor of category OUTIN
140	Specified input device is not present on workstation
142	Input device is not in SAMPLE mode

——————————————— *FORTRAN-Interface* ———————————————

CALL GSMLC (WKID,LCDNR,TNR,PX,PY)

Parameters:

Input	WKID	workstation identifier		(1..n)	INTEGER
Input	LCDNR	locator device number		(1..n)	INTEGER
Output	TNR	normalization transformation nb		(0..n)	INTEGER
Output	PX,PY	LOCATOR position	WC		2xREAL

Example 8.7   Moving objects using the SAMPLE LOCATOR function

This part of a program moves an object (a group of segments) depending on the actual state of a LOCATOR device. We assume, that the group of segments is determined by other program parts, e.g., as in Example 8.5.

Transformations are performed on NDC level, i.e., in the unit square [0,1]x[0,1]. To ensure the LOCATOR device delivers NDC coordinates, transformation number zero (the unity transformation) is given highest priority.

This program is incomplete in that it never stops. For proper control, Example 8.5 may be taken.

——————————————————————— *Pascal* ———————————————————————

```
......
                        {get list of normalization transform. nbs. The first one has}
                        {highest priority. Give transformation zero highest priority}
L10   INQUIRE_LIST_OF_NORMALIZATION_TRANSFORMATION_NUMBERS
      (ERROR,LENGTH, TRANSFORMATION_NUMBERS);
L20   SET_VIEWPORT_INPUT_PRIORITY
      (0,TRANSFORMATION_NUMBERS[1],HIGHER);
                        {select transformation 0, set initial transformation matrix}
L30   SELECT_NORMALIZATION_TRANSFORMATION (0);
L40   EVALUATE_TRANSFORMATION_MATRIX ((0,0),(0,0),0,(1,1),NDC,M);
                        {enable LOCATOR and get reference point for relative shifts}
L50   SET_LOCATOR_MODE (DISPLAY,LC1,SAMPLE,ECHO);
L60   SAMPLE_LOCATOR (DISPLAY,LC1,STATUS,TNR,P);
                        {loop of transformations}
L70   REPEAT
L80      SAMPLE_LOCATOR (DISPLAY,LC1,STATUS,TNR,Q);
L90      ACCUMULATE_TRANSFORMATION_MATRIX
         (M,(0,0),Q-P,0,(1,1),NDC,M);
```

```
L100    P := Q;
L110    FOR I := 1 TO NUMB_SEG DO
L120       SET_SEGMENT_TRANSFORMATION (SEGMENTS[I] ,M);
L130    UNTIL (STOP);
.....
```

──────────────────────────── *Fortran* ────────────────────────────

```
.........
       C                        *** get normalization transformation nb one; this has
       C                        *** highest priority. Give transformation zero highest priority
L10             CALL GQENTN (1,ERRIND,ACTL,TNRL)
L20             CALL GSVPIP (0,TNRL,GHIGHR)
       C                        *** select transformation 0, set initial transformation matrix
L30             CALL GSELNT (0)
L40             CALL GEVTM (0.0,0.0,0.0,0.0,0.0,1.0,1.0,NDC,M)
       C                        *** enable LOCATOR and get reference point for relative shifts
L50             CALL GSLCM (DISP,LC1,GSAMPL,GECHO)
L60             CALL GSMLC (DISP,LC1,TNR,PX,PY)
       C                        *** loop of transformations
L70       70    CONTINUE
L80             CALL GSMLC (DISP,LC1,TNR,QX,QY)
L90             CALL GACTM (M,0.0,0.0,PX-QX,PY-QY,0.0,1.0,1.0,NDC,M)
L100            PX = QX
L105            PY = QY
       C                        *** transform group of segments (stored in segl(1..nbseg)
L110            DO 120 I=1,NBSEG
L120      120   CALL GSSGT (SEGL(I),M)
L130            IF (.NOT. STOP) GOTO 70
...
L990      990   CONTINUE
L998            STOP
```

───

SAMPLE STROKE   WSOP,WSAC,SGOP   L0c

Parameters:

Input	workstation identifier		N
Input	stroke device number	(1..n)	I
Output	normalization transformation number	(0..n)	I
Output	number of points	(0..n)	I
Output	points in stroke	WC	nxP

Effect:

The logical input value, which is the current measure of the specified STROKE device, is returned. The measure consists of a sequence of points in world coordinates and the normalization transformation number used in the conversion to world coordinates. The points in the stroke all lie within the window of the normalization transformation.

Note:

If an operator enters more points than the stroke input buffer size (in the workstation state list) allows, the additional points are lost. It is anticipated that the operator would be informed of this situation.

Errors:

7	GKS not in proper state: GKS shall be in one of the states WSOP, WSAC or SGOP
20	Specified workstation identifier is invalid
25	Specified workstation is not open
38	Specified workstation is neither of category INPUT nor of category OUTIN
140	Specified input device is not present on workstation
142	Input device is not in SAMPLE mode

———————————————— *FORTRAN-Interface* ————————————————

CALL GSMSK (WKID,SKDNR,MNB,TNR,NB,PX,PY)

Parameters·

Input	WKID	workstation identifier	(1..n)	INTEGER
Input	SKDNR	stroke device number	(1..n)	INTEGER
Input	MNB	maximum number of points	(1..n)	INTEGER
Output	TNR	normalization transformation nb	(0..n)	INTEGER
Output	NB	number of points in stroke	(0..n)	INTEGER
Output	PX(MNB),PY(MNB)			
		STROKE positions	WC	nx2xREAL

SAMPLE VALUATOR		WSOP,WSAC,SGOP	L0c

Parameters:

Input	workstation identifier		N
Input	valuator device number	(1..n)	I
Output	value		R

Effect:

The logical input value, which is the current measure of the specified VALUATOR device, is returned. The value delivered is in the range specified in the workstation state list entry (for this device) in the data record.

Errors:

7	GKS not in proper state: GKS shall be in one of the states WSOP, WSAC or SGOP
20	Specified workstation identifier is invalid
25	Specified workstation is not open
38	Specified workstation is neither of category INPUT nor of category OUTIN
140	Specified input device is not present on workstation
142	Input device is not in SAMPLE mode

———————————————— *FORTRAN-Interface* ————————————————

CALL GSMVL (WKID,VLDNR,VAL)

Parameters:

Input	WKID	workstation identifier	(1..n)	INTEGER
Input	VLDNR	valuator device number	(1..n)	INTEGER
Output	VAL	value		REAL

Example 8.8   Rotation of objects using the SAMPLE VALUATOR function

This part of a program rotates an object (a group of segments) dynamically, depending on the actual state of a VALUATOR device. Rotation is relative to a fixed point. Transformation takes place in NDC space.

We assume, that the group of segments is determined by other program parts, e.g., as in Example 8.5.

―――――――――――――――――――――――― *Pascal* ――――――――――――――――――――――――

```
......
                                {set fixed point and initial segment transformation matrix}
L10    FIXP := (.5,.5);
L20    EVALUATE_TRANSFORMATION_MATRIX (FIXP,(0,0),0,(1,1),NDC,M);
                        {initialise valuator to range [-1 : +1], initial value 0}
L30    DATARECORD := (-1,+1);
l40    INITIALISE_VALUATOR
          (DISPLAY,VL1,0,1,ECHO_AREA,DATARECORD);
                        {put VALUATOR into SAMPLE mode, switch echo off}
L50    SET_VALUATOR_MODE (DISPLAY,VL1,SAMPLE,NOECHO);
                                                           {loop of rotation}
L60    REPEAT
L70      SAMPLE_VALUATOR (DISPLAY,VL1,VAL);
L80      ACCUMULATE_TRANSFORMATION_MATRIX
            (M,FIXP,(0,0),VAL,(1,1),M);
                                        {transform group of segments}
L90      FOR I := 1 TO NUMB_SEG DO
L100       SET_SEGMENT_TRANSFORMATION (SEGMENTS[I],M);
L110     UNTIL (STOP);
.....
```

―――――――――――――――――――――――― *Fortran* ――――――――――――――――――――――――

```
.........
       C                    *** set fixed point and initial segment transformation matrix
L10           FX = 0.5
L15           FY = 0.5
L20           CALL GEVTM (FX,FY,0.0,0.0,0.0,1.0,1.0,NDC,M)
       C                    *** initialise valuator to range [-1 : +1], initial value 0 *)
L40           CALL GINVL (DISP,VL1,0.0,1,EX1,EX2,EY1,EY2,-1.,1.,1,EMPTD)
       C                    *** put VALUATOR into SAMPLE mode, switch echo off *)
L50           CALL GSVLM (DISP,VL1,GSAMPL,GNECHO)
       C                                              *** loop of rotation
L60      10   CONTINUE
L70           CALL GSMVL (DISP,VL1,VAL)
L80           CALL GACTM (M,FX,FY,0.0,0.0,VAL,1.0,1.0,NDC,M)
       C                    *** transform group of segments (stored in segl(1..nbseg)
L90           DO 100 I=1,NBSEG
L100     100  CALL GSSGT (SEGL(I),M)
L110          IF (.NOT. STOP) GOTO 10
...
L990     990  CONTINUE
L998          STOP
```

―――

SAMPLE CHOICE   WSOP,WSAC,SGOP   L0c

Parameters:

Input	workstation identifier		N
Input	choice device number	(1..n)	I
Output	choice number	(0..n)	I

Effect:

The logical input value, which is the current measure of the specified CHOICE device, is returned. The choice number zero means "no choice".

Errors:

7	GKS not in proper state: GKS shall be in one of the states WSOP, WSAC or SGOP
20	Specified workstation identifier is invalid
25	Specified workstation is not open
38	Specified workstation is neither of category INPUT nor of category OUTIN
140	Specified input device is not present on workstation
142	Input device is not in SAMPLE mode

———————————————— *FORTRAN-Interface* ————————————————

CALL GSMCH (WKID,CHDNR,CHNR)

Parameters:

Input	WKID	workstation identifier	(1..n)	INTEGER
Input	CHDNR	choice device number	(1..n)	INTEGER
Output	CHNR	choice number	(0..n)	INTEGER

Example 8.9   Scaling objects using the SAMPLE CHOICE function

The following program part demonstrates a SAMPLE CHOICE application. As long as specific buttons are depressed, the application program performs certain actions dependent on the actual CHOICE number. In this case, an object is dynamically reduced (respectively expanded) in size, depending on the depressing of button 1 or button 2.

A CHOICE device is put into SAMPLE mode. In SAMPLE mode, the state of the CHOICE device always indicates whether buttons are actually depressed (then the CHOICE number is greater than 0), and which button (or combination of buttons) is actually depressed.

A typical implementation might use a function keyboard with at least two buttons. These are mapped to the CHOICE numbers 0 to 3.

The operator interface looks like the following:
— no buttons are pressed: CHOICE number = 0; nothing happens;
— button 1 is pressed: CHOICE number = 1; reduce object in size dynamically;
— button 2 is pressed: CHOICE number = 2; expand object dynamically;
— both buttons are pressed: CHOICE number = 3; stop program.

———————————————— *Pascal* ————————————————

......

```
                                              {select transformation 0 }
L10    SELECT_NORMALIZATION_TRANSFORMATION (0);
                        {set fixed point and initial segment transformation matrix}
L20    FIXP := (.5,.5);
L30    EVALUATE_TRANSFORMATION_MATRIX (FIXP,(0,0),0,(1,1),NDC,M);
                        {put CHOICE into SAMPLE mode; no echo, since direct feedback}
L40    SET_CHOICE_MODE (DISPLAY,CH1,SAMPLE,NOECHO);
                                              {loop of transformations}
```

```
L50    REPEAT
L60       SAMPLE_CHOICE (DISPLAY,CH1,CHNB);
L70       CASE CHNB OF
L80       0: GOTO 170;
L90       1: {reduce object in size};
L100         ACCUMULATE_TRANSFORMATION_MATRIX
                (M,FIXP,(0,0),0,(1-DELTA_X,1-DELTA_Y),M);
L110      2: {expand object};
L120         ACCUMULATE_TRANSFORMATION_MATRIX
                (M,FIXP,(0,0),VAL,(1+DELTA_X,1+DELTA_Y),M);
L130      3: GOTO 170;
L140      END {end case};
L150      FOR I := 1 TO NUMB_SEG DO
L160         SET_SEGMENT_TRANSFORMATION (SEGMENTS[I],M);
L170      170 UNTIL (CHNB = 3);
.....
```

───────────────────────────── *Fortran* ─────────────────────────────

```
.........
       C                                              *** select transformation 0
L10           CALL GSELNT (0)
       C                 *** set fixed point and initial segment transformation matrix
L20           FX = 0.5
L25           FY = 0.5
L30           CALL GEVTM (FX,FY,0.0,0.0,0.0,1.0,1.0,NDC,M)
       C                       *** put CHOICE into SAMPLE mode, no echo needed
L40           CALL GSCHM (DISP,CH1,GSAMPL,GNECHO)
       C                                              *** loop of transformations
L50      50   CONTINUE
L60           CALL GSMCH (DISP,CH1,CHNB)
L65           CHNB = CHNB + 1
L70           GOTO (170,90,110,170), CHNB
L90      90   CONTINUE
       C                                              *** reduce object in size
L100          CALL GACTM (M,FX,FY,0.0,0.0,0.0,1.0-DX,1.0-DY,M)
L105          GOTO 150
L110     110  CONTINUE
       C                                              *** expand object
L120          CALL GACTM (M,FX,FY,0.0,0.0,0.0,1.0+DX,1.0+DY,M)
       C                   *** transform group of segments (stored in segl(1..nbseg)
L150     150  DO 160 I = 1,NBSEG
L160     160  CALL GSSGT (SEGL(I),M)
L170     170  IF (CHNB .NE. 3) GOTO 50
...
L990     990  CONTINUE
L998          STOP
```

──

SAMPLE PICK		WSOP,WSAC,SGOP L1c

Parameters:

Input	workstation identifier		N
Input	pick device number	(1..n)	I

Output	status	(OK,NOPICK)	E
Output	segment name		N
Output	pick identifier		N

Effect:

If the current measure of the specified PICK device is indicating no pick, status will be returned NOPICK; otherwise, OK will be returned together with the segment name and the pick identifier associated with the primitive, within the segment, that was picked.

Errors:

7	GKS not in proper state: GKS shall be in one of the states WSOP, WSAC or SGOP
20	Specified workstation identifier is invalid
25	Specified workstation is not open
37	Specified workstation is not of category OUTIN
140	Specified input device is not present on workstation
142	Input device is not in SAMPLE mode

———————————————— *FORTRAN-Interface* ————————————————

CALL GSMPK (WKID,PCDNR,STAT,SGNA,PCID)

Parameters:

Input	WKID	workstation identifier	(1..n)	INTEGER
Input	PCDNR	pick device number	(1..n)	INTEGER
Output	STAT	status	(0 = NOPICK,1 = OK)	INTEGER
Output	SGNA	segment name		INTEGER
Output	PCID	pick identifier		INTEGER

Example 8.10   Identifying segments via the SAMPLE PICK function

A PICK input device is put into SAMPLE mode. Then, moving a suitable physical device (e.g. a lightpen) over the screen, the PICK device state is changed. The logical PICK device always contains the segment name and pick identifier belonging to the primitive which the physical input device currently indicates.

Certain physical devices may only change the PICK device state when an internal trigger is set. In such implementations, a ligthpen switch, for example, is considered as an internal trigger; it is used to change the logical PICK device measure in SAMPLE mode.

This example demonstrates the following application:

— the operator identifies primitives on the screen by moving a suitable input device, e.g., a lightpen or a cursor, over the display;

— the state of the logical PICK device changes, always indicating the segment name and the pick identifier to which the currently identified primitive belongs. The segment may be echoed, e.g., highlighted, as long as the input device points at one of its primitives;

— the application program reads the current PICK device state via the SAMPLE PICK function;

— the application program checks, whether the delivered segment fulfills certain application-specific rules (e.g., belongs to a specific object), and, if it does,

feedback is generated (e.g., the segment is permanently highlighted), the segment name is put into a segment list for further use, and it is set to "non-detectable" in order to not detect it a second time;
— the loop is terminated when the specified CHOICE device (which is also in SAMPLE mode) changes its value from zero to one.

────────────────────────── *Pascal* ──────────────────────────

```
......
L10   SET_PICK_MODE (DISPLAY,PC1,SAMPLE,ECHO);
L20   SET_CHOICE_MODE (DISPLAY,CH1,SAMPLE,ECHO);
L30   INDEX := 1;
L40   REPEAT
L50     SAMPLE_CHOICE (DISPLAY,CH1,CHNB);
L60     IF (CHNB = 0) THEN
L70       SAMPLE_PICK (DISPLAY,PC1,STATUS,SEGMENT_NAME,PICK_ID);
L80       CHECK_RULES (SEGMENT_NAME,ADMISSIBLE);
L90       IF (ADMISSIBLE) THEN
L100        SEGMENT_LIST[INDEX] := SEGMENT_NAME;
L110        INDEX := INDEX + 1;
L120        SET_DETECTABILITY (SEGMENT_NAME,UNDETECTABLE);
L130        SET HIGHLIGHTING (SEGMENT_NAME,HIGHLIGHTED);
L140      END;
L150    END;
L160  UNTIL (CHNB = 1);
.....
```

────────────────────────── *Fortran* ──────────────────────────

```
......
      C                         *** set PICK and CHOICE devices into SAMPLE mode
L10           CALL GSPKM (DISP,PC1,GSAMPL,GECHO)
L20           CALL GSCHM (DISP,CH1,GSAMPL,GECHO)
L30           INDEX = 1
      C                                    *** start segment gathering loop
L40   40      CONTINUE
L50           CALL GSMCH (DISP,CH1,CHNB)
L60           IF (CHNB .EQ. 1) GOTO 999
L70           CALL GSMPK (DISP,PC1,STATUS,SEGN,PCID)
L80           CALL CHECK_RULES (SEGN,ADMISS)
L90           IF (.NOT. ADMISS) GOTO 40
L100          SEGL(INDEX) = SEGN
L110          INDEX = INDEX + 1
L120          CALL GSDTEC (SEGN,GUNDET)
L130          CALL GSHLIT (SEGN,GHILIT)
L160          GOTO 10
.....
L990  999     STOP
L999          END
```

SAMPLE STRING   WSOP,WSAC,SGOP   L0c

Parameters:

Input	workstation identifier		N
Input	string device number	(1..n)	I
Output	character string		S

Effect:

The logical input value, which is the current measure of the specified STRING device, is returned. The length of the returned string is less than or equal to the buffer size specified in the workstation state list entry (for this device) in the data record.

Errors:

7	GKS not in proper state: GKS shall be in one of the states WSOP, WSAC or SGOP
20	Specified workstation identifier is invalid
25	Specified workstation is not open
38	Specified workstation is neither of category INPUT nor of category OUTIN
140	Specified input device is not present on workstation
142	Input device is not in SAMPLE mode

——————————————————— *FORTRAN-Interface* ———————————————————

CALL GSMST (WKID,STDNR,LC,STR)

Parameters:

Input	WKID	workstation identifier	(1..n)	INTEGER
Input	STDNR	string device number	(1..n)	INTEGER
Output	LC	actual length of string in characters	(0..n)	INTEGER
Output	STR	string		CHARACTER*(*)

8.7 Event Input

8.7.1 Input Queue and Current Event Report

The input queue contains zero or more event reports. Event reports contain device identifier/logical input value pairs resulting from trigger firings. Event reports can be added to the input queue when logical input devices in EVENT mode are triggered by the operator. Events can be removed from the input queue by invocations of AWAIT EVENT, FLUSH DEVICE EVENTS and CLOSE WORKSTATION. The input queue can overflow, in which case it must be emptied before any further event reports will be added.

When a trigger that is part of one or more logical input devices in EVENT mode fires, the resulting event reports are entered into the queue and marked as a group of simultaneous event reports. An event report for each device is added to the input queue, if and only if, there is room for the whole group of simultaneous event reports.

The order of reports within a group of simultaneous event reports is undefined.

If there is not room in the queue for all event reports when a trigger fires, input queue overflow has occurred. Input queue overflow is not reported to

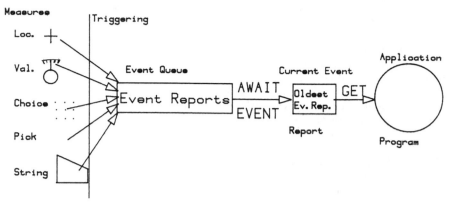

Figure 8.7 Model of event input

the application program immediately. It is reported via the error mechanism during the next invocation of any GKS function that can remove event reports from the input queue (AWAIT EVENT, FLUSH DEVICE EVENTS, and CLOSE WORKSTATION). Between the detection of input queue overflow and the next time AWAIT EVENT is invoked with the input queue being empty, no events are generated by trigger firings. (This permits the application program to determine how many events were in the queue when overflow occurred by calling AWAIT EVENT with zero timeout.)

When the "input queue overflow" error is reported, the trigger causing the overflow is indicated by placing into the error state list the identification of any one of the logical input devices using that trigger which was in EVENT mode at the time the overflow was detected.

AWAIT EVENT, if the queue is not empty, removes the first event report after copying the logical input value into the current event report in the GKS state list. The workstation identifier and device number are returned to the application program directly by AWAIT EVENT. If the queue is empty, AWAIT EVENT suspends execution until an event report is queued or until the specified timeout period has elapsed.

The application program may obtain the contents of the current event report by calling the appropriate GET <input class> function.

If, after removing the event report, there remains in the queue other reports in the same group of simultaneous events as the removed report, the "more simultaneous events" flag in the GKS state list is set to be MORE. Otherwise, it is set to NOMORE.

FLUSH DEVICE EVENTS removes all event reports for a specific device from the input queue. CLOSE WORKSTATION removes from the input queue all event reports for all logical devices on that workstation.

If the "more simultaneous events" flag has the value MORE, when either FLUSH DEVICE EVENTS or CLOSE WORKSTATION is invoked, and they remove all the remaining reports in the group of simultaneous event reports at the head of the queue, then the flag is set to NOMORE.

8.7.2   Functions to Await and Delete Event Queue Entries

AWAIT EVENT   WSOP,WSAC,SGOP   L0c
Parameters:
  Input   timeout (seconds)   R
  Output   workstation identifier   N
  Output   input class
            (NONE,LOCATOR,STROKE,VALUATOR,CHOICE,PICK,STRING)   E
  Output   logical input device number   (1..n)   I
Effect:
  If the input queue is empty, GKS is set into a wait state until an input event is
  written into the queue or the time specified in the timeout parameter has elapsed.
  If a timeout occurs and there is still no entry in the queue, a NONE value is returned
  for input class.
  If there is at least one entry in the queue, the oldest event report is moved from
  the event queue to the current event report in the GKS state list. The workstation
  identifier, the input class, and the logical input device number are returned and the
  corresponding values are made available for subsequent interrogation by the GET
  < device class > functions.
Note:
  The operation is performed even if error 148 (input queue has overflowed) has occurred.
  Note that a timeout of zero causes an immediate inspection of the queue, and a
  NONE value for input class is returned if the queue is empty. Note also that some
  operating systems may not provide a reliable timeout facility. In this case, a timeout
  different from zero may never cause a timeout at all. Repeated calls of the AWAIT
  EVENT function overwrite event reports which have already been stored in the current
  event report as result of previous calls of AWAIT EVENT (see also Example 8.7.1).
Errors:
  7   GKS not in proper state: GKS shall be in one of the states WSOP, WSAC
           or SGOP
  147   Input queue has overflowed
  151   Timeout is invalid

———————————————— *FORTRAN-Interface* ————————————————

CALL GWAIT (TOUT,WKID,INCL,INDNR)
Parameters:
  Input   TOUT   time out (in seconds)   REAL
  Input   WKID   workstation identifier   (1..n)   INTEGER
  Output   INCL   input class
                    (0 = NONE,1 = LOCATOR,2 = STROKE,   INTEGER
                    3 = VALUATOR,4 = CHOICE,5 = PICK,6 = STRING)
  Output   INDNR   logical input device number   (1..n)   INTEGER

Example 8.11   Waiting for specific input data via AWAIT EVENT

This part of a program awaits a logical input datum of a specific data type
(INPUT_CLASS), from a specific input device (WK_ID, INPUT_DEVICE).
All other input data, possibly being stored in the event queue, are ignored
and deleted.

──────────────────────── *Pascal* ────────────────────────

....
L10   TIMEOUT := 28800;   {8 hour working day }
L20   REPEAT
L30   AWAIT_EVENT (TIMEOUT,WKID,CLASS,DEV);
L40   IF (CLASS = NONE) THEN GOTO 999;
L50   UNTIL (WKID = WK_ID AND CLASS = INPUT_CLASS AND
          DEV = INPUT_DEVICE)
                                      {at this stage, the current event report contains an}
                                                        {entry of the desired type.}

......
L999 999 END;

──────────────────────── *Fortran* ────────────────────────

....
        C   *** set time out = 8 hours
L10   TOUT = 28800.
L20   20   CONTINUE
L30   CALL GWAIT (TOUT,WKID,INCL,INDV)
L40   IF (INCL.EQ.0) GOTO 999
L50   IF(WKID.NE.SWKID .OR. INCL.NE.SINCL .OR.
                 INDV.NE.SINDV)GOTO 20
        C   *** at this stage, the current event report contains an
        C   *** entry of the desired type
...
L999   999 STOP
L1000   END

───

FLUSH DEVICE EVENTS   WSOP,WSAC,SGOP   L0c
Parameters:
    Input   workstation identifier   N
    Input   input class
             (LOCATOR,STROKE,VALUATOR,CHOICE,PICK,STRING)   E
    Input   logical input device number   (1..n)   I
Effect:
All entries in the input queue from the specified logical input device are removed.
The operation is performed even if error 148 has occurred.
Errors:
    7   GKS not in proper state: GKS shall be in one of the states WSOP, WSAC
           or SGOP
    20   Specified workstation identifier is invalid
    25   Specified workstation is not open
    38   Specified workstation is neither of category INPUT nor of category OUTIN
    140   Specified input device is not present on workstation
    147   Input queue has overflowed

──────────────────── *FORTRAN-Interface* ────────────────────

CALL GFLUSH (WKID,INCL,INDNR)

Parameters:

Input	WKID	workstation identifier	(1..n)	INTEGER
Input	INCL	input class		INTEGER
		(0 = NONE,1 = LOCATOR,2 = STROKE,		
		= VALUATOR,4 = CHOICE,5 = PICK,6 = STRING)		
Input	INDNR	logical input device number	(1..n)	INTEGER

Example 8.12   FLUSH DEVICE EVENTS

The following examples show how to delete specific event reports in the event queue. The following cases are distinguished:

— all event reports of a specific input class (INPUT_CLASS), originated from a specific workstation (WKID), are deleted in the event queue.

———————————————————— *Pascal* ————————————————————

....
```
                    {get workstation type and number of input devices connected}
                                          {to this type of workstation}
L10   INQUIRE_WORKSTATION_CONNECTION_AND_TYPE
         (WKID,ERROR,CON_ID,WK_TYPE);
L20   INQUIRE_NUMBER_OF_AVAILABLE_LOGICAL_INPUT_DEVICES
         (WK_TYPE,ERROR,NUMB[LOC],NUMB[STO],NUMB[VAL],
         NUMB[CHO],NUMB[PIC],NUMB[STR]);
L30   IF (NUMB[INPUT_CLASS] < > 0) THEN BEGIN
L40      FOR I := 1 TO NUMB[INPUT_CLASS] DO
L50      FLUSH_DEVICE_EVENTS (WKID,INPUT_CLASS,I);
L60   END;
```
......

— all entries of a specific input class are deleted in the input queue. Note, that there can be several input devices of the same input class on one or several workstations. Then the following instructions are to be added:

———————————————————— *Pascal* ————————————————————

....
```
L3    INQUIRE_SET_OF_OPEN_WORKSTATIONS
         (ERROR,NUMB_WK,SET_WK);
L5    FOR J := 1 TO NUMB_WK BEGIN
L7    WKID := SET_WK[J];
...
L55   END;
```

— finally all entries in the event queue are deleted; this is done by adding the following two instructions:

———————————————————— *Pascal* ————————————————————

....
L25 FOR INPUT_CLASS := 1 TO 6 BEGIN
....
L52 END;

The last case, (flush event queue), reads completed:

———————————————————— *Pascal* ————————————————————

....
L3 INQUIRE_SET_OF_OPEN_WORKSTATIONS
        (ERROR,NUMB_WK,SET_WK);
                                              { delete for all open workstations }
L5 FOR J := 1 TO NUMB_WK DO BEGIN
L7   WKID := SET_WK[J];
                      { get workstation type and number of input devices connected }
                                              { to this type of workstation }
L10   INQUIRE_WORKSTATION_CONNECTION_AND_TYPE
           (WKID,ERROR,CON_ID,WK_TYPE);
L20   INQUIRE_NUMBER_OF_AVAILABLE_LOGICAL_INPUT_DEVICES
           (WK_TYPE,ERROR,NUMB[LOC],NUMB[STO],NUMB[VAL],
           NUMB[CHO],NUMB[PIC],NUMB[STR]);
                                              { delete for all input classes }
L25   FOR INPUT_CLASS := 1 TO 6 BEGIN
L30   IF (NUMB[INPUT_CLASS] < > 0) THEN
                                              { delete for all input devices }
L40   FOR I := 1 TO NUMB[INPUT_CLASS] DO
L50   FLUSH_DEVICE_EVENTS (WKID,INPUT_CLASS,I);
L52   END;
L55   END;
L60 END;

———————————————————— *Fortran* ————————————————————

(Gather list of open workstations (due to some cryptic FORTRAN interface design decisions)

```
L2               DO 10 J =1, MAXL
L3        10     CALL GQOPWK (J,ERR,NWK,SETWK(J))
          C                         *** delete for all open workstations
L5               DO 60 J = 1,NWK
L7               WKID = SETWK(J)
          C          *** get workstation type and number of input devices connected
          C                         *** to this type of workstation
L10              CALL GQWKC (WKID,ERR,CONID,WKTYPE)
L20              CALL GQLI
          +      (WKTYPE,ERR,NDV(1),NDV(2),NDV(3),NDV(4),NDV(5),NDV(6))
          C                         *** delete for all input classes
L25              DO 55 CLASS = 1,6
L30              IF (NDV(CLASS).EQ.0) GOTO 200
L35              N = NDV(CLASS)
          C                         *** delete for all input devices
L40              DO 52 I = 1,N
```

L52   52   CALL GFLUSH (WKID,CLASS,I)
L55   55   CONTINUE
L60   60   CONTINUE
...

8.7.3   Get Input Functions

GET LOCATOR   WSOP,WSAC,SGOP   L0c
Parameters:
Output   normalization transformation number   (0..n)   I
Output   locator position   WC   P
Effect:
The LOCATOR logical input value in the current event report is returned. This consists
of a LOCATOR position in world coordinates and the normalization transformation
number which was used in the conversion to world coordinates.
Errors:
7   GKS not in proper state: GKS shall be in one of the states WSOP, WSAC
           or SGOP
150   No input value of the correct class is in the current event report

———————————————— *FORTRAN-Interface* ————————————————
CALL GGTLC (TNR,PX,PY)
Parameters:
Output   TNR   normalization transformation number   (0..n)   INTEGER
Output   PX,PY   locator position   WC   2xREAL

Example 8.13   Asynchronous input and processing of curves

This program part demonstrates an application consisting of the following components:
— the operator enters a series of positions into the GKS event queue;
— they are read from the GKS event queue using the AWAIT EVENT and
   the GET LOCATOR functions; and they are gathered in an application
   program data record;
— when a series is completed, a resulting curve is calculated and displayed.

While the curve is processed, the operator may continue entering positions
into the GKS event queue where they are buffered. Each series of coordinates
is terminated via a special alternative of a CHOICE device.

A typical implementation may use a cursor device (tablet) with at least
one button, and a button device with at least two buttons. The two devices
might be physically connected, e.g., a cursor on a tablet with three buttons
attached.

The LOCATOR is implemented using the positioning facility as measure
value and the button as trigger. The CHOICE device is realized by the two
buttons of a keyboard or by the two remaining buttons of the cursor.

Further solutions of mapping logical to physical devices are shown in Chapter 8.8; more, flexible implementation structures are detailed in Chapter IV.2.

The operator interface looks as follows:
— the cursor is moved, no buttons are pressed: an echo indicates the current value of the LOCATOR device;
— button 1 (the button attached to the LOCATOR device) is pressed: the actual state of the LOCATOR device is put into the event queue as LOCATOR event report;
— button 2 (button 1 of the CHOICE device) is pressed: a CHOICE event report with choice number 1 is generated and put into the event queue. When this event report is read by the application program, it is used to terminate the actual series of positions, and to start further processing them;
— button 3 (button 2 of the CHOICE device) is pressed: a CHOICE event report with choice number 2 is put into the event queue; when it is read, the program terminates.

─────────────────────────── Pascal ───────────────────────────

```
........
L10    SET_LOCATOR_MODE (DISPLAY,LC1,EVENT,ECHO);
L20    SET_CHOICE_MODE (DISPLAY,CH1,EVENT,NOECHO);
L30    INDEX := 1;
L40    TIMEOUT := 28800;
L50    CHNB := 0;
L60    REPEAT
L70      AWAIT_EVENT (TIMEOUT,WKID,CLASS,DEVICE);
L80      CASE CLASS OF
L90        NONE: GOTO 999;
L100       LOCATOR: BEGIN
L110         GET_LOCATOR (TNR,POINTS(INDEX));
L120         INDEX := INDEX + 1;
L130       END;
L140       CHOICE: BEGIN
L150         GET_CHOICE (CHNB);
L160         IF (CHNB = 1) THEN BEGIN
L170           CALCULATE_CURVE (POINTS,CURVE);
L180           POLYLINE (URVE,CURVE);
L190         END;
L200       END;
L210     END;
L220   UNTIL (CHNR = 2);
....
L1000 999 END;
```

─────────────────────────── Fortran ───────────────────────────

```
.........
     C              *** set LOCATOR and CHOICE devices into EVENT mode
L10           CALL GSLCM (DISP,LC1,GEVENT,GECHO)
L20           CALL GSCHM (DISP,CH1,GEVENT,GNECHO)
L30           INDEX = 1
L40           TOUT = 28800
```

L50		CHNB = 0
L60	60	CONTINUE
	C	*** await event of type LOCATOR or CHOICE
L70		CALL GWAIT (TOUT,WKID,CLASS,DEV)
L75		CLASS = CLASS + 1
	C	*** case NONE,LOCATOR,STROKE,VALUATOR,CHOICE,PICK,
		and STRING
L80		GOTO (999,100,999,999,140,999,999),CLASS
	C	*** case LOCATOR
L100	100	CONTINUE
L110		CALL GTLC (TNR,P(INDEX))
L120		INDEX = INDEX + 1
L130		GOTO 60
	C	*** case CHOICE
L140	140	CONTINUE
L150		CALL GTCH (CHNB)
L160		IF (CHNB .EQ. 2) GOTO 999
	C	*** case CHOICE number 1: process curve
L170		CALL CALCULATE_CURVE (INDEX-1,P,LEN,CURVE)
L180		CALL GPL (LEN,CURVE)
L220		IF (CHNR .NE. 2) GOTO 60
....		
L999	999	STOP
L1000		END

GET STROKE   WSOP,WSAC,SGOP   L0c

Parameters:

Output	normalization transformation number	(0..n)	I
Output	number of points	(0..n)	I
Output	points in stroke	WC	nxP

Effect:

The STROKE logical input value from the current event report is returned. This consists of a sequence of points in world coordinates and the normalization transformation number used in the conversion to world coordinates. The normalization transformation number is determined (when the event was queued).

Note:

The number of points in the stroke is less than or equal to the stroke buffer size specified in the workstation state list for this device.

Errors:

7	GKS not in proper state: GKS shall be in one of the states WSOP, WSAC or SGOP
150	No input value of the correct class is in the current event report

———————————————————— *FORTRAN-Interface* ————————————————————

CALL GGTSK (MNB,TNR,NB,PX,PY)

Parameters:

Input	MNB	maximum number of points	(1..n)	INTEGER
Output	TNR	normalization transformation nb	(0..n)	INTEGER

Output NB   number of points in stroke   (0..n)   INTEGER
Output PX(MNB),PY(MNB)   WC   nx2xREAL
                STROKE positions

GET VALUATOR   WSOP,WSAC,SGOP L0c

Parameters:
Output value   R
Effect:
The VALUATOR logical input value in the current event report is returned. The value delivered is in the range specified in the workstation state list entry (for the device) in the data record.
Errors:
   7   GKS not in proper state: GKS shall be in one of the states WSOP, WSAC or SGOP
 150   No input value of the correct class is in the current event report

———————————————— *FORTRAN-Interface* ————————————————

CALL GGTVL (VAL)
Parameters:
Output VAL   value   REAL

GET CHOICE   WSOP,WSAC,SGOP L0c

Parameters:
Output choice number   (0..n)   I
Effect:
The CHOICE logical input value in the current event report is returned. The choice number zero means "no choice".
Errors:
   7   GKS not in proper state: GKS shall be in one of the states WSOP, WSAC or SGOP
 150   No input value of the correct class is in the current event report

———————————————— *FORTRAN-Interface* ————————————————

CALL GGTCH (CHNR)
Parameters:
Output CHNR   choice number   (0..n)   INTEGER

GET PICK   WSOP,WSAC,SGOP L1c

Parameters:
Output status   (OK,NOPICK)   I
Output segment name   N
Output pick identifier   N
Effect:
The PICK logical input value in the current event report is returned. This consists of a PICK status, a segment name and the pick identifier associated with the primitive within the segment that was picked.

Errors:

7	GKS not in proper state: GKS shall be in one of the states WSOP, WSAC or SGOP
150	No input value of the correct class is in the current event report

─────────────────── *FORTRAN-Interface* ───────────────────

CALL GGTPK (STAT,SGNA,PCID)

Parameters:

Output	STAT	status	(0 = OK, 1 = NOPICK)		INTEGER
Output	SGNA	segment name		(1..n)	INTEGER
Output	PCID	pick identifier		(1..n)	INTEGER

Example 8.14   Identifying segments for copying them to a plotter

This example allows for interactively identifying segments and putting their names into the event queue where the application program reads them.

Each segment identified on an interactive workstation is copied to a plotter workstation. Since the process of copying lasts considerably longer than identifying segments, the facility of event report queuing is of benefit: the operator can enter data without waiting for program states.

The program part ends when the operator does not enter a PICK input for more than 10 seconds after the last segment is copied to the plotter, or if the operator generates others than PICK input data.

──────────────────────── *Pascal* ────────────────────────

```
........
L10   OPEN_WORKSTATION (PLOTTER,CONNECTION,PLOTTERTYPE);
L20   SET_PICK_MODE (DISPLAY,PC1,EVENT,ECHO);
L30   REPEAT
L40     AWAIT_EVENT (10,WKID,CLASS,DEVICE);
L50     IF (CLASS = PICK) THEN BEGIN
L60       GET_PICK (SEGMENT_NAME,PICK_ID);
L70       IF (STATUS = OK) THEN BEGIN
L80         SET_HIGHLIGHTING (SEGMENT_NAME,HIGHLIGHTED);
L90         SET_DETECTABILITY (SEGMENT_NAME,UNDETECTABLE);
L100        COPY_SEGMENT_TO_WORKSTATION
              (PLOTTER,SEGMENT_NAME);
L110      END;
L120    END;
L130  UNTIL (CLASS < > PICK)
                              {disable pick device (put it into request mode)}
L140  SET_PICK_MODE (DISPLAY,PC1,REQUEST,ECHO);
L150  CLOSE_WORKSTATION (PLOTTER);
....
```

──────────────────────── *Fortran* ────────────────────────

```
.........
      C              *** open plotter workstation and set pick device into event mode
L10           CALL GOPWK (PLOT,CONID,PLTYP)
L20           CALL GSPKM (DISP,PC1,GEVENT,GECHO)
L30     30    CONTINUE
```

```
      C                    *** await pick event input (all other input leads to termination
L40                CALL GWAIT (10.0,WKID,CLASS,DEVICE)
L50                IF (CLASS .NE. GPICK) GOTO 140
L60                CALL GTPK (SEGN,PCID)
L70                IF (STATUS .EQ. GNPICK) GOTO 140
      C                        *** highlight segment, make it undetectable, and copy it to
      C                                                    *** plotter workstation
L80                CALL GSHLIT (SEGN,GHILIT)
L90                CALL GSDTEC (SEGN,GUNDET)
L100               CALL GCSGWK (PLOT,SEGN)
L130               IF (CLASS .EQ. GPICK) GOTO 30
      C                                *** disable pick device (put it into request mode)
L140      140      CALL GSPKM (DISP,PC1,GREQU,GECHO)
L150               CALL GCLWK (PLOT)
........
L998               STOP
L999               END
```

GET STRING   WSOP,WSAC,SGOP   L0c
Parameters:
   Output   character string   S
Effect:
   The STRING logical input value in the current event report is returned. The length
   of the returned string is less than or equal to the buffer size specified in the workstation
   state list entry (for this device) in the data record at the time the event was queued.
Errors:
   7   GKS not in proper state: GKS shall be in one of the states WSOP, WSAC
            or SGOP
   150   No input value of the correct class is in the current event report

———————————————————— *FORTRAN-Interface* ————————————————————

CALL GGTST (LC,STR)
Parameters:
   Output   LC   length of returned string   (0..n)   INTEGER
   Output   STR   string   CHARACTER*(*)

8.8   A Compound Example of Using the GKS-Input Functions

An interactive job reads segments from long term storage (the GKSM) and
displays them on the display surface (instructions L10 to L170). It allows the
operator to pick one of the segments (instructions L180 to L340), to place
and transform it on the screen (instructions L360 to L880), and to output
it on a plotter into the picture he constructs (instruction L850). It lets him
do this until he hits an end of picture key (instruction L880). The program
is then properly terminated (instructions L890 to L970).

The segments may be, for example, flowchart symbols. They appear on the top or bottom or at the side of the screen and then are used to build the flowchart.

The logical input devices used in this example are:
— PICK device PC1 in event mode;
— LOCATOR device LC1 in event and sample mode;
— Valuator device VL1 in sample mode;
— CHOICE device CH1 with at least 6 alternatives (0 to 5) in event mode.

This program is written in such a way, that its correct performance is independent of the particular physical input devices used in a given installation. All logical input devices might be implemented on distinct physical input devices like,
— the PICK device on a lightpen with a tip switch;
— the LOCATOR device on a trackball or thumb wheels, etc. with one button connected;
— the VALUATOR device on a potentiometer or via simulations using a lightpen, a position device, a function keyboard, etc.
— and the CHOICE device on function or alphanumeric keyboards or screen menus.

It is also possible that several logical input devices can be realized on the same physical input device. An extreme example is given in which all logical devices are implemented on a three-button puck of a tablet. This allows the operator to deal with only one physical input tool and appropriate echos which indicate the respective logical values.

The PICK and the LOCATOR devices are both mapped to the pointing device. For the PICK device, its position is used to calculate a segment name which in turn is the measure value for the PICK device; for the LOCATOR device, its position serves directly (after appropriate transformations are applied) as LOCATOR device measure value.

If both devices are simultaneously in EVENT mode, then one operator action, namely pressing one of the three buttons, puts two event reports into the queue, i.e., the identified segment and the identified position. This is caused by the instructions L180 to L340 in the program. The position for identifying the segment is used as segment reference point at the same time.

The VALUATOR device is implemented using the puck position; the CHOICE device uses the 3 buttons of the puck. With the instructions L360 to L650, the CHOICE device is set into EVENT mode, and either none, or the LOCATOR or the VALUATOR device is in SAMPLE mode; the VALUATOR device delivers values either in the range 0 to 10 (for scaling), or in the range 0 to 3.14 (for rotating). The actual alternative is dependent on the last CHOICE alternative entered by the operator:
— Button 1 was pressed: move segment by moving the pointing device on the tablet. The LOCATOR is in SAMPLE mode;
— Button 2 was pressed: scale the segment by moving the pointing device. The VALUATOR is in SAMPLE mode (range 0 to 10);

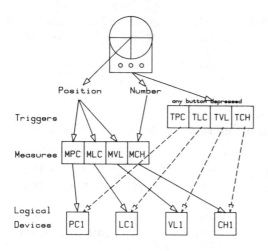

Figure 8.8 Mapping of logical input devices to a data tablet puck

— Buttons 1 and 2 were pressed: rotate segment by moving the pointing device. The VALUATOR is also in SAMPLE mode. The range is from 0 to 3.14;
— Button 3 was pressed: the segment is copied to the plotter. PICK and LO-CATOR devices are set into EVENT mode, VALUATOR and CHOICE devices are disabled. Pointing at a segment and pressing one of the buttons starts the loop again;
— Buttons 1 and 3 are pressed: the program is terminated.

Example 8.15   A compound input program

———————————————— *Pascal* ————————————————

```
L10   OPEN_GKS;
L20   OPEN_WORKSTATION (DISPLAY,DDDIS,REFRESH);      {display workst.}
L30   OPEN_WORKSTATION (PLOTTER,DDPLT,PLOTTYP);      {plotter workst.}
L40   OPEN_WORKSTATION (GKSM_IN,FILE1,GKSM_INPUT);  {Metafile input}
                              {device-independent segment storage}
L50   OPEN_WORKSTATION (SEGSTORE,DDSEG,WISS);
L60   INQUIRE_MAXIMUM_DISPLAY_SURFACE_SIZE
         (REFRESH,ERROR,UNITS,MSIZE);
L70   DX := MSIZE.X / 20;                              {size of an echo area}
L80   DY := MSIZE.Y / 20;
                     {the contents of the Metafile are displayed on the display}
                     {segments, if present, are stored on segment storage}
L90   ACTIVATE_WORKSTATION (DISPLAY);                    {output on display}
L100  ACTIVATE_WORKSTATION (SEGSTORE);                        {output on DIS}
L110  REPEAT                                             {reading the GKSM}
L120  GET_ITEM_TYPE_FROM_GKSM (GKSM_IN,ITEM_TYPE,ITEM_LENGTH);
L130    READ_ITEM_FROM_GKSM (GKSM_IN,ARRAY_LENGTH,ARRAY);
L140    INTERPRET_ITEM (ITEM_TYPE,ITEM_LENGTH,ARRAY);
L150  UNTIL (ITEM_TYPE=EOFTYPE);
```

```
L160  CLOSE_WORKSTATION (GKSM_IN);                    {Metafile released}
L170  DEACTIVATE_WORKSTATION (SEGSTORE);    {no more output on WISS}
               {By now the picture contained in the Metafile is visible on the display.}
                      {The segments contained in this data can be used for}
                      {creating a new picture which will be output on a plotter}
L180  REPEAT                           {each loop transition handles one segment}
                      {A segment is identified and provided with a reference point}
                          {set pick PC1 and locator LC1 both in EVENT mode}
L190  SET_PICK_MODE (DISPLAY,PC1,EVENT,ECHO);
L200  SET_LOCATOR_MODE (DISPLAY,LC1,EVENT,ECHO);
L210  FOR I: = 1 TO 2 DO
L220  BEGIN
                      {read one pick and one locator event in arbitrary sequence}
L230     TIMEOUT = 8_HOURS;                         {standard working day}
                                          {wait for pick and locator input}
L240     AWAIT_EVENT (TIMEOUT,WKID,CLASS,DEV);
L250     IF (CLASS = PICK) THEN
L260     BEGIN                                     {SEGNAME received}
L270        GET_PICK (STATUS,SEGNAME,PICKID);
L280        SET_PICK_MODE (DISPLAY,PC1,REQUEST,ECHO);    {disable pick}
L290     END ELSE
L300     BEGIN                          {segment ref. point POINT1 received}
L310        GET_LOCATOR (TNR1,POINT1);
L320        SET_LOCATOR_MODE (DISPLAY,LC1,REQUEST,ECHO);
L330     END;                                       {disable locator}
L340  END;
L350  SELECT_NORMALIZATION_TRANSFORMATION (TNR1);
                      {subsequent points are expected to be in viewport of}
                      {normalization transformation TNR1.}
                   {This would be zero, since no transformations have}
                   {been set up explicitly}
                      {set choice CH1 in EVENT mode}
L360  SET_CHOICE_MODE (DISPLAY,CH1,EVENT,ECHO);
                          {inquire initial segment transformation matrix}
L370  INQUIRE_SEGMENT_ATTRIBUTES
      (SEGNAME,ERROR,M,VIS,HIGH,PRIOR,DETEC);
      CHNB := 0;                          {wait for first CHOICE alternative}
L380  REPEAT                      {each loop transition for one transformation}
                          {step or a program control change}
L390  TIMEOUT := 0;
L400  AWAIT_EVENT (TIMEOUT,WKID,CLASS,DEV);
L410  IF (CLASS = CHOICE) THEN              {change of program control}
L420  BEGIN
                   {disable locator and valuator to initialize them anew}
L430  SET_VALUATOR_MODE (DISPLAY,VL1,REQUEST,ECHO);
L440  SET_LOCATOR_MODE (DISPLAY,LC1,REQUEST,ECHO);
L450  GET_CHOICE (CHNB);
L460  CASE CHNB OF
L470  1: BEGIN                                       {switch to shift}
L480     ECHO_AREA := (0, MSIZE.X, 0, MSIZE.Y);
                   {LC1 has initial value = segment refpoint and crosshairs}
```

```
L490        INITIALISE_LOCATOR
              (DISPLAY,LC1,REFP,TNR1,2,ECHO_AREA,EMPTD);
L500        SET_LOCATOR_MODE (DISPLAY,LC1,SAMPLE,ECHO);
L510        SAMPLE_LOCATOR (DISPLAY,LC1,TNR1,POINT1);
L520        END;                                          {start point}
L530      2: BEGIN                                   {switch to scaling}
L540        DATA_RECORD := (0,10)
L550        ECHO_AREA := (MSIZE.X-DX,MSIZE.X,MSIZE.Y-DY,MSIZE.Y);
L560        INITIALISE_VALUATOR
              (DISPLAY,VL1,1,1,ECHO_AREA,DATA_RECORD);
L570        SET_VALUATOR_MODE (DISPLAY,VL1,SAMPLE,ECHO);
L580        END;
L590      3: BEGIN                                  {switch to rotation}
L600        DATA_RECORD := (0,3.14)
L610        ECHO_AREA :=
              (MSIZE.X-2*DX,MSIZE.X-DX,MSIZE.Y-DY,MSIZE.Y);
L620        INITIALISE_VALUATOR
              (DISPLAY,VL1,1,1,ECHO_AREA,DATA_RECORD);
L630        END;
L640      END;                                            {end case }
L650      END;                                              {end if }
L660      CASE CHNB OF
L670      1: BEGIN                                          {shift }
L680        SAMPLE_LOCATOR (DISPLAY,LC1,TNR2,POINT2);
                                                      {target point}
L690        IF (TNR2 < > TNR1) GOTO 890;
                                {segment is shifted by POINT2 — POINT1}
L700        D := POINT2-POINT1;
L710        ACCUMULATE_TRANSFORMATION_MATRIX
              (M,REFP,D,0,(1,1),WC,M);
L720        SET_SEGMENT_TRANSFORMATION (SEGNAME,M);
L730        END;
L740      2: BEGIN                                          {scale }
L750        SAMPLE_VALUATOR (DISPLAY,VL1,VAL);          {scale factor}
                              {segment is scaled by VAL in x and y direction,}
L760        ACCUMULATE_TRANSFORMATION_MATRIX
              (M,REFP,(0,0),0,
L770          (VAL,VAL),WC,M);
L775        SET_SEGMENT_TRANSFORMATION (SEGNAME,M);
L780        END;
L790      3: BEGIN                                          {rotate}
L800        SAMPLE_VALUATOR (DISPLAY,VL1,VAL);              {angle}
                              {segment is rotated by ANGLE (relative to REFP)}
L810        ACCUMULATE_TRANSFORMATION_MATRIX
              (M,REFP,(0,0),VAL,
L820          (0,0),WC,M);
L830        SET_SEGMENT_TRANSFORMATION (SEGNAME,M);
L840        END;
L850      4: BEGIN                    {copy segment to plotter, disable choice device}
L852        COPY_SEGMENT_TO_WORKSTATION (PLOTTER, SEGNAME);
L854        SET_CHOICE_MODE (DISPLAY,CH1,REQUEST,ECHO);
L856      END
```

L860		END	{end case}
L870		UNTIL CHNB = 4 OR CHNB = 5;	{end of transformation loop}
L880		UNTIL CHNB = 5;	{end of segment handling loop}
L890	890:		

```
L890   890:
                                                   {disable input devices}
L900  SET_LOCATOR_MODE (DISPLAY,LC1,REQUEST,ECHO);
L910  SET_VALUATOR_MODE (DISPLAY,VL1,REQUEST,ECHO);
L920  SET_CHOICE_MODE (DISPLAY,CH1,REQUEST,ECHO);
                           {deactivate and close workstations, close GKS}
L930  DEACTIVATE_WORKSTATION (DISPLAY);
L940  CLOSE_WORKSTATION (PLOTTER);
L950  CLOSE_WORKSTATION (DISPLAY);
L960  CLOSE_WORKSTATION (SEGSTORE);
L970  CLOSE_GKS;
```

———————————————————— *Fortran* ————————————————————

```
L10             CALL GOPKS
      C                  *** Open display, plotter, metafile input, and segment storage
L20             CALL GOPWK (DISP,DDDIS,REFR)
L30             CALL GOPWK (PLOT,DDPLT,PLTYP)
L40             CALL GOPWK (GKSMIN,FILE1,GMI)
L50             CALL GOPWK (SEGS,DDSEG,GWISS)
      C                       *** Compute echo areas as part of the display surface
L60             CALL GQMDS (REFR,ERR,UNIT,SZLX,SZLY,SZRX,SZRY)
L70             DX = SZLX / 20.
L80             DY = SZLY / 20.
      C                  *** The contents of the Metafile are displayed on the display.
      C                     *** Segments, if present, are stored on segment storage.
      C                       *** Activate display and segment storage workstations
L90             CALL GACWK (DISP)
L100            CALL GACWK (SEGS)
L110    110     CONTINUE
L120            CALL GGTITM (GKSMIN,TYPE,LENGTH)
L130            CALL GRDITM (GKSMIN,MAXL,ARLEN,AR)
L140            CALL GIITM (TYPE,ARLEN,AR)
L150            IF (TYPE .NE. EOFTYP) GOTO 110
      C                       *** Close metafile and deactivate segment storage
L160            CALL GCLWK (GKSMIN)
L170            CALL GDAWK (SEGS)
      C               *** By now the picture contained in the Metafile is visible on
      C             *** the display. The segments contained in this data can be used
      C             *** for creating a new picture which will be output on a plotter
      C                       *** Each loop transition handles one segment
L180    180     CONTINUE
      C             *** A segment is identified and provided with a reference point.
      C                  *** Set pick PC1 and locator LC1 both in EVENT mode
L190            CALL GSPKM (DISP,PC1,GEVENT,GECHO)
L200            CALL GSLCM (DISP,LC1,GEVENT,GECHO)
L210            DO 330 I=1,2
      C                  *** Read one pick and one locator event in arbitrary sequence
L230            TOUT = 28800.
      C                           *** Wait for pick and locator input
```

```
L240                 CALL GWAIT (TOUT,WKID,CLASS,DEV)
L250                 IF (CLASS .NE. GPICK) GOTO 290
L270                 CALL GGTPK (STAT,SEGN,PCID)
      C                                              *** Disable pick
L280                 CALL GSPKM (DISP,PC1,GREQU,GECHO)
L290        290      IF (CLASS .NE. GLOCAT) GOTO 330
L310                 CALL GGTLC (TNR1,RX,RY)
      C                                              *** Disable locator
L320                 CALL GSLCM (DISP,LC1,GREQU,GECHO)
L330        330      CONTINUE
L350                 CALL GSELNT (TNR1)
      C                         *** Subsequent points are expected to be in viewport of
      C                   *** normalization transformation TNR1. This would be zero, since
      C                         *** no transformations have been set up explicitly
      C                                     *** Set choice CH1 in EVENT mode
L360                 CALL GSCHM (DISP,CH1,GEVENT,GECHO)
      C                              *** Inquire initial segment transformation matrix
L370                 CALL GQSGA (SEGN,ERR,M,VIS,HIGH,PRIOR,DET)
      C                                     *** Wait for first CHOICE alternative
L375                 CHNB = 0
      C                             *** Each loop transition causes one transformation step
      C                                     *** or a change of program control
L380        380      CONTINUE
L390                 TOUT = 0
L400                 CALL GWAIT (TOUT,WKID,CLASS,DEV)
L410                 IF (CLASS .NE. GCHOIC) GOTO 640
L410  C                                     *** Change of program control
      C                       *** Disable locator and valuator to initialize them anew
L430                 CALL GSVLM (DISP,VL1,GREQU,GECHO)
L440                 CALL GSLCM (DISP,LC1,GREQU,GECHO)
L450                 CALL GGTCH (CHNB)
L455                 CHNB = CHNB + 1
L460                 GOTO (640,470,530,590,640,640),CHNB
L470        470      CONTINUE
      C                       *** Switch to shift, set echo area for LOCATOR device
L480                 EX1 = 0.
L481                 EY1 = SZLX
L482                 EX2 = 0.
L483                 EY2 = SZLY
      C                  *** LC1 has initial value = segment refpoint and crosshairs echo
L490                 CALL GINLC
                         (DISP,LC1,TNR1,RX,RY,2,EX1,EX2,EY1,EY2,1,EMPTD)
      C                       *** Set locator LC1 into sample mode and sample starting point
L500                 CALL GSLCM (DISP,LC1,GSAMPL,GECHO)
L510                 CALL GSMLC (DISP,LC1,TNR1,PX1,PY1)
L520                 GOTO 640
L530        530      CONTINUE
      C                                              *** Switch to scaling
      C                       *** Pack data record with initial values: range 0 to 10
      C                                     *** Set echo area for VALUATOR device
L550                 EX1 = SZLX − DX
L551                 EX2 = SZLX
```

```
L552                EY1 = SZLY − DY
L553                EY2 = SZLY
     C                                    *** Initialise valuator and put it into sample mode
L560                CALL GINVL (DISP,VL1,1,1,EX1,EX2,EY1,EY2,0.,10.,1,EMPTD)
L570                CALL GSVLM (DISP,VL1,GSAMPL,GECHO)
L580                GOTO 640
L590        590     CONTINUE
     C                                                    *** Switch to rotation
     C                                    *** Set echo area for VALUATOR device
L610                EX1 = SZLX − 2*DX
L611                EX2 = SZLX − DX
L612                EY1 = SZLY − DY
L613                EY2 = SZLY
L620                CALL GINVL (DISP,VL1,1,1,EX1,EX2,EY1,EY2,0.,3.14,1,EMPTD)
L640        640     CONTINUE
L660                GOTO (870,670,740,790,850,870),CHNB
L670        670     CONTINUE
     C                                            *** Shift segment; sample target point
L680                CALL GSMLC (DISP,LC1,TNR2,PX2,PY2)
L690                IF (TNR2 .NE. TNR1) GOTO 890
     C                                        *** Segment is shifted by POINT2 − POINT1
L700                DX = PX2 − PX1
L701                DY = PY2 − PY1
L710                CALL GACTM (M,RX1,RY1,DX,DY,0.0,1.0,1.0,GWC,M)
L720                CALL GSSGT (SEGN,M)
L730                GOTO 870
L740        740     CONTINUE
     C                                            *** Scale segment; sample scale factor
L750                CALL GSMVL (DISP,VL1,VAL)
L760                CALL GACTM (M,RX,RY,0.0,0.0,0.0,VAL,VAL,GWC,M)
L775                CALL GSSGT (SEGN,M)
L780                GOTO 880
L790        790     CONTINUE
     C                                            *** Rotate segment; sample angle
L800                CALL GSMVL (DISP,VL1,VAL)
L810                CALL GACTM (M,RX,RY,0.0,0.0,VAL,0.0,0.0,GWC,M)
L830                CALL GSSGT (SEGN,M)
L840                GOTO 870
L850        850     CONTINUE
     C                                    *** Copy segment to plotter, disable CHOICE device
L852                CALL GCSGWK (PLOT,SEGN)
L854                CALL GSCHM (DISP,CH1,GREQU,GECHO)
     C                            *** End of transformation loop if CHNB = 4 or CHNB = 5
L870        870     IF (CHNB .NE. 4 .AND. CHNB .NE. 5) GOTO 380
     C                            *** End of segment handling loop if CHNB = 5
L880                IF (CHNB .NE. 5) GOTO 180
L890        890     CONTINUE
     C                                                *** Disable input devices
L900                CALL GSLCM (DISP,LC1,GREQU,GECHO)
L910                CALL GSVLM (DISP,VL1,GREQU,GECHO)
L920                CALL GSCHM (DISP,CH1,GREQU,GECHO)
     C                                    *** Deactivate and close workstations, close GKS
```

L930	CALL GDAWK (DISP)
L940	CALL GCLWK (PLOT)
L950	CALL GCLWK (DISP)
L960	CALL GCLWK (SEGS)
L970	CALL GCLKS

8.9   Exercises

Exercise 8.1   Interactive construction of polygons

Develop a program which allows for interactively constructing polygons. Use the REQUEST LOCATOR function for this purpose. Program the same application using the REQUEST STROKE function.

Exercise 8.2   Using rubber band echo

Extend the program of Exercise 8.1: use rubber band echo and provide a useful operator feedback for the positions of the current polygon which are already entered. The feedback output should disappear when the polygon is finally displayed.

Exercise 8.3   Interactive construction of FILL AREA primitives

Write a program which allows for generating FILL AREA primitives with different attributes: colour and interior style (hollow, solid, pattern, and hatch) should be adjustable.
— Decide which logical input devices are needed and are suitable for entering the specific data.
— Develop a control structure which minimizes operator actions under the assumption that several FILL AREA primitives will be constructed, and that attributes do not change for a series of FILL AREA primitives.

Exercise 8.4   Graphical symbols for choice input

Program an example using the prompt/echo type 5 of the CHOICE input device (an application-specified segment is used to represent a screen menu). The screen menu should contain four graphically represented alternatives, namely four symbols for a triangle, a rectangle, a circle, and a rhombus.

Exercise 8.5   Simple picture construction

Extend program 8.4: by identifying one of the buttons using the REQUEST CHOICE function, an operator may construct a picture which is made up of the four symbols. The operator should be able to position the symbols on the screen, the program should automatically connect the currently processed symbol with the last generated symbol at predefined connection points. Facilities for modifying already generated parts of the picture need not be provided.

Exercise 8.6   Adding inscriptions

Extend program of Exercise 8.3: add a facility to inscribe the FILL AREA picture components, by additionally using the REQUEST STRING function. The text attributes, colour and character height, should be interactively adjustable.

Exercise 8.7   Sampling curve positions

A LOCATOR should be put into SAMPLE mode and polygons be constructed by sampling the positions. For taking over positions from the input device to the application program, the following two constraints should be applied:
— a position is only taken over, if there is a certain distance to the lastly accepted point (DELTA_X, DELTA_Y);
— a certain time slice (DELTA_T) has to be elapsed, before the next point is sampled.

Exercise 8.8   Using rubber band echo for curve input

Extend the program of Exercise 8.7 by adding proper feedback. Rubber band echo should be provided; when a point is taken over by the application program, this position is fixed on the screen as the next starting position for the rubber band echo. Between the last and the next to last points, a connection line has to be displayed as feedback. All generated connection lines disappear when the final polygon is generated.

Exercise 8.9   Dynamic zoom of pictures

Dependent on a VALUATOR device in SAMPLE mode, the scale of a picture should be adjusted on a workstation display surface. This should both be performed on the workstation viewport level (pure scaling), and on the workstation window level (dynamic windowing). The GKS constraints have to be obeyed (the workstation viewport must be within the display surface; the workstation window must be within the NDC space).

Exercise 8.10   Recognizing text command input

A STRING device is set into SAMPLE mode; an operator tries to enter text commands which he does not exactly know or which can be uniquely recognized by the system before being typed in completely.
    Write a program which samples the currently typed in string, tries to recognize a possible command and, if it succeeds, gives the operator a suitable message.

Exercise 8.11   Handling the GKS event queue

Delete all entries in the GKS event queue, which are originated from all input devices of a specific workstation, without closing the workstation.

Exercise 8.12   Guiding an operator when event queue has overflowed

When an AWAIT EVENT function was called, an "event queue has over-flowed" error has been reported. Write a program which processes all event reports and which tells the operator where to restart input after the queue is eventually emptied.

Exercise 8.13   Entering curves from a digitizer

Develop a digitizing application, where points are entered by a LOCATOR device (pen or puck of a digitizer with at least two buttons). The points entered have different meanings to the application program dependent on which button (combination of buttons) was pressed to enter the point. The single CHOICE alternatives which are logically connected to each point entered, should have the following meaning:
— choice number = 1: draw line from last point to this one;
— choice number = 2: display a marker symbol at this position; no connection line between the last point and this one should be drawn;
— choice number = 3: this point is the last one of a series; a new series will start;
— choice number = 4: this point is the last one of a series; process it and terminate the program.

Program several alternatives for solving this problem with logical input device combinations and discuss their impacts:

The alternatives are:
— LOCATOR in REQUEST or EVENT mode, CHOICE in SAMPLE mode;
— LOCATOR in SAMPLE mode; CHOICE in REQUEST or EVENT mode;
— both LOCATOR and CHOICE devices in REQUEST mode;
— both LOCATOR and CHOICE devices in SAMPLE mode;
— both LOCATOR and CHOICE devices in EVENT mode.

9   ERROR HANDLING

9.1   Strategy

For each GKS function, a finite number of error situations is specified, any of which will cause the ERROR HANDLING procedure to be called. Every GKS implementation must support this error checking. The ERROR HANDLING procedure provides an interface between GKS and the application program.

Figure 9.1 demonstrates the structural organization of the error handling components:

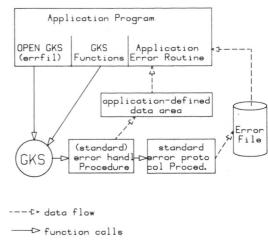

--- ⊏> data flow

———⊳ function calls

Figure 9.1 Organization of error handling

— The application programs call GKS functions;
— If the GKS functions detect error situations, they perform the effect as described in Section 9.4 and call the ERROR HANDLING procedure;
— The ERROR HANDLING procedure is either provided as a standard facility or supplied by the application program. If provided by the application program, it may interpret the information about the error (supplied by GKS via parameters and INQUIRY functions) and may store data in a data area. The ERROR HANDLING procedure provided by GKS just calls the ERROR LOGGING procedure.
— The ERROR LOGGING procedure writes the error message and the function identification on the error file and returns to the ERROR HANDLING procedure which in turn returns to the GKS function which called it;
— The application program may inspect the contents of the data area and of the error file after it has regained control from GKS again. It may react to the error situation reported.

The GKS error handling strategy is derived from the following classification of errors:
I   errors resulting in a precisely defined reaction;
II errors resulting in an attempt to save the results of previous operations;
III errors which cause unpredictable results including the loss of information.
   GKS recognizes several situations in which errors are detected:
A   error detected in GKS procedures;
B   error detected outside GKS (driver procedures and operating system procedures called by GKS, and application programs).

If errors are detected outside GKS (situation B), either the application program may regain control over the execution or program execution will be terminated abnormally. In the latter case, results are unpredictable (case III) and in the worst situation, all graphical information produced so far in this job may be lost. If, however, the application program obtains control, it may attempt to close GKS properly or at least attempt an emergency closure by calling the EMERGENCY CLOSE GKS procedure. Similarly, if the error occurs in procedures called by GKS and control is not returned properly to GKS, the effects are unpredictable.

All errors which are listed explicitly as part of the definition of GKS functions belong to class I. Either they are detected within GKS itself (situation A) or a procedure called from GKS has returned control to the corresponding GKS procedure with the appropriate error information (situation B). In all these class I cases, GKS calls the error handling procedure. If a GKS function is called with more than one error condition applicable, at least one error is reported.

9.2   The Emergency Closure Procedure

The EMERGENCY CLOSE GKS procedure is an implementation-dependent facility. Its purpose is to save as much of the graphical information produced as possible. It may be called directly from the application program and also by GKS itself as an error reaction.

The way in which the graphical information is saved by the EMERGENCY CLOSE GKS procedure is mainly done by properly closing the workstations which are active or open when the error condition occurs. Metafile output workstations, for example, are deactivated, suitable "END records" are written to the files, and they are properly released. Similar things may happen if certain workstations produce intermediate graphical files (e.g., the buffers of microfilm and plotter workstations). Implementations of the emergency closure procedure should take care that such files are properly closed in order to subsequently produce pictures from them.

The definition of the emergency closure procedure is as follows:

EMERGENCY CLOSE GKS   GKCL,GKOP,WSOP,WSAC,SGOP   L0a
Parameters: none
Effect:
  GKS is emergency closed. The following actions are performed (if possible):
    — CLOSE SEGMENT (if open);
    — UPDATE for all open workstations;
    — DEACTIVATE all active workstations;
    — CLOSE all open workstations;
    — CLOSE GKS.
Note:
  This function may be called even if the error state is ON.
———————————————————— *FORTRAN-Interface* ————————————————————

CALL GECLKS
Parameters: none

9.3 The ERROR HANDLING and ERROR LOGGING Procedures

The application program may either provide its own error handling procedure or may use the standard ERROR HANDLING procedure provided as part of GKS. The error handling procedure is called by GKS in any of the error situations listed in Section 9.6. The following information is passed to it:
— the identification of the error condition (error number as listed in Section 9.6);
— the identification of the GKS function called by the application program which called the ERROR HANDLING procedure (procedure names as defined in the GKS document or in a language binding);
— the error file;

The ERROR HANDLING procedure provided by GKS just calls the ERROR LOGGING procedure using the same set of parameters. The latter performs the following actions:
a) prints an error message and GKS function identification on the error file;
b) returns to the calling procedure.

The definition of the ERROR HANDLING procedure is as follows:

ERROR HANDLING   GKCL,GKOP,WSOP,WSAC,SGOP   L0a
Parameters:

Input	error number as listed in Section 9.6	I
Input	identification of the GKS procedure called by the application program which caused the error detection	N
Input	error file	N

Note:
The last parameter has been defined in OPEN GKS.
Effect:
The ERROR HANDLING procedure is called by GKS in any of the error situations listed in Section 9.6. The standard procedure just calls the ERROR LOGGING procedure with the same parameters.
Note:
The ERROR HANDLING procedure may be replaced by an application program supplied procedure to allow specific reaction to some error situations. Any application program supplied error handling procedure should at least perform the effect of the standard error handling procedure.

――――――――――――― *FORTRAN-Interface* ―――――――――――――

CALL GERHND (ERRNR,FCTID,ERRFIL)
Parameters:

Input	ERRNR	error number	(1..n)	INTEGER
Input	FCTID	function identification	(1..n)	INTEGER
Input	ERRFIL	error message file		INTEGER

An application-supplied error handling procedure which replaces the standard one, may define a COMMON area that can be accessed both by the error handling routine and the application program. Examples are given below.

It has access to the GKS state table information via the GKS inquiry functions. The actual GKS states correspond to the GKS operating state prior to the GKS function call which caused the error. However, no modification of GKS states is possible during error handling, i.e., only GKS INQUIRY functions, the ERROR LOGGING procedure and the EMERGENCY CLOSE GKS procedure may be called by the ERROR HANDLING procedure. This is achieved by setting the error state to ON prior to calling the ERROR HANDLING procedure from GKS and resetting the error state to OFF afterwards. An inquiry function cannot generate an error; if one is called in an erroneous situation, it reports the error condition in a specific output parameter.

The definition of the ERROR LOGGING procedure is as follows:

ERROR LOGGING   GKCL,GKOP,WSOP,WSAC,SGOP   L0a

Parameters:
   Input   error number as listed in Section 9.6   I
   Input   identification of the GKS procedure called by the   N
             application program which caused the error detection
   Input   error file   N

Note:
The last parameter has been defined in OPEN GKS.

Effect:
The ERROR LOGGING procedure prints an error message and GKS function identification on the error file and returns to the calling procedure.

———————————————— *FORTRAN-Interface* ————————————————

CALL GERLOG (ERRNR,FCTID,ERRFIL)
Parameters:
   Input   ERRNR   error number   (1..n)   INTEGER
   Input   FCTID   function identification   (1..n)   INTEGER
   Input   ERRFIL   error message file   INTEGER

An example of an application program supplied error handling procedure follows:

Example 9.1   Error handling (special treatment)

———————————————————— *Pascal* ————————————————————

L10   PROCEDURE ERROR HANDLING
        (ERROR_NUMBER,FUNCTION_IDENT, ERROR_FILE)
                             {call ERROR LOGGING procedure}
L20   ERROR_LOGGING
        (ERROR_NUMBER, FUNCTION_IDENT, ERROR_FILE)
                  {interpret GKS FUNCTION IDENTIFICATION
                          and ERROR NUMBER to select}
                         {case of special treatment via procedure ST }
L30   SPECIAL_TREATMENT = ST(FUNCTION_IDENT, ERROR_NUMBER);

L40 IF SPECIAL_TREATMENT THEN BEGIN
{gather more relevant information about the error environment}
{using inquiry functions};
L50 INQUIRE ....;
L60 INQUIRE ....;
{store information in application program provided global area};
L70 GLOBAL_VARIABLE_A := ;
L80 GLOBAL_VARIABLE_B := ;
L90 END {end if};
L100 END {return to calling GKS procedure};

───────────────────────── *Fortran* ─────────────────────────

L10		SUBROUTINE GERHND (ERRNB,FCTID,ERRFIL)
L11		INTEGER ERRNB,FCTID,ERRFIL
	C	*** common data area for communication with application program
L12		COMMON /GKCERR/ COMA,COMB
	C	*** call ERROR LOGGING procedure
L20		CALL GERLOG (ERRNB,FCTID,ERRFIL)
	C	*** interpret GKS function identification and error number to
	C	*** select a special case of treatment
L30		IF (.NOT. ST (FCTID,ERRNR) RETURN
	C	*** gather more relevant information about the error environment
	C	*** using the GKS inquiry functions
L50		CALL GQ...........
L60		CALL GQ...........
	C	*** store information in application program provided
	C	*** COMMON AREA variables
L70		COMA = ...
L80		COMB = ...
L90		RETURN
L100		END

9.4 Error Detection Within GKS Procedures

All GKS procedures perform the following actions after detecting an error condition:
— set error state to ON;
— call error handling procedure with parameters as described above;
— reset error state to OFF;
— Perform built-in error reaction (normally, a function causing an error has no effect; to accomplish this in some cases requires clean-up operations).

All GKS procedures must check on entry (in the following order):
— that GKS is in the correct state;
— that the values of input parameters are valid.

At least the first error detected must be reported.

9.5   Reaction of Application Programs to Error Detections

An application program is notified of an error detection by entries in the error communication area. Usually, the application program has to provide higher, application-specific error handling parts to process possibly occurring erroneous situations.

Within the application program, error checking parts of code should be provided at all places, where errors are expected or where possibly occurred errors might cause damage for further processing. This may range from checking error states after each call of a GKS function (or a group of those) in highly interactive applications, to only checking a possible error occurrence at the end of a program execution. The latter case might be supported by Example 9.1. Some typical error situations and reactions are listed in the following Section 9.6.

9.6   List of GKS Error Numbers and Messages

GKS recognizes several types of error situations. A classification is shown in this chapter. One specific type of errors should be mentioned particularly: the invalid parameters. This type of error occurs if restrictions to certain ranges of the data are ignored; examples are:
— Negative or zero integer numbers are used, when only positive numbers are allowed, like restricting polyline indices to the integer range 1 to n; These restrictions are listed with the parameter definitions of the GKS function specifications;
— language-dependent restrictions are violated. Enumeration types in FORTRAN for example, are mapped to a range of integer values starting with 0.

Thus, besides the GKS function definitions, the language binding rules have to be taken into account when determining parameter values. With each FORTRAN GKS function in this textbook, these additional rules are listed.

9.6.1   States

In every implementation for each GKS function, the first error to be checked is whether or not the function is applied in the correct state. If an operating state error occurs, it has to be reported first. All other possibly following errors might be meaningless. For each GKS function, the appropriate operating states are listed with the function name. If this error occurs, the program should be aborted and carefully corrected.

Some examples of error causing situations are:
— The first call to GKS is not OPEN GKS (errors 2 to 8, especially 2 and 8);
— It was forgotten to OPEN a WORKSTATION, before accessing attached input devices and workstation states like attributes (errors 6 and 7);

— The program has missed to ACTIVATE a WORKSTATION, before producing output and generating segments (errors 3,5,7);
— A segment is not OPEN, when CLOSE SEGMENT is called (error 4);
— It is attempted to re-OPEN GKS, when GKS is open (error 1).

Errors:

1	GKS not in proper state: GKS shall be in the state GKCL
2	GKS not in proper state: GKS shall be in the state GKOP
3	GKS not in proper state: GKS shall be in the state WSAC
4	GKS not in proper state: GKS shall be in the state SGOP
5	GKS not in proper state: GKS shall be either in the state WSAC or in the state SGOP
6	GKS not in proper state: GKS shall be either in the state WSOP or in the state WSAC
7	GKS not in proper state: GKS shall be in one of the states WSOP, WSAC or SGOP
8	GKS not in proper state: GKS shall be in one of the states GKOP, WSOP, WSAC or SGOP

9.6.2 Workstations

A variety of errors can be produced by erroneously addressing workstations. Besides invalid names for workstation identifiers (error 20), for connection identifiers (error 21), and for workstation types (error 22), a desired workstation type may not be available in an installation (error 23) or cannot be opened (error 26). The latter case might, for example, occur when the workstation is assigned to another user (GKS program).

The further errors are caused in most cases by access to workstation states either when the workstation is not in a suitable operating state (open, not open, active, not active), or if the workstation is not of a suitable type. An example of the latter case is the definition of workstation attributes or workstation transformations for segment storage and metafile input workstations.

In most cases, workstation errors occur for three reasons:
— They are not available;
— A wrong workstation identifier is used (editing mistake);
— A series of GKS functions is applied to all open or all active workstations without inspecting and distinguishing their type.

Errors:

20	Specified workstation identifier is invalid
21	Specified connection identifier is invalid
22	Specified workstation type is invalid
23	Specified workstation type does not exist
24	Specified workstation is open
25	Specified workstation is not open
26	Specified workstation cannot be opened
27	Workstation Independent Segment Storage is not open
28	Workstation Independent Segment Storage is already open

29	Specified workstation is active
30	Specified workstation is not active
31	Specified workstation is of category MO
32	Specified workstation is not of category MO
33	Specified workstation is of category MI
34	Specified workstation is not of category MI
35	Specified workstation is of category INPUT
36	Specified workstation is Workstation Independent Segment Storage
37	Specified workstation is not of category OUTIN
38	Specified workstation is neither of category INPUT nor of category OUTIN
39	Specified workstation is neither of category OUTPUT nor of category OUTIN
40	Specified workstation has no pixel store readback capability
41	Specified workstation type is not able to generate the specified generalized drawing primitive

9.6.3   Transformations

Most of the transformation errors occur because of violating specific boundaries:
— The viewport and the workstation window have to be within NDC space (errors 52 and 53);
— The workstation viewport has to be within the maximum display surface size (error 54) which can be inquired via the INQUIRE MAXIMUM DISPLAY SURFACE SIZE;
— The order of the parameters is wrong (XMIN,XMAX,YMIN,YMAX) (error 51).

Errors:

50	Transformation number is invalid
51	Rectangle definition is invalid
52	Viewport is not within the Normalized Device Coordinate unit square
53	Workstation window is not within the Normalized Device Coordinate unit square
54	Workstation viewport is not within the display space

9.6.4   Output Attributes

Besides violating data restrictions (polyline, polymarker, text, fill area, and pattern indices have to be within 1 to n), the other errors typically occur when inquiry functions for non-existing attribute representations are issued.

Errors:

60	Polyline index is invalid
61	A representation for the specified polyline index has not been defined on this workstation
62	Linetype is less than or equal to zero

63	Specified linetype is not supported on this workstation
64	Polymarker index is invalid
65	A representation for the specified polymarker index has not been defined on this workstation
66	Marker type is less than or equal to zero
67	Specified marker type is not supported on this workstation
68	Text index is invalid
69	A representation for the specified text index has not been defined on this workstation
70	Text font is less than or equal to zero
71	Requested text font is not supported for the required precision on this workstation
72	Character expansion factor is less than or equal to zero
73	Character height is less than or equal to zero
74	Length of character up vector is zero
75	Fill area index is invalid
76	A representation for the specified fill area index has not been defined on this workstation
77	Specified fill area interior style is not supported on this workstation
78	Style (pattern or hatch) index is less than or equal to zero
79	Specified pattern index is invalid
80	Specified hatch style is not supported on this workstation
81	Pattern size value is not positive
82	A representation for the specified pattern index has not been defined on this workstation
83	Interior style PATTERN is not supported on this workstation
84	Dimensions of colour array are invalid
85	Colour index is less than zero
86	Colour index is invalid
87	A representation for the specified colour index has not been defined
88	Colour is outside range [0,1]
89	Pick identifier is invalid

9.6.5 Output Primitives

Errors:

100	Number of points is invalid
101	Invalid code in string
102	Generalized drawing primitive identifier is invalid
103	Content of generalized drawing primitive data record is invalid
104	At least one active workstation is not able to generate the specified generalized drawing primitive

9.6.6 Segments

Errors:

120	Specified segment name is invalid
121	Specified segment name is already in use

122   Specified segment does not exist
123   Specified segment does not exist on specified workstation
124   Specified segment does not exist on Workstation Independent Segment Storage
125   Specified segment is open
126   Segment priority is outside the range [0,1]

9.6.7   Input

Errors:
140   Specified input device is not present on workstation
141   Input device is not in REQUEST mode
142   Input device is not in SAMPLE mode
143   EVENT/SAMPLE input mode is not available at this level of GKS
144   Specified prompt and echo type is not supported on this workstation
145   Echo area is outside display space
146   Contents of input data record are invalid
147   Input queue has overflowed
148   Input queue has not overflowed since GKS was opened or the last invocation of INQUIRE INPUT QUEUE OVERFLOW
149   Input queue has overflowed, but associated workstation has been closed
150   No input value of the correct class is in the current event report
151   Timeout is invalid
152   Initial value is invalid
153   Length of initial string is greater than the implementation defined maximum

9.6.8   Metafiles

Errors:
160   Item type is not allowed for user items
161   Item length is invalid
162   No record is left in GKS metafile input
163   Metafile item is invalid
164   Item type is not a valid GKS item
165   Content of item data record is invalid for the specified item type
166   Maximum item data record length is invalid
167   User item cannot be interpreted

9.6.9   Escape

Errors:
180   Specified function is not supported
181   Contents of escape data record is invalid

9.6.10   Implementation-Dependent Errors

The following error detections depend on the particular GKS implementation, the operating system, the linkage editor, the run-time support system, etc. They are candidates for causing an emergency closure of GKS as in many cases unpredictable results may have been produced when these errors are detected. GKS functions may already have changed states and performed operations which cannot be reverted when the error occurs.

Error 300 is usually reported during linkage editor time in the form of unsatisfied references to non-existing library elements (also error 307). Erroneously bound programs cannot or should not be executed, except when it is ensured that the non-existing functions are not called during program execution.

Errors 301 and 302 report internal storage overflow. These errors can only be handled if programs react immediately after their occurrence. A reaction, for example, might be
— to close the open segment,
— to delete it (since its contents are unsafe);
— to swap other existing segments to metafiles or to plot and delete them;
— and possibly, to increase the storage space.

Errors 303 to 309 usually lead to abnormal program termination; if control is returned to GKS properly, it could either try to send or receive data repeatedly, or stop the program by calling the emergency closure procedure.

Typical situations producing I/O errors arise when devices and communication lines do not work properly, are not connected, are interrupted, etc.

Errors:

300	Specified function is not supported in this level of GKS
301	Storage overflow has occurred in GKS
302	Storage overflow has occurred in segment storage
303	Input/Output error has occurred while reading
304	Input/Output error has occurred while writing
305	Input/Output error has occurred while sending data to a workstation
306	Input/Output error has occurred while receiving data from a workstation
307	Input/Output error has occurred during program library management
308	Input/Output error has occurred while reading workstation description table
309	Arithmetic error has occurred

9.6.11   Other Errors

Other errors are numbered from 900 onwards; examples of those are:

Errors:

998   not yet implemented:
if GKS implementations are not yet completed and the application program demands not-existing features, this error message should be issued. Examples are missing linetypes 2 to 4, missing marker types up to 5, etc.; in general, facilities which belong to the minimal requirements in a level.

999   Implementation error:
Within a GKS implementation, inconsistent states and operations might be self-checked; if an implementation error is recognized, this message may be issued. Note, that this should be reported to the system's experts.

9.7   Exercises

Exercise 9.1   Emergency closing GKS

Design an EMERGENCY CLOSE GKS procedure as defined in Section 9.2 using GKS functions. Care should be taken, that the GKS functions are only called if necessary according to the current GKS states, e.g., only active workstations should be deactivated.

Exercise 9.2   Reaction to operating state errors

Write an extension to the error handling procedure of Example 9.1 and design a corresponding error reaction of the application program. Assume that the application program calls a POLYLINE function, and error 5 occurs. Program the following actions:
— Within the error handling procedure, record the current operating state in an error communication area.
— Within the application program, check whether an error occurred after the return of the POLYLINE function. Using the INQUIRY functions, correct the GKS state in such a way that the POLYLINE function is applicable.

Exercise 9.3   Reaction to segment storage overflow

Write a program creating segments which reacts to error 302 (storage overflow has occurred in segment storage). It should ensure that the finally produced graphical information is consistent (no output is lost). Use a metafile workstation for your application program.

10   INQUIRY FUNCTIONS

10.1   State Lists and Inquiry Functions

Inquiry functions allow the application program to get information about the current state of GKS. As explained in Chapter 3, the complete state of GKS is stored in a number of state lists and description tables. Every value present in one of the lists can be retrieved by the application program by using inquiry functions. Therefore, the inquiry functions can be divided into the following eight groups:
— an inquiry function for the operating state;
— inquiry functions for the GKS state list;
— inquiry functions for the workstation state lists;
— inquiry functions for the segment state lists;

— inquiry functions for the GKS error state list;
— inquiry functions for the pixel memory of raster type workstations;
— inquiry functions for the GKS description table;
— inquiry functions for the workstation description table.

10.1.1 Error Reports in Inquiry Functions

Since the inquiry functions are the only functions that can be called by an error recovery routine, a recursion could occur if the inquiry routine itself would try to report an error (see Chapter 9). In order to avoid this 'error in the error recovery' situation, the inquiry functions do not report errors by using the normal GKS error handling method, but instead return an additional parameter 'error indicator'. The error indicator has the value zero if no error has been detected by the inquiry function. If an error is to be reported the error number is returned in the error indicator and the values of the other output parameters are implementation-dependent.

10.1.2 Inquiry Functions for the Settable State Lists

The first five groups of inquiry functions generally return values that previously have been set by the application program itself. The question could arise why they are needed, since the application program itself could keep track of the values it has set. One reason for using the inquiry functions advantageously is the following: If an application layer is to be constructed on top of GKS, it will probably consist of a set of subroutines that themselves call GKS functions. If such an application subroutine changes the state of GKS, it might wish to reset it to the previous state before returning control to its caller. This can be done easily by inquiring the GKS state after the subroutine is entered, saving the values, and resetting the state to the values before returning (see Example 10.1, page 390).

The group of inquiry functions for the workstation state list can also be used for another reason: In many cases the workstations are not able to realize the parameters of the functions changing the workstation state in exactly the way they are passed to them, e.g., the SET POLYLINE REPRESENTATION function contains the parameters 'linetype', 'linewidth scale factor', and 'colour index'. The workstation will use a linetype and linewidth as near as possible to the ones desired, and use colour index 1 if the desired colour index is outside the allowed range on the workstation. So there will be a difference between the SET values and the REALIZED values on a workstation. In order to be able to retrieve both types of values most of the inquiry functions for the workstation state list have an input parameter of enumeration type 'type of returned value'. It can be set either to SET or to REALIZED. The inquiry function will return the workstation state list values either as SET by the application program or as REALIZED by the workstation (see Example 10.2, page 393).

10.1.3   Inquiry Functions for the Workstation Description Table

The GKS description table and the workstation description table cannot be changed by the application program, they are set up by the implementation. The GKS description table contains information about the GKS implementation, e.g., GKS level, available workstation types, and number of normalization transformations. The workstation description table contains a set of values describing the capabilities of every workstation type present in the implementation. Therefore, the description tables are the most important source of information for an application program that wants to test its graphical environment. If application programs based on GKS are designed to be portable between a wide range of GKS implementations and graphics devices, they will have to make extensive use of the inquiry functions for the description tables. They will find out whether the GKS implementation and the workstations have sufficient capabilities for the application to be realized, and adjust their behaviour accordingly (see Example 10.3, page 394).

10.1.4   Inquiry Functions for the Error State List and Pixel Memories

The only inquiry function for the GKS error state list is INQUIRE INPUT QUEUE OVERFLOW; it delivers the identification of the input device that caused the queue to overflow. Inquiry functions for the pixel memory of a raster type workstation return the colour indices of one or more pixels from the pixel memory of that workstation. Since there is a GKS rule that inquiry functions only can return values from any one of the GKS state lists, the pixel memories of raster type workstations have to be considered part of the GKS state. Normally, the state of a workstation pixel memory has been set by a number of GKS output functions (e.g., CLEAR WORKSTATION, SET xxx INDEX, SET xxx REPRESENTATION, SET COLOUR REPRESENTATION, POLYLINE, FILL AREA, PIXEL ARRAY, ...). However, the pixel memory could also be filled by a process not under GKS control or by an ESCAPE function call. In this way, the memory of a raster type workstation could be filled with a picture obtained by scanning a photograph. The pixel inquiry functions could be used to read the colour or intensity information into the GKS application program (see example 10.4). Naturally, not all workstations (not even all raster type workstations) will be able to deliver the colour values of pixels. In this case the pixel inquiry functions will return in the error indicator parameter error number 38 ("Specified workstation has no pixel store read-back capability").

10.2   Description of the Inquiry Functions

This section presents all inquiry functions from the GKS document and the FORTRAN interface for them.

In order to reduce the amount of space needed for representing the inquiry functions the 'Effect' in most cases is reduced to the following short form:

Effect:
The inquired values are returned. Possible error numbers:

This form replaces the following sentences that are part of the effect of almost all of the inquiry functions:

Effect:
If the inquired information is available, the error indicator is returned as 0 and values are returned in the output parameters. If the inquired information is not available, the values returned in the output parameters are implementation-dependent and the error indicator is set to one of the following error numbers to indicate the reason for non-availability:

Also, since none of the inquiry functions can raise an error, the phrase "Errors: none" has been omitted from the function definitions.

The error numbers that can be returned in the error indicator parameter by an inquiry function are listed, however, the error message text has been omitted. The message texts corresponding to the error numbers are listed in Chapter 9.6 on page 340 ff.

10.2.1   Inquiry Function for Operating State

INQUIRE OPERATING STATE VALUE
$\qquad\qquad\qquad\qquad\qquad$ GKCL,GKOP,WSOP,WSAC,SGOP   L0a

Parameters:
Output   operating state value (GKCL,GKOP,WSOP,WSAC,SGOP)   E
Effect:
The operating state of GKS is returned.

――――――――――――――― *FORTRAN-Interface* ―――――――――――――――

CALL GQOPS (OPSTA)
Parameters:
Output   OPSTA   operating state value
$\qquad\qquad$ (0 = GKCL,1 = GKOP,2 = WSOP,3 = WSAC,4 = SGOP)   INTEGER

10.2.2   Inquiry Functions for GKS Description Table

INQUIRE LEVEL OF GKS   GKCL,GKOP,WSOP,WSAC,SGOP   L0a
Parameters:
Output   error indicator   I
Output   level of GKS   (0a,0b,0c,1a,1b,1c,2a,2b,2c)   E
Effect:
The inquired values are returned. Possible error numbers: 8.

──────────────── *FORTRAN-Interface* ────────────────

CALL GQLVKS (ERRIND,LEVEL)
Parameters:
| Output | ERRIND | error indicator | | INTEGER |
| Output | LEVEL | level of GKS | | INTEGER |

$(0 = L0a, 1 = L0b, 2 = L0c, 3 = L1a, 4 = L1b,$
$5 = L1c, 6 = L2a, 7 = L2b, 8 = L2c)$

INQUIRE LIST OF AVAILABLE WORKSTATION TYPES
GKCL,GKOP,WSOP,WSAC,SGOP   L0a

Parameters:
Output	error indicator		I
Output	number of available workstation types	(1..n)	I
Output	list of available workstation types		nxN

Effect:
The inquired values are returned. Possible error numbers: 8.

──────────────── *FORTRAN-Interface* ────────────────

CALL GQEWK (N,ERRIND,NUMBER,WKTYPL)
Parameters:
Input	N	list element requested		INTEGER
Output	ERRIND	error indicator		INTEGER
Output	NUMBER	number of workstation types	(1..n)	INTEGER
Output	WKTYPL	n th element of av. workstation types		INTEGER

INQUIRE WORKSTATION MAXIMUM NUMBERS
GKCL,GKOP,WSOP,WSAC,SGOP   L1a

Parameters:
Output	error indicator		I
Output	maximum number of simultaneously open workstations	(1..n)	I
Output	maximum number of simultaneously active workstations	(1..n)	I
Output	maximum number of workstations associated with segment	(1..n)	I

Effect:
The inquired values are returned. Possible error numbers: 8.

──────────────── *FORTRAN-Interface* ────────────────

CALL GQWKM (ERRIND,MXOPWK,MXACWK,MXWKAS)
Output	ERRIND	error indicator		INTEGER
Output	MXOPWK	max. number of simult. open workst.	(1..n)	INTEGER
Output	MXACWK	max. number of simult. active workst.	(1..n)	INTEGER
Output	MXWKAS	max. number of workst. associated with segment	(1..n)	INTEGER

INQUIRE MAXIMUM NORMALIZATION TRANSFORMATION
NUMBER　　　　　　　　　　　　GKCL,GKOP,WSOP,WSAC,SGOP　L0a
Parameters:

Output	error indicator		I
Output	maximum normalization transformation number	(1..n)	I

Effect:

The inquired values are returned. Possible error numbers: 8.

──────────────── *FORTRAN-Interface* ────────────────

CALL GQMNTN (ERRIND,MAXTNR)

Parameters:

Output	ERRIND	error indicator		INTEGER
Output	MAXTNR	max. norm. transformation number	(1..n)	INTEGER

10.2.3　Inquiry Functions for GKS State List

INQUIRE SET OF OPEN WORKSTATIONS
　　　　　　　　　　　GKCL,GKOP,WSOP,WSAC,SGOP　L0a

Parameters:

Output	error indicator		I
Output	number of open workstations	(0..n)	I
Output	set of open workstations		nxN

Effect:

The inquired values are returned. At GKS level 0a, there is a maximum of one workstation in the set. Possible error numbers: 8.

──────────────── *FORTRAN-Interface* ────────────────

CALL GQOPWK (N,ERRIND,OL,WKIDL)

Parameters:

Input	N	set member requested		INTEGER
Output	ERRIND	error indicator		INTEGER
Output	OL	number of open workstations	(0..n)	INTEGER
Output	WKIDL	nth member of set of open workstations		INTEGER

INQUIRE SET OF ACTIVE WORKSTATIONS
　　　　　　　　　　　GKCL,GKOP,WSOP,WSAC,SGOP　L1a

Parameters:

Output	error indicator		I
Output	number of active workstations	(0..n)	I
Output	set of active workstations		nxN

Effect:

The inquired values are returned. Possible error numbers: 8.

──────────────── *FORTRAN-Interface* ────────────────

CALL GQACWK (N,ERRIND,OL,WKIDL)

Parameters:

Input	N	set member requested	INTEGER
Output	ERRIND	error indicator	INTEGER

Output	OL	number of active workstations	(0..n)	INTEGER
Output	WKIDL	nth member of set of active worksta-tions		INTEGER

INQUIRE CURRENT PRIMITIVE ATTRIBUTE VALUES
GKCL,GKOP,WSOP,WSAC,SGOP   L0a

Parameters:

Output	error indicator			I
Output	current polyline index		(1..n)	I
Output	current polymarker index		(1..n)	I
Output	current text index		(1..n)	I
Output	current character height	WC	>0	R
Output	current character up vector	WC		2xR
Output	current text path	(RIGHT,LEFT,UP,DOWN)		E
Output	current text alignment			
	(NORMAL,LEFT,CENTRE,RIGHT;NORMAL,TOP,			
	CAP,HALF,BASE,BOTTOM)			
				2xE
Output	current fill area index		(1..n)	I
Output	current pattern size	WC		2xR
Output	current pattern reference point	WC		P
Output	current pick identifier			N

Effect:

The inquired values are returned. Possible error numbers: 8.

--------------------------- *FORTRAN-Interface* ---------------------------

INQUIRE CURRENT SETTING OF PRIMITIVE ATTRIBUTES
CALL GQPLI (ERRIND,POLYLI)

Parameters:

Output	ERRIND	error indicator		INTEGER
Output	POLYLI)	current polyline index	(1..n)	INTEGER

CALL GQPMI (ERRIND,POLYMI)

Parameters:

Output	ERRIND	error indicator		INTEGER
Output	POLYMI	current polymarker index	(1..n)	INTEGER

CALL GQTXI (ERRIND,TEXTI)

Parameters:

Output	ERRIND	error indicator		INTEGER
Output	TEXTI	current text index	(1..n)	INTEGER

CALL GQCHH (ERRIND,CHARHI)

Parameters:

Output	ERRIND	error indicator		INTEGER
Output	CHARHI	current character height WC	>0	REAL

CALL GQCHUP (ERRIND,CHRUPX,CHRUPY)

Parameters:

Output	ERRIND	error indicator		INTEGER
Output	CHRUPX,CHRUPY	current character up vector WC		2xREAL

CALL GQTXP (ERRIND,TXPATH)
Parameters:

Output	ERRIND	error indicator	INTEGER
Output	TXPATH	current character path	INTEGER
		(0 = right, 1 = left, 2 = up, 3 = down)	

CALL GQTXAL (ERRIND,TXALH,TXALV)
Parameters:

Output	ERRIND	error indicator	INTEGER
Output	TXALH	current horizontal alignment	INTEGER
		(0 = normal, 1 = left, 2 = centre, 3 = right)	
Output	TXALV	current vertical alignment	INTEGER
	(0 = normal, 1 = top, 2 = cap, 3 = half, 4 = base, 5 = bottom)		

CALL GQFAI (ERRIND,FILLAI)
Parameters:

Output	ERRIND	error indicator		INTEGER
Output	FILLAI	current fill area index	(1..n)	INTEGER

CALL GQPA (ERRIND,PATTSX,PATTSY)
Parameters:

Output	ERRIND	error indicator		INTEGER
Output	PATTSX, PATTSY	current pattern size	WC	2xREAL

CALL GQPARF (ERRIND,REFPNX,REFPNY)
Parameters:

Output	ERRIND	error indicator	INTEGER
Output	REFPNX,REFPNY	current pattern reference point WC	REAL

CALL GQPKID (ERRIND,PICKID)
Parameters:

Output	ERRIND	error indicator	INTEGER
Output	PICKID	current pick identifier	INTEGER

INQUIRE CURRENT INDIVIDUAL ATTRIBUTE VALUES

GKCL,GKOP,WSOP,WSAC,SGOP   L0a

Parameters:

Output	error indicator		I
Output	linetype	(1..n)	I
Output	linewidth scale factor		R
Output	polyline colour index	(0..n)	I
Output	marker type	(1..n)	I
Output	marker size scale factor		R
Output	polymarker colour index	(0..n)	I
Output	text font and precision	(1..n;STRING,CHAR,STROKE)	(I;E)
Output	character expansion factor	>0	R
Output	character spacing		R
Output	text colour index	(0..n)	I
Output	fill area interior style		
	(HOLLOW,SOLID,PATTERN,HATCH)		E
Output	fill area style index	(1..n)	I
Output	fill area colour index	(0..n)	I
Output	list of aspect source flags	(BUNDLED,INDIVIDUAL)	13xE

Effect:
The inquired values are returned. Possible error numbers: 8.

———————————————— *FORTRAN-Interface* ——————————————

INQUIRE CURRENT INDIVIDUAL ATTRIBUTE VALUES
CALL GQLN (ERRIND,LNTYPE)

Parameters:

Output	ERRIND	error indicator		INTEGER
Output	LNTYPE	line type	(1..n)	INTEGER

CALL GQLWSC (ERRIND,LNWDSF)

Parameters:

Output	ERRIND	error indicator		INTEGER
Output	LNWDSF	linewidth scale factor		REAL

CALL GQPLCI (ERRIND,PLCOLI)

Parameters:

Output	ERRIND	error indicator		INTEGER
Output	PLCOLI	polyline colour index	(0..n)	INTEGER

CALL GQMK (ERRIND,MKTYPE)

Parameters:

Output	ERRIND	error indicator		INTEGER
Output	MKTYPE	marker type	(1..n)	INTEGER

CALL GQMKSC (ERRIND,MKSZSF)

Parameters:

Output	ERRIND	error indicator		INTEGER
Output	MKSZSF	marker size scale factor		REAL

CALL GQPMCI (ERRIND,PMCOLI)

Parameters:

Output	ERRIND	error indicator		INTEGER
Output	PMCOLI	polymarker colour index	(0..n)	INTEGER

CALL GQTXFP (ERRIND,TXFONT,TXPREC)

Parameters:

Output	ERRIND	error indicator	(1..n)	INTEGER
Output	TXFONT	text font		INTEGER
Output	TXPREC	text precision (0 = string, 1 = char, 2 = stroke)		INTEGER

CALL GQCHXP (ERRIND,CHARXP)

Parameters:

Output	ERRIND	error indicator		INTEGER
Output	CHARXP	character expansion factor	>0	REAL

CALL GQCHSP (ERRIND,CHARSP)

Parameters:

Output	ERRIND	error indicator		INTEGER
Output	CHARSP	character spacing		REAL

CALL GQTXCI (ERRIND,TXCOLI)

Parameters:

Output	ERRIND	error indicator		INTEGER
Output	TXCOLI	text colour index	(0..n)	INTEGER

CALL GQFAIS (ERRIND,FAINTS)

Parameters:

Output	ERRIND	error indicator		INTEGER
Output	FAINTS	fill area interior style		
		(0 = hollow, 1 = solid, 2 = pattern, 3 = hatch)		INTEGER

CALL GQFASI (ERRIND,FASI)

Parameters:

Output	ERRIND	error indicator		INTEGER
Output	FASI	fill area style index	(1..n)	INTEGER

CALL GQFACI (ERRIND,FACOLI)

Parameters:

Output	ERRIND	error indicator		INTEGER
Output	FACOLI	fill area colour index	(0..n)	INTEGER

CALL GQASF (ERRIND,LASP)

Parameters:

Output	ERRIND	error indicator		INTEGER
Output	LASP(13)	list of aspect source flags	(0 = bundled, 1 = individual)	INTEGER

INQUIRE CURRENT NORMALIZATION TRANSFORMATION NUMBER
GKCL,GKOP,WSOP,WSAC,SGOP   L0a

Parameters:

Output	error indicator		I
Output	current normalization transformation number	(0..n)	I

Effect:

The inquired values are returned. Possible error numbers: 8.

───────────────────── *FORTRAN-Interface* ─────────────────────

CALL GQCNTN (ERRIND,CTNR)

Parameters:

Output	ERRIND	error indicator		INTEGER
Output	CTNR	current norm. transf. number	(0..n)	INTEGER

INQUIRE LIST OF NORMALIZATION TRANSFORMATION NUMBERS
GKCL,GKOP,WSOP,WSAC,SGOP   L0a

Parameters:

Output	error indicator		I
Output	list of transformation numbers		nxI

Effect:

The inquired values are returned. The list of transformation numbers is ordered by viewport input priority, starting with the highest priority. Possible error numbers: 8.

───────────────────── *FORTRAN-Interface* ─────────────────────

CALL GQENTN (N,ERRIND,OL,NPRIO)

Parameters:

Input	N	list element requested	INTEGER
Output	ERRIND	error indicator	INTEGER
Output	OL	length of list	INTEGER
Output	NPRIO	n th element of list of transformation numbers, ordered by viewport input priority in decreasing order	INTEGER

INQUIRE NORMALIZATION TRANSFORMATION
GKCL,GKOP,WSOP,WSAC,SGOP   L0a

Parameters:

Input	normalization transformation number	I
Output	error indicator	I

Output	window limits	WC	4xR
Output	viewport limits	NDC	4xR

Effect:
The inquired values are returned. Possible error numbers: 8, 50.

─────────────────────────── *FORTRAN-Interface* ───────────────────────────

CALL GQNT (NTNR,ERRIND,WINDOW,VIEWPT
Parameters:

Input	NTNR	transformation number		INTEGER
Output	ERRIND	error indicator		INTEGER
Output	WINDOW(4)	window limits in world coordinates	WC	REAL
Output	VIEWPT(4)	viewport limits in normalized device coordinates	NDC	REAL

───

INQUIRE CLIPPING INDICATOR
GKCL,GKOP,WSOP,WSAC,SGOP   L0a

Parameters:

Output	error indicator		I
Output	clipping indicator	(CLIP,NOCLIP)	E

Effect:
The inquired values are returned. Possible error numbers: 8.

─────────────────────────── *FORTRAN-Interface* ───────────────────────────

CALL GQCLIP (ERRIND,CLIP)
Parameters:

Output	ERRIND	error indicator	INTEGER
Output	CLIP	clipping indicator	(0 = noclip, 1 = clip) INTEGER

───

INQUIRE SET OF SEGMENT NAMES IN USE
GKCL,GKOP,WSOP,WSAC,SGOP   L1a

Parameters:

Output	error indicator		I
Output	number of segment names	(0..n)	I
Output	set of segment names in use		nxN

Effect:
The inquired values are returned. Possible error numbers: 7.

─────────────────────────── *FORTRAN-Interface* ───────────────────────────

CALL GQSGUS (N,ERRIND,OL,SEGNAM)
Parameters:

Input	N	set member requested		INTEGER
Output	ERRIND	error indicator		INTEGER
Output	OL	number of segment names	(0..n)	INTEGER
Output	SEGNAM	Nth member of set of segment names in use		INTEGER

INQUIRE NAME OF OPEN SEGMENT
GKCL,GKOP,WSOP,WSAC,SGOP   L1a

Parameters:

Output	error indicator	I
Output	name of open segment	N

Effect:
The inquired values are returned. Possible error numbers: 4.

——————————— *FORTRAN-Interface* ———————————

CALL GQOPSG (ERRIND,SEGNAM)

Parameters:

Output	ERRIND	error indicator	INTEGER
Output	SEGNAM	name of open segment	INTEGER

INQUIRE MORE SIMULTANEOUS EVENTS
GKCL,GKOP,WSOP,WSAC,SGOP   L0c

Parameters:

Output	error indicator		I
Output	more simultaneous events	(NOMORE,MORE)	E

Effect:
The inquired values are returned. Possible error numbers: 7.

——————————— *FORTRAN-Interface* ———————————

CALL GQSIM (ERRIND,FLAG)

Parameters:

Output	ERRIND	error indicator	INTEGER
Output	FLAG	more simultaneous events	
		(0 = nomore, 1 = more)	INTEGER

10.2.4   Inquiry Functions for Workstation State List

INQUIRE WORKSTATION CONNECTION AND TYPE
GKCL,GKOP,WSOP,WSAC,SGOP   L0a

Parameters:

Input	workstation identifier	N
Output	error indicator	I
Output	connection identifier	N
Output	workstation type	N

Effect:
The inquired values are returned. Possible error numbers: 7, 20, 25.

——————————— *FORTRAN-Interface* ———————————

CALL GQWKC (WKID,ERRIND,CONID,WTYPE)

Parameters:

Input	WKID	workstation identifier	INTEGER
Output	ERRIND	error indicator	INTEGER
Output	CONID	connection identifier	INTEGER
Output	WTYPE	workstation type	INTEGER

INQUIRE WORKSTATION STATE

GKCL,GKOP,WSOP,WSAC,SGOP   L0a

Parameters:

Input	workstation identifier		N
Output	error indicator⸴		I
Output	workstation state	(INACTIVE,ACTIVE)	E

Effect:
The inquired values are returned. Possible error numbers: 7, 20, 25, 33, 35.

———————————————— *FORTRAN-Interface* ————————————————

CALL GQWKS (WKID,ERRIND,STATE)
Parameters:

Input	WKID	workstation identifier		INTEGER
Output	ERRIND	error indicator		INTEGER
Output	STATE	workstation state	(0 = inactive, 1 = active)	INTEGER

INQUIRE WORKSTATION DEFERRAL AND UPDATE STATES

GKCL,GKOP,WSOP,WSAC,SGOP   L0a

Parameters:

Input	workstation identifier		N
Output	error indicator		I
Output	deferral mode	(ASAP,BNIL,BNIG,ASTI)	E
Output	implicit regeneration mode	(SUPPRESSED,ALLOWED)	E
Output	display surface empty	(EMPTY,NOTEMPTY)	E
Output	new frame action necessary at update	(NO,YES)	E

Effect:
The inquired values are returned. Possible error numbers: 7, 20, 25, 33, 35.

———————————————— *FORTRAN-Interface* ————————————————

CALL GQWKDU (WKID,ERRIND,DEFMOD,REGMOD,EMPTY,NFRAME)
Parameters:

Input	WKID	workstation identifier		INTEGER
Output	ERRIND	error indicator		INTEGER
Output	DEFMOD	deferral mode	(0 = asap, 1 = bnil, 2 = bnig, 3 = asti)	INTEGER
Output	REGMOD	implicit regeneration mode	(0 = suppressed, 1 = allowed)	INTEGER
Output	EMPTY	display surface empty	(0 = empty, 1 = notempty)	INTEGER
Output	NFRAME	new frame action necessary at update	(0 = no, 1 = yes)	INTEGER

INQUIRE LIST OF POLYLINE INDICES

GKCL,GKOP,WSOP,WSAC,SGOP   L1a

Parameters:

Input	workstation identifier		N
Output	error indicator		I

Output	number of polyline bundle table entries	(5..n)	I
Output	list of defined polyline indices	(1..n)	nxI

Effect:
The inquired values are returned. Possible error numbers: 7, 20, 25, 33, 35, 36.

───────────────── *FORTRAN-Interface* ─────────────────

CALL GQEPLI (WKID,N,ERRIND,OL,PLIND)
Parameters:

Input	WKID	workstation identifier		INTEGER
Input	N	list element requested		INTEGER
Output	ERRIND	error indicator		INTEGER
Output	OL	number of polyline bundle table entries	(5..n)	INTEGER
Output	PLIND	Nth element of list of defined polyline indices	(1..n)	INTEGER

INQUIRE POLYLINE REPRESENTATION
GKCL,GKOP,WSOP,WSAC,SGOP   L1a

Parameters:

Input	workstation identifier		N
Input	polyline index	(1..n)	I
Input	type of returned values	(SET,REALIZED)	E
Output	error indicator		I
Output	linetype	(1..n)	I
Output	linewidth scale factor		R
Output	polyline colour index	(0..n)	I

Effect:
The inquired values are returned. Possible error numbers: 7, 20, 25, 33, 35, 36, 60, 61.

───────────────── *FORTRAN-Interface* ─────────────────

CALL GQPLR (WKID,PLI,TYPE,ERRIND,LNTYPE,LWIDTH,COLI)
Parameters:

Input	WKID	workstation identifier		INTEGER
Input	PLI	polyline index	(1..n)	INTEGER
Input	TYPE	type of returned values	(0 = set, 1 = realized)	INTEGER
Output	ERRIND	error indicator		INTEGER
Output	LNTYPE	linetype	(1..n)	INTEGER
Output	LWDITH	linewidth scale factor		REAL
Output	COLI	colour index	(0..n)	INTEGER

INQUIRE LIST OF POLYMARKER INDICES
GKCL,GKOP,WSOP,WSAC,SGOP   L1a

Parameters:

Input	workstation identifier	N
Output	error indicator	I

Output   number of polymarker bundle table entries   (5..n)   I
Output   list of defined polymarker indices   (1..n)   nxI
Effect:
The inquired values are returned. Possible error numbers: 7, 20, 25, 33, 35, 36.

──────────────────────── *FORTRAN-Interface* ────────────────────────

CALL GQEPMI (WKID,N,ERRIND,OL,PMIND)
Parameters:

Input	WKID	workstation identifier		INTEGER
Input	N	list element requested		INTEGER
Output	ERRIND	error indicator		INTEGER
Output	OL	number of polymarker bundle table entries	(5..n)	INTEGER
Output	PMIND	N th element of list of defined polymarker indices	(1..n)	INTEGER

INQUIRE POLYMARKER REPRESENTATION
GKCL,GKOP,WSOP,WSAC,SGOP   L1a

Parameters:

Input	workstation identifier		N
Input	polymarker index	(1..n)	I
Input	type of returned values	(SET,REALIZED)	E
Output	error indicator		I
Output	marker type	(1..n)	I
Output	marker size scale factor		R
Output	polyline colour index	(0..n)	I

Effect:
The inquired values are returned. Possible error numbers: 7, 20, 25, 33, 35, 36, 64, 65.

──────────────────────── *FORTRAN-Interface* ────────────────────────

CALL GQPMR (WKID,PMI,TYPE,ERRIND,MKTYPE,MKSSCF,COLI)
Parameters:

Input	WKID	workstation identifier		INTEGER
Input	PMI	polymarker index	(1..n)	INTEGER
Input	TYPE	type of returned values	(0 = set, 1 = realized)	INTEGER
Output	ERRIND	error indicator		INTEGER
Output	MKTYPE	marker type	(1..n)	INTEGER
Output	MKSSCF	marker size scale factor		REAL
Output	COLI	colour index	(0..n)	INTEGER

INQUIRE LIST OF TEXT INDICES
GKCL,GKOP,WSOP,WSAC,SGOP   L1a

Parameters:

Input	workstation identifier		N
Output	error indicator		I

| Output | number of text bundle table entries | (6..n) | I |
| Output | list of defined text indices | (1..n) | nxI |

Effect:

The inquired values are returned. Possible error numbers: 7, 20, 25, 33, 35, 36.

———————————————— *FORTRAN-Interface* ————————————————

CALL GQETXI (WKID,N,ERRIND,OL,TXIND)

Parameters:

Input	WKID	workstation identifier		INTEGER
Input	N	list element requested		INTEGER
Output	ERRIND	error indicator		INTEGER
Output	OL	number of text bundle table entries	(6..n)	INTEGER
Output	TXIND	Nth element of list of defined text indices	(1..n)	INTEGER

INQUIRE TEXT REPRESENTATION

GKCL,GKOP,WSOP,WSAC,SGOP   L1a

Parameters:

Input	workstation identifier		N
Input	text index	(1..n)	I
Input	type of returned values	(SET,REALIZED)	E
Output	error indicator		I
Output	text font and precision	(1..n;STRING,CHAR,STROKE)	(I;E)
Output	character expansion factor	>0	R
Output	character spacing		R
Output	text colour index	(0..n)	I

Effect:

The inquired values are returned. Possible error numbers: 7, 20, 25, 33, 35, 36, 68, 69.

———————————————— *FORTRAN-Interface* ————————————————

CALL GQTXR
(WKID,TXI,TYPE,ERRIND,FONT,PREC,CHARXP,CHARSP,COLI)

Parameters:

Input	WKID	workstation identifier		INTEGER
Input	TXI	text index	(1..n)	INTEGER
Input	TYPE	type of returned values	(0=set, 1=realized)	INTEGER
Output	ERRIND	error indicator		INTEGER
Output	FONT	text font	(1..n)	INTEGER
Output	PREC	text precision	(0=string, 1=char, 2=stroke)	INTEGER
Output	CHARXP	character expansion factor	>0	REAL
Output	CHARSP	character spacing		REAL
Output	COLI	text colour index	(0..n)	INTEGER

INQUIRE TEXT EXTENT   GKCL,GKOP,WSOP,WSAC,SGOP   L0a

Parameters:

| Input | workstation identifier | | N |
| Input | text position | WC | P |

Input	character string		S
Output	error indicator		I
Output	concatenation point	WC	P
Output	text extent rectangle	WC	4xP

Effect:

The inquired values are returned. The extent of the specified character string is computed using the text font and precision, character expansion factor and character spacing currently selected (either via the bundle or individually, depending upon the corresponding aspect source flag settings) and the current text attributes (CHARACTER HEIGHT, CHARACTER UP VECTOR, TEXT PATH, TEXT ALIGNMENT). The concatenation point can be used as the origin of a subsequent TEXT output primitive for the concatenation of character strings. For LEFT and RIGHT text path directions, the offset of the concatenation point from the text position is the character string width plus one additional CHARACTER SPACING along the text path direction. For UP and DOWN text paths, it is the character string height plus one additional CHARACTER SPACING along the text path. The text extent rectangle points define the rectangle which completely encloses the character bodies of the string (see Figure 10.1). For UP and DOWN text paths, the widest character body available in the font has to be enclosed. The text extent points are given in counterclockwise order. Possible error numbers: 7, 20, 25, 39, 101.

———————————————— *FORTRAN-Interface* ————————————————

CALL GQTXX (WKID,PX,PY,STR,ERRIND,CPX,CPY,TXEXPX,TXEXPY)

Parameters:

Input	WKID	workstation identifier		INTEGER
Input	PX,PY	text position	WC	2xREAL
Input	STR	character string		CHARACTER*(*)
Output	ERRIND	error indicator		INTEGER
Output	CPX,CPY	concatenation point	WC	2xREAL
Output	TXEXPX(4),TXEXPY(4)			
		text extent rectangle	WC	REAL

INQUIRE LIST OF FILL AREA INDICES

GKCL,GKOP,WSOP,WSAC,SGOP   L1a

Parameters:

Input	workstation identifier		N
Output	error indicator		I
Output	number of fill area bundle table entries	(5..n)	I
Output	list of defined fill area indices	(1..n)	nxI

Effect:

The inquired values are returned. Possible error numbers: 7, 20, 25, 33, 35, 36.

———————————————— *FORTRAN-Interface* ————————————————

CALL GQEFAI (WKID,N,ERRIND,OL,FAIND)

Parameters:

Input	WKID	workstation identifier		INTEGER
Input	N	list element requested		INTEGER
Output	ERRIND	error indicator		INTEGER

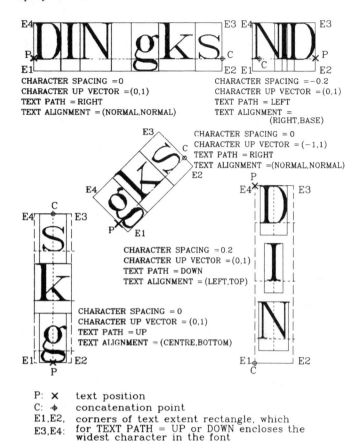

CHARACTER SPACING = 0
CHARACTER UP VECTOR = (0,1)
TEXT PATH = RIGHT
TEXT ALIGNMENT = (NORMAL,NORMAL)

CHARACTER SPACING = -0.2
CHARACTER UP VECTOR = (0,1)
TEXT PATH = LEFT
TEXT ALIGNMENT =
                (RIGHT,BASE)

CHARACTER SPACING = 0
CHARACTER UP VECTOR = (-1,1)
TEXT PATH = RIGHT
TEXT ALIGNMENT =(NORMAL,NORMAL)

CHARACTER SPACING = 0.2
CHARACTER UP VECTOR = (0,1)
TEXT PATH = DOWN
TEXT ALIGNMENT = (LEFT,TOP)

CHARACTER SPACING = 0
CHARACTER UP VECTOR = (0,1)
TEXT PATH = UP
TEXT ALIGNMENT = (CENTRE,BOTTOM)

P: ✗   text position
C: ✦   concatenation point
E1,E2,   corners of text extent rectangle, which
E3,E4:   for TEXT PATH = UP or DOWN encloses the
          widest character in the font

Figure 10.1 Examples for INQUIRE TEXT EXTENT

| Output | OL | number of fill area bundle table entries | (5..n) | INTEGER |
| Output | FAIND | Nth element of list of defined fill area indices | (1..n) | INTEGER |

INQUIRE FILL AREA REPRESENTATION
GKCL,GKOP,WSOP,WSAC,SGOP   L1a

Parameters:

Input	workstation identifier		N
Input	fill area index	(1..n)	I
Input	type of returned values	(SET,REALIZED)	E
Output	error indicator		I
Output	interior style	(HOLLOW,SOLID,PATTERN,HATCH)	E
Output	fill area style index	(1..n)	I
Output	fill area colour index	(0..n)	I

Effect:

The inquired values are returned. Possible error numbers: 7, 20, 25, 33, 35, 36, 75, 76.

──────────────── *FORTRAN-Interface* ────────────────

CALL GQFAR (WKID,FAI,TYPE,ERRIND,STYLE,STYLID,COLI)

Parameters:

Input	WKID	workstation identifier		INTEGER
Input	FAI	fill area index	(1..n)	INTEGER
Input	TYPE	type of returned values	(0 = set, 1 = realized)	INTEGER
Output	ERRIND	error indicator		INTEGER
Output	STYLE	interior style		
		(0 = hollow, 1 = solid, 2 = pattern, 3 = hatch)		INTEGER
Output	STYLID	style index	(1..n)	INTEGER
Output	COLI	colour index	(0..n)	INTEGER

INQUIRE LIST OF PATTERN INDICES

GKCL,GKOP,WSOP,WSAC,SGOP   L1a

Parameters:

Input	workstation identifier	N
Output	error indicator	I
Output	number of pattern table entries	(0..n)	I
Output	list of pattern indices	(1..n)	nxI

Effect:

The inquired values are returned. Possible error numbers: 7, 20, 25, 33, 35, 36.

──────────────── *FORTRAN-Interface* ────────────────

CALL GQEPAI (WKID,N,ERRIND,OL,PAIND)

Parameters:

Input	WKID	workstation identifier		INTEGER
Input	N	list element requested		INTEGER
Output	ERRIND	error indicator		INTEGER
Output	OL	number of pattern table entries	(0..n)	INTEGER
Output	PAIND	N th element of list of pattern indices	(1..n)	INTEGER

INQUIRE PATTERN REPRESENTATION

GKCL,GKOP,WSOP,WSAC,SGOP   L1a

Parameters:

Input	workstation identifier		N
Input	pattern index	(1..n)	I
Input	type of returned values	(SET,REALIZED)	E
Output	error indicator		I
Output	pattern array dimensions l,m	(1..n)	2xI
Output	pattern array	(0..n)	lxmxI

Effect:

The inquired values are returned. Possible error numbers: 7, 20, 25, 33, 35, 36, 79, 82, 83.

──────────────── *FORTRAN-Interface* ────────────────

CALL GQPAR (WKID,PAI,TYPE,NMX,MMX,ERRIND,N,M,PARRAY)

Parameters:

Input	WKID	workstation identifier		INTEGER
Input	PAI	pattern index	(1..n)	INTEGER

Input	TYPE	type of returned values	(0 = set, 1 = realized)	INTEGER
Input	NMX,MMX	maximum pattern array dimensions		INTEGER
Output	ERRIND	error indicator		INTEGER
Output	N,M	pattern array dimensions	(1..n)	INTEGER
Output	PARRAY(NMX,MMX)			
		pattern array	(0..n)	INTEGER

INQUIRE LIST OF COLOUR INDICES
GKCL,GKOP,WSOP,WSAC,SGOP   L0a

Parameters:

Input	workstation identifier		N
Output	error indicator		I
Output	number of colour table entries	(2..n)	I
Output	list of colour indices	(0..n)	nxI

Effect:

The inquired values are returned. Possible error numbers: 7, 20, 25, 33, 35, 36.

——————————————— *FORTRAN-Interface* ———————————————

CALL GQECI (WKID,N,ERRIND,OL,COLIND)
Parameters:

Input	WKID	workstation identifier		INTEGER
Input	N	list element requested		INTEGER
Output	ERRIND	error indicator		INTEGER
Output	OL	number of colour table entries	(2..n)	INTEGER
Output	COLIND	N th element of list of colour indices	(0..n)	INTEGER

INQUIRE COLOUR REPRESENTATION
GKCL,GKOP,WSOP,WSAC,SGOP   L0a

Parameters:

Input	workstation identifier		N
Input	colour index	(0..n)	I
Input	type of returned values	(SET,REALIZED)	E
Output	error indicator		I
Output	colour (red/green/blue intensities)	[0,1]	3xR

Effect:

The inquired values are returned. Possible error numbers: 7, 20, 25, 33, 35, 36, 86, 87.

——————————————— *FORTRAN-Interface* ———————————————

CALL GQCR (WKID,COLI,TYPE,ERRIND,RED,GREEN,BLUE)
Parameters:

Input	WKID	workstation identifier		INTEGER
Input	COLI	colour index	(0..n)	INTEGER
Input	TYPE	type of returned values	(0 = set, 1 = realized)	INTEGER
Output	ERRIND	error indicator		INTEGER
Output	RED,GREEN,BLUE			
		red/green/blue intensities	[0,1]	REAL

INQUIRE WORKSTATION TRANSFORMATION
GKCL,GKOP,WSOP,WSAC,SGOP   L0a

Parameters:

Input	workstation identifier	N
Output	error indicator	I
Output	workstation transformation update state	
	(NOTPENDING,PENDING)	E
Output	requested workstation window	NDC	4xR
Output	current workstation window	NDC	4xR
Output	requested workstation viewport	DC	4xR
Output	current workstation viewport	DC	4xR

Effect:

The inquired values are returned. The workstation transformation update state is PENDING if a workstation transformation change has been requested but not yet provided. Possible error numbers: 7, 20, 25, 33, 36.

––––––––––––––––––––––– *FORTRAN-Interface* –––––––––––––––––––––––

CALL GQWKT
(WKID,ERRIND,TUS,RWINDO,CWINDO,RVIEWP,CVIEWP)

Parameters:

Input	WKID	workstation identifier		INTEGER
Output	ERRIND	error indicator		INTEGER
Output	TUS	workstation transformation update		
		state (0 = notpending, 1 = pending)		INTEGER
Output	RWINDO(4)	requested workstation window	NDC	REAL
Output	CWINDO(4)	current workstation window	NDC	REAL
Output	RVIEWP(4)	requested workstation viewport	DC	REAL
Output	CVIEWP(4)	current workstation viewport	DC	REAL

INQUIRE SET OF SEGMENT NAMES ON WORKSTATION
GKCL,GKOP,WSOP,WSAC,SGOP   L1a

Parameters:

Input	workstation identifier		N
Output	error indicator		I
Output	number of segment names	(0..n)	I
Output	set of stored segments for this workstation		nxN

Effect:

The inquired values are returned. Possible error numbers: 7, 20, 25, 33, 35.

––––––––––––––––––––––– *FORTRAN-Interface* –––––––––––––––––––––––

CALL GQSGWK (WKID,N,ERRIND,OL,SEGNAM)

Parameters:

Input	WKID	workstation identifier		INTEGER
Input	N	set member requested		INTEGER
Output	ERRIND	error indicator		INTEGER
Output	OL	number of segment names	(0..n)	INTEGER
Output	SEGNAM	Nth set member of list of stored		
		segments for this workstation		INTEGER

INQUIRE LOCATOR DEVICE STATE
GKCL,GKOP,WSOP,WSAC,SGOP   L0b

Parameters:

Input	workstation identifier		N
Input	locator device number	(1..n)	I
Input	type of returned values	(SET,REALIZED)	E
Output	error indicator		I
Output	operating mode	(REQUEST,SAMPLE,EVENT)	E
Output	echo switch	(NOECHO,ECHO)	E
Output	initial normalization transformation number	(0..n)	I
Output	initial locator position	WC	P
Output	prompt/echo type	(1..n)	I
Output	echo area	DC	4xR
Output	locator data record		D

Effect:

The inquired values are returned. Possible error numbers: 7, 20, 25, 38, 140.

――――――――――――― *FORTRAN-Interface* ―――――――――――――

CALL GQLCS(WKID,LCDNR,TYPE,ILI,ERRIND,MODE,ESW,ITNR,ILPX,
ILPY,PET,EAREA,IL,IA)

Parameters:

Input	WKID	workstation identifier		INTEGER
Input	LCDNR	locator device number	(1..n)	INTEGER
Input	TYPE	type of returned values	(0 = set, 1 = realized)	INTEGER
Input	ILI	dimension of data record		INTEGER
Output	ERRIND	error indicator		INTEGER
Output	MODE	mode	(0 = request, 1 = sample, 2 = event)	INTEGER
Output	ESW	echo switch	(0 = noecho, 1 = echo)	INTEGER
Output	ITNR	init. norm. transformation number	(0..n)	INTEGER
Output	ILPX,ILPY	initial locator position	WC	2xREAL
Output	PET	prompt/echo type	(1..n)	INTEGER
Output	EAREA(4)	echo area	DC	REAL
Output	IL	length of data record		INTEGER
Output	IA(ILI)	data record		CHARACTER*80

INQUIRE STROKE DEVICE STATE
GKCL,GKOP,WSOP,WSAC,SGOP   L0b

Parameters:

Input	workstation identifier		N
Input	stroke device number	(1..n)	I
Input	type of returned values	(SET,REALIZED)	E
Output	error indicator		I
Output	operating mode	(REQUEST,SAMPLE,EVENT)	E
Output	echo switch	(ECHO,NOECHO)	E
Output	initial normalization transformation number	(0..n)	I
Output	initial number of points	(0..n)	I
Output	initial points in stroke	WC	nxP
Output	prompt/echo type	(1..n)	I

Output	echo area	DC	4xR
Output	stroke data record		D

Effect:

The inquired values are returned. Possible error numbers: 7, 20, 25, 38, 140.

———————————————— *FORTRAN-Interface* ————————————————

CALL GQSKS(WKID,SKDNR,TYPE,N,ILI,ERRIND,MODE,ESW,ITNR,
NP,PX,PY,PET,EAREA,BUFLEN,IL,IA)

Parameters:

Input	WKID	workstation identifier		INTEGER
Input	SKDNR	stroke device number	(1..n)	INTEGER
Input	TYPE	type of returned values	(0 = set, 1 = realized)	INTEGER
Input	N	maximum number of points		INTEGER
Input	ILI	dimension of stroke data record		INTEGER
Output	ERRIND	error indicator		INTEGER
Output	MODE	mode	(0 = request, 1 = sample, 2 = event)	INTEGER
Output	ESW	echo switch	(0 = noecho, 1 = echo)	INTEGER
Output	ITNR	init. norm. transformation number	(0..n)	INTEGER
Output	NP	number of points	(0..n)	INTEGER
Output	PX,PY	initial points in stroke	WC	nx2xREAL
Output	PET	prompt/echo type	(1..n)	INTEGER
Output	EAREA(4)	echo area	DC	REAL
Output	BUFLEN	buffer length for STROKE		INTEGER
Output	IL	length of data record		INTEGER
Output	IA(ILI)	data record		CHARACTER*80

INQUIRE VALUATOR DEVICE STATE

GKCL,GKOP,WSOP,WSAC,SGOP   L0b

Parameters:

Input	workstation identifier		N
Input	valuator device number	(1..n)	I
Output	error indicator		I
Output	operating mode	(REQUEST,SAMPLE,EVENT)	E
Output	echo switch	(ECHO,NOECHO)	E
Output	initial value		R
Output	prompt/echo type	(1..n)	I
Output	echo area	DC	4xR
Output	valuator data record		D

Effect:

The inquired values are returned. Possible error numbers: 7, 20, 25, 38, 140.

———————————————— *FORTRAN-Interface* ————————————————

CALL GQVLS (WKID,VLDNR,ILI,ERRIND,MODE,ESW,IVAL,PET,EAREA,
LOVAL,HIVAL,IL,IA)

Parameters:

Input	WKID	workstation identifier		INTEGER
Input	VLDNR	valuator device number	(1..n)	INTEGER
Input	ILI	dimension of data record		INTEGER
Output	ERRIND	error indicator		INTEGER

Output	MODE	mode	(0 = request, 1 = sample, 2 = event)	INTEGER
Output	ESW	echo switch	(0 = noecho, 1 = echo)	INTEGER
Output	IVAL	initial value		REAL
Output	PET	prompt/echo type	(1..n)	INTEGER
Output	EAREA(4)	echo area	DC	REAL
Output	LOVAL, HIVAL	minimal and maximal value		2xREAL
Output	IL	length of data record		INTEGER
Output	IA(ILI)	data record		CIIARACTER*80

INQUIRE CHOICE DEVICE STATE
GKCL,GKOP,WSOP,WSAC,SGOP   L0b

Parameters:

Input	workstation identifier		N
Input	choice device number	(1..n)	I
Output	error indicator		I
Output	operating mode	(REQUEST,SAMPLE,EVENT)	E
Output	echo switch	(ECHO,NOECHO)	E
Output	initial choice number	(0..n)	I
Output	prompt/echo type	(1..n)	I
Output	echo area	DC	4xR
Output	choice data record		D

Effect:

The inquired values are returned. Possible error numbers: 7, 20, 25, 38, 140.

─────────────── *FORTRAN-Interface* ───────────────

CALL GQCHS (WKID,CHDNR,ILI,ERRIND,MODE,ESW,ICHNR,PET, EAREA,IL,IA)

Parameters:

Input	WKID	workstation identifier		INTEGER
Input	CHDNR	choice device number	(1..n)	INTEGER
Input	ILI	dimension of data record		INTEGER
Output	ERRIND	error indicator		INTEGER
Output	MODE	mode	(0 = request, 1 = sample, 2 = event)	INTEGER
Output	ESW	echo switch	(0 = noecho, 1 = echo)	INTEGER
Output	ICHNR	initial choice number	(0..n)	INTEGER
Output	PET	prompt/echo type	(1..n)	INTEGER
Output	EAREA(4)	echo area	DC	REAL
Output	IL	length of data record		INTEGER
Output	IA(ILI)	data record		CHARACTER*80

INQUIRE PICK DEVICE STATE GKCL,GKOP,WSOP,WSAC,SGOP   L1b

Parameters:

Input	workstation identifier		N
Input	pick device number	(1..n)	I
Input	type of returned values	(SET,REALIZED)	I
Output	error indicator		I
Output	operating mode	(REQUEST,SAMPLE,EVENT)	E
Output	echo switch	(ECHO,NOECHO)	E

Output	initial status	(NONE,OK,NOPICK)		E
Output	initial segment			N
Output	initial pick identifier			N
Output	prompt/echo type		(1..n)	I
Output	echo area	DC		4xR
Output	pick data record			D

Effect:

The inquired values are returned. Possible error numbers: 7, 20, 25, 37, 140.

———————————————— *FORTRAN-Interface* ————————————————

CALL GQPKS (WKID,PCDNR,TYPE,ILI,ERRIND,MODE,ESW,ISTAT,
ISGNA,IPCID,PET,EAREA,IL,IA)

Parameters:

Input	WKID	workstation identifier		INTEGER
Input	PCDNR	pick device number	(1..n)	INTEGER
Input	TYPE	type of returned values	(0 = set, 1 = realized)	INTEGER
Input	ILI	dimension of data record		INTEGER
Output	ERRIND	error indicator		INTEGER
Output	MODE	mode	(0 = request, 1 = sample, 2 = event)	INTEGER
Output	ESW	echo switch	(0 = noecho, 1 = echo)	INTEGER
Output	ISTAT	initial status	(0 = none, 1 = ok, 2 = nopick)	INTEGER
Output	ISGNA	initial segment		INTEGER
Output	IPCID	initial pick identifier		INTEGER
Output	PET	prompt/echo type	(1..n)	INTEGER
Output	EAREA(4)	echo area	DC	REAL
Output	IL	length of data record		INTEGER
Output	IA(ILI)	data record		CHARACTER*80

INQUIRE STRING DEVICE STATE

                                              GKCL,GKOP,WSOP,WSAC,SGOP   L0b

Parameters:

Input	workstation identifier			N
Input	string device number		(1..n)	I
Output	error indicator			I
Output	operating mode	(REQUEST,SAMPLE,EVENT)		E
Output	echo switch	(ECHO,NOECHO)		E
Output	initial string			S
Output	prompt/echo type		(1..n)	I
Output	echo area	DC		4xR
Output	string data record			D

Effect:

The inquired values are returned. Possible error numbers: 7, 20, 25, 38, 140.

———————————————— *FORTRAN-Interface* ————————————————

CALL GQSTS (WKID,STDNR,ILI,ERRIND,MODE,ESW,LISTR,ISTR,
PET,EAREA,BUFLEN,INIPOS,IL,IA)

Parameters:

Input	WKID	workstation identifier		INTEGER
Input	STDNR	string device number	(1..n)	INTEGER
Input	ILI	dimension of string data record		INTEGER

Output	ERRIND	error indicator		INTEGER
Output	MODE	mode (0 = request, 1 = sample, 2 = event)		INTEGER
Output	ESW	echo switch (0 = noecho, 1 = echo)		INTEGER
Output	LISTR	character count (ISTR)		INTEGER
Output	ISTR	initial string		CHARACTER*(*)
Output	PET	prompt/echo type (1..n)		INTEGER
Output	EAREA(4)	echo area	DC	REAL
Output	BUFLEN	buffer length of string		INTEGER
Output	INIPOS	initial cursor position		INTEGER
Output	IL	length of data record		INTEGER
Output	IA(ILI)	data record		CHARACTER*80

10.2.5 Inquiry Functions for Workstation Description Table

INQUIRE WORKSTATION CATEGORY
                                    GKCL,GKOP,WSOP,WSAC,SGOP   L0a

Parameters:

Input	workstation type	N
Output	error indicator	I
Output	workstation category	
	(OUTPUT,INPUT,OUTIN,WISS,MO,MI)	E

Effect:
The inquired values are returned. Possible error numbers: 8, 22, 23.

——————————————— *FORTRAN-Interface* ———————————————

CALL GQWKCA (WTYPE,ERRIND,WKCAT)
Parameters:

Input	WTYPE	workstation type	INTEGER
Output	ERRIND	error indicator	INTEGER
Output	WKCAT	workstation category	
		(0 = output, 1 = input, 2 = outin, 3 = wiss, 4 = mo, 5 = mi)	INTEGER

INQUIRE WORKSTATION CLASSIFICATION
                                    GKCL,GKOP,WSOP,WSAC,SGOP   L0a

Parameters:

Input	workstation type	N
Output	error indicator	I
Output	vector/raster/other type (VECTOR,RASTER,OTHER)	E

Effect:
The inquired values are returned. Possible error numbers: 8, 22, 23, 31, 33, 35, 36.

——————————————— *FORTRAN-Interface* ———————————————

CALL GQWKCL (WTYPE,ERRIND,VRTYPE)
Parameters:

Input	WTYPE	workstation type	INTEGER
Output	ERRIND	error indicator	INTEGER
Output	VRTYPE	vector/raster/other type	
		(0 = vector, 1 = raster, 2 = other)	INTEGER

INQUIRE MAXIMUM DISPLAY SURFACE SIZE
GKCL,GKOP,WSOP,WSAC,SGOP   L0a

Parameters:

Input	workstation type			N
Output	error indicator			I
Output	device coordinate units		(METRES,OTHER)	E
Output	maximum display surface size	DC	>0	2xR
Output	maximum display surface size in raster units		(1..n)	2xI

Effect:

The inquired values are returned. Possible error numbers: 8, 22, 23, 31, 33, 36.

──────────────────── *FORTRAN-Interface* ────────────────────

CALL GQMDS (WTYPE,ERRIND,DCUNIT,RX,RY,LX,LY)

Parameters:

Input	WTYPE	workstation type		INTEGER
Output	ERRIND	error indicator		INTEGER
Output	DCUNIT	device coordinate units		
		(0 = metres, 1 = other)		INTEGER
Output	RX,RY	maximum display surface size	DC >0	REAL
Output	LX,LY	maximum display surface size (raster units)		INTEGER

INQUIRE POLYLINE FACILITIES
GKCL,GKOP,WSOP,WSAC,SGOP   L0a

Parameters:

Input	workstation type			N
Output	error indicator			I
Output	number of available linetypes		(4..n)	I
Output	list of available linetypes		(1..n)	nxI
Output	number of available linewidths		(0..n)	I
Output	nominal linewidth	DC	>0	R
Output	range of linewidths (minimum,maximum)	DC	>0	2xR
Output	number of predefined polyline indices		(5..n)	I

Effect:

The inquired values are returned. If the number of linewidths is returned as 0, the workstation supports a continuous range of linewidths. Possible error numbers: 8, 22, 23, 39.

──────────────────── *FORTRAN-Interface* ────────────────────

CALL GQPLF (WTYPE,N,ERRIND,NLT,LT,NLW,NOMLW,RLWMIN,
RLWMAX,NPPLI)

Parameters:

Input	WTYPE	workstation type		INTEGER
Input	N	list element requested		INTEGER
Output	ERRIND	error indicator		INTEGER
Output	NLT	number of available linetypes	(4..n)	INTEGER
Output	LT	N th element of list of available linetypes	(1..n)	INTEGER
Output	NLW	number of available linewidths	(0..n)	INTEGER
Output	NOMLW	nominal linewidth	DC >0	REAL

Output	RLWMIN,RWLMAX				
		range of linewidths	DC	>0	REAL
Output	NPPLI	number of predefined polyline indices		(5..n)	INTEGER

INQUIRE PREDEFINED POLYLINE REPRESENTATION
GKCL,GKOP,WSOP,WSAC,SGOP   L0a

Parameters:

Input	workstation type		N
Input	predefined polyline index	(1..n)	I
Output	error indicator		I
Output	linetype	(1..n)	I
Output	linewidth scale factor		R
Output	polyline colour index	(0..n)	I

Effect:

The inquired values are returned. Possible error numbers: 8, 22, 23, 39, 60.

──────────────── *FORTRAN-Interface* ────────────────

CALL GQPPLR (WTYPE,PLI,ERRIND,LNTYPE,LWIDTH,COLI)

Parameters:

Input	WTYPE	workstation type		INTEGER
Input	PLI	predefined polyline index	(1..n)	INTEGER
Output	ERRIND	error indicator		INTEGER
Output	LNTYPE	linetype	(1..n)	INTEGER
Output	LWIDTH	linewidth scale factor		REAL
Output	COLI	colour index	(0..n) R	INTEGER

INQUIRE POLYMARKER FACILITIES
GKCL,GKOP,WSOP,WSAC,SGOP   L0a

Parameters:

Input	workstation type			N
Output	error indicator			I
Output	number of available marker types		(5..n)	I
Output	list of available marker types		(1..n)	nxI
Output	number of available marker sizes		(0..n)	I
Output	nominal marker size	DC	>0	R
Output	range of marker sizes (minimum,maximum)	DC	>0	2xR
Output	number of predefined polymarker indices		(5..n)	I

Effect:

The inquired values are returned. If the number of marker sizes is returned as 0, the workstation supports a continuous range of marker sizes. Possible error numbers: 8, 22, 23, 39.

──────────────── *FORTRAN-Interface* ────────────────

CALL GQPMF (WTYPE,N,ERRIND,NMT,MT,NMS,NOMMS,RMSMIN,
RMSMAX,NPPMI)

Parameters:

Input	WTYPE	workstation type	INTEGER
Input	N	list element requested	INTEGER

Output	ERRIND	error indicator			INTEGER
Output	NMT	number of available marker types		(5..n)	INTEGER
Output	MT	Nth element of list of available marker types		(1..n)	INTEGER
Output	NMS	number of available marker sizes		(0..n)	INTEGER
Output	NOMMS	nominal marker size	DC	>0	REAL
Output	RMSMIN,RMSMAX	range of marker sizes	DC	>0	REAL
Output	NPPMI	number of predefined polymarker indices		(5..n)	INTEGER

INQUIRE PREDEFINED POLYMARKER REPRESENTATION
GKCL,GKOP,WSOP,WSAC,SGOP   L0a

Parameters:

Input	workstation type		N
Input	predefined polymarker index	(1..n)	I
Output	error indicator		I
Output	marker type	(1..n)	I
Output	marker size scale factor		R
Output	polymarker colour index	(0..n)	I

Effect:
The inquired values are returned. Possible error numbers: 8, 22, 23, 39, 64.

──────────────────── *FORTRAN-Interface* ────────────────────

CALL GQPPMR (WTYPE,PMI,ERRIND,MKTYPE,MKSSCF,COLI)
Parameters:

Input	WTYPE	workstation type		INTEGER
Input	PMI	predefined polymarker index	(1..n)	INTEGER
Output	ERRIND	error indicator		INTEGER
Output	MKTYPE	marker type	(1..n)	INTEGER
Output	MKSSCF	marker size scale factor		REAL
Output	COLI	colour index	(0..n)	INTEGER

INQUIRE TEXT FACILITIES   GKCL,GKOP,WSOP,WSAC,SGOP   L0a

Parameters:

Input	workstation type		N
Output	error indicator		I
Output	number of font and precision pairs	(1..n)	I
Output	list of font and precision pairs	(1..n;STRING,CHAR,STROKE)	nx(I;E)
Output	number of available character heights	(0..n)	I
Output	minimum character height	>0	R
Output	maximum character height	>0	R
Output	number of available character expansion factors	(0..n)	I
Output	minimum character expansion factor	>0	R
Output	maximum character expansion factor	>0	R
Output	number of predefined text indices	(2..n)	I

Effect:
The inquired values are returned. If the number of character heights is returned as 0, the workstation supports a continuous range of character heights. Possible error numbers: 8, 22, 23, 39.

———————————————— *FORTRAN-Interface* ————————————————

CALL GQTXF (WTYPE,N,ERRIND,NFPP,FONT,PREC,NCHH,MINCHH,
MAXCHH,NCHE,MINCHE,MAXCHE,NPTXI)

Parameters:

Input	WTYPE	workstation type		INTEGER
Input	N	list element requested		INTEGER
Output	ERRIND	error indicator		INTEGER
Output	NFPP	number of text font/precision pairs	(1..n)	INTEGER
Output	FONT	Nth element of list of available text fonts	(1..n)	INTEGER
Output	PREC	Nth element of list of available text precisions (0=string, 1=char, 2=stroke)		INTEGER
Output	NCHH	number of available character heights	(0..n)	INTEGER
Output	MINCHH,MAXCHH	range of character heights	>0	2xREAL
Output	NCHE	number of available character expansion factors	(0..n)	INTEGER
Output	MINCHE,MAXCHE	range of character expansion factors		2xREAL
Output	NPTXI	number of predefined text indices	(2..n)	INTEGER

INQUIRE PREDEFINED TEXT REPRESENTATION
                                        GKCL,GKOP,WSOP,WSAC,SGOP   L0a

Parameters:

Input	workstation type		N
Input	predefined text index	(1..n)	I
Output	error indicator		I
Output	text font and precision	(1..n;STRING,CHAR,STROKE)	(I;E)
Output	character expansion factor	>0	R
Output	character spacing		R
Output	text colour index	(0..n)	I

Effect:
The inquired values are returned. Possible error numbers: 8, 22, 23, 39, 68.

———————————————— *FORTRAN-Interface* ————————————————

CALL GQPTXR (WTYPE,PTXI,ERRIND,FONT,PREC,CHARXP,CHARSP,COLI)

Parameters:

Input	WTYPE	workstation type		INTEGER
Input	PTXI	predefined text index	(1..n)	INTEGER
Output	ERRIND	error indicator		INTEGER
Output	FONT	text font	(1..n)	INTEGER
Output	PREC	text precision (0=string, 1=char, 2=stroke)		INTEGER

Output	CHARXP	character expansion factor	> 0	REAL
Output	CHARSP	character spacing		REAL
Output	COLI	colour index	$(0..n)$	INTEGER

INQUIRE FILL AREA FACILITIES
GKCL,GKOP,WSOP,WSAC,SGOP   L0a

Parameters:

Input	workstation type		N
Output	error indicator		I
Output	number of available fill area interior styles	$(1..n)$	I
Output	list of available fill area interior styles		
	(HOLLOW,SOLID,PATTERN,HATCH)		nxE
Output	number of available hatch styles	$(1..n)$	I
Output	list of available hatch styles		nxI
Output	number of predefined fill area indices	$(5..n)$	I

Effect:

The inquired values are returned. Possible error numbers: 8, 22, 23, 39.

──────────────── FORTRAN-Interface ────────────────

CALL GQFAF (WTYPE,NI,NH,ERRIND,NIS,IS,NHS,HS,NPFAI)

Parameters:

Input	WTYPE	workstation type		INTEGER
Input	NI	list element of IS requested		INTEGER
Input	NH	list element of HS requested		INTEGER
Output	ERRIND	error indicator		INTEGER
Output	NIS	number of fill area interior styles	$(1..n)$	INTEGER
Output	IS	NIth element of list of fill area interior styles		
		$(0 = \text{hollow}, 1 = \text{solid}, 2 = \text{pattern}, 3 = \text{hatch})$		INTEGER
Output	NHS	number of fill area hatch styles	$(1..n)$	INTEGER
Output	HS	NHth element of list of fill area hatch styles		INTEGER
Output	NPFAI	number of predefined fill area indices	$(5..n)$	INTEGER

INQUIRE PREDEFINED FILL AREA REPRESENTATION
GKCL,GKOP,WSOP,WSAC,SGOP   L0a

Parameters:

Input	workstation type		N
Input	predefined fill area index	$(1..n)$	I
Output	error indicator		I
Output	fill area interior style		
	(HOLLOW,SOLID,PATTERN,HATCH)		E
Output	fill area style index	$(1..n)$	I
Output	fill area colour index	$(0..n)$	I

Effect:

The inquired values are returned. Possible error numbers: 8, 22, 23, 39, 75.

———————————————— *FORTRAN-Interface* ————————————————

CALL GQPFAR (WTYPE,PFAI,ERRIND,STYLE,STYLID,COLI)
Parameters:

Input	WTYPE	workstation type		INTEGER
Input	PFAI	predefined fill area index	(1..n)	INTEGER
Output	ERRIND	error indicator		INTEGER
Output	STYLE	interior style		
		(0 = hollow, 1 = solid, 2 = pattern, 3 = hatch)		INTEGER
Output	STYLID	style index	(1..n)	INTEGER
Output	COLI	colour index	(0..n)	INTEGER

INQUIRE PATTERN FACILITIES
GKCL,GKOP,WSOP,WSAC,SGOP   L0a

Parameters:

Input	workstation type		N
Output	error indicator		I
Output	number of predefined pattern indices	(0..n)	I

Effect:
The inquired values are returned. Possible error numbers: 8, 22, 23, 39.

———————————————— *FORTRAN-Interface* ————————————————

CALL GQPAF (WTYPE,ERRIND,NPPAI)
Parameters:

Input	WTYPE	workstation type		INTEGER
Output	ERRIND	error indicator		INTEGER
Output	NPPAI	number of predef. pattern indices	(0..n)	INTEGER

INQUIRE PREDEFINED PATTERN REPRESENTATION
GKCL,GKOP,WSOP,WSAC,SGOP   L0a

Parameters:

Input	workstation type		N
Input	predefined pattern index	(1..n)	I
Output	error indicator		I
Output	pattern array dimensions l,m	(1..n)	2xI
Output	pattern array	(0..n)	lxmxI

Effect:
The inquired values are returned. Possible error numbers: 8, 22, 23, 39, 79, 83.

———————————————— *FORTRAN-Interface* ————————————————

CALL GQPPAR (WTYPE,PPAI,NMX,MMX,ERRIND,N,M,PARRAY)
Parameters:

Input	WTYPE	workstation type		INTEGER
Input	PPAI	predefined pattern index	(1..n)	INTEGER
Input	NMX,MMX	maximum pattern array dimensions		INTEGER
Output	ERRIND	error indicator		INTEGER
Output	N,M	pattern array dimensions	(1..n)	INTEGER
Output	PARRAY(NMX,MMX)	pattern array	(0..n)	INTEGER

INQUIRE COLOUR FACILITIES GKCL,GKOP,WSOP,WSAC,SGOP   L0a
Parameters:

Input	workstation type		N
Output	error indicator		I
Output	number of colours or intensities	(0,2..n)	I
Output	colour available	(MONOCHROME,COLOUR)	E
Output	number of predefined colour indices	(2..n)	I

Effect:

The inquired values are returned. Possible error numbers: 8, 22, 23, 39.

———————————————— *FORTRAN-Interface* ————————————————

CALL GQCF (WTYPE,ERRIND,NCOLI,COLA,NPCI)
Parameters:

Input	WTYPE	workstation type		INTEGER
Output	ERRIND	error indicator		INTEGER
Output	NCOLI	number of colours or intensities	(0,2..n)	INTEGER
Output	COLA	colour available		
		(0 = monochrome, 1 = colour)		INTEGER
Output	NPCI	number of predef. colour indices	(2..n)	INTEGER

INQUIRE PREDEFINED COLOUR REPRESENTATION
GKCL,GKOP,WSOP,WSAC,SGOP   L0a
Parameters:

Input	workstation type		N
Input	predefined colour index	(0..n)	I
Output	error indicator		I
Output	colour (red/green/blue intensities)	[0,1]	3xR

Effect:

The inquired values are returned. Possible error numbers: 8, 22, 23, 39, 86.

———————————————— *FORTRAN-Interface* ————————————————

CALL GQPCR (WTYPE,PCI,ERRIND,RED,GREEN,BLUE)
Parameters:

Input	WTYPE	workstation type		INTEGER
Input	PCI	predefined colour index	(0..n)	INTEGER
Output	ERRIND	error indicator		INTEGER
Output	RED,GREEN,BLUE	colour (RGB values)	[0,1]	REAL

INQUIRE LIST OF AVAILABLE GENERALIZED DRAWING PRIMI-TIVES
GKCL,GKOP,WSOP,WSAC,SGOP   L0a
Parameters:

Input	workstation type		N
Output	error indicator		I
Output	number of available generalized drawing primitives	(0..n)	I
Output	list of GDP identifiers		nxN

Effect:

The inquired values are returned. Possible error numbers: 8, 22, 23, 39.

———————————————————— *FORTRAN-Interface* ————————————————————

CALL GQEGDP (WTYPE,N,ERRIND,NGDP,GDPL)

Parameters:

Input	WTYPE	workstation type		INTEGER
Input	N	list element requested		INTEGER
Output	ERRIND	error indicator		INTEGER
Output	NGDP	number of available generalized drawing primitives	(0..n)	INTEGER
Output	GDPL	N th element of list of GDP identifiers		INTEGER

INQUIRE GENERALIZED DRAWING PRIMITIVE
GKCL,GKOP,WSOP,WSAC,SGOP   L0a

Parameters:

Input	workstation type		N
Input	GDP identifier		N
Output	error indicator		I
Output	number of sets of attributes used	(0..n)	I
Output	list of sets of attributes used (POLYLINE,POLYMARKER,TEXT,FILL AREA)		nxE

Effect:

The inquired values are returned. Possible error numbers: 8, 22, 23, 39, 39, 41.

———————————————————— *FORTRAN-Interface* ————————————————————

CALL GQGDP (WTYPE,NB,ERRIND,MB,BUNTAB)

Parameters:

Input	WTYPE	workstation type		INTEGER
Input	GDP	GDP identifier		INTEGER
Output	ERRIND	error indicator		INTEGER
Output	MB	number of sets of attributes used	(0..4)	INTEGER
Output	BUNTAB(4)	list of bundle tables used (0 = polyline, 1 = polymarker, 2 = text, 3 = fill area)		INTEGER

INQUIRE NUMBER OF SEGMENT PRIORITIES SUPPORTED
GKCL,GKOP,WSOP,WSAC,SGOP   L1a

Parameters:

Input	workstation type		N
Output	error indicator		I
Output	number of segment priorities supported	(0..n)	I

Effect:

The inquired values are returned. If a value of 0 is returned, the workstation supports an infinite number of segment priorities. Possible error numbers: 8, 22, 23, 39.

———————————————————— *FORTRAN-Interface* ————————————————————

CALL GQSGP (WTYPE,ERRIND,NSG)

Parameters:

Input	WTYPE	workstation type	INTEGER

Output	ERRIND	error indicator		INTEGER
Output	NSG	number of segment priorities supported	(0..n)	INTEGER

INQUIRE MAXIMUM LENGTH OF WORKSTATION STATE TABLES
GKCL,GKOP,WSOP,WSAC,SGOP   L1a

Parameters:

Input	workstation type		N
Output	error indicator		I
Output	maximum number of polyline bundle table entries	(20..n)	I
Output	maximum number of polymarker bundle table entries	(20..n)	I
Output	maximum number of text bundle table entries	(20..n)	I
Output	maximum number of fill area bundle table entries	(10..n)	I
Output	maximum number of pattern indices	(0..n)	I
Output	maximum number of colour indices	(20..n)	I

Effect:

The inquired values are returned. Possible error numbers: 8, 22, 23, 39.

———————————————— *FORTRAN-Interface* ————————————————

CALL GQLWK (WTYPE,ERRIND,MPLBTE,MPMBTE,MTXBTE,MFABTE,
MPAI,MCOLI)

Parameters:

Input	WTYPE	workstation type		INTEGER
Output	ERRIND	error indicator		INTEGER
Output	MPLBTE	length of polyline bundle table	(20..n)	INTEGER
Output	MPMBTE	length of polymarker bundle table	(20..n)	INTEGER
Output	MTXBTE	length of text bundle table	(20..n)	INTEGER
Output	MFABTE	length of fill area bundle table	(10..n)	INTEGER
Output	MPAI	maximum number of pattern indices	(0..n)	INTEGER
Output	MCOLI	maximum number of colour indices	(20..n)	INTEGER

INQUIRE DYNAMIC MODIFICATION OF WORKSTATION ATTRIBUTES
GKCL,GKOP,WSOP,WSAC,SGOP   L1a

Parameters:

Input	workstation type		N
Output	error indicator		I
Output	polyline bundle representation changeable	(IRG,IMM)	E
Output	polymarker bundle representation changeable	(IRG,IMM)	E
Output	text bundle representation changeable	(IRG,IMM)	E
Output	fill area bundle representation changeable	(IRG,IMM)	E
Output	pattern representation changeable	(IRG,IMM)	E
Output	colour representation changeable	(IRG,IMM)	E
Output	workstation transformation changeable	(IRG,IMM)	E

Effect:

The inquired values are returned. IRG means that implicit regeneration is necessary; IMM means the action is performed immediately. Possible error numbers: 8, 22, 23, 39.

——————————————— *FORTRAN-Interface* ———————————————

CALL GQDWKA (WTYPE,ERRIND,PLBUN,PMBUN,TXBUN,FABUN,PAREP,
   COLREP,WKTR)

Parameters:

Input	WTYPE	workstation type		INTEGER
Output	ERRIND	error indicator		INTEGER
Output	PLBUN	polyline bundle representation changeable	(0 = irg, 1 = imm)	INTEGER
Output	PMBUN	polymarker bundle represent. changeabl¹	(0 = irg, 1 = imm)	INTEGER
Output	TXBUN	text bundle representation changeable	(0 = irg, 1 = imm)	INTEGER
Output	FABUN	fill area bundle represent. changeable	(0 = irg, 1 = imm)	INTEGER
Output	PAREP	pattern representation changeable	(0 = irg, 1 = imm)	INTEGER
Output	COLREP	colour representation changeable	(0 = irg, 1 = imm)	INTEGER
Output	WKTR	workstation transformation changeable	(0 = irg, 1 = imm)	INTEGER

INQUIRE DYNAMIC MODIFICATION OF SEGMENT ATTRIBUTES
GKCL,GKOP,WSOP,WSAC,SGOP   L1a

Parameters:

Input	workstation type		N
Output	error indicator		I
Output	segment transformation changeable	(IRG,IMM)	E
Output	visibility changeable from 'visible' to 'invisible'	(IRG,IMM)	E
Output	visibility changeable from 'invisible' to 'visible'	(IRG,IMM)	E
Output	highlighting changeable	(IRG,IMM)	E
Output	segment priority changeable	(IRG,IMM)	E
Output	adding primitives to the open segment	(IRG,IMM)	E
Output	segment deletion immediately visible	(IRG,IMM)	E

Effect:

The inquired values are returned. IRG means that implicit regeneration is necessary; IMM means the action is performed immediately. Possible error numbers: 8, 22, 23, 39.

——————————————— *FORTRAN-Interface* ———————————————

CALL GQDSGA (WTYPE,ERRIND,SGTR,VONOFF,VOFFON,HIGH,SGPR,
   ADD,SGDEL)

Parameters:

Input	WTYPE	workstation type		INTEGER
Output	ERRIND	error indicator		INTEGER
Output	SGTR	segment transformation changeable	(0 = irg, 1 = imm)	INTEGER
Output	VONOFF	visibility changeable from on to off	(0 = irg, 1 = imm)	INTEGER
Output	VOFFON	visibility changeable from off to on	(0 = irg, 1 = imm)	INTEGER

Output	HIGH	highlighting changeable	$(0 = \mathrm{irg}, 1 = \mathrm{imm})$	INTEGER
Output	SGPR	segment priority changeable		
			$(0 = \mathrm{irg}, 1 = \mathrm{imm})$	INTEGER
Output	ADD	adding primitives to the open segment		
			$(0 = \mathrm{irg}, 1 = \mathrm{imm})$	INTEGER
Output	SGDEL	segment deletion immediately visible		
			$(0 = \mathrm{irg}, 1 = \mathrm{imm})$	INTEGER

INQUIRE DEFAULT DEFERRAL STATE VALUES
GKCL,GKOP,WSOP,WSAC,SGOP   L1a

Parameters:

Input	workstation type		N
Output	error indicator		I
Output	default value for deferral mode	(ASAP,BNIL,BNIG,ASTI)	E
Output	default value for implicit regeneration mode		
		(SUPPRESSED,ALLOWED)	E

Effect:
The inquired values are returned. Possible error numbers: 8, 22, 23, 39.

──────────────── *FORTRAN-Interface* ────────────────

CALL GQDDS (WTYPE,ERRIND,DEFMOD,REGMOD)

Parameters:

Input	WTYPE	workstation type		INTEGER
Output	ERRIND	error indicator		INTEGER
Output	DEFMOD	default value for deferral mode		
			$(0 = \mathrm{asap}, 1 = \mathrm{bnil}, 2 = \mathrm{bnig}, 3 = \mathrm{asti})$	INTEGER
Output	REGMOD	default value for implicit regeneration		
		mode	$(0 = \mathrm{suppressed}, 1 = \mathrm{allowed})$	INTEGER

INQUIRE NUMBER OF AVAILABLE LOGICAL INPUT DEVICES
GKCL,GKOP,WSOP,WSAC,SGOP   L0b

Parameters:

Input	workstation type		N
Output	error indicator		I
Output	number of locator devices	$(0..n)$	I
Output	number of stroke devices	$(0..n)$	I
Output	number of valuator devices	$(0..n)$	I
Output	number of choice devices	$(0..n)$	I
Output	number of pick devices	$(0..n)$	I
Output	number of string devices	$(0..n)$	I

Effect:
The inquired values are returned. Possible error numbers: 8, 22, 23, 38.

──────────────── *FORTRAN-Interface* ────────────────

CALL GQLI (WTYPE,ERRIND,NLCD,NSKD,NVLD,NCHD,NPCD,NSTD)

Parameters:

Input	WTYPE	workstation type		INTEGER
Output	ERRIND	error indicator		INTEGER
Output	NLCD	number of locator devices	$(0..n)$	INTEGER

Output	NSKD	number of stroke devices		(0..n)	INTEGER
Output	NVLD	number of valuator devices		(0..n)	INTEGER
Output	NCHD	number of choice devices		(0..n)	INTEGER
Output	NPCD	number of pick devices		(0..n)	INTEGER
Output	NSTD	number of string devices		(0..n)	INTEGER

INQUIRE DEFAULT LOCATOR DEVICE DATA
GKCL,GKOP,WSOP,WSAC,SGOP L0b

Parameters:

Input	workstation type			N
Input	logical input device number		(1..n)	I
Output	error indicator			I
Output	default initial locator position for locators	WC		P
Output	number of available prompt/echo types		(1..n)	I
Output	list of available prompt/echo types		(1..n)	nxI
Output	default echo area	DC		4xR
Output	default locator data record			D

Effect:

The inquired values are returned. Possible error numbers: 8, 22, 23, 38, 140.

———————————————— *FORTRAN-Interface* ————————————————

CALL GQDLC (WTYPE,IDCNR,N,JL,ERRIND,DPX,DPY,OL,PETL,EAREA,
DL,LDAT)

Parameters:

Input	WTYPE	workstation type			INTEGER
Input	IDCNR	logical input device number		(1..n)	INTEGER
Input	N	list element requested			INTEGER
Input	JL	dimension of array LDAT			INTEGER
Output	ERRIND	error indicator			INTEGER
Output	DPX,DPY	default init. locator position	WC		2xREAL
Output	OL	number of av. prompt/echo types		(1..n)	INTEGER
Output	PETL	N th element of list of av. prompt/echo types		(1..n)	INTEGER
Output	EAREA(4)	default echo area	DC		REAL
Output	DL	length of locator data record			INTEGER
Output	LDAT(JL)	default locator data record			CHARACTER*80

INQUIRE DEFAULT STROKE DEVICE DATA
GKCL,GKOP,WSOP,WSAC,SGOP L0b

Parameters:

Input	workstation type			N
Input	logical input device number		(1..n)	I
Output	error indicator			I
Output	maximum input buffer size		(64..n)	I
Output	number of available prompt/echo types		(1..n)	I
Output	list of available prompt/echo types		(1..n)	nxI
Output	default echo area	DC		4xR
Output	default stroke data record			D

Effect:

The inquired values are returned. Possible error numbers: 8, 22, 23, 38, 140.

──────────────────── *FORTRAN-Interface* ────────────────────

CALL GQDSK (WTYPE,IDCNR,N,JL,ERRIND,BUFSIZ,OL,PETL,EAREA,
  BUFLEN,DL,SDAT)

Parameters:

Input	WTYPE	workstation type		INTEGER
Input	IDCNR	logical input device number	(1..n)	INTEGER
Input	N	list element requested		INTEGER
Input	JL	dimension of array SDAT		INTEGER
Output	ERRIND	error indicator		INTEGER
Output	BUFSIZ	maximum input buffer size	(64..n)	INTEGER
Output	OL	number of av. prompt/echo types	(1..n)	INTEGER
Output	PETL	Nth element of list of av. prompt/echo types	(1..n)	INTEGER
Output	EAREA(4)	default echo area	DC	REAL
Output	BUFLEN	buffer length for stroke		INTEGER
Output	DL	length of stroke data record		INTEGER
Output	SDAT(JL)	default stroke data record		INTEGER

INQUIRE DEFAULT VALUATOR DEVICE DATA
                              GKCL,GKOP,WSOP,WSAC,SGOP   L0b

Parameters:

Input	workstation type		N
Input	logical input device number	(1..n)	I
Output	error indicator		I
Output	default initial value		R
Output	number of available prompt/echo types	(1..n)	I
Output	list of available prompt/echo types	(1..n)	nxI
Output	default echo area	DC	4xR
Output	default valuator data record		D

Effect:

The inquired values are returned. Possible error numbers: 8, 22, 23, 38, 140.

──────────────────── *FORTRAN-Interface* ────────────────────

CALL GQDVL (WTYPE,IDCNR,N,JL,ERRIND,VALUE,OL,PETL,EAREA,
  LOVAL,HIVAL,DL,VDAT)

Parameters:

Input	WTYPE	workstation type		INTEGER
Input	IDCNR	logical input device number	(1..n)	INTEGER
Input	N	list element requested		INTEGER
Input	JL	dimension of array VDAT		INTEGER
Output	ERRIND	error indicator		INTEGER
Output	VALUE	default initial value		REAL
Output	OL	number of av. prompt/echo types	(1..n)	INTEGER
Output	PETL	Nth element of list of av. prompt/echo types	(1..n)	INTEGER
Output	EAREA(4)	default echo area	DC	REAL
Output	LOVAL,HIVAL	minimal and maximal value		2xREAL

Output	DL	length of valuator data record		INTEGER
Output	VDAT(JL)	default valuator data record		CHARACTER*80

INQUIRE DEFAULT CHOICE DEVICE DATA
GKCL,GKOP,WSOP,WSAC,SGOP   L0b

Parameters:

Input	workstation type		N
Input	logical input device number	(1..n)	I
Output	error indicator		I
Output	maximum number of choice alternatives		I
Output	number of available prompt/echo types	(1..n)	I
Output	list of available prompt/echo types	(1..n)	nxI
Output	default echo area	DC	4xR
Output	default choice data record		D

Effect:
The inquired values are returned. Possible error numbers: 8, 22, 23, 38, 140.

——————————————— *FORTRAN-Interface* ———————————————

CALL GQDCH (WTYPE,IDCNR,N,JL,ERRIND,NUMBER,OL,PETL,EAREA,
DL,CDAT)

Parameters:

Input	WTYPE	workstation type		INTEGER
Input	IDCNR	logical input device number	(1..n)	INTEGER
Input	N	list element requested		INTEGER
Input	JL	dimension of array CDAT		INTEGER
Output	ERRIND	error indicator		INTEGER
Output	NUMBER	maximum number of choice alternatives		INTEGER
Output	OL	number of av. prompt/echo types	(1..n)	INTEGER
Output	PETL	N th element of list of av. prompt/echo types	(1..n)	INTEGER
Output	EAREA(4)	default echo area	DC	REAL
Output	DL	length of choice data record		INTEGER
Output	CDAT(JL)	default choice data record		CHARACTER*80

INQUIRE DEFAULT PICK DEVICE DATA
GKCL,GKOP,WSOP,WSAC,SGOP   L0b

Parameters:

Input	workstation type		N
Input	logical input device number	(1..n)	I
Output	error indicator		I
Output	number of available prompt/echo types	(1..n)	I
Output	list of available prompt/echo types	(1..n)	nxI
Output	default echo area	DC	4xR
Output	default pick data record		D

Effect:
The inquired values are returned. Possible error numbers: 8, 22, 23, 38, 140.

—————————————— *FORTRAN-Interface* ——————————————

CALL GQDPK (WTYPE,IDCNR,N,JL,ERRIND,OL,PETL,EAREA,DL,PDAT)
Parameters:

Input	WTYPE	workstation type		INTEGER
Input	IDCNR	logical input device number	(1..n)	INTEGER
Input	N	list element requested		INTEGER
Input	JL	dimension of array PDAT		INTEGER
Output	ERRIND	error indicator		INTEGER
Output	OL	number of av. prompt/echo types	(1..n)	INTEGER
Output	PETL	N th element of list of av. prompt/echo		
		types	(1..n)	INTEGER
Output	EAREA(4)	default echo area	DC	REAL
Output	DL	length of pick data record		INTEGER
Output	PDAT(JL)	default pick data record		CHARACTER*80

INQUIRE DEFAULT STRING DEVICE DATA
GKCL,GKOP,WSOP,WSAC,SGOP   L0b

Parameters:

Input	workstation type		N
Input	logical input device number	(1..n)	I
Output	error indicator		I
Output	maximum string buffer size	(72..n)	I
Output	number of available prompt/echo types	(1..n)	I
Output	list of available prompt/echo types	(1..n)	nxI
Output	default echo area	DC	4xR
Output	default string data record		D

Effect:
The inquired values are returned. Possible error numbers: 8, 22, 23, 38, 140.

—————————————— *FORTRAN-Interface* ——————————————

CALL GQDST (WTYPE,IDCNR,N,JL,ERRIND,MAXBUF,OL,PETL,EAREA,
BUFLEN,DL,TDAT)
Parameters:

Input	WTYPE	workstation type		INTEGER
Input	IDCNR	logical input device number	(1..n)	INTEGER
Input	N	list element requested		INTEGER
Input	JL	dimension of array TDAT		INTEGER
Output	ERRIND	error indicator		INTEGER
Output	MAXBUF	maximum string buffer size	(72..n)	INTEGER
Output	OL	number of av. prompt/echo types	(1..n)	INTEGER
Output	PETL	N th element of list of av. prompt/echo		
		types	(1..n)	INTEGER
Output	EAREA(4)	default echo area	DC	REAL
Output	BUFLEN	buffer length of string		INTEGER
Output	DL	length of string data record		INTEGER
Output	TDAT(JL)	default string data record		CHARACTER*80

10.2.6 Inquiry Functions for Segment State List

INQUIRE SET OF ASSOCIATED WORKSTATIONS
GKCL,GKOP,WSOP,WSAC,SGOP   L1a

Parameters:

Input	segment name		N
Output	error indicator		I
Output	number of associated workstations	(1..n)	I
Output	set of associated workstation identifiers		nxN

Effect:
The inquired values are returned. Possible error numbers: 7, 120, 122.

———————————— *FORTRAN-Interface* ————————————

CALL GQASWK (SGNA,N,ERRIND,OL,WKIDL)

Parameters:

Input	SGNA	segment name		INTEGER
Input	N	set member requested		INTEGER
Output	ERRIND	error indicator		INTEGER
Output	OL	number of associated workstations	(1..n)	INTEGER
Output	WKIDL	N th element of set of associated workstation identifiers		INTEGER

INQUIRE SEGMENT ATTRIBUTES
GKCL,GKOP,WSOP,WSAC,SGOP   L1a

Parameters:

Input	segment name		N
Output	error indicator		I
Output	segment transformation matrix		2x3xR
Output	visibility	(INVISIBLE,VISIBLE)	E
Output	highlighting	(NORMAL,HIGHLIGHTED)	E
Output	segment priority	[0,1]	R
Output	detectability	(UNDETECTABLE,DETECTABLE)	E

Effect:
The inquired values are returned. Possible error numbers: 7, 120, 122.

———————————— *FORTRAN-Interface* ————————————

CALL GQSGA (SGNA,ERRIND,SEGTM,VIS,HIGH,SGPR,DET)

Parameters:

Input	SGNA	segment name		INTEGER
Output	ERRIND	error indicator		INTEGER
Output	SEGTM(6)	segment transformation matrix		REAL
Output	VIS	visibility	(0=invisible, 1=visible)	INTEGER
Output	HIGH	highlighting	(0=normal, 1=highlighted)	INTEGER
Output	SGPR	segment priority	[0,1]	REAL
Output	DET	detectability	(0=undetectable, 1=detectable)	INTEGER

10.2.7   Pixel Inquiries

INQUIRE PIXEL ARRAY DIMENSIONS
GKCL,GKOP,WSOP,WSAC,SGOP   L/a

Parameters:

Input	workstation identifier		N
Input	2 points P,Q	WC	2xP
Output	error indicator		I
Output	dimensions of pixel array	(1..n)	2xI

Effect:

The inquired values are returned. The points P,Q define a rectangle. By transforming P and Q by the current normalization and workstation transformations, the rectangle is mapped onto the display surface. The number of columns and the number of rows of pixels, whose positions lie within the rectangle, are returned. For this calculation no clipping is applied. Possible error numbers: 7, 20, 25, 39.

--------------------- *FORTRAN-Interface* ---------------------

CALL GQPXAD (WKID,PX,PY,QX,QY,ERRIND,N,M)

Parameters:

Input	WKID	workstation identifier		INTEGER
Input	PX,PY,QX,QY			
		lower left and upper right corner	WC	4xREAL
Output	ERRIND	error indicator		INTEGER
Output	N,M	dimensions of pixel array	(1..n)	INTEGER

INQUIRE PIXEL ARRAY   GKCL,GKOP,WSOP,WSAC,SGOP   L0a

Parameters:

Input	workstation identifier		N
Input	point P	WC	P
Input	dimensions of colour index array l,m	(1..n)	2xI
Output	error indicator		I
Output	presence of invalid values	(ABSENT,PRESENT)	E
Output	colour index array	(-1..n)	lxmxI

Effect:

The inquired values are returned. The point P is transformed by the current normalization and workstation transformations and mapped onto the closest pixel of the display surface. This pixel is the upper left pixel of the index array returned. If a colour index cannot be ascertained (for example, the point P was transformed such that the position of a pixel is not on the display surface), the value -1 (i.e. invalid) is assigned will be returned. In this case, the parameter 'presence of invalid values' will be set to PRESENT. Possible error numbers: 7, 20, 25, 39, 40, 84.

--------------------- *FORTRAN-Interface* ---------------------

CALL GQPXA (WKID,PX,PY,DX,DY,NMX,ERRIND,INVVAL,COL)

Parameters:

Input	WKID	workstation identifier		INTEGER
Input	PX,PY	lower left corner	WC	2xREAL
Input	DX,DY	size of requested pixel array		2xINTEGER
Input	NMX	first dimension of colour index array		INTEGER
Output	ERRIND	error indicator		INTEGER

Output	INVVAL	presence of invalid values		
		(0 = absent, 1 = present)		INTEGER
Output	COL(NMX,DY)			
		colour index array	(-1..n)	INTEGER

INQUIRE PIXEL   GKCL,GKOP,WSOP,WSAC,SGOP   L0a
Parameters:

Input	workstation identifier		N
Input	point P	WC	P
Output	error indicator		I
Output	colour index	(-1..n)	I

Effect:
The inquired values are returned. By transforming P by the current normalization and workstation transformations, it is mapped onto a pixel of the display surface. The colour index of this pixel is returned. If a colour index cannot be ascertained, the value -1 (i.e. invalid) is returned. Possible error numbers: 7, 20, 25, 39, 40.

———————————————— *FORTRAN-Interface* ————————————————

CALL GQPX (WKID,PX,PY,ERRIND,COLI)
Parameters:

Input	WKID	workstation identifier		INTEGER
Input	PX,PY	point	WC	REAL
Output	ERRIND	error indicator		INTEGER
Output	COLI	colour index	(-1..n)	INTEGER

10.2.8   Inquiry Function for GKS Error State List

INQUIRE INPUT QUEUE OVERFLOW
                                             GKCL,GKOP,WSOP,WSAC,SGOP   L0c
Parameters:

Output	error indicator		I
Output	workstation identifier		N
Output	input class (LOCATOR,STROKE,VALUATOR,CHOICE,		
	PICK,STRING)		E
Output	input device number	(1..n)	I

Effect:
The inquired values are returned. If the input queue has overflowed, the error indicator is returned as 0 and the identification of the logical input device that caused the overflow is returned. The entry is removed from the error state list. Possible error numbers: 7, 148, 149.

———————————————— *FORTRAN-Interface* ————————————————

CALL GQIQOV (ERRIND,WKID,ICL,IDN)
Parameters:

Output	ERRIND	error indicator		INTEGER
Output	WKID	workstation identifier		INTEGER
Output	ICL	input class		
	(1 = locator, 2 = stroke, 3 = valuator, 4 = choice, 5 = pick, 6 = string)		INTEGER
Output	IDN	input device number	(1..n)	INTEGER

10.3   Examples

Example 10.1   Inquiry for GKS state list

GKS state list variables are inquired and saved. At a later time they are reset to the saved values. Saving and restoring state list values is required in cases where an application subroutine changes those values. The values are saved upon entry to the subroutine and restored before returning to the calling program.

───────────────────────── *Pascal* ─────────────────────────

```
                            {Saving values:   save normalization transformations}
L10   INQUIRE_CURRENT_NORMALIZATION_TRANSFORMATION
         NUMBER (ERR_IND,CNUM);
L20   INQUIRE_LIST_OF_NORMALIZATION_TRANSFORMATION_NUMBERS
         (ERR_IND,LENGTH,NUMS);
L30   FOR I:= 1 TO LENGTH DO
L40   BEGIN
L50      INQUIRE_NORMALIZATION_TRANSFORMATION
            (NUMS[I],ERR_IND,WINDOWS[I],VIEWPORTS[I]);
L60   END;
                                              {save primitive attributes}
L70   INQUIRE_CURRENT_PRIMITIVE_ATTRIBUTE_VALUES
            (ERR_IND,IPOLYL,IPOLYM,ITEXT,CH_HEIGHT,CH_UP,TX_PATH,
                            TX_ALIGN,IFILL,P_SIZE,P_REFP,IPICK);
L80   INQUIRE_CURRENT_INDIVIDUAL_ATTRIBUTE_VALUES
            (ERR_IND,LTYPE,LWIDTH,ICPOLYL,MTYPE,MSIZE,ICPOLYM,
             TXFONP, CH_EXP,CH_SP,ICTEXT,STYLE,ISFILL,ICFILL,ASF);

      {Resetting the values:                 reset normalization transformations}
L100  FOR I:= 1 TO LENGTH(NUMS) DO
L110  BEGIN
L120     SET_WINDOW (NUMS[I],WINDOWS[I]);
L130     SET_VIEWPORT (NUMS[I],VIEWPORTS[I]);
L140  END;
                                  {order transformations by viewport input priority}
L150  FOR I:= 2 TO LENGTH(NUMS) DO
L160  BEGIN
L170     SET_VIEWPORT_INPUT_PRIORITY (NUMS[I],NUMS[I-1],LOWER);
L180  END;
                                              {reset current transformation}
L190  SELECT_NORMALIZATION_TRANSFORMATION (CNUM);
                                              {reset bundle indices}
L200  SET_POLYLINE_INDEX (IPOLYL);
L210  SET_POLYMARKER_INDEX (IPOLYM);
L220  SET_TEXT_INDEX (ITEXT);
L230  SET_FILL_AREA_INDEX (IFILL);
                                              {reset POLYLINE attributes}
L240  SET_LINETYPE (LTYPE);
L250  SET_LINEWIDTH_SCALE_FACTOR (LWIDTH);
```

L260 SET_POLYLINE_COLOUR_INDEX (ICPOLYL);

{reset POLYMARKER attributes}

L270 SET_MARKER_TYPE (MTYPE);
L280 SET_MARKER_SIZE_SCALE_FACTOR (MSIZE);
L290 SET_POLYMARKER_COLOUR_INDEX (ICPOLYM);

{reset TEXT attributes}

L300 SET_CHARACTER_HEIGHT (CH_HEIGHT);
L310 SET_CHARACTER_UP_VECTOR (CH_UP);
L320 SET_TEXT_PATH (TX_PATH);
L330 SET_TEXT_ALIGNMENT (TX_ALIGN);
L340 SET_TEXT_FONT_AND_PRECISION (TXFONP);
L350 SET_CHARACTER_EXPANSION_FACTOR (CH_EXP);
L360 SET_CHARACTER_SPACING (CH_SP);
L370 SET_TEXT_COLOUR_INDEX (ICTEXT);

{reset FILL AREA attributes}

L380 SET_PATTERN_SIZE (P_SIZE);
L390 SET_PATTERN_REFERENCE_POINT (P_REFP);
L400 SET_FILL_AREA_INTERIOR_STYLE (STYLE);
L410 SET_FILL_AREA_STYLE_INDEX (ISFILL);
L420 SET_FILL_AREA_COLOUR_INDEX (ICFILL);

{reset aspect source flags}

L430 SET_ASPECT_SOURCE_FLAGS (ASF);

{resct PICK identifier}

L440 SET_PICK_IDENTIFIER (IPICK);

─────────────────────────────── *Fortran* ───────────────────────────────

```
       C          *** save normalization transformation
L10               CALL GQCNTN(ERRIND,CNUM)
L20               CALL GQENTN(1,ERRIND,LENGTH,NUMS(1))
L30               DO 60 I = 1,LENGTH
L31                 CALL GQENTN(I,ERRIND,LENGTH,NUMS(I))
L50                 CALL GQNT(NUMS(I),ERRIND,WINDO(I,1),VIEWP(I,1))
L60               CONTINUE
       C          *** save primitive attributes
L61               CALL GQPLI (ERRIND,IPOLYL)
L62               CALL GQPMI (ERRIND,IPOLYM)
L63               CALL GQTXI (ERRIND,ITEXT)
L64               CALL GQCHH (ERRIND,CHHEIG)
L65               CALL GQCHUP (ERRIND,CHUPX,CHUPY)
L66               CALL GQTXP (ERRIND,TXPATH)
L67               CALL GQTXAL (ERRIND,TXALH,TXALV)
L68               CALL GQFAI (ERRIND,IFILL)
L69               CALL GQPA (ERRIND,PSIZX,PSIZY)
L70               CALL GQPARF (ERRIND,PREFX,PREFY)
L71               CALL GQPKID (ERRIND,IPICK)
L80               CALL GQLNA (ERRIND,LTYPE)
L81               CALL GQLWSC (ERRIND,LWIDTH)
L82               CALL GQPLCI (ERRIND,ICPL)
L83               CALL GQMK (ERRIND,MTYPE)
L84               CALL GQMKSC (ERRIND,MSIZE)
L85               CALL GQPMCI (ERRIND,ICPM)
```

L86		CALL GQTXFP (ERRIND,TXFONT,TXPREC)
L87		CALL GQCHXP (ERRIND,CHEXP)
L88		CALL GQCHSP (ERRIND,CHSP)
L89		CALL GQTXCI (ERRIND,ICTEXT)
L90		CALL GQFAIS (ERRIND,STYLE)
L91		CALL GQFASI (ERRIND,ISFILL)
L92		CALL GQFACI (ERRIND,ICFILL)
L93		CALL GQASF (ERRIND,ASF)

Resetting the values:

```
         C        *** reset normalization transformations
L100              DO 140 I = 1,LENGTH
L120                 CALL GSWN(NUMS(I),WINDO(I,1),WINDO(I,2),WINDO(I,3),
                        WINDO(I,4))
L130                 CALL GSVP(NUMS(I),VIEWP(I,1),VIEWP(I,2),VIEWP(I,3),
                        VIEWP(I,4))
L140        140   CONTINUE
L150              DO 180 I = 2,LENGTH
L170                 CALL GSVPIP(NUMS(I),NUMS(I-1),LOWER)
L180        180   CONTINUE
         C        *** reset current transformation
L190              CALL GSELNT(CNUM)
         C        *** reset bundle indices
L200              CALL GSPLI(IPOLYL)
L210              CALL GSPMI(IPOLYM)
L220              CALL GSTXI(ITEXT)
L230              CALL GSFAI(IFILL)
         C        *** reset POLYLINE attributes
L240              CALL GSLN(LTYPE)
L250              CALL GSLWSC(LWIDTH)
L260              CALL GSPLCI(ICPL)
         C        *** reset POLYMARKER attributes
L270              CALL GSMK(MTYPE)
L280              CALL GSMKSC(MSIZE)
L290              CALL GSPMCI(ICPM)
         C        *** reset TEXT attributes
L300              CALL GSCHH(CHHEIG)
L320              CALL GSCHUP(CHUPX,CHUPY)
L320              CALL GSTXP(CHPATH)
L330              CALL GSTXAL(TXALH,TXALV)
L340              CALL GSTXFP(TXFONT,TXPREC)
L350              CALL GSCHXP(CHEXP)
L360              CALL GSCHSP(CHSP)
L370              CALL GSTXCI(ICTEXT)
         C        *** reset FILL AREA attributes
L380              CALL GSPA(PSIZX,PSIZY)
L390              CALL GSPARF(PREFX,PREFY)
L400              CALL GSFAIS(STYLE)
L410              CALL GSFASI(ISFILL)
L420              CALL GSFACI(ICFILL)
         C        *** reset aspect source flags
```

L430   CALL GSASF(ASF)
    C   *** reset PICK identifier
L440   CALL GSPKID(IPICK)

Example 10.2   Inquiry for colour table

The colour table of an output type workstation is inspected. The colour indices having colour values closest to pure red and pure green are to be found. "Close" means in this context that the sum of the difference of the RGB values of the inspected colour and the desired colour will be a minimum. E.g., if the desired colour is green, it has RGB values of (0,1,0). So the difference of a given colour from green is given by R + (1-G) + B. The colour index pointing to that entry in the colour table whose RGB values yield the minimal difference is the index "closest to green". The colour values REALIZED by the workstation will be tested. The differences of the tested colours from red and green are held in the variables DIFRED and DIFGRN. The indices closest to red and green are held in variables INDRED and INDGRN.

——————————————— *Pascal* ———————————————
                                          {get list of colour indices}
L10   INQUIRE_LIST_OF_COLOUR_INDICES (WSID,ERR_IND,NUMBER,LIST);
                              {initialise differences to maximal value}
                              {(colour values R,G,B are in the range 0..1)}
L20   DIFRED:=3; DIFGRN:=3;

                                          {initialise indices to -1}
L30   INDRED:=-1; INDGRN:=-1;
L40   FOR I:=1 TO NUMBER DO   {inspect all colour table entries}
L41   BEGIN

                                          {inquire colour table}
L50   INQUIRE_COLOUR_REPRESENTATION
          (WSID,LIST[I],REALIZED,ERR_IND,COLOUR);
                                  {test if colour is closer to red}
L60   IF (1-COLOUR.RED)+COLOUR.GREEN+COLOUR.BLUE < DIFRED
          THEN DO
L70   BEGIN
L80   DIFRED:=(1-COLOUR.RED)+COLOUR.GREEN+COLOUR.BLUE;
L90   INDRED:=LIST[I];
L100   END;
                                  {test if colour is closer to green}
L110   IF COLOUR.RED+(1-COLOUR.GREEN)+COLOUR.BLUE < DIFGRN
          THEN DO
L120   BEGIN
L130   DIFGRN:=COLOUR.RED+(1-COLOUR.GREEN)+COLOUR.BLUE;
L140   INDGRN:=LIST[I];
L150   END;
L160 END;
                                  {if INDRED or INDGRN are not equal -1,}
                        {they contain colour indices closest to red resp. green}

──────────────────────────── *Fortran* ────────────────────────────

```
        C           *** get number of colour indices
L10                 CALL GQECI(WSID,1,ERRIND,NUMBER,LIST(1))
        C           *** initialize differences to maximal values possible
L20                 DIFRED = 3.0
L21                 DIFGRN = 3.0
        C           *** initialize indices to -1
L30                 INDRED = -1
L31                 INDGRN = -1
L40                 DO 160 I = 1,NUMBER
        C              *** get colour index
L45                 CALL GQCI(WSID,I,ERRIND,NUMBER,LIST(I))
        C              *** test inquire colour table
L50                 CALL GQCR(WSID,LIST(I),REALIZED,ERRIND,RED,
                    GREEN,BLUE)
        C              *** test if colour is closer to red
L60                 IF ((1.0-RED)+GREEN+BLUE.GE.DIFRED) GOTO 110
L80                 DIFRED = (1.0-RED)+GREEN+BLUE
L90                 INDRED = LIST(I)
        C              *** test if colour is closer to green
L110       110      IF (RED+(1.0-GREEN)+BLUE.GE.DIFGRN) GOTO 160
L130                DIFGRN = RED+(1.0-GREEN)+BLUE
L140                INDGRN = LIST(I)
L160       160   CONTINUE
```

──

Example 10.3   Inquiry for workstation description table

The workstation description table of a workstation type WSTYPE is inspected.
The following GKS function calls deliver:
— whether or not colour is available;
— if colour is available, the number of colour table entries.

Then the POLYLINE and FILL AREA bundles will be set up according
to the inquired values.

──────────────────────────── *Pascal* ────────────────────────────

```
                                              {test if colour available}
L10   INQUIRE_COLOUR_FACILITIES
          (WSTYPE,ERR_IND,ICOLOURS,CAVAIL,NINDEX) ;
L20   IF CAVAIL = COLOUR THEN DO
L30   BEGIN
L50      IF NINDEX > = 3 THEN DO
L60      BEGIN              {set first three polyline bundles to colours red, green, blue}
L70        SET_POLYLINE_REPRESENTATION (WSID,1,1,1.0,1);
L80        SET_POLYLINE_REPRESENTATION (WSID,2,1,1.0,2);
L90        SET_POLYLINE_REPRESENTATION (WSID,3,1,1.0,3);
L100       SET_COLOUR_REPRESENTATION (WSID,1,1.0,0.0,0.0);          {red}
L110       SET_COLOUR_REPRESENTATION (WSID,2,0.0,1.0,0.0);        {green}
L120       SET_COLOUR_REPRESENTATION (WSID,3,0.0,0.0,1.0);         {blue}
L130   END;
```

L140 END;
L150 ELSE DO
L160 BEGIN   {set first three polyline bundles to three linetypes}
L170   SET_POLYLINE_REPRESENTATION (WSID,1,1,1.0,1);
L180   SET_POLYLINE_REPRESENTATION (WSID,2,2,1.0,1);
L190   SET_POLYLINE_REPRESENTATION (WSID,3,3,1.0,1);
L200 END;

———————————————————— *Fortran* ————————————————————

```
        C          *** test if colour available
L10                CALL GQCF(WSTYPE,ERRIND,ICOLS,CAVAIL,NINDEX)
L20                IF (CAVAIL.NE.COLOUR) GOTO 170
L50                IF (NINDEX.LT.3) GOTO 200
        C          *** set first three polyline bundles to colours
        C          *** red, green, blue
L70                CALL GSPLR(WSID,1,1,1.0,1)
L80                CALL GSPLR(WSID,2,1,1.0,2)
L90                CALL GSPLR(WSID,3,1,1.0,3)
L100               CALL GSCR(WSID,1,1.0,0.0,0.0)
L110               CALL GSCR(WSID,2,0.0,1.0,0.0)
L120               CALL GSCR(WSID,3,0.0,0.0,1.0)
L130               GOTO 200
        C          *** set first three polyline bundles
        C          *** to three linetypes
L170        170    CALL GSPLR(WSID,1,1,1.0,1)
L180               CALL GSPLR(WSID,2,2,1.0,1)
L190               CALL GSPLR(WSID,3,3,1.0,1)
L200        200    CONTINUE
```

Example 10.4   Pixel inquiry

The pixel memory of a workstation is inspected using pixel inquiry functions. It is assumed in this example that an ESCAPE function is used to fill the pixel memory and the colour table of a workstation with values obtained from outside GKS (e.g., from an external file set up by a scanner). Then the pixel inquiries are used to find out a pixel with a given colour (yellow in the example, yellow has RGB values $(1,1,0)$). All yellow pixels will then be set to the background colour by using the CELL ARRAY output primitive function. The background colour index in GKS is always zero. The window and the viewport of the normalization transformation are both set to the workstation window. In this way it is ensured that the pixel array sent to the workstation will overlay the pixel array read in.

———————————————————— *Pascal* ————————————————————

```
                                          {get workstation window CWW}
L10    INQUIRE_WORKSTATION_TRANSFORMATION
          (WSID,ERR_IND,WS,RWW,CWW,RWV,CWV);
                              {set window and viewport to workstation window CWW}
```

```
L20    SET_WINDOW (1,CWW);
L30    SET_VIEWPORT (1,CWW);
L35    SELECT NORMALISATION TRANSFORMATION (1);
               {get dimensions N,M of pixel array covering the whole workstation}
                        {window. Points P,Q are set to window corners.}
L40    P[1]:=CWW[1]; P[2]:=CWW[3];
L50    Q[1]:=CWW[2]; Q[2]:=CWW[4];
L60    INQUIRE_PIXEL_ARRAY_DIMENSIONS (WSID,P,Q,ERR_IND,N,M);
               {start traversing picture at lower left corner with pixel array of}
                        {dimension 5x5 until upper right corner is reached}
L70    PP[2]:=P[2];                    {y-value of lower left corner of 5x5 pixel array}
L80    REPEAT
L90      PP[1]:=P[1];                  {x-value of lower left corner of 5x5 pixel array}
L100     REPEAT
                                                          {upper right corner}
L110       QQ[1]:=PP[1]+5*(CWW[2]-CWW[1])/N;
L120       QQ[2]:=PP[2]+5*(CWW[4]-CWW[3])/M;
L130       CHANGED:=FALSE;
                                                          {inquire 5x5 pixel array}
L140       INQUIRE_PIXEL_ARRAY (WSID,PP,5,5,ERR_IND,PRES,CIND);
                                                          {look for yellow pixels}
L150       FOR I:=1 TO 5 DO
L160         FOR J:=1 TO 5 DO
L170         BEGIN
L180           INQUIRE_COLOUR_REPRESENTATION (WSID,CIND[I,J],
L190           VTYPE,ERR_IND,RED,GREEN,BLUE);
                                                {if yellow set colour index to 0}
L200           IF RED>0.95 & GREEN>0.95 & BLUE<0.05 THEN DO
L210           BEGIN
L220             CIND[I,J]:=0;
L230             CHANGED:=TRUE
L240           END
L250         END;
                        {if indices changed send changed pixel array back to workstation}
L260       IF CHANGED THEN DO
L270         CELL_ARRAY (PP,QQ,5,5,CIND);
                                                {increment x of lower left corner}
L280       PP[1]:=PP[1]+5*(CWW[2]-CWW[1])/N;
L290     UNTIL QQ[1] > = Q[1];
                                                {increment y of lower left corner}
L300     PP[2]:=PP[2]+5*(CWW[4]-CWW[3])/M;
L310   UNTIL QQ[2] > = Q[2];
```

---------------------------------- *Fortran* ----------------------------------

```
       C        *** get workstation window
L10             CALL GQWKT(WSID,ERRIND,WS,RWINDO,CWINDO,
                RVIEW,CVIEW)
       C        *** set window and viewport to workstation window
L20             CALLGSWN(1,CWINDO(1),CWINDO(2),CWINDO(3),CWINDO(4))
L30             CALL GSVP(1,CWINDO(1),CWINDO(2),CWINDO(3),CWINDO(4))
L35             CALL GSELNT(1)
```

```
        C              *** get dimensions N,M of pixel array covering the
        C              *** whole workstation window. Points P,Q are set to
        C              *** window corners.
L40                    PX = CWINDO(1)
L41                    PY = CWINDO(3)
L50                    QX = CWINDO(2)
L51                    QY = CWINDO(4)
L60                    CALL GQPXAD(WSID,PX,PY,QX,QY,ERRIND,N,M)
        C              *** start traversing picture at lower left corner with
        C              *** pixel array of dimension 5x5 until upper right
        C              *** corner is reached.
        C              *** y-value of lower left corner of 5x5 pixel array
L70                    PPY = PY
        C              *** repeat until ymax is reached
L80        80   CONTINUE
        C              *** x-value of lower left corner of 5x5 pixel array
L90                    PPX = PX
        C              *** repeat until xmax is reached
L100      100    CONTINUE
        C              *** calculate upper right corner of 5x5 array
L110                   QQX = PPX + 5*(CWINDO(2)-CWINDO(1))/N
L120                   QQY = PPY + 5*(CWINDO(4)-CWINDO(3))/M
L130                   CHANGED = .FALSE.
        C              *** inquire 5x5 pixel array
L140                   CALL GQPXA(WSID,QQX,QQY,5,5,5,ERRIND,PRES,CIND)
        C              *** look for yellow pixels
L150                   DO 250 I = 1,5
L160                      DO 240 J = 1,5
L180                         CALL GQCR(WSID,CIND(I,J),
L190             +              VTYPE,ERRIND,RED,GREEN,BLUE)
        C                     *** if yellow set colour index to 0
L200                         IF (RED.LE.0.95 .OR. GREEN.LE.0.95. .OR.
L201             +              BLUE.GE.0.05) GOTO 240
L220                         CIND(I,J) = 0
L230                         CHANGED = .TRUE.
L240       240        CONTINUE
L250       250   CONTINUE
        C              *** if indices changed send changed pixel array
        C              *** array back to workstation
L260                   IF (CHANGED) THEN
L270             +        CALL GCA(PPX,PPY,QQX,QQY,5,5,5,CIND)
        C              *** increment x of lower left corner
L280                   PPX = PPX + 5.0*(CWINDO(2)-CWINDO(1))/N
L290              IF (QQX.LT.QX) GOTO 100
        C              *** increment y of lower left corner
L300                   PPY = PPY + 5.0*(CWINDO(4)-CWINDO(3))/M
L310              IF (QQY.LT.QY) GOTO 80
```

10.4   Exercises

Exercise 10.1   Saving workstation state list values

Extend the program parts in example 10.1 in a way that not only GKS state list values but also workstation state list values of a workstation given by its workstation identifier are saved and restored. Design, realize and test two general purpose subroutines for saving and restoring state list values.

Exercise 10.2   Search lines in raster picture

Imagine a pixel memory is filled by an ESCAPE function as in example 10.4. The picture consists of a number of irregular line segments, one pixel wide, of different colours. Change example 10.4 in a way that lines of a given colour index c1 are followed and all the pixels are set to colour index c2 (c2 $\neq$ c1).

Exercise 10.3   Search lines in raster picture

Change the program resulting from exercise 10.2 in a way that not lines of a given colour index, but lines of a given colour bandwidth (Rmin..Rmax, Gmin..Gmax,Bmin..Bmax) are followed and set to colour index c2.

11   METAFILE INTERFACE

11.1   Overview

The GKS Metafile (GKSM) is the GKS facility for long term storage of pictures. Whereas the GKS workstation-independent segment storage is available for storage of segments only during a GKS application, between OPEN GKS and CLOSE GKS, the metafile is retained for an unlimited time. The most important applications of the metafile are:
— storage of graphical data from one GKS application to the next one;
— storage of graphical data for archiving purposes;
— transport of graphical data to a different installation;
— transmission of graphical data to a different graphics system;
— saving the state of a GKS application for continuation of the session or run at a later time;
— device-independent storage of graphical data for deferred transmission to an output device;
— storage of non-graphical, application-defined data that are logically connected to the graphics data.

GKS provides functions for routing data to the metafile for long term storage. When the metafile is written in this way, it is called a *GKSM output* workstation. But GKS also provides functions for reading the metafile back into the system, and displaying the graphical contents on an output workstation, or storing segments contained in the metafile in the workstation-dependent segment storage. In this case, the metafile is used as a *GKSM input* workstation.

When generating output on the GKSM, GKS functions will cause units of data to be written on the file. These units are called GKSM *items*. In most cases, a GKS function will cause one item to be recorded on the metafile. When reading a metafile, one item will be retrieved from the metafile at a time. The different item types are identified by an item number.

While the contents and the format of the metafile, as described in Annex E of the GKS document, are not part of the international standard, the functional interface to the metafile has been integrated into the GKS standard. As soon as an international graphics metafile standard will be established, the GKS metafile interface will be used for the communication of GKS with the ISO standard metafile. However, the GKS metafile format defined in Annex E is suitable for all GKS applications, and this format will be used in this chapter when format specific questions are addressed. The contents and the format of the GKS metafile are described in detail in Chapter IV.6 and in Appendix 1.

11.2 The Metafile Workstation

In order to use the metafile in a consistent and easy-to-use fashion, it is addressed in GKS like a workstation. Two workstation types for metafiles are defined in an implementation: the GKSM output and GKSM input workstation.

The following workstation control functions are used to control GKSM output workstations:

GKS name	FORTRAN name
OPEN WORKSTATION	GOPWK
CLOSE WORKSTATION	GCLWK
ACTIVATE WORKSTATION	GACWK
DEACTIVATE WORKSTATION	GDAWK
SET DEFERRAL STATE	GSDFS
CLEAR WORKSTATION	GCLWK
UPDATE WORKSTATION	GUWK
REDRAW ALL SEGMENTS ON WORKSTATION	GRSGWK
MESSAGE	GMSG
ESCAPE	GESC

Any number of GKSM output workstations can be open or active at a time (unless restricted by the implementation). As with other workstations, output will be sent to a GKSM output workstation as long as it is active. CLEAR WORKSTATION, UPDATE WORKSTATION, REDRAW ALL SEG-

MENTS and MESSAGE are valid as long as the workstation is open or active. Not only output, but also control and segment functions will be recorded on the metafile as they are called, making the GKSM output workstation an *audit trail* for output related GKS functions.

For GKSM input workstations, only the workstation control functions OPEN WORKSTATION and CLOSE WORKSTATION are valid. Any number of GKSM input workstations can be open at one time (unless restricted by implementation). Input can be obtained from the metafile, using the GKSM input functions, only when the GKSM input workstation is open. All other control functions will cause error no. 33 ("Specified workstation is of category GKSM input") to be generated.

The GKSM output workstation and the GKSM input workstation only have a very restricted workstation description table. Since the characteristics of these workstations are specified completely by the workstation interface of the GKS standard, they cannot vary from one installation to the other.

Conceptionally the GKSM output workstation is a completely equipped output-type workstation. It is capable of both VECTOR and RASTER output, device coordinate units are METRES, and the display area size is undefined (limited by the NDC range). The deferral mode can be considered to be ASAP (all output effects visible immediately) and implicit regeneration will not occur. The function SET DEFERRAL STATE is valid for a GKSM output workstation, however, it will not create any output on the GKSM, but will set the deferral state of the metafile workstation itself.

11.3   GKSM Output

Output is generated on a GKSM output workstation as long as it is active, i.e., GKS is in one of the operating states WSAC or SGOP. Figure 11.1 shows

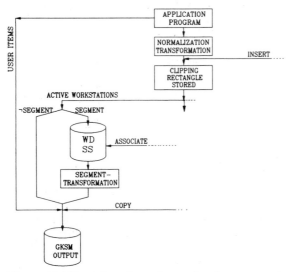

Figure 11.1 Data flow from the application program to the GKS metafile

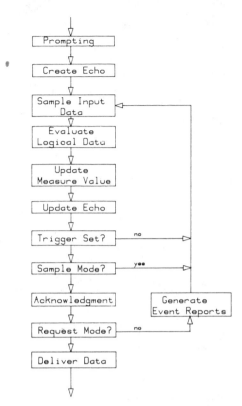

Figure 2.4
Flow diagram of interaction processes

Note that two global states are defined, namely TRIGGER and OPERAT-ING MODE. The TRIGGER state indicates whether the trigger part for that device is set, the OPERATING MODE state determines the current operating mode for that device.

The parsing of this syntax leads to the following flow diagram (Figure 2.4).

2.5.2 Generating Logical Input Device Implementations

The generation of executable programs representing interaction processes is done by a bottom-up parsing of the given syntax. It is controlled by the user-defined requirement and system property tables. Properties are identified for graphics input and output devices and for all modules used by higher modules once they are configured. The parser selects the appropriate productions of the syntax above according to the given tables. The appropriate program modules are chosen and instructions are generated to activate these modules and supply them with parameters. The parsing is performed in a bottom-up manner starting with the terminal symbols. Some examples for choosing the appropriate productions, and thereby, selecting the corresponding program modules are shown in Table 2.2:

Table 2.2 Deriving program modules from descriptions

Physical device characteristics	→ Physical device identifier
Physical device identifier	→ Input data types, contents and meanings
Input data types and contents	→ Sample input data function
Input data types, contents and meaning + desired logical input device	
	→ function to evaluate the logical device data
Output device facilities + desired prompt/echo type	
	→ functions to create and update the echo

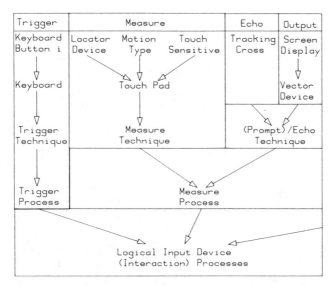

Figure 2.5 Deriving an interaction process from requirements

A small example is given to illustrate the description of requirements and the resulting stepwise generation of the interaction process. Starting from the requirements (upper part of Figure 2.5) the physical input device is selected and the corresponding input sampling function is chosen. The format and meaning of the input data obtained from the input device is taken from the interface description tables. Now the simulation module can be selected for the required logical device; this module maps the physical to logical data. In parallel, the required prompt/echo technique "tracking cross" and the output device facilities of the given device determine the program module which exactly performs this task. With the simulation function and the prompt/echo functions the final interaction program can be set up. Note that some details about initialising and terminating the interaction device and also about the handling of the trigger device are omitted.

2.6 Some Examples of Logical Input Device Realizations

In this chapter, we describe some examples how logical input devices can be implemented on physical input tools and which simulation software is possibly needed. We also describe some of the device characteristics influencing the operator interface.

2.6.1 LOCATOR and STROKE Devices

The logical input device LOCATOR delivers a pair of coordinates and the number of the world coordinate system used. The STROKE device expands this logical data to a sequence of coordinates. With regard to physical input devices, the two logical input devices being related, we will consider the LO-CATOR device further. For any physical input device, the computation from device to the appropriate world coordinate system has to be done by software. LOCATORs can be implemented on a variety of input devices; some of them are:

Data Tablets or Digitizers with Stylus or Hand Cursor (Puck)
These devices deliver absolute positions rather than motions. Relative movements, however, can easily be simulated by software keeping an actual position, sampling the device position in a given time slice, calculating the differences between the two positions and reporting them whenever a certain time has passed or a distance is exceeded, and finally updating the actual position.

An interesting aspect of the pens (stylus) of data tablets and digitizers is the use of their pressure-sensitive switch. Three states can be distinguished: 'normal state' when the device is on the surface and its position can be inquired but its switch is not set, 'push down' when the pen is depressed on the surface in order to indicate positions of interest, 'lift off' when the device is removed from the surface and thus no positions can be sensed.

The same functional behaviour is frequently implemented with a lightpen, a hand cursor, or a mouse if at least one button is associated with them, or with a touch tablet, touch panel, etc.

Lightpens Mostly with Tip Switches
Most lightpens deliver a screen position which can be used to calculate a position in world coordinates. Advantageous, when using lightpens is the direct working on the output medium; i.e., the operator can give full attention to the screen and indicate positions on it directly rather than moving a screen cursor to the desired position. On the other hand, working with a lightpen can be very tiring for an operator who must pick it up, point to a screen position, and put it down again. Therefore, the use of lightpens can be expected to decrease in the near future.

Mouse
Another very popular device is the mouse because of its simplicity, user friendliness, and inexpensiveness. Based on potentiometers being adjusted by rollers at the bottom of the mouse, this hand-held device reports relative movements.

While it is very natural to be handled (moving the mouse can be directly translated into moving an object) it is not very suitable for precise working.

Trackballs, Joysticks and Thumb Wheels
All three device types are rigidly mounted and have facilities to adjust values. Rather than moving the device itself, either a ball is rotated within its mount or a stick is moved left or right, forward or backward, or two wheels are turned. Thereby, potentiometers are adjusted and relative movements are reported.

Function Keyboard
Cheap workstations often have only a keyboard as input device. If a function keyboard is available (the depressing of a button can be sampled), a convenient simulation of a LOCATOR can be done using at least five buttons. Depending on which one is actually depressed, a cursor is moved left or right, up or down. The fifth button is needed to indicate whether the actual cursor position is significant. Four additional buttons might be used for diagonal directions and also for controlling the velocity of the cursor movement.

Alphanumeric Keyboard
In the worst case, positions can be typed in on a keyboard. While this allows for entering coordinates very precisely it is a rather inconvenient way of working.

Touch Tablet, Touch Screen
Two less common but innovative and upcoming device types should be mentioned briefly: touch tablets and touch screens. Some are based on light emitting and sensing diodes, others on sound emitting and reflection measuring techniques, still others measure the changes of electrical capacity, and so on. They all allow an operator to indicate a position with her/his finger or to move the finger over the surface to indicate a motion. These device types provide a very immediate way of interactive working and can therefore be applied especially well for occasional and unskilled users.

2.6.2 VALUATOR

VALUATORS are used to enter real numbers as scalar values. Typical input devices suitable for VALUATOR implementations are rotary and slide potentiometers. If available, they should be applied in accordance with the semantic interpretation of the values they deliver. For example, a rotary potentiometer should be used to rotate objects, a slide potentiometer to scale them.

With most graphics workstations VALUATORs have to be simulated by some of the devices mentioned in the chapter before. Thereby, either one dimension of their two is taken to calculate a scalar value or their two dimensions are used to serve two associated VALUATORs.

The simulation might be done in various ways, e.g., one of the dials or scales shown in Figure 2.6 is displayed. Using a lightpen, a trackball, a mouse,

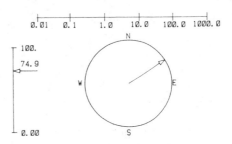

Figure 2.6 Valuator device simulations

a hand cursor, or another suitable device, a mark on the scale is moved to a new position or a pointer is turned clockwise or counterclockwise. The currently indicated value, and possibly the lowest and highest possible values, should be displayed in numeric form. As with the potentiometer types (rotary or slide), the kind of simulation should be in accordance with the semantic interpretation of the values.

Obviously, VALUATOR values can also be typed on a alphanumeric keyboard. Unlike LOCATOR input this is a more reasonable way of working if highly precise numbers have to be entered.

2.6.3 CHOICE

Most commonly, CHOICE devices are implemented on function keyboards where each button is assigned a choice alternative. The choice alternative is a number between 1 and N, N being either the number of buttons or the number of button combinations. The latter is true for chord devices where an arbitrary number and combination of buttons can be pressed at the same time thus delivering a combined number. A chord device with 4 buttons can thus produce numbers between 1 and 15. A choice alternative is typically interpreted as a command or an enumeration type value. This realization is often called 'programmable function keyboard'. Usually, coded overlays are put onto the keyboard to indicate the meaning of the buttons.

More advanced implementations of the CHOICE device use menu techniques. Menus are either displayed on a screen or put on a tablet as an overlay. Using a positioning or a picking device (hand cursor, lightpen, thumb wheels) an alternative is selected. The single choice alternatives are displayed either as text strings or as graphics symbols.

Another solution is to use alphanumeric keyboards to type text strings. A string is compared against the menu definition. If it matches a choice alternative its number is reported.

An upcoming input device also fits into this scheme: word recognizer. A number of words is stored internally and speech input is compared against them. The number of the recognized word is delivered.

Another interesting simulation should be mentioned briefly: choice alternatives can be recognized from hand-written patterns entered by the operator.

A hand-written symbol 'd', e.g., could be interpreted to the command 'delete' after being recognized as d. Suitable input devices are the hand-held devices of Chapter 2.6.1, especially hand cursors, pens and the mouse.

2.6.4 PICK

The only true pick device is the lightpen of vector displays. From a display file address (the address where the display processor stops when the lightpen detects the beam) the identifier is calculated.

In most cases, it is necessary to simulate the PICK. For that purpose, all positioning devices can be used. A cursor is moved to the object to be identified and the position is entered. When interpreting an internal display file (segment storage), all output primitives are checked whether the position entered lies on or near to them. If several objects are detected the segment priority is used to determine the desired one.

Several techniques can be used to accelerate this computation. One is to store for each segment a surrounding rectangle or area in order to avoid the interpretation of segments which cannot have been hit. Another technique is to divide the screen into regions and to store for each region the segment names which fall into it. Then only those segments have to be considered which belong to the region the position entered lies in.

2.6.5 STRING

The only string device is the alphanumeric keyboard. There is a lot of literature about the ergonomics of keyboards treating aspects like pressure needed to depress a button, point of contact when a key is accepted, suitability of delimiter and correction button handling, the separation of 'dangerous' keys such as clear screen (see, for example, [FRAE77]).

Two simulation types should be mentioned: one is the display of characters and short character sequences on a screen or as overlay of a tablet. The operator composes the text string by identifying the single characters or character sequences with some identification technique.

Another realization is via pattern recognition of hand written input. The operator typically writes at a tablet using a pen. The resulting stream of positions is input to the character recognizer. This compares characteristic features of the characters drawn against a stored dictionary of each character's features. The stored characters are previously defined by the operator as samples.

3 IMPLEMENTATION ASPECTS

3.1 Feasibility of GKS Implementations

GKS is defined in a device- and processor-independent way. It is possible to implement GKS on nearly all computers starting with 8 bit microprocessors and to support most of the common graphics devices. Only those device facilities cannot be utilized that do not fit within the GKS functionality like three-dimensional primitives and projection hardware. At the time of writing this book, we know of implementations for the following processor types: SIEMENS (BS2000), SIEMENS R30, UNIVAC V77, CDC MODCOMP, IBM, VAX 11/780, PDP 11, PRIME, DEC10, MOTOROLA 68000, KONTRON-PSI 80, HP1000, and others. More detailed information can be obtained from [GKSVER]. Some of the graphics devices supported by these implementations are: HEWLETT PACKARD plotters and displays, CALCOMP, VERSATEC and TEWIDATA plotters, IDIIOM and FERRANTI vector displays, TEK-TRONIX storage tubes, MEGATEK 7000, DEC VT100, and many others. Depending on the level of GKS, the facilities within the supported level, and depending on the intelligence of the connected graphics devices, the memory sizes needed are between 4 K bytes and 200 K bytes. The size, of course, also depends on the quality of the particular compiler and the facilities of the available linkage editor.

3.2 Generality of GKS Implementations

The device and processor independence of the GKS definition does not necessarily mean a particular implementation should be independent from the actual graphics devices and processors. On the contrary, GKS installations should be as environment-adapted as possible. They should utilize the particular device and processor properties in optimal ways in order to decrease software overhead and improve execution characteristics. On the other hand, it is obviously not sensible in most cases to implement a new GKS system for every new graphical environment. Three strategies should be briefly discussed how to develop GKS implementations.

3.2.1 Environment-Specific Systems

These types of GKS implementations are device- and/or processor-specific as a consequence of the whole design process. That means they are developed with very specific installation characteristics for one unique hardware configuration in mind. A particular (set of) graphics device(s) is chosen and thus a set of device functions is determined. The GKS implementation realizes the GKS functions by either using the device functions directly or by emulating them via existing device functions. An example may clarify this approach:

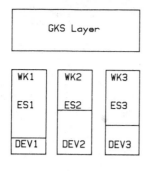

WKi: Workstation i
ESi: Emulation Software i
DEVi: Device i

Figure 3.1 Device-specific implementations

Let us take a storage tube (e.g., TEKTRONIX 4014) or a graphics device which offers a similar interface (e.g., DEC VT100). Then POLYLINE and low precision TEXT can be directly mapped by generating the corresponding character codes. Also functions for clearing the screen and entering positions, function codes, and keyboard strings are used. All other GKS output and the attribute functions must be emulated on the basis of lines or characters. For higher GKS levels a segment storage is required to simulate the segment functions and retroactive attribute bundle and workstation transformation modifications. The segment storage may be device-dependent with regard to the function items it stores and to the length of the coordinate data representations.

Several disadvantages occur with a pure approach like this. Almost no real graphics configuration will have only one type of devices. GKS deals with workstations. Every workstation covers a graphics device or a metafile or a segment storage. A typical interactive system will have a display device, a plotter for hard copying, a metafile for long term filing, and a segment storage for the transport of segments between the workstations. All these workstations base on different devices and thus use different device functions. The above approach thus needs a duplication of emulation software as is shown in Figure 3.1.

Another major disadvantage are the high costs involved when connecting a new different device to the system. This would require development of a new workstation with the necessary emulation software (e.g., another device-dependent segment storage).

Summarizing, this approach is only meaningful if very simple GKS installations are intended (level 0 systems with one workstation) and no exchange of the graphics device is demanded.

3.2.2 Device-Independent Systems

To overcome the above mentioned shortcomings another approach was undertaken: the development of a DI/DD interface [DIN81]. This separates the de-

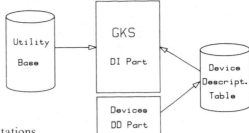

Figure 3.2 Device-independent implementations

vice-dependent part (DD) from the device-independent system (DI). Each particular device defines its own different DI/DD interface. Details of this approach can be read in Chapter 5. A set of utilities and emulations is identified, each one performing a transformation step within the mapping process from logical to physical functions.

The facilities of each particular device are described in a device description table or can be inquired from the respective driver. The DI part uses this information for selecting the appropriate simulation and emulation modules and maps the GKS functions to the actually available device functions. This approach is sketched out in Figure 3.2. It ensures maximum flexibility.

Only one workstation driver is needed to control any graphics device whose functionality is supported by the DI part. Any new device can be connected to the system without a modification. Only its facilities must be described in the table. By adding more utilities, the scope of the implementation can be expanded with regard to applications as well as to graphics device types.

The problems of this approach lie in two aspects: one is, the generality of the implementation may lead to some overhead for a particular installation (devices and applications may be supported that are not needed in a particular case). The other problem is, the general simulations may not be optimal for certain devices (e.g., a circle might be mapped to lines even if circular arcs are available).

3.2.3 Configurable Systems

One step further in this development is the generation of configurable systems. Because of the large number of different graphics devices and the wide range of application requirements, the effort to program a dedicated GKS system for each particular case does not seem to be feasible. A multi-purpose GKS implementation (as described above) may be developed such that environment and application-specific GKS installations can be deduced. In [PFAF82a] an approach is described in which a dedicated system is automatically generated from a description of the requirements, a set of utility modules, and the specification of the DI part. Figure 3.3 illustrates this approach.

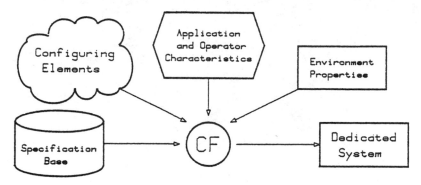

Figure 3.3 Configuration model

3.3 Some Implementation Concepts

The GKS functions can be distinguished into 4 classes: output, state setting, state inquiring, and input functions. They are embedded in a GKS system as shown in Figure 3.4.

3.3.1 Output

One interesting concept is that of the output pipelining. Any output primitive realization can be seen as a sequence of modular steps transforming the primitive from the logical level to the physical device functions. The intermediate steps are controlled by GKS states (e.g., attributes) which themselves are set prior to the output function activation. One possible transformation sequence for a polyline pipeline is shown in Figure 3.5.

Other valid polyline pipelines can be obtained by exchanging some of these modules without changing the function's effect. The above example addresses a simple device where all attribute emulations and coordinate transformations are performed by software. Other realizations could omit modules in their DI part because the corresponding effect is guaranteed by the device.

A lot of issues arise around the output concept. Some of these are:

— The software pipeline can be translated into hardware pipelines where each module may work independently from each other. This is relevant both for distributing a GKS system on a multiprocessor system and for designing a special GKS processor by VLSI techniques. While in the first case the modules could directly be distributed, they have to be broken up into smaller pieces for VLSI [ENCA82b].

— Obviously, attributes may be sent to the driver each time they are set by the application program. For code optimising reasons, they may be stored in the DI part and sent to the driver only when a significant output primitive is processed. Otherwise, e.g., a large amount of output information may be clipped by GKS but the associated attributes are sent to the drivers and stored on metafiles and the segment storage.

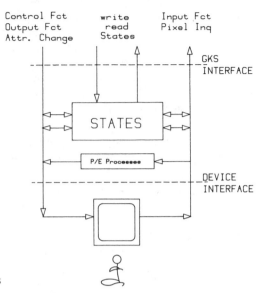

Figure 3.4 Distinction of GKS functions

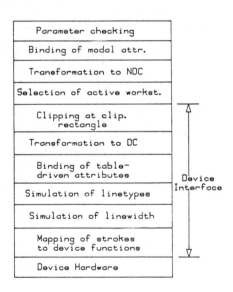

Figure 3.5 Output pipelining

3.3.2 Input

The input model is exhaustively treated in Chapter 2. Here we want to discuss three implementation strategies of asynchronous input (sample and event input).

The most important requirement is the facility of multitasking, i.e., several processes should exist and be active in parallel. If the operating system provides true multitasking, then all input processes and the one output process may exist simultaneously. Each time a logical device is set into sample or event mode, a new process is created. It terminates when the logical device is reset into request mode. Synchronization has to be established for access to the event queue, to common state lists, and to commonly used physical devices.

A second solution is that only two processes exist, one handling the output, the other one the input functions. The input process is in existence as long as at least one logical input device is in sample or event mode. It handles all input devices sequentially (e.g., in a polling loop).

If the operating system does not provide multitasking, an input handling routine has to be implemented. It has to be activated each time an interrupt generating device "fires" as result of an operator triggering, and each time a given time slice has passed. Then the output task has to be suspended (deactivated and saved). The input handling routine processes the prompting, echoing, acknowledgement, and input data computation for all logical input devices which are currently in event or sample mode. Afterwards, it returns control to the output process again.

3.4   Allowable Differences Between GKS Implementations

A number of details of the Standard has been left deliberately unspecified, so as to provide the freedom to adapt implementations to different environments and different requirements. In particular, the Standard is described in abstract terms, so that it can be useful to application programs written in a wide range of programming languages. In a language binding, the abstract GKS functions are embedded in a language-dependent layer, according to a number of rules. These rules are set out in Chapter 4 and are not considered further here. Other allowable differences fall into two categories:
— Global differences.
— Workstation-dependent differences.

The documentation accompanying a particular implementation should list, for each allowable difference, the specific choices made in that implementation.

3.4.1   Global Differences

A number of differences are global in the sense of applying to an implementation as a whole rather than to a particular workstation. These global differences are itemized below (see Table 3.1).

3.4.2   Workstation Dependent Differences

This group of allowable differences provides for a range of workstations to be used in a GKS implementation. The major group of differences are listed as the Workstation Description Table, specified in Chapter III.3, which forms

Table 3.1 Global differences

Functional Scope
    GKS level
Capacity
    Maximum normalization transformation number
    Number of available workstation types
    List of available workstation types
    Maximum number of simultaneously open workstations
    Maximum number of simultaneously active workstations
    Maximum number of workstations associated with a segment
    Maximum size of input queue
    Number of fonts available
    Number of GDPs
    Number of ESCAPE functions
Miscellaneous
    Initial setting of associated source flags (ASFs)
    EMERGENCY CLOSE GKS behaviour
    Value returned by inquiry if information is unavailable
    GKSM format used by each GKSM workstation type
    Font definitions
Note:
    The GKS level and the first capacity items are held in the GKS description table, and can be inquired by an application program. At different GKS levels, certain minimal capabilities are defined in Chapter III.2.

part of the GKS data structures. Entries in this table can be inquired by an application program.

There are restrictions, however, on the values of some entries: at different GKS levels, certain minimal capabilities of a workstation are defined. In addition, a number of further workstation-dependent differences are listed here:

Control Functions
Realization of the GKS functions: MESSAGE, ESCAPE, Buffering of deferred actions in deferral modes BNIL, BNIG and ASTI

Output Functions and Attributes

POLYLINE: Whether linetype is continuous or restarted, at the start of a polyline, at the start of a clipped piece of a polyline and at each vertex of a polyline. Graphical representation of available linetypes (with the restrictions that linetypes 1-4 must be recognizable as solid, dashed, dotted and dashed-dotted, and that other linetypes must have similar appearance on all workstations on which they are available).

POLYMARKER: Graphical representation of available markers (with the restrictions that markers 1-5 must be recognizable as dot, plus sign, asterisk, circle and diagonal cross, and that other markers must have similar appearance on all workstations on which they are available).

TEXT: Clipping of STRING and CHAR precision text. For STRING precision, how current settings of text attributes are taken into account. For CHAR precision, evaluation of the attributes CHARACTER HEIGHT, CHARACTER UP VECTOR, CHARACTER EXPANSION FACTOR and TEXT ALIGNMENT.

FILL AREA: Whether and how the interior styles SOLID, PATTERN and HATCH are supported; and if not supported, the simulation of these interior styles (minimal action required is interior style HOLLOW). Whether patterns and hatching are affected by transformations. Linetype and linewidth for interior style HOLLOW.

CELL ARRAY: Simulation (minimal action required is to draw the transformed boundaries of the cell rectangle, using implementation-dependent colour, linetype and linewidth).

GDP: Realization of each GDP.

All primitives: Colour index used if an output primitive is displayed with a colour index that is not present in the colour table.

Segments
Picking segments of equal priority. Display of overlapping segments of equal priority. Realization of highlighting.

Input Functions
Realization of logical input devices (for each logical input device, its measure and trigger must be described in terms of the physical devices available on a workstation).

Default prompt/echo realization. Use of input data record for optional parameters (see also Section 3.5).

Inquiry
Values returned by INQUIRE TEXT EXTENT
Values returned by PIXEL inquiry functions
Answers returned by Inquiry when the "REALIZED" flag is set.

3.5 Documentation of an Implementation

A GKS implementation is a module or library written in a programming language which conforms to a GKS language binding. The following rules should be followed when implementing GKS. The objective is to provide all the functions of a particular level of GKS, and none of the functions of higher levels of GKS, in an efficient manner using the facilities available from the host machine and operating system.

Rule I1

The documentation of a GKS implementation should include a list of all identifiers for procedures, functions, global data aggregates, and files that are visible either to an application program or to the underlying operating system.

Because this set of identifiers will, in general, be a superset of the names specified by the language binding, programs transported to an implementation from other implementations of the same binding might have used names that clash. Documentation is required to enable potential clashes to be detected (see also Chapter 4).

Rule I2

Implementations should not restrict an application program's use of any I/O facilities provided by the host language or operating system. However, implementations should prevent applications bypassing GKS and accessing graphical resources directly.

An implementation will need to assume that it has exclusive control over the graphical resources it is managing. However, as few restrictions as possible should be placed upon the use of other resources.

Rule I3

The documentation of an implementation should specify, for each of the implementation and workstation dependencies, how the dependencies have been resolved.

Several details of the Standard have been left deliberately unspecified, so as to provide implementors with sufficient freedom to adapt to particular computers and operating systems. These are indicated in the text by the words "implementation-dependent". Others have been left unspecified to allow for adaptation to particular graphics devices. These are indicated in the text by the words "workstation-dependent". A list of all such details is given in Section 3.4. The resolution of each of these details should be documented so that the behaviour of application programs may be predicted.

Rule I4

The documentation of each workstation of an implementation should specify the correspondence between physical input devices and operator actions, and the logical input devices on that workstation (if any).

The correspondence between physical input devices and operator actions, and the logical input devices on a workstation is static, and not under the control of the application program. These correspondences should be documented. Also, it is desirable that workstation implementors provide means whereby these correspondences may be changed, perhaps during a GKS configuration phase (see also Chapter 2). However, any such means lie outside the scope of the Standard.

4   LANGUAGE INTERFACES
AND THEIR IMPLEMENTATION

4.1   Guidelines for the Definition of Language Bindings

The Standard is described in abstract terms, in order that it may be useful
to applications written in a wide range of programming languages (host languages). Before it can be used by a particular application program written
in a particular language, two further stages of specification are required:
— The abstract functions and data types of the Standard must be instantiated
   in terms of the constructs available in the host language.
— This set of language-specific facilities must then be provided using the facilities of a particular machine and operating system.

The objective of the standard are the portability of application programs
between different implementations and the portability of programming knowledge for different languages. Therefore, restrictive rules for the definition of
language interfaces are developed with regard to the language binding (4.1.1)
and to its implementations (4.1.2).

4.1.1   Language Binding Rules

A GKS language binding is a document describing the functions that can be
accessed by programs written in a specific language. The following rules should
be observed when binding GKS to a host language. The objective of a binding
is to provide the functions and data types of GKS in a natural and efficient
manner using the facilities of the host language.

Rule L1
All GKS functions, other than inquiry functions, must appear atomic to the
application program.
   This rule forbids the binding to map single GKS functions into sequences
of language functions called by the application program, except possibly for
inquiry functions, which in certain language bindings may need to be called
once for each element of a structured data type.

Rule L2
The language binding should specify, for each GKS abstract function name,
exactly one identifier acceptable to the language.
   The names used for GKS functions in the Standard are merely tools for
describing the semantics of the Standard; they should be replaced by actual
identifiers conforming to the restrictions of the host language. There must be
a one-to-one mapping from language functions to abstract functions.

Rule L3

The language binding should specify, for each of the GKS data types, a corresponding data type acceptable to the language. Other data types may be specified as convenient, in terms of the GKS data types.

The data types used in the Standard are merely tools for describing the semantics of the standard, they should be replaced by actual data types conforming to the restrictions of the host language.

Rule L4

The language binding should specify, for each GKS abstract function, how the corresponding language function is to be invoked, and the means whereby each of the abstract parameters is transmitted to or from the language function.

The abstract functions will normally be mapped onto language functions or procedures. The parameters will normally be transmitted via a parameter list. The items in such a list may either be, or be references to, items of the data types corresponding to the GKS data types, or aggregates of these types.

Rule L5

The language binding should specify a set of identifiers, acceptable to the language, which may be used by an implementation for internal communication.

An implementation will normally be unable to restrict its use of externally visible identifiers to those specified as a consequence of the preceding rules. Applications should, therefore, avoid using identifiers in this internal set.

4.1.2 Implementation of the Language Interface

A GKS implementation is a module or library written in a programming language which conforms to a GKS language binding. The following rules should be followed when implementing GKS. The objective is to provide all the functions of a particular level of GKS, and none of the functions of higher levels of GKS, in an efficient manner using the facilities available from the host machine and operating system.

Rule I1

The documentation of a GKS implementation should include a list of all identifiers for procedures, functions, global data aggregates, and files that are visible either to an application program or to the underlying operating system.

Because this set of identifiers will, in general, be a superset of the names specified by the language binding, programs transported to an implementation from other implementations of the same binding might have used names that clash. Documentation is required to enable potential clashes to be detected (see also rule L5).

Rule I2

Implementations should not restrict an application program's use of any I/O facilities provided by the host language or operating system. However, implementations should prevent applications bypassing GKS and accessing graphical resources directly.

An implementation will need to assume that it has exclusive control over the graphical resources it is managing. However, as few restrictions as possible should be placed upon the use of other resources.

4.2   The GKS FORTRAN Interface

This chapter contains the GKS language binding for FORTRAN 77 [FORT77]. The complete specification of the GKS FORTRAN subroutines is given together with the specification of the GKS functions in Chapter III. The FORTRAN 77 GKS interface is designed in a way that GKS application programs can be transported between full FORTRAN 77, FORTRAN 77 Subset, and ANSI FORTRAN 66 [FORT66] installations without many modifications.

In the following, the decisions taken when designing the interface are explained. Thereby, we refer to the rules listed in the chapter before.

Rule L1
The mapping from GKS functions to FORTRAN subroutines is done in a one-to-one correspondence. Each GKS function has a unique FORTRAN subroutine name by which it can be invoked. Some GKS inquiry functions however, are splitted into several FORTRAN subroutines to ease the GKS application programming.

Rule L2
All FORTRAN subroutine names start with the letter 'G'. The remaining letters after the first one are chosen by deriving a unique abbreviation of the single words of the function names. For example, ACTIVATE becomes AC, WORKSTATION becomes WK; hence the FORTRAN subroutine name of ACTIVATE WORKSTATION becomes GACWK. A complete list of all subroutine names is given in Table 4.1. The method described eases the training of programmers since relatively few names have to be memorized to construct all GKS FORTRAN functions. It therefore was preferred to the alternative of giving each GKS function a more pronounceable name which does not fit into a unique abbreviation concept.

Rule L3
The Standard uses several types of parameters most of which cannot be realized directly in FORTRAN. Table 4.2 shows the correspondence between the types used in the GKS document and their realization in FORTRAN implementations.

Generally, the parameters in the FORTRAN subroutines are in the same order as in the GKS document. For some subroutines however, there are additional parameters which may intervene the normal parameter sequence (e.g., maximum array length for arrays being output parameters). This is shown in detail in Appendix 1.

Some of the GKS data types need special attention beyond their treatment in Table 4.2:

— The GKS data type STRING is mapped onto the FORTRAN 77 data type CHARACTER*(*). In a FORTRAN 77 Subset implementation CHARACTER*const and an additional parameter N are used where N is the number of characters. In FORTRAN 66 GKS implementations all occurrencies of CHARACTER*const declarations in application programs have to be changed to INTEGER array (M) declarations. The length M of the INTEGER array can be computed as the next greater whole number of [N/K] where K is the number of characters per INTEGER word.

The packing density (number of characters per INTEGER) is the usual one for the particular FORTRAN 66 implementation. This would be the packing density used for the Hollerith string literals.

— The GKS data type ENUMERATION is mapped to INTEGER. The values start with zero. Except for null values, the order of the ENUMERATION alternatives is the same as in the GKS document: null values always appear in the first position (e.g., GNONE, GNCLAS, GNCLIP).

In Table 4.3 a list of FORTRAN names is devised for each enumeration type value. It is not required that these mnemonics must be used in application programs. Installations should provide convenient means of incorporating the definitions of the names, for example by an INCLUDE or INSERT statement.

— The GKS data type RECORD cannot be implemented in FORTRAN in convenient ways. Therefore, two special utility functions have been defined to pack any data of the FORTRAN data types INTEGER, REAL and CHARACTER into a CHARACTER*80 array and to unpack the CHARACTER*80 array into the individual data items.

An example is given to illustrate their use: In GKS, the VALUATOR resolution has to be given in the VALUATOR DATA RECORD when the INITIALISE VALUATOR function is invoked. This reads in a FORTRAN program as follows:

```
RA1(1) = 0.00001
CALL GPREC (1,EMPTI,1,RA,1,EMPTC,MAXLD,
   ACTLD,D)
CALL GINVL (DISP,VAL1,INITVL,1,EXMIN,EXMAX,EYMIN,
   EYMAX,0.,3.14159,ACTLD,D)
```

Note that if a FORTRAN array is empty, its corresponding length parameter has to be set to '1' to facilitate the use of the adjustable dimension feature. The first element of the array has to be set to an implementation-dependent value signaling invalid data. In the example above, we use the names EMPTI and EMPTC to indicate the INTEGER array and the CHARACTER datum be empty. EMPTR would indicate an empty REAL array. The data record D delivered by the subroutine GPREC is passed to GKS as an input parameter of the subroutine GINVL when this is called.

Table 4.1 List of the GKS function names and their FORTRAN abbreviations

Control Functions

GOPKS (ERRFIL)	OPEN GKS
GCLKS	CLOSE GKS
GOPWK (WKID,CONID,WTYPE)	OPEN WORKSTATION
GCLWK (WKID)	CLOSE WORKSTATION
GACWK (WKID)	ACTIVATE WORKSTATION
GDAWK (WKID)	DEACTIVATE WORKSTATION
GCLRWK (WKID,COFL)	CLEAR WORKSTATION
GRSGWK (WKID)	REDRAW ALL SEGMENTS ON WORKSTATION
GUWK (WKID,REGFL)	UPDATE WORKSTATION
GSDS (WKID,DEFMOD,REGMOD)	SET DEFERRAL STATE
GMSG (WKID,MESS)	MESSAGE
GESC (FCTID,IL,IA)	ESCAPE

Output Functions

GPL (N,PX,PY)	POLYLINE
GPM (N,PX,PY)	POLYMARKER
GTX (X0,Y0,CHARS)	TEXT
GFA (N,PX,PY)	FILL AREA
GCA (PX,PY,QX,QY,N,M,DIMX,COLIA)	CELL ARRAY
GGDP (N,PX,PY,PRIMID,IL,IA)	GENERALIZED DRAWING PRIMITIVE

Output Attributes

GSPLI (INDEX)	SET POLYLINE INDEX
GSLN (LTYPE)	SET LINETYPE
GSLWSC (LWSC)	SET LINEWIDTH SCALE FACTOR
GSPLCI (PLCI)	SET POLYLINE COLOUR INDEX
GSPMI (INDEX)	SET POLYMARKER INDEX
GSMK (MKTYPE)	SET MARKER TYPE
GSMKSC (MKSC)	SET MARKER SIZE SCALE FACTOR
GSPMCI (PMCI)	SET POLYMARKER COLOUR INDEX
GSTXI (INDEX)	SET TEXT INDEX
GSTXFP (FONT,PREC)	SET TEXT FONT AND PRECISION

Table 4.1 (continued)

GSCHXP (CHXP)	SET CHARACTER EXPANSION FACTOR
GSCHSP (CHSP)	SET CHARACTER SPACING
GSTXCI (TXCI)	SET TEXT COLOUR INDEX
GSCHH (CHH)	SET CHARACTER HEIGHT
GSCHUP (CHUX,CHUY)	SET CHARACTER UP VECTOR
GSTXP (TXP)	SET TEXT PATH
GSTXAL (TXALH,TXALV)	SET TEXT ALIGNMENT
GSFAI (INDEX)	SET FILL AREA INDEX
GSFAIS (FAIS)	SET FILL AREA INTERIOR STYLE
GSFASI (FASI)	SET FILL AREA STYLE INDEX
GSFACI (FACI)	SET FILL AREA COLOUR INDEX
GSPA (SZX,SZY)	SET PATTERN SIZE
GSPARF (RFX,RFY)	SET PATTERN REFERENCE POINT
GSASF (LASF)	SET ASPECT SOURCE FLAGS
GSPKID (PCID)	SET PICK IDENTIFIER

Workstation Attributes (Representations)

GSPLR (WKID,PLI,LTYPE,LWIDTH,COLI)	SET POLYLINE REPRESENTATION
GSPMR (WKID,PMI,MTYPE,MSZSF,COLI)	SET POLYMARKER REPRESENTATION
GSTXR (WKID,TXI,FONT,PREC,CHXP,CHSP,COLI)	SET TEXT REPRESENTATION
GSFAR (WKID,FAI,INTS,STYLI,COLI)	SET FILL AREA REPRESENTATION
GSPAR (WKID,PAI,N,M,COLIA)	SET PATTERN REPRESENTATION
GSCR (WKID,CI,CR,CG,CB)	SET COLOUR REPRESENTATION

Transformation Functions

GSWN (TNR,XMIN,XMAX,YMIN,YMAX)	SET WINDOW
GSVP (TNR,XMIN,XMAX,YMIN,YMAX)	SET VIEWPORT
GSVPIP (TNR,RTNR,RELPRI)	SET VIEWPORT INPUT PRIORITY
GSELNT (TNR)	SELECT NORMALIZATION TRANSFORMATION
GSCLIP (CLSW)	SET CLIPPING INDICATOR
GSWKWN (WKID,XMIN,XMAX,YMIN,YMAX)	SET WORKSTATION WINDOW
GSWKVP (WKID,XMIN,XMAX,YMIN,YMAX)	SET WORKSTATION VIEWPORT

Table 4.1 (continued)

Segment Functions

GCRSG (SGNA)	CREATE SEGMENT
GCLSG	CLOSE SEGMENT
GRENSG (OLD,NEW)	RENAME SEGMENT
GDSG (SGNA)	DELETE SEGMENT
GDSGWK (WKID,SGNA)	DELETE SEGMENT FROM WORKSTATION
GASGWK (WKID,SGNA)	ASSOCIATE SEGMENT WITH WORKSTATION
GCSGWK (WKID,SGNA)	COPY SEGMENT TO WORKSTATION
GINSG (SGNA,M)	INSERT SEGMENT
GSSGT (SGNA,M)	SET SEGMENT TRANSFORMATION
GSVIS (SGNA,VIS)	SET VISIBILITY
GSHLIT (SGNA,HIL)	SET HIGHLIGHTING
GSSGP (SGNA,PRIOR)	SET SEGMENT PRIORITY
GSDTEC (SGNA,DET)	SET DETECTABILITY

Input Functions

GINLC (WKID,LCDNR,TNR,IPX,IPY, * PET,XMIN,XMAX,YMIN,YMAX,IL,IA)	INITIALISE LOCATOR
GINSK (WKID,SKDNR,TNR,N,IPX,IPY, * PET,XMIN,XMAX,YMIN,YMAX,BUFLEN,IL,IA)	INITIALISE STROKE
GINVL (WKID,VLDNR,IVAL,PET,XMIN, * XMAX,YMIN,YMAX,LOVAL,HIVAL,IL,IA)	INITIALISE VALUATOR
GINCH (WKID,CHDNR,IVAL,PET,XMIN, * XMAX,YMIN,YMAX,IL,IA)	INITIALISE CHOICE
GINPK (WKID,PCDNR,ISTAT,ISGNA,IPCID,PET, * XMIN,XMAX,YMIN,YMAX,IL,IA)	INITIALISE PICK
GINST (WKID,STDNR,ISTR,PET,XMIN, * XMAX,YMIN,YMAX,IBUFLN,INIPOS,IL,IA)	INITIALISE STRING
GSLCM (WKID,IDNR,MODE,ESW)	SET LOCATOR DEVICE MODE
GSSKM (WKID,IDNR,MODE,ESW)	SET STROKE DEVICE MODE
GSVLM (WKID,IDNR,MODE,ESW)	SET VALUATOR DEVICE MODE
GSCHM (WKID,IDNR,MODE,ESW)	SET CHOICE DEVICE MODE
GSPKM (WKID,IDNR,MODE,ESW)	SET PICK DEVICE MODE

Table 4.1 (continued)

GSSTM (WKID,IDNR,MODE,ESW)	SET STRING DEVICE MODE
GRQLC (WKID,LCDNR,STAT,TNR,PX,PY)	REQUEST LOCATOR
GRQSK (WKID,SKDNR,N,STAT,TNR,NP,PX,PY)	REQUEST STROKE
GRQVL (WKID,VLDNR,STAT,VAL)	REQUEST VALUATOR
GRQCH (WKID,CHDNR,STAT,CHNR)	REQUEST CHOICE
GRQPK (WKID,PCDNR,STAT,SGNA,PCID)	REQUEST PICK
GRQST (WKID,STDNR,STAT,RNCH,CHARS)	REQUEST STRING
GSMLC (WKID,LCDNR,TNR,LPX,LPY)	SAMPLE LOCATOR
GSMSK (WKID,SKDNR,N,TNR,NP,PX,PY)	SAMPLE STROKE
GSMVL (WKID,VLDNR,VAL)	SAMPLE VALUATOR
GSMCH (WKID,CHDNR,CHNR)	SAMPLE CHOICE
GSMPK (WKID,PCDNR,STAT,SGNA,PCID)	SAMPLE PICK
GSMST (WKID,STDNR,RNCH,CHARS)	SAMPLE STRING
GWAIT (TOUT,WKID,ICL,IDNR)	AWAIT EVENT
GFLUSH (WKID,ICL,IDNR)	FLUSH DEVICE EVENTS
GGTLC (TNR,LPX,LPY)	GET LOCATOR
GGTSK (N,TNR,NP,PX,PY)	GET STROKE
GGTVL (VAL)	GET VALUATOR
GGTCH (CHNR)	GET CHOICE
GGTPK (STAT,SGNA,PCID)	GET PICK
GGTST (RNCH,CHARS)	GET STRING

Metafile Functions

GWITM (WKID,TYPE,IL,IA)	WRITE ITEM TO GKSM
GGTITM (WKID,TYPE,IL)	GET ITEM TYPE FROM GKSM
GRDITM (WKID,IIL,IOL,IA)	READ ITEM FROM GKSM
GIITM (TYPE,IL,IA)	INTERPRET ITEM

Inquiry Function for Operating State Value

GQOPS (OPSTA)	INQUIRE OPERATING STATE VALUE

Table 4.1 (continued)

Inquiry Function for GKS Description Table

GQLVKS (IERR,JLEVEL)	INQUIRE LEVEL OF GKS
GQEWK (N,IERR,NB,WKTYP)	INQUIRE LIST element of AVAILABLE WK TYPES
GQWKM (IERR,MXOPWK,MXACWK,MXWKAS)	INQUIRE WORKSTATION MAXIMUM NUMBERS
GQMNTN (IERR,MAXTNR)	INQUIRE MAXIMUM NORM.TRANS. NUMBER

Inquiry Functions for GKS State List

GQOPWK (N,IERR,NB,IWKID)	INQUIRE SET member of OPEN WORKSTATIONS
GQACWK (N,IERR,NB,IWKID)	INQUIRE SET member of ACTIVE WORKSTATIONS

Inquire Current Primitive Attribute Values (splitted into 11 individual subroutines)

GQPLI (IERR,INDEX)	INQUIRE POLYLINE INDEX
GQPMI (IERR,INDEX)	INQUIRE POLYMARKER INDEX
GQTXI (IERR,INDEX)	INQUIRE TEXT INDEX
GQCHH (IERR,CHH)	INQUIRE CHARACTER HEIGHT
GQCHUP (IERR,CHUX,CHUY)	INQUIRE CHARACTER UP VECTOR
GQTXP (IERR,JTXP)	INQUIRE TEXT PATH
GQTXAL (IERR,JTXALH,JTXALV)	INQUIRE TEXT ALIGNMENT
GQFAI (IERR,INDEX)	INQUIRE FILL AREA INDEX
GQPA (IERR,SZX,SZY)	INQUIRE PATTERN SIZE
GQPARF (IERR,RFX,RFY)	INQUIRE PATTERN REFERENCE POINT
GQPKID (IERR,IPKID)	INQUIRE PICK IDENTIFIER

Inquire Current Setting of Individual Attributes (splitted into 14 individual subroutines)

GQLN (IERR,ILTYPE)	INQUIRE LINETYPE
GQLWSC (IERR,RLWID)	INQUIRE LINEWIDTH SCALE FACTOR
GQPLCI (IERR,INDEX)	INQUIRE POLYLINE COLOUR INDEX
GQMK (IERR,IMTYPE)	INQUIRE MARKERTYPE
GQMKSC (IERR,RMSZSF)	INQUIRE MARKER SIZE SCALE FACTOR

Table 4.1 (continued)

GQPMCI (IERR,ICI)	INQUIRE POLYMARKER COLOUR INDEX
GQTXFP (IERR,IFONT,JPREC)	INQUIRE TEXT FONT AND PRECISION
GQCHXP (IERR,CHXP)	INQUIRE CHARACTER EXPANSION FACTOR
GQCHSP (IERR,CHSP)	INQUIRE CHARACTER SPACING
GQTXCI (IERR,ICI)	INQUIRE TEXT COLOUR INDEX
GQFAIS (IERR,JINTS)	INQUIRE FILL AREA INTERIOR STYLE
GQFASI (IERR,ISTYLI)	INQUIRE FILL AREA INTERIOR STYLE
GQFACI (IERR,ICI)	INQUIRE FILL AREA COLOUR INDEX
GQASF (IERR,LJASF)	INQUIRE ASPECT SOURCE FLAGS
GQCNTN (IERR,ICTNR)	INQUIRE CURRENT NORM.TRANS. NUMBER
GQENTN (N,IERR,NB,INPRIO)	INQUIRE LIST element OF NORM.TRANS. NBS
GQNT (ITNR,IERR,WINDOW,VIEWPT)	INQUIRE NORMALIZATION TRANSFORMATION
GQCLIP (IERR,JCLIP)	INQUIRE CLIPPING INDICATOR
GQOPSG (IERR,ISEGNA)	INQUIRE NAME OF OPEN SEGMENT
GQSGUS (N,IERR,NB,ISEGNA)	INQUIRE SET member OF SEGMENT NAMES IN USE
GQSIM (IERR,JFLAG)	INQUIRE MORE SIMULTANEOUS EVENTS

Inquiry Functions for the Workstation State List

GQWKC (IWKID,IERR,ICONID,IWTYPE)	INQUIRE WK CONNECTION AND TYPE
GQWKS (IWKID,IERR,JSTATE)	INQUIRE WORKSTATION STATE
GQWKDU (IWKID,IERR,JDFM,JRGM,JEMPT,JNF)	INQUIRE WK DEFERRAL AND UPDATE STATES
GQEPLI (IWKID,N,IERR,NB,PLI)	INQUIRE LIST element OF POLYLINE INDICES
GQPLR (IWKID,IPLI,JTYP,IERR,ILT,RLWSF,ICI)	INQUIRE POLYLINE REPRESENTATION
GQEPMI (IWKID,N,IERR,NB,PMI)	INQUIRE LIST element OF POLYMARKER INDICES
GQPMR (IWKID,IPMI,JTYP,IERR,IMT,RMSZS,ICI)	INQUIRE POLYMARKER REPRESENTATION
GQETXI (IWKID,N,IERR,NB,TXI)	INQUIRE LIST element OF TEXT INDICES
GQTXR (IWKID,ITXI,JTYP,IERR,IFT,JPREC,CHX,CHSP,ICI)	INQUIRE TEXT REPRESENTATION
GQTXX (IWKID,SX,SY,KSTR,IERR,CPX,CPY,EXRX,EXRY)	INQUIRE TEXT EXTENT (F77)
GQTXXS (IWKID,SX,SY,NCH,KSTR,IERR,CPX,CPY,EX,EX)	INQUIRE TEXT EXTENT (F77-SUBSET)
GQEFAI (IWKID,N,IERR,NB,FAI)	INQUIRE LIST element OF FILL AREA INDICES
GQFAR (IWKID,IFAI,JTYP,IERR,JINST,ISTIN,ICI)	INQUIRE FILL AREA REPRESENTATION

Table 4.1 (continued)

GQEPAI (IWKID,N,IERR,NB,PAI)	INQUIRE LIST element OF PATTERN INDICES
GQPAR (IWKID,IPAI,JTYPE,NMX,MMX,IERR,N,M,ICIA)	INQUIRE PATTERN REPRESENTATION
GQECI (IWKID,N,IERR,NB,COLI)	INQUIRE LIST element OF COLOUR INDICES
GQCR (IWKID,ICI,JTYP,IERR,RR,RG,RB)	INQUIRE COLOUR REPRESENTATION
GQWKT (IWKID,IERR,ITUS,RWINDO,CWINDO,RVIEWP, * CVIEWP)	INQUIRE WORKSTATION TRANSFORMATION
GQSGWK (IWKID,N,IERR,NB, ISEGNA)	INQUIRE SET member OF SEGMENT NAMES ON WK
GQLCS (IWKID,ILCDNR,JTYP,MLDR,IERR, JMODE,JESW, * ITNR,IPX,IPY,IPET,EAREA,ILDR,KDR)	INQUIRE LOCATOR DEVICE STATE
GQSKS (IWKID,ISKDNR,JTYP,N,MLDR,IERR,JMODE,JESW, * ITNR,NP,PX,PY,IPET,EAREA,IBUFLN,ILDR,KDR)	INQUIRE STROKE DEVICE STATE
GQVLS (IWKID,IVLDNR,MLDR,IERR,JMODE,JESW, * RIVAL,IPET,EAREA,RLOVAL,RHIVAL,ILDR,KDR)	INQUIRE VALUATOR DEVICE STATE
GQCHS (IWKID,ICHDNR,MLDR,IERR,JMODE,JESW, * ICHNR,IPET,EAREA,ILDR,KDR)	INQUIRE CHOICE DEVICE STATE
GQPKS (IWKID,IPCDNR,JTYP,MLDR,IERR,JMODE,JESW, * JSTAT,ISGNA,IPKID,IPET,EAREA,ILDR,KDR)	INQUIRE PICK DEVICE STATE
GQSTS (IWKID,ISTDNR,MLDR,IERR,JMOD,JESW, * IRNCH,KISTR,IPET,EAREA,IBUFLN,INIPOS,ILDR,KDR)	INQUIRE STRING DEVICE STATE (F77)
GQSTSS (IWKID,ISTDNR,MNCH,MLDR,IERR,JMOD,JESW, * NRCH,KISTR,IPET,EAREA,IBUFLN,INIPOS,ILDR,KDR)	INQUIRE STRING DEVICE STATE (SUBSET)

Inquiry Functions for Workstation Description Table

GQWKCA (IWTYP,IERR,JWKCAT)	INQUIRE WORKSTATION CATEGORY
GQWKCL (IWTYP,IERR,JVRTYP)	INQUIRE WORKSTATION CLASSIFICATION
GQMDS (IWTYP,IERR,JDCUN,RX,RY,ILX,ILY)	INQUIRE MAXIMUM DISPLAY SURFACE SIZE
GQDWKA (IWTYP,IERR,JPLBUN,JPMBUN,JTXBUN, * JFABUN,JPAREP,JCOLR,JWKTR)	INQUIRE DYNAMIC MODIFICATION OF WORKSTATION ATTRIBUTES
GQDDS (IWTYP,IERR,JDEFMO,JREGMO)	INQUIRE DEFAULT DEFERRAL STATE VALUE
GQPLF (IWTYP,N,IERR,NLT,LT,NLW,NOMLW, * RLWMIN,RLWMAX,NPPLI)	INQUIRE POLYLINE FACILITIES

Table 4.1 (continued)

GQPPLR (IWTYP,IPLI,IERR,ILN,RLWSF,ICI)	INQUIRE PREDEFINED POLYLINE REPRES.
GQPMF (IWTYP,N,IERR,NMT,MT,NMS,NOMMS, * RMSMIN,RMSMAX,NPPMI)	INQUIRE POLYMARKER FACILITIES
GQPPMR (IWTYP,IPMI,IERR,IMTYP,RMSZ,ICI)	INQUIRE PREDEFINED POLYMARKER REPRES.
GQTXF (IWTYP,N,IERR,NFPP,IFT,JPREC,NCCH, * RMIKH,RMAKH,NCHX,RMIKX,RMAKX,NPTXI)	INQUIRE TEXT FACILITIES
GQPTXR (IWTYP,IPTXI,IERR,IFT,JPR,CHX,CHSP,ICI)	INQUIRE PREDEFINED TEXT REPRES.
GQFAF (IWTYP,NI,NH,IERR,NIS,IS,NHS,IHS,NPFAI)	INQUIRE FILL AREA FACILITIES
GQPFAR (IWTYP,IPFAI,IERR,JINST,ISTI,ICI)	INQUIRE PREDEFINED FILL AREA REPRES.
GQPAF (IWTYP,IERR,NPPAI)	INQUIRE PATTERN FACILITIES
GQPPAR (IWTYP,IPPAI,NM,MM,IERR,N,M,ICIA)	INQUIRE PREDEFINED PATTERN REPRES.
GQCF (IWTYP,IERR,NCOLI,JCOLA,NPCI)	INQUIRE COLOUR FACILITIES
GQPCR (IWTYP,IPCI,IERR,RR,RG,RB)	INQUIRE PREDEFINED COLOUR REPRES.
GQEGDP (IWTYP,N,IERR,NGDP,IGDP)	INQUIRE LIST element OF AVAILABLE GDPs
GQGDP (IWTYP,IGDP, IERR,NSET,JLSET)	INQUIRE GENERALIZED DRAWING PRIMITIVE
GQLWK (IWTYP,IERR,MPLB,MPMB,MTXB,MFAB,MPAI, * MCOLI)	INQUIRE MAXIMUM LENGTH OF WORKSTATION STATE TABLES
GQSGP (IWTYP,IERR,NSG)	INQUIRE NUMBER OF SEGMENT PRIORITIES
GQDSGA (IWTYP,IERR,JSGTR,JVONOF,JVOFON,JHIGH, * JSGPR,JADD,JSGDEL)	INQUIRE DYNAMIC MODIFICATION OF SEGMENT ATTRIBUTES
GQLI (IWTYP,IERR,NLC,NSK,NVL,NCH,NPK,NST)	INQUIRE NB OF AVAILABLE INPUT DEVICES
GQDLC (IWTYP,IDNR,NP,MLDR,IERR,RIPX,RIPY, * NPL,IPET,EAREA,LDR,KDR)	INQUIRE DEFAULT LOCATOR DEVICE DATA
GQDSK (IWTYP,IDNR,NP,MLDR,IERR,MBFSZ, * NPL,IPET,EAREA,IBUFLN,LDR,KDR)	INQUIRE DEFAULT STROKE DEVICE DATA
GQDVL (IWTYP,IDNR,NP,MLDR,IERR,DVAL, * NPL,IPET,EAREA,RLOVAL,RHIVAL,LDR,KDR)	INQUIRE DEFAULT VALUATOR DEVICE DATA
GQDCH (IWTYP,IDNR,NP,MLDR,IERR,MAXALT, * NPL,IPET,EAREA,LDR,KDR)	INQUIRE DEFAULT CHOICE DEVICE DATA
GQDPK (IWTYP,IDNR,NP,MLDR,IERR, * NPL,IPET,EAREA,LDR,KDR)	INQUIRE DEFAULT PICK DEVICE DATA

Table 4.1 (continued)

460   4 Language Interfaces and Their Implementation

GQDST (IWTYP,IDNR,NP,MLDR,IERR,MBFSZ,   INQUIRE DEFAULT STRING DEVICE DATA
* NPL,IPET,EAREA,IBUFLN,LDR,KDR)

Inquiry Functions for Segment State List

GQASWK (ISGNA,N,IERR,NB,IWKID)   INQUIRE SET member OF ASSOCIATED WORKSTAT.
GQSGA (ISGNA,IERR,RSEGM,JVIS,JHIGH,SGPR,JDET)   INQUIRE SEGMENT ATTRIBUTES

Pixel Inquiries

GQPXAD (WKID,PX,PY,QX,QY,ERR,N,M)   INQUIRE PIXEL ARRAY DIMENSIONS
GQPXA (WKID,PX,PY,NMX,MMY,IDIMX,ERR,INVVAL,COL)   INQUIRY PIXEL ARRAY
GQPX (WKID,PX,PY,ERR,COLI)   INQUIRE PIXEL

Inquiry Function for GKS Error State List

GQIQOV (ERR,WKID,ICL,IDN)   INQUIRE INPUT QUEUE OVERFLOW

Utility Functions

GEVTM (X0,Y0,DX,DY,PHI,FX,FY,SW,MOUT)   EVALUATE TRANSFORMATION MATRIX
GACTM (MIN,X0,Y0,DX,DY,PHI,FX,FY,SW,MOUT)   ACCUMULATE TRANSFORMATION MATRIX

Error Handling

GECLKS   EMERGENCY CLOSE GKS
GERHND (ERRNB,FCTID,ERRFIL)   STANDARD ERROR HANDLING PROCEDURE
GERLOG (ERRNB,FCTID,ERRFIL)   STANDARD ERROR LOGGING PROCEDURE

Utility Functions not defined in GKS

GPREC (IL,IA,RL,RA,NST,KSTR,NLDR,LDR,KDR)   PACK DATA RECORD
GUREC (LDR,KDR,MIL,MRL,MSL,IL,IA,RL,RA,NST,KSTR)   UNPACK DATA RECORD

Table 4.2 Correspondence of the GKS data types to the FORTRAN data types

GKS Data Type	FORTRAN Data Representation
INTEGER	INTEGER
INTEGER ARRAY	INTEGER giving the length of the INTEGER array INTEGER array (length)
REAL	REAL
REAL ARRAY	INTEGER giving the length of the REAL array REAL array (length)
const x REAL	List of REALS, or REAL array (const) in INQUIRY functions where const. > 3
STRING	INTEGER giving the number of characters (for output string argument only) CHARACTER*(*) containing the string In a FORTRAN 77 Subset implementation: INTEGER giving the number of characters input INTEGER giving the number of characters returned (for output string argument only) CHARACTER*const containing the string In a FORTRAN 66 implementation: INTEGER giving the number of characters input INTEGER giving the number of characters returned (for output string argument only) INTEGER array (length) containing the string length = the next greater whole number of N/y; y = number of chars per integer word
POINT	REAL,REAL giving the X- and Y- values
POINT ARRAY	INTEGER giving the length of the POINT ARRAY REAL array1 (length), REAL array2 (length) containing the X- and Y- values
NAME	INTEGER
ENUMERATION	INTEGER. All values are mapped to the range zero to N-1, where N is the number of enumeration alternatives. Except for null values, the order of the enumeration alternatives is the same as in the GKS document: null values always appear in the first position.
RECORD	Represented as a set of scalar values and an array of CHARACTER*80 containing the remainder of the data. Note: The set of scalar values is empty, except where the data record contains values which are compulsary in GKS. Data can be written into the data record with the FORTRAN READ and WRITE statements. Special utility functions are defined to pack INTEGER, REAL and CHARACTER data into the data record and to unpack the data record to the individual data items (GPREC,GUREC).

The representation of CELL ARRAY, PIXEL ARRAY, and PATTERN allows the user of the routines requiring a cell array parameter to store his data in either a one or two dimensional array, and pass any portion of the array as an argument. Two examples should make this clear. Note however that passing only part of the array relies on call-by-address parameter passing and the FORTRAN standard array storage convention.

Certainly the user can pass an entire two-dimensional array. In this case the number of columns of the cell array is the same as the first dimension of the FORTRAN array:

```
INTEGER        DX,DY,CELLS(DX,DY)
CALL GCA       (X1,Y1,X2,Y2,DX,DY,DX,CELLS)
```

(1,1)	(2,1)	(3,1)	...	(DX,1)
(1,2)	(2,2)	(3,2)	...	(DX,2)
⋮	⋮	⋮		⋮
(1,DY)	(2,DY)	(3,DY)	...	(DX,DY)

To use an arbitrary portion of an array the user passes the upper left corner of the portion as starting address and the first dimension of the entire array for the right treatment of addresses. The area inside the plus-signs the cell array being passed:

```
INTEGER        DX,DY,DIMX,DIMY,CELLS(DIMX,DIMY)
DATA           DX/2/,DY/3/
CALL GCA       (X1,Y1,X2,Y2,DX,DY,DIMX,CELLS(3,6))
```

(1,1)	(2,1)	(3,1)	(4,1)	...	(DIMX,1)
(1,2)	(2,2)	(3,2)	(4,2)	...	(DIMX,2)
⋮	⋮	⋮	⋮		⋮
(1,6)	(2,6)	(3,6)	(4,6)	...	(DIMX,6)
(1,7)	(2,7)	(3,7)	(4,7)	...	(DIMX,7)
(1,8)	(2,8)	(3,8)	(4,8)	...	(DIMX,8)
⋮	⋮	⋮	⋮		⋮
(1,DIMY)	(2,DIMY)	(3,DIMY)	(4,DIMY)	...	(DIMX,DIMY)

All the enumeration types of GKS are mapped to FORTRAN INTEGERS. The correspondence between GKS scalars and FORTRAN INTEGERS is shown in this table in a list of symbolic FORTRAN constants which may be included in any application program. The following section contains a method of mapping GKS Enumeration types to FORTRAN variable names. In a full FORTRAN 77 implementation, this mapping could also be accomplished by the PARAMETER statement. However, the following method would ensure compatibility between full FORTRAN 77 and FORTRAN 77 subset. Also, a numbering of all GKS functions is given for use in the error handling procedures.

Note that due to space limitations, only the DATA statements are listed. All of these variables have to be declared as INTEGERS additionally.

Table 4.3 Mnemonic FORTRAN names for the GKS ENUMERATION type values

INCLUDE FILE containing the mnemonic FORTRAN names and their values for all GKS ENUMERATION type values

aspect source:	bundled, individual	
DATA GBUNDL,GINDIV		/0,1/
clear control flag:	conditionally, always	
DATA GCONDI,GALWAY		/0,1/
clipping indicator:	noclip, clip	
DATA GNCLIP,GCLIP		/0,1/
colour available:	monochrome, colour	
DATA GMONOC,GCOLOR		/0,1/
coordinate switch:	WC, NDC	
DATA GWC,GNDC		/0,1/
deferral mode:	asap, bnil, bnig, asti	
DATA GASAP,GBNIL,GBNIG,GASTI		/0,1,2,3/
detectability:	undetectable, detectable	
DATA GUNDET,GDETEC		/0,1/
device coordinate units: /	metres, other	
DATA GMETRE,GOTHU		/0,1/
dynamic modification:	irg,imm	
DATA GIRG,GIMM		/0,1/
echo switch:	noecho, echo	
DATA GNECHO,GECHO		/0,1/
fill area interior style:	hollow, solid, pattern, hatch	
DATA GHOLLO,GSOLID,GPATTR,GHATCH		/0,1,2,3/
highlighting:	normal, highlighted	
DATA GNORML,GHILIT		/0,1/
input device status:	none, ok, nopick	
DATA GNONE,GOK,GNPICK		/0,1,2/
input class:	none, locator, stroke, valuator, choice, pick, string	
DATA GNCLAS,GLOCAT,GSTROK,GVALUA		/0,1,2,3/
DATA GCHOIC, GPICK,GSTRIN		/4,5,6/
implicit regeneration mode:	suppressed, allowed	
DATA GSUPPD,GALLOW		/0,1/
level of GKS:	L0a, L0b, L0c, L1a, L1b, L1c, L2a, L2b, L2c	
DATA GLOA,GLOB,GLOC,GL1A,GL1B,		/0,1,2,3,4/
DATA GL1C,GL2A,GL2B,GL2C		/5,6,7,8/
new frame action necessary:	no, yes	
DATA GNO,GYES		/0,1/
operating mode:	request, sample,event	
DATA GREQU,GSAMPL,GEVENT		/0,1,2/
operating state value:	GKCL, GKOP, WSOP, WSAC, SGOP	
DATA GGKCL,GGKOP,GWSOP,GWSAC,GSGOP		/0,1,2,3,4/
presence of invalid values:	absent, present	
DATA GABSNT,GPRSNT		/0,1/
regeneration flag:	suppress, perform	
DATA GSUPP,GPERFO		/0,1/
relative input priority:	higher, lower	
DATA GHIGHR,GLOWER		/0,1/

Table 4.3 (continued)

INCLUDE FILE containing the mnemonic FORTRAN names and their values for all GKS ENUMERATION type values

simultaneous events flag: nomore, more
   DATA GNMORE,GMORE   /0,1/
text alignment horizontal: normal, left, center, right
   DATA GAHNOR,GALEFT,GACENT,GARITE   /0,1,2,3/
text alignment vertical: normal, top, cap, half, base, bottom
   DATA GAVNOR,GATOP,GACAP,GAHALF,GABASE,GABOTT
                                                    /1,2,3,4,5/
text path: right, left,up,down
   DATA GRIGHT,GLEFT,GUP,GDOWN   /0,1,2,3/
text precision: string, char, stroke
   DATA GSTRP,GCHARP,GSTRKP   /0,1,2/
type of returned values: set,realized
   DATA GSET,GREALI   /0,1/
update state: notpending, pending
   DATA GNPEND,GPEND   /0,1/
vector/raster/other type: vector,raster,other
   DATA GVECTR,GRASTR,GOTHWK   /0,1,2/
visibility: invisible, visible
   DATA GINVIS,GVISI   /0,1/
workstation category: output, input, outin, wiss, mo, mi
   DATA GOUTPT,GINPUT,GOUTIN,GWISS,GMO,GMI   /0,1,2,3,4,5/
workstation state: inactive, active
   DATA GINACT,GACTIV   /0,1/
list of GDP attributes:
   DATA GPLBND,GPMBND,GTXBND,GFABND   /0,1,2,3/
line type: solid, dashed, dotted, dash-dotted
   DATA GLSOLI,GLDASH,GLDOT,GLDASD   /1,2,3,4/
marker type: point, plus, asterisk, o-mark, x-mark
   DATA GPOINT,GPLUS,GAST,GOMARK,GXMARK   /1,2,3,4,5/
GKS functions (for error handling). The names are the same as the GKS function names except that the sentinel character 'G' is replaced by 'E'.
DATA EOPKS,ECLKS,EOPWK,ECLWK,EACWK,EDAWK   /0,1,2,3,4,5/
DATA ECLRWK,ERSGWK,EUWK,ESDS,EMSG,EESC   /6,7,8,9,10,11/
DATA EPL,EPM,ETX,EFA,ECA,EGDP   /12,13,14,15,16,17/
DATA ESPLI,ESLN,ESLWSC,ESPLCI,ESPMI,ESMK   /18,19,20,21,22,23/
DATA ESMKSC,ESPMCI,ESTXI,ESTXFP,ESCHXP,ESCHSP   /24,25,26,27,28,29/
DATA ESTXCI,ESCHH,ESCHUP,ESTXP,ESTXAL,ESFAI   /30,31,32,33,34,35/
DATA ESFAIS,ESFASI,ESFACI,ESPA,ESPARF,ESASF   /36,37,38,39,40,41/
DATA ESPKID,ESPLR,ESPMR,ESTXR,ESFAR,ESPAR   /42,43,44,45,46,47/
DATA ESCR,ESWN,ESVP,ESVPIP,ESELNT,ESCLIP   /48,49,50,51,52,53/
DATA ESWKWN,ESWKVP,ECRSG,ECLSG,ERENSG,EDSG   /54,55,56,57,58,59/
DATA EDSGWK,EASGWK,ECSGWK,EINSG,ESSGT,ESVIS   /60,61,62,63,64,65/
DATA ESHLIT,ESSGP,ESDTEC,EINLC,EINSK,EINVL   /66,67,68,69,70,71/
DATA EINCH,EINPK,EINST,ESLCM,ESSKM,ESVLM   /72,73,74,75,76,77/
DATA ESCHM,ESPKM,ESSTM,ERQLC,ERQSK,ERQVL   /78,79,80,81,82,83/
DATA ERQCH,ERQPK,ERQST,ESMLC,ESMSK,ESMVL   /84,85,86,87,88,89/

the data flow from the application program to the GKSM. (The complete GKS data flow diagram is shown in Figure I.9.2 on page 31).

Three main paths can be identified in this figure: user data, passed from the application program directly to the metafile, output outside segments and information contained in segments.

11.3.1   User Data

The user data is passed to the GKSM by a GKS function only applicable to GKSM output workstations. In all other cases error 32 ("Specified workstation is not of category GKSM output") will be generated.

WRITE ITEM TO GKSM   WSAC,SGOP   L0a
Parameters:

Input	workstation identifier		N
Input	item type		I
Input	item data record length	(0..n)	I
Input	item data record		D

Effect:

A record containing non-graphical data provided by the application program is written to the GKSM. The parameters 'item data record' and 'item data record length' define the data to be output whilst 'item type' specifies its type.

Note:

This function will be used only to transfer non-graphical information to the GKSM. Graphical data will be sent automatically after GKSM output has been activated.

Errors:

5	GKS not in proper state: GKS shall be either in the state WSAC or in the state SGOP
20	Specified workstation identifier is invalid
30	Specified workstation is not active
32	Specified workstation is not of category MO
160	Item type is not allowed for user items
161	Item length is invalid

——————————————— *FORTRAN-Interface* ———————————————

CALL GWITM (WKID,TYPE,LINT,ITEM)
Parameters:

Input	WKID	workstation identifier		INTEGER
Input	TYPE	item type		INTEGER
Input	LINT	item dimension	(1..n)	INTEGER
Input	ITEM(LINT)	item data record		CHARACTER*80

The WRITE ITEM TO GKSM function will pass non-graphical data to the metafile. Item types > 100 are reserved for this purpose. The intent of this function is to allow user data, related to the graphics data, to be stored on the same file for the convenience of archiving and processing by the application program. It is recommended that the 'item' should contain a key in its first part identifying the kind of user data stored. In this way, unknown user data items can be identified if the metafile is processed by a different application program or a different system.

11.3.2 Graphical GKSM Output

Output is passed to the GKSM after the normalization transformation has
been applied to all geometrical parameters. If clipping is on, the viewport of
the selected normalization transformation is stored as a clipping rectangle on
the metafile along with the output primitives. The following control functions
are recorded on the metafile:

GKS name	FORTRAN name	item created
OPEN WORKSTATION	GOPWK	file header
CLOSE WORKSTATION	GCLWK	end item
CLEAR WORKSTATION	GCLRWK	item no 1
REDRAW ALL SEGMENTS ON WORKSTATION	GRSGWK	item no 2
UPDATE WORKSTATION	GUWK	item no 3
SET DEFERRAL STATE	GSDS	item no 4
MESSAGE	GMSG	item no 5
ESCAPE	GESC	item no 6

The transformation functions:

SET VIEWPORT	GSVP
SELECT NORMALIZATION TRANSFORMATION	GSELNT
SET CLIPPING INDICATOR	GSCLIP

cause a clipping rectangle to be stored on the metafile (item no 61), if the
clipping rectangle is changed by one of these functions. This can occur by
switching clipping on or off, by selecting a normalization transformation with
a different viewport while clipping is on, or by changing the viewport of the
currently selected normalization transformation while clipping is on. If clipping
is turned off, the clipping rectangle on the metafile is set to the NDC range.
This is also the default clipping rectangle.

The parameters of the following output primitive functions and attribute
setting functions will be recorded on the GKSM:

GKS name	FORTRAN name	item created
POLYLINE	GPL	item no 11
POLYMARKER	GPM	item no 12
TEXT	GTX	item no 13
FILL AREA	GFA	item no 14
CELL ARRAY	GCA	item no 15
GENERALIZED DRAWING PRIMITIVE	GGDP	item no 16
SET POLYLINE INDEX	GSPLI	item no 21
SET LINETYPE	GSLN	item no 22
SET LINEWIDTH SCALE FACTOR	GSLWSC	item no 23
SET POLYLINE COLOUR INDEX	GSPLCI	item no 24
SET POLYMARKER INDEX	GSPMI	item no 25
SET MARKER TYPE	GSMK	item no 26

SET MARKER SIZE SCALE FACTOR	GSMKSC	item no 27
SET POLYMARKER COLOUR INDEX	GSPMCI	item no 28
SET TEXT INDEX	GSTXI	item no 29
SET TEXT FONT AND PRECISION	GSTXFP	item no 30
SET CHARACTER EXPANSION FACTOR	GSCHXP	item no 31
SET CHARACTER SPACING	GSCHSP	item no 32
SET TEXT COLOUR INDEX	GSTXCI	item no 33
SET CHARACTER HEIGHT	GSCHH	item no 34
SET CHARACTER UP VECTOR	GSCHUP	item no 34
SET TEXT PATH	GSTXP	item no 35
SET TEXT ALIGNMENT	GSTXAL	item no 36
SET FILL AREA INDEX	GSFAI	item no 37
SET FILL AREA INTERIOR STYLE	GSFAIS	item no 38
SET FILL AREA STYLE INDEX	GSFASI	item no 39
SET FILL AREA COLOUR INDEX	GSFACI	item no 40
SET PATTERN SIZE	GSPA	item no 41
SET PATTERN REFERENCE POINT	GSPARF	item no 42
SET ASPECT SOURCE FLAGS	GSASF	item no 43
SET PICK IDENTIFIER	GSPKID	item no 44

The following workstation attribute functions are recorded, if the addressed workstation is the GKSM output workstation:

GKS name	FORTRAN name	item created
SET POLYLINE REPRESENTATION	GSPLR	item no 51
SET POLYMARKER REPRESENTATION	GSPMR	item no 52
SET TEXT REPRESENTATION	GSTXR	item no 53
SET FILL AREA REPRESENTATION	GSFAR	item no 54
SET PATTERN REPRESENTATION	GSPAR	item no 55
SET COLOUR REPRESENTATION	GSCR	item no 56
SET WORKSTATION WINDOW	GSWKWN	item no 71
SET WORKSTATION VIEWPORT	GSWKVP	item no 72

11.3.3 Segment Functions

Some segment functions are simply recorded on the metafile. As can be seen from Figure 11.1, other functions are evaluated before a recording on the metafile takes place. All segment functions related to the workstation-dependent segment storage (present in GKS output level 1) are recorded on the metafile, whereas the segment functions making use of the workstation-independent segment storage (present only in output level 2) are evaluated. Recorded segment functions are:

GKS name	FORTRAN name	item created
CREATE SEGMENT	GCRSG	item no 81
CLOSE SEGMENT	GCLSG	item no 82
RENAME SEGMENT	GRENSG	item no 83

DELETE SEGMENT	GDSG	item no 84
DELETE SEGMENT FROM WORKSTATION		
(GKSM)	GDSGWK	item no 84
SET SEGMENT TRANSFORMATION	GSSGT	item no 91
SET VISIBILITY	GSVIS	item no 92
SET HIGHLIGHTING	GSHLIT	item no 93
SET SEGMENT PRIORITY	GSSGP	item no 94
SET DETECTABILITY	GSDTEC	item no 95

The DELETE SEGMENT FROM WORKSTATION function will cause item no 84 to be written to the GKSM only if the workstation addressed by the function is the GKSM output workstation. Evaluated segment functions are:

ASSOCIATE SEGMENT WITH WORKSTATION (GKSM)	GASGWK
COPY SEGMENT TO WORKSTATION (GKSM)	GCSGWK
INSERT SEGMENT	GINSG

The ASSOCIATE SEGMENT TO WORKSTATION function, if addressed to a GKSM output workstation, causes all functions that previously have been called to build the segment to be recorded on the metafile. The effect is the same as if the GKSM output workstation had been active at the time the segment was built, i.e., between CREATE SEGMENT and CLOSE SEGMENT. Thus the sequence of recorded items will comprise CREATE SEGMENT (item no 81), output primitives, clipping, attribute functions, segment attribute functions, and CLOSE SEGMENT (item no 82).

The COPY SEGMENT TO WORKSTATION function will record the output contained in a segment to the metafile. Only output primitive functions, clipping, and output primitive output functions will be recorded. As with other workstations, COPY SEGMENT TO WORKSTATION uses the clipping rectangle that was in effect when the primitives in the segment were created.

INSERT SEGMENT behaves much the same way as COPY, except for the treatment of clipping and the additional INSERT-transformation. INSERT will apply the INSERT-transformation to the geometrical information contained in the segment, then use the clipping that is in effect when the INSERT takes places, and then will send the clipping rectangle and the transformed contents of the segment to the GKSM. If a segment is open when the INSERT takes place, the inserted output primitives and their attributes will be collected in the open segment (this behaviour is the same for all output type workstations).

Table 11.1 summarizes the GKS functions causing items to be written to the GKS metafile.

Example 11.1   GKSM Output

Copying all existing segments from the workstation-independent segment storage to the GKSM. The segment structure will be recorded on the GKSM. A procedure SAVPIC is used to copy the segments. Both the workstation-independent segment storage and the output metafile have to be OPEN when

Table 11.1 GKS functions causing items to be recorded on the GKSM

GKS functions which apply to GKSM output	FORTRAN name	GKSM item or effect
OPEN WORKSTATION (GKSM-OUT,...)	GOPWK	— (file header) 1
CLOSE WORKSTATION (GKSM-OUT)	GCLWK	0 (end item)
ACTIVATE WORKSTATION (GKSM-OUT	GACWK	enable output
DEACTIVATE WORKSTATION (GKSM-OUT)	GDAWK	disable output
CLEAR WORKSTATION (GKSM-OUT,...)	GCLRWK	1
REDRAW ALL SEGMENTS ON WORKSTATION (GKSM-OUT)	GRSGWK	2
UPDATE WORKSTATION (GKSM-OUT,...)	GUWK	3
SET DEFERRAL STATE (GKSM_OUT,...)	GSDS	4
MESSAGE (GKSM-OUT,...)	GMSG	5 (message)
ESCAPE	GESC	6
POLYLINE	GPL	11 (output
POLYMARKER	GPM	12 primitives)
TEXT	GTX	13
FILL AREA	GFA	14
CELL ARRAY	GCA	15
GENERALIZED DRAWING PRIMITIVE	GGDP	16
SET POLYLINE INDEX	GSPLI	21 (attributes
SET LINETYPE	GSLN	22 for output
SET LINEWIDTH SCALE FACTOR	GSLWSC	23 primitives)
SET POLYLINE COLOUR INDEX	GSPLCI	24
SET POLYMARKER INDEX	GSPMI	25
SET MARKER TYPE	GSMK	26
SET MARKER SIZE SCALE FACTOR	GSMKSC	27
SET POLYMARKER COLOUR INDEX	GSPMCI	28
SET TEXT INDEX	GSTXI	29
SET TEXT FONT AND PRECISION	GSTXFP	30
SET CHARACTER EXPANSION FACTOR	GSCHXP	31
SET CHARACTER SPACING	GSCHSP	32
SET TEXT COLOUR INDEX	GSTXCI	33
SET CHARACTER HEIGHT	GSCHH	34
SET CHARACTER UP VECTOR	GSCHUP	34
SET TEXT PATH	GSTXP	35
SET TEXT ALIGNMENT	GSTXAL	36
SET FILL AREA INDEX	GSFAI	37
SET FILL AREA INTERIOR STYLE	GSFAIS	38
SET FILL AREA STYLE INDEX	GSFASI	39
SET FILL AREA COLOUR INDEX	GSFACI	40
SET PATTERN SIZE	GSPA	41
SET PATTERN REFERENCE POINT	GSPARF	42
SET ASPECT SOURCE FLAGS	GSASF	43
SET PICK IDENTIFIER	GSPKID	44
The following functions, if applied to the workstation GKSM Output:		

Table 11.1 (continued)

GKS functions which apply to GKSM output	FORTRAN name	GKSM item or effect
SET POLYLINE REPRESENTATION	GSPLR	51 (workstation
SET POLYMARKER REPRESENTATION	GSPMR	52 attributes)
SET TEXT REPRESENTATION	GSTXR	53
SET FILL AREA REPRESENTATION	GSFAR	54
SET PATTERN REPRESENTATION	GSPAR	55
SET COLOUR REPRESENTATION	GSCR	56
SET WORKSTATION WINDOW	GSWKWN	71
SET WORKSTATION VIEWPORT	GSWKVP	72
SET VIEWPORT of current normalization transformation	GSVP	.61 (clipping rectangle)
SELECT NORMALIZATION TRANSFORMATION	GSELNT	61
SET CLIPPING INDICATOR	GSCLIP	61
CREATE SEGMENT	GCRSG	81 (segment
CLOSE SEGMENT	GCLSG	82 mani-
RENAME SEGMENT	GRENSG	83 pulation)
DELETE SEGMENT	GDSG	84
DELETE SEGMENT FROM WORKSTATION (GKSM-OUT)	GDSGWK	84
ASSOCIATE SEGMENT WITH WORKSTATION (GKSM-OUT)	GASGWK	81,(21-44, 11-16,61),82
COPY SEGMENT TO WORKSTATION	GCSGWK	(21-44,11-16,61)
INSERT SEGMENT	GINSG	(21-44,11-16,61)
SET SEGMENT TRANSFORMATION	GSSGT	91 (segment
SET VISIBILITY	GSVIS	92 attributes)
SET HIGHLIGHTING	GSHLIT	93
SET SEGMENT PRIORITY	GSSGP	94
SET DETECTABILITY	GSDTEC	95
WRITE ITEM TO GKSM	GWITM	>100

the procedure is called. The GKSM will be activated and deactivated within the procedure.

─────────────────────── *Pascal* ───────────────────────

```
L10   PROCEDURE SAVPIC(GKSM_OUT:STRING);
                                        {GKSM_OUT is GKSM identifier}
L20   VAR I,IERROR,NSEGS: INTEGER;
L30     SEGNAMES: ARRAY[1..250] OF INTEGER;
L31   BEGIN
                                        {route output to GKSM output}
```

L40   ACTIVATE_WORKSTATION (GKSM_OUT);

{get all segments' names}
L50   INQUIRE_SET_OF_SEGMENT_NAMES_IN_USE
          (IERROR,NSEGS,SEGNAMES);
L60   FOR I:= 1 TO NSEGS DO {for all segments copy the segment and its contents}
L70   ASSOCIATE_SEGMENT_WITH_WORKSTATION
          (GKSM_OUT,SEGNAMES[I]);
L80   END;
L90   DEACTIVATE_WORKSTATION (GKSM_OUT);

If, in this example, the segment structure is not to be recorded on the metafile, the ASSOCIATE SEGMENT function function has to be replaced by the COPY SEGMENT function. In this case, the metafile will contain an unstructured picture.

Fortran

```
L10         SUBROUTINE SAVPIC (GKSMID)
     C                          *** copies all segments to GKSM via GKSMID
L20         INTEGER NSEGS,GKSMID,IERROR,I
L30         INTEGER SEGNAM(250)
     C                          *** ACTIVATE, INQUIRE SEGMENTS
L40         CALL GACWK(GKSMID)
L50         CALL GQSGUS(1,IERROR,NSEGS,SEGNAM)
     C             *** test if error or too many segments for array SEGNAM
L51         IF (IERROR) 52,52,55
L52    52   WRITE(6,1000) IERROR
L53   1000  FORMAT(' ERROR NO ',I3,' IN SAVPIC')
L54         RETURN
L55    55   IF (NSEGS.LE.250) GOTO 60
L56         WRITE(6,2000) NSEGS
L57   2000  FORMAT(' NO OF SEGMENTS IN SAVPIC = ',I3,' >250')
L58         NSEGS=250
     C                          *** send segments to GKSM
L60    60   DO 71 I=1,NSEGS
L61         CALL GQSGUS(I,IERROR,NSEGS,SEGNAM(I))
L70            CALL GASGWK(GKSMID,SEGNAM(I))
L71    71   CONTINUE
     C                          *** DEACTIVATE metafile
L80         CALL GDAWK(GKSMID)
L81         RETURN
L90         END
```

11.4 GKSM Input

Data can be retrieved from a GKS metafile by special GKS functions valid only for an open GKSM input workstation. These functions cause the data in the metafile to be passed to the application program in a data record. Then

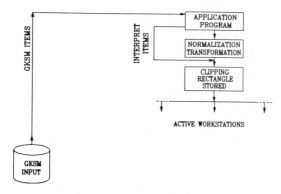

Figure 11.2 Data flow for GKSM input

the data record can be passed back to GKS for interpretation. The interpretation of a GKSM item will normally cause the same effect as the function that caused the GKSM item to be recorded during writing time of the GKSM. The data flow from the GKSM to the application program is shown in Figure 11.2.

After the GKSM input workstation has been opened, the following functions can be used to retrieve data from the metafile:

GET ITEM TYPE FROM GKSM   WSAC,SGOP,SGOP   L0a

Parameters:

Input	workstation identifier		N
Output	item type		I
Output	item data record length	(0..n)	I

Effect:
GKS inspects the type of the next record and its length in the GKSM and returns type and length back to the application program.

Errors:

7	GKS not in proper state: GKS shall be in one of the states WSOP, WSAC or SGOP
20	Specified workstation identifier is invalid
25	Specified workstation is not open
34	Specified workstation is not of category MI
162	No record is left in GKS metafile input
163	Metafile item is invalid

FORTRAN-Interface

CALL GGTITM (WKID,TYPE,LITM)

Parameters:

Input	WKID	workstation identifier		INTEGER
Output	TYPE	item type		INTEGER
Output	LITM	item length	(0..n)	INTEGER

This function delivers the type of the next item on the metafile in an integer variable. The types are given in Table 11.1. Together with the type, the function delivers the length of the GKSM item, this is the length of the data record needed for the subsequent retrieval of the item. In FORTRAN, the item length is given in number of 80-characterelements needed to contain the item. After the GET ITEM TYPE function was called, the item itself can be retrieved from the GKSM by the READ ITEM function:

READ ITEM FROM GKSM   WSAC,SGOP   L0a
Parameters:
Input	workstation identifier		N
Input	maximum length of item data record	(0..n)	I
Output	item data record		D

Effect:
GKS returns the next item on the GKSM back to the application program. If its data record length is greater than the maximum length specified, excess parts of the item are lost.

Note:
By specifying 'maximum item data record length' = 0, the next item can be skipped without reading.

Errors:
7	GKS not in proper state: GKS shall be in one of the states WSOP, WSAC or SGOP
20	Specified workstation identifier is invalid
25	Specified workstation is not open
34	Specified workstation is not of category MI
162	No record is left in GKS metafile input
163	Metafilc item is invalid
165	Content of item data record is invalid for the specified item type
166	Maximum item data record length is invalid

———————————————————— *FORTRAN-Interface* ————————————————————

CALL GRDITM (WKID,LMAX,LITM,ITEM)
Parameters:
Input	WKID	workstation identifier		INTEGER
Input	LMAX	dimension of item data record	(0..n)	INTEGER
Output	LITM	actual item data record length	(1..n)	INTEGER
Output	ITEM(LMAX)	item data record		CHARACTER*80

If the application program wishes to ignore (skip) an item on the metafile, ⹀is can be done by specifying a maximum length of zero. After the application program knows the item type and has retrieved the item itself in a data record (CHARACTER*80 array in FORTRAN), it has the choice to perform any calculations it wishes. Especially user records can only be dealt with by the application program. But if the format of the GKSM is known to the application program, it could also extract the information from the graphical GKSM items and inspect or modify them. The normal case, however, will be to pass the graphical GKSM items back to GKS for interpretation. The GKS function for this purpose is the INTERPRET ITEM function:

INTERPRET ITEM   GKOP,WSOP,WSAC,SGOP   L0a

Parameters:

Input	item type		I
Input	item data record length	(0..n)	I
Input	item data record		D

Effect:

The item is interpreted. The effect normally will be the same as if the function that generated the GKSM item were invoked again. Functions used to control the output workstation in creating the metafile are applied to all active workstations. Attribute items referring to attributes stored in the GKS state list will not change the GKS state list, however, they will be used for interpreting subsequent primitive items on the metafile.

Note:

Apart from errors noted below, other GKS errors may occur as a result of interpreting the item.

Errors:

7	GKS not in proper state: GKS shall be in one of the states WSOP, WSAC or SGOP
161	Item length is invalid
163	Metafile item is invalid
164	Item type is not a valid GKS item
165	Content of item data record is invalid for the specified item type
167	User item cannot be interpreted

───────────────────────── *FORTRAN-Interface* ─────────────────────────

CALL GIITM (TYPE,LITM,ITEM)

Parameters:

Input	TYPE	item type		INTEGER
Input	LITM	item data record dimension	(0..n)	INTEGER
Input	ITEM(LITM)	item data record		CHARACTER*80

Table 11.2 gives lists the functions internally called by GKSM items. There are two exceptions from a one-to-one correspondence between metafile items and GKS functions:

— Output primitives are not transformed by the currently selected normalization transformation. Since the coordinates of the items stored on the metafile are already in NDC units, they do no need to be normalized once more during interpretation. Thus, the normalization transformation applies to them which was in effect when the GKSM was written. The functions are marked "(b)" in Table 11.2.

— All items containing workstation attribute settings cause the corresponding attribute setting function to be executed for all active workstations. In this way, attribute bundles, the deferral state, and the workstation transformation can be stored on the metafile. During interpretation, the items are used to set the workstation attributes of the workstations on which the metafile contents are displayed. The functions are marked "(a)" in Table 11.2.

Table 11.2 GKS functions called for interpretation of GKSM items

metafile item	resulting GKS functions by INTERPRET ITEM	
— (file header)	interpretation parameters set	
0 (end item)	condition for error 'no record left in GKSM input' set	
1	CLEAR WORKSTATION	(a)
2	REDRAW ALL SEGMENTS ON WORKST.	(a)
3	UPDATE	(a)
4	SET DEFERRAL STATE	(a)
5 (message)	MESSAGE	(a)
6	ESCAPE	
11 (output	POLYLINE	(b)
12 primitives)	POLYMARKER	(b)
13	TEXT	(b)
14	FILL AREA	(b)
15	CELL ARRAY	(b)
16	GENERALIZED DRAWING PRIMITIVE	(b)
21 (attributes	SET POLYLINE INDEX	
22 for output	SET LINETYPE	
23 primitives)	SET LINEWIDTH SCALE FACTOR	
24	SET POLYLINE COLOUR INDEX	
25	SET POLYMARKER INDEX	
26	SET MARKER TYPE	
27	SET MARKER SIZE SCALE FACTOR	
28	SET POLYMARKER COLOUR INDEX	
29	SET TEXT INDEX	
30	SET TEXT FONT AND PRECISION	
31	SET CHARACTER EXPANSION FACTOR	
32	SET CHARACTER SPACING	
33	SET TEXT COLOUR INDEX	
34	SET CHARACTER HEIGHT and SET CHARACTER UP VECTOR	
35	SET TEXT PATH	
36	SET TEXT ALIGNMENT	
37	SET FILL AREA INDEX	
38	SET FILL AREA INTERIOR STYLE	
39	SET FILL AREA STYLE INDEX	
40	SET FILL AREA COLOUR INDEX	
41	SET PATTERN SIZE	
42	SET PATTERN REFERENCE POINT	
43	SET ASPECT SOURCE FLAGS	
44	SET PICK IDENTIFIER	
51 (workstation	SET POLYLINE REPRESENTATION	(a)
52 attributes)	SET POLYMARKER REPRESENTATION	(a)
53	SET TEXT REPRESENTATION	(a)

Table 11.2 (continued)

metafile item	resulting GKS functions by INTERPRET ITEM	
54	SET FILL AREA REPRESENTATION	(a)
55	SET PATTERN REPRESENTATION	(a)
56	SET COLOUR REPRESENTATION	(a)
61 (clipping rectangle)	SET VIEWPORT of current normalization transformation; SET CLIPPING INDICATOR to 'CLIP'	
71 (workstation 72 trans- formation)	SET WORKSTATION WINDOW SET WORKSTATION VIEWPORT	(a) (a)
81 (segment 82 mani- 83 pulation) 84	CREATE SEGMENT CLOSE SEGMENT RENAME SEGMENT DELETE SEGMENT	
91 (segment 92 attributes) 93 94 95	SET SEGMENT TRANSFORMATION SET VISIBILITY SET HIGHLIGHTING SET SEGMENT PRIORITY SET DETECTABILITY	

In the normal case, the application program will pass the graphical items obtained by the READ ITEM function on to the INTERPRET ITEM function without touching them. It is no violation of any GKS rule, however, to modify the items, e.g. to change attribute values or apply transformations to the coordinates of the primitives. The application program may even generate GKSM items by itself without reading them from any GKSM input workstation. In these cases, the application program makes use of information not contained in the GKS standard, but defined by the implementation. It is sensible, therefore, that implementors use the GKSM format in Annex E of the GKS document as long as there is no metafile standard defined.

Example 11.2   GKSM-input

The procedure GETPIC will read a GKSM and display it on an output workstation. Only output primitive items, attribute items and segment items will be interpreted. If a new picture starts (CLEAR WORKSTATION item), the program will wait for a CHOICE obtained by the REQUEST CHOICE input function before continuing to process the metafile. The output workstation must be OPEN but INACTIVE when the procedure is called. The input metafile workstation is opened and closed in the procedure itself.

—————————————————— *Pascal* ——————————————————

```
L10   PROCEDURE GETPIC(GK_FILE:FILE OF CHAR,DISPLAY:STRING);
                                    {read GKSM from file GK_FILE and}
                                    {display it on workstation DISPLAY}
L20   CONST GKSM_IN = 'GKSM_IN';        {name for GKSM input workstation}
L30   VAR TYPE,LENGTH,CH_NO: INTEGER;
L40     ITEM: STRING[1..1000];
                                    {string to hold GKSM item}
L50     NONE: STRING[1..1];
L60   BEGIN
                                    {OPEN metafile input}
                                    {assume ws-type 1 = GKSM input}
L70   OPEN_WORKSTATION (GKSM_IN,GK_FILE,1);
                                    {display output on DISPLAY}
L80   ACTIVATE_WORKSTATION (DISPLAY);
L90   REPEAT                            {until end of GKSM input}
                                    {get type and length of item}
L100    GET_ITEM_TYPE_FROM_GKSM (GKSM_IN,TYPE,LENGTH);
L110    IF TYPE = 1 THEN                {CLEAR WORKSTATION item}
L120    BEGIN
                                    {wait for any CHOICE or break}
L130      REQUEST_CHOICE (DISPLAY,1,STATUS,CH_NO);
                                    {skip item}
L140      READ_ITEM_FROM_GKSM (GKSM_IN,0,NONE);
L150    END;
L160    ELSE IF TYPE > = 11 AND TYPE < = 95 THEN
L170    BEGIN              {output primitive, attribute or segment item}
                                    {READ and INTERPRET item}
L180      READ_ITEM_FROM_GKSM (GKSM_IN,LENGTH,ITEM);
L190      INTERPRET_ITEM (TYPE,LENGTH,ITEM);
L200    END;
L210    ELSE
                                    {skip item}
L220      READ_ITEM_FROM_GKSM (GKSM_IN,0,NONE);
L230    UNTIL TYPE = 0;                    {end record}
                                    {DEACTIVATE output workstation}
L240    DEACTIVATE_WORKSTATION (DISPLAY);
                                    {CLOSE input metafile}
L250    CLOSE_WORKSTATION (GKSM_IN);
L260  END;
```

—————————————————— *Fortran* ——————————————————

```
L10           SUBROUTINE GETPIC(FILNO,DISID)
      C                   *** reads GKSM via file no FILNO and displays it on
      C                   *** workstation with identifier DISID
L30           INTEGER STATUS,CHNO,LENGTH,FILNO,GKSMID,
              DISID,TYPE
L40           CHARACTER*80 ITEM(250)
L20           GKSMID = 777
      C                                   *** OPEN input metafile
L70           CALL GOPWK(GKSMID,FILNO,1)
      C                                   *** ACTIVATE display
L80           CALL GACWK(DISID)
```

```
         C                                      *** DO UNTIL end record
L90      90    CONTINUE
L100           CALL GGTITM(GKSMID,TYPE,LENGTH)
         C                                      *** test if item too long
L101               IF (LENGTH.LE.250) GOTO 110
L102                   WRITE(6,2000) LENGTH
L103     2000          FORMAT( 'ITEM LENGTH IN GETPIC = ',I3,' > 250')
L104                   GOTO 220
         C                                      *** CLEAR WORKSTATION item ?
L110     110   IF (TYPE.NE.1) GOTO 160
         C                                      *** wait for CHOICE
L130               CALL GRQCH (DISID,1,STATUS,CHNO)
L131               GOTO 220
         C                                      *** output, attribute or segment item?
L160     160   IF (TYPE.LT.11.OR.TYPE.GT.95) GOTO 210
         C                                      *** READ and INTERPRET item
L180               CALL GRDITM(GKSMID,250,LENGTH,ITEM)
L190               CALL GIITM(TYPE,LENGTH,ITEM)
L191               GOTO 230
L210     210   CONTINUE
         C                                      *** skip item
L220     220   CALL GRDITM(GKSMID,0,LENGTH,ITEM)
L230     230   IF (TYPE.NE.0) GOTO 90
         C                                      *** DEACTIVATE display
L240           CALL GDAWK(DISID)
         C                                      *** CLOSE input metafile
L250           CALL GCLWK(GKSMID)
L251           RETURN
L260           END
```

11.5   Program Examples

The following two examples demonstrate saving and restoring the state of a GKS session. In example 11.3, a subroutine named SAVEGK is used to save the current state of an interactive GKS session on an output metafile. In example 11.4, the subroutine RESTGK restores the state of the session from the metafile. The two examples make use of the subroutines SAVPIC and GETPIC in the examples 11.1 and 11.2 (pages 404 and 412). It is assumed that the workstation-independent segment storage was active during the session to be saved, and that one workstation was used for output and input (it is referenced by the workstation identifier DISID). When saving and restoring the state of the session two sets of information have to be considered:
— the workstation state of the interactive workstation;
— the segments currently in existence and the primitives and attributes contained therein.

Within the subroutine SAVEGK the workstation state is inquired and then sent to the GKSM output workstation. Then all segments with the primitives and attributes contained therein are sent to the GKSM output workstation by calling subroutine SAVPIC. The subroutine RESTGK calls GETPIC where the restoration of the workstation state of the display workstation and the recreation of segments will be performed automatically by the READ and IN-TERPRET functions. Note, however, that the GKS state list will not be restored to the values at the saving time (calling time of SAVEGK). The reason for this is the fact that the GKS function INTERPRET ITEM will not change the values of attribute values in the GKS state list, but will remember the values for subsequent calls to INTERPRET ITEM when output primitives are to be created.

Example 11.3   Save state

———————————————————————— *Pascal* ————————————————————————
```
L10    PROCEDURE SAVEGK(DISID:STRING;MFILE:FILE OF CHAR);
                            {DISID is the workstation identifier of the interactive}
                                            {workstation, MFILE the metafile}
L20    CONST GKSM_OUT = 'GKSM_OUT';
L30    TYPE DMODE = (ASAP,BNIL,BNIG,ASTI);
L31      IMODE = (SUPPRESSED,ALLOWED);
L32      NFRAME = (YES,NO);
L33      SURF = (EMPTY,NOTEMPTY);
L34      USTATE = (PENDING,NOTPENDING);
L35      VTYPE = (SET,REALIZED);
L40    VAR ERR_IND,NIND,I,LTYPE,CIND: INTEGER;
L41      LWIDTH : REAL;
L42      DM : DMODE;
L43      IM : IMODE;
L44      NF : NFRAME;
L45      EM : SURF;
L46      US : USTATE;
L50      LIST : ARRAY[1..250] OF INTEGER;
L60      RWW,CWW,RWV,CWV : ARRAY[1..4] OF REAL;
L70    BEGIN
                    {OPEN metafile output, assume output metafile has type 2}
L80    OPEN_WORKSTATION (GKSM_OUT,MFILE,2);
                                        {output routed to GKSM output}
L90    ACTIVATE_WORKSTATION (GKSM_OUT);
                            {get deferral mode and implicit regeneration mode}
L100   INQUIRE_WORKSTATION_DEFERRAL_AND_UPDATE_STATES
          (DISID,ERR_IND,DM,IM,EM,NF);
                                            {send the modes to metafile}
L110   SET_DEFERRAL_STATE (GKSM_OUT,DM,IM);
                                        {get workstation transformation}
L120   INQUIRE_WORKSTATION_TRANSFORMATION
          (DISID,US,RWW,CWW,RWV,CWV);
                            {send current transformation to the metafile}
L130   SET_WORKSTATION_WINDOW (GKSM_OUT,CWW);
```

L140 SET_WORKSTATION_VIEWPORT (GKSM_OUT,CWV);
                                                              {get polyline indices}
L150 INQUIRE_LIST_OF_POLYLINE_INDICES (DISID,ERR_IND,NIND,LIST);
L160 FOR I: = 1 TO NIND DO   {for all POLYLINE indices}
L161 BEGIN
                                                              {get polyline bundle}
L170   INQUIRE_POLYLINE_REPRESENTATION
            (DISID,LIST[I],SET,ERR_IND, LTYPE,LWIDTH,CIND);
                                                              {send bundle to metafile}
L180   SET_POLYLINE_REPRESENTATION
            (GKSM_OUT,LIST[I], LTYPE,LWIDTH,CIND);
L190 END;

                                             {repeat lines L150 through L190 for POLYMARKER,
                                                          TEXT, FILL AREA bundles}
                                             {and for PATTERN and COLOUR tables}

L200 DEACTIVATE_WORKSTATION (GKSM_OUT);
                                                   {now call SAVPIC to save segments}
L210 CALL SAVPIC (GKSM_OUT);
                                                              {CLOSE output metafile}
L220 CLOSE_WORKSTATION (GKSM_OUT);
                                                   {CLOSE interactive workstation}
L230 CLOSE_WORKSTATION (DISID);
L240 END;

───────────────────────────────── *Fortran* ─────────────────────────────────

```
L10              SUBROUTINE SAVEGK (DISID, MFILE)
      C                      *** stores state of workstation DISID on file MFILE
L20              INTEGER GKSMID
L21              DATA GKSMID /777/
L40              INTEGER MFILE,DISID,I,ERRIND,NIND,LTYPE,CIND
L41              INTEGER DM,IM,EM,NF,US
L50              INTEGER LIST(250)
L60              REAL RWINDO(4),CWINDO(4),RVIEWP(4),CVIEWP(4)
      C                      *** OPEN and ACTIVATE output metafile
L80              CALL GOPWK(GKSMID,MFILE,2)
L90              CALL GACWK(GKSMID)
      C                      *** get workstation state and send it to GKSM
L100             CALL GQWKDU(DISID,ERRIND,DM,IM,EM,NF)
L110             CALL GSDS(GKSMID,DM,IM)
      C                      *** get and send workstation transformation
L120             CALL GQWKT(DISID,ERRIND,US,RWINDO,CWINDO,
     +    RVIEWP,CVIEWP)
L130             CALL GSWKWN(GKSMID,CWINDO(1),CWINDO(2),
     +    CWINDO(3),CWINDO(4))
L140             CALL GSWKVP(GKSMID,CVIEWP(1),CVIEWP(2),
     +    CVIEWP(3),CVIEWP(4))
      C                      *** get polyline indices
L150             CALL GQEPLI(DISID,1,ERRIND,NIND,LIST)
```

```
L160                 DO 190 I = 1,NIND
      C                                     *** get and send all POLYLINE bundles
L165                 CALL GQPLI(DISID,I,ERRIND,NIND,LIST(I))
L170                  CALL GQPLR(DISID,LIST(I),0,ERRIND,LTYPE,
             +        LWIDTH,CIND)
L180                  CALL GSPLR(GKSMID,LIST(I),LTYPE,LWIDTH,CIND)
L190      190    CONTINUE
      C      .
      C      .                    *** repeat lines L150 through L190 for POLYMARKER,
      C      .                                     TEXT, FILL AREA bundles
      C      .                           *** and for PATTERN and COLOUR tables
      C      .
      C      .
      C              *** DEACTIVATE metafile
L200            CALL GDAWK(GKSMID)
      C              *** call SAVPIC to save segments
L210            CALL SAVPIC(GKSMID)
      C                                                  *** CLOSE metafile
L220            CALL GCLWK(GKSMID)
      C                                       *** CLOSE output workstation
L230            CALL GCLWK(DISID)
L231            RETURN
L240            END
```

Example 11.4 Restore state

──────────────────────────── *Pascal* ────────────────────────────

```
L10   PROCEDURE RESTGK(DISID:STRING;DFILE,MFILE:FILE OF CHAR);
                        {DISID is the workstation identifier and DFILE the file}
                        {identifier for the interactive workstation. MFILE is the}
                                            {file identifier for the metafile}
L20   BEGIN
                                        {OPEN the interactive workstation}
                                                    {assume it has type 5}
L30   OPEN_WORKSTATION (DISID,DFILE,5);
                                            {now call GETPIC to restore state}
L40   CALL GETPIC (MFILE,DISID);
                                        {ACTIVATE interactive workstation}
L50   ACTIVATE_WORKSTATION (DISID);
L60   END;
```

──────────────────────────── *Fortran* ────────────────────────────

```
L10             SUBROUTINE RESTGK (DISID, MFILE)
      C              *** restores the state of workstation DISID from
      C              *** metafile. DISID: workstation identifier
      C              *** DFILE: file number of interactive workstation
      C              *** MFILE: file number of input metafile
L11             INTEGER MFILE,DISID,DFILE
```

```
      C                                      *** OPEN interactive workstation
L30             CALL GOPWK(DISID,DFILE,5)
      C                                      *** call GETPIC to restore state
L40             CALL GETPIC(MFILE,DISID)
      C                                      *** ACTIVATE interactive workstation
L50             CALL GACWK(DISID)
L51             RETURN
L60             END
```

Example 11.5   User item

In this example a user item is used to store the current normalization transformation on the metafile. When reading the metafile back into GKS, these values can be used to restore the values in the GKS state list. In this way example 11.3 and 11.4 could be extended to include saving and restoring of GKS state list values. Appropriate program parts would have to be inserted after line L210 in example 11.2 and before line L200 in example 11.3.

———————————————————————————— *Pascal* ————————————————————————————

```
                                                  {Definitions and declarations:}
L10   TYPE TRANS = RECORD KEY: STRING [1..8]; TRANS_NO:INTEGER;
L11       WINDOW,VIEWPORT: ARRAY [1..4] OF REAL;
L12   END;
L20   VAR CT : TRANS;
                                       {Storing the normalization transformation:}
                                   {insert before line L200 in example 11.3, page 416}
                                         {get normalization transformation}
L30   INQUIRE_CURRENT_NORMALIZATION_TRANSFORMATION_
          NUMBER (ERR_IND,CT.TRANS_NO);
L40   INQUIRE_NORMALIZATION_TRANSFORMATION
          (CT.TRANS_NO,ERR_IND,CT.WINDOW,CT.VIEWPORT);
                           {use the string variable as key for identifying the user item}
L50   CT.KEY = 'NORMTRAN';
                                  {send user item to GKSM, item type = 177, length = 44
                                                       (implementation dependent)}
L60   WRITE_ITEM_TO_GKSM (GKSM_OUT,177,44,CT);


                                          {Retrieving the user item from the metafile:}
                                     {insert after line L210 in example 11.2, page 413}
L30   ELSE IF TYPE = 177 THEN                               {user item type 177}
L40   BEGIN
L50     READ_ITEM_FROM_GKSM (GKSM_IN,44,CT);        {read item into record}
L60     IF CT.KEY = 'NORMTRAN' THEN                         {test correct key}
L70     BEGIN
L80       SET_WINDOW (CT.TRANS_NO,CT.WINDOW);
                                              {set WINDOW and VIEWPORT}
L90       SET_VIEWPORT (CT.TRANS_NO,CT.VIEWPORT);
```

L100   SELECT_NORMALIZATION_TRANSFORMATION
               (CT.TRANS_NO);   {select transformation}
L110   END;
L120 END;

─────────────────────────── *Fortran* ───────────────────────────

L10   REAL WIN(4),VIEW(4)
L11   INTEGER NO
L13   CHARACTER*80CT(2)

        C   ***Storing the normalization transformation:
        C   ***insert before line L200 in example 11.3, page 417
        C   *** get normalization transformation
L30   CALL GQCNTN(ERRIND,NO)
L40   CALL GQNT(NO,ERRIND,WIN,VIEW)
        C   *** store key and transformation in record
L50   WRITE(CT(1),'(A8,I4,4E14.7)')'NORMTRAN',NO,WIN
L51   WRITE(CT(2),'(4E14.7)')VIEW
        C   *** send user item to GKSM, item type=177, length=2
L60   CALL GWITM(GKSM_OUT,177,2,CT)

        C   ***Retrieving the user item from the metafile:
        C   ***insert after line L210 in example 11.2, page 414
        C   *** user item 177?
L30   IF (TYPE.NE.177) GOTO 220
        C   *** read item into array CT
L50   CALL GRDITM(GKSMID,2,LENGTH,CT)
        C   *** test correct length and key
L60   IF (LENGTH.NE.2) GOTO 220
L61   READ(CT(1),'(8×,I4,4E14.7)')NO,WIN
L62   READ(CT(2),'(4E14.7)')VIEW
L63   IF (CT(1)(1:8).NE.'NORMTRAN' GOTO 220
        C   *** set WINDOW and VIEWPORT
L80   CALL GSWN(NO,WIN)
L90   CALL GSVP(NO,VIEW)
L100   CALL GSELNT(NO)
L120   220 CONTINUE

11.6   Exercises

Exercise 11.1   Display metafile

Design, realize and test a procedure that reads an input metafile given by a
file identifier and displays its contents on an output workstation given by its
workstation identifier. All items referring to capabilities not present in GKS
level 0a are to be discarded.

Exercise 11.2   Backup copy on metafile

Design, realize and test two procedures for using the metafile as a backup copy of the pictures created on an output workstation. One procedure is to be called after OPEN GKS, the other one before CLOSE GKS. Which deferral state would you choose for the GKSM output workstation and why?

Exercise 11.3   Concatenate metafiles

Design, realize and test a procedure for concatenating two input metafiles and copying them to one output metafile. All three metafiles are identified by their file identifier. The metafiles may contain user items.

PART IV

THE GKS ENVIRONMENT

Part IV is devoted to the elaboration of the various interfaces of GKS within the Computer Graphics environment. The first two chapters outline methods for implementing the GKS standard with the aims of utilizing most existing features of a variety of graphical devices. It is outlined how the GKS functionality can be realized by using emulation and simulation software to tailor a system to the particular device functions. In Chapter 3, several implementation styles are explained to produce GKS systems in an efficient manner. This chapter also gives allowable differences between implementations. Chapter 4 treats the topics of language interfaces. It contains the rules for designing a GKS language binding, details the GKS FORTRAN interface (which is already very close to a standard) and also contains the list of GKS FORTRAN subroutines which might be used by a non-beginner GKS programmer as very concise reference material. Chapter 5 handles the interfaces of GKS implementations to graphical devices — a topic which is subject to standardization. This chapter is both important for GKS implementors and those people developing device drivers and connecting them to GKS.

From Chapter 6 onwards, more general information in the area of Computer Graphics is given. Also in this chapter, we introduce the major activities concerning graphics metafiles, the aim of which is to standardize the interfaces between different graphics systems for exchanging graphical information. Chapter 7 is devoted to the important projects of checking and proving the conformity of GKS implementations to the standard. It can be argued that without means for validation and certification, standardization is mostly useless because the major goal of standardization, the portability of programs, pictures and training knowledge, will not be reached. Chapter 8 mentions the international efforts to develop a common terminology and indeed, in Appendix 2, we list the most important international computer graphics terms.

Finally, in Chapter 9, we introduce a first (and compatible!) concept of extending the two-dimensional GKS definition to a 3-D standard.

1   MAPPING OF OUTPUT PRIMITIVES
AND ATTRIBUTES ON PHYSICAL WORKSTATIONS

An important concept within the GKS standard is the concept of input/output primitives as capabilities of logical input/output devices. To a certain extent, the abstraction of physical devices to logical devices allows a device-independent access to physical devices. However, the implementor of logical input/output devices has to go back this abstracting process and has to map the logical devices on the capabilities of the available physical devices. This chapter describes major aspects of this mapping process for output primitives and attributes. The subsequent chapter will discuss the mapping process for input primitives.

The details of mapping logical to physical devices intentionally has been left undefined within the standard to give the implementor sufficient freedom to take profit of specific hardware capabilities and to elaborate more comfortable features required by the constituency of an implementation. The result of the design decisions of the implementor has to be made transparent to the users. The major aspects have to be listed in the workstation description table; other decisions have to be documented in the implementation manual.

1.1   POLYLINE Primitive and Attributes

Line drawing facilities will be available on almost all graphical output devices and mapping of POLYLINE, therefore, will be straightforward. Raster devices need a description of linear objects in terms of pixel structures. The conversion of lines to pixels (line-to-scan conversion) will be done within the device or must be provided by the driver. Due to the pixel structure, lines may differ in appearance when drawn horizontally, diagonally, or vertically.

Lines can be drawn with different LINETYPES. LINETYPES solid, dashed, dotted and dashed-dotted are mandatory; they must be implemented even for devices like colour raster displays which usually will use colour to distinguish lines of different classes.

LINETYPE includes some geometric features, e.g., the length of dash and gap for LINETYPE dashed. However, GKS regards LINETYPE a non-geometric attribute and, deliberately, does not address this question. This allows on one hand the use of any available hardware capability and on the other hand the generation of LINETYPES by software routines which, very carefully, may consider requirements necessary for some applications like technical drawings and cartography, e.g.:

— LINETYPE patterns which are continuous over vertices of a POLYLINE or even from one POLYLINE to a subsequent one;
— LINETYPE patterns which are generated for a whole POLYLINE before clipping instead of starting the pattern for the visible parts only;
— securing that starting point and endpoint do not lie within a gap by slight modification of the LINETYPE pattern.

If such a comfortable LINETYPE is implemented, it is advisable to assign a new linetype number to it and associate the cheapest method to the mandatory linetypes.

For the LINEWIDTH attribute, the implementor has full freedom to realize it or not. This is due to the fact that most devices have a fixed linewidth only and can achieve other linewidths only by drawing several lines side by side which may be too expensive, e.g., on vector refresh displays.

1.2 POLYMARKER Primitive and Attributes

The POLYMARKER primitive is a facility to identify points rather than a symbol facility which allows the generation of transformable symbols. It has been designed such that some hardware character generators may be used provided the symbols dot, plus sign, asterisk, circle, and diagonal cross can be drawn centred to a given position.

The clipping convention for POLYMARKER reflects the fact that points are to be identified. A POLYMARKER symbol is drawn if, and only if, the marker position is inside the clipping rectangle. If the marker position is inside, but some part of the marker symbol outside the clipping rectangle, clipping may occur or not.

1.3 TEXT Primitive and Attributes

GKS provides a very comfortable TEXT generation facility which can usually be supported by software text generators only. This full comfort must be present in GKS output levels 1 and 2. Even if such modules are present, it may be reasonable to use less flexible built-in capabilities for efficiency reasons. A special TEXT PRECISION attribute allows the selection of cheaper TEXT generation facilities:

— STRING text precision may ignore all geometric attributes except the initial position specified in the primitive's invocation, thus allowing the use of simple character generators capable of generating text in fixed size and in horizontal direction only;
— CHAR text precision evaluates all TEXT attributes to position precisely each character individually. The geometry of each character may be ignored, thus allowing the use of any available generator for each individual character.

— STROKE text precision fully obeys all TEXT attributes. TEXT is transformed and clipped as if expanded to POLYLINES in WC. However, this does not prevent raster character generating facilities as long as they behave accordingly.

STROKE text precision usually can be realized by a software character generator only. This generator may be included in the GKS nucleus; more efficiency may be achieved by decentralization of the generator to reduce data transfer rates. If decentralized character generators are used, the following rules must be obeyed:

— Font 1 containing the full ASCII character set (ISO 646) must be present on all workstations with output capabilities. More fonts may be defined within a GKS implementation.
— Not all fonts must be present on each workstation but the same font number must be used to select that font on all workstations of a particular installation.
— Not all workstations need to support a specific font with the same text precision. However, if text precision STROKE is required, i.e., in GKS output levels 1 and 2, any workstation must at least support STROKE text precision for font 1.

1.4 FILL AREA Primitive and Attributes

The FILL AREA primitive has been inspired by raster devices which possess a true area representation capability. Vector devices genuinely cannot generate areas and have to use some simulation technique. Therefore, the implementation of FILL AREA strongly will depend on the type of output device. Four different FILL AREA INTERIOR STYLES have been defined which allow each device type to realize FILL AREA according to its capabilities. The following list gives some typical combinations of INTERIOR STYLE and device classes:

SOLID intended for colour raster displays; a solid area in a specified colour is generated.

PATTERN intended for black-and-white and colour raster displays; a solid area is generated; different areas are distinguished by different definable patterns.

HATCH intended for plotters and storage tubes; areas are hatched; different areas are distinguished by different hatch styles selected from a list provided by the implementor.

HOLLOW intended for vector refresh displays; only the outline of the area is drawn. This is the minimum simulation. It reflects the fact that hatching is expensive in terms of computing time for calculation of hatch lines and in terms of number of vectors to be drawn, which is important for displays with limited number of displayable vectors.

1.5 CELL ARRAY Primitive

CELL ARRAY is a typical raster primitive which, in contrast to the FILL AREA primitive, cannot sensibly be simulated on non-raster devices. For those devices, the minimum simulation required is the drawing of the transformed CELL ARRAY boundary.

Whereas the patterns used for FILL AREA generation may be transformed or not, a CELL ARRAY must fully undergo all transformations, e.g., a segment transformation may result in rotation and shearing of the CELL ARRAY. This will include some implementation effort. Furthermore, mapping of a transformed CELL ARRAY to physical pixels includes round off errors which may become visible due to the limited resolution.

Although there might be problems in transforming CELL ARRAYS, for consistency reasons CELL ARRAYS must be defined in WC and must undergo transformations. It is left to the responsibility of the application program to select reasonable transformations which do not show irritating effects.

1.6 GENERALIZED DRAWING PRIMITIVE (GDP)

The GDP is a means for an implementor to introduce non-standard primitives for his implementation only. The original motivation for GDP was to give access to output capabilities of some workstations like circle generator, interpolator, etc. Also, an implementor may decide to provide special output functions within the driver of some workstation which, from the GKS point of view, will be regarded as a GDP. A GDP may not belong to the GKS nucleus.

The attributes used for a specific GDP may be selected arbitrarily among the attributes specified for other primitives. However, this choice must be documented in the implementation manual.

1.7 Colour Attribute

Colour is specified as red, green and blue intensity (RGB) where the intensity is normalized to the interval [0,1]. This RGB colour model has been chosen to serve the most common colour raster devices.

From the application program's point of view, the RGB model is far from being the best choice. There are other models like HLS, HLV [SMIT78] and models based on colour names as used in spoken languages [BERK82] which allow an operator to specify a desired colour more easily and more precisely. These models can be built on top of GKS.

1.8 Transformability of Geometric Aspects of Non-Geometric Attributes

GKS distinguishes geometric and non-geometric attributes. Geometric attributes are

— CHARACTER HEIGHT;
— CHARACTER UP VECTOR;
— TEXT PATH;
— TEXT ALIGNMENT;
— PATTERN SIZE;
— PATTERN REFERENCE POINT.

These attributes in conjunction with the attributes
— TEXT FONT AND PRECISION;
— CHARACTER EXPANSION FACTOR;
— CHARACTER SPACING;
— FILL AREA INTERIOR STYLE

define the geometry of the TEXT and FILL AREA primitive in WC. The geometry is subject to the same transformations as the geometric data in the definition of the primitive. For example, if a rectangle is drawn around a TEXT, TEXT should be transformed in a way that the transformed rectangle always is filled by the TEXT primitive. Transformation requirements may be relaxed by the TEXT PRECISION for TEXT. For FILL AREA, a workstation which can implement pattern but not transformed patterns may refuse to transform patterns.

However, a closer look to the so-called non-geometric attributes
— LINEWIDTH;
— LINETYPE (length of dash and gap);
— MARKER SIZE;
— FILL AREA INTERIOR STYLE (hatch geometry)

shows that they contain also some geometrical aspects which could be affected by transformations.

LINEWIDTH and MARKER SIZE are specified relatively to a nominal size which is defined in DC. This implies that these geometric aspects cannot be transformed by any transformation but can be changed only by resetting the appropriate entry of a bundle table.

The transformation and clipping of dashing geometry deliberately has been left undefined to allow the implementor the use of capabilities of available hardware and requirements of his constituency.

Hatching compares well with pattern filling and, therefore, hatch lines should be transformed like patterns. If FILL AREA is transformed but the hatching remains static, a viewer has the impression of a moving outline before a wall with a stationary wall-paper. However, it is left to the workstation whether hatch lines are transformed or not. Furthermore, the PATTERN REFERENCE POINT can be used with advantage for positioning the same hatch pattern in different areas. For example, in cartography, it is annoying if hatch lines are not aligned if the same hatch pattern is used for adjacent areas. In business graphics, hatched rectangles are frequently used where the hatch lines are parallel to a rectangle side. In this case it is of importance whether the first hatch line coincides with this rectangle side or the hatch lines are centred in between two rectangle sides.

1.9 Segment Attributes

Segments can be manipulated dynamically. The dynamic capabilities primarily are modelled after capabilities present with vector refresh displays. Other devices will have serious difficulties in providing the same functionality. The extent to which dynamic changes are supported by the workstation is described in the workstation description table. If dynamic changes require an 'implicit regeneration', they may be postponed as specified by the workstation attribute 'deferral state'.

If dynamic changes are postponed, the state of the display surface remains undefined for a certain period of time. This intermediate state intentionally is left undefined giving the implementor freedom for appropriate alternate actions. For example, if a line has to be deleted on a storage tube, the implementor may choose to leave the line but cross it out to indicate a postponed deletion.

Highlighting is provided by a small class of devices only. Devices without intensity control may redraw the segment several times (storage tube) or assign a special colour (colour raster displays).

2   THE MAPPING OF LOGICAL TO PHYSICAL INPUT DEVICES

2.1   The Role of Logical Input Devices

To unify the great variety of hardware input devices, a small number of well-defined abstract input devices is identified. The concept of virtual input devices was enunciated by Wallace [WALL76] as a means whereby interactive graphics applications could be insulated from the peculiarities of the input devices of particular terminals.

As can be deduced from the popular discussions about the construction of user interfaces [GUED80, SIGG82, PFAF82b], the basic mistake when designing a graphics package is to regard the input and output functions as two independent concepts rather than seeing their tight coupling. Input alone is rather useless for solving interactive problems. Rather than input functions, interaction functions should be defined. Two contradictory approaches are shown in the Figures 2.1a and 2.1b. In Figure 2.1a, input and output functions are separated up to a rather high level leaving the coupling of both to application layers. The problem with this approach is that logical input devices at that level hide most physical characteristics of actual devices which are needed to build interaction techniques. Both the goals of developing suitable interaction

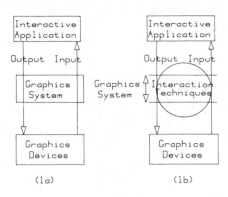

Figure 2.1 Output/input vs. output/interaction

techniques and the portability of interactive application programs normally fail if no well-defined access to physical input devices and their characteristics is available. A reason for that is the significance of physical device characteristics to human behaviour. For example, an interaction technique working with a LOCATOR device which is realized on a joystick will not work equally well if the LOCATOR is implemented via a keyboard or a lightpen device.

The original goal of standard input devices was to have their *final* effect being the same on all installations (e.g., a LOCATOR should deliver a pair of coordinates); however, also the *way* to achieve the final effect is important, i.e., the interaction technique.

Therefore, another approach must be taken: In Figure 2.1b the interaction techniques are integrated in the graphics system. Rather than input functions, interaction functions are identified. They provide a well-defined standardizable interface which enables portability of application programs. Their *realization* can be device-dependent since physical input devices instead of logical input devices can be used at this level.

A model containing both, a fixed set of six logical input devices and the facility to control interaction techniques was included in the final versions of GKS. Moreover, the model of input devices was refined such that it allows to control details of the operator interface like the definition and selection of interaction techniques (prompt/echo types) and the grouping of logical input devices [ROSE82]. This, of course, demands appropriate implementation structures. A concept of a GKS implementation which can be configured to actual hardware devices and application and operator needs was described in [PFAF82b].

2.2 Properties of Logical Input Devices

The set of logical input devices consists of LOCATOR, STROKE, VALUATOR, CHOICE, PICK, and STRING. All the logical devices have certain properties which can be controlled by the application program or a dialogue component (such as in [BORU80b] and [BORU82]) via parameters. Some of them are:

Simulation: how the implementation simulates the logical device using physical devices;

Prompting: how the operator is informed that a physical input device is available for manipulation;

Echo: how the operator is informed of the current logical data value of the device;

Acknowledgement: how the operator is informed that the current logical data value is significant. Then it satisfies a REQUEST function invocation or adds event reports to the input queue;

Operating mode: (REQUEST, SAMPLE, EVENT);

Initial values: a logical device is started with specific initial values each time an interaction begins;

Prompt/echo switch: the display of prompting and echoing information may be switched on or off.

The selection of attribute values for each of these attribute classes describes an instantiation of a logical device.

2.3 Properties of Physical Input Devices

The logical device attributes are not sufficient to describe interactions with human operators. Also the characteristics of physical devices have to be identified and described in a unified concept. The term "pragmatics" [BAEC82] seems adequate to us to describe the physical properties of input tools. Some of these attributes are:

Data contents: the number, type, and meaning of data delivered by an input device.

Category: a generic name describing the type of devices (e.g., joystick representing a group of similar devices).

Number of dimensions a device allows to handle simultaneously (e.g., a thumb wheel has 1 dimension, tablets have 2 dimensions; 3 dimensions are provided by some joysticks and track balls).

Operating mode: whether a device delivers discrete values (e.g, keyboards) or continuous values (e.g., joysticks, data tablets).

What is sensed: position with tablet and lightpen (absolute values), motion with trackball and mouse (relative movements), pressure with pressure pads and isometric joysticks;

How is it sensed: mechanically with joysticks and thumb wheels, touch-sensitively with touch tablets and touch screens.

Note that many devices are aggregates of more than one different type of simple devices. Their power often derives directly from their integration; it cannot be simulated equally well by a collection of simple devices (e.g., the four-button puck can be managed with one hand and is, therefore, more powerful than a puck without buttons and a separate four-button function keyboard).

2.4 The Model of Logical Input Devices

Every logical input device consists of two components, a measure part and a trigger part. The two components are responsible for performing the desired interaction. They map from physical devices (i.e., data obtained from them) to logical values (i.e., a pair of coordinates, a sequence of points, a real value, an integer number, a segment name and pick identifier, and a character string). The measure part determines how the operator controls the logical data value, and the trigger part determines how the operator indicates that the current value is significant.

The measure part of a logical device is only active when the device is taking part in an interaction (i.e., is enabled). It may be seen as a process using the states and changes of state of various physical input devices to calculate a logical data value. It is important that a single physical input device may affect the measures of several logical input devices. Figure 2.2 shows a 4-button puck of a data tablet used for controlling the measure parts of a LOCATOR and a CHOICE device. It may simultaneously deliver a pair of coordinates and a choice number between 1 and 15. At the same time, it may control the trigger process.

The trigger part of a logical device may accept two states: either it fires or it remains quiescent. Its reaction is dependent on state changes of the physical device. In the example above, the trigger part may be implemented using the four buttons of the puck. If one of the buttons is depressed the trigger fires.

Many logical input devices may have their trigger part in common. The trigger part itself may be seen as an independent process. When the trigger of a logical device fires, it sends a message to all measure processes it is associated with. The current value of each measure part is treated depending on the operating state of the logical device:

— In REQUEST mode, the measure process returns its data value to the application program and then stops;
— In SAMPLE mode, trigger processes are always ignored. The application program may obtain the data value from the measure process whenever it wants;
— In EVENT mode, the measure process attempts to add an event record, containing its identification and data value, to the input queue.

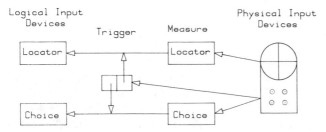

Figure 2.2 Configuration of logical devices on a four-button puck of a data tablet

If caused by a single trigger firing, several event reports are generated they are marked as a "group of simultaneous event reports". This may be inquired by the application program during the dequeuing process.

Most ambitious interaction techniques need input device associations like that of the example above. These requirements should be part of the description of each interaction technique. During a configuration phase, these associations may be set up. Each association is described as a tuple consisting of two logical devices the second of which will refer to the trigger of the first device. The description of the first device is taken from its specification as described in the next chapter.

2.5 Means for Defining Logical Input Device Realizations

Given the measure/trigger model of logical input devices and the attributes introduced above, the binding of logical to physical devices can be defined. As described in [PFAF82b], the definition could be input to a configuration generator. Using a set of programmed modules, a syntax by which each interaction process can be described and some description tables, executable programs can be generated. These implement the desired interaction processes.

Figure 2.3 shows the components of the configuration method. The desired realization of a logical device is described in terms of the logical and physical device attributes wanted. They are input to the configuration generator in form of tables. Controlled by these requirement tables and system description tables the generator applies the appropriate productions and replaces symbols by program modules. Eventually, an executable program representing the whole interaction process is generated.

2.5.1 A Syntax for the Specification of Interaction Processes

A syntactic notation to describe interaction processes is chosen for two reasons: First, the syntax could serve as input for a parser which generates the desired

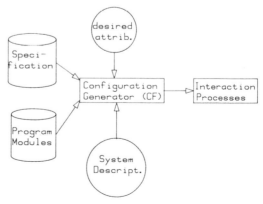

Figure 2.3 Components of the configuration method

Table 2.1 Syntax for the specification of interaction processes

< interaction >	: : = < start > < prompting > < adjustment > < stop >
< start >	: : = determine source of input data, set initial state of measure process, add measure identification to trigger list, < create echo item >
< prompting >	: : = empty | display message | ....
< adjustment >	: : = < sample input data > < evaluate logical data > < reaction >
< stop >	: : = delete echo, delete prompt, remove measure identification from the trigger list
< create echo item >	: : = begin segment, < output primitives >, end segment | .... | ....
< sample input data >	: : = read puck (x,y,i) | read lightpen (x,y,display_file_address) | read keyboard (string) | ....
< evaluate logical data >	: : = < evaluate measure value >, < evaluate trigger value >
< evaluate measure value >	
	: : = COORDINATE : = F(x,y) | SEGMENT_NAME,PICK_ID : = P(display_file_address) | ALTERNATIVE : = i | ....
< evaluate trigger value >	: : = TRIGGER = T1(x,y,i) | TRIGGER = T2(x,y,TIME) | ....
< reaction >	: : = < update measure value > < update echo >, IF TRIGGER = 'NOTSET' THEN < adjustment > ELSE < trigger >
< update measure value >	: : = LOCATOR : = COORDINATE | PICK : = SEGMENT_NAME, PICK_ID | CHOICE : = ALTERNATIVE | ....
< update echo >	: : = shift segment | delete segment, < create echo item > | ... | ...
< trigger >	: : = CASE OPERATING MODE OF
REQUEST:	< acknowledgement >,deliver measure value
SAMPLE:	< adjustment >
EVENT:	< acknowledgement >, for each measure id in the trigger list: generate one event report, < adjustment > END

executable program. The grammar thus determines the sequencing of modules to be generated. Secondly, by using this syntax a dialogue author can easily extend the set of program modules. He just has to define new productions and (terminal) symbols and develop the corresponding program modules (Table 2.1).

Table 4.3 (continued)

INCLUDE FILE containing the mnemonic FORTRAN names and their values for all GKS ENUMERATION type values

---

DATA ESMCH,ESMPK,ESMST,EWAIT,EFLUSH,EGTLC	/90,91,92,93,94,95/
DATA EGTSK,EGTVL,EGTCH,EGTPK,EGTST	/96,97,98,99,100/
DATA EWITM,EGTITM,ERDITM,EIITM	/101,102,103,104/
DATA EEVTM,EACTM,EPREC,EUREC	/105,106,107,108/

The following three entries are useful for utilizing the adjustable dimension feature passing 'empty' arrays of length '1' as parameters.

INTEGER	EMPTI	/i.d./
REAL	EMPTR	/i.d./
CHARACTER*1	EMPTC	/i.d./

Note: 'i.d.' means implementation-dependent

Rule L4
Since all GKS functions are mapped to FORTRAN subroutines their invocation is done by FORTRAN CALLS. The corresponding parameters are passed to and obtained from them according to the FORTRAN parameter passing conventions.

Rule L5
For internal communication purposes, a GKS implementation may need reserved names, e.g., for internal subroutines, functions and common blocks. Since these are known outside GKS, e.g., during linking, name conflicts have to be taken care of. Therefore, it is recommended that internal names should start with the letters 'GK'; other programs should not use such names. GKS installations should provide means to rename globally known internal names when necessary.

Other Features
Every GKS installation has to provide a standard error handling routine, named GERHND. The user may replace this standard error handling routine by his own one using the same name GERHND and passing the same parameters. Means has to be provided to perform this replacement (e.g., by library management utilities).

4.3 Other Language Interfaces

While at the time of writing this book only the FORTRAN 77 language binding has been internationally discussed and agreed upon, other language bindings are being developed on a more personal or institutional basis. Most important of these bindings are a PASCAL [JUNG83] and a C [ROSE82b] language interface. Generally, language bindings may differ in two aspects: how the abstract data types used in the GKS document are mapped onto language data types, and how the abstract GKS function names and argument lists are mapped onto language functions.

When defining a language binding there is, depending on the capacity of the language, a tradeoff between the number of functions and the number of data types used. The FORTRAN language binding represents the one extreme choice: only the very basic FORTRAN data types can be used and all GKS functions are implemented as FORTRAN subroutines, leaving the error checking and the achievement of the functions' effects to the subroutine-based implementation. The other extreme is given by a pure specification language using abstract data types such as the Wide Spectrum Language [BAUE81] or the specification language used by Carson for the PMIG specification [CARS82]. All GKS functions would correspond to an abstract data type, expressing the error checking and the effect of the functions by operators on the data types.

Taking the GKS abstract function SET POLYLINE INDEX (INDEX), the first solution leads to a FORTRAN subroutine which is called as CALL GSPLI (INDEX). INDEX is an input parameter of type INTEGER. The check whether INDEX is greater than 1 is left to the implementation as well as its effect on the GKS state list. In the second case, POLYLINE INDEX would be an abstract data type which operates on an INTEGER value restricted to the range [1..n]. One more operator is to set the GKS state POLYLINE_INDEX to the given value. Given a powerful compiler (which would process the specifications), one could simply write POLYLINE_INDEX := 4; in the application program.

The actual implementation of a language interface will obviously depend on the language elements available and on the extensibility of the system, e.g., by macros. The C language binding proposed by Rosenthal [ROSE82b] features 92 functions compared with 157 FORTRAN subroutines and 62 data types instead of 8 FORTRAN data types (this is true for the GKS version 7.0; one may extrapolate for the final GKS version).

The PASCAL binding [JUNG83] developed within the GMD uses, for compatibility reasons, the same number and names of procedures as the FORTRAN binding does. However, to allow for data type checking at compile time and to make PASCAL programs more readable some more data types were defined. Some of these are:

Table 4.4 Pascal data types

INTERIORSTYLE	= (hollow,solid,pattern,hatch);
INPCLASS	= (noclass,locator,stroke,valuator,choice,pick,string);
STRING	= RECORD ltext:INTEGER;
	text:PACKED ARRAY(.1..80.) OF CHAR END;
POINT	= ARRAY (.1..2.) OF REAL;
POINTS	= ARRAY (.1..101.) OF POINT;
RANGE	= ARRAY (.1..2.) OF REAL;
SIZEI	= ARRAY (.1..2.) OF INTEGER;

Table 4.4 (continued)

BOX	= ARRAY (.1..2.)	OF POINT;
BOXES	= ARRAY (.1..10.)	OF BOX;
LISTI	= ARRAY (.1..12.)	OF INTEGER;
LISTIL	= ARRAY (.1..80.)	OF INTEGER;
TRMATRIX	= ARRAY (.1..6.)	OF REAL;
METAREC	= ARRAY (.1..80.)	OF INTEGER;
MATRIX	= ARRAY (.1..2.)	OF INTEGER;
COLOURS	= ARRAY (.1..3.)	OF REAL;
LINTERIORSTYLES	= ARRAY (.1..12.)	OF INTERIORSTYLE;

5   INTERFACES TO GRAPHICS DEVICES

5.1   Principles

GKS is based on the concept of abstract workstations. A workstation of GKS represents a unit consisting of zero or one display surfaces and zero or more input devices, such as keyboard, tablet and lightpen. The workstation presents these devices to the application program as a configuration of abstract devices, thereby, shielding the hardware peculiarities. Workstations provide the logical interface through which the application program controls physical devices. Certain special workstations provide facilities for the storage and exchange of graphical information. In Table 4.3 in Chapter III.4.4 on page 129, all GKS functions applying to the single workstation categories directly or indirectly are listed. Output functions, attribute, transformation and segment functions, e.g., apply to all output, output/input, and metafile output workstations, whereas they do not apply to input and metafile input workstations.

Rather than implementing the logical workstation interfaces, GKS systems will normally realize interfaces to physical devices for the exchange of graphical data. In order to provide a certain amount of independence of a GKS system from the various devices, a well-defined interface between them should be identified. Workstations are based on physical devices of various capabilities. They map the logical GKS functions to physical device functions. The interaction with physical devices is done via a set of device functions which, in total, form device interfaces. They address capabilities being directly supported by the low-level device drivers.

The GKS standard does not define the set of functions for possible device interfaces, nor the way those functions can be used by a GKS implementation. Also no prescriptions are made that any interfaces to devices must be provided at all.

However, there exist good reasons for explicitly providing interfaces to devices in a GKS implementation:

— Often GKS implementations have to support multiple workstations connected at the same time, or to adjust themselves to different workstations in different installations. Using a modular structure and providing interfaces helps to reduce the complexity. It allows for developing drivers independently of the GKS system and of other drivers even by different teams.
— In many application areas, workstations have to be easily modifiable and exchangeable. This can be supported via "connection points" provided by well-defined interfaces. This is a most important element ensuring device-independence of the major part of a GKS implementation.
— Interfaces provide means for distributing a GKS system on a multiprocessor system, e.g., fully or largely equipped workstations can be implemented on remote microprocessors with local software. Data exchange is performed at the interface levels.
— If a GKS implementation shall be certified by testing methods, interfaces are needed to measure the data sent to and received from actual devices. This is explained in Chapter 7.

Besides the implementational aspects, interfaces and their functional elements are needed to describe or "formally specify" the effect of the GKS functions more completely than the GKS document does. Most of the effect of the GKS functions lies in producing the correct data for a graphical device. This is not such difficult a task if it is performed for abstract workstations of about equal functionality. But most physically existing graphical devices have different capabilities. The mapping of the logical GKS functions to the various physically existing functions makes up the real problem of a GKS definition. This is addressed in the Chapters 1, 2, and 7 of this Part IV. Moreover, the interface design as explained in this chapter reflects this task.

It can be expected that for the reasons listed above, a small number of device interfaces will evolve reflecting the facilities of typical graphics devices. This is a kind of standardization on a low level: if new graphics devices are developed, their number and kind of functions can be chosen from the existing set. They can then be driven almost directly by existing GKS software.

The following Section 5.2 describes a logical structure within GKS systems. Section 5.3 introduces the background of the DI/DD interface construction. In Section 5.4, we list some DI/DD functions, and in Section 5.5, introduce description tables to describe the capabilities of device drivers.

5.2 Separation of the Device-Independent from the Device-Dependent Code Parts

Logically, a GKS system can be subdivided into 3 hierarchically organized subsystems, each one adding certain functionality to the overall system. As shown in Figure 5.1, we distinguish the device-dependent, the workstation-dependent, and the workstation-independent parts.

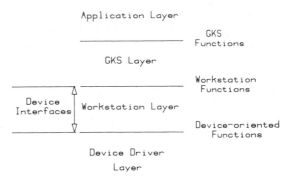

Figure 5.1 Logical structure of GKS systems

The device-dependent part of a GKS system serves graphics devices at a very low interface (e.g., generating control commands for display processors). Generally, this level should reduce the various device- and supplier-specific functions to a low level logical function set. In order to keep requirements of device driver construction very small, GKS demands only very few, low level functions, e.g., draw line, draw pixel, sample input datum, clear screen. Almost no restrictions are made to extend the device driver function set by new capabilities. One restriction would be that those capabilities fit into the GKS functionality, i.e., GKS functions should be able to utilize them. Some proposals to extend this interface by more sophisticated functions are derived from existing device capabilities and the GKS workstation design, e.g., SET COLOUR REPRESEN-TATION to allow the use of colour tables, CREATE and CLOSE SEGMENT to support devices with own structured display files, SET SEGMENT TRANS-FORMATION to utilize devices with hardware transformation capabilities.

The next logically higher level is constituted by workstations. These establish a comparable level of intelligence of graphics functions by introducing device independence [ENCA80]. Software is needed to implement higher logical functions on different device driver functions, e.g., clipping algorithms, area fill functions, attribute simulations, and logical input device implementations. These solutions can be implemented in device-independent ways, i.e., they reduce the higher functions to the minimally required low-level device driver functions. Thus, they can be applied in many different device environments. This is the reason why we call this part of the system the device-independent (DI) part, the device drivers the device-dependent (DD) part, and the interface between the two of them the DI/DD interface. An example of a device-independent solution of a GKS function on various device-dependent interfaces is shown in Figure 5.2.

The workstation-independent part of GKS finally contains all functions of a required level, regardless of actual device capabilities and workstation simulations. This level is mainly responsible for "dynamics" in GKS. All problems of segment handling, dynamic attribute changes, dynamic windowing, etc. may be handled by redrawing primitives out of a workstation-independent segment storage if no workstation-dependent segment storage is available for that device.

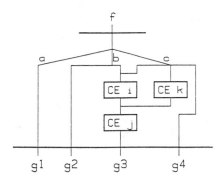

Figure 5.2 Different mappings of the function f to device functions gi

How the effects are achieved is largely hidden from the application programmer and program. Only differences in the behaviour of the program performance may be visible. Redrawing of pictures, e.g., may occur at different moments for different workstations or the appearance of attributes may be more or less precise.

An example follows how the effect of the function f of the GKS interface, e.g., SET SEGMENT TRANSFORMATION, can be achieved differently using combinations of the functions gi of three different device interfaces. The gi-functions might represent SET SEGMENT TRANSFORMATION, DELETE SEGMENT, CLEAR DISPLAY SURFACE, and "draw primitives". The CEi stand for device-independent simulations and utilities, e.g., TRANSFORM CO-ORDINATES, READ AND INTERPRET PRIMITIVES FROM SEGMENT STORAGE.

In case a in Figure 5.2, the device driver is able to perform the GKS-function f in the way required by GKS. In the second and third case (b and c), the drivers have simpler graphical interfaces than the GKS-function at the application layer. The DI-part has to analyse the 'complexer' function f and to map it onto a sequence of 'simpler' functions g determined by the real capabilities of the driver. In case b), the combination g2 and g3, in case c) g3 and g4 are used.

5.3 DI/DD Interfaces

As can be deduced from the previous sections, actual DI/DD interfaces are not fixed at all. They may range from supporting very few and simple functions to providing a fully equipped GKS workstation. For one-workstation implementations, this may be even almost the GKS interface. Additionally, they may contain any device-specific functions at all logical levels lower than the GKS level in order to be used by a GKS implementation in flexible and efficient ways.

For constructing DI/DD interfaces, we need the definitions of the DI/DD function set and of minimal DI/DD interfaces.

5.3.1 DI/DD Function Set

The DI/DD function set consists of an extensible set of functions (given by the names of routines and the list or range of parameters for each routine). Every function defines a possible logical capability of a device driver. The functions are realized directly by the device driver in device-dependent ways.

The DI/DD function set is listed in Section 5.4. It consists of two parts:
— the workstation function set (5.4.1) is a fixed set of functions which is determined by the GKS functions applicable to workstations.
— The device-oriented function set (5.4.2) addresses more device-oriented facilities like the setting of static unbundled, static bundled, and dynamic unbundled attributes, the drawing of device-specific primitives, the control of physical input devices, etc. It may be extended by any new device-specific function which can be used by a GKS implementation.

5.3.2 Minimal DI/DD Interfaces

Minimal sets of functions can be chosen out of the DI/DD function set, according to the device types. Every device driver has to support the corresponding required set of functions. It is ensured that the functions of the minimal interface are sufficient for implementing any GKS function on top of them. Device types anticipated at the moment are vector types, raster types and input types; they can be combined arbitrarily. Minimal DI/DD interfaces consist of the following functions:

OPEN DEVICE	
CLOSE DEVICE	
CLEAR SURFACE	(for output type devices)
LINE	(for vector-output type devices)
PIXEL	(for raster-output types)
SAMPLE INPUT DATUM	(for input type devices)

If a device is an aggregate of several types, the minimal required functions of this list have to be added.

5.3.3 Constructing DI/DD Interfaces

Each particular DI/DD interface represents a logical description of the capabilities of a particular device driver, expressed in terms of a number of functions and a DI/DD interface description table. The functions are chosen from the DI/DD function set. A particular DI/DD interface might consist of
— the workstation function set. All functions of a fully equipped workstation (of a particular GKS level) are supported by the device driver. There is no need for simulation software in the device-independent part. The workstation driver is identical with the device driver and is completely implemented

in device-dependent form (DD-part). Such solutions are feasible if the graphical device used provides powerful facilities such as a structured display file (device-dependent segment storage), hardware transformations and clipping, attribute tables, etc. It may also be adopted if device-dependent solutions can be developed with reasonable efforts and are more powerful than device-independent solutions. This is especially true for remote GKS workstations with slow connection lines to a time-shared host, and for one-workstation systems.

suitable subsets, chosen from one or both of the workstation function set and the device-oriented function set. In order to provide the application program with powerful workstations on less powerful devices without implementing special software solutions in device-dependent form, a particular DI/DD interface may omit most of the functions required by a workstation. Then device-independent (DI) solutions can be realized on top of the device drivers (output, input, attribute simulations, segment handling, redrawing, retroactive attribute changes, and workstation windowing). The term "suitable subset" means that it must include at least the minimal DI/DD interface, and that duplication of functions of different complexity at different levels should be avoided.

5.4   The DI/DD Function Set

5.4.1   The Workstation Function Set

The following list of functions (Table 5.1) is directly deduced from the GKS functions. Their effect is either the same as in the GKS document or self-explaining.

Table 5.1 Workstation function set

Workstation Control Functions	
OPEN WORKSTATION	CLOSE WORKSTATION
CLEAR WORKSTATION	REDRAW ALL SEGMENTS
UPDATE WORKSTATION	SET DEFERRAL STATE
MESSAGE	ESCAPE

Output Functions	
POLYLINE	POLYMARKER
TEXT	FILL AREA
CELL ARRAY	GEN. DRAWING PRIMITIVE

Setting of Modal Attributes	
SET POLYLINE INDEX	SET POLYMARKER INDEX
SET TEXT INDEX	SET CHARACTER HEIGHT
SET CHARACTER UP VECTOR	SET TEXT PATH
SET FILL AREA INDEX	SET PATTERN SIZE
SET PATTERN REF. POINT	SET PICK IDENTIFIER
SET TEXT ALIGNMENT	SET ATTRIB. SOURCE FLAGS

Table 5.1 (continued)

SET LINETYPE	SET LINEWIDTH SCALE FACTOR
SET POLYLINE COLOUR INDEX	SET MARKER TYPE
SET MARKER SIZE SCALE FAC.	SET POLYMARKER COLOUR INDEX
SET TEXT FONT AND PREC.	SET CHAR EXPANSION FAC.
SET CHARACTER SPACING	SET TEXT COLOUR INDEX
SET INTERIOR STYLE	SET STYLE INDEX
SET FILL AREA COLOUR INDEX	

Setting of Attribute Bundles (Retroactive Modification possible)

SET POLYLINE REPRESENTATION	SET POLYMARKER REPRESENTATION
SET TEXT REPRESENTATION	SET FILL AREA REPRESENTATION
SET PATTERN REPRESENTATION	SET COLOUR REPRESENTATION

Transformations and Clipping

SET NORMALIZATION TRANSFORM.	SET CLIPPING RECTANGLE
SET WORKSTATION WINDOW	SET WORKSTATION VIEWPORT

Segmentation Functions

CREATE SEGMENT	CLOSE SEGMENT
RENAME SEGMENT	DELETE SEGMENT
SET SEGMENT TRANSFORMATION	SET VISIBILITY
SET HIGHLIGHTING	SET SEGMENT PRIORITY
SET DETECTABILITY	

Input Functions (for input and output/input types only)

INITIALISE < input device >	SET < input device > MODE
REQUEST < input device >	SAMPLE < input device >

Inquire Functions

All INQUIRIES except those to the GKS state list

Additional Metafile Output Function

WRITE ITEM TO GKSM

Metafile Input Functions

GET ITEM TYPE FROM GKSM	READ ITEM FROM GKSM

5.4.2 Device-Oriented Function Set

The device-oriented function set (Table 5.2) is directly deduced from existing low level device drivers. It, therefore, should not be seen from a point of conceptual cleanness but from a pragmatic point of view: as many device facilities should be utilizable by GKS systems as possible. It is very important to mention that this list of functions can be extended if need arises. It should serve as starting point only.

Table 5.2 Device-oriented function set

Device Control Functions

OPEN DEVICE   CLOSE DEVICE
CLEAR SURFACE   OUTPUT BUFFER

Output Functions

LINE   LINETO
MOVETO   VECTOR_SET
DRAW_CHARACTER

The following functions allow for controlling raster devices on a pixel stream basis; i.e., the raster scan conversion is above the DI/DD interface.

PIXEL   PIXEL STREAM
FILLED RECTANGLE   DRAW PATTERN

Some more static unbundled Attributes

The following group of functions is to support some more static unbundled attributes.

SET CURRENT LINEWIDTH   SET CURRENT MARKER SIZE
SET CURRENT CHARACTER SIZE   SET CURRENT CHARACTER ROTA-
                                     TION
SET CURRENT PATTERN   SET CURRENT COLOUR ATTRIBUTES

Setting of Unbundled Attribute Tables

The following group of functions allows the support of drivers with additional unbundled attribute tables (other than colour and pattern tables such as linetype tables).

SET LINETYPE REPRESENTATION   SET LINEWIDTH REPRESENTATION
SET MARKER TYPE REPRESEN-
   TATION   SET TEXT FONT REPRESENTATION
SET FILL AREA STYLE REPRESEN-
   TATION

Setting of Predefined Attributes (no modification possible)

Driver-predefined attributes or attribute-combinations may be used also. This is to address, specific plotter pens, device-specific linetypes, text fonts, etc.

SET PREDEFINED ATTRIBUTE INDEX

Input Control

The following function addresses physical input devices with specific data formats and contents. This allows — together with some segment manipulation functions — the realization of logical input devices above the DI/DD interface.

SAMPLE INPUT DATUM

Segment Storage Functions

SELECT SEGMENT   GET NEXT RECORD

5.5 DI/DD Interface Description Tables

The capabilities of every GKS device driver can be described in the DI/DD interface description table (DIDT). Depending on the GKS implementation it has to be set up each time a new device is connected to or integrated in the system. It may be used for several purposes:
— Implementations may be developed in a device-independent way so that they can adjust themselves to the particular device driver peculiarities [BORU80a]. In their device-independent part, they may use simulation software to increase the device capabilities to the required workstation functions. Of course, this may be limited to certain device types, e.g., a plotter, a storage tube, and a refresh display.
— Implementations may be adjusted to actual device driver capabilities by software adaptations. The DI/DD interface description table will not be available during the run time of GKS programs in that case. Rather it is used by a system expert to tailor the implementation. It may also be used as parameters to control an automated configuration phase. Approaches like this are based on "conditional code" [SCHO81], source code modelling, or program generation techniques [PFAF82a].
— In any case, the DI/DD interface description table serves as basis for establishing the workstation description table (WDT). Most of the entries of the DIDT are directly taken over to the WDT. The workstation description tables are completed by the DI part of the GKS implementation according to the simulation facilities available and applicable.

All capabilities lined up in the DI/DD interface description table are either available by device hardware or at least performable by the software of the device driver.

A proposed DI/DD interface description table contains the entries listed in Table 5.3. Obviously, its final format and contents has to be fixed by each GKS implementation using it.

Table 5.3 A device description table

Workstation type:
— sequence number
— output/input type
— raster/vector type
Type of device coordinate units
Maximum display surface in length or device units
Default value for deferral and implicit regeneration mode
Availability of primitives:
— Polyline
— Polymarker
— Text
— Fill area
— Pixel array

Table 5.3 (continued)

— Pixel array read back
— others (e.g., line, move, pixel)
Number and table of predefined bundles for:
— Polyline
— Polymarker
— Text
— Fill area
— Pattern
— Colour
Number of intensities and colours
Availability of transformation and clipping: (none, static, dynamic)
Type of attribute handling (static unbundled, static bundled, dynamic unbundled, dynamic bundled)
— Polyline
— Polymarker
— Text
— Fill area
— Pattern
— Colour
Number and list of available linetypes
Number of linewidths and nominal/minimal/maximal linewidths
Number and list of different marker types
Number of marker sizes and nominal/minimal/maximal marker size
Number and list of (text fonts and associated precisions)
Number of character heights and minimum/maximum character height
Number and list of interior styles
Number and list of hatch styles
Number and list of (gdp id's and associated bundle types)
Number of segments and segment priorities supported
Technique of attribute modification realized for:
— segment transformation (full matrix, shift, zoom, combinations, not-supported)
— visibility (on to off and off to on)
— highlighting
— segment priority
— adding primitives to open segment of lower priority
— segment deletion (direct, inverse overwriting, not-supported)
— detectability
Number of logical input devices supported
List of logical input devices supported
— input class
— input device number
— available operating mode
— maximum and default values
— default echo area
— Number and list of prompt/echo types
Number of physical input devices supported
List of physical input devices supported
— connection identification
— data format

It should be mentioned that GKS systems developed for specific devices normally integrate the DI/DD description table in their program code. It therefore is not visible to a user of the system nor is it possible to describe a new (different) device and connect it to the system.

6   METAFILES

6.1   Introduction

Graphics metafiles have been used for a considerable time for storing and transmitting pictures. GKS includes a metafile interface as part of the standard (see Chapter III.11). An appendix of the GKS document gives the definition of the GKS metafile that can be used together with this interface. However, it is not part of the ISO standard. Efforts have been started within ISO to standardize a single graphics metafile. The metafile subgroup of ISO TC97/SC5/WG2 gave the following general definition for graphics metafiles:
"A graphics metafile is a mechanism for the transfer and storage of graphics data that is both device- and application-independent".

Additionally, some basic design principles for graphics metafiles were stated: "The minimal capability of a graphics metafile must include all functions necessary to describe pictures independently of each other. The pictures in graphics metafiles must be storable on different media, transportable between different graphics systems, and displayable on different graphics devices. The graphics metafile should not require non-sequential access to graphics primitives in order to display the picture. The basic set of functions should not preclude the addition of application-dependent data or picture structure information. The specification of functionality will be separated from the specification of coding formats."

6.2   Graphics Metafiles Proposals

In many application areas, a variety of graphics metafile formats is being used together with different graphics systems and on different levels of functionality. The spectrum reaches from very simple and very general designs containing few graphics primitives and attributes, to very sophisticated data formats for specific application areas. Examples for recent graphics metafile proposals are:
— GKS metafile, developed together with GKS;
— GSPC metafile, developed by the "Graphics Standards Planning Committee" of ACM-SIGGRAPH, 1977 [GSPC79];

— Videotex, a graphics metafile format for routing graphical data to television sets connected to the VIDEOTEX-network, developed by the Canadian Department of Communication, 1980 [BRIE80];
— AGF plotfile, a graphics data exchange format developed by German research centers (and used as the base for the GKS metafile), 1976 [ENDE78].

The GSPC metafile, the Videotex metafile, the AGF plotfile, as well as lower levels of the GKS metafile, are very basic formats for the description of pictures.

Another metafile standard should be mentioned: IGES (Initial Graphics Exchange Specification), developed under the supervision of the US-National Bureau of Standards, ANSI-Standard 1981 [ANSI81]. It is not a graphics metafile, but a product definition data file for the CAD/CAM field. It provides a very complex, application-oriented schema for describing CAD/CAM design objects together with their attributes and properties. Although IGES contains graphics entities, the scope of IGES was considered to be sufficiently distinct from the scope of graphics metafiles, that up to now both developments were independent of each other. However, CAD-files will surely have an influence on the development of graphics metafiles in the future.

6.3   GKS Metafile

The Graphical Kernel System GKS has an interface to a graphics metafile called GKS Metafile (GKSM). As part of the standard, the document contains a complete definition of the interface to and from the GKSM.

The contents and the format of the GKSM are described in an appendix that is not part of the standard. This separation was done in order to allow for a development of standardized graphics metafile independently from specific systems or devices. The metafile interface of GKS, and how the metafile is written or read, is presented in Chapter III.11.

6.3.1   Contents of the GKS Metafile

The GKS metafile contains two dimensional pictures. Every picture is represented by a series of data records ("items") that are generated as the result of GKS functions invoked. The GKS functions are grouped in upward compatible levels with increasing capabilities. Although not explicitly stated, the GKS levels imply corresponding GKSM levels. In its simplest form, the GKSM thus contains only twelve types of records comprising the output primitives polyline, polymarker and text, simple attributes, together with file header, picture header and end record. Higher levels include more elaborate attribute setting functions (e.g., colour, linewidth, text font), raster primitives and segment functions. Additional to the graphics records, the GKSM may contain non-graphical, application-dependent data.

6.3.2   Format of the GKS Metafile

The GKSM is built from a sequence of logical variable length data records. Every record starts with a key denoting the record type. It is followed by the length of the data record so it can be skipped easily if an interpreter is not interested in a particular record type. The key can be between one and eight bytes long; the data format for real and integer values can be chosen in a flexible way. Internal machine code representation is possible as well as formatted representation by ASCII strings. Which format a given GKSM uses is specified in the file header, which is the first record of each metafile. The logical data records are arranged one after the other on physical records that have card image format. The complete description of the GKS metafile format is given in Appendix 1 of this book.

6.4   The ISO Standard Metafile

In October 1981, ISO TC97/SC5/WG2 "Computer Graphics" established a metafile subgroup that was charged with:
— developing a framework in which graphical metafiles can be studied, developed and related to other standards;
— designing a metafile standard proposal and recommending whatever 'work items' are needed in this area to produce the desired standard.

The metafile subgroup had its first meetings in 1982. The goal of this project is to create a system-independent graphics metafile that can be used with a wide range of systems and devices. The subgroup can base its work on experiences with various metafiles and with GKS and its metafile (e.g., [ENDE80,ROSE80,REED81]). However, the most impact will come from the metafile group of the American National Standards Institute, ANSI X3H33. This group is currently developing a national U.S. standard for a metafile called "Virtual Device Metafile, VDM" [ANSI82]. In cooperation with the WG2 metafile subgroup, VDM will be processed into an international standard.

The status of the metafile standard is as follows (December 1982):
— agreement was reached to concentrate on a "Basic Metafile" that contains the basic functionality. The minimal set of required functions for a metafile was identified. Later, more complex metafile levels or additional modules can be defined;
— a formal grammar for graphics metafile was sketched, that gives a formal definition of the metafile structure, allows for generation of metafile parsers, and offers a framework for extensions;
— it was agreed that a metafile standard may have different bindings, i.e. coding formats and physical file formats, but that at least one binding should be specified as part of the standard. This could serve as a general communication format.

Table 6.1 contains the set of basic metafile elements that has been set up in the draft. It includes output primitives, output primitive attributes, some

Table 6.1 Elements of the basic metafile

Metafile descriptor elements:
METAFILE VERSION	Version of the metafile (there may be more than one version in the future)
METAFILE DESCRIPTION	Description of the metafile contents in free format text (person-readable)
METAFILE DIMENSIONALITY	Dimensionality of current version is 2D, future versions may be 3D
COORDINATE TYPE	Selection of integer or real values to represent coordinates on the metafile
METAFILE ELEMENT LIST	List of all elements used in a metafile
METAFILE DEFAULTS	At BEGIN PICTURE the state of the metafile interpreter will be reset to these default values

Control elements:
BEGIN METAFILE	Start of metafile
END METAFILE	End of metafile
BEGIN PICTURE	Begin of picture
END PICTURE	End of picture
CLEAR VIEW SURFACE	Erase device display surface
DATA PRECISION	Precision of real and integer data used within the metafile, including precision for coordinate values, for enumerated values, for indices, and for colours
VIRTUAL DEVICE COORDINATE EXTENT	Specifies which part of the metafile coordinate space is used for primitives
CLIP RECTANGLE	Rectangle used for clipping
CLIP INDICATOR	Switches clipping on or off
DESIGNATE CHARACTER SET	Specifies a mapping from character codes to characters
CHARACTER SET INDEX	Selects a character code mapping

Output primitives:
POLYLINE	Vector sequence
POLYMARKER	Set of marker symbols
TEXT	Text string
CELL ARRAY	Array of cells of different colours
FILL AREA	Filled, hatched or patterned area

The following primitives will be included in the metafile description, either explicitly or as GDP elements:
CIRCLE	Behaves like a polyline or a fill area
ARC	Behaves like a polyline
ARC CLOSED	Behaves like a fill area

Attributes:
Colour:
COLOUR TABLE	Table for associating RGB values to colour indices

Table 6.1 (continued)

COLOUR SPECIFICATION	Selects colour specification by index or direct by RGB values
BACKGROUND INDEX	Colour index used for the background colour

Polyline attributes:

LINEWIDTH	Width of line
LINETYPE	Solid, dashed, ...
LINE.COLOUR	Colour, either by index or by RGB values
POLYLINE BUNDLE INDEX	Index of predefined polyline bundle
POLYLINE ASPECT SOURCE FLAGS	ASF settings for polyline attributes

Marker attributes:

MARKER TYPE	Type of marker symbol
MARKER SIZE	Height of marker symbol
MARKER COLOUR	Colour, either by index or by RGB values
POLYMARKER BUNDLE INDEX	Index of predefined polymarker bundle
POLYMARKER ASPECT SOURCE FLAGS	ASF settings for polymarker attributes

Text attributes:

CHARACTER HEIGHT	Height of characters
CHARACTER EXPANSION FACTOR	Deviation from nominal width/height ratio
CHARACTER SPACING	Intercharacter space
CHARACTER UP VECTOR	Up-direction of characters
TEXT PATH	LEFT-RIGHT-UP-DOWN
TEXT FONT INDEX	Number of text font
TEXT PRECISION	Degree of fidelity for text attribute evaluation
TEXT ALIGNMENT	Position of text relative to reference point
TEXT COLOUR	Colour, either by index or by RGB values
TEXT BUNDLE INDEX	Index of predefined text bundle
TEXT ASPECT SOURCE FLAGS	ASF settings for text attributes

Fill area attributes:

INTERIOR STYLE	Fill-style for area
HATCH INDEX	Selects type of hatching
PATTERN INDEX	Index referring pattern table entry
PATTERN TABLE	Pattern table
PATTERN SIZE	Size of pattern
FILL AREA COLOUR	Colour, either by index or by RGB values
FILL AREA BUNDLE INDEX	Index of predefined fill area bundle
FILL AREA ASPECT SOURCE FLAGS	ASF settings for fill area attributes

Other:

ESCAPE	General escape-function
MESSAGE	Text that may be used for communication with the operator
APPLICATION DATA	Data generated and processed by the application program.

Table 6.2 Formal grammar for the basic metafile

\<metafile\>	::= \<BEGIN METAFILE\> \<metafile descriptor\>
	\<metafile element\>* \<END METAFILE\>
\<metafile descriptor\>	::= \<identification elements\>
	\<characteristics elements\>
\<identification elements\>	::= \<METAFILE VERSION\> \<character list\>
	\<METAFILE DESCRIPTION\> \<character list\>
\<characteristics elements\>	::= \<METAFILE DIMENSIONALITY\> \<value\>
	\<METAFILE ELEMENT LIST\> \<element list\>
	\<METAFILE DEFAULTS\> \<default list\>
	\<METAFILE COORDINATE TYPE\> \<ctype\>
\<metafile element\>	::= \<picture\> | \<external element\>
\<picture\>	::= \<BEGIN PICTURE\> \<identifier\>
	\<picture element\> \<END PICTURE\>
\<picture element\>	::= \<graphical element\> | \<external element\>
\<graphical element\>	::= \<output element\> | \<attribute element\> |
	\<control element\> | \<escape element\>
\<external element\>	::= \<application element\> | \<message element\>
\<output element\>	::= \<polyline element\> | \<polymarker element\> |
	\<text element\> | \<pixel element\> |
	\<fill area element\> | ....
\<polyline element\>	::= \<POLYLINE\> \<point list\>
\<polymarker element\>	::= \<POLYMARKER\> \<point list\>
\<text element\>	::= \<TEXT\> \<point\> \<character list\>
\<pixel element\>	::= \<PIXELS\> \<rectangle\> \<pixel list\>
\<attribute element\>	::= \<COLOUR TABLE\> \<index\> \<colour list\>|
	\<COLOUR SPECIFICATION\> \<colour spec\> |
	\<BACKGROUND INDEX\> \<index\> |
	\<LINEWIDTH\> \<value\> |
	\<LINETYPE\> \<line type\> |
	\<LINE COLOUR\> \<colour\> |
	\<POLYLINE BUNDLE INDEX\> \<index\> |
	\<POLYLINE ASPECT SOURCE FLAGS\>
	\<flags\> |
	\<MARKER TYPE\> \<marker type\> |
	.
	.
	.
\<control element\>	::= \<CLEAR VIEW SURFACE\> |
	\<REAL PRECISION\> \<real prec\>|
	\<INTEGER PRECISION\> \<integer prec\>|
	\<REAL COORDINATE PRECISION\>
	\<real coord prec\>|
	\<INTEGER COORDINATE PRECISION\>
	\<integer coord prec\>|
	\<ENUMERATED PRECISION\>
	\<enumerated prec\>|
	\<INDEX PRECISION\> \<index prec\>|
	\<COLOUR PRECISION\> \<colour prec\>|
	\<COLOUR INDEX PRECISION\>
	\<colour index prec\>|

Table 6.2 (continued)

	< VIRTUAL DC EXTENT > < rectangle > |
	< CLIP RECTANGLE > < rectangle > |
	< CLIP INDICATOR > < switch >
< escape element >	:: = < ESCAPE > < escape code > < value list >
< application element >	:: = APPLICATIONS DATA < identifier > < value list >
< message element >	:: = MESSAGE < character list >
.	.
.	.
.	.

control elements, and application data. The extent of the functional capabilities is coincident with the functions in the lowest GKS level L0a.

The metafile supports two colour models: the direct colour specification by Red-Green-Blue (RGB) values or indirect by an index pointing into a colour table containing RGB values. There are devices and applications for either one of the models. In the above list the PIXELS-primitive uses only the indirect specification via colour indices, whereas the colour of the other primitives can be specified either by index or by RGB. The selection is done once for a picture with the COLOUR SPECIFICATION element.

The ISO metafile will take the same approach with respect to clipping as the GKS metafile. Primitives can be stored unclipped, but the clipping rectangle is included along with the primitives in the metafile. Clipping can be turned on and off at any time between two primitives.

The basic productions of a formal grammar for graphics metafiles is given in Table 6.2.

In these productions, the main constructs of a basic metafile are included. The ISO metafile standard will contain, as a part of the standard, a formal definition. This adds to the conciseness of the standard document. Moreover, such a formal specification can give help for extending a definition, e.g., it is a difference whether segment information is included by a new right side of the < picture element >, of the < attribute element >, or of the < control element > production.

The ISO metafile standard will be the description of a basic device- and system-independent file for storage and transmission of pictures. An ISO Draft Proposal can be expected in 1983. However, for higher levels of metafiles, the areas of intersection with other standards (e.g., IGES, OSI [ISO82b]) will become larger, and thus, agreements will be more difficult to achieve.

6.5 Levels of Metafiles

The metafile to be processed by WG2 to create an international standard will, in the first step, include graphical functions only. On the other hand, there is a need for the integration of graphics metafiles and high-level, application-

LEVEL	CONTENTS
L3 application level	L2+ application oriented data (CAD design objects, their geometry and properties)
L2 definition mechanism	L1+ definition and referencing of subpictures, macros, and text fonts
L1 structured picture	L0+ picture segmentation: naming and transformation of subpictures
L0 picture	graphics primitives graphics attributes

Figure 6.1 Graphics metafile level-structure

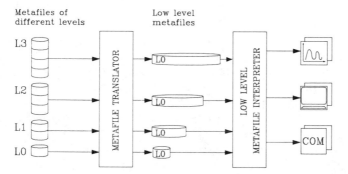

Figure 6.2 Extracting basic graphics information from higher level metafiles

dependent metafiles, grouped in upward compatible levels. At the highest level, application-dependent files like the IGES file could be based on graphical metafile formats for the graphics parts of their contents. One way of including higher levels of functionality without loosing the generality of a simple graphics metafile would be an explicit level-structure for metafiles, just as the level-structure defined for GKS (see Figure 6.1). While the lower three levels in Figure 6.1 are levels with growing graphical functionality, the top level is application-dependent, e.g., the CAD information contained in IGES. While only a CAD system can work on the data contained in the CAD level, an interpreter can be designed to extract the graphics information contained in metafile and to produce a base level metafile. The information contained in the base level metafile then can be displayed on any available graphics output device (see Figure 6.2).

7   CERTIFICATION/VALIDATION OF GKS

7.1   Introduction

Following the GKS definition process, a closely related activity was started in 1981: the certification of graphics systems. A special subgroup on certification was formed within ISO/TC97/SC5/WG 2 and the EEC decided to sponsor a number of workshops with the aim to develop a certification/validation scheme and to guide the GKS reviewing process in its final stages. It was recognized that a standard is largely worthless unless there is a procedure to test the conformity of implementations to it. Two major goals were identified: the more or less informal specification of GKS should be improved and eventually a formal specification of the GKS functions should be developed which could accompany the standard and help implementors of GKS systems with more precise definitions. A sub-subgroup concentrated on the topics of formal specification for graphics standards. Some of their results are contained in [EEC82d]. In this chapter we focus on the second goal, i.e., to test and ensure that an implementation of GKS adheres to the standard. We refer to results of formal specification research were appropriate.

From the very beginning, two approaches to the problem were identified and work was undertaken in both areas [EEC81a]. Those can be described as a verification approach using formal correctness proving methods, and a falsification approach which is based on a suite of test programs [BROD82].

7.1.1   Verifying GKS Implementations

Verification is the attempt to prove that an implementation is correct, i.e., that it conforms exactly to the standard. The problem of verification seems hard to solve in the area of computer software — especially if larger packages are involved. This is undoubtly the case with GKS which even in the smallest level covers quite a number of functions; also, since it is defined in a device-independent way, different implementations for different devices might look quite different. Verification might be done by taking a formal specification of GKS, and develop implementations from this specification by a series of program transformations. This is closely connected with program generation techniques [NORM81], [GNAT81]. In the Sections 7.4 and 7.5, we will handle these topics in more detail and show a promising certification concept. This covers both verification and falsification methods and seems to be feasible with reasonable efforts at short notice.

7.1.2   Falsification Approach

Especially in the area of graphics, no certification procedure will be acceptable without applying testing procedures. We will prove this statement later on.

Falsification is the attempt to prove that an implementation is incorrect. To that purpose, a set of test programs is applied and the results produced by the GKS implementation are compared against expected results. If the two sets of results are not "identical", the GKS implementation to be tested is assumed to be incorrect. Of course, this process yields no guarantee of correctness, but confidence is at least inspired in any implementation which survives the rigours of test procedures. However, several problems remain which we try to solve in this chapter:

— When are two sets of results "identical"? A picture description, e.g., for a storage tube will look quite different from that for a raster plotter.
— how can expected results (reference results) be obtained and how reliable with regard to correctness are they?
— how many test programs have to be applied and which features of GKS have to be tested until a "certificate of correctness" can be issued for a candidate implementation?

Leaving these issues to the next sections, the necessity of falsification testing should be emphasized.

— Formal verification of complete packages must be seen as a distant target — yet there is an immediate requirement for some means of validating implementations.
— Formal verification is based on a formal specification of GKS and on program generation techniques. There are and will be GKS implementations which are not derived from a common source and which are developed completely independent from any certification centre. Those will be available as "black boxes" only, not allowing any internal checking.
— There are graphics aspects which are not exactly specified by the GKS document but deliberately left free to the implementors' decisions. Examples are the appearance of attributes such as linetypes and of characters. Those can only be tested by looking at their visible appearance in pictorial form.
— Formal verification can only cover that part of the system which is above the device driver implementations. A GKS system however includes device drivers and even the device hardware. The correct functioning of the whole system can only be checked by test programs producing pictures and sequences of interactions.

7.2   A Model for Certification

A reference model of the test environment for GKS implementations is shown in Figure 7.1 [BROD81, PFAF81b]. Its main components can be identified as:

— A suite of test programs;
— The implementation under test, termed the candidate implementation;
— A reference implementation;
— A set of results, generated by applying the test suite to the reference implementation;

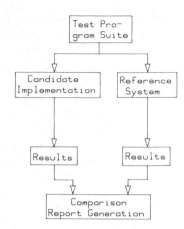

Figure 7.1 Model of testing

— A set of results, generated by applying the test suite to the candidate implementation;
— A tool for comparing the two sets of results and generating messages.

7.2.1   Test Programs

The deliberate design of a test program suite is the most important demand to succeed with certifying by testing. Test methods naturally lack the completeness of verification methods since testing of all the different combinations of functions, parameters, and configurations of GKS implementations would need huge sources of time and costs. To overcome this drawback, very carefully designed test cases have to be applied to a candidate. Following, there are some guidelines for the development of test programs, a more detailed list can be found in [MAGU81].

— Employ many test programs containing few tests (then errors can be easily detected);
— Identify potential implementation deficiencies and device tests to detect their presence;
— Design test programs to cover normal, extreme and erroneous cases;
— Ensure that the test suite covers the graphics standard;
— Check the order dependency of functions; e.g., the following calling sequence should produce three errors when started in the GKS operating state "workstation active":

CLOSE SEGMENT	error
CREATE SEGMENT (1)	
CREATE SEGMENT (2)	error
CLOSE SEGMENT	
CLOSE SEGMENT	error

Further important aspects when designing the test programs are:

— The test programs should be designed in a language-independent fashion (e.g., in a PASCAL-like notation). Then they can relatively easily be translated into several languages for particular implementation sites. This eases maintaining of the suite of test programs.

— To keep the test program suite small, test programs should be defined in a device-independent way as far as possible. If device-dependent features are to be tested (such as attributes), the test programs should adjust themselves by using inquire functions to the workstation description table.

— The test suite should be dynamically extensible. In order to be able to publish the test suite and to give implementors maximal benefit from the certification, and in order to integrate test programs developed by other sites into the test suite, there have to be means for extensibility. The test suite is adapted at some intervals; all programs have to be classified using a given scheme.

7.2.2   Candidate Implementations

Ideally, candidate implementations should be verified during their development from a GKS specification. Since this is not feasible in most cases such implementations will be provided more or less as "black boxes" allowing testing only at their interfaces. As shown in Section 7.5, we also expect implementors to describe their internal program steps — at least on a logical basis, and the elements of the interfaces their implementation is using.

Normally, a GKS implementation covers the whole graphics system between the GKS/application program interface and the graphics devices. As is explained in the next section, this alone is not suitable for a complete testing procedure. An automated testing has to be supported at a functional device interface that is just above the level of the device hardware functions. There we may distinguish between implementations tailored to specific devices and those being largely device-independent. In the first case, certification with respect to a particular set of devices is required, in the second case the correctness of the device-independent part should be checked, i.e, the ability to drive any customer-supplied device drivers.

Taking the GKS workstation concept into consideration, one recognizes that implementations of the second kind also drive devices: they control virtual (idealized) devices which are similar to the GKS metafile and segment storage workstations. The adaptation to real devices is done below in the device-dependent parts. Thus, the two kinds of implementations can be tested with the same means, comparing picture descriptions for a real device or a virtual device with a suitable reference picture description.

7.2.3   Reference Implementations

It must be inexpensive to compare reference results with results produced by a candidate implementation. That means, both sets of results should be on the same logical level, i.e., use the same language elements to describe a picture. Three ways of achieving this were identified:

— Reference results can be produced manually. The actual device (real or virtual) determines its interface elements which the candidate implementation uses. For simple cases, the expected output of a test program can be derived from the GKS definition.

— A reference implementation supporting a fixed set of devices may be developed. Test programs are applied to it and the resulting output is stored on a file. If a candidate supports the same set of devices its output can be directly compared, otherwise, it has to connect "transformers" which map the candidate's device-specific output to the logical level of the reference output.

— Using the candidate description, a reference implementation can be configured from a specification. This should automatically produce output on the same level, (i.e., uses the same picture description elements) as the candidate output. This is detailed in Section 7.5.

While the first two methods of producing reference output are rather inflexible and problems exist with how to prove their correctness, the third method allows to leave the candidate unchanged, to test exactly its output, and to prove the correctness of the reference output by formal verification methods.

7.3 Interfaces for Testing

This section will explore which features of a GKS implementation can be tested and to identify the interfaces at which testing can take place. As shown in Figure 7.2, three interfaces can be identified [EEC81b] at which results from the candidate and reference implementations can be compared.

7.3.1 Application Program Interface

This interface consists of all GKS functions defined in the standard. It is the appropriate point at which to verify the GKS 'set functions', inquiry functions, input functions and the error handling function. GKS provides well-defined data structures. These provide a detailed record of the current state of a GKS program. Many of the GKS functions are defined in terms of their effect on the state lists. In a first step, a test suite has been developed to check that those state lists are manipulated correctly. The test suite consists of several layers, the lowest one being a one-to-one correspondence to the GKS functions [EEC82a]. These functions either perform the GKS-defined effect or report possibly occurred errors. Thus, in any application program, the GKS function calls can be replaced by the corresponding test function calls without changing the effect of the application program.

The test functions are self-checking. Each one basically consists of the steps:

— the current states of GKS are inquired and stored in the test function,
— the GKS function is invoked,

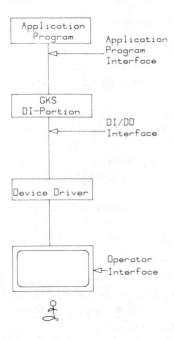

Figure 7.2 Testing interfaces

— the corresponding changes of the GKS states are calculated, the state lists stored in the test function are changed, and thus a set of expected results is generated,
— using specially designed test-inquiry functions, it is checked that the GKS states after the GKS function call are identical with the expected ones. That means, the GKS-defined state changes must have been performed and no other state changes must have occurred.

In higher layers, groups of GKS functions and specific features of GKS are tested with regard to their dependencies.

A similar approach is applied for checking the correct error behaviour. For every GKS function, the GKS system is driven into erroneous situations for that function. The function is called in each of these situations, and it is tested whether the expected errors have occurred and no non-expected errors are reported.

7.3.2 Operator Interface

This interface is on a pictorial level between graphics devices and an operator to check visual output and to input data into the system. There are features in GKS that can only be checked by human judgement such as the representation of characters and the echoing of operator actions, generally, the suitability of the visual representations. Furthermore, operator interface checking is the only way to ensure that the complete system works correctly (the device-independent and the device-dependent parts).

Pictorial testing is what manufacturers of GKS implementations will apply at first. A lot of test programs already exist for GKS and other graphics packages such as GSPC which serve as starting points. Concerning GKS and our test model, the problem is not the quantity of test programs. The art is in designing the tests to highlight the appearance of any errors in the picture or in the interaction sequence in order to help the human judgement.

7.3.3 Device Interface

To ease the testing of pictorial output and input, the checking of data passing to and from physical devices should be automated. An interface to devices has been identified just above the level of the pictorial form which still can be uniquely described and therefore be compared. On the other hand, it became clear very early that the elements of a particular interface cannot be lower (more atomic) than the capabilities of the specific device. As an example, if a device provides appropriate clipping hardware, then it should be served with unclipped coordinates in order to utilize its capabilities. Obviously then the correct clipping behaviour cannot be checked at the device interface; but it can be checked that suitable data for defining the clipping rectangle is passed to the driver.

From a GKS implementation's point of view, the device interface usually also separates the device-independent portion (which provides general software for missing device capabilities) from the device-dependent parts (i.e., the device drivers). In this sense, this chapter is related to Chapter 5 (Interfaces to Graphics Devices). Using the definitions of "device driver function set", "minimal device interfaces", and the "construction of device interfaces" given in Chapter 5, it is obvious that there are a number of device interfaces to actual devices, their functionality depending on the availability of driver functions.

As will be explained in more detail in Section 7.5, a GKS candidate implementation must identify the particular device interface(s) it is supporting. By determining the elements of an interface, also the syntax for the description of pictures for that device is fixed. Reference pictures using the same syntax can then be produced and comparison of the two be performed.

Regarding the three interfaces, it became clear that each one provides very specific suitability for testing purposes. Certain testing problems typically can be solved at a certain interface relatively easily and cause big problems at another interface, e.g., the appearance of a fill area hatch style displayed as strokes or as patterns can best be tested at the operator interface. On the other hand, if importance is laid on the correct computation of coordinates, on large number of picture sequences, or on large data sets to be handled, then the device interface should be used. The different kinds of testing should complement each other.

7.4 Certification by Program Construction

There is a strong relationship between software methodology and the formal specification of a system. Todays software development methodology centres around program specification systems. Starting from a very short and highly abstract specification, methods of "stepwise refinement" are applied. This is either done automatically (automated program generation) or by guided program transformations where a programmer decomposes higher program constructs into lower ones. The original abstract specification is in programming language-independent form. It does not contain algorithmic details.

At some stage of the refinement process, a real program is generated, e.g., such as a FORTRAN or PASCAL program. Applying different program transformations for variable environments (e.g., graphics devices), different end products will arise. This corresponds to the model of device-independent GKS definitions on the one hand, and device-dependent GKS implementations for the peculiarities of a given graphics environment on the other hand.

At some intermediate stage, the program transformation process reaches the final level which is still device-independent; in GKS, this is the functional interface to the device independent segment storage and the GKS metafile. Both workstations contain real pictures, but in a completely device-independent fashion. At this stage, there might already exist a real GKS program. This would accept the GKS functions and control GKS workstations all of which have the same capabilities (i.e., they are fully equipped workstations). However, such an implementation is rather useless, since it leaves the real programming work to external workstation drivers (the mapping of logical functions to physical device capabilities), and it does not contain anything really worth proving for correctness.

Taking the characteristics of actual graphics devices into consideration, the workstation-dependent part can be constructed by further program transformations in an either automated or manual configuring process. This is explained in the next section.

Obviously, there is a logical connection to the reference implementation mentioned in the sections before. For our model, a reference implementation would be quite useless that either implements one certain device-dependent case or that stops at the GKS workstation level (i.e., does not support any real device). We recognized this fact very early [PFAF81a] and proposed the approach of a "configurable reference implementation". This approach was refined in further discussions so that the following model resulted:

A suitable syntax for the specification of GKS is developed and an initial specification is undertaken. The terminal symbols of the grammar are atomic modules such as coordinate transformation, clipping, prompt/echo generation and transformation programs. Additionally, the dependencies of basic module invocations from specific device capabilities are available in form of tables. From this specification a real program can be derived by program transformations. This is able to drive a real device. Changing the device properties a new, different reference implementation is generated from the same specification chosing other parsing trees.

The initial reference specification only supports a common set of graphics devices. If a new device should be supported, or if an implementor finds solutions other than already contained in the specification this is extended in an implementor/certifier dialogue.

The certification problem now is split into two aspects:
— the specification has to be correct; this is a process of achieving agreement within a responsible authority;

— the generation of programs from the syntax must be proven for being correct. This is made easier by using simple known parsing techniques.

7.5 A Combined Model of Verification and Testing

The intention is to test a candidate GKS implementation, in part, by automatically comparing output from the candidate generated by a "certification workstation", with output from a reference implementation. What information should this output from the implementations, which is input to the comparator, contain? Two objectives in designing this certification data stream were selected [EEC82b]:

— The comparator must not change between varying candidate implementations. The criteria must be derived only from information contained in the GKS document.
— The comparator should be simple enough to warrant a high degree of confidence in its correctness.

Two immediate consequences of these objectives were:

— Both streams of comparator input must be at the same logical level. The comparator must not be asked, for example, to determine that a POLYLINE and its dissection into a set of lines are the same.
— The input streams must be compared item-by-item. These items will typically correspond to GKS functions. Each item in either stream must be self-contained; the comparator must not be expected to maintain a context of attribute values in which to interpret input items.

These consequences imply that the reference implementation must be configurable; capable of being adapted to mimic the behaviour of the candidate. Clearly, it is impossible to predict in advance all the adaptations which will need to be made. The certification process, however, is not to be viewed as static, in which the certification criteria are imposed and are unchanging. It is, rather, a dialogue between implementors and certifiers, with the implementors being aided by experience from the certification process and vice versa. It is only necessary to start the process by identifying the common adaptations and building a reference implementation capable of performing them. To perform testing based on this approach, three things are required:

— A format must be specified for the certification data stream which the comparator will accept; the comparator must be implemented.
— A format must be specified for the information that describes the candidate to the configurable reference implementation. This information will be supplied by the candidate and used by certifiers to adapt their reference implementation.
— A reference implementation must be constructed. A technique has been identified for doing so.

7.5.1 Format of Certification Data

A certification data stream has many similarities with a graphical metafile, such as that produced and interpreted by the GKS metafile workstation. However, the goals in designing a metafile and a certification data stream are diametrically opposed. A metafile must be as insensitive as possible to differences between implementations, because it will be used to transport information between them. The certification data stream, on the other hand, must be as sensitive as possible to differences between implementations; these are what it will be used to detect.

Input to the comparator must be capable of representing:

a) The GKS output and input primitives;
b) The device-oriented primitives, into which they may be decomposed;
c) The properties which are assigned to these primitives, in terms of coordinates, transformations, and attributes;
d) Potentially retro-active modifications of attributes.

In order for the items of comparator input to be self-contained, each primitive should carry with it all the properties it has been assigned. The outline design of the certification data may be expressed as a grammar, using BNF (Table 7.1):

Table 7.1 Grammar for describing certification data

\<picture\>	::= \<item\>*
\<item\>	::= \<start\> \<item name\> \<prop list\>
	\<item\>* \<end\>
\<item name\>	::= \<GKS primitive\>
	| \<device primitive\>
	| set attr
\<prop list\>	::= \<prop name\>* \<value\>
\<value\>	::= \<GKS data type\> \<data\>
\<prop name\>	::= \<GKS attr name\>
	| coords
	| transform
	| clip rect
	| pixel array
	| chars

Note, that it is not necessary to specify that the COORDS are in NDC or DC, nor that TRANSFORM maps, for example, from WC to NDC. This information is supplied from the candidate to the reference implementation and does not affect the comparison process. Note, also, that as is shown in a later example, this grammar can be used to express the state of a primitive at any stage in its progress from the GKS interface to the device.

7.5.2 Describing the Candidate Implementation

In order for the reference implementation to mimic the operations of the candidate implementation, it must operate on the same workstation description table. Although this ensures that the coordinate spaces will be the same, that the same amounts of resources will be used and that regenerations will occur at appropriate times, this is not sufficient. The particular set of operations and properties to be applied to the "device" by the candidate will be determined by the "device" capabilities. For example, if the "device" provides linetypes a LINETYPE property will be applied to it, but if it does not, the POLYLINE primitives will be dissected into sets of lines. Thus, the candidate must supply not only the workstation description table, but also information describing the capabilities of the "device" the workstation is driving. Some of the information required is shown in the example at the end of this section, other information needed was identified by classifying the dependencies flagged in the GKS document.

7.5.3 Reference Implementation

A technique for constructing a reference implementation was identified. In this, we basically distinguish between functions setting GKS states, output functions which — implemented as pipelines — eventually generate output items of a picture description, and input functions which perform interaction sequences in form of processes (see Chapter 2).

The implementation of every function is dependent on the particular characteristics of a graphics device, while the function's interface remains constant. For some capabilities of a common set of devices the different implementation possibilities are already identified. These served for the initial GKS specification. Restricting ourselves to the pipelines of output primitives, the following model was established:

A set of basic modules such as coordinate transformations, clipping and attribute emulation functions was identified. Each function is specified using basic modules such that it generates items of the syntax above. Thereby, a skeleton specification is written. Each choice of device capabilities is expressed as a conditional statement. The information from the candidate determines a path through these conditional statements, which in fact, is a specific pipeline of transformations. The implementation is configured by selecting and permuting these modules.

In each pipeline, the comparator format's generality is exploited by generating it at the GKS interface. Each step in the transformation and attribute binding pipeline reads the input from preceding stages, identifies the keywords in the stream with which this stage is concerned, alters them and passes the result on to the next stage. For example, one stage might be to apply the TRANSFORM to the COORDS, another might be to replace the POLYLINE INDEX attribute by LINETYPE, LINEWIDTH and COLOUR INDEX attributes.

Besides serving for the construction of the reference implementation, the specification also provides valuable guidance for implementors, if published.

Note, that to ensure confidence in the correctness of the reference implementation, it is important that the executable form of the implementation be as close as possible to the notation used to describe it. This is ensured if the

A Polyline Pipeline

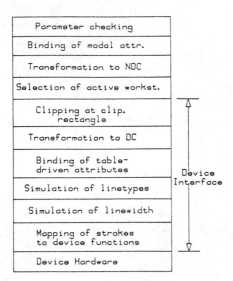

Figure 7.3 A polyline pipeline

program transformation steps to a real programming language are very few and simple. The reference implementation does not have to be in the same language as the candidate because its only use is to generate reference output for comparison.

The following pipeline as shown in Figure 7.3 describes the effect of the GKS output function POLYLINE. At the GKS interface, a picture item is generated containing the name of the item and all relevant attributes such as coordinates, transformations, clipping rectangle, etc. Each box applies a specific transformation to the elements of the item. For each box, the transformation applied and the changes to the item's data set are described. At every point of the pipeline stream, the actual item contents can be tested. Each capability of a specific candidate device represents such a point in the stream; when certain transformations are applied, others are not. A particular candidate device may, for example, take over a polyline with coordinates being in NDC and the polyline bundle index bound to it (P4). Another one might be controlled by polylines in DC and the linetype and colour index of the current polyline bundle bound to it (P10). A third one will take over the polyline after attribute simulation is performed (after P12).

7.6   GKS Certification in Practice

As the technical problems in certifying GKS become resolved, it is appropriate to consider how a certification scheme might operate in practice.

7.6.1   Test Centres

It is expected that for practical reasons, there will be a number of test centres situated at different locations throughout the world. It makes good sense, however, for one central authority to have the responsibility of monitoring the test software; copies of the software would be distributed to all the test centres. This should cause few problems if the test software is updated at intervals of say, one year. Certification of course, could be carried out by any of the centres.

7.6.2   Test Program Suite

The test program suite will have three main parts:
1. application interface tests
2. device interface tests
3. operator interface tests

according to the three interfaces that have been identified for checking. The suite ought to be regarded not as something fixed, but dynamic: it will be regularly updated to improve the thoroughness of its coverage. The suite will be configurable to GKS implementations of different capabilities, e.g., different GKS levels, different numbers of workstations supported.

Some reference implementation must be available that can be configured according to different candidate implementations.

The results of applying the test suite to the candidate are evaluated in different ways for the three types of tests. For application interface results, the test programs themselves can verify the results. For operator interface tests, the evaluation is done visually, by comparison against some reference hard-copy output. For device interface tests, the evaluation is performed automatically by a comparator program that compares data generated by the candidate and reference implementations.

7.6.3   Certification Procedure

The certification of a candidate GKS implementation might proceed in the following way:
— The implementor contacts the test centre to indicate that he wishes to have his implementation certified.
— The test centre sends the implementor a form, in which he enters full details of his implementation.
— This information enables the test centre to select (generate) an appropriate language version of the test suite and to configure both the test suite and the reference implementation appropriately.
— A set of reference results at the device interface is generated at the test centre, together with suitable pictorial output for checking of the operator interface.

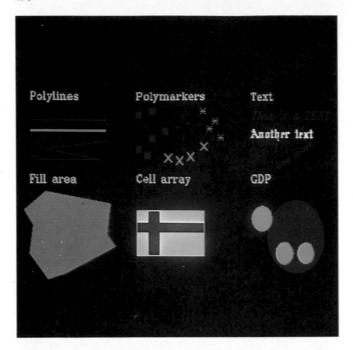

Figure C1 GKS primitives displayed on a colour raster workstation

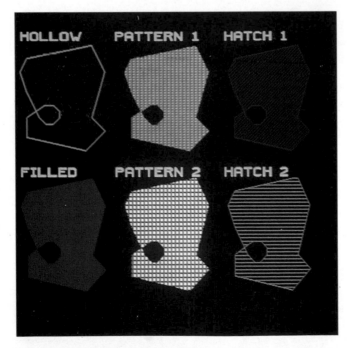

Figure C2 Examples for FILL AREA attributes on a colour raster workstation

Figure C3 Example for PIXEL ARRAY

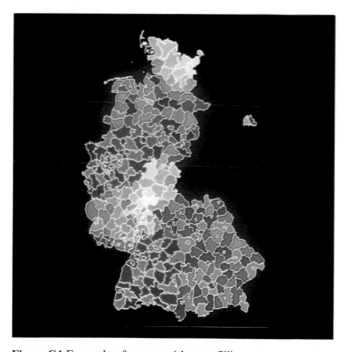

Figure C4 Example of a map with area filling

— When the implementor indicates he is ready for his implementation to be certified, a representative of the test centre visits the implementor and runs the test suite against the candidate implementation. Comparison of results is made, and a certificate is issued listing any errors detected.
— The implementor may ask to be re-tested at any time and in any case, a certificate would remain valid only for a certain length of time.

7.6.4 Assistance for an Implementor

The implementor may contact the test centre at an early stage in the development of his software. The reference specification, the configured test suite, reference results and comparator can then be made available to him and can be used to assist in the debugging of the implementation. A representative of the test centre would still be responsible for the actual test run for which a certificate is issued.

8 TERMINOLOGY

Human communication needs, in order to succeed, a common language. Naturally, in a new and fastly developing field like Computer Graphics, different groups will develop their own communication base. Many conflicts and misunderstandings in the course of GKS design and review were caused by the missing common language. Different terms were used for the same object, or different objects were given the same name by different people. This was true not only in the international field, where English is used as the main communication language, but also in various other languages. In order to avoid difficulties from designing GKS in two languages in parallel, DIN had decided in a very early stage to develop the GKS standard in English, and later translate the finished document into German.

When a task force was set up within TC97 to develop a standardized data processing vocabulary, one of the chapters of the anticipated standard was devoted to a computer graphics vocabulary. The working group ISO TC97/SC5/WG2 took part in this task and commented the first draft and recommended changes and additions. This process has been influenced to a great extent by the ongoing GKS review. Since, for reviewing GKS, a common terminology had to be used (in many cases, it evolved after considerable discussions), this terminology could serve as a basis for the graphics part of the data processing vocabulary. In 1982, Section 13 "Computer Graphics" of the ISO data processing vocabulary reached the state of a Draft International Standard (ISO DIS 2382/13, [ISO82a]). Appendix 2 of this book gives the terms and definitions from this standard.

Like every other ISO Draft Standard, the data processing vocabulary can only become an International Standard when an approved French Translation is available. Therefore the graphics terms and definitions of Section 13 of ISO DIS 2382 were translated into French. The presence of a French graphics vocabulary was a valuable help for the translation of the GKS document into French. GKS also can only become an International Standard after the French translation is finished. Within DIN, a graphics vocabulary was developed which was used as the basis for the German version of the GKS standard document. Appendix 2 lists the German terms together with the English and French ones. For many of the terms in French and German, no suitable words were available and new terms had to be coined.

The computer graphics vocabulary developed by ISO as an International Standard will contribute considerably to establishing an equal base for the communication between computer graphics experts. It will ease the education in computer graphics and it will facilitate international cooperation in this field.

9   3D EXTENSIONS TO GKS

About 90% of all computer graphics applications only need a two-dimensional (2D) system. This was one reason for designing GKS as a purely 2D graphics standard. The other reason was that it was considered to be easier to design a 2D system first, without the problems related to three dimensions (3D). But now, as the 2D GKS is an international standard, it seems that a straightforward extension of GKS to three dimensions is possible and desirable. Therefore, the ISO working group TC97/SC5/WG2 "Computer Graphics" decided that:
"ISO TC97/SC5/WG2 recommends that a 3D subgroup be established with the following terms of reference:
1. to prepare a document setting out the scope, purpose, goals and underlying model of a 3D graphics standard that is an extension to GKS;
2. to start the process of obtaining a work item and a sponsoring body and to prepare a document setting out an outline of the functionality of such a standard."

Meanwhile, the subgroup has started its work, the first issues concerning design decisions for a 3D extension have been generated. One of the most important aspects of a 3D extension of GKS is that of the viewing pipeline in 3D and its relation to the current 2D GKS viewing pipeline.
One possible solution is sketched in Figure 9.1. It stems from the following assumptions:
1. One complete viewing pipeline is present for 2D primitives to a 2D display surface (lower part) and another pipeline for 3D primitives to a 3D display

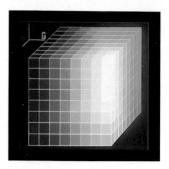

Figure C5 RGB colour model visualized by colour cube

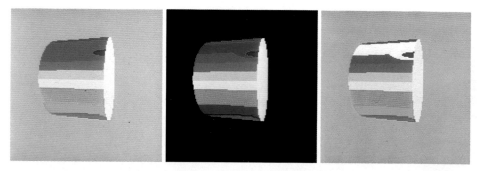

Figure C6 Effect of a change of the colour table on a raster image

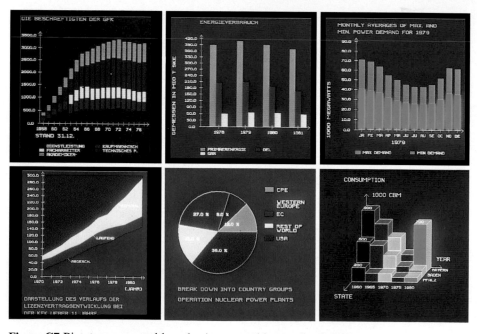

Figure C7 Pictures generated by a business graphics application layer

Figure C8 Picture generated by an application layer for mapping

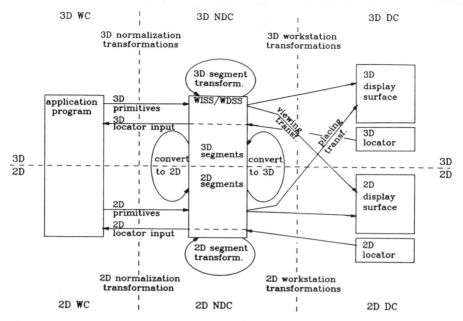

Figure 9.1 Transformations and viewing pipelines in a 3D GKS extension

surface. A 3D display surface belongs to a workstation that either has a
real 3D display capability, or it is a workstation that receives 3D device
coordinates and performs the viewing transformation to 2D locally under
local control by the workstation operator.

2. 3D primitives are a separate set of primitives. They are extensions of the
GKS 2D primitives to 3D.

3. 3D primitives use the 2D attributes where appropriate. Additional attributes
are only used where needed (e.g., 3D text attributes, more advanced area
attributes like colour as function of coordinate or colour interpolation between corner points).

4. Segments are either 2D-segments or 3D segments. Dimensionality is a static
segment attribute. If a 2D segment is open, only 2D primitives are allowed;
if a 3D segment is open, only 3D primitives are allowed. The WISS contains
2D and 3D segments. Also, the WDSS contains both 2D and 3D segments.
Segment transformations are either 2D (for 2D segments) or 3D (for 3D-
segments).

5. There exist a number of normalization transformations to map 2D WC
to 2D NDC for 2D primitives. This includes clipping at the 2D window.
There exist a number of normalization transformations to map 3D WC to
3D NDC for 3D primitives. In analogy to 2D this is done by mapping
a rectangular volume onto another rectangular volume. This includes clipping
at the 3D window.

6. There exists a workstation transformation that maps 2D NDC to a 2D
workstation display surface. This includes 2D workstation clipping. There

exists a workstation transformation that maps 2D NDC to a 3D workstation display surface. This can be done by adding a z-coordinate. There exists a workstation transformation that maps 3D NDC to a 3D workstation display surface. This includes 3D workstation clipping. There exists a workstation transformation that maps 3D NDC to a 2D workstation display surface. This is the transformation usually referred to as viewing transformation (3D→2D). It includes clipping at a view volume. The parameters of the viewing transformation can be taken from viewing models already existent in other 3D systems, e.g. in GSPC.

7. There are 2D locators and 3D locators. They may be present at 2D and 3D workstations. A 2D locator delivers as its input value 2D coordinates and a 2D transformation number. A 3D locator delivers as its input value 3D coordinates and a 3D transformation number.

8. There are two functions for taking a segment off the WISS, convert it from 2D to 3D or from 3D to 2D and putting it back into the WISS. It is not stated yet if it should replace the old segment in the WISS or if a new segment with a new name is to be created. The conversion from 3D NDC to 2D NDC is a viewing transformation, the conversion 2D to 3D could place the 2D segment in 3D space by means of a transformation matrix.

9. The list of functions contained in Table 9.1 could be a base for a 3D-extension of GKS. It was set up using as much analogy to the 2D functions as possible.

Table 9.1 Functions of a GKS 3D-extension

3D Output Functions
POLYLINE 3D
  defined by a sequence of 3D positions.
POLYMARKER 3D
  defined by a set of 3D positions.
TEXT 3D
  defined by a starting position and a text string. The text plane is defined in an additional attribute function.
FILL AREA 3D
  defined by a sequence of 3D positions. The polygon defined by them is filled according to the interior style of the referenced fill area bundle table entry. The FILL AREA 3D primitive is a planar area. The plane is derived from suitable points. All other points are projected onto the plane in the direction of the plane's normal. If all points lie on a straight line, the area degenerates to a straight 3D polyline.
CELL ARRAY 3D
  defined by a cell rectangle and a colour index array.
GENERALIZED DRAWING PRIMITIVE 3D (GDP 3D)
  used in analogy to the 2D GDP.

Table 9.1 (continued p.506)

Table 9.1 (continued)

Output Attributes 3D
  SET CHARACTER PLANE 3D
    used to define the plane and the character-up-vector for 3D text
  SET PATTERN 3D
    used for FILL AREA 3D primitives with interior style PATTERN, defines origin
    and orientation of the pattern.

Transformation Functions 3D
  SET WINDOW 3D
    defines the window volume of a 3D normalization transformation.
  SET VIEWPORT 3D
    defines the viewport volume of a 3D normalization transformation.
  SET VIEWPORT INPUT PRIORITY 3D
    defines the viewport input priority of a 3D normalization transformation.
  SELECT NORMALIZATION TRANSFORMATION 3D
    selects the normalization transformation for the 3D viewing pipeline.
  SET CLIPPING INDICATOR 3D
    switches clipping at the 3D view volume on or off.
  SET WORKSTATION WINDOW 3D
    defines the workstation window volume of the 3D workstation transformation for
    a 3D workstation.
  SET WORKSTATION VIEWPORT 3D
    defines the workstation viewport volume of the 3D workstation transformation for
    a 3D workstation.
  SET VIEWING TRANSFORMATION
    defines the viewing transformation (3D/2D workstation transformation) for a 2D
    workstation.
  SET PLACING TRANSFORMATION
    defines the workstation transformation parameters for displaying 2D primitives on
    3D workstations.

Segment Functions 3D
  CREATE SEGMENT 3D
    creates a 3D segment.
  SET SEGMENT TRANSFORMATION 3D
    sets the segment transformation for a 3D segment (in 3D NDC).
  CONVERT SEGMENT TO 2D
    converts a 3D segment to 2D by applying a given viewing transformation.
  CONVERT SEGMENT TO 3D
    converts a 2D segment to 3D by applying a given transformation.

3D Input Functions
  INITIALISE LOCATOR 3D
  SET LOCATOR MODE 3D
  REQUEST LOCATOR 3D
  SAMPLE LOCATOR 3D
  GET LOCATOR 3D
    above functions are used for logical 3D LOCATOR input devices.

Table 9.1 (continued)

INITIALISE STROKE 3D
SET STROKE MODE 3D
REQUEST STROKE 3D
SAMPLE STROKE 3D
GET STROKE 3D
    above functions are used for logical 3D STROKE input devices.

Inquiry functions
    A number of inquiry functions are needed in analogy to the 2D part of GKS.

Utility Functions 3D
    EVALUATE TRANSFORMATION MATRIX 3D
        used to create a transformation matrix for a 3D segment transformation from given
        transformation parameters.
    ACCUMULATE TRANSFORMATION MATRIX 3D
        used to create a transformation matrix for a 3D segment transformation from a
        given matrix and given transformation parameters.

Appendix 1
GKS METAFILE FORMAT

1.1 Status of the Metafile Definition

The specification of the format and content of a metafile is not part of GKS. However, as a metafile standard does not exist, in the following a specification of a metafile is given which can be used as an implementation guide for a metafile which satisfies all GKS requirements.

1.2 File Format and Data Format

The GKS metafile is built up as a sequence of logical data records. The file starts with a FILE HEADER in fixed format which describes the origin of the metafile (author, installation), the format of the following records, and the number representation. The file ends with an END record indicating the logical end of the file. In between these two records the following information is recorded in the sense of an audit trail: workstation control records and message records; output primitive records, describing elementary graphics objects; attribute information, including output primitive attributes, segment attributes, and workstation attributes; segment records, describing the segment structure and dynamic segment manipulations; user records. The overall structure of the GKS metafile is shown in Figure 1.1.

All data records except the file header have a record header containing: the character string 'GKSM' (optional) which has been introduced to improve legibility of the file and to provide an error control facility; the item type identification number which indicates the kind of information that is contained

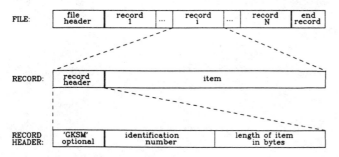

Figure 1.1 GKS metafile structure

in the record; the length of the item. The length of each of these subfields of the record header may be implementation dependent and is specified in the file header. The content of the item is fully described below for each item type.

The metafile contains characters, integer numbers, and real numbers marked (c), (i), (r) in the record description. Characters in the metafile will be represented according to ISO 646 and ISO 2022. Numbers will be represented according to ISO 6093 using format F1 for integers and format F2 for reals. (Remark: Formats F1 and F2 can be written and read via FORTRAN formats I and F respectively.)

Real numbers describing coordinates and length units will be stored as normalized device coordinates. The workstation transformation, if specified in the application program for the GKSM-OUT workstation will not be performed but WORKSTATION WINDOW and WORKSTATION VIEWPORT will be stored in data records for later usage. Real numbers may be stored as integers. In this case, transformation parameters are specified in the file header to allow proper transformation of integers into normalized device coordinates.

For reasons of economy, numbers can be stored using an internal binary format. As no standard exists for binary number representation, this format will limit the portability of the metafile. The specification of such a binary number representation is outside the scope of this document.

When exchanging metafiles between different installations, the physical structure of data sets on specific storage media should be standardized. Such a definition is outside the scope of this standard. However, as an appropriate standard is missing, the following specifications are recommended:

Metafiles should be exchanged using unlabelled 9-track 1600 bpi tapes. Data should be stored in fixed blocks with length 960 bytes, each block composed of 12 physical records of 80 bytes, each byte containing 8 bits.

1.3 Generation and Interpretation of Metafile

The generation and interpretation of metafiles is described in Chapter III.11 of this book.

1.4 Control Items

FILE HEADER | GKSM | N | D | V | H | T | L | I | R | F | RI | ZERO | ONE |

All fields in the file header record have fixed length. Numbers are formatted according to ISO 6093 Format F1.

General Information:

GKSM	4 bytes	containing string 'GKSM'
N	40 bytes	containing name of author/installation
D	8 bytes	date (year/month/day, eg., 83/03/13)
V	2 bytes	version number: the metafile described here has version number 1

Specification of Field Length

H	2 bytes	integer specifying how many bytes of the string 'GKSM' are used in the record header. Possible values: 0, 1, 2, 3, 4.
T	2 bytes	length of item type indicator field
L	2 bytes	length of item length indicator field
I	2 bytes	length of field for each integer in the item (applies to all data marked (i) in the record description)
R	2 bytes	length of field for each real in the item (applies to all data marked (r) in the record description)

Specification of Number Representation:

F	2 bytes	Possible values: 1, 2. This applies to all data in the items marked (i) or (r) and to item type and item length: 1: all numbers are formatted according to ISO 6093 2: all numbers (except in the file header) are stored in an internal binary format
RI	2 bytes	Possible values: 1, 2. This is the number representation for data marked (r): 1 = real, 2 = integer
ZERO	11 bytes	integer equivalent to 0., if $RI = 2$
ONE	11 bytes	integer equivalent to 1., if $RI = 2$

After the file header, which is in fixed format, all values in the following records are in the format defined by file header. For the following description, the setting:

$$H = 4; \ T = 3; \ F = 1$$

is assumed. In addition to formats (c), (i) and (r), which are already described, (p) denotes a point represented by a pair of real numbers (2r). The notation allows the single letter to be preceded by an expression, indicating the number of values of that type.

END ITEM | 'GKSM   0' | L |

Last item of every GKS Metafile

CLEAR WORKSTATION | 'GKSM   1' | L | C |

Requests clearing of all active workstations
C(i):   clearing control flag (0 = CONDITIONAL, 1 = ALWAYS)

REDRAW ALL SEGMENTS ON WORKSTATION

                                      | 'GKSM   2' | L |

Requests redrawing of all segments

UPDATE WORKSTATION | 'GKSM   3' | L | R |

Requests update
R(i):   regeneration flag (0 = PERFORM, 1 = SUSPEND)

SET DEFERRAL STATE | 'GKSM 4' | L | D | R |

Requests setting of deferral state
D(i): deferral mode (0 = ASTI, 1 = BNIG, 2 = BNIL, 3 = ASTI)
R(i): implicit regeneration mode (0 = ALLOWED, 1 = SUPPRESSED)

MESSAGE | 'GKSM 5' | L | N | T |

N(i): number of characters in string
T(Nc): string with N characters

ESCAPE | 'GKSM 6' | L | FI | L | M | I | R |

FI(i): escape function identifier
L(i): length of integer data in data record
M(i): length of real data in data record
I(Li): integer data
R(Mr): real data

1.5 Items for Output Primitives

POLYLINE | 'GKSM 11' | L | N | P |

N(i): number of points of the polyline
P(Np): list of points

POLYMARKER | 'GKSM 12' | L | N | P |

N(i): number of points
P(Np): list of points

TEXT | 'GKSM 13' | L | P | N | T |

P(p): starting point of character string
N(i): number of characters in string
T(Nc): string with N characters from the set of ISO 646

FILL AREA | 'GKSM 14' | L | N | P |

N(i): number of points
P(Np): list of points

CELL ARRAY | 'GKSM 15' | L | P | Q | R | N | M | CT |

P(p),Q(p),R(p): coordinates of corner points of cell array
N(i): number of rows in array
M(i): number of columns in array
CT(MNi): array of colour indices stored row by row

GENERALIZED DRAWING PRIMITIVE

| 'GKSM 16' | L | GI | N | P | L | M | I | R |

GI(i):   GDP identifier
N(i):   number of points
P(Np):   list of points
L(i):   length of integer data in data record
M(i):   length of real data in data record
I(Li):   integer data
R(Mr):   real data

1.6   Items for Output Primitive Attributes

POLYLINE INDEX

| 'GKSM 21' | L | M |

M(i):   polyline index

LINETYPE

| 'GKSM 22' | L | T |

T(i):   linetype

LINEWIDTH SCALE FACTOR

| 'GKSM 23' | L | S |

S(r):   linewidth scale factor

POLYLINE COLOUR INDEX

| 'GKSM 24' | L | I |

I(i):   polyline colour index

POLYMARKER INDEX

| 'GKSM 25' | L | M |

M(i):   polymarker index

MARKER TYPE

| 'GKSM 26' | L | T |

T(i):   marker type

MARKER SIZE SCALE FACTOR

| 'GKSM 27' | L | S |

S(r):   marker size scale factor

POLYMARKER COLOUR INDEX

| 'GKSM 28' | L | C |

C(i):   polymarker colour index

TEXT INDEX | 'GKSM 29' | L | I |

I(i):   text index

TEXT FONT AND PRECISION | 'GKSM 30' | L | TF | TP |

TF(i):   text font
TP(i):   text precision (0=STRING, 1=CHAR, 2=STROKE)

CHARACTER EXPANSION FACTOR

| 'GKSM 31' | L | E |

E(r):   character expansion factor

CHARACTER SPACING | 'GKSM 32' | L | S |

S(r):   character spacing

TEXT COLOUR INDEX | 'GKSM 33' | L | C |

C(i):   text colour index

CHARACTER VECTORS | 'GKSM 34' | L | CH | CW |

CH(2r):   character height vector
CW(2r):   character width vector

TEXT PATH | 'GKSM 35' | L | P |

P(i):   text path (0=RIGHT, 1=LEFT, 2=UP, 3=DOWN)

TEXT ALIGNMENT | 'GKSM 36' | L | HA | VA |

HA(i):   horizontal alignment (0=NORMAL, 1=LEFT, 2=CENTRE,
                   3=RIGHT)
VA(i):   vertical alignment (0=NORMAL, 1=TOP, 2=CAP, 3=HALF,
                   4=BASE, 5=BOTTOM)

FILL AREA INDEX | 'GKSM 37' | L | M |

M(i):   fill area index

FILL INTERIOR STYLE | 'GKSM 38' | L | S |

S(i):   fill area interior style (0=HOLLOW, 1=SOLID, 2=PATTERN,
                   3=HATCH)

FILL AREA STYLE INDEX | 'GKSM 39' | L | N |

N(i):   fill area style index

FILL AREA COLOUR INDEX | 'GKSM 40' | L | C |

C(i):   fill area colour index

PATTERN SIZE | 'GKSM 41' | L | PW | PH |

PW(2r):   pattern width vector
PH(2r):   pattern up vector

PATTERN REFERENCE POINT | 'GKSM 42' | L | P |

P(p) reference point

ASPECT SOURCE FLAGS | 'GKSM 43' | L | F |

F(13i):   aspect source flags (0 = BUNDLED, 1 = INDIVIDUAL)

PICK IDENTIFIER | 'GKSM 44' | L | P |

P(i):   pick identifier

1.7 Items for Workstation Attributes

POLYLINE REPRESENTATION | 'GKSM 51' | L | I | LT | LW | CI |

I(i):   polyline index
LT(i):   linetype number
LW(r):   linewidth scale factor
CI(i):   colour index

POLYMARKER REPRESENTATION

| 'GKSM 52' | L | I | MT | MF | CI |

I(i):   polymarker index
MT(i):   marker type
MF(r):   marker size scale factor
CI(i):   colour index

TEXT REPRESENTATION | 'GKSM 53' | L | I | F | P | E | S | CI |

I(i):   text index
F(i):   text font
P(i):   text precision (0 = STRING, 1 = CHAR, 2 = STROKE)
E(r):   character expansion factor
S(r):   character spacing
CI(i):   text colour colour index

FILL AREA REPRESENTATION | 'GKSM 54' | L | I | S | SI | CI |

I(i):   fill area index
S(i):   interior style (0 = HOLLOW, 1 = SOLID, 2 = PATTERN, 3 = HATCH)
SI(i):   style index
CI(i):   colour index

PATTERN REPRESENTATION | 'GKSM 55' | L | I | N | M | CT |

I(i):   pattern index
N(i):   number of columns in array
M(i):   number of rows in array
CT(MNi):   table of colour indices stored row by row

COLOUR REPRESENTATION | 'GKSM 56' | L | CI | RGB |

CI(i):   colour index
RGB(3r):   red/green/blue intensities:

1.8   Item for Clipping Rectangle

CLIPPING RECTANGLE | 'GKSM 61' | L | C |

C(4r):   clipping rectangle XMIN, XMAX, YMIN, YMAX

1.9   Items for Workstation Transformation

WORKSTATION WINDOW | 'GKSM 71' | L | W |

W(4r):   limits of workstation window (XMIN, XMAX, YMIN, YMAX)

WORKSTATION VIEWPORT | 'GKSM 72' | L | V |

V(4r):   limits of workstation viewport (XMIN, XMAX, YMIN, YMAX)

1.10   Items for Segment Manipulation

CREATE SEGMENT | 'GKSM 81' | L | S |

S(i):   segment name

CLOSE SEGMENT | 'GKSM 82' | L |

Indicates end of segment

RENAME SEGMENT | 'GKSM 83' | L | SO | SN |

SO(i):   old segment name
SN(i):   new segment name

DELETE SEGMENT | 'GKSM 84' | L | S |

S(i):   segment name

1.11   Items for Segment Attributes

SET SEGMENT TRANSFORMATION

| 'GKSM 91' | L | S | M |

S(i):   segment name
M(6r):   transformation matrix M11,M21,M31,M21,M22,M23,M31,M32,M33

SET VISIBILITY | 'GKSM 92' | L | S | V |

S(i):   segment name
V(i):   visibility (0 = INVISIBLE, 1 = VISIBLE)

SET HIGHLIGHTING | 'GKSM 93' | L | S | H |

S(i):   segment name
H(i):   highlighting (0 = NORMAL, 1 = HIGHLIGHTED)

SET SEGMENT PRIORITY | 'GKSM 94' | L | S | P |

S(i):   segment name
P(r):   segment priority

SET DETECTABILITY | 'GKSM 95' | L | S | D |

S(i):   segment name
D(i):   detectability (0 = UNDETECTABLE, 1 = DETECTABLE)

1.12   User Items

USER ITEM | 'GKSMXXX' | L | D |

XXX > 100
D: user data (L bytes)

Appendix 2
VOCABULARY

This appendix contains the computer graphics terms from ISO/DIS 2382/13. For every concept, the English term, the French term, and the German term are given. The English definition of the concept is added. The entries are arranged in alphabetical sequence of the English terms.

English	French	German
ABSOLUTE COMMAND ABSOLUTE INSTRUCTION	COMMANDE ABSOLUE	ABSOLUTER BEFEHL

A display command that causes the display device to interpret the data following the command as absolute coordinates.

| ABSOLUTE COORDINATE | COORDONNEE ABSOLUE | ABSOLUTE KOORDI-
NATE |

One of the coordinates that identify tne position of an addressable point with respect to the origin of a specified coordinate system.

| ABSOLUTE VECTOR | VECTEUR ABSOLU | ABSOLUTER VEKTOR |

A vector whose start and end points are specified in absolute coordinates.

| ADDRESSABILITY
in Computer Graphics | CAPACITE D'ADRESSAGE | ADRESSBEREICH |

The number of addressable points in each axis of a specified device space.

| ADDRESSABLE POINT | POSITION ADRESSABLE | ADRESSIERBARER
PUNKT |

Any point of a device that can be addressed.

| AIMING SYMBOL
AIMING CIRCLE
AIMING FIELD | CHAMP DE VISEE | ZIELSYMBOL
ZIELKREIS
PICKBEREICH |

On a display surface, a circle or other pattern of light used to indicate the area in which the presence of a light pen can be detected at a given time.

English	French	German

BACKGROUND IMAGE
  STATIC IMAGE

FOND D'IMAGE
  ARRIERE PLAN D'IMAGE

HINTERGRUNDBILD
  STATISCHES BILD

That part of a display image, such as a form overlay, that is not changed during a particular sequence of transactions.

BLANKING

EXTINCTION

UNSICHTBAR MACHEN

The suppression of the display of one or more display elements or segments.

BLINKING

CLIGNOTEMENT

BLINKEN

An intentional periodic change in the intensity of one or more display elements or segments.

CALLIGRAPHIC
  DISPLAY DEVICE
  DIRECTED BEAM
  DISPLAY DEVICE

VISU A BALAYAGE
  CAVALIER

LINIENGRAPHIKGERÄT
  KALLIGRAPHISCHES
  GERÄT

A display device in which the display elements of a display image may be generated in any program-controlled sequence.

CHARACTER GENERATOR

GENERATEUR DE
  CARACTERES

ZEICHENGENERATOR

A functional unit that converts the coded representation of a character into the graphic representation of the character for display.

CLIPPING

DETOURAGE, DECOUPAGE

KLIPPEN

Removing those parts of display elements that lie outside a given boundary.

CODED IMAGE

IMAGE CODEE

KODIERTES BILD

A representation of a display image in a form suitable for storage and processing.

CHOICE DEVICE

SELECTEUR

AUSWÄHLER

An input device providing one value from a set of alternatives.

COMPUTER GRAPHICS

INFOGRAPHIE

COMPUTERGRAPHIK
  GRAPHISCHE DATEN-
  VERARBEITUNG

Methods and techniques for converting data to or from a graphical display via computers.

English	French	German

CONTROL BALL   BOULE ROULANTE   ROLLKUGEL
  TRACK BALL

A ball, rotatable about its center that is used as an input device, normally as a locator.

COORDINATE GRAPHICS   INFOGRAPHIE AU TRAIT   KOORDINATEN-
  LINE GRAPHICS   GRAPHIK
                                                   LINIENGRAPHIK

Computer graphics in which display images are generated from display commands and coordinate data.

CURSOR   CURSEUR   SCHREIBMARKE
                                                   POSITIONSMARKE

A movable, visible mark used to indicate the position on which the next operation will occur on a display surface.

CURVE GENERATOR   GENERATEUR DE COURBES   KURVENGENERATOR

A functional unit that converts a coded representation of a curve into the graphic representation of the curve for display.

DETECTABLE SEGMENT   SEGMENT DETECTABLE   PICKBARES SEGMENT

A segment that can be detected by a pick device.

DEVICE COORDINATE   COORDONNEE D'APPAREIL   GERÄTEKOORDINATE

A coordinate specified in a coordinate system that is device dependent.

DEVICE SPACE   ESPACE ECRAN   GERÄTE-
                                                   KOORDINATENRAUM

The space defined by the complete set of addressable points of a display device.

DISPLAY   AFFICHAGE   DARSTELLUNG

A visual presentation of data.

DISPLAY COMMAND   COMMANDE D'AFFICHAGE   DARSTELLUNGS-
  DISPLAY INSTRUCTION   BEFEHL

A command that controls the state or action of a display device.

English	French	German

DISPLAY CONSOLE · VISU, VISUEL CONSOLE DE VISUALISATION · GRAPHISCHER ARBEITSPLATZ

A console that includes at least one display surface and may also include one or more input devices.

DISPLAY ELEMENT GRAPHIC PRIMITIVE OUTPUT PRIMITIVE · ELEMENT GRAPHIQUE PRIMITIVE GRAPHIQUE · GRAPHISCHES GRUNDELEMENT DARSTELLUNGS-ELEMENT

A basic graphic element that can be used to construct a display image.

DISPLAY IMAGE · IMAGE · GRAPHISCHE DAR-STELLUNG BILD

A collection of display elements or segments that are represented together at any one time on a display surface.

DISPLAY SPACE OPERATING SPACE · ESPACE D'AFFICHAGE · BILDBEREICH DARSTELLUNGS-BEREICH

That portion of the device space corresponding to the area available for displaying images.

DISPLAY SURFACE · SURFACE D'AFFICHAGE SURFACE DE VISUALI-SATION · DARSTELLUNGS-FLÄCHE SICHTFLÄCHE

In a display device, that medium on which display images may appear.

DOT MATRIX CHARACTER GENERATOR · GENERATEUR DE CARACTERES PAR POINTS · RASTER-ZEICHEN-GENERATOR

A character generator that generates character images composed of dots.

DRAGGING · ENTRAINEMENT D'IMAGE · NACHZIEHEN

Moving one or more segments on a display surface by translating it along a path determined by a locator.

DRUM PLOTTER · TRACEUR A ROULEAU · TROMMELPLOTTER

A plotter that draws a display image on a display surface mounted on a rotating drum.

English	French	German

ECHO   ECHO   ECHO

The immediate notification of the current values provided by an input device to the operator at the display console.

ELECTROSTATIC PLOTTER   TRACEUR ELECTRO-   ELEKTROSTATISCHER
                          STATIQUE   PLOTTER

A raster plotter that uses a row of electrodes to fix the inks electrostatically on the paper.

FLATBED PLOTTER   TABLE TRACANTE   TISCHPLOTTER
                          TABLE A TRACER   ZEICHENTISCH

A plotter that draws a display image on a display surface mounted on a flat surface.

FLICKER   PAPILLOTEMENT   FLICKERN

An undesirable pulsation of a display image on a cathode ray tube.

FOREGROUND IMAGE   PREMIER PLAN D'IMAGE   VORDERGRUNDBILD
DYNAMIC IMAGE   DYNAMISCHES BILD

That part of a display image that can be changed for every transaction.

FORM FLASH   AFFICHAGE DE GRILLE   FORMULAREINBLEN-
                                                   DUNG

The display of a form overlay.

FORM OVERLAY   GRILLE DE SAISIE   FORMULAR

A pattern such as a report form, grid or map used as a background image.

HIDDEN LINE   LIGNE CACHEE   VERDECKTE KANTE

A line segment that represents an edge obscured from view in a two-dimensional projection of a three-dimensional object.

HIGHLIGHTING   MISE EN EVIDENCE   HERVORHEBEN

Emphasizing a display element or segment by modifying its visual attributes.

IMAGE REGENERATION   REGENERATION D'IMAGE   BILDWIEDERHOLUNG

The sequence of events needed to generate a display image from its representation in storage.

INCREMENTAL   COORDONNEE RELATIF   INKREMENTELLE
COORDINATE   KOORDINATE

A relative coordinate where the previously addressed point is the reference point.

INCREMENTAL VECTOR   VECTEUR RELATIF   RELATIVER VEKTOR

A vector whose end point is specified as a displacement form its start point.

English	French	German

INCREMENT SIZE   PAS, INCREMENT   INKREMENT

The distance between adjacent addressable points on the display surface.

INKING   TRACE   SPUR ZEICHNEN

Creating a line by moving a locator over the display surface leaving a trail behind the locator in the manner of a pen drawing a line on paper.

INPUT PRIMITIVE   PRIMITIVE D'ENTREE   EINGABEELEMENT

An item of data obtained from an input device such as a keyboard, choice device, locator, pick device, stroke device, or valuator.

JOY STICK   MANCHE A BALAI   STEUERKNÜPPEL

A lever with at least two degrees of freedom that is used as an input device, normally as a locator.

LIGHT PEN   PHOTOSTYLE   LICHTGRIFFEL

A light-sensitive pick device that is used by pointing it at the display surface.

LIGHT PEN DETECTION   DETECTION PAR   LICHTGRIFFEL-
  LIGHT PEN HIT   PHOTOSTYLE   DETEKTION

The sensing by a light pen of light generated by a display element on a display surface.

LOCATOR   RELEVEUR DE   LOKALISIERER
          COORDONNEES

An input device providing coordinates of a position.

MARKER in Computer Graphics   MARQUE   MARKE

A glyph with a specified appearance which is used to indicate a particular location.

MIRRORING   REFLEXION   SPIEGELN

Reflection of display elements about a line or plane.

MOUSE   SOURIS   MAUS

A hand held locator operated by moving it on a surface.

NORMALIZED DEVICE   COORDONNEE ECRAN   NORMALISIERTE
  COORDINATE   NORMEE   GERÄTEKOORDINATE

A coordinate specified in a device-independent intermediate coordinate system normalized to some range, typically 0 to 1.

PANNING   PANORAMIQUE   SCHWENKEN

Progressively translating the entire display image to give the visual impression of lateral movement of the image.

English	French	German

PICK DEVICE DISPOSITIF DE DESIGNATION PICKER

An input device used to specify a particular display element or segment.

PIXEL PIXEL PIXEL
  PICTURE ELEMENT   BILDELEMENT

The smallest element of a display surface that can be independently assigned a colour or intensity.

PLASMA PANEL ECRAN A PLASMA PLASMABILDSCHIRM
  GAS PANEL

A part of a display device that consists of a grid of electrodes in a flat, gas-filled panel.

PLOTTER STEP SIZE PAS (DE TRACEUR) PLOTTER-
      SCHRITTWEITE

The increment size on a plotter.

PLOTTING HEAD TETE TRACANTE ZEICHENKOPF

That part of a plotter used to create marks on a display device.

RASTER DISPLAY DEVICE VISU A POINTILLAGE RASTERGERÄT

A display device in which display images are generated on the display surface by raster graphics.

RASTER GRAPHICS INFOGRAPHIE PAR IMAGE RASTERGRAPHIK

Computer graphics in which display images are composed of an array of pixels arranged in rows and columns.

RASTER PLOTTER TRACEUR PAR LIGNE RASTERPLOTTER

A plotter that generates a display image on a display surface using a line-by-line scanning technique.

RASTER UNIT UNITE DE TRAME RASTEREINHEIT

The unit of measure determined by the distance between adjacent pixels.

REFRESH RAFRAICHISSEMENT BILDWIEDERHOLUNG

The process of repeatedly producing a display image on a display surface so that the image remains visible.

REFRESH RATE FREQUENCE DE BILDWIEDERHOL-
    REFRAICHISSEMENT FREQUENZ

The number of times per second at which a display image is produced for refresh.

RELATIVE COMMAND COMMANDE RELATIVE RELATIVER BEFEHL
  RELATIVE INSTRUCTION

A display command that causes the display device to interpret the data following the command as relative coordinates.

English	French	German
RELATIVE COORDINATE	COORDONNEE RELATIVE	RELATIVE KOORDINATE

One of the coordinates that identify the position of an addressable point with respect to some other addressable point.

ROLLING	DEFILEMENT VERTICAL	ROLLEN

Scrolling restricted to an upward or downward direction.

ROTATION	ROTATION	DREHUNG

Turning display elements about an axis.

RUBBER-BAND	TRACE ELASTIQUE	GUMMIBAND

An method of echoing a locator position by moving the common ends of a set of straight lines while the other ends remain fixed.

SCALING	CHANGEMENT D'ECHELLE	SKALIERUNG

The application of a multiplicative factor to one or more display elements.

SCROLLING	DEFILEMENT	BLÄTTERN

Moving a window vertically or horizontally in such a manner that new data appear within the viewport as the old data disappears.

SEGMENT in Computer Graphics	SEGMENT	SEGMENT

A collection of display elements that can be manipulated as a whole.

SHIELDING REVERSE CLIPPING	MASQUAGE	AUSBLENDEN

Suppression of all or parts of display elements falling within a a specified region.

SOFT COPY	IMAGE-VIDEO IMAGE SUR ECRAN	BILDSCHIRM-DARSTELLUNG

A nonpermanent display image.

STORAGE TUBE	TUBE A MEMOIRE	SPEICHERSCHIRM

A type of cathode ray tube that retains a display image without requiring refresh.

STROKE CHARACTER GENERATOR	GENERATEUR DE CARACTERES PAR TRAITS	LINIEN-ZEICHEN-GENERATOR

A character generator that generates character images composed of line segments.

STROKE DEVICE	LECTEUR DE COURBES	LINIENGEBER

An input device providing a set of coordinates that records the path of the device.

English	French	German
TABLET	TABLETTE	TABLETT

A special flat surface with a mechanism for indicating positions thereon, normally used as a locator.

THUMB WHEEL	MOLETTE	DAUMENRAD

A wheel, rotatable about its axis, that provides a scalar value.

TO DISPLAY	AFFICHER	DARSTELLEN
	VISUALISER	

To represent data visually.

TRACKING	POURSUITE	VERFOLGUNG

Moving a tracking symbol.

TRACKING SYMBOL	SYMBOLE DE POURSUITE	VERFOLGUNGSSYMBOL

A symbol on the display surface that indicates the position corresponding to the coordinate data produced by the locator.

TRANSLATION	TRANSLATION	VERSCHIEBUNG

The application of a constant displacement to the position of one or more display elements.

TUMBLING	CULBUTE	TAUMELN

Dynamic display of the rotation of display elements about an axis the orientation of which is continuously changing in space.

USER COORDINATE	COORDONNEE	ANWENDER-
	D'UTILISATEUR	KOORDINATE

A coordinate specified by a user and expressed in a coordinate system that is device independent.

VALUATOR	VALUATEUR	WERTGEBER

An input device providing a scalar value.

VECTOR GENERATOR	GENERATEUR DE VECTEURS	VEKTORGENERATOR

A functional unit that generates directed line segments.

VIEWPORT	CLOTURE	DARSTELLUNGSFELD

A predefined part of a display space.

VIRTUAL PUSH BUTTON	ELEMENT DE MENU	MENÜELEMENT
LIGHT BUTTON	TOUCHE VIRTUELLE	

Display elements used to simulate a function key by means of a pick device.

VIRTUAL SPACE	ESPACE VIRTUEL	VIRTUELLER
in Computer Graphics		KOORDINATENRAUM

A space in which the coordinates of the display elements are expressed in a device-independent manner.

English	French	German

WINDOW   FENETRE   FENSTER

A predefined part of a virtual space.

WINDOW/VIEWPORT   TRANSFORMATION   NORMALISIERUNGS-
  TRANSFORMATION   FENETRE CLOTURE   TRANSFORMATION
  NORMALIZATION   TRANSFORMATION DE
  TRANSFORMATION   NORMATION

A transformation that maps the boundary and contents of a window into the boundary and interior
of a viewport.

WIRE FRAME   REPRESENTATION FIL   DRAHTRAHMEN-
  REPRESENTATION   DE FER   DARSTELLUNG
                                                                 DRAHTMODELL

A mode of display showing all edges of a three-dimensional object without distinguishing hidden
lines.

WORLD COORDINATE   COORDONNEE UNIVERSELLE WELTKOORDINATE

A device independent cartesian coordinate used by the application program for specifying graphical
input and output.

WRAPAROUND   BOUCLAGE   UMLAUF

The display at some point on the display surface of the display elements whose coordinates normally
lie outside of the display space.

ZOOMING   VARIATION DE FOCALE   ZOOMEN
                                  EFFET DE LOUPE

Progressively scaling the entire display image to give the visual impression of movement of one or
more segments toward or away from an observer.

REFERENCES

[ANSI81]   American National Standards Institute:
             Engineering Drawing and Related Documentation Practices — Digital
             Representation for Communication of Product Definition Data (IGES).
             American National Standard ANS Y14.26M (1981).

[ANSI82]   American National Standards Institute:
             Draft Proposed American National Standard for the Virtual Device Meta-
             file.
             Working document X3H33 82-15R5 (1982).

[BAEC82]   R. Baecker and W. Buxton:
             Lexical and Pragmatic Considerations of Input Structures.
             Computer System Research Group, University of Toronto, Toronto,
             Ontario, Canada M5S 1A1 (1982).

[BAUE81]   F. L. Bauer et al.:
             Report on a Wide Spectrum Language for Program Specification and
             Development (Tentative Version).
             TU München, Institut für Informatik, TUM-I8104 (Mai 1981).

[BERK82]   T. Berk, L. Brownston, A. Kaufman:
             A Human Factors Study of Colour Notation Systems for Computer
             Graphics.
             CACM 25(1982) 547-550.

[BO79]   Ketil Bö:
             IDIGS — Interactive Device Independent Graphic System.
             Report RUNIT Trondheim (1979).

[BORU80a]   H. G. Borufka, H. Kuhlmann, and G. Pfaff:
             Implementation of the Graphics Standard Proposal GKS.
             In: P. ten Hagen (ed.): Lecture Notes of Eurographics '80 Tutorials.
             published by EUROGRAPHICS Association.

[BORU80b]   H. G. Borufka and G. Pfaff:
             The Design of a general-purpose Command Interpreter for Man-Machine
             Communication.
             Proc. IFIP WG 5.2-5.3 Conf., Tokyo (1980) 161-175.

[BORU82]   H. G. Borufka, P. ten Hagen, H. Kuhlmann:
             Defining Interactions by Dialogue Cells.
             IEEE Computer Graphics and Applications (July 1982) 25-33.

[BOS77]   J. van den Bos, L. C. Caruthers, and A. van Dam:
             GPGS: A Device-Independent General Purpose Graphic System.
             Proc. Conf. SIGGRAPH 1977, Computer Graphics 11,2 (1977) 112-119.

[BRIE80]   C. D. O'Brien, H. Newman:
             Picture Description Instructions for Geometric and Photographic Image
             Codings in Videotex Systems.
             Dept. of Communications, Canada (1980).

[BROD81]   K. W. Brodlie:
              Certification Testing at the DI/DD Interface.
              Report G2, Computer Laboratory, University of Leicester (1981).
[BROD82]   K. W. Brodlie, M. C. Maguire, and G. E. Pfaff:
              A Practical Strategy for Certifying GKS Implementations.
              Proc. Eurographics '82, North-Holland (1982).
[CARS82]   S. Carson:
              A Formal Specification of the Programmers Minimal Interface to Graph-
              ics.
              X3H3/82-43(1982).
[DIN79]   Deutsches Institut für Normung:
              Proposal of Standard DIN 66 252, Information Processing,
              Graphical Kernel System (GKS), Functional Description (1979).
[DIN81]   Deutsches Institut für Normung:
              DI/DD-Interface for GKS (Preliminary Version).
              DIN-NI/UA-5.9/40-81(1981).
[DIN82a]   Deutsches Institut für Normung:
              Entwurf DIN ISO 7942, Informationsverarbeitung, Graphisches
              Kernsystem (GKS), Funktionale Beschreibung (1982).
[DIN82b]   Deutsches Institut für Normung:
              FORTRAN Interface of GKS 7.2.
              DIN-NI/UA-5.9/40-82 (1982).
[EEC81a]   Report on EEC Workshop on Graphics Certification, Rixensart-Brussels.
              University of Leicester (May 1981).
[EEC81b]   Report on EEC Workshop on Graphics Certification, Darmstadt.
              Report G1, University of Leicester (Sept 1981).
[EEC82a]   Initial Development of GKS Test Suite.
              Report on EEC Workshop on Graphics Certification, Leicester.
              Report G6, University of Leicester (Febr 1982).
[EEC82b]   Defining a Device Interface for Certification.
              Report on EEC Workshop on Graphics Certification, Miltenberg/ Darm-
              stadt.
              GRIS-Report 82-4, Technische Hochschule Darmstadt (April 1982).
[EEC82c]   Formal Specification of Graphics Software Standards.
              Report on EEC Workshop on Graphics Certification, Steensel/ Eindhoven
              (June 82).
[EEC82d]   Testing at the Device Interface.
              Report on EEC Workshop on Graphics Certification, Leicester,
              GRIS-Report 82-11, Technische Hochschule Darmstadt (Sept 1982).
[ENCA80]   J. Encarnacao, G. Enderle, K. Kansy, G. Nees, E. G. Schlechtendahl,
              J. Weiss, and P. Wißkirchen:
              The Workstation Concept of GKS and the Resulting Conceptual Differ-
              ences to the GSPC Core System.
              Computer Graphics 14,3 (1980) 226-230.
[ENCA81a]   J. Encarnacao, W. Straßer (Eds.):
              Geräteunabhängige graphische Systeme.
              Oldenbourg (1981).
[ENCA81b]   J. Encarnacao:
              Entstehung und Entwicklung des Graphischen Kernsystems GKS.
              In: J. Encarnacao, W. Straßer (Eds.):
              Geräteunabhängige graphische Systeme.
              Oldenbourg (1981) 13-34.

[ENCA82a]   J. Encarnacao, E. G. Schlechtendahl:
             Computer Aided Design, Fundamentals and System Architecture.
             Springer Verlag (1982).
[ENCA82b]   J. Encarnacao, R. Lindner, M. Mehl, G. Pfaff, W. Straßer:
             Realisierung des graphischen Standards GKS durch VLSI-Technologie.
             Technische Hochschule Darmstadt, GRIS-Report (1982).
[ENDE78]   G. Enderle, I. Giese, M. Krause, H. P. Meinzer:
             The AGF Plotfile — Towards a Standardization for Storage and Transpor-
             tation of Graphics Information.
             Computer Graphics 12,4 (1978) 92-113.
[ENDE80]   G. Enderle:
             A Distributed Graphics System Based on a Standard Graphics File.
             ASME-PVP Conference, August 1980.
[ENDE81]   G. Enderle, P. ten Hagen:
             GKS Principles and Goals. DIN-NI/UA-5.9/15-81 (1981).
[FORT66]   FORTRAN 66.
             ISO/R 1539 (1972), ANSI X3.9 (1966), DIN 66 027 (1979).
[FORT77]   FORTRAN 77.
             ISO 1539 (1980), ANSI X3.9 (1978), DIN 66 027 (1980).
[FRAE77]   J. Fraedrich:
             Mensch-Maschine Kommunikation in Leitständen, Teil 1.
             Gesellschaft für Kernforschung mbH Karlsruhe, KFK-PDV 131 (Oktober
             77) Kap. 5.
[GILO72]   W. K. Giloi, J. Encarnacao, W. Kestner:
             APL-G, APL Extended for Graphics.
             Proc. Online '72 (1972).
[GILO78]   W. K. Giloi:
             Interactive Computer Graphics.
             Prentice Hall (1978).
[GINO75]   GINO-F User Manual.
             CAD-Centre, Cambridge (1975).
[GKS82]   Information Processing — Graphical Kernel System (GKS) — Functional
             Description.
             ISO DIS 7942 (1982).
[GKSVER]   GKS Verein, Kaiserstr. 179a, 7500 Karlsruhe
[GNAT81]   R. Gnatz:
             Certification by Program Constructions from Specifications.
             Institut für Informatik der Technischen Universität München.
[GSPC77]   Status Report of The Graphics Standards Planning Committee.
             Computer Graphics 11,3 (1977).
[GSPC79]   GSPC '79, Status Report of The Graphics Standards Planning Committee.
             Computer Graphics 13,3 (1979).
[GUED76]   R. A. Guedj, H. A. Tucker (Eds.):
             Methodology in Computer Graphics.
             Proc. IFIP WG5.2 Workshop SEILLAC I, May 1976.
             North-Holland, Amsterdam (1979).
[GUED80]   R. Guedj et al. (Eds.):
             Methodology of Interaction.
             North-Holland, Amsterdam (1980).
[HAGE79]   P. ten Hagen, F. R. A. Hopgood:
             Towards Compatible Graphic Standards.
             Mathematical Centre Report IN17, Amsterdam 1979.

[HAGE81]   P. J. W. ten Hagen: The GKS Reviewing Process.
             In: J. Encarnacao, W. Straßer (Eds.):
             Geräteunabhängige graphische Systeme.
             Oldenbourg Verlag, München (1981) 75-96.

[HURW67]   A. Hurwitz, J. P. Citron, J. B. Yeaton:
             GRAF: Graphic Additions to FORTRAN.
             Proc. SJCC (1967).

[ISO73]   International Organization for Standardization:
             7-Bit-Code. ISO 646 (1973), DIN 66 003 (1974).

[ISO80]   International Organization for Standardization:
             ISO/TC97/SC5/WG2 — GKS Review: First Active Issues List.
             Document ISO/TC97/SC5/WG2 — N92 (1980).

[ISO81a]   International Organization for Standardization:
             ISO/TC97/SC5/WG2 — Minutes of experts' meeting in Melbourne, Flor-
             ida, 1981.
             Document ISO TC97/SC5/WG2 — N100 (1981).

[ISO81b]   International Organization for Standardization:
             ISO/TC97/SC5/WG2 — GKS Review: Second Active Issues List.
             Document ISO/TC97/SC5/WG2 — N102 (1981).

[ISO81c]   International Organization for Standardization:
             ISO/TC97/SC5/WG2 — GKS Review: Third Active Issues List.
             Document ISO/TC97/SC5/WG2 — N106 (1981).

[ISO81d]   International Organization for Standardization:
             ISO/TC97/SC5/WG2 — GKS Review: Resolved Issues List.
             Document ISO/TC97/SC5/WG2 — N103 (1981).

[ISO82a]   International Organization for Standardization:
             Data Processing Vocabulary, Section 13: Computer Graphics.
             ISO/DIS 2382/13 (1982).

[ISO82b]   International Organization for Standardization:
             Open Systems Interconnection.
             ISO DIS 7498 (1982).

[JUNG83]   H. Jungblut, K. H. Klein, G. Schmitgen:
             GKS-300, GMD-Implementierung des grafischen Kernsystems GKS auf
             SIEMENS Arbeitsplatzrechnern.
             Arbeitspapiere der GMD (ISSN 0723-0508) Nr.12 (1983)

[MAGU81]   M. C. Maguire:
             The Design of Test Programs for the Certification of Graphics Standards.
             Report G3, University of Leicester (November 1981).

[MICH78]   J. C. Michener, J. D. Foley:
             Some Major Issues in the Design of the Core Graphics System.
             Computing Surveys 10,4 (1978) 445-463.

[NAKE72]   F. Nake, A. Rosenfeld (Eds.): Graphic Languages.
             Proc. IFIP Working Conference on Graphic Languages, Vancouver,
             Canada, 1972.
             North-Holland, Amsterdam (1972).

[NEWM78]   W. M. Newman, A. v. Dam:
             Recent Efforts Towards Graphics Standardization.
             Computing Surveys 10,4 (1978) 365-380.

[NORM81]   L. S. Norman:
             Software Methodology and Formal Specification Systems.
             Research Department Sperry Univac, Blue Bell, Pa 19424 (ANSI-X3H3/
             81-93).

[PARN75]   D. L. Parnas:
            On the Design and Development of Program Families.
            TH Darmstadt, FB Informatik, 6100 Darmstadt, Forschungsbericht BS1
            75/2.
[PFAF81a]   G. Pfaff:
            Certification's Support by a Configurable Reference Implementation of
            GKS.
            Position Paper for EEC-Workshop May 1981.
            Technische Hochschule Darmstadt (May 1981).
[PFAF81b]   G. Pfaff:
            On Testing Methods for the Certification of Graphics Systems.
            GRIS-Report 81-3, Technische Hochschule Darmstadt (July 1981).
[PFAF82a]   G. Pfaff, G. Maderlechner:
            Tools for Configuring Interactive Picture Processing Systems.
            Computer Graphics and Applications (July 1982).
[PFAF82b]   G. Pfaff, H. Kuhlmann, H. Hanusa:
            Constructing User Interfaces based on Logical Input Devices.
            IEEE, Computers (Nov 82) pp.62-68.
[REED81]   T. Reed:
            Experiences in the Design and Support of a Graphics Device Driver Inter-
            face.
            Proc. Eurographics '81, Darmstadt, North-Holland (1981).
[ROSE80]   D. Rosenthal:
            On the Design of Graphics Metafiles.
            ISO TC97/SC5/WG2 N86 (1980).
[ROSE80]   D. Rosenthal: Procedure for Technical Comments on GKS.
            Document ISO/TC97/SC5/WG2 — N83 (1980).
[ROSE82]   D. Rosenthal, J. Michener, G. Pfaff, R. Kessener, M. Sabin:
            The Detailed Semantics of Graphics Input Devices.
            Computer Graphics 16,3 (1982) 33-38.
[ROSE82b]   D. Rosenthal, P. ten Hagen:
            GKS in C.
            Proc. Eurographics '82, North-Holland (1982) 359-370.
[SCHO81]   J. Schönhut:
            Portabilität und Effizienz graphischer Software — ein Widerspruch?
            In: J. Encarnacao, W. Straßer (Eds.):
            Geräteunabhängige Graphische Systeme.
            Oldenburg Verlag (1981) 217-233.
[SIGG82]   Graphical Input Interaction Technique (GIIT).
            Summary of a SIGGRAPH Workshop, Seattle 1982.
            Computer Graphics 17,1 (1983) 5-30.
[SMIT71]   D. N. Smith:
            GPL/I — A PL/1 Extension for Computer Graphics.
            Proc. SJCC (1971).
[SMIT78]   A. R. Smith: Colour Gamut Transform Pairs.
            Proc. SIGGRAPH '78 / Computer Graphics 12,3 (1978) 12-19.
[SOOP72]   K. Soop:
            The Design and Use of a PL/1 Based Graphical Programming Language.
            Proc. Online '72 (1972).
[WALL76]   V. L. Wallace:
            The Semantics of Graphics Input Devices.
            Computer Graphics 10,1 (1976) 61-65.

[WIRT71]   Niklaus Wirth:
              The Programming Language PASCAL.
              ACTA INFORMATICA 1 (1971) 35-63.
[WISS78]   P. Wißkirchen, K. H. Klein, P. Seuffert, G. Woetzel:
              Implementation of the Core Graphics System GKS in a Distributed
              Graphics Environment.
              Proc. Int. Conf. Interactive Techniques in CAD, Bologna (1978) 249-254.
[WISS79]   P. Wißkirchen, K. Kansy:
              Experiences with the Implementation of the GKS Standard Proposal.
              Proc. SEAS Spring Technical Meeting, Nijmegen (1979) 135-144.

INDEX

Symbolic Computation

Managing Editors:
J. Encarnação, P. Hayes

Computer Graphics

Editors: K. Bø,
J. D. Foley, R. Guedj,
J. W. ten Hagen,
FRA Hopgood,
M. Hosaka, M. Lucas,
A. G. Requicha

Springer-Verlag
Berlin
Heidelberg
New York
Tokyo

J. Encarnação, E. G. Schlechtendahl

Computer Aided Design

Fundamentals and System Architectures

1983. 176 figures (12 of them in color).
IX, 348 pages. ISBN 3-540-11526-9

Contents: Introduction. – History and Basic Components of CAD. – The Process Aspect of CAD. – The Architecture of CAD Systems. – Implementation Methodology. – Engineering Methods of CAD. – CAD Application Examples. – Trends. – Subject Index. – Author Index. – Color Plates.

This outstanding work is a thorough introduction to the fundamentals of CAD. Both computer science and engineering sciences contribute to the particular flavor of CAD. Design is interpreted as an interactive process involving specification, synthesis, analysis, and evaluation, with CAD as a tool to provide computer assistance in all these phases.
The book is intended primarily for computer scientists and engineers seeking to become proficient in CAD. It will help them obtain the necessary expertise in designing, evaluating or implementing CAD systems and embedding them into existing design environments. Major topics of the book are: system architecture, components and interfaces, the data base aspects in CAD, man-machine communication, computer graphics for geometrical design, drafting and data representation, the interrelationship between CAD and numerical methods, simulation, and optimization. Economic, ergonomic, and social aspects are considered as well.

Symbolic Computation

Managing Editors:
J. Encarnação, P. Hayes

Artificial Intelligence

Editors: L. Bolç,
A. Bundy, J. Siekmann,
A. Sloman

Springer-Verlag
Berlin
Heidelberg
New York
Tokyo

Automation of Reasoning 1

Classical Papers on Computational Logic 1957–1966

Editors: **J. Siekmann, G. Wrightson**
1983. XII, 525 pages
ISBN 3-540-12043-2

Automation of Reasoning 2

Classical Papers on Computational Logic 1967–1970

Editors: **J. Siekmann, G. Wrightson**
1983. XII, 637 pages
ISBN 3-540-12044-0

M.M. Botvinnik

Solving Inexact Search Problems

Translated from the Russian by A. A. Brown
1983. 48 figures. Approx. 255 pages
ISBN 3-540-90869-2

The Design of Interpreters, Compilers, and Editors for Augmented Transition Networks

Editor: **L. Bolç**
1983. 72 figures. XI, 214 pages
ISBN 3-540-12789-5

N. J. Nilsson

Principles of Artificial Intelligence

1982. 139 figures. XV, 476 pages
ISBN 3-540-11340-1
(Originally published by Tioga Publishing Company, 1980)